KW-433-960

1- 1- 71

Photo by W. F. Little

E. Estyn Evans, CBE MA DSc *Wales* Hon. ScD *Bowdoin* FSA MRIA Hon. MTPI

Irish Geographical Studies

in honour of

E. Estyn Evans

Irish Geographical Studies

in honour of

E. Estyn Evans

Edited by

Nicholas Stephens

and

Robin E. Glasscock

Published by the Department of Geography, The Queen's University of Belfast

1970

LIVERPOOL INSTITUTE
OF HIGHER EDUCATION
THE MARKLAND LIBRARY

Accession No.
SK 21097

Class No. 914.295
STE

Catal.

© The Queen's University of Belfast

This book or any part thereof
must not be reproduced in any
form without written permission

Set in Monotype Bembo 11 on 12 point

ST. KATHARINE'S
COLLEGE

CLASS: 914.295
STE

VOLUME:

PRICE:

ACCESSION 1|1|41
NUMBER:

BOUND:

Printed in England by James Townsend & Sons Limited, Exeter

PREFACE

This volume represents the wishes of twenty-five people to honour E. Estyn Evans after his forty years at The Queen's University of Belfast. During this time he lectured in Geography, 1928–1945, held the first Chair 1945–1968, and was the first Director of the newly-established Institute of Irish Studies from 1968 until his retirement in 1970.

Every contributor has had contact with him in various ways, some as undergraduates in Queen's, some as members of his staff, some as academic colleagues, and others as friends of many years standing. They would readily acknowledge the debt which geography, and especially Irish geographical studies owe to Professor Evans. All have at some time enjoyed his writings and lectures; many have also had the pleasure of his company in the field, where his penetrating observations have contributed so much to the enjoyment and training of generations of students. Others have joined in conversations with him around the fireside and enjoyed his deep and special love of the Irish countryside and its people. These informal gatherings have taken place in all parts of Ireland, but most often in his small cottage over-looking the Bloody Bridge River on the flanks of the Mourne mountains or at home in Belfast where he and Mrs Evans have entertained so generously for many years.

The editors are members of a small organising committee established to make arrange-ments for marking his retirement, but they alone decided upon the form of this book and the selection of contributors, all of whom are responsible for the views expressed in their respective chapters. It is, of course, unfortunate that not everyone who might have wished to contribute an essay was able to do so, and we regret that some who were invited were already committed to other pieces of work. The difficulty of producing a balanced selection of material was made more difficult by the very large number of potential contributors among Professor Evans's friends all over the world.

The list of contents makes it quite clear that *Irish Geographical Studies* is not a textbook on the geography of Ireland. We have endeavoured to draw upon the knowledge and recent work of academics extending across a wide field of geography, as we believe Professor Evans would wish. The book falls into three parts: chapters I-VIII are concerned mainly with the physical landscape, chapters IX–XV with historical aspects of the cultural landscape, and chapters XVI–XXIII with contemporary geographical problems. Although all con-tributors were asked to write, as far as possible, on subject matter dealing with the whole of Ireland, or at least a large part of it, we recognised that there was a place for a small number of more restricted studies, for example those on the cities of Dublin and Belfast.

Acknowledgements can never cover adequately all who have made some contribution to a venture of this kind, but there are some, especially in The Queen's University of Belfast, who deserve the special thanks of the editors for their part in the production of this volume: Professor J. J. Pritchard, Head of the Department of Anatomy, and chairman of the organising committee; Professor W. Kirk, Head of the Department of Geography; Dr R. Common, Reader in Geography, and Honorary Secretary to the organising committee; and Mr V. C. R. Ford, Senior Lecturer and Acting-Head of the Department of Geography, 1968–9.

We should also like to thank Miss Eileen Duncan, Senior Cartographer in the Department of Geography, who has been responsible for drawing almost all the line diagrams, and Mrs Dora McCarthy, Mrs Dorothy Stephens, and Mr R. Nelson who have assisted her; Mrs Velma Atcheson, for the final typing and assembly of the text, and Miss Ann Crawford, Mrs Margaret Kennedy, Mrs Joan Kenny, Mrs Rosemary Logan, and Mr R. Lester, all of the Geography department, who assisted in various ways. The advice and guidance of Mr D. J. Morgan of Messrs James Townsend & Sons Ltd, has been invaluable throughout the printing and publication of this book, and his help is gratefully acknowledged.

We are indebted to The Queen's University of Belfast for the financial backing of this volume.

Finally, the editors would like to place on record their own pleasure in producing this volume of essays in honour of a man for whom we have the highest academic regard. We are both indebted to Estyn Evans for his assistance and support of our respective teaching and research, and in many other ways, and we wish him many years of good health, good writing and active geographical discovery.

NICHOLAS STEPHENS
ROBIN E. GLASSCOCK

Belfast, July 1970

NOTES

1 Metrication
  Metric measurements (and Imperial equivalents) have been used wherever the editors considered it desirable. It was judged inadvisable to metricate those chapters dealing with historical aspects.

2 All manuscripts were submitted to the Editors between May 1968 and March 1969.

CONTENTS

CONTENTS

LIST OF FIGURES

LIST OF PLATES

ACKNOWLEDGEMENTS

We wish to acknowledge the permission given to reproduce the following photographic plates:—

XII, XV and XVI	Aerofilms Ltd., London
XVII, XVIII and XX	J. K. St. Joseph, Director of Aerial Photography, University of Cambridge
XXII	Lensmen, Dublin
XXIV	B. K. S. (Technical Services Ltd.), Dublin

The frontispiece is reproduced from a photograph specially taken by W. F. Little, ARPS FRSA, 70 Beech Hill Park West, Belfast 8

THE ENIGMA OF THE IRISH TERTIARY

G. L. Davies

It seems, indeed, not a little curious, that notwithstanding the amount of geological knowledge diffused through this country regarding the origin of the various systems and formations which lie beneath the surface, so much ignorance and uncertainty should exist with respect to the origin of the surface itself.

Sir Archibald Geikie, *The Scenery of Scotland Viewed in Connexion with its Physical Geology,* London and Cambridge, 1865

Although they were written more than a century ago and with Scotland in mind, Geikie's words ring only too true in Ireland today. In Ireland deposits belonging to two geological systems far exceed all others in the extent of their outcrop; Carboniferous rocks underlie more than 40 per cent of the island (Fig. 1.1) and Pleistocene deposits are represented almost everywhere. It is therefore hardly surprising that both Ireland's Carboniferous and Pleistocene stratigraphy have received close attention, but about the history of Ireland during the interval which separates the deposition of the Coal Measures from the advance of the Pleistocene glaciers—an interval of not less than 250 million years—we know remarkably little. In the north-east, the presence of the plateau basalts, the Mourne granites, and other igneous masses—all evidently of Eocene age—and the Lough Neagh Clays (Oligocene?) has admittedly allowed some interpretation of the region's Tertiary history. Elsewhere, however, the almost total absence of Permian, Mesozoic, and Tertiary rocks has made it impossible for the geologist to even begin the reconstruction of Ireland's history during the aeon lying between the Carboniferous and the Pleistocene. Yet it was during that interval that the physique of modern Ireland was blocked out.

Geomorphologists seeking an understanding of Ireland's landforms have valiantly tried to devise their own interpretation of Ireland's history during the missing eras. As their geological brethren stand watchfully by, unable to tackle the problem themselves for want of stratigraphical evidence, the geomorphologists press boldly forward with little more to guide them than the evidence afforded by the island's erosional features. Such a procedure is hazardous in the extreme; with almost his first step forward the geomorphologist finds himself plunged deeply into the realms of mere speculation. He may be likened to a scholar seeking to reconstruct the history of some society by using nothing more substantial than a rudimentary knowledge of the society's existing social institutions.

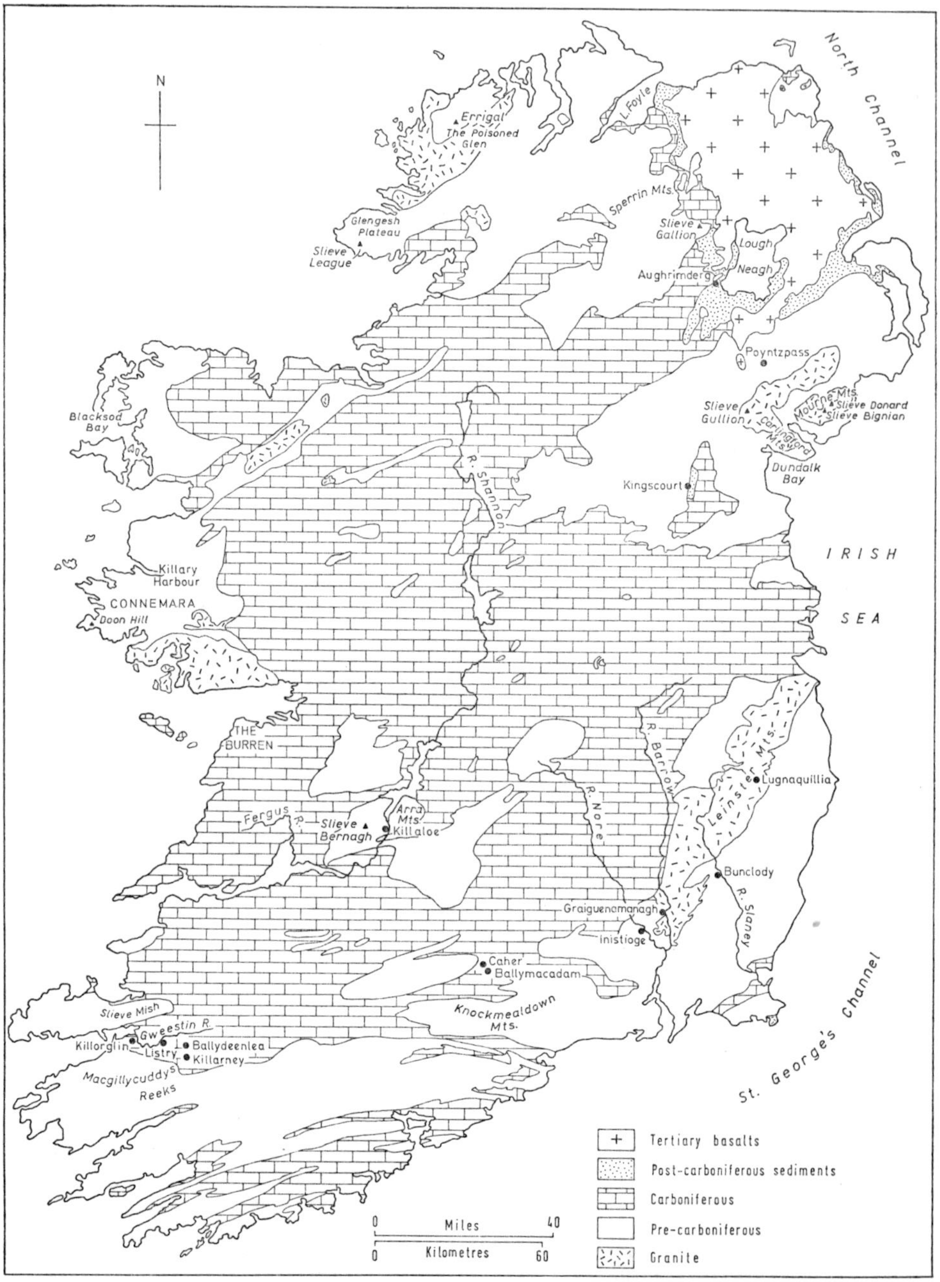

Fig. 1.1 Simplified geological map and important site locations in Ireland

In view of the paucity of the evidence available to them, the unanimity of the Irish geomorphologists over the last hundred years at first sight seems quite remarkable, but first impressions are perhaps misleading. Here, surely, is a case where the very scarcity of the evidence has encouraged a general consensus of opinion. Early writers based their speculations upon the barest minimum of field evidence, and later workers, finding themselves with little fresh evidence to contribute and with almost no evidence to reinterpret, have been only too happy to conform with an interpretation already arrived at. Perhaps in Ireland over the last hundred years we have done little more than erect a geomorphic house of cards. It is sobering to reflect that many theories which once seemed securely grounded upon field-evidence, have in the long run proved to be entirely false. Such was the fate, for example, of both the Wernerian system of geology which dominated the geological scene for forty years after 1775, and the Glacial Submergence theory which proved so popular in nineteenth-century Britain. Yet in their day these two theories seemed to be supported by a much greater body of field-evidence than has ever been available to back up the traditional interpretation of Ireland's Mesozoic and Tertiary history. Had only a little more evidence been available in Ireland, differences of opinion must surely have been generated, leading perhaps to the formulation of rival hypotheses. Such a development can be postponed no longer. It is the object of this essay to trace the history of the traditional and still widely current interpretation of the Irish Tertiary, and to emphasise the lesson of a recent paper by George[1], namely that a fundamental re-examination of our thinking upon this important subject is already long overdue.

THE TRADITIONAL INTERPRETATION

One evening in May 1862 the members of the Geological Society of Dublin gathered in the Museum Building of Trinity College to hear Joseph Beete Jukes, the Local Director of the Geological Survey of Ireland, read his now famous paper "On the Mode of Formation of some of the River-Valleys in the South of Ireland".[2] In the paper Jukes sought to explain certain anomalies in the drainage pattern of southern Ireland, and in the course of so doing he outlined a pioneer interpretation of the post-Carboniferous history of southern Ireland.[3] For Jukes the Carboniferous transgression was the *terminus a quo* of Irish landscape evolution. He believed that during the transgression Ireland had received a thick coat of Coal Measure strata lined beneath with Millstone Grit and limestone.

> I am, in fact, unable to escape the conviction that at the close of the Carboniferous Period one great plain of Coal-measures extended horizontally over all Ireland, with the exception perhaps of the loftier peaks of Connemara, Donegal, Down, and Wicklow, even if any parts of those mountains remained uncovered by the highest Coal-measure beds.

This Carboniferous-mantled block, Jukes claimed, emerged from the sea at the close of the Carboniferous, and as it did so the newly-formed Variscan folds were planed away by wave-action to leave an expansive surface of marine denudation. This surface stood at least as high as the summits of Ireland's modern mountains, and he believed that on its southward dipping surface there had been initiated the ancestors of such modern southward-flowing rivers as the Shannon, Slaney, Barrow, and Nore. He maintained that apart from the brief episode of the Glacial Submergence, Ireland had stood above sea-level throughout the post-Carboniferous period, and he regarded the modern Irish landscape as essentially the result of subaerial denudation effected during Mesozoic and Tertiary time. During this prolonged period of denudation, he claimed, the once ubiquitous Coal Measure strata were reduced to the few outliers existing today, while the gradual wasting of the surface over which they flowed allowed the ancient consequent rivers to superimpose themselves into their present anomalous positions. In this way he sought to explain the passage of the Shannon across the Old Red Sandstone and Silurian rocks of the inlier which forms Slieve Bernagh and the Arra Mountains around Killaloe, and the courses of the Slaney, Barrow, and Nore across the granite, schist, and Ordovician rocks of the Leinster Mountains via three narrow and picturesque valleys at Bunclody, Graiguenamanagh, and Inistioge.

The presence of Tertiary igneous rocks in north-eastern Ireland, together with faults and flexures of similar age, makes it abundantly clear that the north-east has experienced a turbulent recent history. So far as the remainder of Ireland is concerned, however, Jukes's interpretation of Irish Mesozoic and Tertiary history as a tranquil period of continuous subaerial denudation soon found general acceptance. His successor as Local Director in Dublin, Edward Hull, certainly agreed that Ireland had been dry land throughout the greater part of post-Carboniferous time.

> Throughout this inconceivably prolonged lapse of time, our island was more or less
> unsubmerged, its surface being swept by subaerial waters, and its strata carried little
> by little into the adjoining ocean to form perhaps some of those which were being
> piled up over the submerged British area.[4]

The Irish mountains, Hull observed, "were therefore developed, not so directly by the process of upheaval, as by the lowering of the neighbouring tracts of Carboniferous strata".[5] In October 1887, when on a tour of inspection in Ireland, Archibald Geikie, the Director-General of the Geological Survey, was taken to see two recently discovered outliers of Carboniferous sandstone resting atop the quartzite mass of Slieve League, co. Donegal, he felt well satisfied that here was impressive evidence that Ireland had indeed been carved from a Carboniferous-coated block.

> What a picture was here presented of the stupendous denudation which the surface
> of the island has undergone! The Carboniferous system, including, perhaps, its
> coal-bearing portion, may once have spread over this north-west region of Ireland,
> but it has now been worn away and washed into the Atlantic Ocean, leaving only
> this little patch of its lowest platform on the top of Slieve League, as a memorial of
> its presence.[6]

Jukes had placed both the final emergence of Ireland and the formation of the wave-cut surface as far back as the late Palaeozoic for two reasons. Firstly, he believed that no post-Carboniferous marine sediments were to be found anywhere in southern Ireland, and, like many a later geologist, he took the modern absence of rocks of some particular formation to mean that those rocks had never been laid down in the region in question. Able geologist though he was, it never seems to have occurred to him that rocks of Mesozoic or Tertiary age might once have existed in southern Ireland only to be completely removed by subsequent denudation. Secondly, in the May of 1862 Jukes was a convert to fluvialism of only a few months standing, and impressed as he was by the slowness with which rain and rivers perform their destructive work, he considered that the reduction of Ireland's Upper Carboniferous rocks to their present very limited outcrops could not have been accomplished in anything less than the entire post-Carboniferous interval. Interestingly, Jukes seriously overestimated the duration of this interval. He was one of the geologists who considered that Darwin had made a mistake in 1861 when in the third edition of *The Origin of Species* he withdrew his earlier suggestion that post-Mesozoic time alone amounted to not less than 300 million years.[7]

The Survey officer who conducted Geikie to the summit of Slieve League in the autumn of 1887 was J. R. Kilroe[8] and it was he who twenty years later suggested that traces of Jukes's postulated plain of marine erosion actually survive in the modern Irish landscape.[9] Kilroe pointed out that many Irish mountains, developed in a wide variety of rocks, attain heights of between 600 and 900 metres (2,000 and 3,000 feet), and he claimed that this general accordance of summit altitude exists because the mountains in question rise to the level of a wave-cut surface that was bevelled across Ireland during its final emergence. Like Jukes, Kilroe believed that this surface had been cut chiefly in Palaeozoic strata, but he differed from Jukes in one important respect. Instead of regarding the postulated surface as the product of late Carboniferous wave attack, Kilroe argued that Ireland had made its final emergence from the sea during the Miocene and that the wave-cut surface tangent to the Irish mountains was therefore very much younger than Jukes had supposed. Kilroe modified Jukes's hypothesis in this respect because he believed the summits of Slieve Donard (847 metres, 2,796 feet) and Slieve Bignian (740 metres, 2,449 feet) in co. Down both to be a part of the ancient wave-cut surface which must therefore post-date the Eocene granites in which the two mountains are developed. Otherwise he left Jukes's hypothesis intact; he merely compressed into the Tertiary those events which Jukes believed to have occupied the entire post-Carboniferous period.

Kilroe found few disciples, but his writing marked the appearance of a fresh approach to the problem of Ireland's Tertiary evolution. Kilroe and his contemporaries far surpassed Jukes in their appreciation of the true rate of subaerial denudation; no longer was it necessary to suppose that Ireland had been under subaerial attack ever since the Upper Palaeozoic. In place of the old Jukesian interpretation of Ireland's physiographic history, there arose the fresh belief that the island's final emergence had taken place not in the late Carboniferous but at the close of the Mesozoic, and that the region's consequent drainage had taken its origin not upon the dusky, wave-trimmed Coal Measure strata, but upon a southward-dipping sedimentary surface developed in sparkling Cretaceous chalk.

Apart from the increased appreciation of the efficacy of the fluvial processes to effect major topographic changes within so "limited" a period as the Tertiary, there were three factors which encouraged the belief that Ireland had been carved from a high-standing, chalk-surfaced block. Firstly, and very obviously, the existence of Cenomanian, Senonian and Maestrichtian deposits in north-eastern Ireland beneath the protective black mantle of the subaerial Eocene basalts makes it clear that at least one portion of the island was submerged during the Cretaceous. Secondly, there was increasing evidence that the Cretaceous transgression had been much more extensive than earlier workers had supposed. As early as 1878, for example, G. H. Kinahan reminded his readers that in counties Wicklow and Wexford the flint content of the drifts increases southward, thus suggesting the presence of a chalk outlier on the bed of St George's Channel.[10] Between 1901 and 1907 dredging operations off the west coast of Ireland actually brought up chalk-flints, seemingly of local origin, from the bed of the Atlantic.[11] Even onshore in the west of Ireland flints had been found in the drifts of co. Limerick.[12]

The final reason for the growth of a belief in a former Irish chalk mantle is less tangible, namely the influence of drainage pattern studies being made elsewhere. Increasingly it was becoming the practice to invoke now lost sedimentary formations in explaining modern drainage patterns. Ramsay had employed such a device in a none too happy paper on the rivers of England and Wales presented to the Geological Society of London as early as 1872[13], but much more influential was W. M. Davis's famous paper "The Development of Certain English Rivers" which appeared in *The Geographical Journal* in 1895.[14] In this context it is worth noting that Davis himself visited Ireland twice soon after the turn of the century. In September 1908 he attended the British Association meeting in Dublin as a Vice-President of both Sections C and E, and he read papers to both Sections (on glacial erosion in North Wales and on the physiographic subdivisions of the Appalachians) in addition to delivering an evening discourse upon "The Lessons of the Colorado Canyon".[15] Three years later he returned to Ireland on the first stage of his 1911 European pilgrimage, and he and his companions travelled through the southern portion of the island (counties Kerry, Cork, Waterford etc.) under the guidance of Grenville Cole, the Director of the Geological Survey of Ireland.[16] These two visits clearly provided Irish geologists with excellent opportunities of ascertaining their distinguished visitor's views on the recent geomorphic history of Ireland, and, more especially, on the problems presented by the Irish rivers. It may be significant that it is in a paper read to the Royal Irish Academy in June 1912, the year after Davis's Irish tour, that we encounter the earliest attempt to explain Irish geomorphic features by invoking the former presence of a Cretaceous cover.[17] The author of the attempt was none other than Cole himself.

The concept of a former Irish chalk mantle soon earned general acceptance, and since 1912 the device has been used by many authors. Indeed, so securely was the concept established that in the 1950's geomorphologists began to speculate about the level at which the base of the chalk must have stood following Ireland's emergence from the floor of the Cretaceous sea. In 1951 Linton suggested that the sub-Cenomanian surface had risen westwards across England and Wales to attain a height of almost 1,100 metres (3,600 feet) in Snowdonia and a still higher elevation across the St George's Channel in Ireland.[18] Linton surmised that the existence of chalk at very low elevations in north-eastern Ireland today must be the result of the Cretaceous deposits there having been let down some 1,500 metres (5,000 feet) by late Mesozoic or Tertiary earth-movements. Six years later Whittow tentatively concluded that the Cretaceous rocks in southern Ireland had been folded into a south-westward trending geanticline (the 'Kerry-Wicklow Ridge') in which the sub-Cenomanian surface attained a maximum elevation of almost 1,000 metres (3,300 feet) along an axis extending from co. Wicklow to Dingle Bay.[19] Finally, in 1960 the present writer suggested that in south-eastern Ireland, at least, the surface of the chalk could hardly have stood lower than the summit of Lugnaquillia (927 metres, 3,039 feet), the highest peak in Leinster.[20] Such interpretations of the altitude of the base of the now lost chalk perhaps never earned universal acceptance among geologists, but they certainly have obtained general currency among geomorphologists.

Today what is here termed the 'traditional' interpretation of Ireland's Tertiary history has a respectable pedigree extending back to the days of Cole and Kilroe if not still further back to the days of Jukes himself. One of the most recent presentations of the traditional interpretation is to be found in Charlesworth's standard text on the geology of Ireland published in 1963.[21] As epitomised therein the traditional interpretation is that Ireland finally emerged from the sea at the close of the Mesozoic and that its newly elevated surface, carpeted with chalk, stood some thousand metres (3,300 feet) or more above modern sea-level. Gradually, we are told, this high-standing block was ground down to yield Ireland's modern topography while the ancient consequent rivers were slowly superimposed into their present positions. Over the greater part of Ireland all this is supposed to have been effected without any interference from diastrophism. It seems that it was only in the north-east that the relentless work of the agents of denudation was hindered by the obtrusion of the endogenetic forces which caused both major faulting and flexuring and the outpouring of the great pile of plateau basalts. Thus if we subscribe to the traditional interpretation we are forced to conclude that Ulster first showed its independence of the remainder of Ireland as far back as the Eocene!

EVIDENCE SUPPORTING THE TRADITIONAL INTERPRETATION

The suggestion that Ireland formerly possessed a mantle of sedimentary strata younger than the Carboniferous limestone—whether those strata be Jukes's Coal Measures or Cole's chalk—arose largely because many anomalies in the Irish drainage pattern may be explained conveniently by the superimposition hypothesis. Thus to invoke the drainage anomalies as evidence of the former presence of a sedimentary cover rising higher than the summits of Ireland's modern mountains can only lead into a dangerous cyclical argument. We must therefore seek elsewhere for more secure evidence suggesting that Ireland really has been sculpted from some high-standing block as a result of prodigious Tertiary denudation. This evidence takes five forms: the reduction of the plateau basalts to their present extent and thickness; the exposure of three Tertiary plutons in north-eastern Ireland; the presence of dykes of evident Tertiary age outcropping on either side of deep modern valleys; the widespread presence of planation surfaces of supposed Tertiary or later date; and finally there is what Linton has aptly termed "the fragmentation" of Ireland's upland topography.

The plateau basalts

Today the basalts underlie some 4,000 square kilometres (1,550 sq. miles) of north-eastern Ireland, but the existence of basaltic outliers in co. Down to the east of Poyntz Pass, on Slieve Gallion, co. Londonderry, and elsewhere, proves that the basalts once extended far beyond their present limits. They have clearly been reduced to their existing outcrop as a result of post-Eocene circum-denudation. Similarly, thick as the basaltic pile still is (more than 900 metres, 3,000 feet) many of the younger flows have obviously been stripped off by denudation. Indeed Charlesworth has suggested that eastern co. Antrim may have lost some 450 metres (1,500 feet) of its higher lavas in this manner.[22]

The Tertiary plutons

In the Slieve Gullion area and in the Carlingford and Mourne mountains three early Tertiary plutons have been laid bare by the removal of the rocks into which the igneous bodies were emplaced. Especially interesting is the case of the Mourne Mountains which are formed of a series of closely synchronous granites emplaced in Silurian slates and greywackes, and a recent dating of one of the granites by the potassium-argon method has yielded an age of 75 ± 7 million years.[23] Now the emplacement of the granites took the form of ring-dyke formation and cauldron subsidence, and according to Richey there was little or no associated doming of the adjacent Silurian strata.[24] Thus if we discount the possibility of differential post-Eocene uplift of the Mourne pluton, we must regard the difference in altitude between the highest granite peak in the Mournes (Slieve Donard, 847 metres, 2,796 feet) and the surrounding Silurian country (averaging about 75 metres, 250 feet) as affording some indication of the minimum thickness of Silurian rocks removed from the region during the last 75 million years.

The Tertiary dykes

Dykes of presumed Tertiary age are widespread in Ireland to the north of a line drawn from Blacksod Bay, co. Mayo, to Dundalk Bay, co. Louth, and in many cases the local topography has obviously been completely changed since the intrusions were formed. Nowhere is this fact better demonstrated than around The Poisoned Glen in co. Donegal. As Dury has pointed out, the glen is essentially a subsequent feature aligned along a series of Tertiary dykes.[25] Many such dykes outcrop on the walls around the head of the glen while another member of the suite can be traced across the crest of nearby Errigal Mountain. Clearly the excavation of the glen, the floor of which lies 680 metres (2,200 feet) below the peak of Errigal, must post-date the intrusion of the dykes. The two dolerite plugs in the vicinity of Donegal town, and the tholeiitic neck of Doon Hill to the south-west of Ballyconneely, co. Galway, again all intrusions of presumed Tertiary age, seem to afford similar evidence of Tertiary denudation on a grand scale.

The planation surfaces

Workers in many parts of Ireland have described series of planation surfaces rising to heights of several hundred metres above sea-level, and nowhere are such features better displayed than in co. Waterford and eastern co. Cork. There, in the country to the south of the Knockmealdown Mountains, the tough Old Red Sandstone of the Dromana Forest and Watergrasshill anticlines has been worn down to form a series of remarkable upland plains which Miller regarded as the remnants of a South Ireland Peneplane (180 to 240 metres, 600 to 800 feet) and a Coastal Peneplane (60 to 120 metres, 200 to 400 feet).[26] The precise nature of these surfaces is in Ireland, as elsewhere, something of a mystery. Some have urged that the Irish examples are ancient features exhumed from beneath a sedimentary cover and that they therefore have little relevance to the subject of Tertiary denudation.[27] Such a view, however, is difficult to sustain, and most authors have accepted the features as the work of Tertiary and later processes. Almost fifty years ago Hallissy advocated a subaerial origin for the South Ireland Peneplane[28], and Farrington has consistently urged the justice of such an interpretation.[29] The overwhelming majority of authors have nevertheless preferred Miller's view that most of the Irish planation surfaces were cut by waves during Tertiary (Pliocene?) marine transgressions. This despite the fact that not a single Tertiary marine deposit is known anywhere in Ireland. Whatever their origin may be, however, and assuming that they are not exhumed features, the planation surfaces stand as further mute testimony to the effectiveness of Tertiary denudation.

The fragmentation of the Irish uplands

Around the margins of Ireland, where the Carboniferous coat has become frayed and worn, pre-Carboniferous rocks are widely exposed at the surface. Many of these rocks are of precisely the same age and type as the rocks which elsewhere in the British Isles form such features as the Scottish Highlands, the Southern Uplands of Scotland, and the Welsh plateau. In Ireland, however, as Linton has pointed out[30], these rocks, instead of forming extensive uplands, merely give rise to scattered mountain ridges separated by lowland corridors. Nowhere is this fragmentation of the Irish uplands better displayed than in the region centred upon Killary Harbour. There, in counties Mayo and Galway, in an area of less than 800 square kilometres (300 sq. miles), the mountains are arranged into ten relatively compact, steep-sided units, all but two of them rising to over 500 metres (1,500 feet), and each disjoined from its neighbours by valleys and lowlands lying within 100 metres (300 feet) of sea-level. Linton has made the interesting suggestion that this fragmentation of Ireland's uplands is evidence not only of monumental Tertiary denudation, but also of denudation at a rate much more rapid than the rate which prevailed elsewhere in the British Isles. Is is possible, Linton asks, that the high humidity of the Irish climate has allowed denudation to carry the Irish uplands to a very much more advanced stage of destruction than that attained in other less humid parts of the British Isles?

This, then is the evidence that Tertiary denudation took place in Ireland upon a grand scale. It is the testimony to which geomorphologists have repeatedly resorted in order to support the traditional view that modern Ireland is merely a delicate bas-relief sculpted from a massive late Mesozoic block. Until recently the general tenor of the evidence seemed clear and in almost entire accord with the traditional view, but during the last fifteen years fresh geological evidence has come to light casting grave suspicion upon the validity of the traditional interpretation. It is to this new evidence that we must next turn our attention.

SOME FRESH ILLUMINATION

In 1857 one of Jukes's Survey officers, Arthur B. Wynne, described a deposit of pipeclay containing organic material and lying at Ballymacadam, near Caher in co. Tipperary.[31] A hundred years later Watts re-examined the organic material contained in the clay and on the evidence of its pollen content he concluded that the deposit is of early Tertiary (Upper Eocene?) age.[32]

This age-determination had a twofold interest. Firstly, the deposit is of freshwater origin and it therefore confirms the traditional view that southern Ireland had already emerged from the sea before the dawn of the Tertiary. Secondly—and this was very difficult to reconcile with the traditional interpretation—the Ballymacadam clays lie in a hollow in the Carboniferous limestone at an altitude of only 75 metres (250 feet), and Watts's dating thus seemed to suggest that the surface of co. Tipperary had been lowered to something approaching its present low level as far back as the early Tertiary. True, the presence of limestone beneath the deposit may have allowed the clays to be lowered through many metres as a result of solution subsidence, but the amount of such subsidence can hardly be of the order of several hundred metres. Thus, in the light of Ballymacadam, is there room any longer for the traditional belief in an early Tertiary southern Irish land-surface standing perhaps thousands of metres above present sea-level? Unfortunately for the traditionalists, Ballymacadam cannot be dismissed as a freak; there are in the same area two other similar but as yet undated deposits, and both of these also lie at about 75 metres (250 feet) O.D.

Not for long did Watts's discovery remain the sole thorn in the side of the traditional interpretation. In June 1960 Walsh announced the discovery of an outcrop of Cretaceous (later clarified as Senonian) chalk with flints in a disused quarry in the basin of the Gweestin River in Ballydeenlea townland, 10 kilometres (6 miles) to the north of Killarney, co. Kerry.[33] Again the discovery at once both delighted and dismayed the traditionalists. On the one hand Walsh had confirmed that the Cretaceous transgression had indeed extended over at least a part of southern Ireland.[34] On the other hand jubilation was severely tempered because the Ballydeenlea chalk lies not at the height which had been postulated for the basal chalk surface—namely many hundreds of metres above sea-level—but, rather, in a hollow in the local Namurian shales at a mere 90 metres (300 feet) O.D. The Irish chalk was never a very thick deposit (the thickest known in Ireland today is an unbottomed section of 146 metres (476 feet) at Aughrimderg, co. Tyrone) and it is therefore difficult to see how a late Mesozoic surface in co. Kerry could have stood at the height demanded by the traditional interpretation. Walsh himself believes that there is indirect evidence suggesting that the floor of the chalk sea at Ballydeenlea can have lain no more than some 100 metres (330 feet) above the present topography and at a height of barely 200 metres (660 feet) O.D.

Walsh followed up his startling discovery at Ballydeenlea with some further interesting finds elsewhere in the Gweestin valley.[35] About a mile east-north-east of Listry he found in two localities a breccia lying close to the junction between the Carboniferous limestone and the overlying Namurian shales. The breccia, he suggests, is the result of the collapse and brecciation of the roofs of former limestone caverns, and although the matrix of the breccia contains no fossils, Walsh regards the breccia as a terrestrial deposit of Tertiary age formed soon after the equivalent of the Ballydeenlea chalk had been stripped from the lower portion of the valley. The final noteworthy feature of the breccia is the altitude at which it occurs; it lies at only 43 metres (140 feet) O.D. Again, how can the presence of this deposit at such a low level be reconciled with the traditional interpretation of Ireland's Tertiary history?

THE DILEMMA

The discoveries at Ballymacadam and in the Gweestin valley have fixed Irish geomorphologists squarely upon the horns of a dilemma. On the one hand, seeking to adhere to the traditional interpretation, they envisage Ireland's post-Mesozoic history as a period of continuous denudation which saw the steady reduction of a high-standing late Cretaceous block. As we have seen there is considerable evidence seeming to support such a view. As uniformitarians, convinced that the present is the key to the past, they note Williams's estimate that in the Fergus basin of co. Clare the limestone is today wasting at a rate equivalent to the loss of a thickness of 51 mm (2 inches) of rock from the entire basin every 1,000 years,[36] and they conclude that a mere 5 million years ago the limestone surface of Ireland may well have stood some 250 metres (830 feet) higher than it does today. On the other hand, the deposits at both Ballymacadam and in the Gweestin valley suggest that the notion of a high-level early Tertiary surface is only a figment of the geomorphic imagination. Indeed, the two deposits would seem to indicate that the modern Irish landscape, far from being the product of prodigious post-Mesozoic denudation, is really a feature of great antiquity which has suffered little exogenetic modification during the last eighty million years. Clearly neither of these conflicting and mutually exclusive alternatives can possibly hold a monopoly of the truth. They represent extreme viewpoints and some form of compromise is obviously called for.

Hitherto the traditional interpretation of the Irish Tertiary has proved very resilient, but geomorphologists must be cautioned against trying to explain away the deposits at Ballymacadam and Ballydeenlea while still adhering to the old creed. Already geomorphologists in Ireland are vulnerable to the criticism that they have formulated their hypotheses with scant regard to the facts of geology. Long before Watts made his investigations at Ballymacadam, geological evidence was to hand which should have raised some doubts as to the validity of the traditional interpretation. For example, more attention should have been paid to the relationship between Ireland's surviving chalk and her pre-Cretaceous rocks. It is generally admitted that the chalk must have been deposited upon a surface of very low relief, and in north-eastern Ireland the overlap of the chalk on to Liassic, Triassic, Carboniferous, Devonian, and Dalradian rocks amply demonstrates that strata of a wide variety of ages were exposed at the surface during the early and middle Cretaceous. Now if the pre-chalk denudation in north-eastern Ireland was sufficiently profound to lay bare the region's Pre-Cambrian foundations, one may legitimately ask whether it is really likely that great thicknesses of Carboniferous and later strata survived elsewhere to constitute the sedimentary courses necessary to raise Ireland's chalk roof to a height of at least a thousand metres (3,300 feet) above present sea-level. George has recently taxed Irish geomorphologists with this very pertinent question.[37]

Quite apart from the geological evidence, there is one simple geomorphic fact which should perhaps have brought the traditional interpretation into question long ago. This interpretation was originally adopted in order to explain the anomalous and supposedly superimposed courses of many Irish rivers. The superimposition hypothesis, however, involves the belief that such rivers as the Shannon, Slaney, Barrow, and Nore have all assumed their present courses as a result of the steady wasting of a mantle of sedimentary strata containing thick beds of Carboniferous limestone. When these limestones were extensively exposed, karstic conditions perhaps prevailed over wide areas, and as Murphy has shown, large caverns may still be present beneath the drifts of counties Meath, Westmeath, and Offaly.[38] The survival of ancient consequent rivers amidst such karstic terrain is at best open to doubt. Surely, as today in the Burren of co. Clare, the drainage during such a phase would be largely subterranean following lines of structural weakness within the limestone.

One final criticism of the traditional interpretation deserves mention: it is too simple. A neat and plain hypothesis certainly has its attractions, but as Thornbury has reminded students, complexity of geomorphic evolution is much more common than simplicity.[39] The notion that the greater part of Ireland has been the victim of 100 million years of almost continuous denudation with scarcely any interference from other of nature's forces is so simple as to be almost naïve. Assailed by all these doubts and difficulties the geomorphologist must surely seek for some hypothesis more rational than that embodied in the traditional interpretation.

TOWARDS A FRESH INTERPRETATION

As we have seen, the traditional interpretation of Ireland's more recent geological history disregards the possible impact of Tertiary diastrophism outside the north of Ireland. Earth-movements may nevertheless be the key which will enable the conflicting geological and geomorphic evidence to be reconciled. If we suppose that some areas of Ireland have been uplifted and subjected to vigorous denudation while other areas have been downwarped and largely protected from nature's attack, then we have seemingly resolved the dilemma which at present confronts the student of the Irish Tertiary. Donegal, Connemara, and the Mourne Mountains, for example, may be regions of uplift, while localities such as those around Ballymacadam and Ballydeenlea may be areas that were lowered below Tertiary base-levels. If such movements did occur, then it follows that the ghost of the basal chalk surface is not a gently sloping high-level plane as envisaged by the traditional interpretation, but rather a tectonised surface with an amplitude of several hundred metres. Did it still exist, the surface would perhaps in many places lie far below the level of Ireland's modern mountain peaks.

There is of course ample evidence of large-scale Tertiary earth-movement in north-eastern Ireland, but elsewhere the virtual absence of Mesozoic and Tertiary strata makes impossible the positive identification of post-Armorican deformation. In co. Donegal, however, the Barnes Lough fault is of possible Tertiary age[40], as is some of the faulting in the Triassic inlier at Kingscourt, co. Cavan. Similarly Gill has tentatively suggested that some of the shear deformation in the south of Ireland may be Alpine in age.[41]

Feeble though the evidence of recent deformation may be, a number of workers have already invoked differential Tertiary movements in explaining both geological and geomorphic phenomena in various parts of Ireland. Dury has suggested that central Donegal was uplifted during the Tertiary, that the Foyle valley was down-warped, and that the Glengesh Plateau was tilted to the south.[42] Hartley believed that the Sperrin Mountains may have undergone Tertiary uplift[43], and Dewey and McKerrow have boldly claimed that the area around Killary Harbour was uplifted perhaps as recently as the Miocene or Pliocene.[44] In co. Kerry Walsh admitted the possibility of a recent 750 metres (2,500 feet) uplift of the Old Red Sandstone mountains (the Slieve Mish range and Macgillycuddy's Reeks) in relation to the neighbouring Killorglin plain over which the Gweestin river flows. He immediately dismissed the suggestion for want of confirmatory evidence, but in the ensuing discussion at the Geological Society Hollingworth observed that the absence of any detrital Old Red Sandstone material in the Ballydeenlea deposit was indeed negative evidence that the local mountains had not existed during the Cretaceous.[45] Finally, in co. Cork, Farrington has found it necessary to invoke slight and recent warping to explain certain aspects of the region's present morphology.[46]

At the moment any detailed discussion of the nature of this postulated and widespread Irish Tertiary diastrophism is clearly impossible but one suggestion may be proffered. Today Ireland has a lowland heart developed in Carboniferous limestone and set within an upland frame formed in most places of pre-Carboniferous rocks. It is therefore tempting to suggest that the broad pattern of the movements involved the sinking of the Irish mid-lands and the elevation of the island's peripheral regions.

Since the chalk was evidently involved in the warping in co. Kerry it seems that there, at least, the earth-movements must have occurred no later than the early Tertiary, but in south-eastern Ireland the evidence afforded by the Caledonian Leinster batholith suggests that the movements there may have been much more recent. The presence of pebbles of Leinster granite in the Old Red Sandstone of counties Kilkenny and Waterford, the overlap of the Devonian and Carboniferous rocks on to the granite in counties Kilkenny and Carlow, and the existence of fragments of the granite in the Viséan limestone of co. Dublin, all serve to show that the granite was unroofed as early as the Upper Palaeozoic. Yet, surprisingly, there is conclusive proof that today, some 300 million years after the unroofing, the agents of denudation are still working in the highest zone of the batholith.[47] Indeed, in central Wicklow fragments of the batholith's schist roof are still preserved on Lugnaquillia and other mountains. Clearly the batholith must have been protected from denudation through-out the greater part of post-Carboniferous time, but in the light of the Ballymacadam deposit it seems hardly likely that a protective Mesozoic mantle could have survived until very recently atop the 800-metre (2,600 feet) peaks of central Wicklow. It is more probable that the granite and its protective mantle lay at a low level and that the mantle was rapidly stripped off following the uplift of the granite to its present elevation. That so little granite has been lost from many portions of the batholith despite the ravages of Upper Palaeozoic and later denudation strongly suggests that the uplift and re-exposure of the granite was a very recent event.

If the Irish Tertiary is to be re-interpreted as a period of denudation combined with diastrophism, then what explanation can be offered to account for the anomalies in the Irish drainage pattern? Clearly if the high-level late Mesozoic surface demanded by the traditional interpretation is a fiction, then Jukes's century-old superimposition hypothesis is invalidated. Its demise may be no great loss. Quite apart from the difficulty of allowing the persistence of the ancient Irish consequent rivers during a late Tertiary karstic phase, it must be doubted whether the major Irish rivers have really had the simple history implied by the traditional interpretation. Again, have we not been guilty of the implicit acceptance of an over-simple hypothesis? This certainly seems to be the lesson taught by recent work on the Shannon, which has for long been regarded as the arch-type of an Irish superimposed consequent river. Farrington has now shown that in the crucial section around Killaloe the Shannon has had a complex recent history, and that the old notion of the river having superimposed itself across the rocks of the Slieve Bernagh-Arra Mountains inlier must be abandoned.[48] Perhaps no general theory will be found adequate to explain all the anomalies present in the Irish drainage, but if Ireland was really the scene of widespread Tertiary diastrophism, then there remains the possibility that some of the rivers which Jukes claimed as superimposed in 1862 are in fact of antecedent origin.

The anomalies of Ireland's drainage constitute but one of a multitude of Irish geomorphic problems and it will be a long time before Ireland's Tertiary history loses its present enigmatic character. When Geikie and Kilroe made their way up Slieve League in October 1887 they must have felt confident that they understood both the broad outline of Ireland's post-Carboniferous history and the geomorphic significance of the Carboniferous outlier which was their immediate destination. This confidence long persisted in the minds of later geologists but it has been rudely shaken by the discoveries of the last fifteen years. It will be some decades before a new certainty is arrived at and Geikie's words which opened this essay are likely to remain true of Ireland for many years to come.

REFERENCES

1 T. N. George, Landform and structure in Ulster, *Scottish J. Geol.*, 3 (1967), 413–48
2 Gordon L. Davies, Joseph Beete Jukes and the rivers of southern Ireland – a century's retrospect, *Irish Geography*, 4 (1962), 221–33, and *The Earth in decay* (1969), 325–31
3 *Quart. J. Geol. Soc. London*, 18 (1862), 378–403
4 Edward Hull, *The physical geology & geography of Ireland* (1891), 197
5 Ibid., 195
6 Sir Archibald Geikie, *A long life's work* (1924), 221. See also Geikie's, *Landscape in history* (1905), 58–64
7 Sir Francis Darwin, *The life and letters of Charles Darwin* (1887), II, 296
8 *Sci. Proc. Roy. Dublin Soc.*, n.s., 6 (1888–90), 63–6
9 James R. Kilroe, The river Shannon: its present course and geological history, *Proc. Roy. Irish Acad.*, 26 B (1907), No. 8, 74–96; *A description of the soil-geology of Ireland*, (1907), 93–8
10 George H. Kinahan, *Manual of the geology of Ireland* (1878), 262
11 A. J. Grenville Cole and T. Crook, *On rock-specimens dredged from the floor of the Atlantic off the coast of Ireland*, Mem. Geol. Surv. Ireland (1910)
12 George W. Lamplugh, *et al.*, *The geology of the country around Limerick*, Mem. Geol. Surv. Ireland (1907), 64
13 On the river-courses of England and Wales, *Quart. J. Geol. Soc. London*, 28 (1872), 148–60
14 *Geogr. J.*, 5 (1895), 127–46
15 *Rep. Brit. Ass., Dublin 1908, passim*
16 *Ann. Ass. Amer. Geogr.*, 2 (1912), 73–100
17 G. A. J. Cole, The problem of the Liffey valley, *Proc. Roy. Irish Acad.*, 30 B (1912), No. 2, 8–19
18 D. L. Linton, Problems of Scottish scenery, *Scot. Geog. Mag.*, 67 (1951), 65–85
19 J. B. Whittow, The structure of the southern Irish Sea area, *Adv. Science*, 14 (1957–8) 381–385
20 G. L. Davies, The age and origin of the Leinster mountain chain, *Proc. Roy. Irish Acad.*, 61 B (1960), No. 5, 79–107
21 J. K. Charlesworth, *Historical geology of Ireland*, (1963)
22 Ibid., 372
23 *Geol. Mag.*, 100 (1963), 93
24 J. E. Richey, The structural relations of the Mourne granites, *Quart. J. Geol. Soc. London*, 83 (1927), 653–88
25 G. H. Dury, A contribution to the geomorphology of central Donegal, *Proc. Geol. Ass.*, 70 (1959), 1–27
26 A. A. Miller, River development in southern Ireland, *Proc. Roy. Irish Acad.*, 45 B (1939), 321–54
27 See for example W. E. Nevill, *Geology and Ireland*, (1963), 237–8
28 Timothy Hallissy, *Barytes in Ireland*, Mem. Geol. Surv. Ireland, (1923)
29 A. Farrington, Notes on the geomorphology of the Kinsale District, *Irish Geography*, 2 (1951), 124–28; The South Ireland Peneplane, *Ibid.*, 2 (1953), 211–17; The Lee Basin: Part 2, The Drainage Pattern, *Proc. Roy. Irish Acad.*, 61 B (1961), No. 14, 233–53
30 D. L. Linton, Tertiary landscape evolution in J. W. Watson and J. B. Sissons, eds., *The British Isles: a systematic geography*, (1964), 110–130
31 *Rep. Brit. Ass., Dublin 1857*, 94–5
32 W. A. Watts, A Tertiary deposit in county Tipperary, *Sci. Proc. Roy. Dublin Soc.*, n.s. 27 (1957), 309–11
33 *Proc. Geol. Soc.* (1959–60), No. 1581, 112–3; P. T. Walsh, Cretaceous outliers in south-west Ireland and their implications for Cretaceous palaeogeography, *Quart. J. Geol. Soc. London*, 122 (1966), 63–84
34 In September 1966 Upper Cretaceous chalk was also found *in situ* some 60 kilometres south of Cork harbour. See *Proc. Geol. Soc.*, (1967), No. 1640, 134–6

35 P. T. Walsh, Possible Tertiary outliers from the Gweestin valley, co. Kerry, *Irish Nat. Jour.*, 15 (1965), 100–04

36 P. W. Williams, An initial estimate of the speed of limestone solution in County Clare, *Irish Geography*, 4 (1963), 432–41

37 T. N. George, (1967), op. cit.

38 T. Murphy, Some unusual low Bouguer Anomalies of small extent in central Ireland and their connection with geological structure, *Geophys. Prospect,* 10 (1962), 258–70

39 W. D. Thornbury, *Principles of geomorphology,* (1954), 21

40 G. P. Leedal and G. P. L. Walker, Tear faults in the Barnesmore area, Donegal, *Geol. Mag.*, 91 (1954), 116–120

41 W. D. Gill, The Variscan Fold Belt in Ireland, in Kenneth Coe, ed., *Some aspects of the Variscan Fold Belt,* (1962), 49–64

42 G. H. Dury, (1959), op. cit.

43 J. J. Hartley, The Dalradian rocks of the Sperrin mountains and adjacent areas in Northern Ireland, *Proc. Roy. Irish Acad.,* 44 B (1938), No. 8, 141–71

44 J. F. Dewey and W. S. McKerrow, An outline of the geomorphology of Murrisk and north-west Galway, *Geol. Mag.,* 100 (1963), 260–75

45 P. T. Walsh, (1966), op. cit.

46 A. Farrington, (1961), op. cit.

47 G. L. Davies, (1960), op. cit.

48 A. Farrington, Suggestions towards a history of the Shannon, *Irish Geography,* 5 (1968), 402–07

II

TERTIARY AND INTERGLACIAL FLORAS IN IRELAND

W. A. Watts

TERTIARY FLORAS

The Interbasaltic rocks

This account attempts to draw together and evaluate the somewhat scrappy and dispersed information that is now available about Ireland's Tertiary floras. It will help initially to place them in a chronological framework, the outlines of which are provided by the review articles of Casey and Funnell.[1]

The youngest Mesozoic rocks in Ireland are Upper Cretaceous chalks which outcrop extensively in north-east Ireland. The chalk is mainly Senonian in age and sedimentation is known to have continued into the lower Maestrichtian.[2] A very small outlier of Senonian chalk also occurs near Killarney in co. Kerry[3] more than 300 km (186 miles) south-west of the main outcrop. From this, a Senonian marine invasion of south-west Ireland can be inferred, nearly all trace of which has been removed by subsequent erosion. Radiometric dates for the Maestrichtian lie between 69 million (early Maestrichtian) and 63 million (uppermost Maestrichtian) years ago.[4] It can be concluded that the youngest Cretaceous marine sediments in northern Ireland lie within this age range.

The chalk is overlain and largely preserved by basalt which covers some 390,000 ha (1,500 square miles), chiefly in counties Antrim and Londonderry. Over most of the area the basalts of the Antrim lava series[5] can be divided into two series, the Lower and Upper Basalts, which are separated by a major zone of weathering termed the Interbasaltic Bed. In northern co. Antrim a Tholeiitic Basalt occurs between the Lower and Upper Basalts from each of which it is separated by a weathering horizon, the 'Lower Interbasaltic Bed' and the 'Upper Interbasaltic Bed'.[6] The basalts are of considerable thickness, the Lower Basalt alone reaching a thickness of 250 m (807 ft) in the Mire House, co. Tyrone, borehole. Around the coastline of north-east Ireland from Belfast Lough to Lough Foyle, the basalts form a bold escarpment often with high cliffs in which successive strata of black basalt, red interbasaltic layers, white chalk and red Triassic sandstone make for spectacular scenery. Inland, the basalt makes an upland plateau in co. Antrim which dips towards Lough Neagh (Fig. 2.1).

C

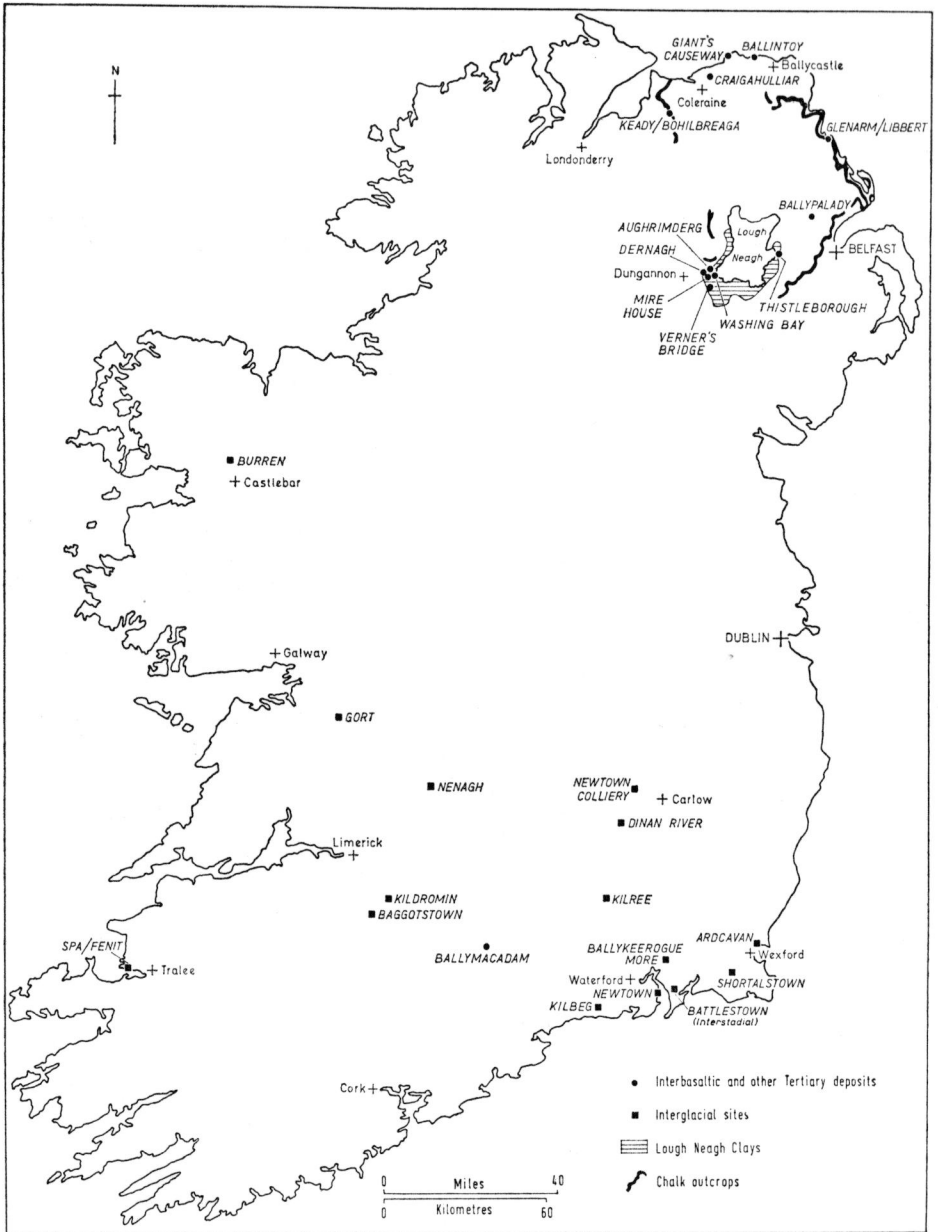

Fig. 2.1   Location map of Tertiary and Interglacial sites in Ireland

The basalt seems to have been extruded over a land surface of weathered chalk;[7] 140 cm (56 in) of clay-with-flints was found between chalk and basalt in the Dernagh No. 1 borehole, near Coalisland, co. Tyrone.[8] Similar sections are known from exposures at Keady Mountain and Bohilbreaga, co. Derry.[9] At Bohilbreaga a lignite bed up to 50 cm (20 in) thick is recorded at the basalt-chalk contact, but it is possible that the overlying basalt belongs to the upper series, so that the lignite may be stratigraphically in the interbasaltic horizon.[10] If this assumption is true there is no evidence, such as exists in Scotland at Ardnamurchan, for pre-basaltic plant-bearing deposits.[11]

Radiometric dates of 74 million years (average of 13 dates) are available for basalt of the Upper Lava Series,[12] but it is suggested that these dates may require re-examination[13] because of possible technical difficulties caused by the presence of zeolites. The dates seem irreconcilable with a Maestrichtian age for the top of the chalk. The same is true of a date of 75 ± 7 million years for the earliest intrusion of the Mourne granites.[14] A series of dates for granites and quartz-porphyry sills in Arran[15] centres on 60 million years, and the Lundy Island granites, centring on 52 million years, provide the youngest available dates for Tertiary igneous activity in Britain.[16] The scatter of the published dates does not allow for great precision in the chronology of the basalts as yet. Some 20 radiometric dates from the Tertiary volcanic province in Britain and Ireland[17] make it reasonable to suggest provisionally that volcanic activity, beginning around the Cretaceous-Tertiary boundary, was centred on the Paleocene, and continued into the earliest Eocene. On this basis the fossiliferous interbasaltic lignites may well be of Paleocene age.

The interbasaltic horizon is variable in lithology. Characteristically it is a purple or reddish sticky clay or 'bole'. Locally, there are concentrations of iron-ore and bauxite which were worked as small mines in the nineteenth century. There are occasional local 'lignite' beds, seldom more than 1 m (3 ft) in thickness, and often very thin. The lignite is either compressed peat or compressed lake muds which often are rich in fine mineral particles. There are also local occurrences of fossilised tree stumps and logs, in some cases charred at the basalt-interbasaltic upper contact. It is widely agreed that the interbasaltic bed is the result of decomposition of basalt caused by sub-aerial weathering, perhaps under tropical or warm-temperate forested conditions. The red clays may be compared to lateritic soils. The lignites represent a variety of kinds of organic sedimentation on the interbasaltic land surface. The majority of the recorded exposures were seen during nineteenth century mining operations. The mines are now abandoned and overgrown and conditions are much less favourable for study than a century ago. It should be made clear that although there is much emphasis in the literature on the single main interbasaltic horizon, both the upper and lower basalt series were extruded as a series of flows, each separated from the next by a period of subaerial erosion, so that lateritic horizons other than the main interbasaltic are well known. This is well illustrated from the Washing Bay, co. Tyrone, borehole,[18] where the main interbasaltic horizon reaches the exceptional thickness of 27 m (88 ft) with twenty-three recognizable lava-flows in the Upper Basalt, separated from one another by weathering horizons up to 6 m (20 ft) in thickness. A similar situation exists in the Lower Basalt in Washing Bay. In the circumstances, lignites might be expected in horizons other than the main interbasaltic although none are known, with the possible exception of a lignite "associated with the Upper Basalt" at the Giant's Causeway.[19] This lignite, which has not been studied, is probably in the "Upper Interbasaltic Bed" above the local tholeiitic basalt.[20]

What is known of the Irish interbasaltic macroflora was reviewed effectively by Moss.[21] Since then no important further publication has appeared. Macroscopic plant remains have been published from Ballypalady, a mile north of Templepatrick railway station, from the iron-ore and bauxite mine at Libbert, near Glenarm, and from a 'leaf-bed' at Ballintoy in northern co. Antrim. Although Cole and others[22] make it clear that lignite with tree trunks, twigs and other plant debris occur at many places in the interbasaltic horizon, the three sites named appear to be the only ones from which collections were made. Ballypalady was always the most important of the three sites and collections from it are to be found in several museums. At Ballypalady the plant remains were found in a "reddish-yellow ferrugineo-arenaceous shale, distinctly laminated, with fragments of plants along the planes of bedding"; Tate and Holden describe the section in detail.[23] At Libbert the "leaf-bed" occurred as a 30 cm (12 in) thick patch of dark clay-rich sand interbedded with bauxite and sand, and at Ballintoy leaves were found in a laminated lignite.[24]

Gardner[25] published lists of ferns and gymnosperms from Ballypalady and Libbert. The ferns were determined as *Gleichenia hibernica* sp. nov. and *Gleichenia,* sp. indeterminable. The *Gleichenia* identification was based on venation characteristics and the position of what was thought to be the scar of the sorus. Among the gymnosperms *Pinus plutonis* Baily, *P. Bailyi* sp. nov., *Tsuga heerii* sp. nov. *Cupressus pritchardii* Goepp., *Cryptomeria Sternbergii* Goeppert and *Taxus Swanstoni* sp. nov. were determined. Of the six, *Pinus plutonis* Baily, *Cupressus pritchardii* Goepp. and *Cryptomeria Sternbergii* Goeppert are the most abundant and best characterised. It can hardly be doubted that these three at least correspond to well-defined taxonomic entities, whatever problems may surround their nomenclature or true taxonomic position. Cones of *Pinus plutonis,* a two-needle species, were frequent at Bally-palady and pine cones may still be collected at Craigahulliar, near Portrush, co. Antrim,[26] where a quarry is operated in basalt and exposes lignite in the interbasaltic horizon. In more recent literature[27] *Cryptomeria Sternbegii* Goeppert is discussed. A case can be made that the species is an araucarian which should properly be named *Araucarites Sternbergii* Goeppert. Seward and Holttum also prefer *Cupressites MacHenryi* Bail. as a name for *Cupressus pritchardii* Goepp. in recognition of the priority of the description of the species by Baily.[28] Baily, who was the first to publish lists of plant fossils from the interbasaltic beds, determined a species as *Sequoia du Noyeri* Baily. It seems likely that this is identical with *Araucarites Sternbergii* Goeppert. Baily's work was reviewed and published in greater detail by Gardner.[29] To sum up, a two-needle pine like the living *Pinus pinaster,* a cypress, and an araucarian similar in appearance to the living *Araucaria excelsa* are frequent fossils of the interbasaltic horizon. Other conifers may occur. No particular stratigraphic signifi-cance can be attached to the occurrence of *Araucarites Sternbergii* as it may have a long vertical range. Chandler[30] records it from the Bournemouth Freshwater Beds which are of Eocene (Cuisian or Lutetian) age, but it also has a wider range in the Eocene.[31]

Very little is known about the interbasaltic angiosperms. They have never been published as fully as the gymnosperms, and the few available illustrations are to be found in papers by Baily.[32] Leaves of dicotyledonous type occur which clearly belong to several species on grounds of diversity of venation and leaf margin morphology. Baily[33] was very cautious in his angiosperm determinations. Having named some gymnosperms, he states, "the remaining specimens, principally leaves, the author did not attempt to identify positively, but, after careful comparison with the works of Unger, Massalongo, Heer, etc., merely ventured to suggest the possibility of their belonging to certain genera and species figured by these authors from probably contemporaneous deposits." His list of determinations was *? Rhamnus, ? Olea, ? Andromeda, ? Fagus, ? Quercus* and *? Platanus.* Tate and Holden[34] report further species from Ballypalady, namely, *Eucalyptus oceanica* Ung., *Hakea* sp., *Celastrus* sp., *Daphnogene Kanii* Heer? It is not clear whether further species reported by Tate and Holden come from the interbasaltic horizon or the Lough Neagh clays. Yet more species were added to the list by Baily in Reports to the British Association.[35] These included *Populus* sp., *Alnus Kefersteinii?* Goepp., *Viburnum Whymperi* Heer, *M'Clintockia trinervis* Heer, *Juglans acuminata* (?) A. Br., *Salix* sp., and *Magnolia glauca?* Heer. Gardner[36] states that the majority of the leaves at Ballintoy, co. Antrim, belong to "a peculiar triple-nerved form, whose affinities are not yet understood, named *MacClintockia* by Heer". Johnson[37] published illustrations of a supposed *Sassafras* from the Libbert mine. These records are included for completeness rather than in any belief that they can be considered well founded. In view of the well-known difficulties in dealing with Tertiary leaf-floras[38] it is probable that the records indicate little more than that dicotyledonous leaves of varied venation type, shape and size were found, and that a flora of at least moderate diversity might be inferred from this. If *MacClintockia* is correctly determined, it is of some importance, as this is an Upper Cretaceous and Paleocene genus which disappeared before London Clay times.[39]

It is interesting to compare the Antrim records with those from Ardtun in Mull.[40] Seward and Holttum express themselves very conservatively in determination of angiosperms but *Cupressites MacHenryi* Baily and *Araucarites Sternbergii* Goeppert are common to the Scottish and Irish interbasaltic sites, as may also be *Platanus. Ginkgo* and *Platanus,* recognised at Ardtun, are characteristic of, but not exclusive to Paleocene floras.[41] To sum up, the interbasaltic macroflora of Ireland is not well known and its angiosperm fossils have never been published effectively. The flora is too little studied to be characterised or dated with much confidence.

It is remarkable that with the growth of the science of palynology, so little work has been done with Tertiary and Cretaceous plant micro-fossils in Great Britain and Ireland in spite of the twin attractions of the Tertiary Volcanic Province and the London and Hampshire Basins. The work of J. B. Simpson[42] is the only published information from Scotland, and a very brief note of the author's[43] the only information from the Irish interbasaltics. Simpson[44] published pollen floras from Ardslignish, Ardnamurchan, from the base of the basalt series, and from two sites, Shiaba and Bremanoir, within the Mull lava succession. Shiaba and Bremanoir were considered by Simpson to be at the same stratigraphic level as the Ardtun macroflora, that is to say, within the basalt series, but much nearer the base than the top. All three may be, but are not necessarily, at an equivalent stratigraphic horizon to the interbasaltic horizon of north-east Ireland, which is much thicker and more continuous over a wide area. Unfortunately, Simpson's work was incomplete at the time of his death in 1960, and it was published without a discussion and with only very general observations on the quantitative occurrence of different pollen types. He was mainly concerned to establish the botanical affinity of the fossils he found, so that he attempted to describe them in relation to living genera, rather than as form genera which would probably be considered a more correct approach by present day workers. Nevertheless, Simpson's last paper contains information of great interest and value in that it is the only effective publication of an interbasaltic pollen flora.

No gymnosperms are recorded from Ardslignish. Angiospermous pollen grains occur which are predominantly triporate and tricolpate-reticulate of several kinds. The author has compared Simpson's photographs with the illustrations in the review of Upper Cretaceous and Tertiary pollen groups by Krutzsch.[45] The species described as *Haloragis scotica* n. sp. by Simpson compared closely with the '*thiergarti*-group' which is regarded by Krutzsch as one of the most important groups characterising the Paleocene. The '*thiergarti*-group' is also present in the Bremanoir interbasaltic deposit. Specimens referred to by Simpson as *Engelhardtia* may belong to Krutzsch's '*Oculopollis*' and '*Trudopollis*' types. *Alnus* is present. According to Krutzsch, the earliest *Alnus*-like forms date to the upper Paleocene. As the *thiergarti, Oculopollis* and *Trudopollis* types scarcely persist into the Eocene it may be claimed that the evidence, such as it is, is consistent with a Paleocene age for the flora.

The interbasaltic flora from Shiaba and Bremanoir has abundant gymnospermous pollen, including papillate pollen referable to the Taxodiaceae and several kinds of saccate pollen. Angiospermous pollen occurs with considerable diversity, but there are few forms in common with the Ardslignish flora. As Simpson concluded, the interbasaltic and sub-basaltic floras are very different indeed and it is reasonable to suggest that they must be of different age. The pollen type named *Taurocephalus* by Simpson, supposedly an extinct genus of the Proteaceae, appears to be a species of *Aquilapollenites*,[46] a primarily Cretaceous genus which was already in decline in the Paleocene. In the course of preparation of this chapter the author became aware that the observation that '*Taurocephalus*' was in fact a species of *Aquilapollenites* had been made independently by Martin.[47] Martin's general conclusions about the age of the Scottish floras agree with the author's. *Ulmus*-like grains, which occur in the interbasaltic horizon, are known in quantity as early as the late-Cretaceous in eastern Asia.[48]

Two interbasaltic floras from Ireland were examined by the author, at Craigahulliar near Portrush, co. Antrim and at Ballypalady. In an earlier report[49] it was stated that the preservation of Craigahulliar pollen did not permit detailed study. Since then further lignite samples have yielded better material. Samples of a reddish-purple mudstone with macroscopic plant debris from Ballypalady proved rich in moderately well-preserved pollen. These samples, with further material from Ballypalady, are preserved in the collection of the Department of Geology, Trinity College, Dublin. Both sites have abundant conifer pollen. Papillate pollen of the Taxodiaceae is the predominant pollen at Craigahulliar, but is infrequent at Ballypalady. At both sites saccate pollen similar to modern *Pinus* is common, and a further saccate type is common at Ballypalady in which there is no constriction where the wing base joins the body cell, as in some modern *Picea* or *Podocarpus* species. Pollen of *Sciadopitys* type is frequent at both sites, as is *Alnus*. Pollen, apparently of the '*atumescens*' group of Krutzsch is frequent at Ballypalady; its main range is Paleocene and basal Eocene. Examples of frequent pollen types from Ballypalady are shown in Plate I.

Much the same range of conifer pollen types occurs at the Irish and Scottish inter-basaltic localities, although *Sciadopitys* is not recorded from Scotland. '*Taurocephalus*' has not been observed in Ireland, nor have the Scottish *Ulmus*-like grains. Conversely the '*Atumescens*' group is not on record from Scotland. A type very similar to the delicately reticulate tricolpate pollen called '*Corylopsis*' by Simpson is common in the Irish sites which also have a variety of triporate, tricolpate and tricolporate types, most of which would not seem out of place in a modern pollen assemblage. There is a broad floristic similarity between the Irish and Scottish interbasaltic sites which suggests approximate contemporaneity, but there are differences in detail between Scotland and Ireland, and even quite important differences between the two Irish sites, which suggest at least a difference of facies between the sites, if not also a difference of age. The Lower Tertiary floras of Spitsbergen described by Manum[50] have much in common with the Irish interbasaltic floras and the floras must have been broadly similar in character and, presumably, contemporaneous. It is interesting that a broadly homogeneous Lower Tertiary flora appears to have existed throughout the basalt province of the North Atlantic.

None of the evidence available conflicts with the supposition that the Scottish sub-basaltic lignite and the Irish and Scottish interbasaltic deposits can be broadly classified as Paleocene, the age suggested by radiometric dates. The data available are, however, so rudimentary, that a dating to Paleocene cannot be further refined and must be regarded as a tentative conclusion until both the pollen and macrofloras are studied and published at an acceptable modern standard.

The Lough Neagh clays and Ballymacadam lignitic clay

The Lough Neagh Clays consist of a series of white or bluish clays, sandy clays and sands with occasional beds of compressed peat (lignite) which often contain wood, and some brown humic clays. The Clays are exposed around the southern half of Lough Neagh (Fig. 2.1). They occupy a narrow strip on each side of the lake, southward from Kiltagh Point on the west side and from Langford Lodge on the east. There is a broader exposure on the southern, particularly the south-western margin of the lake. The total surface exposure is about 21,000 ha (80 square miles), and it is probable that the Clays underlie a still larger area beneath the waters of Lough Neagh.[51] The Clays are covered over much of their area by boulder clay and post-glacial peat bogs so that the outcrops are few and unsatisfying. Much of our information is derived from boreholes put down at the south-west corner of Lough Neagh in the area of Coalisland, co. Tyrone, in an effort to find eastward extensions of the Tyrone Carboniferous coalfield. E. T. Hardman[52] published a useful body of information about the Clays in 1875 and had come to the conclusion that they were post-basaltic. Some authors at this time did not distinguish them clearly from the interbasaltic rocks and for this reason care must be taken with older plant macrofossil records where determinations from interbasaltic beds and Lough Neagh Clays were published together. This problem was clarified by the Washing Bay, co. Tyrone, borehole[53] which remains the most important single item of information available about the Clays. Tragically, the Washing Bay cores were discarded after a period in storage and only small scraps of the core still remain in museum collections.

Wright was able to show that the Clays had the astonishing and unexpected thickness of 350 m (1,145 ft) and that they overlie the Upper Basalt from which they are separated by 22 m (72 ft) of weathered basalt. This is the only site where the weathered top of the basalt has been preserved. Evidently the Clays were deposited after a period of undefined length during which the basalts were weathered and eroded. The Washing Bay core was divided into three units by Wright. The Upper Clays and Sands (253 m or 830 ft) consist of blue, grey and white clays and sands with thin lignites and beds of iron carbonate. Some poorly-preserved macroscopic plant remains occur. The Middle Shales (39 m or 127 ft) consist of brown shaly clays with well preserved plant macrofossils and freshwater molluscs. The Lower Clays and Sands (57 m or 185 ft) are of the same general character as the Upper, but lignites are much more frequent and a thick series (10 m or 32 ft) of lignites and humic clays lies at the transition to the Middle Shales. No other borehole has produced as thick deposits or as detailed stratigraphy as Washing Bay, but valuable auxiliary borehole information is assembled in Fowler and Robbie.[54] Hartley[55] describes a borehole at Aughrimderg, two miles north-west of Washing Bay where basalt was found some 60 m (194 ft) below surface: the Lough Neagh Clays in a lignitic facies, with one bed 3 m (10 ft) thick, were found in the core from 43–60 m (140–194 ft). At Thistleborough near Crumlin, co. Antrim, on the east side of Lough Neagh a lignite bed 120 cm (48 in) thick is exposed in a stream section. This exposure is the best existing one for palaeobotanical purposes for most of the exposures described in the older literature are now unavailable. There is some question whether the thicker lignite beds all lie at one stratigraphic horizon, in which case the Lower Clays and Sands at Washing Bay would be equivalent to the Aughrimderg and Thistleborough lignites. The palynological evidence (see below) suggests that the Washing Bay and Thistleborough lignites are not of the same age. It seems possible that lignite beds are of quite local occurrence and that their presence is of little value for purposes of correlation.

The most important studies of Lough Neagh Clay macrofossils are a series of papers by Johnson and Gilmore[56] and Johnson.[57] A substantial list of plants has been named mainly from leaf impressions, preserved leaf fragments, and, in some cases, from pollen or spores. It is difficult to evaluate, and some determinations appear to be erroneous or inadequately based. They cannot, however, be dismissed out of hand. What emerges from Johnson's work is that well-preserved plant macrofossils occur below about 200 m (658 ft) in the Washing Bay core. Coniferous wood is present and this, together with some foliage shoots, is considered to belong most probably to *Sequoia Couttsiae* Heer.[58] It is interesting that pollen of the Taxodiaceae occurs in the Mire House borehole at 118 m (388 ft) (see below). At the lower levels of the Washing Bay core saccate pollen is the only conifer pollen observed by the author. It is possible that the wood and foliage described by Johnson belong to a non-taxodiaceous species producing saccate pollen. Johnson and Gilmore[59] figured finely preserved leaves of a genus referred to as *Dewalquea*. It was considered possible that this was an extinct genus of the Juglandaceae and a comparison was made with *Engelhardtia*. Pollen certainly referable to *Engelhardtia* occurs in the lower part of the Washing Bay core so that the determination is not inherently improbable. Johnson[60] refers fern spores from Washing Bay to *Mohria* in the Schizaeaceae. Schizaeaceous spores are, of course, well known from Cretaceous and older Tertiary floras but they are very infrequent in samples from the Lough Neagh Clays and Ballymacadam which the author has studied. Although they undoubtedly occur, they cannot be regarded as characteristic elements of the flora. Finally, the significance attached to *Sphagnum* by Johnson[61] cannot be sustained, as it is known fossil at least as far back as the Lower Jurassic.[62]

Recently the author[63] recorded the occurrence of seeds of *Eurya stigmosa* (Ludw.) Mai from the Lough Neagh Clays, about 35 m (112 ft) below surface at Verner's Bridge, co. Tyrone. The genus *Eurya,* of which the species is an extinct member, is in the family Theaceae. It is now found in East Asia, chiefly in tropical regions. Seeds of *Eurya stigmosa* occur at many horizons in the Paleocene and Eocene deposits of the London and Hampshire basins. Chandler[64] refers to it as "this widely distributed Eocene species". The species may, however, have a still longer stratigraphic range in the younger Paleogene so that it is not absolutely diagnostic of age.

There is no published information on the fossil pollen of the Lough Neagh Clays other than a brief note by the author[65] which concluded that they were probably of Lower or Middle Oligocene age. In preparing this review the author attempted to characterise the pollen flora from samples from an exposed lignite bed 120 cm (48 in) thick at Thistleborough, co. Antrim, from the Washing Bay core at 283 m (929 ft) and 309 m (1,014 ft), and from the Mire House core at 118 m (388 ft). Several other samples from the lower part of the Washing Bay core were also examined.

The Thistleborough exposure has abundant well preserved pollen in lignite which has two facies, one a clayey homogeneous dark-brown lignite, the other lighter in colour and almost completely organic. The flora contains no ferns and very sparse saccate conifer pollen. *Quercus*-like pollen of several kinds is overwhelmingly dominant. Ericaceae are frequent. There are rare *Nyssa*-like and *Clethra*-like forms. There are sparse non-quercoid tricolpate and tricolporate pollen grains. No other types are present in significant abundance.

At Mire House ferns and saccate conifers are absent but papillate pollen of the Taxodiaceae is frequent in a thin-walled form resembling *Taxodium* rather than *Sequoia*. *Quercus*-like pollen is the predominant angiosperm type. *Alnus* is frequent and triporate pollen sparse. *Engelhardtia, Ilex, Nyssa* and cf. *Tilia* were observed.

At Washing Bay the 309 m (1,014 ft) sample is a lignite with abundant organic debris and little pollen. It might be compared to a modern wood-peat. The 283 m (929 ft) sample occurs in Wright's Middle Shales.[66] It is a greyish-olive clay-mud with abundant pollen, moderately well preserved. Saccate pollen is abundant in the form in which the wings merge into the body cell without a constriction, as is seen in some species of *Picea* or

Podocarpus. Associated with the saccate pollen is essentially the same assemblage as in the Mire House sample. A sample at 240 m (786 ft) near the base of the Upper Clays and Sands has sparse saccate pollen and is largely '*Quercus*'-dominated.

Much work will be required before the Lough Neagh Clay pollen floras can be published satisfactorily. Discussion is necessarily at a very crude level. The pollen floras have little in common with the interbasaltic floras. The common occurrence in both of Taxodiaceous and saccate pollen should not obscure the completely different character of the angiospermous floras and the absence of indicators of Cretaceous or Paleocene age in the Clays. At the other end of the time scale the flora is unfamiliar to persons familiar with the German Miocene brown-coals so that a Neogene age can be ruled out.[67] The Eocene and Oligocene remain. The essential absence of archaic pollen types might be held to confirm that the later Eocene or Oligocene is the most probable date for the Lough Neagh Clays, as was suggested earlier.[68]

A small Tertiary deposit at Ballymacadam, co. Tipperary[69] has abundant excellently preserved pollen. The assemblage is similar to the Lough Neagh Clays, in that it is predominantly quercoid with sparse saccate pollen of the same type as occurs in the Washing Bay core. There are some tricolporate forms and *Engelhardtia, Symplocos,* Ericaceae and Palmae occur sparsely. There are very rare occurrences of genera which might suggest an older Eocene age such as spores of the Schizaeaceae and plicatoid triporate pollen. This suggests that the Ballymacadam site may predate the Lough Neagh Clays but the flora is plainly of the same general character and Ballymacadam may be contemporary with part of the Lough Neagh Clay sequence.

The time span occupied by the Lough Neagh Clays is of considerable interest. The flora is broadly homogeneous but differs from place to place in important details. It could represent a rather long period of time in which major changes did not take place. Equally, it could represent rapid sedimentation in a short period in which the differences between pollen spectra relate more to facies than to broad floristic change. Until the flora has been studied properly in relation to known well-dated floras only statements of a very general character can be made. A very large problem awaits the interested research-worker and a new Washing Bay core will be needed as one element of a badly-needed major study.

INTERGLACIAL FLORAS

In Ireland interglacial floras have been published from Gort (Gorteenaniska Townland), co. Galway[70], Kilbeg Td., co. Waterford,[71] Baggotstown Td., co. Limerick[72], and Kildromin Td., co. Limerick.[73] At each of these substantial portions of a warm interglacial cycle were found. Temperate interglacial deposits have also been discovered recently in Ballykeerogue More Td., near New Ross, co. Wexford and in Burren Td., near Castlebar, co. Mayo. These are being investigated by Professor G. F. Mitchell and the author. In addition, deposits with boreal floras are known from Newtown Td., co. Waterford[74] and from a recently discovered coastal deposit between Spa and Fenit on the north shore of Tralee Bay, co. Kerry. Both sites appear to represent the end of an interglacial cycle. The Kilbeg,

Baggotstown and Kildromin sites are known only from drilling. The Gort deposit cannot be seen at present because of slumping, and the Ballykeerogue More site is poorly exposed in the base of a sand pit. The newly discovered site in Burren Td. is well exposed in a stream section and is particularly important as the only well-exposed temperate interglacial site which can be demonstrated at the moment in Ireland. The Spa deposit is also exposed in a very satisfactory section (Fig. 2.1).

Ireland is unfortunate that there was no Clement Reid to record and study interglacial deposits at the turn of the century, as was so well done in Britain. It may be considered certain that some deposits in temporary sections have gone unrecorded and that exposed sections similar to those at Burren and Spa remain to be found. It is nevertheless probably true that interglacial deposits are more numerous in south-eastern Britain than in Ireland, perhaps because Ireland was more severely glaciated during the Last Glaciation, with consequent destruction or burying of interglacial sediments. Some deposits were noted by older observers. G. H. Kinahan, who first discovered the Gort interglacial deposit and understood its significance more than a century ago, deserves special mention.[75] Kinahan published numerous short notes on Irish glacial geology and it is due to his sustained interest that most of our few records of probable interglacial deposits are due. Oldham[76] recorded a peat mass under 13 m (43 ft) of till at Nenagh, co. Tipperary. At Newtown Colliery, co. Laois, peat 1 m (3 ft) thick, with associated clays, was found under 29 m (96 ft) of till during drilling for coal. The site is exactly recorded and could be re-sampled. Buried peats are known from several places in the immediate area.[77] In addition, 3 m (10 ft) of peat were found under 10 m (32 ft) of till at Kilree, near Stonyford, co. Kilkenny.[78] Kinahan[79] also records a "peaty accumulation" under till in the valley of the Dinan River between Dysart and Coalcullen, co. Kilkenny. The author has attempted to re-locate this deposit without success. There are post-glacial peaty deposits under alluvium in the valley which may have been confused with interglacial deposits.

Interglacial deposits are studied for a variety of reasons. To the biologist their contained fossils and the inferences that can be made from them about palaeoclimates, ecology, biogeography and evolution are of great interest. If a deposit represents a substantial period of time and shows a number of successive kinds of temperate vegetation it can usually be dated. This may prove of great assistance to geologists in glaciated regions such as Ireland where the dating of tills is often difficult and controversial. A dated interglacial deposit between tills helps place both the underlying and overlying strata in their correct time-stratigraphic position.

To understand how interglacial deposits are dated it is necessary to understand the concept of the interglacial cycle. This has recently been elaborated by Iversen[80] and further discussed in relation to zonation of pollen diagrams by Turner and West.[81] Essentially, an interglacial cycle in north-west Europe is the record of invasion of the landscape by vegetation immediately after a glaciation with a succession of progressively more demanding types of forest, and the ultimate return to glacial conditions. Iversen[82] distinguishes four stages in an idealised interglacial cycle. There is first a 'cryocratic' stage with arctic temperatures, solifluction of unleached soils, and a limited cover of shade-intolerant herbs. In the second 'protocratic' stage temperatures rise and tolerant pioneer trees, shrubs and herbs form a closed cover over base-rich soils. In the succeeding 'mesocratic' stage, at the warmest period of the interglacial, broad-leaved mesic forest predominates over fertile, slightly acid, brown forest soils in which leaching has begun. At the end of the cycle in the 'telocratic' stage, temperatures have begun to fall, but species-rich forest of different composition from the mesocratic stage now predominates over acid podsols. In this stage bogs and heaths develop in a cool oceanic climate. There is then a rapid regression through boreal forest to cryocratic conditions preceding the next glaciation.

The details of development of vegetation in the post-glacial period in north-west Europe, the Eemian (Last) Interglacial and Holsteinian (Penultimate) Interglacial are well known. The post-glacial has the general characteristics of an interglacial cycle. The most important distinction between the three lies in the order of immigration of climatically demanding tree species in the mesocratic and telocratic stages and their relative importance in the pollen percentages at each stage. In dating, the total species list is often less significant than order of appearance and relative abundance of the leading tree genera in the pollen rain. Few species have any value as indicators for particular interglacial periods, although *Azolla filiculoides* (water fern), is not known in Europe after the Holsteinian, to which it is virtually confined.

All the known Irish interglacial sites are of the same age. They are Gortian, which is equivalent to the Hoxnian of Britain or the Holsteinian of the North European Plain. The Gortian resembles the Hoxnian in several important respects, (1) the abundance of *Hippophae* (sea-buckthorn) in the protocratic stage, (2) the association of abundant *Taxus* (yew), *Alnus* (alder), *Abies* (silver fir) and sparse *Picea* (spruce) in the telocratic stage; *Rhododendron ponticum* (rhododendron) is common at this stage in Ireland but is not recorded from Britain, (3) the presence of *Azolla filiculoides* at several sites. It differs from the Hoxnian in having low percentages for pollen of trees and shrubs of 'mixed oak-forest' throughout the interglacial. Only *Quercus* (oak), with up to 10 per cent of the pollen total, is important, whereas *Ulmus* (elm) and *Corylus* (hazel) are rare throughout, in striking contrast to their post-glacial abundance. *Pinus* (pine) is much more abundant in the Gortian than in the Hoxnian cycle. Finally, all Irish Gortian sites are characterised by the presence in the telocratic stage of macrofossils of ericaceous plants of species which now have extreme oceanic distributions in Western Europe. They are not recorded from Britain. Although the Gortian and Hoxnian cycles differ in these details, their common characteristics suggest that they must be contemporaneous and that the Gortian, as one would expect from Ireland's geographical position, is an oceanic version of the Hoxnian.

It is interesting to compare the Gortian with the Ipswichian (Eemian, Last Interglacial) of Britain. In the Ipswichian *Azolla* is unknown, *Abies* and *Hippophae* are present, if at all, as isolated pollen grains, and *Alnus* and *Taxus* play subordinate roles. In their place, *Carpinus* (hornbeam) is the distinctive telocratic tree species and *Acer* (maple) is important at some sites in the mesocratic stage. These two genera are known only as rare isolated pollen grains in the Gortian cycle. All the botanical evidence, in fact, points to the equivalence of the Gortian and Hoxnian cycles. A detailed description on the development of vegetation during the Gortian in Ireland has been published by the author[83] and it is not proposed to repeat it here.

Of the new sites at present under study, Burren contains the mesocratic and telocratic stages of the Gortian cycle. The deposit is truncated at a level where wood peat contains very abundant *Rhododendron* pollen. Underlying peats have the characteristic *Alnus-Taxus-Abies* flora and a good development of the mesocratic *Pinus-Quercus* flora. At Ballykeerogue More large peat and gyttja masses, convoluted and distorted by ice pressure, contain an *Abies-Taxus* flora. The Spa deposit is very significant stratigraphically. It consists of up to 2 m (6 ft) of alternating beds of peat and silt, well exposed in coastal cliff sections of considerable length between Spa and Fenit on the north shore of Tralee Bay. The deposits overlie beach sands and gravels on a wave-cut rock platform which is evidently the 'Pre-Glacial' platform of Wright and Muff.[84] This occurs extensively around the coasts of Ireland. The interglacial sediments are overlain by soliflucted 'head' and this in turn is covered by till. The lower peats have a pine-dominated flora, the upper have a grass-sedge flora with diverse herbs. The sequence plainly represents the end of an interglacial cycle in which tolerant boreal forest is replaced by herbaceous vegetation under cryocratic conditions. The silts between the peats contain pollen of temperate genera with an assemblage strongly reminiscent of the telocratic stage of the Gortian.[85] Mitchell argues that the silts represent solifluction of soils formed late in the Gortian with redeposition of temperate pollen. As the peats are plainly autochthonous and contain only pollen of boreal trees or herbs, this seems a satisfactory explanation. If it is accepted, it also indicates strongly that the Spa deposits can be dated to the extreme end of the Gortian cycle. The similar deposit at Newtown, co. Waterford[86] is probably of the same age. A recent radiocarbon date shows that it lies outside the range of radiocarbon dating.[87]

No interglacial deposits of Eemian age have been found in Ireland, for the Ardcavan deposit, co. Wexford[88] is no longer considered to be interglacial. It is anomalous and puzzling, but is probably a late-glacial and early post-glacial kettle-hole deposit, much oxidised, and buried by till during farm levelling operations. Recently, a large erratic of marine shelly clay some 31 m (100 ft) long was exposed during drainage work in a till section in Shortalstown Td., near Johnstown Castle, co. Wexford. The clay, which is evidently a temperate interglacial deposit, contains pollen appropriate to a mesocratic stage of an interglacial cycle. The pollen spectra are not very distinctive, but there is much more *Ulmus* than is normally found in the Gortian cycle. This clay is possibly the only deposit with serious claims to be regarded as of Last Interglacial (Eemian or Ipswichian) age in Ireland. This is a very astonishing situation. In principle, it should be easier to find Eemian than Gortian deposits. They should lie at the surface, covered only by solifluction earths in areas not covered by ice during the Last Glaciation. Consequently, they should be found readily during building or construction operations and exposed in shallow stream or coastal sections. Unfortunately, this has not proved to be the case and, indeed, some Gortian deposits are covered by as little as 5 m (16 ft) of till in areas with an ice cover during the last glaciation. This is true of Baggotstown and Kildromin, and the Burren Td. site, although with a thicker overburden, is covered by deposits of a local end-moraine of the last glaciation which shows no evidence for the presence of two tills. This very curious situation naturally suggests that the interglacial deposits are, in fact, of Eemian age. However, the very strong botanical reasons for referring them to the penultimate interglacial have already been discussed. It has therefore become a very critical issue in Pleistocene stratigraphy in Ireland to find an interglacial deposit which clearly differs from the Gortian cycle and could represent the Eemian.

In an effort to find Eemian deposits, a drilling programme organised by Professor G. F. Mitchell has recently been carried out in enclosed hollows in an area of co. Wexford which is believed to have been free of ice during the last glaciation. To date, this has yielded no new interglacial material, but a number of thin interstadial deposits with arctic plants and animals have been found under barren silts up to 5 m (16 ft) thick in south-west co. Wexford. At the same time it has become clear that the unglaciated area has particularly long and fine late-glacial sequences. The immediate consequence of the drilling programme appears to be that it will be possible to establish a good sequence of Weichselian inter-stadials and of the Weichselian-late-glacial transition in counties Wexford and Waterford but, at least for the present, we are as far as ever from solving the mystery of the missing Eemian deposits.

REFERENCES

1 R. Casey, The Cretaceous period, *in* the Phanerozoic Time Scale, *Quart. J. Geol. Soc. London,* Supplementary Volume 120, (1964), 193–202.
   B. M. Funnell, The Tertiary Period, *in* the Phanerozoic Time Scale, *Quart. J. Geol. Soc. London,* Supplementary Volume 120, (1964), 179–92

2 C. J. Wood, Some new observations on the Maestrichtian stage in the British Isles, *Bull. Geol. Surv. Gt. Britain,* 27 (1967), 271–88

3 P. T. Walsh, Cretaceous outliers in south-west Ireland and their implications for Cretaceous palaeogeography, *Quart. J. Geol. Soc. London,* 122 (1966), 63–84

4 R. Casey, (1964), op. cit.

5 A. Fowler and J. A. Robbie, *Geology of the Country around Dungannon,* Mem. Geol. Surv., (1961), 274 p.

6 H. E. Wilson and J. A. Robbie, *Geology of the Country around Ballycastle,* (1966), 370 p.

7 H. E. Wilson and J. A. Robbie, (1966), op. cit.

8 A. Fowler and J. A. Robbie, (1961), op. cit.

9 G. A. J. Cole, et al., *The Interbasaltic rocks of north-east Ireland,* Mem. Geol. Surv. Ireland, (1912), 129 p.

10 G. A. J. Cole, et alia, (1912), op. cit.

11 J. B. Simpson, The Tertiary pollen flora of Mull and Ardnamurchan, *Trans. Roy. Soc. Edinburgh,* 64 (1961), 421–68

12 J. A. Miller and P. E. Brown, On dating the British Tertiary igneous province, *Geol. Mag.,* 100 (1963), 381–83

13 P. A. Sabine and J. V. Watson, Isotopic age determinations of rocks from the British Isles, 1955–64, *Quart. J. Geol. Soc. London,* 121 (1965), 477–533

14 J. A. Miller and P. E. Brown, An absolute age determination on the Mourne Mountain granite, *Geol. Mag.,* 100 (1963), 93

15 J. A. Miller and W. B. Harland, Age of some Tertiary intrusive rocks in Arran, *Miner. Mag.,* 33 (1963), 521–23

16 M. H. Dodson and L. E. Long, Age of Lundy Granite, Bristol Channel, *Nature*, 195 (1962), 975–76

17 P. A. Sabine and J. V. Watson, Isotopic age determinations of rocks from the British Isles, 1955–64, *Quart. J. Geol. Soc. Lond*, 121 (1965), 477–533, 122 (1966), 443–459, 123 (1968), 379–93

18 W. B. Wright, Age and origin of the Lough Neagh Clays, *Quart. J. Geol. Soc. London*, 80 (1924), 468–88

19 G. A. J. Cole, et al (1912), op. cit.

20 H. E. Wilson and J. A. Robbie, (1966), op. cit.

21 C. E. Moss, The plant remains of the interbasaltic rocks of co. Antrim, in Cole, G. A. J. et al., (1912), op. cit.

22 G. A. J. Cole, et al., (1912), op. cit.

23 R. Tate and J. S. Holden, On the iron-ores associated with the basalts of the north-east of Ireland, *Quart. J. Geol. Soc. London*, 26 (1870), 151–65

24 J. S. Gardner, On the Lower Eocene Plant-beds of the basaltic formation of Ulster, *Quart. J. Geol. Soc. London*, 41 (1885 a), 82–92

25 J. S. Gardner, A. Monograph of the British Eocene Flora, 2, Gymnospermae, *Palaeontographical Soc. London*, (1885 b), 69–90
J. S. Gardner, Eocene ferns from the basalts of Ireland and Scotland, *J. Linn. Soc.* (Bot.), 21, (1885 c), 655–64

26 G. A. J. Cole, et al., (1912), op. cit.

27 A. C. Seward and R. E. Holttum, Tertiary plants from Mull in Tertiary and Post-Tertiary Geology of Mull, *Mem. Geol. Surv. Scotland,* (1924), 445 p.
M. E. J. Chandler, The lower Tertiary flora of southern England III, *British Museum, London,* (1963), 169 p.

28 W. H. Baily, Notice of plant-remains from the beds interstratified with the basalt of the County of Antrim, *Quart. J. Geol. Soc. London*, 25 (1869), 357–62

29 J. S. Gardner, (1885), op. cit.

30 M. E. J. Chandler, (1963), op. cit.

31 M. E. J. Chandler, The lower Tertiary flora of southern England IV, *British Museum, London,* (1964), 151 p.

32 W. H. Baily, (1869), op. cit.
W. H. Baily, Report of the Committee appointed for the purpose of collecting and reporting on the Tertiary (Miocene) Flora etc. of the Basalt of the North of Ireland, *Report British Ass.,* (1880), 107–09
W. H. Baily, Report of the Committee appointed for the purpose of collecting and reporting on the Tertiary (Miocene) Flora etc. of the Basalt of the North of Ireland, *Report British Ass.,* (1881), 152–54

33 W. H. Baily, (1869), op. cit.

34 R. Tate and J. S. Holden, On the iron-ores associated with the basalts of the north-east of Ireland, *Quart. J. Geol. Soc. London*, 26 (1870), 151–65

35 W. H. Baily, Report of the Committee appointed for the purpose of collecting and reporting on the Tertiary (Miocene) Flora etc. of the Basalt of the North of Ireland, *Report British Ass.,* (1879), 162–164
W. H. Baily, (1880), op. cit.
W. H. Baily, (1881), op. cit.

36 J. S. Gardner, (1885 b), op. cit.

37 T. Johnson, A fruiting *Sassafras* from N.E. Ireland, *Mem. and Proc. Manchester Lit. and Phil. Soc.,* 82 (1938), 43–47

38 A. C. Seward and R. E. Holttum, (1924), op. cit.

39 M. E. J. Chandler, The lower Tertiary flora of southern England IV *British Museum, London,* (1964), 151 p.

40 A. C. Seward and R. E. Holttum, (1924), op. cit.

41 M. E. J. Chandler, (1964), op. cit.

42 J. B. Simpson, Fossil pollen in Scottish Tertiary coals, *Proc. Roy. Soc. Edinburgh*, 56 (1936), 90–108
   J. B. Simpson, (1961), op. cit.

43 W. A. Watts, Early Tertiary pollen deposits in Ireland, *Nature*, 193 (1962), 600

44 J. B. Simpson, (1961), op. cit.

45 W. Krutzsch, Sporen- und Pollengruppen aus der Oberkreide und dem Tertiär Mitteleuropas und ihre stratigraphische Verteilung, *Z. für angewandte Geol.*, 11/12 (1957), 509–48

46 J. Funkhouser, Pollen of the genus *Aquilapollenites*, *Micropaleontology*, 7 (1961), 193–98

47 A. R. H. Martin, *Aquilapollenites* in the British Isles, *Palaeontology*, 11 (1968), 549–553

48 S. R. Samoilovitch, Tentative botanico-geographical subdivision of northern Asia in late Cretaceous time, *Rev. Palaeobot. and Palynol.*, 2 (1967), 127–139

49 W. A. Watts, (1962), op. cit.

50 S. Manum, Studies in the Tertiary flora of Spitsbergen, with notes on Tertiary floras of Ellesmere Island, Greenland and Iceland, *Norsk Polarinstitutt*, Nr. 125 (1962), 119 p.

51 A. Fowler and J. A. Robbie, (1961), op. cit.

52 E. T. Hardman, On the age and mode of formation of Lough Neagh, Ireland; with notes on the physical geography and geology of the surrounding country, *J. Roy. Geol. Soc. Ireland*, 14 (1875), 170–199

53 W. B. Wright, Age and origin of the Lough Neagh Clays, *Quart. J. Geol. Soc. London*, 80 (1924), 468–88

54 A. Fowler and J. A. Robbie, (1961), op. cit.

55 J. J. Hartley, The Post-Mesozoic Succession south of Lough Neagh, co. Antrim, *Irish Nat. Jour.*, 9 (1948), 115–21

56 T. Johnson and J. G. Gilmore, The occurrence of a *Sequoia* at Washing Bay, *Sci. Proc. Roy. Dublin Soc.*, 16 (1921 a), 345–52
   T. Johnson and J. G. Gilmore, The occurrence of *Dewalquea* in the coalbore at Washing Bay, *Sci. Proc. Roy. Dublin Soc.*, 16 (1921 b), 323–33
   T. Johnson and J. G. Gilmore, The lignite of Washing Bay, co. Tyrone, *Sci. Proc. Roy. Dublin Soc.*, 17 (1922), 59–64

57 T. Johnson, The occurrence of the genus *Platanus* in the Lough Neagh Clays and other Tertiary deposits of the British Isles, *Mem. and Proc. Manchester Lit. and Phil. Soc.*, 77 (1933), 109–16
   T. Johnson, *List of Fossil Plants from co. Tyrone*, in the National Museum, Dublin (1941), 13 p.
   T. Johnson, Fossil Plants from Washing Bay, co. Tyrone, II, Sphagnaceae, *Irish Nat. Jour.*, 10 (1951), 150

58 T. Johnson and J. G. Gilmore, (1921 a), op. cit.
   T. Johnson and J. G. Gilmore, (1922), op. cit.

59 T. Johnson and J. G. Gilmore, (1921 b), op. cit.

60 T. Johnson, (1941), op. cit.

61 T. Johnson, (1951), op. cit.

62 W. S. Lacey, Fossil Bryophytes, *Biol. Rev.*, 44 (1969), 189–206

63 W. A. Watts, Fossil seeds from the Lough Neagh Clays, *Irish Nat. Jour.*, 14 (1963), 117–18

64 M. E. J. Chandler, (1961), op. cit.

65 W. A. Watts, (1962), op. cit.

66 W. B. Wright, (1924), op. cit.

67 W. A. Watts, (1962), op. cit.

68 W. A. Watts, (1962), op. cit.

69 W. A. Watts, A Tertiary deposit in County Tipperary, *Sci. Proc. Roy. Dublin Soc.*, 27 (1957), 309–311

70 K. Jessen, S. T. Andersen and A. Farrington, The Interglacial deposit near Gort, co. Galway, Ireland, *Proc. Roy. Irish Acad.*, 60 B (1958), 1–77

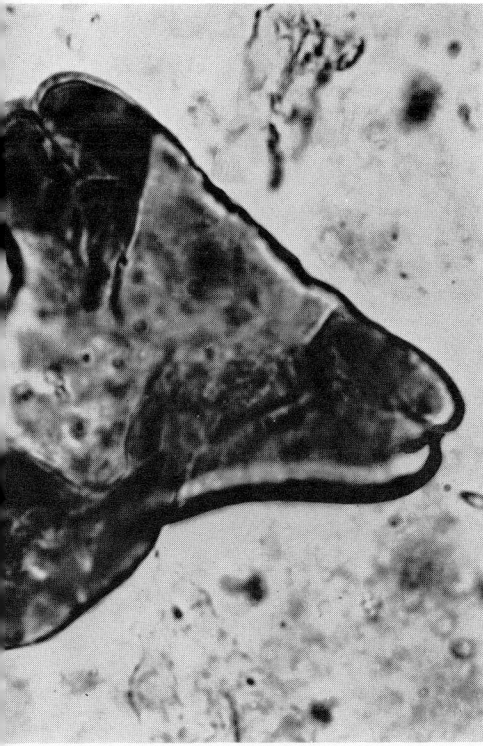

a. Pollen of Thiergarti—group × 1,200

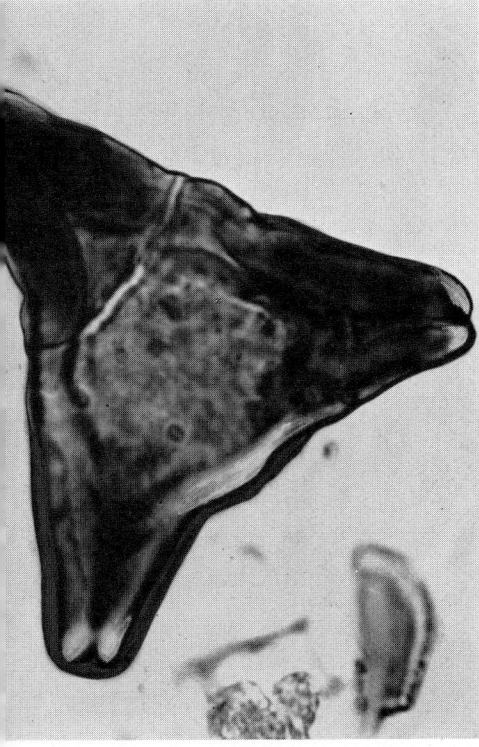

b. Pollen of Thiergarti—group × 1,200

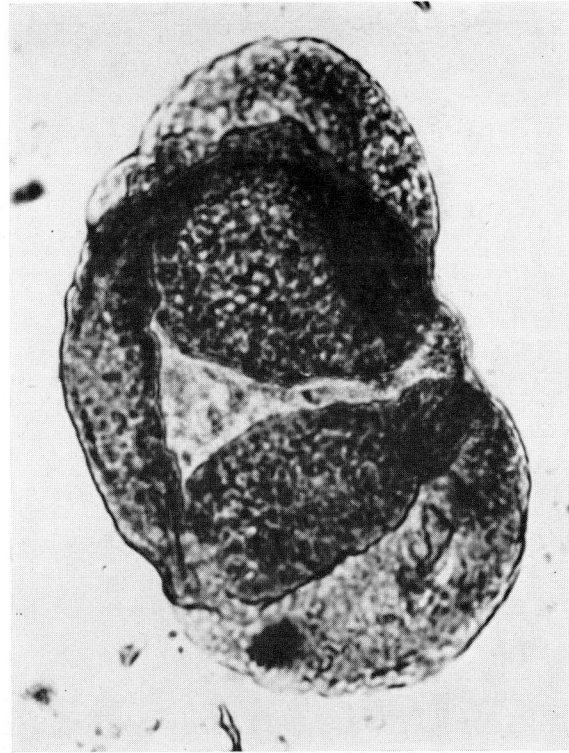

c. Pollen of Pinus type × 525

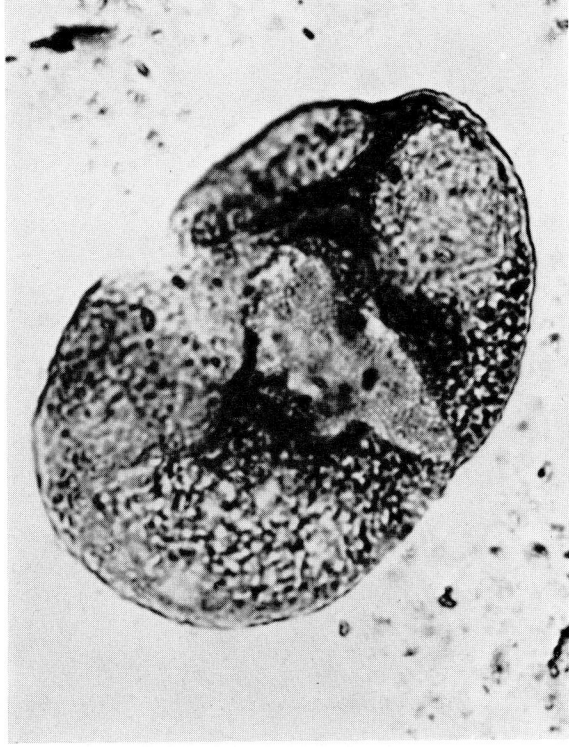

d. Pollen of Picea type × 525

I Frequent pollen types from Ballypalady, co. Antrim, Interbasaltic deposit

71 W. A. Watts, Interglacial deposits at Kilbeg and Newtown, co. Waterford, *Proc. Roy. Irish Acad.*, 60 B (1959), 79–134
72 W. A. Watts, Interglacial deposits at Baggotstown, near Bruff, co. Limerick, *Proc. Roy. Irish Acad.*, 63 B (1964), 167–89
73 W. A. Watts, Interglacial deposits in Kildromin Townland, near Herbertstown, co. Limerick, *Proc. Roy. Irish Acad.*, 65 B (1967), 339–48
74 W. A. Watts, (1959), op. cit.
75 G. H. Kinahan, *Explanation to accompany Sheet 115 and 116,* Memoirs of the Geol. Surv., (1865 a), 43 p.
76 T. Oldham, On the more recent geological deposits in Ireland, *J. Geol. Soc. Dublin,* 3 (1844), 61–71
77 G. H. Kinahan, On preglacial (?) drift in Queen's County, Ireland, *Geol. Mag.,* 2 (1865 b), 442–44
78 J. R. Kilroe, *A description of the Soil Geology of Ireland,* Dept. of Agric. and Technical Instruction for Ireland, (1907), 300 p.
79 J. R. Kilroe, (1907), op. cit.
80 J. Iversen, The bearing of glacial and interglacial epochs on the formation and extinction of plant taxa, *Uppsala Univ. Arsskr.,* 6 (1958), 210–15
81 C. Turner and R. G. West, The subdivision and zonation of interglacial periods, *Eiszeitalter und Gegenwart,* 19 (1968), 93–101
82 J. Iversen, (1958), op. cit.
83 W. A. Watts, (1967), op. cit.
84 W. B. Wright and H. B. Muff, The pre-glacial raised beach of the south coast of Ireland, *Sci. Proc. Roy. Dublin Soc.,* 10 (1904), 250–324
85 G. F. Mitchell, *in manuscript*
86 W. A. Watts, (1959), op. cit.
87 F. W. Shotton, *in correspondence*
88 G. F. Mitchell, Two interglacial deposits in south-east Ireland, *Proc. Roy. Irish Acad.,* 52 B (1948), 1–14

D

III

THE IRISH QUATERNARY: CURRENT VIEWS 1969

F. M. Synge

Ireland, like the greater part of northern Europe, has been covered by ice several times during the past one or two million years. The simple monoglacial view of the early investigators has now given way to the concept of multiple glaciations, each separated from the other by an interglacial period with a temperate climate. In Ireland the glacial deposits are all generally regarded as belonging to the last two cold stages of the Quaternary period. They consist of an older series of drifts which are broadly the equivalent of those of the Saale glaciation of northern Europe, the Riss of the Alps and the Gipping in England; and a younger series which is correlated with the Weichsel glaciation of northern Europe, the Würm of the Alps and the Last glaciation in England.[1] The older and more extensive of these glaciations engulfed the whole of Ireland, with the possible exception of some mountain summits in the south and south-west (Fig. 3.1). In contrast, the younger, or last glaciation was represented by an ice sheet that covered the northern and central parts of Ireland, but failed to inundate the southern third of the island.[2]

The relationship between the deposits of the two glaciations was worked out by means of a series of investigations carried out by Farrington in the vicinity of Dublin (Table 1). The general till associated with the older drift series—a purple clay containing fragments of marine shell and few stones—represents glaciation from the east and north-east, that is, from the Irish Sea; hence the name, Eastern General, has been applied to this glaciation. Deposits of the younger drift series—characterised by a stony limestone till from the north-west—represent the Midland General glaciation.[3] During both of these glacial periods local glaciers transported granite drift from the Wicklow Mountains. Thus, following the retreat of the Eastern General ice sheet, a local mountain glacier carrying granitic materials advanced down the Liffey valley to Brittas, on the border between co. Dublin and co. Wicklow, across terrain previously occupied by the former ice.[4] During the maximum of the Midland General glaciation the ice sheet front impounded Lake Blessington, with a level at 280 to 283 m (920 to 930 ft), in the valley of the upper Liffey.[5] The fresh glacial outwash of the local mountain ice in this valley extended some metres below this former lake level at Athdown, co. Wicklow, some 9 km (5.5 miles) from the

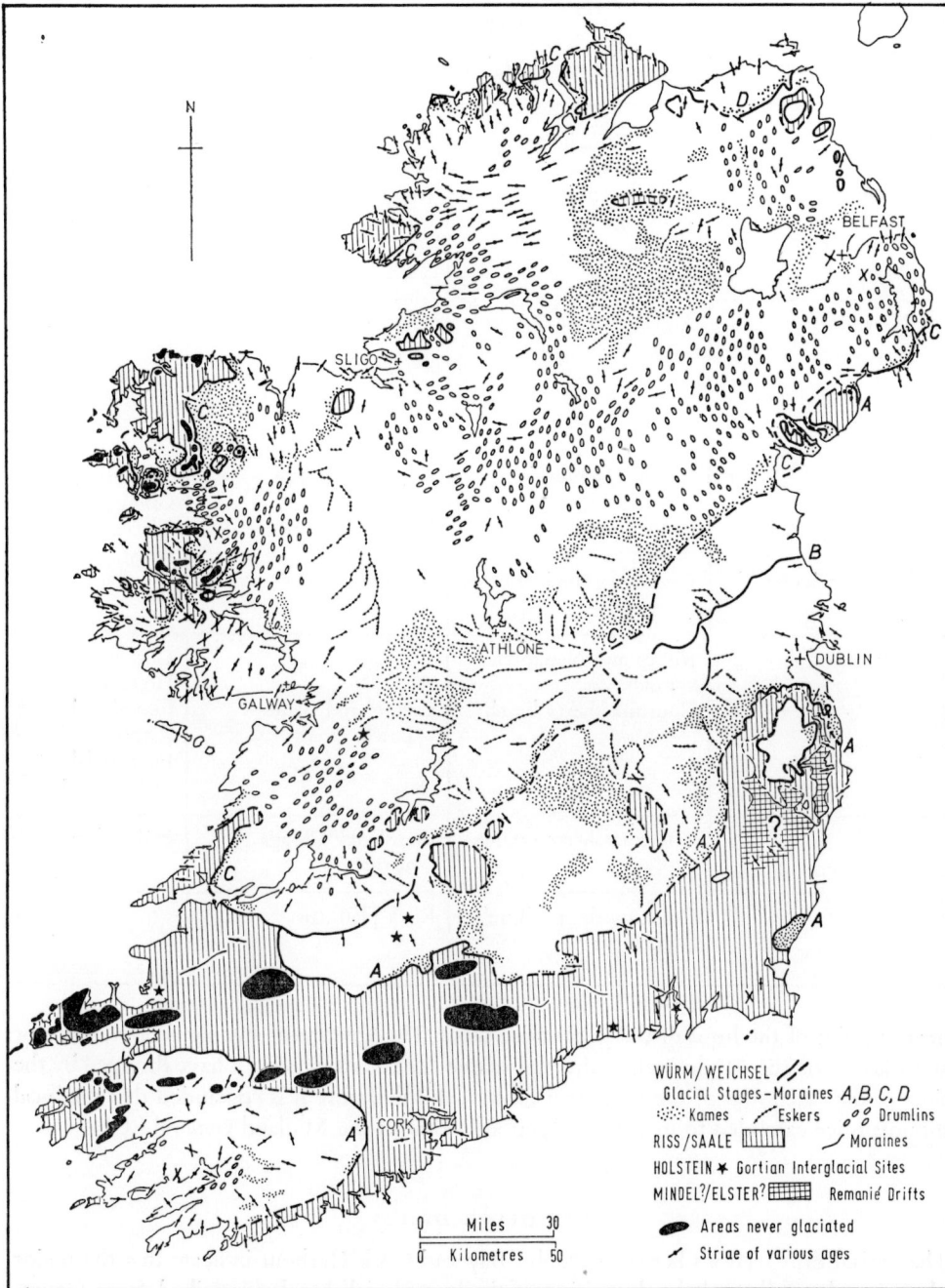

Fig. 3.1   Quaternary geology of Ireland, based largely upon records and recent fieldwork of the Geological and Soil Surveys of Ireland, and the published works of J. K. Charlesworth, A. Farrington, G. F. Mitchell, W. A. Watts, N. Stephens, and F. M. Synge

TABLE I

Glacials and interglacials of the Irish Pleistocene

A. Farrington (1954)	G. F. Mitchell (1960)	F. M. Synge (1964)	General names
Athdown Mt. Glacn. Midland Gen. Glacn. Mt. Glacn.	Athdown moraine Tipperary moraine —	Athdown advance (local) Screen Hills moraine —	Last or Weichselian Glaciation (Würm)
Ardcavan Interglacial	Ardcavan (now rejected, 1968)		Last or Ipswichian Interglacial (Eemian)
Brittas Mt. Glacn. Eastern Gen. Glacn. Enniskerry/Clogga Gl. Solifluction	Brittas, Garryvoe boulder clays Ballycroneen boulder clays Enniskerry boulder clays	Brittas advance (local) Bannow advance (general) Macamore advance (general)	Saale or Gipping Glaciation (Riss)
Gort Interglacial	Kilbeg and Newtown muds Courtmacsherry beach	Cahore and Bannow beach	Gortian or Hoxnian Interglacial (Great Interglacial or Holstein)
	Courtmacsherry erratics	Enniskerry/Clogga advance	Early Glacn.
	Courtmacsherry shore platform	Rock platform	

nearest point of the limit of the general ice sheet. The absence of any signs of washing or wave action on the Athdown moraine shows that the lake waters must have dropped by the time of the expansion of the mountain glacier, and therefore it is concluded that the local mountain ice extended to its furthest limit after that of the Midland General ice.[6]

THE OLDER DRIFTS

The coastal drift sections between Dublin Bay and Cork Harbour indicate that the major glaciation that followed the deposition of the 'pre-glacial' beach (described from Courtmacsherry Bay, co. Cork, and other sites)[7], consisted of ice streams from three main centres. The largest ice stream was that from the Firth of Clyde, which flowed along the bed of the Irish Sea, and the east side of co. Wicklow and deposited the shelly, calcareous, Irish Sea till which extends inland to a western limit of limestone pebbles, then declines southwards from approximately 244 m (800 ft) at Enniskerry to 90 m (300 ft) near Arklow.[8] This coastal drift extends southwards to cover the whole east side of co. Wexford as a surface deposit, except in the area of the Screen Hills, where the terminal lobe of the Midland General ice front pushed across the present coastline from the east (Fig. 3.1). The western margin of the Irish Sea till crosses the south coast of Wexford at Kilmore Quay, and continues westwards along the south coast to the mouth of Cork Harbour, where the till contains marine shells and more far distant erratics such as Ailsa Craig microgranite.[9]

There is, however, a break in the succession in east co. Waterford where the place of the Irish Sea shelly till is taken by a boulder clay which came from country immediately to the north. The inland ice streamed southwards across the Irish midlands to deposit the Bannow till in south co. Wexford[10], also known as the Ballyvoyle till on the co. Waterford coast.[11] At Kilmore Quay, cliff sections show that the Irish Sea shelly till was co-extensive with this local till derived from the Irish midlands. On account of the presence of boulders of Leinster granite this drift of inland origin has been equated with the Brittas advance, and it has also been termed the Munster General till. The shelly Irish Sea till, known in the past as Eastern General till, has been renamed the Ballycroneen till, from the most westerly exposure in co. Cork.[12]

A third ice-stream emanated from a centre in west co. Cork and co. Kerry, and has been called the Greater Cork-Kerry glaciation. An extensive deposit of rubbly boulder clay has been weathered and reduced to give smooth slope profiles, lacking the fresh, hummocky forms of the younger drift country. The greater Cork-Kerry boulder clay has been named the Garryvoe till, from a site in Ballycotton Bay where the following sequence is seen in the cliff sections and has been interpreted as:

Garryvoe till	Greater Cork-Kerry glaciation
Shell-bearing sands	Outwash from the decaying Ballycroneen ice
Shelly Ballycroneen till	Irish Sea, Eastern General or Ballycroneen glaciation

Several acres of frost-shattered limestone rock, with polygonal structures, can be seen below the Ballycroneen till near Garryvoe; this cryoturbation is equivalent to the lower head, which elsewhere on this coast occurs in the same stratigraphic position and overlies a wave-cut rock platform.[13] In places such as Howe Strand, in Courtmacsherry Bay, and in Ballycotton Bay, and many other sections along the south coast, the rock platform is overlain by beach gravels containing far-travelled erratics. This is the oldest Pleistocene deposit known in Ireland, and while well-rounded pebbles predominate, several authors have described sections where considerable amounts of angular rock (head?) is inter-bedded with the beach. The included erratics and head deposits make it difficult to determine the exact climatological-chronological sequence represented by the beach gravels, which have counterparts in other areas of south-west Britain.[14]

There are, however, further complications in the stratigraphy of the older drifts, for

Farrington[15] also recorded the presence of a till deposited by ice moving eastwards from the Wicklow Mountains. This till occurs below the Irish Sea or Ballycroneen till, and was first recognised at Clogga, near Arklow, co. Wicklow, but has been observed also on the Wexford coast as far south as Cahore Point.[16]

The position of the Clogga till in the Pleistocene sequence is somewhat problematical. At some localities this till rests upon a low level wave-cut platform, but has never been observed overlying beach gravels. However, at Cahore, co. Wexford, rounded gravels remarkably like a beach gravel intervene between the Clogga till and the overlying Bally-croneen till. On this evidence the Clogga till should be placed in the earlier Enniskerry mountain glaciation. The only reason why the Clogga till has been placed in the same glaciation as that which laid down the Ballycroneen till is because no weathering horizon has been found between the two tills. This, however, may not be surprising if strong marine or glacial erosion occurred. If the Clogga till does indeed belong to a distinct and separate early glaciation, the presence of erratics in the 'pre-glacial' beach may be readily explained.

A number of organic horizons have been found in association with these older drifts (Fig. 3.1). Such deposits at Kilbeg and Newtown, co. Waterford give a pollen curve that is characteristic, not of the Last Interglacial (Eemian), but of the one that precedes the Saale or Gippingian glaciation in England.[17] This interglacial is known as the Gortian (Hoxnian in England and Holstein on the continent) from a site near the town of Gort, co. Galway.[18] At Newtown, co. Waterford, the organic deposits rest partly upon beach gravel and partly on a wavecut rock-platform overlain by the same beach deposits; in places, the top of the rock platform has been completely shattered by frost action and the angular fragments arranged in festoons.[19]

THE YOUNGER DRIFTS

Since 1950 a search has been made for organic deposits belonging to the Last or Eemian Interglacial period. To date no such organic remains have been recognised with certainty for the Ardcavan deposits in co. Wexford are not now regarded as unequivocally represen-tative of the Eemian Interglacial.[20] Some organic beds found recently in the drift, at Meenbog in the Corraun peninsula, co. Mayo[21], and at Shortalstown, near Bridgetown, co. Wexford[22] might belong to this period. The significance of these sites will be discussed later.

Despite the absence of organic deposits progress has been made in delimiting the extent of glaciation. The methods used have been both morphological and stratigraphical. Also, the close association between the parent drifts and the soils produced from them has enabled geographers, geologists and pedologists to establish significant drift boundaries from the maps produced by the National Soil Survey of Ireland. Such maps are available for the counties of Wexford[23], Limerick and Carlow[24], and those for co. Clare and co. Mayo are almost complete.

The drift limit of the last glaciation (Farrington's Midland General[25]) has been mapped in detail in the south-eastern part of co. Limerick as the southern limit of fresh limestone till banked against the northern slope of the Old Red Sandstone hills that extend as

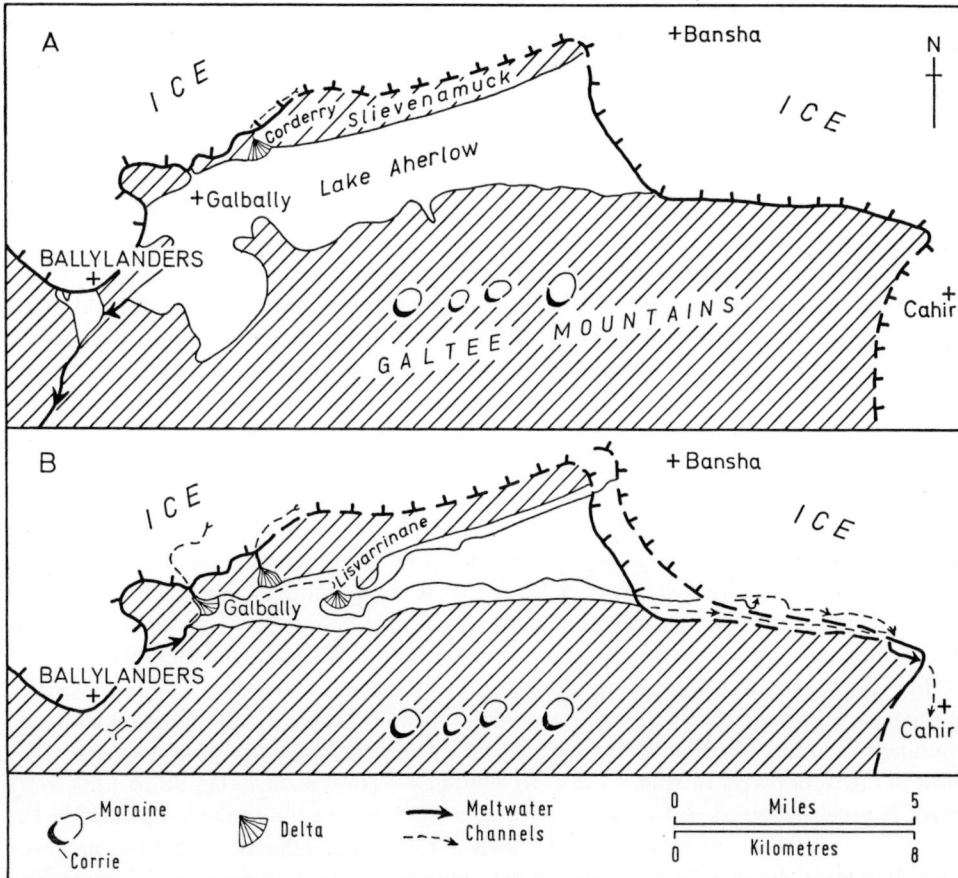

Fig. 3.2(A)   The extent of the proglacial lake that occupied the Glen of Aherlow during the maximum of the Last Glaciation.

Fig. 3.2(B)   Stages in the shrinkage of proglacial Lake Aherlow during the waning of the Last Glaciation.

northern foothills of the Galtee Mountains (Fig 3.2A). Wherever gaps occur in this hill range, this drift limit lobed southwards, as at the east end of the Vale of Aherlow, and into the Ballylanders depression.[26] Hummocky kame-moraine is associated with each of these lobes, between which the drift limit rises on the steep hill slopes to 230 m (750 ft).[27] In the Glen of Aherlow a proglacial lake was impounded, the highest outlet of which, is represented by the intake of a small rock-cut gorge at 166 m (545 ft), draining west, just south of Ballylanders, into the Funshion, a tributary of the Blackwater. This level accords with the level of the highest ice-marginal delta, the Corderry delta in the Glen of Aherlow, at 168 m (550 ft). The lake level fell to 122 m (400 ft) (Galbally delta), and then to 90 m (295 ft)

(Lissvarrinane delta). These delta levels are associated with subglacial drainage channels that carried waters along the north-east flank of the Galtee mountains to the Suir valley (Fig. 3.2B; Plate II).

There is little evidence to support the idea that the drift south of this glacial limit, here termed the Ballylanders moraine, can be regarded as an earlier stage of the same glaciation. The older drift sheet is much dissected, and lacks constructional landforms, although a few isolated features survive. On the western flank of the Galtee mountains this older drift is associated with glacial erratics that reach 320 m (1,050 ft), but no higher. Stone counts made from the till fabric of the two drifts also support the contention that they represent different glaciations; thus while the younger till contains 45 to 60 per cent limestone, the older one contains only 35 per cent or less. As all till samples were collected at depths well below that of the surface soil, such differences could be due to some phase of weathering or to a different direction of glaciation. The first explanation is preferred because it accounts for morphological differences as well as for variations in the degree of weathering of the drifts.

Further evidence is provided by consideration of a series of corrie glaciations in the Galtee mountains which were independent of the main ice sheets. The oldest of these mountain glaciations was also the largest one, and is represented by an ancient line of moraines hardly recognisable as topographic features. These contrast markedly with the arcs of fresh moraine found at higher levels across the mouths of the corries; this latter series consists of two distinct moraine stages which may be compared with the Athdown and late-glacial stages of corrie glaciation moraines in the Wicklow mountains.

In co. Mayo numerous exposures of older till were observed in coastal sections especially in the north-west and south-west of the county; these were readily distinguished from the younger tills in that the stone fabric was affected by periglacial activity to such a degree that most of the stones were rearranged so as to stand in a vertical plane to depths of 3 m (10 ft) or so. No such wholesale rearrangement of the stone fabric in tills of the last glaciation has been observed elsewhere by the writer. Such a till fabric, referred to by the name of 'glacialoid drift' by Kinahan[28] must not be confused with individual fossil ice wedges, which are known to occur within the limits of the last glaciation.[29] In these areas of older drift there is a marked absence of constructional features except isolated kames, probably because of the erosion that occurred during the following phases of interglacial and peri-glacial climates.

Certain of the higher summits, in west co. Mayo, may never have been covered by ice at any time. On Achill Island erratics are found up to an altitude which corresponds with the upper limit of glacial action. Above that limit thick scree and frost-shattered buttresses abound.[30] The highest erratic limit observed inclines northwards from Mweelrea at 580 m (1,900 ft) to 335 m (1,100 ft) on the Corraun peninsula. This represents a gradient of 7 m per km (40 ft per mile). This gradient is steeper than that of the ice sheet of the last glaciation, represented by the fine lateral moraine which marks the upper limit of fresh drift topography along the north side of Clew Bay, sloping at 5 m per km (27 ft per mile), from 380 m (1,250 ft) on Nephin mountain to 200 m (650 ft) in the Corraun peninsula.[31] This drift is closely associated with the great drumlin swarm at the head of Clew Bay and overlies an organic horizon at Meenbog in the Corraun peninsula. Here some 5 m (16 ft) of glacio-fluvial sand and gravel overlie a sandy series containing organic horizons with much pine pollen, but with little deciduous tree pollen. These organic beds, which may indicate part of an interglacial deposit, rest upon red till which is derived from Old Red Sandstone, and probably represents the older drift of the area.

In co. Sligo the western edge of the Carboniferous Limestone escarpment also appears to have escaped inundation during the last glaciation; here thick screes and landslips abound above a marked 'trim-line'. At this time nunataks were also present in the south on the Slievefelim Mountains and the Castlecomer plateau. These discoveries were mentioned in a description of the Irish Quaternary published in 1960[32], and subsequently the coastal highlands of the Slieve League peninsula (where screes and buttresses represent severe periglacial denudation), Bloody Foreland, and the northern part of Inishowen in co. Donegal were shown to lie outside this glacial limit. The presence of raised beaches up to 25 m (81 ft) in north-east co. Donegal show that isostatic downwarping of the earth's crust by the nearby Scottish ice cap must have been considerable. As the highest shorelines terminate southwards at the ice limit, both in Lough Swilly and Lough Foyle, isostatic recovery was already taking place before the ice had receded from that position.[33]

East of Lough Foyle the ice of the last glaciation would appear to have covered the entire coast of north-east Ulster. The tentative suggestion put forward in 1960 for an ice-free zone along the north-east coast of Antrim[34] must now be withdrawn, as fresh drift associated with a northward movement of Irish coastal ice has since been discovered in this area.[35] It is still likely that parts of the Antrim plateau remained as nunataks above the general ice-limit. In some valleys, such as Glendun and Glenaan, small local plateau glaciers extended to sharply defined limits and were not in contact with the general ice.[36]

In co. Clare also, the position of this suggested glacial limit has had to be modified. The new line runs north (not west), from Kilrush to Miltown Malbay, as a large moraine at the eastern edge of a featureless sheet of older drift.[37] Although this moraine represents the outermost limit of the last glaciation in west co. Clare, north co. Kerry, and west co. Limerick, it appears to be a younger feature than the Ballylanders moraine. This later glacial stage, named the Fedamore moraine, overlaps the older ice-limit in the vicinity of Ardagh in co. Limerick.

The changes in the interpretation of the stages of the last glaciation limit indicated above were first shown on a map prepared by the writer for the International Geographical Congress in 1964 (Excursion E.17, the Irish Pleistocene). This map, reproduced in figure 3.1, shows three major stages of the Last or Midland General Glaciation (Weichsel of northern Europe).

A   South Ireland, Tipperary or Ballylanders end-moraine

B   Galtrim moraine

C   The Drumlin (Kells and Fedamore) re-advance moraine, and

D   Armoy re-advance moraine

The oldest stage, 'A', has already been described. Stage 'B', the Galtrim moraine, extends across co. Meath as a narrow belt of ice marginal deltas laid down in proglacial lakes.[38] This moraine has been followed for a distance of 70 km (43.5 miles) from Benhead, south of Drogheda, to the vicinity of Edenderry, co. Offaly. Another moraine of slightly different age forms the eastern margin of the Bog of Allen and is associated with an extensive sheet of outwash at the Curragh in co. Kildare.

Stage 'C', the 'Drumlin' re-advance moraine, clearly marks an important stage of deglaciation. The great drumlin belt that crosses the northern half of Ireland from coast to coast, is bounded on the south by this moraine, and the large eskers of the Irish midlands lie within this line. In north-east Ireland there is some evidence that this re-advance occurred during, or just before, the time of the highest late-glacial marine transgression. Outside this glacial limit evidence of marine wave-action is found at 25 m (81 ft) at Malin Head, Inishowen[39]; at 21 m (68 ft) near Ardglass, co. Down, and at 15 m (49 ft) in the Carlingford peninsula.[40]

Stage 'D', represented by the Armoy moraine in co. Antrim, was laid down by Scottish ice advancing south in the Sound of Jura and Firth of Clyde, and westwards across the north coast of Antrim, while part of the east coast of co. Antrim was still covered by Irish ice flowing north from the vicinity of Larne.[41] The possible continuation of the Armoy moraine into Kintyre and Islay has been observed. This ice seems to have excluded the marine waters responsible for the highest shoreline in east Antrim (24 m or 80 ft at Torr Head), as the marine limit on Rathlin is lower, being at 21 m (68 ft)[42]—thus implying a waning of the Irish ice. Scottish ice may have extended its western limit in response to a withdrawal of Irish ice from the coast of east co. Antrim[43], and remained at the Armoy moraine while the Irish ice withdrew somewhat to the line of moraines noted at Kilrea, at Dunmurry close to Belfast, and just north of Newry.

During the last cold climatic phase (Pollen Zone III), which occurred some twelve thousand years ago when a considerable ice-sheet was still present in the Highlands of Scotland[44], only small corrie glaciers were present in some of the mountains of Ireland. To this stage belong the youngest series of corrie moraines, as very fresh block moraines in certain of the larger corries of co. Mayo[45], the Wicklow Hills[46], and co. Kerry. This stage is also represented throughout the peat sequence of the Irish midlands as a distinct horizon, indicating cooler conditions (Pollen Zone III), preceded by less cold conditions (Allerød or Pollen Zone II), and followed by even milder post-glacial conditions beginning in Pollen Zone IV.[47] A similar sedimentary record has been found in a coastal situation by the sequence of deposits described at Roddans Port, co. Down.[48]

DISCUSSION

In the past few years conflicting views have been put forward concerning the nature and character of the Irish glaciations. In this connection the discussion on this subject, presented by J. K. Charlesworth in 1963, is important, because of the basic concepts involved.[49] In this paper the view was put forward, that, in each glaciation, the ice built up initially in the mountains of the western seaboard, that is, in the highlands of co. Donegal, west co. Mayo and Connemara, and in co. Kerry, and from these centres the ice radiated in all directions. From such a hypothesis it follows that ice-free areas could not have survived in these highlands and western peninsulas. This argument, however, runs contrary to field evidence. Both the landforms and the absence of erratics on certain highlands in the west and south-west suggest unglaciated enclaves.[50] Although in certain areas the complete removal of erratic drift material by subsequent erosion is a possibility, the survival of such material even on steep slopes is known. For instance, numerous erratics of Old Red Sandstone may be observed on the steep scree-covered slopes of the quartzite hills of north Corraun, co. Mayo.[51]

If unglaciated nunataks did occur in the west, then the build-up of last glaciation ice must have taken place further east, over the Irish midlands. Such a view seems reasonable when the low altitude (700 to 915 m or 2,300 to 3,000 ft), and the discontinuous nature of the western highlands is taken into consideration. In no sense do these highlands constitute a topographic barrier similar to that of the European Alps, or the Rockies of North America. The moisture bearing westerly winds approaching Ireland would have had little difficulty in penetrating into the central lowland by the broad corridors of Galway Bay and Donegal Bay. Snow would tend to accumulate in this lowland, well to the east of the present west coast, as the westerly winds would be forced to precipitate their load when cooled on their passage eastwards. Such a situation of an ice-sheet surrounded by a rim of unglaciated mountain peaks prevails today in Greenland. But there is no reason to suppose that the ice axis remained in the same position throughout the last glaciation, for there is evidence to suggest that it moved, first eastwards, and later westwards, as deglaciation progressed. This evidence is discussed below.

The presence of nunataks within the limits of the last glaciation has been questioned on the grounds that such upland areas stand at too low an elevation to have escaped inundation by the ice. This criticism may be valid in the case of certain isolated hill masses such as Slieve Croob in co. Down[52], and the Sperrin mountains[53], but does not seem applicable to other uplands, such as the Mourne, Carlingford, and Slievefelim mountains. It may be argued that if the ice had moved south from the Carlingford mountains (640 m or 2,100 ft) and reached 336 m (1,100 ft) on the north flank of the Dublin hills, there is little doubt that both the Mourne and Carlingford mountains would have been covered. This is shown by the fact that an ice sheet possesses a gradient of at least 5 m per km (27 ft per mile), the average gradient of the Greenland ice cap.[54] There is, however, no evidence to indicate that the ice at that time flowed south from Carlingford. On the contrary, both striae and erratics show that the ice flowed east and south-east across the present coastline between the mouth of Strangford Lough and Dublin. This being the case, the ice limit on both the Carlingford mountains, and the Dublin Hills should be at comparable altitudes, as this limit represents opposing flanks of the same ice stream, and there is a great deal of field evidence to support this view.

Indications of strong periglacial activity above the limit of the fresh drift that encircles the Carlingford and Mourne Mountains suggests that these summits remained as nunataks above the south-easterly flowing ice at its maximum height. If this is so, the surrounding drift limit, termed the 'Carlingford Re-advance' by Charlesworth[55], must be regarded as the upper glacial limit of the last glaciation ice-sheet. The re-advance moraine associated with the limit of the drumlins in co. Louth, therefore, lies at an even lower level, and coastal sections show that such a re-advance extended across the present coast at Rathcor, co. Louth, associated with a lobe of ice that pushed into Dundalk Bay. At the same time another lobe of ice extended down Carlingford Lough as far as Greenore and Greencastle, and the re-advance drumlin moraine re-appears near Killough and Ardglass in east co. Down.[56]

Similar arguments can be presented to show that the Slievefelim mountains, and the Castlecomer plateau, co. Laois and co. Kilkenny, also stood up as nunataks, while in co. Mayo ice streaming west along Clew Bay has been proved to slope at 5 m per km (27 ft per mile) by the fine lateral moraine extending from Nephin to Corraun.[57] Unlike its counterpart in the east, this part of the drumlin end-moraine transgresses older drift terrain, which can be identified by the periglacial structures present. Such structures are represented by the vertical alignment of the stones in the till to a depth of about 3 m (10 ft).[58] This erection of the stones in the till has been observed throughout the 'older' drifts both in the east (in south-east co. Wexford), and in the north-west (in Inishowen, co. Donegal), as well as in the west. No such structures have been observed in the younger drifts within the limits of the Midland General or last glaciation end-moraine, although occasionally individual fossil ice wedges are present. These extensive periglacial structures in the older drifts appear to be associated with the onset of the last glaciation.

The northward extension of the younger drift limit (the Mulrany-Ballycastle moraine) from west co. Mayo, across Donegal Bay to the south-east side of the highland plateau that forms the Slieve League peninsula, is based on the well-defined drumlin limit in that area, and the presence of a massive moraine at Shalwy, east of Muckros Point, and hugging the hill of Crownarad. This moraine may be linked with the hummocky drift found at the north-east edge of the plateau between Ardara and Aighe.[59] On the coastal slope near Carrigan Head 8 km (5 miles) west of Shalwy exposures of older drift were mapped where periglacial structures were recorded.

In central Ireland the dissolution of the last glaciation ice sheet was associated with the formation of long esker chains. Some of these have been interpreted as retreat moraines, particularly in the vicinity of Athlone, and between Tuam and Swinford.[60] Examination of these eskers, beside Tullamore, and at Kilnalag, in the Tuam-Swinford system, show that all these features are essentially similar. Lengthy portions of each of these esker chains have the sinuous course and narrow crested ridge form so typical of glacio-fluvial deposition within an ice tunnel, and quite unlike the transverse ice-marginal morainic features that cross them in certain places. Typically, an esker system is similar to a river drainage system in arrangement, with tributaries converging downstream. Such a pattern is clearly seen in the esker system that extends east from Loughrea, co. Galway, to the Bog of Allen, co. Offaly. Esker deposition evidently extended westwards as the ice cap shrank, laid down by a subglacial drainage system that flowed east. A similar interpretation of the Tuam-Swinford system argues for a northward flow. Field evidence, however, does not support this interpretation as the disposition of the end-moraine west of Lough Mask, co. Mayo, shows that the ice flowed south-westwards, not northwards.[61] If subsequent work on the structure of this esker system shows that the subglacial drainage flowed south, this system would have to be interpreted as a distributary pattern similar to that encountered on deltas. Clearly, the complex pattern of deglaciation in the central lowland has still to be worked out.

Renewed interest as to the precise limits of the last glaciation ice in south-east Ireland has been revived recently as a result of the considerable work being carried out on the opposite shore of the Irish Sea, in Wales. Hitherto only one shelly till, the Ballycroneen till, has been recognised on the east and south coasts of Ireland, whereas two shelly tills have been claimed for west Wales. What has been termed the 'Upper Irish Sea Till' in Wales is the equivalent of the Ballycroneen till on the east coast of Ireland. In Wales it is generally represented with a southern boundary near Fishguard[62] but has been extended even further south.[63] Radiocarbon dates obtained from the shells contained in this till and in its outwash give an age of about 36,000 years B.P.[64], indicating that the ice which picked up these shells advanced since that time. But it has been pointed out that these dates cannot be regarded as absolutely reliable, because of possible contamination.[65] In fact, with the amount of contamination possible in such material, shells many thousands of years older and belonging to the previous glaciation could give such a date.

In Ireland the discovery of organic material caught up in shelly drift at Shortalstown, in south-east co. Wexford has been used as evidence that this drift belongs to the last glaciation, and post-dates the Ballycroneen till of the south coast.[66] This interpretation is based on the fact that these organic beds may conceivably belong to the Last or Eemian Interglacial, but this cannot be regarded as conclusive as the pollen present in the deposit could equally well belong to the Gortian or Hoxnian Interglacial. As matters stand at the moment there are two theories with regard to the age of the shelly tills of the Irish Sea basin. The first considers that two Irish Sea Shelly tills are represented, the younger of which terminates at a 'newer' drift limit across the St George's Channel or further south[67]; and the second that the shelly Irish Sea, Eastern General or Ballycroneen till represents a single unit of older drift age.[68] This older drift predated the younger drift which is represented by a terminal lobe of gravelly drift that expanded across the Wexford coast at Screen Hills, and may have crossed the Welsh coast between Cardigan and Fishguard.[69]

The presence of a very old drift of Clogga age is suggested on the map (Fig. 3.1) as a surface deposit in the middle part of the Leinster Mountains. The drift cover in this area appears to predate the Ballycroneen till but they could, however, be contemporaneous.

CONCLUSION

Knowledge of the extent and nature of each glacial and interglacial episode can be gained only by means of detailed mapping of the morphology of the deposits, the examination of the stratigraphical succession of the drifts observed in natural sections and boreholes, and through the discovery and analysis of organic deposits found within the drifts. So far, detailed drift maps cover only a very small part of Ireland, the counties of Limerick, Carlow, the west part of co. Mayo and parts of counties Londonderry, Antrim, Tyrone and Down; and soil maps only cover the counties of Wexford, Limerick, Carlow and the west part of co. Cork. The drifts of co. Wexford, on which so much of the Irish chronology is based, have never been mapped in detail, but are in the process of being examined.

Future work will be aimed at the elucidation of the pattern of deglaciation of the last ice sheets, the dating of the main retreat stages, and their correlation with the various stages of the local glaciation in the mountains of west co. Cork and co. Kerry, and in counties Wicklow, Mayo, and Donegal. Beyond the present coastline undersea mapping on the continental shelf will, it is hoped, eventually extend the various glacial limits to Britain, thus establishing a better chronology than that used at present.

REFERENCES

1 R. G. West, *Pleistocene geology and biology,* (1968)

2 H. Carvill Lewis, *The glacial geology of Great Britain and Ireland,* (1894)
J. K. Charlesworth, The glacial retreat from central and southern Ireland, *Quart. Jour. Geol. Soc. London,* 84 (1928), 294–300

3 A. Farrington, The glacial drifts of the district of Enniskerry, co. Wicklow, *Proc. Roy. Irish Acad.,* 50 B (1944), 133–57

4 A. Farrington, The granite drift near Brittas, on the border between co. Dublin and co. Wicklow, *Proc. Roy. Irish Acad.,* 47 B (1942), 279–91

5 A. Farrington, Glacial Lake Blessington, *Irish Geography,* 3 (1957), 216–22

6 A. Farrington, The last glacial episode in the Wicklow mountains, *Irish Nat. Jour.,* 19 (1966), 226–29

7 W. B. Wright and H. B. Muff, The pre-glacial raised beach of the south coast of Ireland, *Sci. Proc. Roy. Dublin Soc.,* 10 (1904), 250–324

8 A. Farrington, (1944), op. cit.

9 G. F. Mitchell, The Pleistocene history of the Irish Sea, *Adv. Science,* 68 (1960), 313–25

10 F. M. Synge, Some problems concerned with the glacial succession in south-east Ireland, *Irish Geography,* 5 (1964), 73–82

11 W. A. Watts, Interglacial deposits at Kilbeg and Newtown, co. Waterford, *Proc. Roy. Irish Acad.,* 60 B (1959), 79–134

12 G. F. Mitchell, Summer field meeting in Wales and Ireland, *Proc. Geol. Ass.,* 73 (1962), 197–213

13 A. Farrington, A note on the correlation of the Kerry-Cork glaciations with those of the rest of Ireland, *Irish Geography,* 5 (1954), 161–72
A. Farrington and N. Stephens, The Pleistocene geomorphology of Ireland, in J. A. Steers, ed., *Field Studies in the British Isles,* (1964), 446–61
A. Farrington, The early-glacial raised beach in co. Cork, *Sci. Proc. Roy. Dublin Soc.,* Ser. A, 2 (1966), 197–219

14 A. Farrington, (1966), op. cit.
N. Stephens and F. M. Synge, Pleistocene shorelines, in G. H. Dury, ed., *Essays in Geomorphology,* (1966), 1–51

15 A. Farrington, A note on the correlation of the Kerry-Cork glaciations with those of the rest of Ireland, *Irish Geography,* 3 (1954), 47–53

16 F. M. Synge, (1964), op. cit.

17 W. A. Watts, (1959), op. cit.

18 K. Jessen, S. T. Andersen, and A. Farrington, The interglacial deposit neart Gort, co. Galway, Ireland, *Proc. Roy. Irish Acad.,* 60 B (1959), 1–77

19 G. F. Mitchell, (1962), op. cit.

20 G. F. Mitchell, quoted in H. E. Wilson, Geology of the Irish Sea area, *Irish Nat. Jour.*, 16 (1968), 102–05

21 F. M. Synge, The glaciation of west co. Mayo, *Irish Geography*, 5 (1968), 372–386

22 G. F. Mitchell, This tentative interpretation was made during a field study tour in co. Wexford in April 1969: a paper is being prepared on this subject by G. F. Mitchell and E. A. Colhoun.

23 M. J. Gardiner, et al., The soils of co. Wexford, *Soil Survey Bulletin No. 1*, National Soil Survey of Ireland (1964), 1–171

24 P. Ryan, et al., The soils of co. Limerick, *Soil Survey Bulletin* No. 16, National Soil Survey of Ireland (1966), 1–199
P. Ryan, et al., The soils of co. Carlow, *Soil Survey Bulletin* No. 17, National Soil Survey of Ireland (1967), 1–204

25 A. Farrington, (1944), op. cit.

26 A. Farrington, Notes on the glacial geology of the glen of Aherlow, *Irish Geography*, 1 (1945), 42–45
F. M. Synge, Glacial geology, in T. Finch and P. Ryan eds., The soils of co. Limerick, *Soil Survey Bulletin* No. 16, National Soil Survey of Ireland (1967)

27 J. K. Charlesworth, The glacial geology of north Mayo and west Sligo, *Proc. Roy. Irish Acad.*, 38 B (1928), 100–15

28 G. H. Kinahan, Glacialoid or re-arranged glacial drift, *Geol. Mag.*, N.S. II, 1 (1874), 111

29 P. Worsley, Fossil frost wedge polygons at Congleton, Cheshire, England, *Geografiska Annaler*, 48 A (1966), 211–19

30 A. Farrington, Local Pleistocene glaciation and the level of the snow line of Croaghaun mountain in Achill Island, co. Mayo, Ireland, *J. Glaciology*, 2 (1953), 262–67

31 F. M. Synge, The glaciation of west Mayo, *Irish Geography*, 5 (1968), 372–386

32 F. M. Synge and N. Stephens, The Quaternary period in Ireland—an assessment, 1960, *Irish Geography*, 4 (1960), 121–30

33 N. Stephens and F. M. Synge, Late-Pleistocene shorelines and drift limits in north Donegal, *Proc. Roy. Irish Acad.*, 64 B (1965), 131–53

34 F. M. Synge and N. Stephens, (1960), op. cit.

35 A. R. Hill and D. B. Prior, Directions of ice movement in north-east Ireland, *Proc. Roy. Irish Acad.*, 66 B (1968), 71–84

36 D. B. Prior, Ice limits in the Cushendun area of north-east co. Antrim. See Chapter IV, 3

37 T. Finch and F. M. Synge, The drifts and soils of west Clare and the adjoining parts of counties Kerry and Limerick, *Irish Geography*, 5 (1966), 161–72

38 F. M. Synge, The glacial deposits around Trim, co. Meath, *Proc. Roy. Irish Acad.*, 53 B (1950), 99–110

39 N. Stephens and F. M. Synge, (1965), op. cit.

40 N. Stephens, Late-glacial sea-levels in north-east Ireland, *Irish Geography*, 4 (1963), 345–59
F. M. Synge and N. Stephens, Late- and post-glacial shorelines and ice limits in Argyll and north-east Ulster, *Trans. Inst. Brit. Geog.*, 39 (1966), 101–25
N. Stephens, Late-glacial and post-glacial shorelines in Ireland and south-west Scotland, *Means of Correlation of Quaternary Successions*, 8 (VII INQUA Congress, 1968), 437–56

41 A. R. Hill and D. B. Prior, (1968), op. cit.

42 D. B. Prior, Late-glacial and post-glacial shorelines in north-east Antrim, *Irish Geography*, 5 (1966), 173–87
F. N. Synge and N. Stephens, (1966), op. cit.

43 D. B. Prior, The late-Pleistocene geomorphology of north-east Antrim, (Unpublished PhD thesis, The Queen's University of Belfast, 1968)

44 J. B. Sissons, *The evolution of Scotland's scenery*, (1967)

45 A. Farrington, (1953), op. cit.
F. M. Synge, The glaciation of the Nephin Beg range, co. Mayo, *Irish Geography*, 4 (1963), 397–403

46 A. Farrington, (1966), op. cit.
47 G. F. Mitchell, The late-glacial flora of Ireland, *Dam. Geol. Unders,* II R, 80 (1954), 73
   G. F. Mitchell, Littleton Bog, Tipperary: an Irish vegetational record, 1–16, in H. E. Wright and
   D. G. Frey, eds., *International Studies on the Quaternary,* (1965)
48 M. E. S. Morrison and N. Stephens, A submerged late-Quaternary deposit at Roddans Port on
   the north-east coast of Ireland, *Phil. Trans. Roy. Soc. London,* 249 (1965), 221–55
49 J. K. Charlesworth, Some observations on the Irish Pleistocene, *Proc. Roy. Irish Acad.,* 62 B (1963),
   295–322
50 A. Farrington, Glacial refuges off the west coast and within the country, *Adv. Science,* 35 (1952), 328
51 F. M. Synge, (1968), op. cit.
52 A. R. Hill, An analysis of the spatial distribution and origin of drumlins in north Down and south
   Antrim, Northern Ireland, (Unpublished PhD thesis, The Queen's University of Belfast, 1968)
53 E. A. Colhoun, The glacial geomorphology of the Sperrin mountains and adjacent areas in co.
   Tyrone, co. Londonderry and co. Donegal, Northern Ireland, (Unpublished PhD thesis, The
   Queen's University of Belfast, 1968)
54 P. Woldstedt, *Das Eiszeitalter,* (1961)
55 J. K. Charlesworth, Some observations on the glaciation of north-east Ireland, *Proc. Roy. Irish
   Acad.,* 45 B (1939), 255–95
56 F. M. Synge and N. Stephens, (1966), op. cit.
57 F. M. Synge (1968), op. cit.
58 A. Guilcher, Observations sur la morphologie littorale de la presquile de Mullet et de la baie le
   Blacksod, Comté de Mayo (Irlande), *Bull. de la Sect. de Géogr.,* 75 (1962), 151–75
59 Memoirs of the Geological Survey of Ireland: sheets 23, 31, (1891)
60 J. K. Charlesworth, (1963), op. cit.
61 J. McManus, The influence of Pleistocene glaciation on the geomorphology of eastern Murrisk,
   co. Mayo, *Sci. Proc. Roy. Dublin Soc.,* Ser. A, 3 (1967), 17–31
   F. M. Synge, (1968), op. cit.
62 J. K. Charlesworth, The south Wales end moraine, *Quart. Jour. Geol. Soc. London,* 85 (1929),
   335–55
   D. Wirtz, Zur stratigraphie des pleistozons in westen die Britischen Inseln, *Neues. Jahrb. Geol. und
   Paläont,* 96 (1953), 267–303
   D. Q. Bowen, On the supposed ice-dammed lakes of South Wales, *Trans. Cardiff Nat. Soc.,* 93
   (1964–66), 1–17
63 B. S. John, Age of raised beach deposits of south-western Britain, *Nature,* 218 (1968), 665–67
64 B. S. John, A possible main Würm glaciation in west Pembrokeshire, *Nature,* 207 (1965), 622–23
65 F. W. Shotton, The problems and contribution of methods of absolute dating within the Pleistocene
   period, *Quart. Jour. Geol. Soc. London,* 122 (1967), 356–83
66 G. F. Mitchell, (1969), op. cit.
67 J. K. Charlesworth, (1929), op. cit.
   D. Q. Bowen, (1966), op. cit.
   B. S. John (1968), op. cit.
68 A. Farrington, (1954), op. cit.
   G. F. Mitchell, (1960), op. cit.
   F. M. Synge, (1964), op. cit.
69 D. Wirtz, (1953), op. cit.

III Ballyduff esker near Tullamore,
co. Offaly, showing the core of the ridge.

IV Flank of Ballyduff esker near Tullamore, co. Offaly,
showing contortions resulting from ice pressures.

V   Till interposed with contorted sands and silts, below blanket peat at Orra Lodge, Glendun, co. Antrim

VI   Details of contortions in till, sand and silts at Orra Lodge, Glendun

IV

THREE LOCAL STUDIES OF THE IRISH PLEISTOCENE

1   The Eskers of the Tullamore district
A. Farrington (with F. M. Synge)

In central Ireland the dissolution of the last ice sheet was associated with the formation of a large number of eskers (Fig. 3.1). There have been few detailed studies of these interesting features, and because conflicting interpretations have been made of the Kilcormac gravel ridge[1] a number of eskers were mapped to the north and south of Tullamore, co. Offaly (Fig. 4.1). It is proposed to describe three eskers and to offer reasons for believing them to have originated in subglacial stream systems during the phased retreat of the ice-front.

THE TULLAMORE ESKERS

Three prominent gravel ridges rise above the alluvial flats and peat bogs of the Central Plain near Tullamore (Fig. 4.1) and each of the sinuous esker ridges will be described in turn.

The Kilcormac (Frankford) esker

This gravel ridge extends almost from the Shannon, past Birr and Kilcormac (Frankford) to Screggan, some 6 km (3.7 miles) south-west of Tullamore; in all the esker runs for 32 km (20 miles), and about 6 km (4 miles) of the north-eastern end of the ridge was examined in detail. The ridge was mapped by the Geological Survey[2] in the nineteenth century, and Sollas[3], in his discussion of the eskers of Ireland, concluded that it was formed by a subglacial stream during the retreat of the ice-front. J. K. Charlesworth[4], however, considered that the ridge was morainic in origin. It is believed that the ridge is a true esker formed by a subglacial stream, thus agreeing with the view expressed by Sollas because, firstly, the portion of the ridge examined was narrow and continuous, and symmetrical in section almost everywhere, secondly, striated stones were absent or very rare, thirdly, belts of end-moraine topography cross the ridge at three points, and fourthly, at its eastern end the ridge terminates in a spread of horizontally bedded gravel.

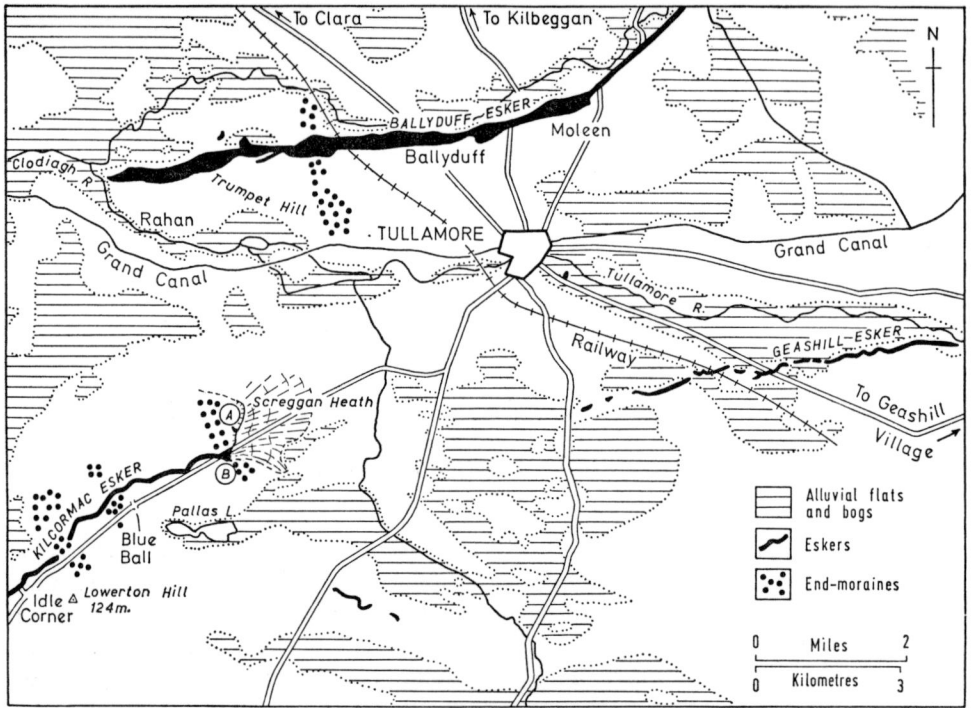

Fig. 4.1   Eskers near Tullamore, co. Offaly

The gravel spread at the end of the esker has a frontal slope of more than 1.6 km (1 mile) and extends in a north-easterly direction to Screggan crossroads. Rather more than 1.6 km (1 mile) across, from north to south, Screggan Heath surface is smooth with a gently inclined slope to the north-east. Here and there shallow winding hollows, like portions of surface valleys, may be seen, and in all the exposures noted the bedding is horizontal.

The crest of the esker is in most places 15 to 18 m (50 to 60 ft) above the surrounding ground: at point A where it joins the gravel spread, there is a deep hollow (Fig. 4.1) which is bounded on the east by a steep escarpment (west-facing) from the top of which the gravels slope gently towards Screggan. The hollow is surrounded on the west and south by a morainic belt, which extends for some distance on either side of the esker. Sollas marked the escarpment on the north as an esker, but the recent fieldwork has led the author to the conclusion that it is not, for it has only one steep side. The escarpment bounding the hollow may be an ice-contact slope. In the hollow there is a jumble of morainic ground, including a small north-south trending gravel ridge, which Sollas showed as continuous with the esker although it lies at right angles to it and at a lower level.

South of the end of the esker at point B the gravel spread is less broken than in the morainic ground in and adjacent to the hollow; nevertheless it is morainic in type and the underlying deposit is gravel. It represents a southern extension of the morainic belt already mentioned. At Blue Ball another morainic belt crosses the esker and consists, on the southern side, of a rough jumble of boulder-strewn mounds passing into a smooth drift ridge beside the rock hill of Lowerton; on the northern side of the esker the terrain consists of rolling hills of drift. Finally near Idle Corner, where the esker rises over the shoulder of Lowerton hill, a morainic belt crosses over the line of the esker and obliterates its characteristic topography for a short distance: but as the morainic topography and the esker topography merge into one another without any recognisable break, it is considered that the deposition was contemporaneous.

It is apparent, from an inspection of the topography in these few miles that the ridge here is a true esker, formed during the retreat stages of the local ice-front, and contemporaneously with the fragments of moraines described. This raises the whole question of the direction of the retreat of the Midland ice-front at this stage: as the observations made are tentative, no final conclusions can be forecast without careful mapping of the whole of the esker and also of the still greater eskers to the north of Tullamore.

The Geashill esker

This small but prominent esker ridge terminates in a peat bog about two miles to the south-east of Tullamore and extends in an easterly direction past Geashill for a total distance of 13 km (8 miles). Of this, 5 km (3 miles) at the western end was mapped in detail. The western end of this ridge is much lower than the other eskers in the area, and averages only 4.5 to 6 m (15 to 20 ft) in height. Both morphologically and structurally it is similar to the Kilcormac esker. Throughout the 5 km (3 miles) examined the ridge was found to follow the southern margin of the peat bogs and alluvial flats that border the Tullamore river; on the side of the esker away from the bogs the ground rises abruptly. Gaps floored by alluvium cut through the ridge in a number of places. Although the Geashill esker terminates at its western end in a bog 6.4 km (4 miles) due east of Screggan, its trend and position suggest that it is related in some way to the Kilcormac esker. At Geashill village, near the south-eastern end of the esker, a moraine crosses the line of the esker and merges into it at the crossing place. This moraine runs north-east—south-west: a second moraine, parallel to it, crosses the esker about 1.6 km (1 mile) south-east of Geashill, at Ballykean.

The Ballyduff esker

The large ridge of gravel, in places 31 m (100 ft) high, that runs from east to west about 3 km (1.8 miles) north of Tullamore has been recorded as the Ballyduff esker by Sollas. The total length of the ridge is 17.6 km (11 miles): the eastern half of it runs from Moleen hill in a north-easterly direction to Judgeville (4 km or 2.5 miles south of Tyrellspass), and this part of the ridge has all the characteristics of a true esker, being a narrow winding ridge of symmetrical cross-section (Plates III and IV).

The esker was examined in detail at three places, Moleen hill, Ballyduff and immediately east of Trumpet hill. Moleen hill and the ridge to the west of it forms a conspicuous feature in places, and reaches a maximum width of a 0.4 km (one quarter mile): the northern slope is steep and in all as much as 31 m (100 ft) high but the southern slopes are much gentler.

Moleen hill, an expansion of the esker, is a steep-sided ridge with a level upper surface pitted by a large number of kettle holes: it is joined to a narrow gravel ridge on the north by several parallel embankments and the depressions between these also resemble kettleholes. At Ballyduff the main road from Tullamore to Clara crosses the esker: here a narrow gravel ridge, typical of esker form is superimposed on a larger ridge which is also of gravel. Immediately to the east of Trumpet hill, the ridge is narrow, and in a large gravel pit perfectly symmetrical arched bedding in sand and fine gravel was revealed. This section shows that the structure is due to initial deposition and there was no sign of slumping. This is the strongest possible indication that the ridge cannot possibly be of morainic origin, as Charlesworth[5] suggested, though the well-defined belt of gravel hillocks that runs transversely across the esker at this point in a north-east—south-west direction is probably morainic. Finally, the western continuation of the esker can be traced as a broad ridge of gravel to the west of Rahan, between the Clodiagh river and the Grand Canal: it terminates abruptly in a bog a short distance farther west.

CONCLUSION

The three gravel ridges described form part of an extensive esker system: each ridge expands and contracts in cross-sectional form, here narrow-crested and sinuous, there plateau-topped and pitted with kettle holes. Arched bedding, sometimes perfectly symmetrical in cross-section, has been recorded, and the ridges appear to be primary depositional features of a type well-known in Ireland.[6] These eskers show considerable similarities with those described near Trim, co. Meath[7], in having associated morainic mounds in contact with them. The disposition of the eskers and associated moraines suggested that near Tullamore the last ice-sheet withdrew towards the west and south-west, the eskers emerging as the ice-edge retreated, and the moraines marking halt-stages in that retreat.

REFERENCES

1 W. J. Sollas, A map to show the distribution of eskers in Ireland, *Sci. Trans. Roy. Dublin Soc.*, Ser. 2, 5 (1896), 785
J. K. Charlesworth, The glacial retreat from central and southern Ireland, *Quart. J. Geol. Soc. London*, 84 (1928), 335
2 Memoirs of the Geological Survey of Ireland, Sheet 109, and 118
3 W. J. Sollas, (1896), op. cit.
4 J. K. Charlesworth, (1928), op. cit.
5 J. K. Charlesworth, (1928), op. cit.
6 G. W. Lamplugh et al., The geology of the country around Belfast, *Memoirs Geol. Survey Ireland,* (1904), 100–103
7 F. M. Synge, The glacial deposits around Trim, co. Meath, *Proc. Roy. Irish Acad.,* 53 B (1950), 99–110

2 The relationship of drumlins to the directions of ice movement in north co. Down

A. R. Hill

The Irish Quaternary Period still presents many unsolved problems to research workers in respect of chronology and of patterns of glaciation and deglaciation. It has been emphasized by F. M. Synge in the previous chapter that many of these problems will only be solved by the application of detailed field work, particularly to certain key areas within the country.

Analysis of the distribution and origin of glacial landforms has been neglected in recent years. The lack of such studies may be attributed in part to the absence of detailed research on the sequences and patterns of glacial episodes. This knowledge constitutes a necessary prerequisite for investigations of a variety of landforms, especially drumlins and eskers, which are important components of the Irish landscape. The following short case study of drumlins in co. Down, Northern Ireland, illustrates that detailed investigations of glacial deposits, using a variety of complementary techniques, can reveal hitherto undiscovered complexities in the sequence of glacial events and also in the formation of glacial landforms.

Recent investigations suggest that two major till sheets are present throughout north Down and south Antrim.[1] A lower and upper till have been differentiated on the basis of colour and texture, carbonate content, erratic content and till fabric analysis. Both tills are probably of last glaciation age. Shells from within the lower till have been radiocarbon dated as 24,050 ± 650 years B.P. (Isotopes Inc. New Jersey I 3268).

Till fabrics, striae and erratics were used to study directions of ice-flow in both tills. They reveal a complex history of ice movement within the area. The lower till was deposited by an ice-sheet flowing from the North Channel and diverging in a fan across north co. Down and south co. Antrim (Fig. 4.2). In north co. Down the main direction of ice movement was from the north and north-east. There is no clear evidence to suggest that there was a direct movement from Scotland across the North Channel and it is therefore inadvisable to refer to the ice-sheet as being of Scottish origin. Instead, this ice movement is described in the following paragraphs as North Channel ice. The upper till in north co. Down and south co. Antrim was deposited by an Irish ice-sheet fanning out from the Lough Neagh basin (Fig. 4.2). In north co. Down ice-flow was from the west and north-west.

The Drumlins

Drumlins are widely distributed throughout north co. Down, occupying an area of 1,600 km² (620 sq miles) containing approximately 3,900 drumlins. The co. Down drumlins form part of a larger drumlin field which extends westwards across counties Armagh, Monaghan and Cavan and north-westwards into counties Fermanagh and Donegal. It is surprising that there has been little investigation of the drumlins in this region, which forms

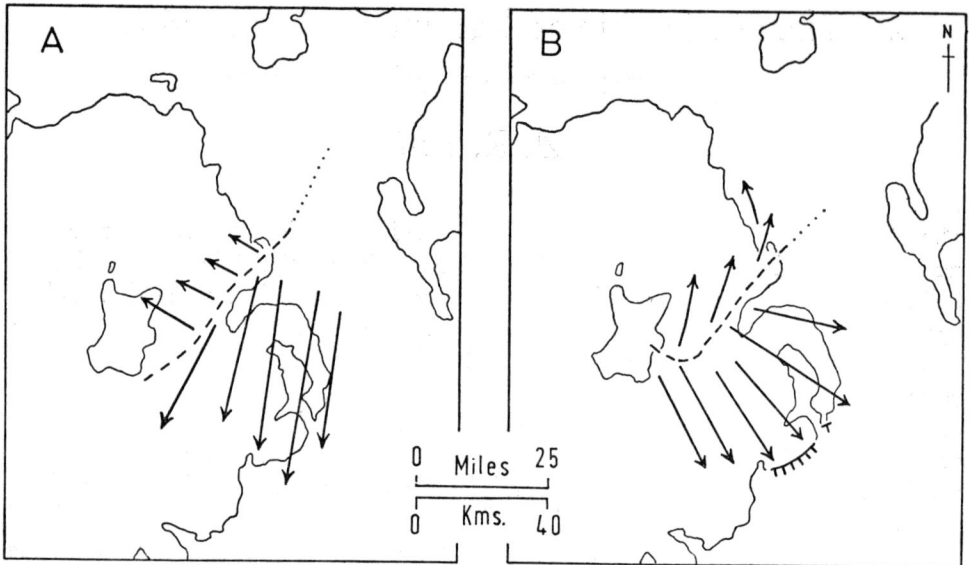

Fig. 4.2   Summary of the directions of ice movement during the Last Glaciation (A—phase 1, Lower
Till, and B—phase 2, Upper Till)

the type area for the drumlin landform. The first general study of drumlins in co. Down
was made by Charlesworth, as part of a wider study on the deglaciation of north-east
Ireland.[2] The drumlins were mapped by ground survey on a scale of one inch to one mile
and a distribution map was subsequently published at a scale of one-quarter inch to one
mile. The drumlins in co. Down were shown to trend north-north-west to south-south-
east and were thought to have been formed during the maximum of the last glaciation
(Plate XV).

More recently a detailed study of the orientation of drumlins in the Ards peninsula and
Strangford Lough area has been made from 1:20,000 air photographs.[3] This study suggested
that a number of zones of different drumlin orientation are present in the area mapped. A
zone of north to south trending drumlins was discovered to the east of Bangor in the north
Ards peninsula. In the remainder of the area the zones of drumlin orientation were west to
east or north-west to south-east. On the basis of drumlin orientation Vernon concluded that
the region was dominated by a strong flow of Irish ice from the north-west, with a weak
flow of Scottish ice present only in the north of the Ards peninsula. These two ice-sheets
were thought to be contemporaneous, the Irish ice forming the drumlins with north-west
to south-east orientations while the Scottish ice formed the north-south trending drumlins.

A detailed investigation has been made of the spatial distribution and origin of drumlins
in north Down and south Antrim.[4] One aspect of this study dealt with the orientation of
drumlins throughout the area. It was hoped that an assessment of the degree of correlation
between drumlin trend and other criteria of ice-flow direction would reveal the time of

drumlin formation within a glaciation, as well as the way in which orientation is modified by variations in ice-flow direction.

The drumlins were mapped from 1:20,000 air photographs on to six inch to one mile base maps. The orientation of all drumlins with a length to width ratio of 3:2 or greater was measured to the nearest 5 degrees on the base maps. This data was then transferred to the corresponding kilometre grid squares of the one inch to one mile maps for the area. The mean orientation was calculated for the drumlin trends within each grid square. There was considerable homogeneity of mean orientation in neighbouring grid cells and it was possible to outline a number of areas of drumlins with similar alignments by inspection (Fig. 4.3).

The drumlins in Area 1 (Fig. 4.3) have a mean orientation of 18.9 degrees and a standard deviation of ± 22.69 degrees. The evidence from till fabrics, erratics and striae suggests that the North Channel ice flowed across this area from the north and north-east, while at a later date Irish ice flowed from the west and north-west. It is obvious therefore that the long axes of the drumlins in Area 1 show a marked lack of correspondence with the flow direction of Irish ice, the most recent ice-sheet to cover the area. On the other hand, the orientation of the drumlins appears to correspond closely with the direction of flow of the North Channel ice. The Kolmogorov-Smirnov Test[5] was used to compare the cumulative frequency curve for the drumlin long axes and the curve for the sixty-four mean orientations of the fabrics analysed within the lower till. The D maximum value is .033 while the 95th percentile for the test is .204. Therefore the null hypothesis is accepted that the lower till fabrics and the drumlin orientations in Area 1 do not differ significantly.

The drumlins in the remainder of north Down can be divided into a number of zones with mean orientations ranging from 290.7° ± 17.82° to 336.2° ± 15.04°. It would appear that the orientation of these drumlins corresponds to the direction of flow of the Irish ice-sheet. Analysis of the internal structure and composition of drumlins confirms this view. These orientation zones have therefore been grouped together in figure 4.3 to differentiate them from the zone of north-south trending drumlins whose history of formation is less easily explained.

The lack of agreement between the drumlin trend in Area 1 and the direction of Irish ice-flow across north co. Down may be explained by a number of hypotheses. Vernon[6] suggested that the drumlins in Area 1 were formed contemporaneously with those in other areas of north Down by North Channel ice which only penetrated into the extreme north of the Ards peninsula and was confluent with the Irish ice-sheet. Detailed field work has not substantiated this view. The upper till deposited by Irish ice, flowing from the west and north-west, rests upon the lower till throughout north co. Down including Area 1. The stratigraphic evidence, together with the uniform direction of ice-flow shown by the mean orientation of the upper till fabrics in the north Ards peninsula, indicates that there was no confluence of the two ice-sheets in this area.

DISCUSSION

A number of other possibilities remain to be examined. Firstly, the features in Area 1 may

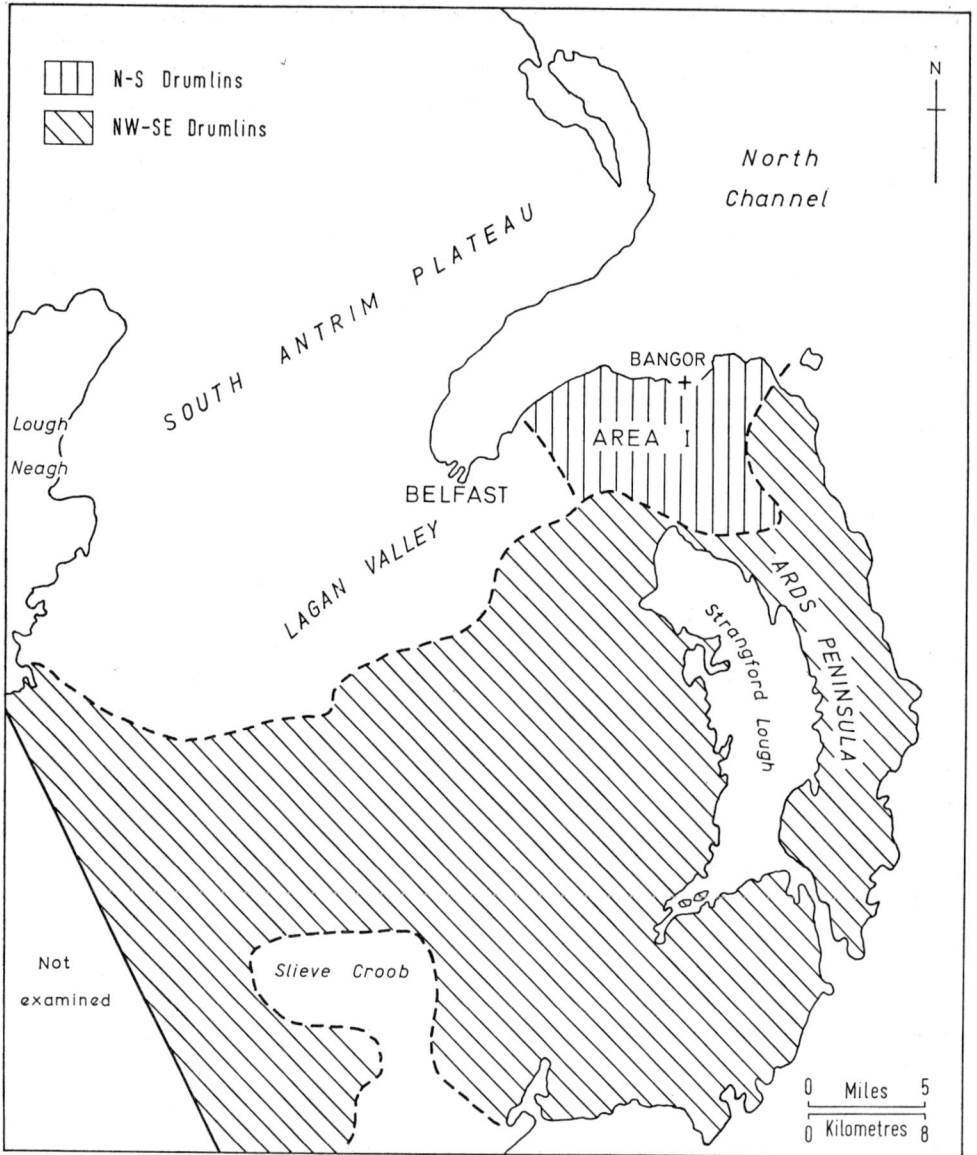

Fig. 4.3   Drumlin orientation zones in northern co. Down

not be drumlins. However, scrutiny of their surface form, dimensions, and internal structure, indicates that these features agree in all respects with the generally accepted definition of the drumlin landform. Secondly, it is possible that there was a late movement of relatively 'clean' Irish ice from the north which re-orientated the drumlins without depositing any till.

But it seems highly probable that ice which could re-orientate the drumlins would also produce a north to south orientation of pebbles in the superficial layers. A third hypothesis is that the drumlins in Area 1 were formed by the North Channel ice and were subsequently covered by Irish ice, which failed to destroy or re-orientate the majority of the drumlins. The possibility that drumlins can be overridden by a later ice-sheet flowing from a different direction without destruction has been advocated occasionally in the literature on drumlins.[7] This hypothesis has been examined in relation to other characteristics of the drumlins in north Down.

Analysis of the stoss ends of drumlins, both in the field and on air photographs, shows that the majority of drumlins in north co. Down have the stoss end facing towards the north-west, from which direction the Irish ice-sheet flowed. In contrast, the drumlins in Area 1 have stoss ends which face towards the north and north-east, and the superficial form of the drumlins is subdued, the features being generally low in height, with gentle side slopes and indistinct basal outlines. Although these characteristics have not been quantified for detailed comparison, they appear to be in sharp contrast to drumlins developed elsewhere in north co. Down. The evidence of form is consistent with the view that these drumlins in Area 1 are somewhat older, and have been overridden by a later ice-sheet, which blurred the original sharpness of their surface form. A number of drumlins, which show evidence of the reshaping of an original north to south axis by ice flowing from the north-west, can be found particularly in the transitional zone separating the drumlins of Area 1 from those further south in co. Down.

A detailed study was made also of the internal composition and structure of drumlins in north co. Down, utilising river sections and railway and road cuttings. Seventy drumlins were examined, eleven of which were located in Area 1. All the drumlins examined in this area were composed mainly of the lower till, the upper till forming only a thin surface layer 0.9 to 1.8 m (3 to 6 ft) in thickness. In contrast, the drumlins examined elsewhere in north co. Down either consisted entirely of the upper till or else contained a core of lower till which was covered by a considerable thickness of the upper till. Till fabrics analysed within the lower till in the drumlins of Area 1 generally exhibited mean orientations ranging between north and north-east, corresponding closely to the long axis trends of the drumlins. A number of till fabrics examined in the thin layer of upper till which covered these drumlins did not display any preferred orientation, the distribution of pebble long axes being non-significant when tested using Chi-Square. In a few cases fabrics were found which displayed north-east to south-west trends, similar to the fabrics in the lower till within the drumlins. However, a large number of fabrics in the upper till had north-west to south-east mean orientations.

The evidence from the internal composition of the drumlins in Area 1 suggests that the features were formed during the earlier advance of North Channel ice, and that a later advance of Irish ice flowed across the area depositing a generally thin layer of till over the pre-existing drumlins and inter-drumlin areas. The detailed fabric analyses indicate that on some portions of the drumlins the Irish ice did not disrupt earlier preferred orientations, while elsewhere disruption resulted in random fabrics in the superficial layers.

There appear to be no significant differences between Area 1 and the remainder of north co. Down in the character of the underlying geology and topography. It is therefore probable that the preservation of older drumlins in Area 1 is related more to the physical and dynamic conditions of the Irish ice-sheet rather than to the characteristics of the underlying terrain. Differences in thickness, velocity or debris load of the Irish ice-sheet between these two areas of north co. Down may have produced the contrast in drumlin development. The failure of the Irish ice to destroy drumlins previously formed by North Channel ice suggests that velocity in particular may have been a significant factor.

The orientation strength of till fabrics can be computed using a Chi-Square test[8], which provides a measure of the concentration of the data in class intervals. This parameter of the till fabric is probably related in part to velocity of ice-flow, high orientation strengths indicating high velocities of flow.[9] The orientation strengths of twenty-five fabrics from the upper till in Area 1 were compared with twenty-six fabrics from the upper till in the remainder of north Down, using the rank-sum test.[10] The results indicate a significant difference at the 95 per cent level, the orientation strengths of the till fabrics in Area 1 being much lower than elsewhere in north co. Down. This suggests that the Irish ice-sheet was flowing at a slower rate in this area compared with the remainder of north co. Down.

CONCLUSION

The majority of drumlins in north co. Down were formed by an Irish ice-sheet radiating outwards from the Lough Neagh lowlands. However, analysis of orientation, morphology and composition indicates that the drumlins in the north Ards peninsula were formed by North Channel ice at an earlier date within the last glaciation. These drumlins have survived the later Irish ice movement across the area.

The currently held view is that the majority of Irish drumlins were formed at a late stage of the last glaciation. This idea is inherent in the concept of a single Drumlin re-advance.[11] The relatively complex history of drumlin development in north Down suggests that detailed research should be undertaken on other drumlin areas within Ireland, before the contemporaneity of the Irish drumlins can be accepted without reservation.

REFERENCES

1 A. R. Hill and D. B. Prior, Directions of ice movement in north-east Ireland, *Proc. Roy. Irish Acad.*, 66 B (1968), 71–84
2 J. K. Charlesworth, Some observations on the glaciation of north-east Ireland, *Proc. Roy. Irish Acad.*, 45 B (1939), 255–95
3 P. Vernon, Drumlins and Pleistocene ice flow over the Ards peninsula/Strangford Lough area, County Down, Ireland, *J. Glaciology*, 6, Part 45 (1966), 401–9
4 A. R. Hill, An analysis of the spatial distribution and origin of drumlins in north Down and south Antrim, Northern Ireland, (Unpublished PhD thesis, Queen's University Belfast, 1968)
5 S. Siegel, *Nonparametric statistics for the behavioural sciences,* (New York, 1956)
6 P. Vernon, (1966), op. cit.

7 S. E. Hollingworth, The glaciation of western Edenside and adjoining areas and the drumlins of Edenside and the Solway basin, *Quart. J. Geol. Soc. London*, 87 (1931), 281–359

L. W. Currier, Tills of eastern Massachusetts, *Bull. Geol. Soc. Am.*, 52 (1941), 1895–6 (abst.)

J. H. Moss, Two tills in Massachusetts, *Bull. Geol. Soc. Am.*, 54 (2) (1943) 1826 (abst.)

8 J. T. Andrews and B. B. Smithson, Till fabrics of the cross-valley moraines of north-central Baffin Island, Northwest Territories, Canada, *Bull. Geol. Soc. Am.*, 77 (1966), 271–90

9 S. A. Harris, Till fabrics and speed of movement of the Arapahoe glacier, Colorado, *Professional Geographer*, 70 (1968), 195–8

10 W. J. Dixon and F. J. Massey, *Introduction to statistical analysis,* (2nd ed., New York, 1951)

11 See F. M. Synge in previous chapter

3   Ice limits in the Cushendun area of north-east co. Antrim

D. B. Prior

The extent of the ice cover in different parts of north-east Ireland has often been debated.[1] Recent work in north-east co. Antrim has located some possible ice limits based upon several distinct types of evidence.[2] Detailed field mapping of a variety of landforms at a scale of 1:10,000 has been supplemented by analysis of till, glacio-fluvial and slope deposits. Samples of approximate weight 2 kg (4 lbs) were sieved and the rock fragments greater than 6 mm (0.24 ins) in diameter were identified and counted. The amount of each rock type present was expressed as a percentage of the total count. The results of this work near Cushendun, co. Antrim will now be discussed (Fig. 4.4).

The area includes two major valleys, Glenaan and Glendun which begin on Tertiary basalt bedrock near Trostan mountain, before crossing a thin outcrop of Cretaceous chalk at approximately 305 m (1,000 ft). The central part of each valley is incised into Dalradian schists while sandstones outcrop along the coast between Cushendun and Cushendall.

The coastal till and its limits

A fresh, unweathered till mantle is confined to the lowland coastal areas between Cushendall and Cushendun. It achieves a maximum thickness of 3 to 5 m (10 to 17 ft) on the slopes of Cross Slieve although, in general, bedrock is near the surface. The till contains up to 60 per cent sandstone fragments, derived from Triassic sandstone near Cushendall and the Old Red Sandstone which forms Cross Slieve hill. The glacial deposits are distinctively bright red in colour and have a sandy texture. Local erratic fans, including a grey felstone porphyry which outcrops south of Cushendall and red Cushendun microgranite suggest that this sediment was deposited by ice moving in a predominantly northward direction along the coast of Antrim. Till fabric analysis supported this interpretation.[3]

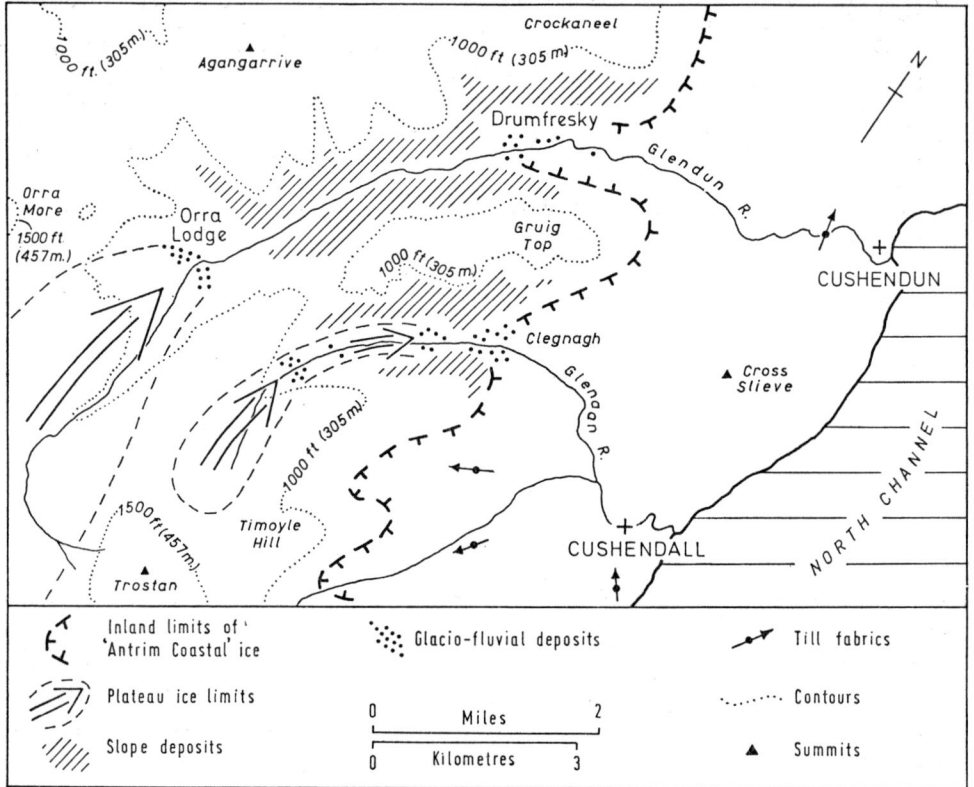

Fig. 4.4 Glacial geomorphology of Glendun and Glenaan, north-east co. Antrim

In addition, analyses of the rock contents of the glacial deposits revealed a carriage of sandstone, porphyry and microgranite erratics inland on to schist bedrock in lower Glenaan and as far as Drumfresky in Glendun. This shows that coastal ice followed the valleys inland, deviating westwards from the main south to north axis of movement.

There is, however, a very distinct inland and upslope limit of this 'Antrim Coastal' till. It is not present on the slopes of Glenaan inland from Clegnagh, nor in Glendun beyond Drumfresky. A sharp till limit was traced southwards from Glenaan along the slopes of Timoyle hill between 150 and 200 m (500 and 650 ft). This limit marks the upslope margins of arable agriculture and the beginning of peaty heath-land where schist and basalt rock outcrops are common. The influence of basalt bedrock at the surface is well seen near Timoyle hill where there are multiple scarps formed by the outcrop of numerous resistant basaltic sheets. Weathering products include coarse angular block accumulations below 'trap' features but till is completely absent. The summit of Trostan mountain shows a pavement of badly weathered basalt debris.

Coastal sandstone, porphyry and granite erratics are absent on the slopes above the till limit and they were not detected in analyses of deposits at nine sites in the valleys inland of Clegnagh and Drumfresky. Likewise, no erratics were observed on the summits of Timoyle hill, Trostan, Gruig Top, Agangarrive and Crockaneel.

Moreover, in both lower Glenaan and lower Glendun there are substantial accumulations of sand and gravel in the valley floors. At Clegnagh a series of sharp-crested ridges cross the valley. They are most pronounced at 60 to 65 m (200 to 218 ft), but hummocky, interbedded sands and gravels continue upvalley to 91 m (300 ft), as revealed by exposures in the banks of the Glenaan river. Sandstone erratics are common in these deposits which are interpreted as ice-marginal morainic accumulations. In Glendun similar deposits fill the valley floor near Drumfresky. There are several large mounds and a distinct, winding ridge which runs parallel to the valley road. Excavations in the ridge showed typical ice-contact glacio-fluvial deposits with interbedded fine sands and coarse gravels accompanied by multiple small scale faults. Analyses revealed up to 4 per cent sandstone fragments some 3 km (1.9 miles) inland from the schist/sandstone contact and a few pieces of Cushendun microgranite were also observed. Neither of these erratics were observed up-valley from Drumfresky and consequently those in the ice-contact gravels represent the maximum inland transport of coastal erratics in Glendun.

The plateau ice and its limits

Another group of glacial sediments is present in the upper parts of the Glendun and Glenaan valleys. These have been interpreted as evidence for the former presence of a local Antrim plateau ice cap.[4] Dark brown, unweathered till was observed over schist bedrock at an altitude of 250 m (720 ft) in the floor of Glenaan. It contained 57 per cent schistose debris with basalt (29 per cent), chalk (11 per cent) and flint (3 per cent). These erratics were apparently derived from the nearby chalk and basalt rocks which outcrop above about 305 m (1,000 ft) in the upper Glenaan valley. Calcareous till with basalt (5 per cent), chalk (1 per cent) and flint (4 per cent), but no coastal sandstone erratics, was also exposed in the valley floor 1.6 km (1 mile) downvalley from the basalt/chalk/schist contacts. This shows that the ice which deposited the till must have moved downvalley, probably from the basin-shaped area on the northern slopes of Trostan mountain. This is supported by the presence of basalt and chalk fragments in the Glenaan valley 0.5 km (0.3 miles) from the chalk outcrop.[5] However, both erratics and till associated with this plateau top ice are confined to the valley floor and were not found below 150 m (500 ft).

The valley floor between 150 and 305 m (500 and 1,000 ft) also contains patches of sand and gravel with basalt and flint. There are several small terrace fragments above 150 m (500 ft) but at 250 m (720 ft) the river cuts through prominent arcuate ridges. There are two main ridges which both make convex curves downvalley. They are also asymmetrical in form with steep inner, up-valley slopes, contrasting with the outer slopes which grade imperceptibly into the adjacent valley sides. These ridges, together with subsidiary hummocks and terraces further downvalley are considered to be associated with the Glenaan valley glacier which distributed the basalt, chalk and flint erratics. The asymmetry of the ridges confirms this, the steeper up-valley sides being interpreted as ice-contact or proximal slopes.

Brown till with basalt, chalk and flint erratics was observed in Glendun between 250 and 290 m (720 and 850 ft) near Orra Lodge. Since the basalt and chalk outcrops lie further up-valley this shows that ice also moved northwards and north-eastwards from the high basin area between Trostan and Orra More. Neither till nor erratics were observed down-valley below Orra Lodge, except those deposits associated with coastal ice at Drumfresky. At Orra Lodge prominent ridges and hummocks fill the valley floor. Recent excavations have revealed blanket peat covering suites of gravels and sands with large masses of intruded till to a total thickness of 7 m (23 ft). The cross-bedded gravels contained large sand and silt lenses, but the main sediment was an extensive sheet of finely bedded silts and sands exhibiting multiple sets of climbing ripples. Where till had been interposed the silts and sands were highly contorted and overthrust (Plates V and VI). Analysis of the gravels showed up to 4 per cent basalt, 2 per cent chalk and 3 per cent flint, with schistose material dominant. While the bedded materials reflect a variety of conditions of water/sediment supply, their close association with the till shows that they may be interpreted as ice-marginal glacio-fluvial deposits.

Slope deposits in Glenaan and Glendun

The smooth, valley-side slopes in both valleys are covered with a stony schistose rubble which is very different in appearance and rock-type content from both the plateau till and the coastal till. It is composed almost entirely of weathered schist fragments and white vein quartz. A few, scattered flint fragments are the only erratics but it is emphasized that these are very scarce. The schist particles are usually subangular and set in a sandy matrix of mica flakes. The deposits are often crudely stratified with poorly defined bedding which consistently dips downslope. Imbrication of the fragments is common but many of the schist particles are badly decomposed.

There are numerous exposures in this slope cover but the best are those cut by tributary streams which flow southwards to the Glendun river between Drumfresky and Orra Lodge. In one of these stream gullies the deposit is 5 m (17 ft) thick. Some stratification was present with a coarse upper layer covering a fine, angular schist gravel, which in turn overlay a basal layer rich in quartz. The junctions between the layers were indistinct but dips of up to 15 degrees downslope were recorded. A large proportion of the fragments in the middle layer were orientated with their long axes parallel to the slope. The angular quartz fragments in the basal layer became more numerous upslope towards a thick quartz vein which crossed the floor of the gully. The basal quartz appeared to have been derived from this source since the fragments decreased in size and number for a distance of 14 m (46 ft) downslope from the vein. This downslope trail of quartz closely resembles 'shoding', and suggests that the slope debris has been subject to mass-movement.[6]

It is notable that this kind of material is restricted to very definite areas within the valleys. It is not found at all in the coastal lowlands or in those areas covered by glacial deposits associated with the plateau ice. Rather it is confined exclusively to the schist slopes in middle

Glenaan and Glendun. It is thickest at the base of the slopes, near the valley floor and thins out against the slopes between 270 and 305 m (790 and 1,000 ft). Above this, blanket peat overlies a weathered schist surface with numerous large, angular schist blocks.

DISCUSSION

The glacial deposits in the Cushendun area are believed to have been produced by ice of the last (Weichsel) glacial period.[7] The depths of weathering and soil development on the till and glacio-fluvial deposits never exceed 1.5 m (5 ft). Also, all the morainic ridges and hummocks are fresh in appearance and have not been extensively dissected since their formation. The evidence from erratics and till fabric analyses also demonstrates the former existence of ice flows from two separate sources. In both Glendun and Glenaan ice moved downvalley from sources on the plateau near Trostan mountain. A flow up-valley was associated with a major ice flow northwards along the coast and inland over the coastal lowlands.

In addition, it would appear that each flow had its own distinct limits. Certainly, the inland and upslope limit of coastal till is very sharp. While this type of evidence has been used to infer the positions of ice margins it is known that till limits alone are not always indicative of ice limits.[8]

However, in the Cushendun area the coastal till limit also represents the maximum inland transport of coastal erratics. There is, in effect, a sharp erratic limit, beyond which sandstone, porphyry and granite fragments are absent. Further, the till/erratic limit is coincident with the location of morainic sands and gravels at Clegnagh and Drumfresky. Since these are interpreted as ice contact kame moraine, the remarkable agreement in the locations of these three different types of evidence is taken to indicate firmly the inland limit of the coastal ice. A similar association of till/erratic limits and morainic glacio-fluvial deposits can also be used to delimit the positions of the margins of the plateau ice, at Orra Lodge in Glendun and downvalley to 150 m (500 ft) in Glenaan.

Parts of the upland plateau surface, including both basalt and schist bedrock areas, do not fall within these ice limits. Thus, if the interpretations are valid, large areas of Glendun and Glenaan were not glaciated either by coastal or plateau ice during the last glaciation. This is substantiated by the distribution and characteristics of the slope deposits in the area above the coastal ice limits and below those of the plateau ice. The trail of quartz downslope points to mass-movement in the basal layers of the slope deposits. The imbrication of the particles and the crude stratification parallel to the slope can also be explained in this way.[9] Contemporary slope processes do not provide sufficient mass-movement to account for the thickness of accumulated debris at the base of the slopes, or the angular, weathered nature of the particles. It seems most probable that these deposits are the combined result of intensive weathering of the schist bedrock together with widespread gravitational creep downslope. Thus, the deposits may be described as 'head'[10], formed in areas free from ice during the last glacial period.

The rare flint fragments found in the slope debris may have been distributed during the more widespread, earlier Saale glaciation.[11] Since flint is extremely resistant to weathering it may have survived to be incorporated into the weathered schist debris.

The total evidence of a variety of landforms and deposits in the Cushendun area suggests that parts of the Antrim plateau escaped glaciation during the Weichsel period. Coastal ice abutted against the eastern edge of the plateau to a maximum of only 200 m (650 ft), but penetrated inland a distance of 5 km (3 miles) in lower Glendun. Two small valley glaciers flowed downvalley but stopped short of the area covered by the coastal ice. Even in Glenaan where the separate ice limits are only 0.2 km (0.1 miles) apart there is no stratigraphical evidence to show whether the coastal ice and the plateau ice were exactly contemporaneous.

REFERENCES

1 F. M. Synge and N. Stephens, The Quaternary period in Ireland—an assessment, *Irish Geography*, 4 (1960), 121–30
J. K. Charlesworth, Some observations on the glaciation of north-east Ireland, *Proc. Roy. Irish Acad.*, 45 B (1939), 255–95
J. K. Charlesworth, Some observations on the Irish Pleistocene, *Proc. Roy. Irish Acad.*, 62 B (1963), 295–322
2 D. B. Prior, The late-Pleistocene geomorphology of north-east Antrim, (Unpublished PhD thesis, Queen's University, Belfast, 1968)
A. R. Hill and D. B. Prior, Directions of ice movement in north-east Ireland, *Proc. Roy. Irish Acad.*, 66 B (1968), 71–84
3 Ibid.
4 A. R. Dwerryhouse, The glaciation of north-east Ireland, *Quart. J. Geol. Soc. London*, 79 (1923), 352–422
J. K. Charlesworth, (1939), op. cit.
D. B. Prior, (1968), op. cit.
5 Geological Survey of Ireland. Manuscript map No. 14, 1886
6 H. G. Dines et al., The mapping of head deposits, *Geol. Mag.*, 77 (1940), 198–226
7 A. R. Hill and D. B. Prior, (1968), op. cit.
8 F. M. Synge, The glaciation of the Nephin Beg range, co. Mayo, *Irish Geography*, 4 (1963), 397–403
9 J. M. Ragg and J. S. Bibby, Frost weathering and solifluction products in southern Scotland, *Geogr. Annaler*, 48 A (1966), 12–23
10 H. G. Dines et al., (1940), op. cit.
11 J. K. Charlesworth, (1939), op. cit.

V

LATE- AND POST-GLACIAL VEGETATIONAL AND CLIMATIC HISTORY OF IRELAND: A REVIEW

A. G. Smith

THE NATURE OF THE EVIDENCE

Any attempt to work out the climatic conditions of the past from biological evidence is fraught with difficulties. This is particularly the case when the periods in question have differed only slightly from the present. Even though we may know that a plant or animal was present during some period of time, it is often almost impossible to be certain that it was absent at some other time. In addition, we have to argue backwards from present biogeography, but the relationship of present climatic conditions to the present distribution of plants and animals is by no means always clear. The climatic tolerances and requirements of organisms may also have changed. The first problem, however, is to discover the nature of the plant and animal communities of the periods under consideration. The macrofossils preserved in peat and lake deposits can generally be taken as reflecting rather local conditions, and often give a specific indication of presence. Nevertheless, even such cumbersome objects as tree trunks or antlers will sometimes have been secondarily deposited. Airborne microfossils, such as pollen, which have been blown into accumulating deposits will probably, in the main, have come from within a few kilometres, although in some cases from much greater distances.

Macroscopic remains, particularly seeds and fruits, have the advantage that they can usually be identified as closely as the species; in many cases they are as characteristic as the whole plant. Identification of pollen, however, can generally be carried only as far as the genus. For instance, it is possible to say that a particular pollen grain belongs to the elm (genus *Ulmus*) but impossible to say whether it belongs to *Ulmus glabra* (the wych elm) or *Ulmus procera* (the English elm). Closer identifications of individual pollen grains will, however, almost certainly be obtained by use of the recently developed scanning electron microscope.[1] Fortunately, the pollen of the native tree genera is readily recognizable under the light microscope, as is the pollen of many genera of herbaceous plants. There are, nevertheless, many instances in which pollen can be identified only to the level of the family.

Despite these limitations, valuable results can be obtained using the technique of pollen analysis. This technique, which should preferably be used in conjunction with a stratigraphic study and analysis of macrofossils, is essentially simple. It consists of taking a series of superposed samples through a suitable deposit and treating them chemically so that as much as possible of the matrix is removed. The pollen and other insoluble material is then mounted on microscope slides and examined systematically. For each sample a record is made of the number of each pollen type present until some predetermined number is reached. All the pollen analytic results for Ireland have so far been expressed on the basis of some particular 'pollen sum' rather than on an absolute basis. The 'pollen sum' generally used has been simply the total number of tree pollen grains. The results have been expressed as a percentage of this number and plotted against depth to form a so-called pollen diagram. Many of the diagrams used in this chapter have, however, been calculated on the basis of total land-plant pollen, a method which has certain advantages.

DIVISIONS OF THE POST-GLACIAL PERIOD

Two schemes of sub-division of the Irish post-glacial are available, though both are to some extent unsatisfactory. Both schemes employ a system of numbered 'zones' based on pollen analytic and lithological criteria. In the scheme devised by Jessen[2] names for these zones were either coined anew, or adopted from the terminology of the early Swedish workers Blytt and Sernander. Their terms—Boreal, Atlantic, Sub-boreal and Sub-atlantic— were intended to have climatic implications and referred essentially to tree-containing and treeless layers in Scandinavian peat mires. The use of these terms became extended to cover periods of vegetational history later distinguished from pollen diagrams. These periods were not precisely the same, but nevertheless the climatic implications, of alternating continental and oceanic conditions, became attached to the periods of vegetational history. Even in the face of the classic world-wide study of Von Post[3], the originator of the pollen analysis technique, showing only a general three-fold division of the post-glacial, these climatic implications have tended to persist in use. In applying the terms to the Irish post-glacial, Jessen made it clear that they were used essentially as names for periods of time and not periods of duration of various types of climate. Because the terms are now entrenched in the literature, and in general use, they will be used again here, but without any climatic implications, and without the implication that the zones are exactly coeval across the country.

The summary in table 1 gives the more important features of the two zonation schemes together with some general notes. The more recent scheme of Mitchell[4] follows Jessen's scheme in all essentials as far as the transition between zones VI and VII, although emphasizing the relationship of high hazel and elm pollen values to calcareous regions. Up to this point only Jessen's scheme is given. After zone VI both schemes are given since they are markedly different. Mitchell's scheme is based entirely on the supposed effects of human activity after Atlantic time.

TABLE I

LATE-GLACIAL TIME

ZONE I   The Older *Salix herbacea* period
Very little pollen. Clayey deposit resting on glacigenous deposits.

ZONE II   The late-glacial birch period, or Allerød period
The base is usually where (partly organic) mud rests on clay. Birch pollen markedly dominant, much willow pollen at the beginning of the period, a little pine pollen throughout; much non-tree pollen. (*Note:* the relative abundance of birch pollen does not necessarily imply abundance of birch trees, and the presence of pine pollen does not signify that pine trees were growing in Ireland at this stage. The boundaries of Zone II have in recent years been drawn with more regard to the changes in the pollen curves than the stratigraphical changes.)

ZONE III   The Younger *Salix herbacea* period
The birch curve is falling, and the pine curve is rising; often a change in the nature of the sediment.

POST-GLACIAL TIME

Pre-boreal time
ZONE IV   The post-glacial birch period
The lower border is not clearly defined but there is often a change in the nature of the sediment. In the zone as a whole birch pollen is dominant and there is much willow pollen. The non-tree pollen decreases markedly.
(*Note:* in some recent detailed studies the zone boundary has been drawn at well defined changes in the pollen curves, or a transition zone III–IV has been delimited.)

Boreal Time
ZONE V   The hazel-birch period
The lower border is at the point where the hazel curve begins markedly to rise (the so-called 'rational border' for hazel); hazel pollen abundant, much birch pollen and a little pine pollen.

ZONE VI   The hazel-pine period
The lower border is at the 'rational border' for the elm curve, where the 'rational border' for the oak curve is often also to be found. The so-called Boreal hazel maximum occurs in the earlier part of the zone, and the maximum for pine somewhat later. Elm pollen is often more frequent than oak pollen. Three sub-zones are distinguished by both Jessen and Mitchell. Their characteristics are given in outline only. Differences occur between calcareous and non-calcareous regions.
    Sub-zone VIa: the hazel curve reaches its highest values.
    Sub-zone VIb: a high proportion of elm pollen, the curve often reaching its highest value.
    Sub-zone VIc: the pine curve is high, often at its maximum. The hazel curve falls, and may reach its minimum in many regions.

JESSEN'S SCHEME

ZONE VII   *Atlantic and Sub-boreal times*
The lower border is at the rational border of the alder curve. Pine pollen is frequent in the lower part of the zone but disappears almost entirely towards the top. A decline of the elm curve takes place in the middle of the zone where the alder curve may rise, and the hazel curve may show a pronounced rise. Two sub-zones are recognized.

MITCHELL'S SCHEME

ZONE VII   *The Atlantic period*
The lower border is placed where the pine curve begins to fall and the alder curve begins to rise. At this point the hazel curve is usually at a minimum. Elm pollen often at high levels in calcareous regions. Often considerable amounts of pine pollen in the lower part. Alder pollen is increasing. The hazel curve rises from the low level at the beginning of the zone.

JESSEN'S SCHEME—*contd.*

Sub-Zone VIIa   Alder-oak-pine period — the Atlantic period

Elm pollen often at a high level. Often less oak pollen than in sub-zone VIIb. The alder curve is rising from its rational border but as a rule is lower than in sub-zone VIIb. The hazel curve often falls to its lowest level.

Sub-zone VIIb   The alder-oak-period — the Sub-boreal period.

The elm curve falls at the beginning of the sub-zone, especially in the north. The pine curve is lower than in sub-zone VIIa and tends to fall, as a rule disappearing at the end of the sub-zone. The birch curve tends to rise. The hazel curve rises strongly from the bottom of the sub-zone and may have a conspicuous maximum at the end.

Sub-atlantic and Historic times

ZONE VIII   The Alder-birch-oak period

The lower border of the zone is placed where the pine curve 'wedges out', very often at the same level as a marked maximum of the oak curve; the border corresponds almost exactly with the oldest recurrence surface 'C'.

(*Note:* Jessen proposed a tentative sub-division of zone VIII, mainly on bog-stratigraphic grounds; but since the validity of the basic division into zones VII and VIII has been challenged, these details will not be repeated.)

MITCHELL'S SCHEME—*contd.*

ZONE VIII   *The pagan period*

The zone boundary is placed where there is evidence of human interference with the woodlands; this is indicated by a fall of the elm curve and a rise of the hazel curve (and sometimes the birch curve) and ribwort plantain pollen appears. The zone ends where the elm curve falls abruptly to low values from which it does not subsequently recover. (The zone as originally described was divided into two sub-zones, VIIIa covering the rise, and VIIIb the fall, of the oak curve; the oak maximum has however been shown probably not to be synchronous across the country.)

ZONE IX   *The Christian period*

The oak curve generally attains a maximum soon after the elm decline with which the zone opens. The hazel curve rises as the elm curve falls. The ribwort plantation curve is at a low level and does not move as the elm curve falls. In the middle of the zone there is often a minimum of the hazel curve. The zone ends where pollen of planted trees first makes its appearance.

ZONE X   Pollen of planted trees present, particularly pine, beech and elm.

THE LATE-GLACIAL PERIOD

Late-glacial deposits usually occur in a three-fold sequence. The sequence starts with laminated or unlaminated clays at the base, then comes a layer of clay-mud (an aquatic deposit, basically mineral with an admixture of organic material). Finally there is another layer of clay which may contain frost-fractured stone fragments. A schematic diagram showing this late-glacial stratigraphy, such as might be found in a small inter-drumlin hollow is given in figure 5.1. The end of the late-glacial period was taken by Jessen to be at the junction between the upper clay and the deposit above, usually a clay-mud. The tendency in recent years, however, has been to rely much more on biostratigraphic criteria.

Evidence from macroscopic remains

A wealth of information is available about the late-glacial flora from macroscopic remains such as seeds and fruits. A geographical analysis, essentially as made by Mitchell[5],

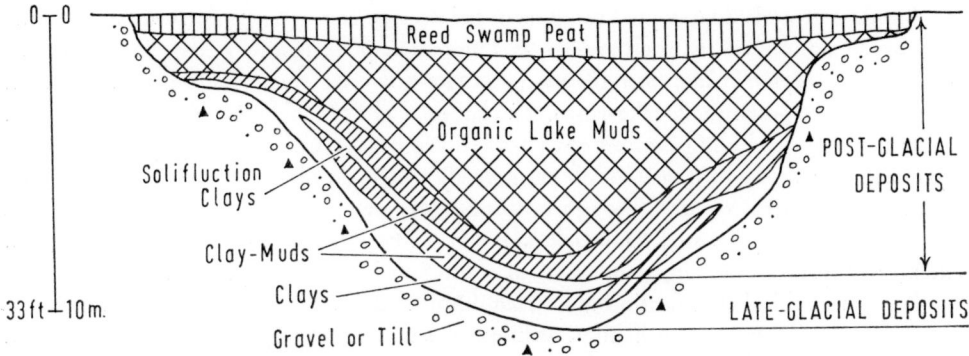

Fig. 5.1   Generalized stratigraphy of inter-drumlin lake deposits.

from his own and Jessen's identifications, is given below. The analysis employs the categories distinguished by Hulten[6], though some are grouped together.

	Number of species	
	Total	Non-aquatic species
Arctic–montane	16	14
Boreal–circumpolar	31	13
Boreal–montane	10	5
Circumpolar shore and sub-oceanic	2	1
Eurasiatic *sensu lato*	24	17
Atlantic and Sub-atlantic	7	1
West European continental	1	1
Continental	3	3
Scattered areas	2	1
Culture	8	7
Not classified	1	—
	105	63

The identifications are essentially from zones II and III of the late-glacial as delimited on lithostratigraphical grounds, relatively few macrofossils having been found in the zone I clays. We should note, however, the occurrence in the zone I clays of the dwarf willow (*Salix herbacea*). It is clear that the arctic-montane element was important in the late-glacial flora, with such species as *Dryas octopetala* (mountain avens), *Thalictrum alpinum* (alpine meadow rue), *Oxyria digyna* (mountain sorrel), *Saxifraga oppositifolia* (purple saxifrage), *Silene acaulis* (moss campion) and *Selaginella selaginoides* (lesser clubmoss). *Luzula spicata* (spiked woodrush) belongs to this group but is not nowadays found in Ireland and has a disjunct distribution in Great Britain; likewise *Minuartia stricta* (bog sand-wort) is now to be found only in Teesdale, Co. Durham.

Another strongly represented category is the oceanic element (the Atlantic/Sub-atlantic category) exemplified by such species as *Littorella uniflora* (shore-weed), *Isoëtes lacustris* (quill-wort), *Myriophyllum alterniflorum* (alternate-flowered water milfoil) and *Eleocharis multicaulis* (many-stemmed spike-rush). The late-glacial flora includes also many species of southern affinity including *Erica tetralix* (cross-leaved heath), *Callitriche stagnalis* (a species of starwort), *Potamogeton crispus* (curled pondweed) which do not nowadays extend further north than southern Sweden (though in some cases having a more northerly distribution along the Norwegian coast), and *Helianthemum canum* (hoary rock-rose) which does **not** extend any further north in Scandinavia than the Swedish island of Öland.

The geographical classification somewhat disguises the fact that many late-glacial species are essentially plants of open habitat. While it is true that among these are some so-called arctic-alpines, which may have a low summer temperature requirement, many are to a large extent indifferent to temperature conditions. *Dryas* and *Selaginella,* for instance, nowadays grow down to sea-level in Ireland. Many late-glacial species are plants of disturbed ground, and today are known as weeds. Among others, we can mention *Atriplex* cf *patula* (common orache), *Cerastium vulgatum* (chickweed), *Chenopodium rubrum* (red goosefoot), *Polygonum nodosum* (a plant of the persicaria type), *Ranunculus repens* (creeping buttercup), *Rumex crispus* (curled dock) and *Taraxacum officinale* agg. (dandelions). Several other species are characteristic of meadows. The aquatic flora must have been a rich one although this aspect of the flora is, of course, emphasized by the conditions of preservation. Mitchell points out that most late-glacial lakes would have had *Myriophyllum alterniflorum* (alternate-leaved water milfoil), *Potamogeton natans* (broad-leaved pondweed), *P. praelongus* (long-stalked pondweed) and *Zannichellia palustris* (horned pondweed) growing in them. Whereas around the margin there would have been sedges, including *Carex rostrata* (the bottle sedge), *Hippuris vulgaris* (mare's tail), *Littorella uniflora* (shore-weed), *Menyanthes trifoliata* (bog bean), *Schoenoplectus lacustris* (bulrush) and many others. Yet other species are today characteristic of sea shores; for instance, *Atriplex glabriuscula* (Babington's orache), *A. hastata* (hastate orache), *Armeria maritima* (sea pink or thrift) and *Cochlearia officinalis* (scurvy grass).

Remains of the following shrubs and trees have been found in late-glacial deposits: the dwarf birch (*Betula nana*) and tree birch (*Betula pubescens*), dwarf willow (*Salix herbacea*), the osier willow (*Salix viminalis*) and the juniper (*Juniperus communis*). No macroscopic remains of pine have been found.

Evidence from pollen

As we have seen, the subdivision of the late-glacial period made by Jessen into three zones, I, II and III rested essentially on stratigraphic criteria. So great is the abundance of the dwarf willow in his zones I and III that he names these zones the 'Older' and 'Younger *Salix herbacea*' periods. The most abundant tree pollen type in zone II appeared to be birch, and Jessen coined the name 'Late-glacial *Betula* Period' for this zone. This period is perhaps more commonly referred to as the Allerød period, however, after the Danish locality from which late-glacial deposits were first described. It will be useful here to summarize, largely in his own words, Jessen's conclusions about the late-glacial zones.

ZONE I   The Older *Salix herbacea* period

The clay is poor in plant remains: the growth of water and swamp plants must have been very sparse. What evidence there is suggests that the country was covered by an open tundra-like vegetation with a limited number of species and was subject to solifluction.

ZONE II   The late-glacial *Betula* period or Allerød period

Ireland was an oceanic sector of the sub-arctic birch region of north-west Europe. There were copses of tree birch and stretches of open country, which in the west were covered by heaths rich in *Empetrum* (the crowberry) and elsewhere by a vegetation of grasses and herbs whose character cannot be closely defined.

ZONE III   The Younger *Salix herbacea* period

The vegetation was clearly more northern in character than in the preceding period, though oceanic influence was maintained. The tree growth was even more restricted but birch copses may have survived in sheltered localities. Solifluction was a common phenomenon and the country for the most part carried an open tundra-like vegetation with patches of sub-arctic heaths containing, among other plants, *Salix herbacea* (dwarf willow), *Dryas octopetala* (the mountain avens) with, in the north-west, much *Empetrum nigrum* (crowberry).

More recent work, particularly the detailed pollen analysis of late-glacial deposits, has emphasized the great richness of the flora. In particular, it has begun to show the important part played by the juniper, whose pollen was not recognized by Jessen. It has been suggested that, because of this, Jessen possibly exaggerated the importance of *Empetrum* in the late-glacial period.[7] Two modern late-glacial pollen digarams, in which the abundance of juniper pollen can be seen, are presented in figures 5.2 and 5.3. The first, worked out by Singh[8], is from Woodgrange, Co. Down, and the second, prepared by Watts[9], is from Long Range, Co. Kerry. It will be noted that the zonation adopted by the authors differs, and relies much more on the biostratigraphy than Jessen's zonation. The early maximum of the juniper curve in both diagrams is perhaps a reflection of ameliorating conditions, and its later decline, although difficult to understand, may also have some climatic implication. A comparison of the two diagrams will exemplify the great disparity found in the behaviour of birch in the Allerød period in Ireland. At The Long Range its pollen is abundant, and presumably betokens the existence of substantial birch woods. At Woodgrange, on the other hand, birch pollen is very sparse. Were it not for the finding of tree-birch seeds in late-glacial deposits in the same area it might even have been suspected that birch trees were not present. What few trees did exist in that area in the late-glacial period were perhaps restricted to sheltered situations. It is of considerable interest to see in the Allerød deposits at Woodgrange pollen of *Cladium mariscus* (the saw sedge). This is a relatively thermophilous species, its distribution extending at present only into the south of Sweden. Its occurrence in Allerød times reinforces the evidence from the other species of southern affinity already mentioned, that conditions could not have been particularly severe. Thus, the poor development of birch in some areas may perhaps be due to a particular, perhaps seasonal, aspect of the prevailing climate, though other reasons could be suggested. Towards the top of both of the

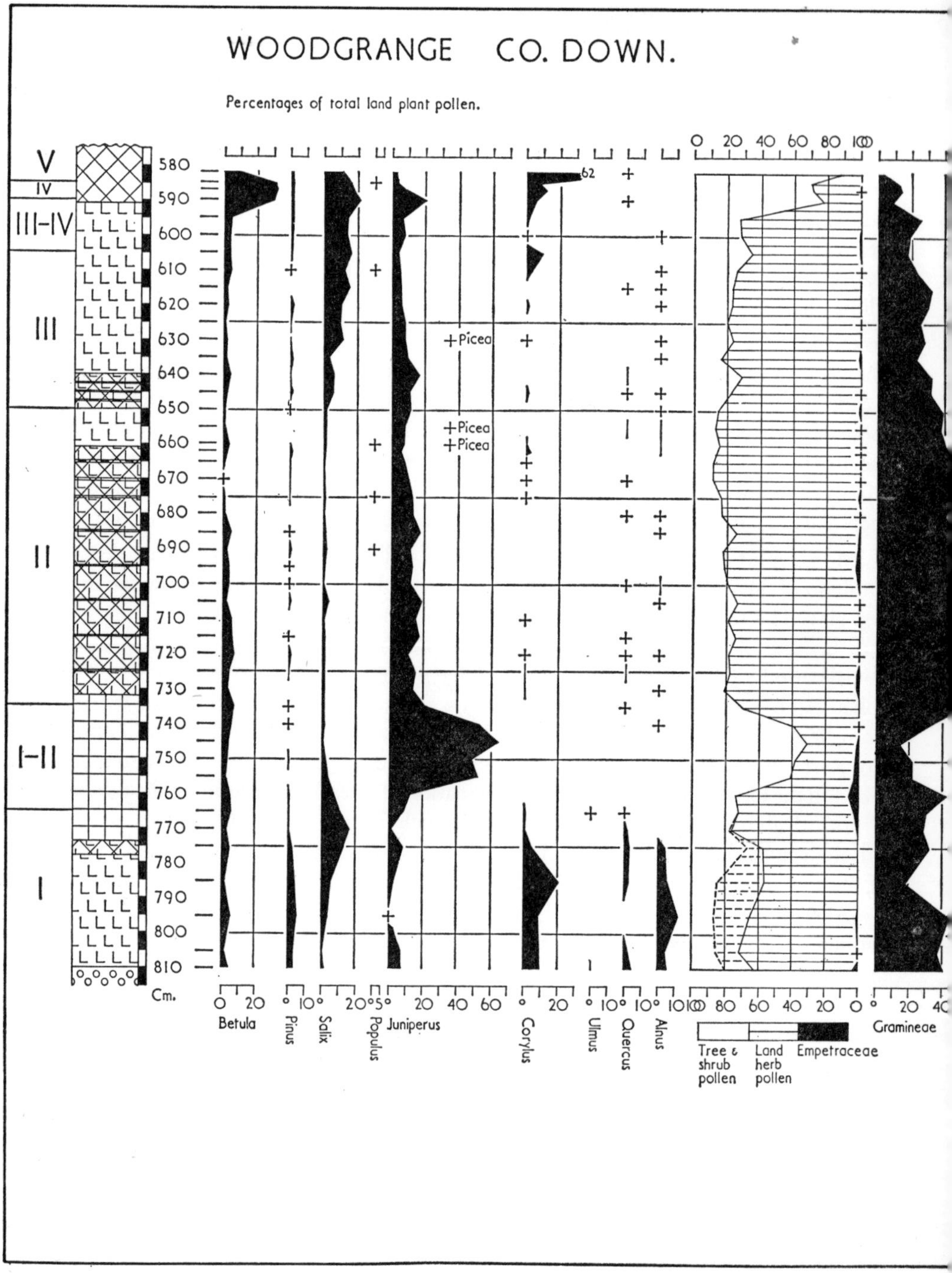

Fig. 5.2   Pollen diagram from late-glacial deposits at Woodrange, co. Down. The percenta
derived from older deposits since derived spores are frequent at that level. (From Singh[8].)

Right-hand column labels (top to bottom):

1271
562 + Lonicera
587
510
404
459 + Engelhardtia
452
445 + Engelhardtia
506
454 + Ephedra
522
457 + Succisa
469 + Juglans
+ Engelhardtia
424
525
567 + Geranium
440
433
448 + Geranium
472
515
424
417
426
420
520
425
411 + Littorella
428
405
442
477
455
477
495 + Littorella
470 + Littorella
448
417
404
231
50
117
45 - 145 1·3 Geranium
268 3·0 Ericaceae
426
414 1·7 Engelhardtia

Bottom axis taxa labels (left to right):

Rumex, Chenopodiaceae, Cladium, Umbelliferae, Caryophyllaceae, Rosaceae, Cruciferae, Ranunculaceae, Tubuliflorae, Liguliflorae, Thalictrum, Helianthemum, Rubiaceae, Boraginaceae, Hippophaë, Epilobium, Polygonaceae, Campanula, Liliaceae, Plantago lanceolata, Plantago maritima, Armeria, Koenigia, Urtica, Centaurea, Filipendula, Typha angustifolia, Alisma, Nuphar, Nymphaea, Myriophyllum alterniflorum, Potamogeton, Menyanthes, Selaginella, Other Filicales, Pteridium, Pediastrum, Derived spores, Land plant pollen

1964 S

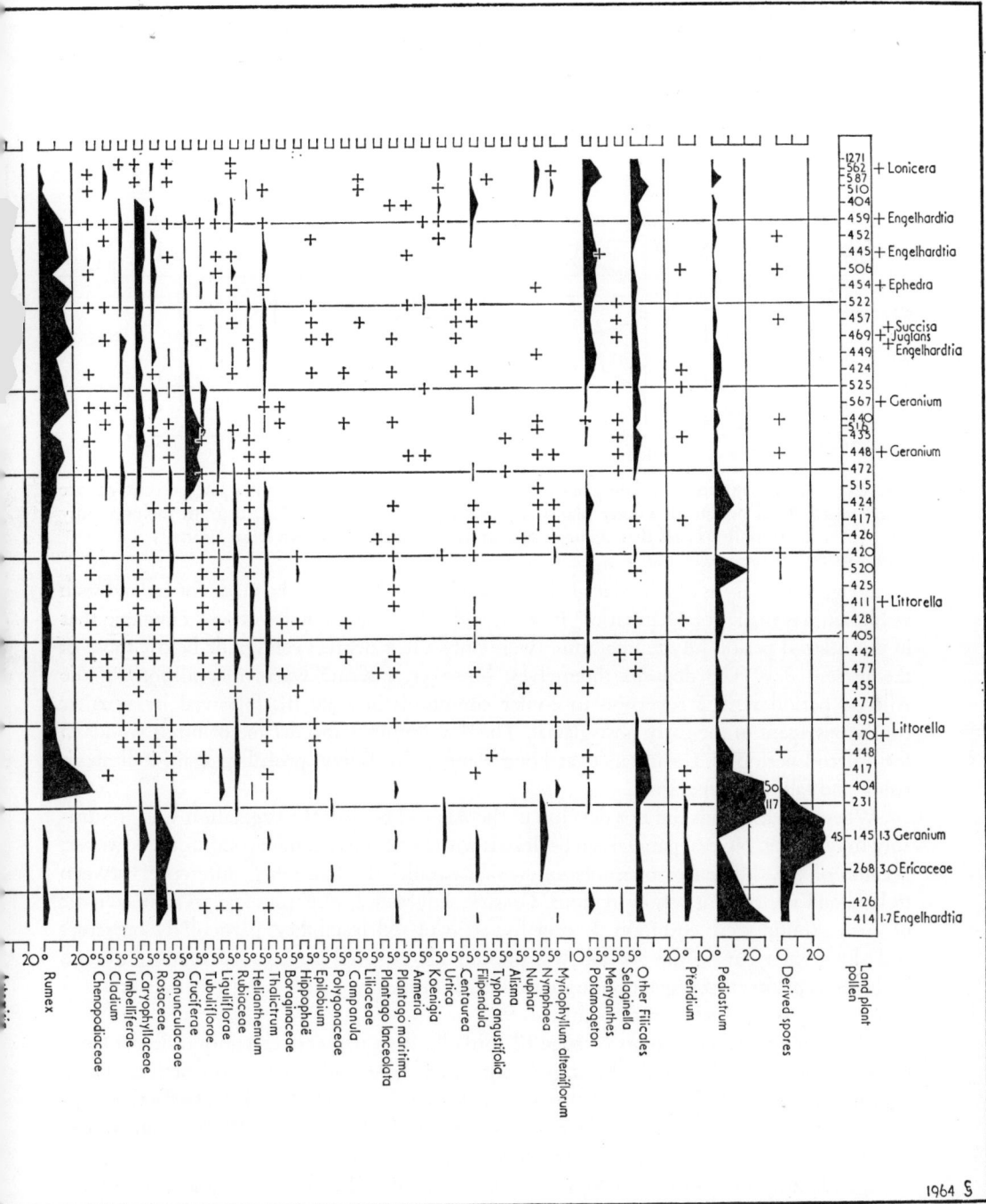

on total land-plant pollen. The pollen of pine, hazel, elm, oak and alder in Zone 1 is almost certainly

late-glacial pollen diagrams given here, the rising curves for tree and shrub pollen betoken the start of the closing of the forests in the early post-glacial period. This development will be discussed in more detail later.

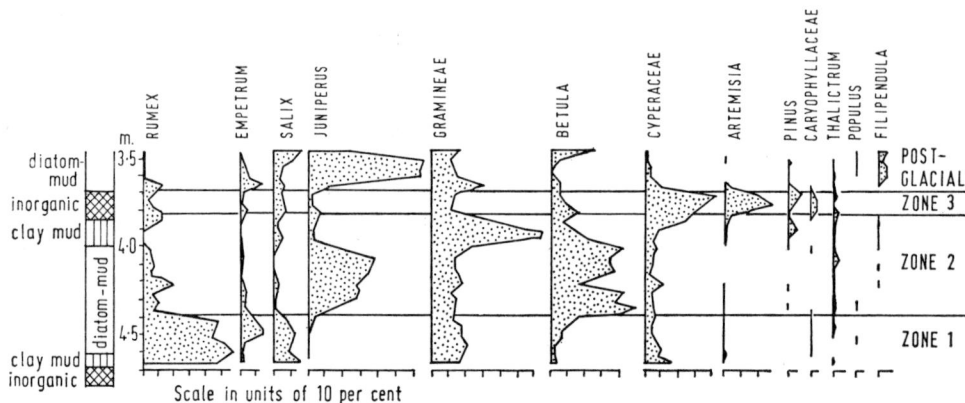

Fig. 5.3 Pollen diagram from late-glacial deposits at Long Range, co. Kerry. The percentages are based on the total pollen of woody plants and wind-pollinated herbs. The diagram includes only those pollen types that occur in substantial quantity. (Redrawn from Watts.[7])

A rigorous analysis of late-glacial climatic conditions has yet to be made for Ireland such as Iversen has made for Denmark.[10] Iversen, and other continental workers, conclude that in the Allerød period July temperatures were only a few degrees centigrade below those of the present day. The deposits themselves, however, indicate warmer conditions in the Allerød period with a reversion to cooler conditions in zone III, followed by warmer conditions again in the early post-glacial. The development and decline of birch woods in the Allerød period as, for instance, at Long Range, Co. Kerry, probably again indicates a rising and falling temperature.

Where birch woods did not develop in the Allerød period, the vegetation was presumably tundra-like. No real parallel can be drawn with present day tundra conditions, however, because of the differences of insolation which parallel the latitudinal difference between Ireland and the present tundra regions. Grasses, sedges and numerous species characteristic of open ground were common. Except for areas of soil instability, particularly on screes and along river banks, the ground was presumably covered by a sward of shrubby and herbaceous plants: this vegetation supported herds of the great Irish deer (Irish elk), reindeer and possibly other herbivorous mammals.[11]

The vegetational conditions of zone III (broadly defined) were certainly different from those of the Allerød period, the soils being much more subject to frost action. There appears characteristically to be more pollen of *Rumex* (sorrels and docks), *Artemisia* (mugworts), *Caryophyllaceae* and, in the west, of *Cyperaceae* (sedges) in zone III. It is unfortunate that the pollen identifications do not allow us to say what actual species were involved though identifications of macroscopic remains from zone III include *Rumex acetosa* (sorrel),

R. acetosella agg. (sheep's sorrel), and some of the *Rumex* pollen almost certainly belongs to these species. *R. acetosa* can act as a snow-patch plant. Caryophyllaceous species identified from macroscopic remains include montane, meadow and ruderal plants. It is impossible to draw any firm conclusion as to the prevailing climatic conditions from the abundance of these pollen types. It is worth noting, however, that Mitchell has found macro-remains of *Armeria maritima* (sea pink or thrift) to be common in zone III deposits; according to Iversen *Armeria maritima* (*sensu lato*) is not now found outside the —8°C January isotherm.[12]

In figure 5.4 the results are given of the radiocarbon dating of late- and early post-glacial

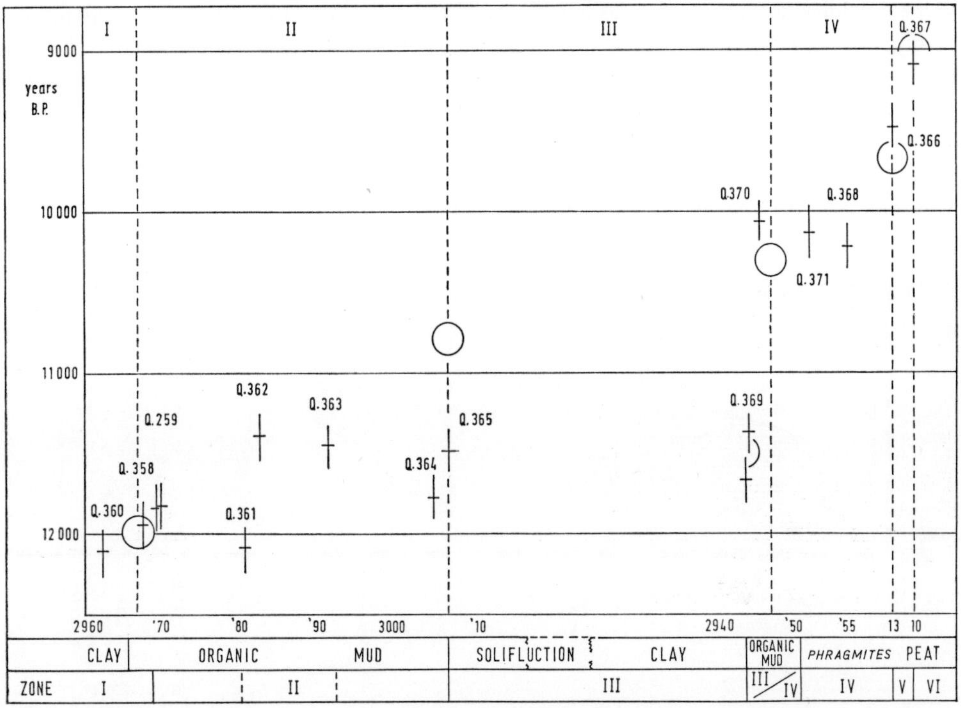

Fig. 5.4 Radiocarbon ages of late-glacial and post-glacial samples from Roddans Port, co. Down. Along the horizontal axis are shown Morrison's sampling index numbers, stratigraphy, and Morrison's pollen zone boundaries. The horizontal line for each dating represents the thickness of the sample slice (1 or 2 cm): the vertical line is the probable error (1 S.D.) of the count. The large open circles give the values to be expected on present knowledge of other British sites for the appropriate zone boundaries.
(Reproduced from figure 11 in M. E. S. Morrison and N. Stephens, 1965.)

deposits at Roddans Port, Co. Down[13], where the pollen diagram, constructed by Morrison, is similar to that from Woodgrange. The open circles in the figure represent the dates that would have been expected by comparison with sites in Great Britain. The late-glacial period is seen to have lasted for some 2,000 years, from roughly 12,000 to 10,000 years ago. But a number of inconsistencies are apparent in the radiocarbon series; in particular, the dates for the top of Morrison's zone II and the beginning of the post-glacial (Morrison's zone III–IV) appear to be too old. This may well be due to the so-called hard-water effect; that is to say, the fixation of carbon by aquatic plants forming part of the deposit dated which was derived in solution—as bicarbonate—from older deposits.

THE LATE-GLACIAL—POST-GLACIAL TRANSITION

As with the late-glacial period, and the later part of the post-glacial period, the actual definition and numbering of pollen zones at the opening of the post-glacial is a matter of some difficulty. Different schemes have been adopted by different authors. The vegetational changes of the earliest post-glacial are, however, very marked, though variable in different areas. The first closed forests of the post-glacial were of birch, pollen of which predominates in all diagrams. In the time intervening between the open conditions of the late-glacial and the closed birch forests of zone IV, there appears in many places to have been a great floruit of juniper. The abundance of juniper pollen can be seen in the top part of the Long Range diagram (Co. Kerry) and in a diagram from Kilrea, Co. Londonderry[14], presented in simplified form in figure 5.5. In this particular diagram the phase covering the development

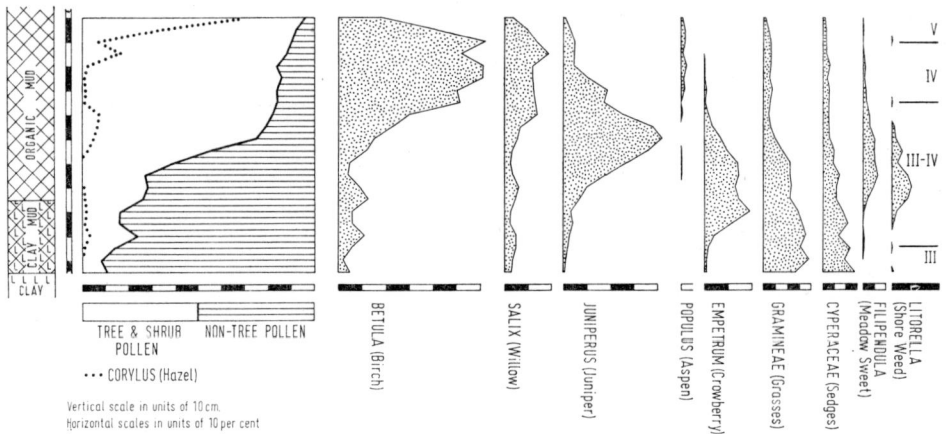

Fig. 5.5   Cannons Lough, Kilrea, co. Londonderry. The upper part of diagram I shown in schematic form. (Based upon Plate XXI, in A. G. Smith, 1961.)

of the birch forest is delimited as zone III–IV. During this zone the late-glacial species, particularly the grasses and sedges virtually disappear; the tree-pollen curve rising from about 10 per cent to 90 per cent of the total pollen demonstrates convincingly the spreading of forest over the countryside. During the middle part of this zone, at the same time as the juniper maximum, the curves for *Filipendula* (meadow sweet), *Littorella* (shore-weed) and *Empetrum* (crowberry) all have a maximum. These are relatively thermophilous species (especially *Littorella*) and it appears likely that, in this instance, as in Denmark, the forest development could not keep pace with the rapidly increasing temperature. Nevertheless, birch eventually came to predominate and the juniper was apparently shaded out. No time scale can as yet be put on these events.

THE POST-GLACIAL PERIOD

There is considerable diversity in the vegetational development of the post-glacial and it is not possible to describe a typical sequence. The diagram from Littleton Bog, Co. Tipperary, published by Mitchell[15], and reproduced as figure 5.6, is perhaps the nearest

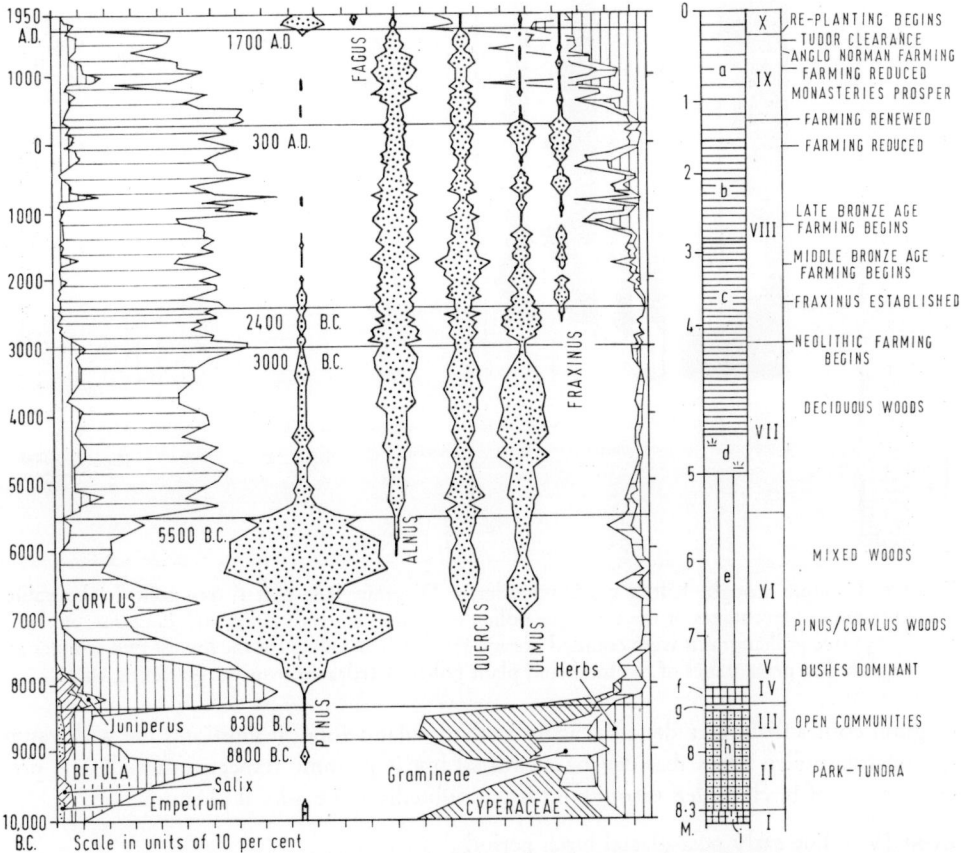

Fig. 5.6 Pollen diagram extending from the Late-glacial period to the present, from Littleton Bog, co. Tipperary. (Redrawn from Mitchell.[15]) The percentages are based on total pollen of non-aquatic plants, though the pollen sum varies in different parts of the diagram. The vertical scale is a time scale based on radiocarbon dates for the horizons indicated by horizontal lines. Some of the dates are derived from work outside Ireland. The radiocarbon dates available for Ireland are given in the text. Key to stratigraphy: (a) light brown fresh *Sphagnum* peat, (b) brown *Sphagnum* peat, more humified, (c) red-brown well humified peat, (d) moss peat, (e) fen peat, (f) grey-green mud, (g) sandy mud with small pebbles, (h) grey-green sandy mud, (i) grey clay

that can be found to a typical lowland pollen diagram. The presentation of this diagram is rather unusual, however, though having a number of advantages. By comparison, the pollen diagram presented in figures 5.7 and 5.8, is drawn in a more conventional manner. This

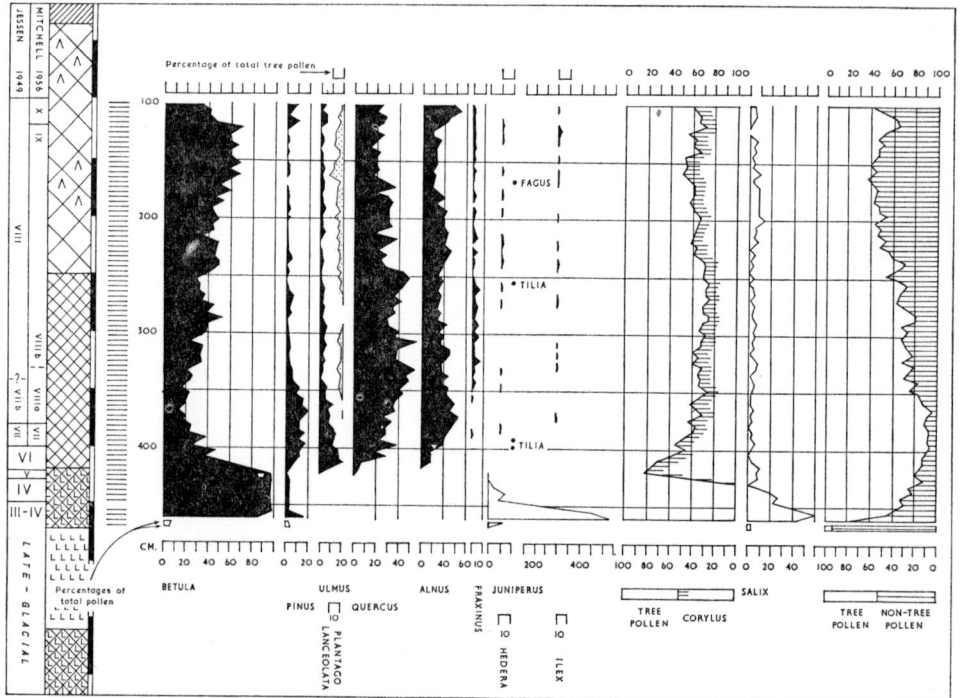

Fig. 5.7 Cannons Lough, Kilrea, co. Londonderry. Diagram IIA, part 1, tree pollen. The values are expressed as percentages of the total tree pollen excluding *Corylus, Salix,* and *Juniperus;* approximately 150 tree pollen grains were counted in each sample. The values for the lowest two samples are expressed as percentages of the total land plant pollen. (Redrawn from A. G. Smith, 1961.)

diagram comes from lake deposits, again in the lowland zone; it illustrates the wide range of non-tree pollen types that can be identified but is in some respects unusual. The preponderance of birch pollen throughout is undoubtedly quite a local phenomenon.

ZONE IV The early post-glacial birch period

In both pollen diagrams the great abundance of birch pollen generally found in zone IV is illustrated. Little pollen of herbaceous plants is found in this zone and the existence of closed birch forest is likely over the whole country. There are few radiocarbon dates for this period in Ireland and the time-scale given by Mitchell must be regarded only as tentative. The C-14 dates from Roddans Port, Co. Down (Q-371), 8180 ± 170 B.C. and (Q-368) 8260 ± 150 B.C. fall within zone IV, and (Q-366) 7480 ± 150 B.C. falls at the zone IV-V boundary, where the hazel curve begins to rise.

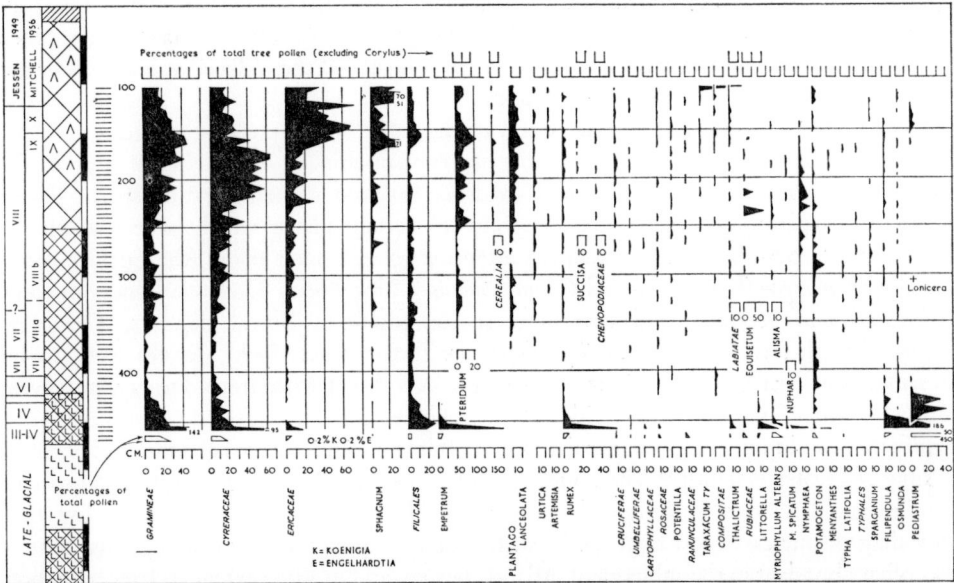

Fig. 5.8   Cannons Lough, Kilrea, co. Londonderry. Diagram IIA, part 2, herb pollen. The method of calculation is as for figure 5.7. (Redrawn from A. G. Smith, 1961.)

Zone V   The hazel-birch period

It will be noted that in the Littleton Bog diagram no distinction can be made between zone IV and V; this is also the case with some other pollen diagrams. Some authors have considered this zone hardly worthy of recognition. Where deposition has been rapid, however, a clear zone V, as defined by Jessen, can be distinguished, although in many cases, as in the Cannon's Lough diagram, zone V covers only that time during which the hazel curve is rising sharply. Hazel, which is shade tolerant and itself casts a dense shade, must have been able to come up through the birch and displace it, birch being a light-demanding species. Thus considerable areas of hazel scrub must have come into existence, but the duration of this period is not known, there being no relevant C-14 dates. From the presence of relatively thermophilous or strongly oceanic species such as the aquatic plants *Naias marina* and *N. flexilis, Erica cinerea* (bell heather), *Cladium mariscus* (saw sedge) and *Osmunda regalis* (royal fern), Jessen concluded that the climate of zone V was rather similar to that of the present day.

Zone VI   The hazel-pine period

The increase of pine pollen and continuing abundance of hazel, from which Jessen took the name of the period, can be seen clearly in both diagrams, but elm and oak also appear. These latter species must have supplanted the birch woods and formed dense forest broken only by rivers and lakes and possibly the higher mountains. Nothing is known of the height of the tree line, however. During zone VI hazel pollen generally becomes much reduced.

Whether this reduction of pollen reflects a real reduction of the amount of hazel is doubtful, although it may give some indication of the reduction of the amount of hazel scrub. Since the pollen productivity of hazel is reduced when it is shaded the reduced values may be the effect of the invasion of scrub by forest trees.

By comparison with the Boreal period of the early Scandinavian geologists, zone VI is sometimes thought of as having a continental type of climate. There is some support for the idea of warm dry summers, though evidence for cold winters is rather sparse. There occur in this period (though not exclusively so) certain plants which have a southerly distribution in Scandinavia. Jessen draws attention to *Viburnum opulus* (the guelder rose), *Crataegus monogyna* (hawthorn) and *Cornus sanguinea* (dogwood). Dogwood does not seem to be native in Scotland, and two other species found in Boreal deposits, *Thelypteris palustris* (marsh fern) and *Rumex hydrolapathum* (great water dock), do not seem to be present in northern Scotland. None of these species is absent from Ireland today, however, and while they may provide evidence of relative warmth, they do not necessarily signify that conditions were warmer than today. Boreal mollusca have been thought possibly to suggest greater warmth.[16] The abundance of Scots pine, a relatively continental species requiring cold winters, is thought by Jessen possibly to suggest a climate more like that prevailing on the east coast than the west. It should be pointed out, however, that pine is also often abundant in the subsequent Atlantic period, and to some extent its later reduction can be attributed to human activity. In general, wood appears to be more common in Boreal deposits than either earlier or later, though this may be due to the particular developmental stage reached by the mires at that time. More striking evidence of warm conditions comes from the submerged Boreal wood peats at both the northern and southern ends of Lough Neagh which suggest a considerably lower water level than in recent times. This idea is supported by the apparent growth of trees on Boreal deposits now submerged in the Downpatrick area.[17]

THE BOREAL–ATLANTIC TRANSITION, AND ATLANTIC PERIOD

The exact definition of the transition between the Boreal and Atlantic periods has been a matter of some diversity of opinion (see Table 1). In general, however, the distinction lies in the expansion of alder in the Atlantic period. In the British Isles as a whole the Boreal-Atlantic transition appears to have taken place somewhere around 5000–5500 B.C.[18]   The relevant C-14 dates for Ireland are:

D-2   Redbog, Co. Louth.   Zone VIc–VII boundary *sensu*
           Jessen   4440 ± 120 B.C.
Y-95   Toome Bay, Co. Londonderry.   Zone VIb   5925 ± 110 B.C.
Q-19   Clonsast, Co. Offaly.   Early zone VII *sensu* Mitchell.
           Also dated by C-358, 3874 ± 300 B.C.   6305 ± 225 B.C.
Q-214   Ballyhalbert, Co. Down.   Zone VIc.   6160 ± 135 B.C.
UB-96 Beaghmore, Co. Tyrone.   Zone VI–VII boundary   5050 ± 90 B.C.
           sensu Jessen

There is a marked discrepancy between the Clonsast dates, which requires further investigation. The remaining dates do not all date the Boreal–Atlantic transition precisely. The apparently late date from Redbog does not appear quite so strange when it is realized that the expansion of alder at one site in the north of Scotland comes between samples dated to 3270 ± 115 B.C. (Q-748) and 2950 ± 105 B.C. (Q-741).[19] In addition, the really marked expansion of alder at two upland sites in Co. Tyrone is dated by UB-93 at 3345 ± 75 B.C. (Beaghmore) and by UB-253 at 3195 ± 70 B.C. (Ballynagilly). Clearly, the phytogeography of the period will become of much interest when more dates are available.

The vegetational changes of the Boreal–Atlantic transition are rather difficult to analyse in detail. It seems unlikely that the simple reading of the pollen diagram as indicating that alder replaced pine, can be correct. In some areas pine pollen remains abundant, and may even increase in proportion in the Atlantic period. A comparison of the diagrams from Littleton Bog and Cannons Lough illustrates this point. It is possible that in general the Boreal-Atlantic transition was a time of the expansion of oak and elm into areas of pine and hazel, with alder invading wetter areas, but there must have been local variations. Further discussion of this period is given in the papers of both Jessen and Mitchell, and of Smith[20] and Oldfield.[21] It is generally assumed that the expansion of alder is an effect of increasing wetness, and indeed, habitats suitable for its growth were almost certainly created at this time by the transgression of the present coastline by the sea. As has long been recognized, however, the lowering of water levels might just as easily have exposed damp soils suitable for colonization by alder. Evidence bearing on this problem is seen in the deposits of the Bann Valley to the north of Lough Neagh. There, diatomite deposits overlie reedswamp peats, apparently at the Boreal-Atlantic transition. The deposition of these clays implies a change of hydrography of the whole of the Lough Neagh basin, presumably with extensive winter flooding. It was also in the early Atlantic period that the widespread mire systems of north Armagh, reaching up to the present southern shore of Lough Neagh were initiated, again suggesting a rise of the water table. Other than this increased wetness there is little evidence from Ireland of changed climatic conditions in the Atlantic period.

The estuarine clays of Belfast Lough are probably post-Boreal in age, though there is some possibility that they began to be deposited in late-Boreal times. It was the study of the molluscan fauna of these clays by Praeger[22] that led to the idea of a post-glacial climatic optimum. From the increased proportion of southern forms, as compared with the present day, it seems clear that in some part of post-Boreal times the waters off the north-east coast were warmer than at present; this may well also be true of Boreal times. The decrease of southern forms in the more recent clays cannot, however, be dated or related to pollen diagrams.

On the whole the Atlantic period seems to have been one of relatively stable vegetational conditions. After the great flux of the earlier post-glacial, and the entry of alder at the beginning of the Atlantic period, the vegetation probably entered into a phase of dynamic equilibrium lasting in different areas some hundreds, or even thousands of years. As in the Boreal period, forests would have covered the countryside, with numerous local variations in composition according to the soil conditions, but again we have no knowledge of the tree line, and there is little evidence of altitudinal variation.

Evidence has recently come to light that this period of equilibrium may have been disturbed by human activity, and that secondary plant communities probably developed in some areas before the forests regenerated.[23] The earliest known human settlements date from the late-Boreal period, though these early, Mesolithic, peoples are generally reckoned to have affected the vegetation only slightly. Accidental burning, or the deliberate use of fire in hunting, could have had severe effects on the forest vegetation, however, and undoubtedly knowledge of any such effects will advance in the next few years.

POST-ATLANTIC TIMES

While the end of the Atlantic period is satisfactorily fixed at the decline of the elm pollen curve, the sub-division of the post-Atlantic period is at present rather difficult. The scheme adopted by Mitchell is given in Table 1, and the results of the application of this scheme can be seen in the Littleton Bog diagram (Fig. 5.6). The main reasons for Mitchell's rejection of the later part of Jessen's zonation scheme were that the features on which the zone VII-VIII boundary depended, the pine decline and the bog stratigraphic change, appeared increasingly difficult to distinguish, and increasingly less likely to be synchronous across the country. Mitchell's new scheme is, in its main features, supported by C-14 dates as providing a chronological division. Based, as it is, on the effects of human activity, it is not surprising to find in practice, however, that in some areas this scheme is just as difficult to apply as Jessen's. Further advances will rely almost entirely on C-14 dating. The difficulties of later post-glacial zonation in Ireland arise to some extent because of the virtual absence of pollen of *Tilia* (lime), *Fagus* (beech), *Carpinus* (hornbeam) and *Picea* (spruce) which provide useful datum points in England and in continental Europe. That these trees did not reach Ireland is probably due to a slow migration rate, and the expansion of the Irish Sea in pre-Boreal and Boreal times. Spruce did not reach England in the post-glacial, although it was abundant, both there and in Ireland, in interglacial times.

As we have seen, the Atlantic period ends at the decline of the elm curve, which took place somewhat before 5,000 radiocarbon years ago. The relevant determinations so far obtained for Ireland are:

D4	Redbog, Co. Louth. Beginning of elm decline	3220 ± 190 B.C.
D-12	Lomcloon Td., Co. Sligo. VII–VIII boundary *sensu* Mitchell	3210 ± 190 B.C.
D13	Treanscrabbagh Td., Co. Sligo. VII–VIII boundary *sensu* Mitchell	3020 ± 180 B.C.
Q-555	Fallahogy Td., Co. Londonderry. Beginning of elm decline	3160 ± 120 B.C. 3380 ± 120 B.C.
Q-653	Fallahogy Td., Co. Londonderry. End of elm decline	3240 ± 120 B.C. 3320 ± 120 B.C.
UB-99	Beaghmore, Co. Tyrone. Beginning of elm decline	3235 ± 70 B.C.
UB-253	Ballynagilly, Co. Tyrone. Beginning of elm decline	3195 ± 75 B.C.

As will be seen from the radiocarbon dates, the elm decline is perhaps the most consistent of all the divisions of the post-glacial and it has been a topic of extensive discussion in recent years.[24] At the elm decline there is little evidence from bog-stratigraphy of any climatic change, and since the elm generally recovers it seems unlikely that a maintained climatic change began at the end of Atlantic times. A shorter-term climatic fluctuation cannot be ruled out and it remains possible that the later decline of elm (which can be seen in the Littleton Bog diagram, and to a lesser extent in the Cannons Lough diagram) is connected with some climatic shift. It is clear, however, that whatever climatic effects there may have been, the early post-Atlantic period is one much affected by the immigration of the Neolithic farmers. The effects of early farming on the forest vegetation were first discovered by Iversen in Denmark.[25] The sequence of changes distinguished by Iversen are typically: (1) a decline of the forest tree pollen (in absolute terms), and especially of the curves for elm and oak, together with an increase in the curves for grasses and certain herbaceous plants, (2) maxima of the herb pollen curves, especially of *Plantago lanceolata* (ribwort plantain) and other weed species; pollen of cereals, a rise of the birch and hazel curves, (3) a decline of the pollen of herbaceous plants, a fall of the birch and finally the hazel curves; the curves of the high forest trees rise roughly to their former levels. This sequence is interpreted by Iversen as representing successive stages of forest clearance, farming and forest regeneration. Such a clearance has become known as a '*landnam*' phase after the old Scandinavian word for 'land taking'. The landnam phase is thought by Iversen to be a rather short episode, representing an attack on the forest by Neolithic farmers using both fire and the axe, followed by a brief period of farming under a system of shifting agriculture. More recently it has been discovered that this type of clearance was not the first due to Neolithic peoples in Denmark. Troels Smith[26] has demonstrated the appearance of weed species exactly at the decline of the elm and ivy curves that mark the transition between the Atlantic and Sub-boreal periods.

Evidence of a landnam type of clearance at the elm decline in Ireland was brought to light first by Mitchell[27], who showed that it was a very widespread phenomenon. In Fig. 5.9 a simplified pollen diagram from Co. Londonderry[28] is given that covers this period and which has been dated by C-14 measurements. Three stages similar to those distinguished by Iversen can be identified, although among the tree pollen it is only elm that shows a decline. No pollen of cereals was found in this instance though traces have been encountered elsewhere. It appears that only hazel was involved in the forest regeneration. The rise of the oak curve seems unlikely to imply an actual increase of oak; it is probably an effect of the percentage type of calculation. The radiocarbon dates show that the clearance began before 3000 B.C. and suggest that the regeneration was complete within a few centuries. The dates are not incompatible with the idea of a quite short phase of agriculture, but more recent work in Co. Tyrone[29] suggests the landnam type of clearance was a more substantial and prolonged affair, possibly involving a series of smaller clearances. When further work is completed this could prove to be more generally the case. Mitchell pictures the country-side at this time as becoming a mosaic, with areas of virgin forest, tillage patches, rough pastures and areas of secondary forest in various stages of regeneration.

The history of the time between the early Neolithic clearances and the present day is one of successive phases of agriculture with varying emphasis on arable and pastoral farming. In figure 5.9 it will be seen that a second clearance, with the re-appearance of weed species, was carried out at about 2500 B.C., although this may not be a general phenomenon. As clearance and grazing pressure increased, the forests began to disappear from the country-side. Evidence for this decline of the woodlands comes from the decreasing proportion of tree pollen in the total. A progressive reduction can be seen, for instance, in the Cannons Lough diagram, although in this particular case some of the non-tree pollen may have come from nearby raised bogs. In the Littleton Bog diagram (Fig. 5.6) the progress of deforestation can be judged from the increasing proportion of grass and herb pollen after *circa* 2400 B.C. A summary of Mitchell's conclusions concerning the major post-Atlantic agricultural phases is included alongside the diagram. He suggests a possible emphasis on cereals and vegetables in Early Christian times, with the ribwort plantain, pollen of which is rather infrequent in the beginning of his zone IX, finding conditions unfavourable. He speculates that later, when the hazel curve is generally at a minimum in the middle of his zone IX, there was an extension of pasture land, dating to Viking times. Nearer the top of many pollen diagrams there is a fall of the alder and rise of the birch curves; these features, Mitchell suggests, could be due to the clearance of wetter, low lying, land following the

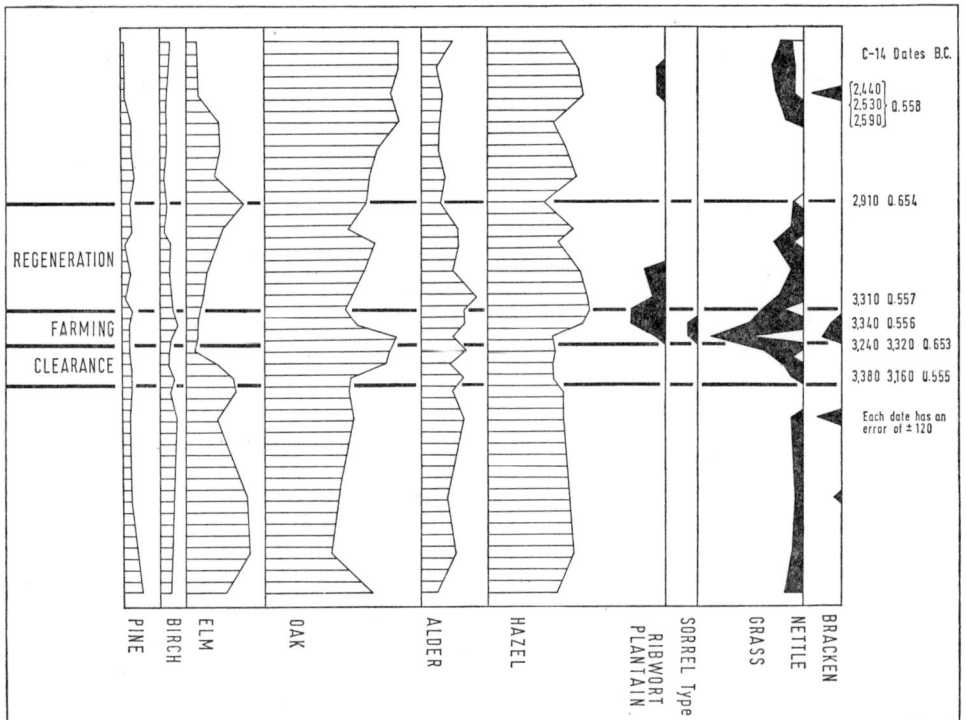

Fig. 5.9 Fallahogy, near Kilrea, co. Londonderry. (The diagram is a schematic representation of the pollen diagram in figure 1 (A. G. Smith and E. H. Willis, 1961), with additions.)

Cistercian foundations and the Norman invasion of the late twelfth century. Mitchell has made several other interesting speculations which hold out hope for a quite detailed analysis once a good chronology is available. At the moment, however, not all the phases are firmly supported by radiocarbon dates or archaeological finds.

Three levels in the post-Atlantic period have been suggested as providing useful datum points:

1   The first appearance of ash pollen in quantity has been suggested as falling between 2500 and 2200 B.C., although the exact point at which this occurs may be difficult to define, as at Redbog, Co. Louth (see D-3 below).[30] Radiocarbon dates which were obtained after this suggestion was made (Q-554, UB-249, UB-250, see below) show that much more information is needed. The relevant C-14 dates are:

D-3	Redbog, Co. Louth	1620 ± 180 B.C.
D-14	Treanscrabbagh, Co. Sligo	2600 ± 180 B.C.
Y-93	Clonsast, Co. Offaly	2195 ± 80 B.C.
Q-554	Fallahogy, Co. Londonderry	2910 ± 120 B.C.
UB-249	Ballynagilly, Co. Tyrone. Just above an increase of ash pollen	2075 ± 65 B.C.
UB-250	Ballynagilly, Co. Tyrone. Just below an increase of ash pollen	2390 ± 65 B.C.

There is little doubt that ash has been favoured by human activity. Its pollen is very infrequent before post-Atlantic times and the later increase is probably due to its entry into secondary woodland. Ash is affected by late frosts, however, and some climatic influence cannot be ruled out.[31]

2   The final decline of the elm curve used by Mitchell to define the opening of his zone IX though not always recognizable, as for instance, in the Cannons Lough diagram, is supported as coming at the beginning of Early Christian times by the following C-14 dates:

D-18	Agher, Co. Meath	340 ± 120 A.D.
Note: a sample 40 cm deeper has a similar date; D-21		300 ± 120 A.D.
D-29	Clonsast, Co. Offaly. Pine stump just below Mitchell's zone VIII–IX boundary (other comparable dates have also been obtained for the same stump)	330 ± 130 A.D.
D-8	Redbog, Co. Louth	235 ± 130 A.D.

3   Towards the top of most pollen diagrams there appears the pollen of exotic trees, especially of beech, and of pine. This pollen is undoubtedly derived from planted trees and its appearance is used by Mitchell to define the beginning of his zone X. Planting was fairly widespread by 1700 A.D., though of course local variations are to be expected. Immediately before this planting, the total tree pollen is often so low (less than 10 per cent at Littleton Bog, for instance) that we can assume an almost treeless landscape. The present-day hedgerows, for instance, produce pollen in amounts that give a value of around 20 per cent of the total pollen rain. Nevertheless, some areas would still have supported scrub. At Cannons Lough, for instance the tree pollen still amounts to some 40 per cent of the total

just before the afforestation period. A large part of this is birch, which from the occurrence of birch seeds in the lake muds, must have been fairly common in the area throughout the post-glacial, either at the lake margin or on the rather poor sandy soils of the area, where it still grows.

The climatic history of the later post-Atlantic period is a matter of considerable interest since it sets the immediate background for present-day conditions. Again it is a difficult period to deal with at the moment in the absence of a good chronology. That there were climatic changes in this period is clear from bog stratigraphy. In lowland raised bogs a distinction can usually be made between a lower, highly humified peat and an upper, less humified, peat. The boundary between these two peat types, sometimes referred to as the boundary horizon, or *grenzhorizont,* is, in fact, only the most pronounced of a series of such changes of humification. The horizons at which the humification becomes less were referred to by Jessen as recurrence surfaces (RS). The third deepest of these (RS-C) is the so-called boundary horizon, and it is this horizon that Jessen used as one of the criteria for his zone VII–VIII boundary. We have seen, however, that this boundary has been difficult to sustain as a generally applicable division of the post-glacial period. Nevertheless, the occurrence of the boundary horizon in Irish bogs is so general that it is difficult to believe that it does not have some climatic significance. That conditions became more oceanic, as Jessen supposed, is not impossible; certainly an increase in atmospheric moisture seems to be the minimum requirement to account for the change in peat humification, accompanied perhaps by a lowering of summer temperature. It is perhaps worth noting here that changes of wind conditions mentioned by Jessen are now hardly necessary to explain vegetational changes in this, or in previous periods. It has been shown by studies on the woodland on islands in Connemara that wind is probably not so restrictive of forest growth as has hitherto been presumed.[32] The date of the boundary horizon is probably not consistent across the country, as Mitchell has supposed, but this does nothing to nullify a climatic explanation.

Jessen found Late-Bronze Age implements generally above the boundary horizon. By comparison with the boundary horizon in England and on the continent, this carried the implication, for Jessen, that the Irish Late-Bronze Age was probably later than the same period elsewhere. This idea is unacceptable from an archaeological standpoint, and the whole problem needs to be re-investigated. The only C-14 date applicable to the problem is for the bog at Fallahogy, Co. Londonderry, Q-558: 2530 ± 120, 2440 ± 120, 2590 ± 120 B.C. which is for a sample immediately above the boundary horizon. Once they have been studied in detail, the other recurrence surfaces and retardation layers (bands of highly humified peat with heather remains) will possibly be a source of further information as to the climatic conditions of the period.

The extensive formation of upland blanket peat on land occupied and farmed in Neolithic and Bronze Age times again may have a climatic explanation. It has been suggested, on the other hand, that forest clearance by man, followed by podsolization and the formation of an impermeable humus layer or iron pan may have been responsible for the initiation of peat growth. Such fossil podsols are not of general occurrence beneath blanket peats, however, and podsolisation is clearly not a pre-requisite for blanket peat formation.

CONCLUSION

It will be apparent that very many problems remain in the study of the post-glacial vegetational and climatic history of Ireland. The problems are, however, reasonably well defined
and amenable to solution. When a more definitive account comes to be written it will
undoubtedly be the geographical aspects of the history that will have been amplified.

REFERENCES

1 J. R. Pilcher, Some applications of scanning electron microscopy to the study of modern and fossil
pollen, *Ulster. J. Arch.,* 31 (1968), 87–91

2 K. Jessen, Studies in Late Quaternary deposits and flora history of Ireland, *Proc. Roy. Irish Acad.,*
52 B (1949), 85–290

3 L. von Post, The prospect for pollen analysis in the study of the earth's climatic history, *New
Phytologist,* 45 (1946), 193–217

4 G. F. Mitchell, Studies in Irish Quaternary deposits: No. 7. *Proc. Roy. Irish Acad.,* 53 B (1951),
111–206
G. F. Mitchell, Post-Boreal pollen diagrams from Irish raised bogs, *Proc. Roy. Irish Acad.,* 57 B
(1956), 185–251

5 G. F. Mitchell, The late-glacial flora of Ireland, *Danm. geol. Unders.,* IIR, No. 80 (1954), 73–86

6 E. Hulten, *Atlas of the distribution of vascular plants in N.W. Europe,* (1950)

7 W. A. Watts, Late-glacial pollen zones in western Ireland, *Irish Geography,* 4 (1963), 367–76

8 G. Singh, Late-glacial vegetational history of Lecale, Co. Down, *Proc. Roy. Irish Acad.,* 69 B
(1970), 189–216

9 W. A. Watts, (1963), op. cit.

10 J. Iversen, The late-glacial flora of Denmark and its relation to climate and soil, *Danm. geol. Unders.,*
IIR, No. 80 (1954), 87–119

11 G. F. Mitchell and H. M. Parkes, The giant deer in Ireland, *Proc. Roy. Irish Acad.,* 52 B (1949),
291–314
G. F. Mitchell, The reindeer in Ireland, *Proc. Roy. Irish Acad.,* 48 B (1941), 183–8
G. Singh, Pollen analysis of a deposit at Roddans Port, Co. Down, N. Ireland, bearing reindeer
antler fragments, *Grana Palynologica,* 4 (1963), 466–474

12 J. Iversen, (1954), op. cit.

13 M. E. S. Morrison and N. Stephens, A submerged Late-Quaternary deposit at Roddans Port on the
north-east coast of Ireland, *Phil. Trans. Roy. Soc.,* B, 249 (1965), 221–55.
H. Godwin and E. H. Willis, Cambridge University Radiocarbon measurements VI, *Radiocarbon,*
6 (1964), 116–37

14 A. G. Smith, Cannons Lough, Kilrea, Co. Derry: stratigraphy and pollen analysis, *Proc. Roy. Irish
Acad.,* 61 B (1961), 369–83

15 G. F. Mitchell, Littleton Bog, Tipperary: an Irish vegetational record, *Geol. Soc. Amer., Special
paper* No. 84 (1965), 1–16
G. F. Mitchell, Littleton Bog, Tipperary, an Irish agricultural record, *J. Roy. Soc. Antiq. Ireland,*
95 (1965), 121–132

16 N. Fisher McMillan, Fauna, pp. 34–37 in H. J. Movius, An early post-glacial archaeological site
at Cushendun, County Antrim, *Proc. Roy. Irish Acad.,* 46 C (1940), 1–84

17 G. Singh, Studies of the Late-Quaternary vegetational history and sea-level changes in Co. Down,
N. Ireland, Unpublished PhD thesis (1964), The Queen's University of Belfast

18 H. Godwin, Radiocarbon dating and Quaternary history in Britain, *Proc. Roy. Soc.,* B, 153 (1960),
287–320

19 N. T. Maor, A radiocarbon dated pollen diagram from north-west Scotland, *New Phytologist, 68* (1969), 209–14
20 A. G. Smith, Problems of inertia and threshold related to post-glacial habitat changes, *Proc. Roy. Soc.,* B, 161 (1965), 331–42
   A. G. Smith, The influence of Mesolithic and Neolithic man on British vegetation: a discussion in D. Walker and R. G. West, ed. *Studies in the Vegetational History of the British Isles,* (1970), 81–96
21 F. Oldfield, Problems of mid-post-glacial pollen zonation in part of north-west England, *J. Ecology, 53* (1965), 247–60
22 R. Ll. Praeger, Report on the estuarine clays of the north-east of Ireland, *Proc. Roy. Irish Acad., 2* (1892), 212
   R. Ll. Praeger, Report on the raised beaches of the north-east of Ireland, with special reference to their fauna. *Proc. Roy. Irish Acad.,* 4 (1897), 30
23 A. G. Smith (1970), op. cit.
24 A. G. Smith, Pollen analytical investigations of the mire at Fallahogy Td., Co. Derry, *Proc. Roy. Irish Acad., 59* B (1958), 329–43
   A. G. Smith, The Atlantic-Sub-boreal transition, *Proc. Linn. Soc. Lond.,* 172 (1961), 38–49
   A. G. Smith, Problems in the study of the earliest agriculture in Northern Ireland, *Rep. VIth Int. Cong. Quat., Warsaw,* 2 (1964), 461–71
   A. G. Smith, (1970), op. cit.
   M. E. S. Morrison, Evidence and interpretation of 'Landnam' in the north-east of Ireland, *Bot. Notiser,* 112 (1959), 185–204
   W. A. Watts, Post-Atlantic forests in Ireland, *Proc. Linn. Soc. Lond.,* 172 (1961), 33–38
   R. McAulay and W. A. Watts, Dublin Radiocarbon Dates I, *Radiocarbon,* 3 (1961), 26–38
25 J. Iversen, Land occupation in Denmark's Stone Age, *Danm. geol. Unders.,* IIR, 66 (1941), 1–68
   J. Iversen, The influence of man on prehistoric vegetation, *Danm. geol. Unders.,* IVR, 3 (1949), 1–25
26 J. Troels Smith, Ertebøllekultur-bondekultur, *Aarb. Nord. Oldkynd. Hist.,* (1953), 1–62
27 G. F. Mitchell, (1951), op. cit.
28 A. G. Smith and E. H. Willis, Radiocarbon dating of the Fallahogy landnam phase. Ulster J. Arch., 24–5 (1962), 16–24
29 J. R. Pilcher, Archaeology, palaeoecology and radiocarbon dating of the Beaghmore stone circle site, *Ulster J. Arch.,* 32 (1969), 73–92
30 W. A. Watts, (1961), op. cit.
   R. McAulay and W. A. Watts, (1961), op. cit.
31 A. G. Smith (1961), op. cit.
32 D. Webb and E. V. Glanville, The vegetation and flora of some islands in the Connemara lakes, *Proc. Roy. Irish Acad.,* 62 B (1962), 31–54

RADIOCARBON DATES

The radiocarbon dates quoted can be traced in the journal *Radiocarbon,* from their index numbers: there are complete indices.

GENERAL REFERENCES

H. Godwin, *The History of the British Flora* (1956)
W. Pennington, *The History of British Vegetation* (1969)
R. G. West, *Pleistocene Geology and Biology* (1968)
G. W. Dimbleby, *Plants and Archaeology* (1967)

VI

SOILS AND PEDOGENESIS IN THE NORTH OF IRELAND

J. G. Cruickshank

The investigation of soils in Ireland lags behind that of most other countries in Western Europe. This is despite a decade of outstanding progress by the new National Soil Survey in the Republic of Ireland[1], and admirable work by a series of lone researchers during this century. It is perhaps even more surprising in view of the pioneer work of J. R. Kilroe in publishing his *Soil Geology of Ireland* in 1907, at a time when there was very little pedological research in progress outside Russia. More than half a century later, this classic work is still on sale and may be used as a reference text. From 1940 onwards, the applied aspects of soil science in Ireland were advanced by T. Walsh and P. H. Gallagher[2], together with other members of the Irish Agricultural Institute. But little was done in Northern Ireland until after the Second World War, when the senior members of the present staff of the Department of Agricultural Chemistry at Queen's University began their work. Scientific staff of the Ministry of Agriculture and the agricultural and biological departments at Queen's University have been responsible for many experimental programmes, both in the field and laboratory. Soil testing and top soil mapping have been carried out as part of the Northern Ireland Government's agricultural advisory work. However, there is at present no soil survey organisation in Northern Ireland, and comparatively little pedological mapping or associated laboratory investigation has been undertaken. The soil survey memoirs being published for counties in the Republic of Ireland may be used as a source of borrowed knowledge, as they report similar soil associations and soil series to some of those found in Northern Ireland. Several of the soil parent materials to be discussed extend generally across the northern half of Ireland observing no political boundary, and the same may be said about the other factors of soil formation.

Soil forming factors

It has been suggested that parent material is the most effective environmental factor in soil development, though this view has been challenged. Elsewhere it has been claimed that soils in the north of Ireland are at an immature stage of development, and for this reason strongly reflect the characteristics of their parent materials.[3] In the view of the author, the latter statement is not the corollary of the first, or vice versa. This unnecessary conflict of interpretation derives from confusion between weathering and pedogenesis.

Because soil parent materials have reached only a youthful or immature stage in weathering in the twenty or thirty thousand years since the Weichsel ice sheets covered two-thirds of Ireland, they must reflect closely the mineral composition of derivative rocks (Fig. 6.1). Pedogenesis is certainly influenced by weathering, but not exclusively so, for the

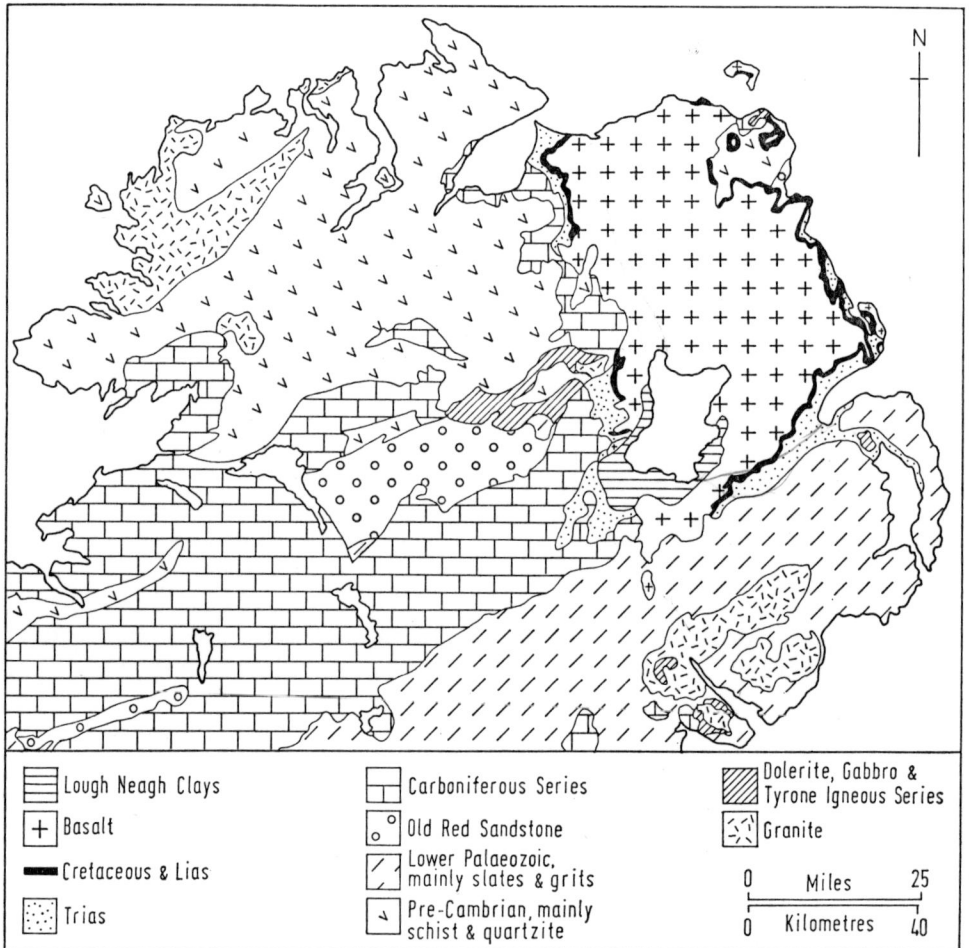

Fig. 6.1 Simplified geology of the north of Ireland.

formation of a soil profile is a compound process. The profile develops relatively quickly in the early stages, lasting a few hundred or as much as a thousand years, and thereafter adjusts more slowly under the conditions of the local environment. There were considerable changes in the natural environment in late- and early post-glacial times, but in the last 8,000–10,000 years these have been relatively minor in respect of pedogenesis. It is inconceivable that a soil profile should fail to reflect soil forming conditions in this period even if the weathering is immature. Since Mesolithic man came into the north of Ireland almost 8,000 years ago[4], perhaps greater changes have occurred in man-modified soils. There will be local exceptions where the soil profile may be regarded as immature, or in other cases 'fossil', but normally it should be in a state of dynamic equilibrium with its soil forming environment.

A map of superficial deposits, including blanket and lowland peat, is basic to the understanding of pedogenesis in the north of Ireland (Fig. 6.2). The glacial deposits of importance are those deposited or reworked during the last glaciation, as earlier tills will be either buried

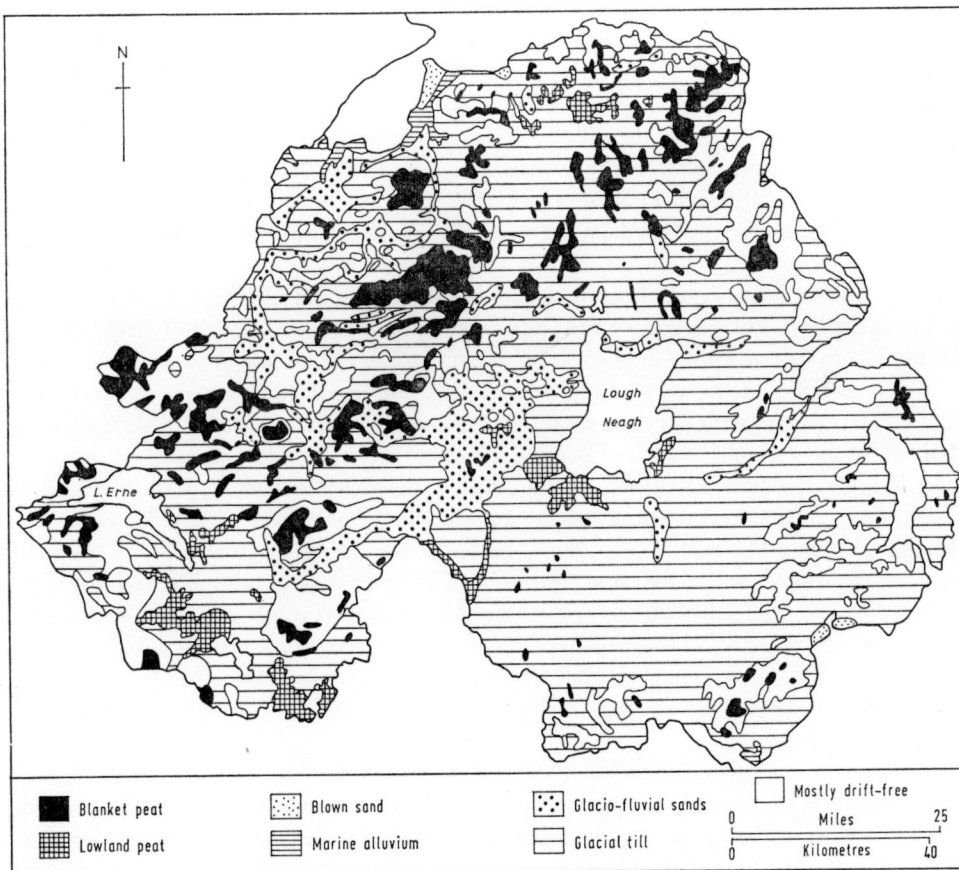

Fig. 6.2   Superficial deposits in Northern Ireland. Areas mostly drift-free lie above 1,000 feet (305 m), but there are exceptions in the west where there are extensive areas of rock outcrop below that height.

or have been modified by periglacial weathering during the last glaciation. There are sites where weathering and pedogenesis are 'fossil' to contemporary processes and where relicts of pre-glacial age are preserved.[5] The latosols of a narrow strip of Tertiary interbasaltic material in co. Antrim, and sub-tropical red loam soils on the older granite in co. Down, are such examples, but these have only sporadic distribution.

In the north of Ireland glacial till usually has a large proportion by weight of clay plus silt fractions in the fine earth material ($<$ 2 mm diameter). The only exceptions are tills derived from quartz-rich granite, schist, Triassic sandstone and Old Red Sandstone rocks. In tills with more than 30 per cent clay, or more than 45 per cent clay plus silt, permeability is reduced markedly and high moisture retention normally leads to gleying of the soil profile. Surface water gleying produced by perched water tables in clayey till is common in the north of Ireland on a variety of parent materials. The greater part of the drumlin-forming tills of the west, in counties Fermanagh, Cavan, Monaghan, Leitrim and in west Tyrone, are strongly gleyed[6], and much of the till derived from basalt and shale is gleyed to some degree. Till may be strongly consolidated and compacted, so that moisture per-colation is further inhibited. Upper limits of glacial till may be identified in some places by the contrast of gleying on the till and free drainage above on less compacted, soliflucted material of similar texture. Drift free areas, and even those where the till cover is only a veneer, are generally well drained, partly due to the greater pore space of the parent materials. Slope is often a secondary factor, improving drainage only in some cases. Glacio-fluvial deposits are almost always well drained. Extensive sand and gravel deposits occur over a wide altitudinal range from the Lagan valley, through most of east Tyrone, and also in the valleys and hill margins of the Sperrin mountains. The full range of freely drained profiles, from brown earths to peaty podsols, can be found only on these deposits.

Relief is expressed as a soil forming factor mainly through altitude and slope. The former is closely associated with climate, while slope combines with parent material to influence drainage in the soil. In the north of Ireland, it is extremely rare to find slopes demonstrating a hydrologic sequence or extensive areas with a climosequence of soil profiles. Sandy textured materials found on slopes in the Mournes and Sperrins are generally too acid to develop anything but podsols. Highly basic basalt and chalk materials do not normally become podsolised under existing climatic conditions; most common of all, are fine-textured parent materials which become gleyed. Steepness of slope is likely to remove the chance of gleying only on the Antrim coast margins of the basalt plateau and the steeper slopes of the Mourne mountains. Cliff slopes occur on Tertiary basalts and Carboniferous Limestone, but steep slopes of 20 to 30 degrees on unconsolidated materials are uncommon in the north of Ireland.

Climate, as a soil forming factor in a relatively small area, is expressed mainly through spatial variation of excess annual precipitation and the temperature regulation of weathering and organic decay. Temperature, wind, humidity and other climatic elements are important in the measure to which they influence average excess precipitation over the normal means of moisture loss from the soil. Monthly potential evapo-transpiration values, calculated by the Penman method, are now available from the Meteorological Office in Belfast for 14 widely spaced stations in the north of Ireland. Despite an altitudinal range from sea level to 273 m (900 ft) these annual potential evapo-transpiration values vary only between 350 and 450 mm (14 and 18 ins) of moisture. The range of actual values is presumably even less. Monthly moisture deficits appear in the summer months at most stations, except in the western uplands, and may occur in two or three consecutive months at lowland stations in the east and north. However, the areal variation of monthly or annual potential evapo-transpiration is small compared with that of mean annual rainfall, and probably is relatively unimportant in explaining areal differences in pedogenesis.[7] The highest potential evapo-transpiration values in the area indicate a moisture loss of less than half the mean annual precipitation. Monthly moisture deficits in summer at lowland stations can be serious for agriculture, but are probably neither long enough nor frequent enough to modify significantly the processes of leaching or gleying, even where the rate of these processes is reduced. In most months there is an excess of precipitation over potential evapo-transpiration and run-off, which allows leaching at freely drained sites. At lowland sites in the north, east and central areas, leaching in freely drained glacio-fluvial sands and sandstone tills could be expected only in winter months and would be limited to the decalcification of brown earths. Brown podsolic profiles are also found on sands and gravels, indicating the early stages of iron movement in podsolisation. In western localities and above about 120 m (400 ft) in the east, podsols of different types appear on freely drained sites. A most useful index of climatic wetness is the lower altitudinal limit of blanket peat, which is discussed in a later section.

Vegetation and man (as part of the biotic factor) are in some ways complementary in influencing soil formation in a long-settled and cultivated landscape. Man has modified the structure and fertility of the upper horizons of most soils by centuries of plough and spade cultivation. Man as a cultivator has been in Ireland for nearly 5,000 years[8], but cultivated land reached a possible maximum only in the last few centuries and probably an acme in the nineteenth century. Today the area of improved land is over 80 per cent of the potential agricultural land in most parts.[9] Cultivation has made a distinct impression in weakening the natural structure of the soil and depleting soil fertility, except on farms with sound management. An unfavourable relationship between man and soil is best demonstrated by puddling or poaching created by cattle trampling a weakened structure. This is a familiar sight where soil disperses easily under physical attack, the product of moisture saturation and depletion of bases. Little remains of even semi-natural vegetation to demonstrate the differential role of plants in pedogenesis. On some of the large estates, such as Clandeboye in north Down, examples can be found of the effect of planted trees on the development of soil profiles on uniform parent material and where there are almost uniform conditions in the other variables. At Cairn Wood, Clandeboye, in a hundred-year-old mixed plantation on thin drift overlying Palaeozoic shales, Scots pine with a heath ground cover has developed strongly horizonated podsols, while adjacent beech stands are associated with brown earths. The rarity of such examples, and the fact that most post-war tree planting involves only one species, Sitka spruce, support the case for a regional approach in examining pedogenesis in the north of Ireland.

A REGIONAL APPROACH TO PEDOGENESIS

Basalt soils of the Antrim plateau

Soils derived from basic igneous rocks have attracted an exceptional degree of research interest in a variety of environments, and have been discussed in a series of papers for Northern Ireland.[10] This parent rock, through the nature of its constituent minerals, exerts an almost unique influence on associated weathered till, and ultimately on the soils developed. Because the parent material is unusual the influence of other soil forming factors may appear to be reduced.

Tertiary basalt lavas covering 4,009 km² (1,548 sq miles) comprise almost one third of the landscape of Northern Ireland. It is the largest continuous unit of basic igneous rock in the British Isles, and for this reason alone, would merit special consideration. The basalt series are divided generally into the earlier, lower flows, which are usually below 305 m (1,000 ft), and the upper flows, which in their eastern remnants form an elevated plateau surface. Within this landscape, soil forming situations range from sea level to over 600 m (1,800 ft), with a mean annual precipitation varying from 750 to 1,750 mm (30 in to 70 in). Most soils of the Tertiary basalts could be classed as variations of brown earths, with the qualification that gleying is common to different degrees. Brown earths are unusually widespread and may be found up to 305 m (1,000 ft), where 1,250 mm (50 in) annual rainfall is recorded and podsolisation would be expected. But podsols are uncommon even in high rainfall areas, and the rare cases are related to a particularly high iron content in the parent material. The basalt soils are characterised by large cation exchange capacities, high content of exchangeable calcium and magnesium cations, an abundance of sesquioxides of iron and aluminium from ferro-magnesian minerals, and a strongly bonded structure which is related to the chemical properties. These properties help to maintain a high base status in basalt soils, producing brown earths under freely drained conditions.

Basalt soils are easily identified by their colour and structure. Freely drained basalt soil has a distinctive chocolate-brown colour which may mask the presence of organic matter. Analyses nearly always show a higher organic matter content than is apparent in the field. A fluctuating water-table, creating gleying, can be identified by bright yellow-orange mottles of ferric iron and a pale purple background of hydrated compounds. Structure is clearly developed into strongly cemented units of crumb or blocky shape, which can be seen as discrete and consolidated aggregates, resisting break-up even under physical attack by hammering with a pestle.

As early as 1907 Kilroe[11] observed the unusual chemical properties of basalt soils, noting that they were rich in calcium and phosphorus, but poor in potassium, being notably deficient in potash feldspars. More recently, research has been concerned with the problem of high cation exchange capacities in basalt soils being less related to the clay and humus content than to the form and nature of the products of weathering. The primary mineral composition of basalt is dominated by labradorite, augite and olivine, to over 80 per cent by weight and volume. Clay minerals produced in chemical weathering are numerous, but olivine weathers early in the sequence to form vermiculite. The particle shape of vermiculite is often larger than clay size (i.e. $> 2\ \mu$) and hence contributes its high cation exchange property to the larger-size silt fraction. These have been referred to as the pseudo-aggregates of silt size which contain some clay minerals.

The cation exchange capacities of basalt soils are usually in the range of 35 to 55 millegram-equivalents per 100 grams of soil, which is regarded as large, and much larger than would be found in similar textures on other parent materials. Normally a cation exchange capacity (C.E.C.) is related to the clay and humus content of the soil, but in basalt soils the C.E.C. may not change and may even increase as the clay and humus decreases with depth. It has been shown that material of sand size may contribute up to 30 per cent of the C.E.C., and the silt fraction up to 50 per cent. The clay fraction contributes up to 80 per cent in the surface horizon but often only 20 to 40 per cent in the deepest horizon. In this zone of initial weathering from the parent material, the clay minerals are in a large size category or are cemented into larger aggregates. The bonding of these aggregates is particularly effective because of the ferric and aluminium oxides and high content of exchangeable bases. Calcium usually dominates the composition of the C.E.C. in any soil (to the extent of 80 to 90 per cent), but in some basalt soils magnesium can make up 40 per cent of the total cations. The high magnesium content is another diagnostic property of weathered basalt, and has been used to trace the direction of movement of glacial drift.

Basaltic brown earths of high base status (pH 6.5 to 7.0) require little lime treatment under cultivation. They are less rich in the other plant nutrients, particularly available phosphate, and will respond to fertiliser treatment. Liming improves the physical condition and increases the availability of phosphate. Brown earths develop on the sandy and loam-textured material of kame-moraine areas between Garvagh and Kilrea, Coleraine and Armoy, and around Ballymena, as well as shallow drift and drift-free slopes on the eastern plateau. Where the clay fraction exceeds 28 to 33 per cent, the soils will retain their own water-table and show gleying features, even on steeply sloping sites. Glacial till in the Bann valley and around Lough Neagh has a clay-loam texture, and the soils are always strongly gleyed. Podsols with iron-pan horizons are restricted to the interbasaltic weathered materials between the upper and lower basalt flows. They are found in the eastern uplands, usually around 305 m (1,000 ft), where the ferric-aluminium oxide material outcrops. They should be regarded as iron-rich soils rather than podsols of a climosequence. By coincidence their occurrence is often peripheral to the blanket peat cover, and in the same altitudinal zone as would be expected for climatically induced iron-pan podsols.

In geological and locational association with the Tertiary basalt, the underlying Cretaceous chalk outcrops in a narrow band along much of the periphery of the basalt plateau. Frequently, the chalk outcrop makes only a minor break of slope, and is usually covered by glacial drift or slope deposits derived from the basalt upslope. 'Chalk soils' are developed on mixed, highly calcareous parent materials, and seldom from chalk alone. Their profiles are well-drained, calcareous brown earths of loam or silt-loam texture. In north-east Antrim, geological faulting has resulted in the separation and elevation (to 212 m or 700 ft) of a chalk block, which has a thin cover of schistose drift with acid, decalcified, iron-pan podsols. Close by, blanket peat covers the chalk, but is probably separated from contact with bedrock by a thin seal of schistose material.

Soils of the north-west

In the Roe valley and north Sperrins of co. Londonderry, Cretaceous, Triassic and Carboniferous rocks are exposed in north-south trending outcrops in a broad depression between Tertiary basalts and Dalradian schists. Ice moved from the central Sperrins in a northerly direction during the last glaciation[12] and was channelled parallel to the various rock outcrops in the Roe valley rather than across them, so glacial till limits coincide almost exactly with their derivative rock types, from which they gain their textural and chemical properties. But in the till derived from Cretaceous chalk and Triassic marl and sandstone, there is a considerable admixture of basalt as a result of solifluction, rock falls, slumping, and downslope creep from elevated positions, rather than by glacial movement. Extensive sand and gravel hills of glacio-fluvial origin occur near the north coast between Ballykelly and Limavady, and there are several cross-valley moraines representing halt stages between the coast and the Sperrins. These kame moraines provide excessively well-drained materials which readily become podsolised. Brown podsolic profiles are the rule below about 91 m (300 ft) and iron podsol profiles occur above that height. The glacio-fluvial sands are mainly found overlying schists on the west side of the valley, and their schistose composition contributes to their podsolisation. Freely drained profiles are found also as shallow brown earths on basalt slopes, on chalk outcrops, and on the most sandy strata of the Triassic sandstones. These brown earths are of medium base status and are confined to the east side of the Roe valley.

Gleying is the rule of pedogenesis in till overlying both sedimentary rocks and schists to the west and south, but there is a difference in the causes of gleying. Dominance of fine particles in the texture is responsible in the sedimentary rock tills and impermeable pan formation in the schist till. The Roe does not have a wide level floor because the river has cut deeply in places into an undulating landscape, so that topography plays a minor part in the development of gleys. There are some alluvial areas where the ground water table is close to the surface, and even above the mineral surface where raised bogs have formed. These are not common in the Roe valley or in co. Londonderry, in general, except in the south-east near Lough Neagh. Gleying is found even on sloping sites, and is associated with perched water tables which may coalesce with the ground water table. Triassic marl out-crops below the Cretaceous chalk on the steep eastern slopes of the Roe valley, but despite their position and the angle of slope, the marl soils are strongly gleyed. High silt plus clay content (40 to 50 per cent) is responsible in this case, a condition found also in the fine grained strata of the Triassic sandstone and Carboniferous calcareous sandstone. The till of the last mentioned rock is distinctive by its large proportion of silt plus fine sand fraction. The proportion of silt (15 to 20 per cent), together with the relative lack of coarse sand and gravel, is probably responsible for gleying in the Carboniferous sandstone till. Till from the Carboniferous sandstone in co. Tyrone has the same texture (clay loam often containing 25 per cent silt plus 30 per cent clay) and the same characteristics of gleying. The surface water gleying of these sedimentary tills is not surprising when related to texture and structure. Less expected is surface water gleying on sloping sites of sandy loam till (usually 65 to 70 per cent sand) on the mica-schists. In the surface horizons of these soils, the consistency is loose and drainage is free. The gleying appears at about 40 cm (15 in) from the surface, just above a strongly cemented and compacted horizon. This indurated or pan horizon has a platy structure, and may be cemented by silicates. The pan is 10 to 15 cm (4 to 6 in) thick, almost impermeable, and promotes surface gleying; below it, drainage is free. The presence of, and the depth and thickness of, the indurated horizon are predictable characteristics of sandy, schist soils in the area around the hill of Loughermore, west of Limavady, and throughout most of the Sperrins. It has also been reported by Hill[13] in the schist soils of agricultural areas in co. Tyrone, with the implication that the induration is a ploughing-pan accentuated by poor management. Preliminary investigations by the author indicate that the compacted horizon is a natural feature of schistose till, and usually occurs well below ploughing depth.

The Sperrin hills are extensively covered with blanket peat. Their morphology, elevation, location, and soil acidity are all conducive to the accumulation of peat which usually overlaps the upper limits of the last glaciation till. Till exposures, both peat covered and cultivated, are sandy, micaceous and stony, and at least slightly mottled by gleying. Soils are a dull grey colour with little indication of oxidised iron. They are naturally of low agricultural fertility, but respond very well with fertiliser treatment; cation exchange capacities are small, and pH values of 4.5 to 5.5 are the most common. Schistose soils are low in available potash, and respond remarkably after potash dressing. Traditionally they are known as productive potato soils. Sandy glacio-fluvial deposits are piled high in the Sperrin valleys, and these develop strongly horizonated podsols.

Soils of the Carboniferous and Old Red Sandstone

The greater area of counties Tyrone and Fermanagh comprises Old Red Sandstone and Carboniferous formations, the latter extending far into the Republic of Ireland. Most of the area of these rock types is deeply mantled by glacial till, frequently moulded into drumlins, which contribute to the complexity of local and regional drainage. Relative relief is small, and there are minimal drainage gradients into the Lough Ernes, the upper Foyle and Lough Neagh systems. Tills derived from Old Red Sandstone and Carboniferous limestone may contain more than 30 per cent clay, which further contributes to the widespread formation of gleyed soils. The soils of drumlin lowlands are strongly gleyed clay loams, and are found in a wedge shape, widening and extending south-westwards from Lough Neagh. Pastures are infested with rushes and wet-site weeds, and the agricultural land is seasonally water-logged and flooded. The western, oceanic presence is strongly expressed in the climate west of Lough Neagh, particularly in higher relative humidity and frequency of rain days.

It is unusual to find Old Red Sandstone till so poorly drained, but in the north of Ireland some series weather to a high proportion of clay, and it has been suggested[14] that 40 per cent of these soils in co. Tyrone are clay loam in texture. It is possible to find 35 per cent clay in the lower horizons of the soils within a radius of 8 km (5 miles) of Dromore, co. Tyrone. These exceptionally clayey soils also have a high proportion of silt, which makes mole-drainage difficult. Towards Lough Erne, the Old Red Sandstone till is much more sandy and

H

stony, and the drumlins are larger. Here it is possible to find brown earths near the drumlin crests, but with gleying on lower slopes. The soils are low in phosphate, relatively low in potash, and a deficiency of lime is related to a lack of calcium compounds in the parent material (pH 4.5 to 5.5). Without artificial drainage and fertilizer treatment, these Old Red Sandstone soils have a low natural fertility.

The Carboniferous series is represented mainly by the Middle and Lower Limestone Series. Till derived from the Middle limestones is a tenacious clay-loam (Calp), blue-grey in colour. Fine-grained sandstones and shales also produce clay-rich till in which the clay proportion is frequently over 35 per cent. Silt content is usually high, and the combined silt and clay may comprise more than half the till by weight. On these parent materials soils are strongly gleyed, and present a serious drainage problem both locally and regionally, with drainage only made possible by using closely spaced stone ditches.[15] Superimposed on the Carboniferous clay till are extensive kame-moraine sands and gravels, well displayed from Caledon to Cookstown, and around Pomeroy. These glacio-fluvial deposits form ridges and hillocks with steep ice-contact faces, making slopes and local soil drainage variable over short distances. Well drained, leached, and podsolised soils are the rule on the sands, but as they are derived from calcareous material, their pH is about 6.0 to 7.0. There is less than 20 per cent clay in these soils, contrasting with the clay-loam till often found intermixed with the sands. The glacio-fluvial material is relatively lime-rich from local Carboniferous limestone rocks, but low in phosphate and potash.

Soils in county Down

In the south-east of the Province, the different rock types may be identified by their clear topographical expression, emphasised by geological faulting, volcanic activity, intrusion of granites, the sharp upper limits of glaciation, and the different degrees of resistance to glacial erosion. The older and newer granites and their respective aureole rocks stand out as the uplands of Slieve Croob and the Mournes. Steep slopes, quartz-rich parent materials, and a sandy texture, promote free drainage and ultimately podsolisation.

The accompanying soil map of the Mournes (Fig. 6.3) displays an arrangement of peat-covered 'flats' and podsolised slopes. Where podsols have developed, the characteristic profile is shallow, has a mor or peaty surface horizon and an incipient or formed iron pan; on the treeless hills, they are associated with heath communities. Elsewhere, slopes greater than 25 degrees have skeletal soils, screes and slope-buttresses or tor formations; at lower elevations, level and gently sloping sites on granite drift, as well as sites on till derived from Palaeozoic shales, develop gley soils with wet site grassland. The greater part of the south-east lowland is composed of Silurian shale till, moulded into drumlins. Slopes are short and variable; parent materials are fine-textured and less acid than the granites.[16] With favourable slopes, and loam textures, it is usual to expect grey-brown podsolic profiles, freely-drained and only slightly acid. Where the shale till is shallow or thinning-out at its upper margins, as on Slieve Croob, it may have a loam texture and become relatively loosely consolidated. In such sites, well drained, low base status soils may also be found. More commonly, the loam soils of the shale till are gleyed to some degree, becoming strongly

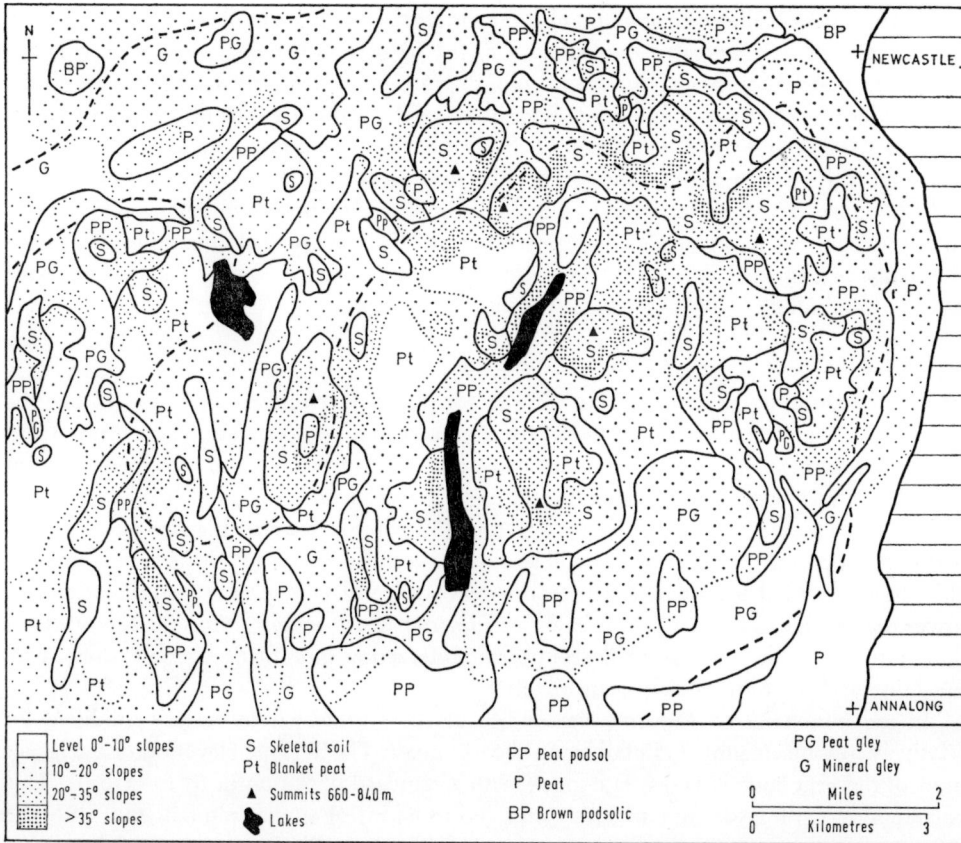

Fig. 6.3 Soils and slopes in the Mourne Mountains, co. Down. The highest summits (range 660–840 metres) are indicated, along with four major slope categories. (Map supplied by E. A. Colhoun) The association between soil and slope is particularly striking in this area of the north of Ireland.

(*Note:* Granite outcrops in the north-west corner of the map, north of the heavy, dashed line. Silurian shales and grits occupy the area between the heavy dashed lines, including a coastal strip from Newcastle to Annalong: granites underlie the greater part of the mountain area in the south-centre of the map).

gleyed downslope and intermixed with waterlogged alluvium and bog in the interdrumlin depressions. Tills derived from chalk and Triassic sandstone, along with glacio-fluvial sands, comprise the well-drained parent materials on which develop brown earths, grey-brown podsolics and brown podsolic profiles in the Lagan-Dundonald lowlands. Clay-alluvium in the Lagan valley, and clay loam till from basalt lavas are strongly gleyed, and extend westward into gleys associated with the Lough Neagh clays and drumlins of the Carboniferous limestones.

An interesting pedological problem in county Down is the development of a deeply weathered regolith on the southern slopes of the older Newry granite complex. On the southern slopes of Slieve Croob and also on the flanks of Slieve Gullion, west of Newry, quarry sections have revealed more than 7 m (23 ft) of weathered granodiorite, which is the parent material of the present soil profile. Exposures occur in protected positions on the lower hill slopes, and yet beyond the upper limits of the drumlins. The distribution of these soils, as a soil complex, on the flanks of Slieve Croob, would cover 13 km² (5 sq miles). Proudfoot[17] has suggested that the soil profiles may be of great age and are relict to present soil formation. The soils are freely drained, iron rich, red or brown in colour, and may be the product of last interglacial chemical weathering. They are related to humid sub-tropical red loams or rotlehms, and should not be confused with adjacent iron-rich brown podsolic soils on granitic till.

PEAT

Climate becomes notable as a soil forming factor in the development of blanket peat. The altitudinal zone of blanket peat is normally associated with excessive surface wetness from a climate in which mean annual rainfall is over 1,250 mm (50 in) and precipitation is at least three times as great as evapo-transpiration. Even in the formation of blanket peat, the influence of climate is modified by topography and parent material. Blanket peat will not form on slopes over 15 degrees, and will be slow to accumulate on any slope having favourable drainage. Acid parent materials tend to encourage blanket peat development and to lower the altitudinal limit, whereas base rich materials act in reverse. Thus the lower altitudinal limit of blanket peat is a reflection of the interaction of climatic wetness, slope, permeability and reaction of the parent material.

In the mountains of Mourne, the acidity of the granite parent rock is modified by relatively low mean annual rainfall along the east coast. The average elevation of the lower limit of the peat zone is 315 m (1,050 ft), with a standard deviation of 63 m (210 ft). This corresponds with 1,500 mm to 1,625 mm (60 to 65 in) of annual rainfall, and with the presence of certain erosion surfaces in the central Mournes. Blanket peat is found on level surfaces with annual rainfall as low as 1,125 mm (45 in), but this is an exceptional case in the southern Mournes. It has accumulated to considerable depths on these limited areas of level ground, and in the past there has been extensive peat cutting for domestic fuel. Cutting may have contributed to the erosion of the exploited cover.[18]

Blanket peat on the Antrim basalts is related to morphology of a different type. The nearly level flows of lava provide ideal surfaces for waterlogging and the development of peat. In south Antrim, the Star Bog over Skeagh Hill has its boundary at an average of 305 m (1,000 ft) and 1,250 to 1,375 mm (50 to 55 in) rainfall, and on Divis Mountain a similar peat boundary coincides with 1,050 to 1,125 mm (42 to 45 in) of rainfall. Farther north, around Carncormick, Collin Top, Trostan, and Parkmore, the lower peat limit continues at 305 m (1,000 ft), but the rainfall is about 1,500 mm (60 in). Thus, at all sites on the basalts, the peat is more closely associated with the form of the lava flows than with any other factor. Steep cliffs falling from about 305 m (1,000 ft) on east and south sides of the plateau prohibit peat developing. The mean annual rainfall of the peat edge is 1,050 to 1,500 mm (42 to 60 in) and does not seem to act as the main control. Lying to the north-east of the basalt is an outlier of Dalradian mica-schist with the similar local climate. Level surfaces and a highly acid rock lower the average height of the blanket peat edge to 210 m (700 ft), standard deviation 31 m (100 ft), corresponding to 1,125 mm to 1,250 mm (45 to 50 in) rainfall. While this much lower boundary of peat can be explained partly by the acidity of the rock and the podsolised mineral soil below the peat, there are chalk outcrops nearby at Greenhill and Goodland where blanket peat is found at 225 m (750 ft). In these apparent anomalies, the peat may be associated with a thin but effective seal of drift over the chalk. Podsol profiles beneath the peat are found where the schistose drift is more than a few inches in depth.

Westwards, across the Bann valley, blanket peat reappears on the western margins of the basalt plateau and on the Sperrin mountains. On the basalt the average height of the peat edge is again 305 m (1,000 ft), with a standard deviation of 69 m (230 ft), associated with about 1,125 to 1,250 mm (45 to 50 in) of rainfall. Much lower peat limits are found in the Loughermore part of the Sperrins, where acid schist and gentle slopes take the peat limit down to an average of 180 m (600 ft), standard deviation 35 m or 117 ft. The peat margins have been cut back for fuel and cleared for cultivation so that the natural lower limit was probably close to 150 m (500 ft) and 1,125 mm (45 in) of rainfall. In the rest of the Sperrins, the average height of the peat edge is 243 m (809 ft) with between 1,250 and 1,375 mm (50 and 55 in) rainfall. The acidity of the schist may have some effect in lowering the peat edge, but in addition these uplands lie west and south-west of the basalt with higher rainfall for the same elevation. On both basalt and schist blanket peat can be expected with 1,250 mm (50 in) mean annual rainfall. Much the same applies in the far west in co. Fermanagh where the peat edge is at 210 m (700 ft) on Millstone Grit (1,250 mm, 50 in rainfall), and slightly higher at 305 m (1,000 ft) on limestone 1,375 mm (55 in) rainfall, On the co. Fermanagh—co. Donegal border, the blanket peat boundary comes down to 120 m (400 ft) on acid schists, but even at this low elevation, annual rainfall is over 1,250 mm (50 in).

In the distribution of blanket peat in Northern Ireland, wetness of site is the main control. Generally, peat is found on all parent materials where there is more than 1,250 mm (50 in) rainfall. The exceptions to this rule are due to slope interference rather more than to parent material. Steep slopes cut off peat in the Mournes and isolate most of it above the 1,500 mm (60 in) isohyet, despite the acidity of the rock. Peat will form on base rich basalt with less than 1,250 mm (50 in) rainfall provided level surfaces exist, as for example on Divis Mountain. The very low altitudinal limits in the Sperrins, 120 to 180 m (400 to 600 ft), are still related to a 1,250 mm (50 in) rainfall, and not necessarily to the acidity of the parent material.

Blanket peat has been cut-over for centuries to supply domestic fuel. In most areas agricultural communities have been close to a local supply of peat and have enjoyed the community right to exploit it. The tools and method of peat cutting are part of Irish heritage and have been fully discussed elsewhere.[19] Blanket peat units in Northern Ireland are usually too small and too irregular in depth to allow commercial development, except for one enterprise on Altahullion, near Dungiven, in co. Londonderry.[20] Such has been the scale of domestic removal that considerable ecological change must be involved. New mineral soil has been exposed for cultivation, and soil profiles have lost their natural peat cover. In many instances, theories of pedogenesis have to be based on speculation in the absence of a complete cover of blanket peat. Natural erosion and bog bursts have also modified the peat cover.[21]

The considerable area of lowland peat in Northern Ireland is widely dispersed in relatively small inter-drumlin depressions and a few raised bogs in the Bann Valley. In the drumlin belt peat areas are small, waterlogged and agriculturally unproductive. Permanent pasture on the lake shore, and inter-drumlin peat around Upper Lough Erne, has now assumed a more than seasonal use since the artificial control of the lake level.[22] Carrots and potatoes are favoured crops in this deep and easily worked soil. Extensive fen peat stretches inland from the south shore of Lough Neagh across low-lying country where Tertiary clays outcrop. There is some commercial exploitation of peat for horticultural purposes near Portadown. Raised bogs in the Bann valley and north co. Antrim carry a canopy of acid peat which makes them suitable only for domestic fuel exploitation.

Lowland bogs preserve in their stratigraphy a valuable record of local ecological conditions since their inception. By pollen analysis and radio-carbon dating of material from a number of sites, a wider impression of the dynamic ecology of the landscape may be reconstructed.[23] Many of these bogs are of great age, their basal sediments dating from late-glacial times, and they record the character of major ecological changes before and after the coming of man. Blanket peat more often spans a much shorter time scale, having greatly extended its distribution only in the sub-Atlantic wetter period, burying monuments of earlier Neolithic and Bronze age settlement. The problem of measuring short-period soil history during and after cultivation is a formidable one, but a beginning has been made by Proudfoot[24] for a site on the chalk in north Antrim.

CONCLUSION

This survey of the spatial variation in soils and pedogenesis in the north of Ireland has concentrated on the contrasting character of soil regions. The principal parent materials are distributed in extensive and continuous units, providing the basis of distinctive soil forming regions. The internal variety of soils in each does not support the concept of parent material as the dominating factor in pedogenesis. Rock mineral composition is reflected in the overlying till, but not necessarily in soil profile development. Each soil region has its own spectrum of soil profiles, brown earths, podsols and gleys being found in several. Properties such as cation exchange capacity and base status are more closely associated with parent material.

There have been several reviews of soils in Northern Ireland[25] from an agricultural viewpoint. It is not surprising that these appraisals emphasised the character of the parent materials, for in the physical and chemical fertility of soil this is most important. The increasing use of fertilisers and other land improvement techniques have meant that soil productivity has been, or can be, brought within a relatively small range over all parent materials. However, this is achieved only at a cost, and the variation in soil or land profitability may be influenced to some degree by the character of the parent material.

The soil geography of the north of Ireland reveals many challenging problems which can be only partly understood at the present stage of knowledge. Pedogenesis of unglaciated and glacially protected areas is one that must borrow information from Pleistocene history and studies in rock weathering. The origins, direction of movement, thickness and limits of glacial till are basic facts to any investigation of soils in Ireland.[26] The role of man has probably been under-estimated in this general review, which draws conclusions on potential natural soil development rather than describing actual conditions after cultivation and management. A detailed record of soils is possible only on a large-scale map, and while the author considers map evidence essential to any discussion of soil geography, the demands of publication preclude incorporation of field maps. Such is the variation of soil profile over small areas in the north of Ireland that field examination and detailed mapping is the necessary preliminary to an understanding of pedogenesis.

REFERENCES

1 M. J. Gardiner and P. Ryan, *Soils of County Wexford,* (An Foras Taluntais, Dublin, 1964)
2 T. Walsh and P. J. Gallagher, Characteristics of Irish soil types I, *Proc. Roy. Irish Acad.,* 47 B (1942), 205–49
3 S. McConaghy and J. S. V. McAllister, Soils in L. J. Symons ed., *Land use in Northern Ireland,* (1963), 93–108
4 G. F. Mitchell, The mesolithic site at Toome Bay, co. Londonderry, *Ulster J. Arch.,* 3rd series, 18 (1955), 1–16
5 V. B. Proudfoot, Relict rotlehm in Northern Ireland, *Nature,* 181 (1958), 1287
6 J. Mulqueen and W. Burke, *Review of drumlin soils research, 1959–66,* (An Foras Taluntais, Dublin, 1967)
7 T. Walker, A study of evapo-transpiration and run-off in Northern Ireland, (Unpublished MA thesis, Queen's University Belfast, 1963)
   Monthly potential evapo-transpiration calculations and other data from Meteorological Office, Belfast
8 W. A. Watts, C-14 dating and the neolithic in Ireland, *Antiquity,* 34 (1960), 111–116
9 L. J. Symons, ed., *Land use in Northern Ireland,* (1963)
10 W. O. Brown, Some soil formations of the basaltic region of north-east Ireland, *Irish Nat. Jour.,* 11 (1954), 120–132
   J. Smith, A mineralogical study of weathering and soil formation from olivine basalt in Northern Ireland, *J. Soil Science,* 8 (1957), 225–239
   D. M. McAleese and S. McConaghy, Studies on the basaltic soils of Northern Ireland, *J. Soil Science,* 8 and 9 (1957–8): i, Cation exchange properties, (1957), 127–34; ii, Contributions from the sand, silt and clay separates to cation-exchange properties, (1957), 135–40; iii, Exchangeable-cation contents of sand, silt and clay separates, (1958), 66–75; iv, Mineralogical study of the clay separates, (1958), 76–80; v, Cation-exchange capacities and mineralogy of the silt separates (2–20 μ), (1958), 81–88; vi, Cation-exchange capacities and mineralogy of the fine sand separates (0.02–0.2 mm), (1958), 289–297
11 J. R. Kilroe, *Soil geology of Ireland,* (1907)
12 E. A. Colhoun, The glacial geomorphology of the Sperrin mountains, (Unpublished PhD thesis, Queen's University, Belfast, 1968)

13 D. H. Hill, Study of the soils of co. Tyrone, (Unpublished MAgr thesis, Queen's University, Belfast, 1960)

14 Ibid.

15 J. G. Cruickshank, Reconnaissance soil survey of co. Fermanagh, *Irish Geography*, 4 (1961), 190–201

16 V. B. Proudfoot and F. W. Boal, Two soil maps of county Down, *Geog. J.*, 126 (1960), 60–6

17 V. B. Proudfoot, (1958), op. cit.

18 L. T. Brown, A survey of turf-working in co. Down, (Unpublished MSc thesis, Queen's University, Belfast, 1968)

19 E. E. Evans, *Irish heritage*, (1942)

20 Ministry of Commerce, Council of Scientific Research and Development, *Northern Ireland peat bog survey; the final report of the preliminary survey*, (1956)

21 E. A. Colhoun, R. Common and M. M. Cruickshank, Recent bog flows and debris slides in the north of Ireland, *Sci. Proc. Roy. Dublin Soc.*, 2 A, (1965), 163–74

22 L. Symons and N. Stephens, The Lough Erne drainage scheme, *Geography*, 41 (1956), 123–26

23 A. G. Smith and E. H. Willis, Radiocarbon dating of the Fallahogy Landnam phase, *Ulster J. Arch.*, 3rd series, 24–5 (1961–2), 16–24

24 V. B. Proudfoot, Problems of soil history, *J. Soil Science*, 9 (1958), 186–98

25 S. McConaghy, The soils of Northern Ireland, in Emrys Jones ed., *Belfast in its regional setting*, (British Ass. Handbook, 1952) J. S. V. McAllister and S. McConaghy, Soils of Northern Ireland and their influence upon agriculture, *Record of Agr. Res.*, Min. of Ag., Northern Ireland, 17 (1968), 101–8

26 F. M. Synge and N. Stephens, The Quaternary period in Ireland—an assessment, *Irish Geography*, 4 (1960), 121–30

P. Ryan and T. Walsh, Character study of soils developed on Weichsel glacial deposits in Ireland, *Proc. Roy. Irish Acad.*, 64 B (1966), 465–507

VII

LIMESTONE MORPHOLOGY IN IRELAND
P. W. Williams

The evolution of the Carboniferous limestone landforms of Ireland dates from the Palaeozoic; but morphological development has not been continuous, having been interrupted by the deposition of various sediments that in turn required eroding before the underlying limestones could be attacked once more. It is therefore hardly surprising, that as a consequence of this complex history of successive stages of erosion, burial, exhumation, and renewed erosion, a diversity of landforms is displayed. This account attempts to explain the varied limestone morphology by relating the landforms to past and present processes.

By far the most common limestones in the country are of Carboniferous age. Their importance to the Irish scene is measurable by their extensive outcrop which covers roughly half the island. A few small patches of other calcareous rocks also occur, some of Cretaceous age and a little of Permian, but their contribution to the total limestone area is slight. This essay will therefore concentrate on landforms developed on Carboniferous formations. Figure 7.1 shows their distribution and names the most important karstic districts.

Not all limestone landforms are karstic phenomena. Many are the products of fluvial erosion and many are at least part the legacy of glaciation. The karst features can be distinguished as those that result from the solution of limestone and subterranean water circulation. In Ireland, limestone landscapes contain elements that are both polygenetic and polycyclic.

GEOLOGICAL BACKGROUND

The Carboniferous limestones were mapped by the Geological Survey during the second half of the last century. The mapping was based mainly on broad lithological divisions that distinguished the relatively pure Lower and Upper limestones from the argillaceous or arenaceous Middle limestones or 'Calp'. Recent work has shown such a system to be geologically inadequate and often misleading for geomorphic purposes, and until information is available on such details as the physical and chemical properties of limestones, any interpretation of the landforms is bound to be provisional.

It is not desirable here to enter into a complex discussion on the regional variations of Lower Carboniferous rocks in Ireland, but some comment is called for because of the

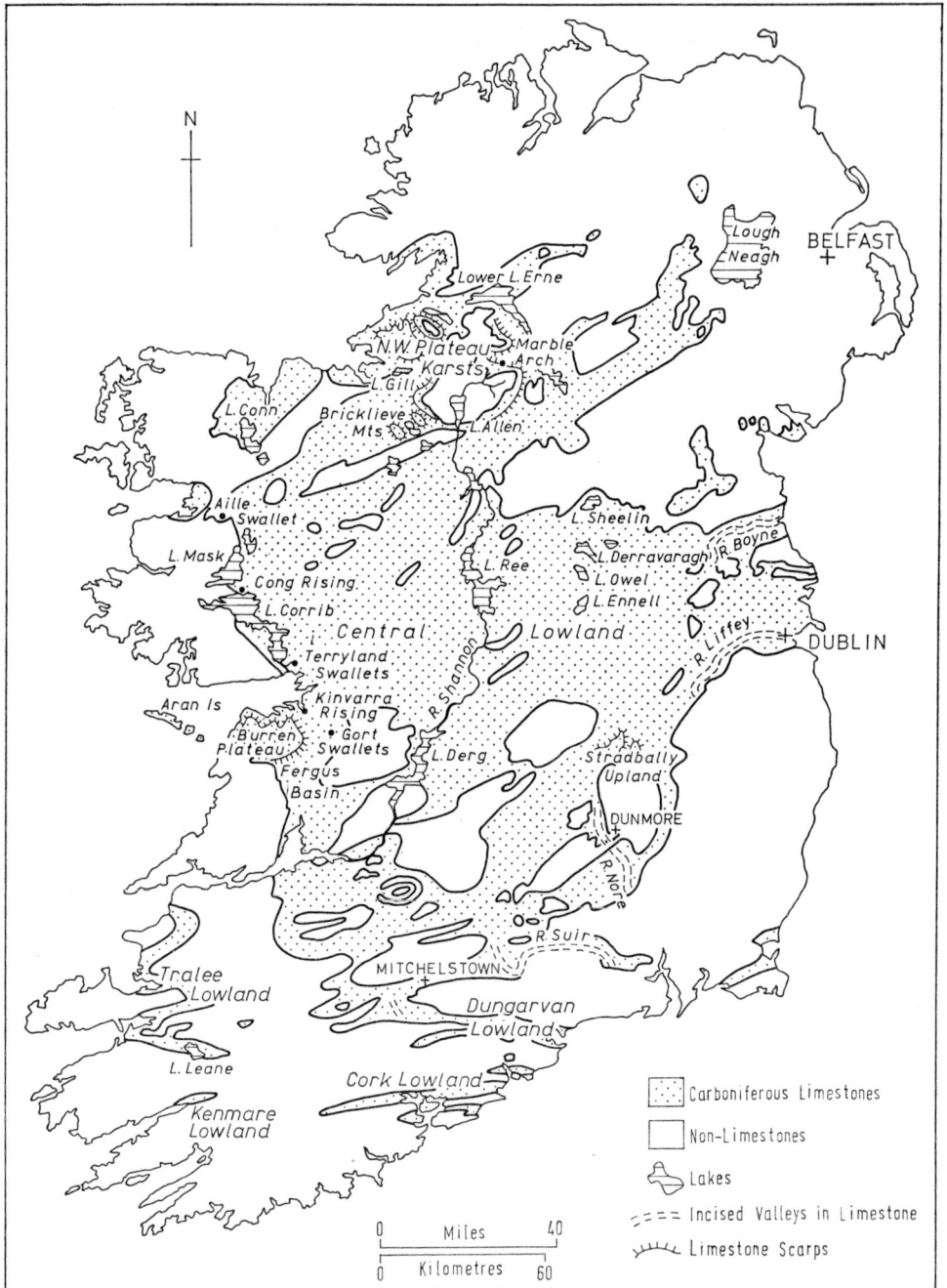

Fig. 7.1　Karstic localities in Ireland

considerable importance of lithology in limestone geomorphology. The sections in figure 7.2 depict the Lower Carboniferous succession as found in three widely spaced parts of Ireland. The first point to notice is that not all the rocks are limestones, despite their designation as such on Geological Survey maps. The Lower and Middle (Calp) limestones of the Survey in particular, are frequently arenaceous or argillaceous, especially in the Donegal and Omagh synclines.[1] However, while the Lower Carboniferous rocks contain frequent non-calcareous elements, particularly north of the 'Highland Boundary' line in the composite Omagh-Mayo troughs, they nevertheless include considerable thicknesses of lime-

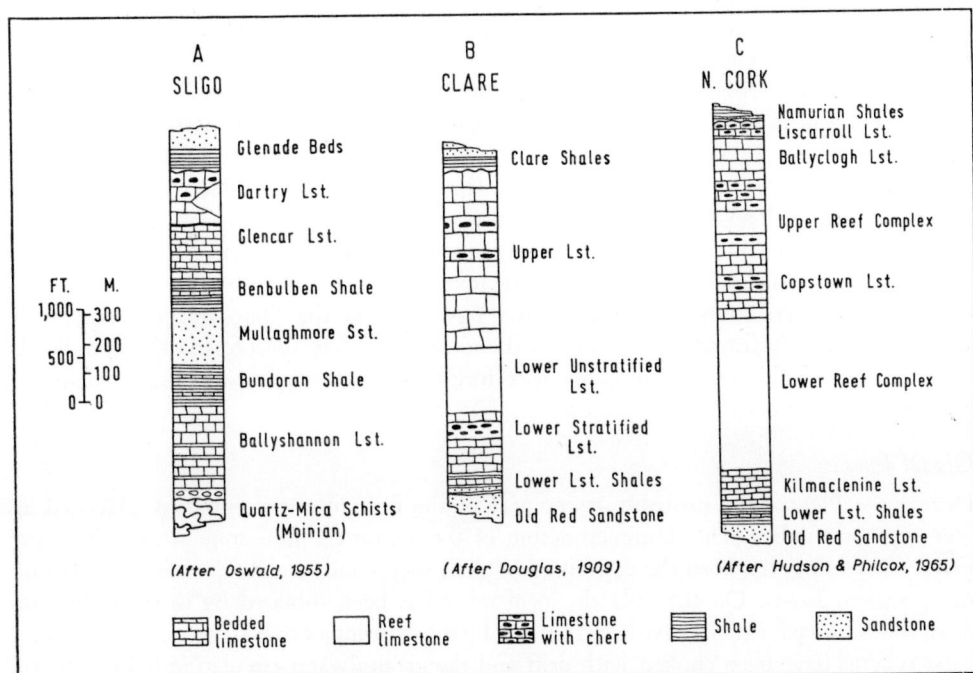

Fig. 7.2 Examples of the Lower Carboniferous succession in Ireland

stones. In the Benbulbin area of the north-west (Fig. 7.2 A), the succession of nearly 1,220 m (4,000 ft) is topped by 365 m (1,200 ft) of massive, relatively pure limestones with chert bands,[2] and within these Upper or Dartry Limestones are occasional very pure, unbedded reef facies, which are of considerable geomorphic significance because of their resistance to erosion. In the Burren of Clare (Fig. 7.2 B), the limestone succession attains a thickness of roughly 1,000 m (3,250 ft) and chemically is much purer than in Sligo. The Lower Stratified Limestone, as designated by Douglas[3], is somewhat argillaceous, but the Lower Unstratified Limestone and the Upper Limestone are generally pure and occupy together a thickness of 700 to 900 m. Interbedded shales are almost unknown in these latter formations, although chert bands and patches of dolomitization occur. South of Clare, in the Buttevant district of north Cork (Fig. 7.2 C), the Lower Carboniferous rocks again change in character. A notable increase in the thickness of unbedded reef limestones is apparent, and in this region they sometimes occupy nearly half of the succession.[4] In the Cork city syncline, pure reef limestones are even more prominent, and attain over 1,220 m (4,000 ft) in thickness.[5] There they rest between relatively thin horizons of dark, argillaceous, cherty limestones below, and well-bedded, pure limestones above.[6]

Before leaving the discussion on lithology, an explanation of the difficult term 'reef' is required, because reef limestones are widespread in Ireland and often produce prominent hills that have been mistaken for hums and even tropical cones (Ger. *Kegel*). Reef limestones are generally recognized as being masses of poorly bedded, pure, dense limestones, with calcite mudstone predominating, although several different lithologies can be found in detail. It is in this sense that the term reef limestone will be used here. Such limestones frequently occur in Ireland in the Upper Tournaisian and Viséan formations, but particular attention has been devoted to them in the Waulsortian phase.[7] Lees has shown that Waulsortian reefs or 'carbonate mudbanks' accumulated in at least two distinct ways, namely as knolls and sheets. The knolls (or knoll-reefs of other workers) are usually circular, sub-circular or elongate in plan and range in diameter from a few metres to more than a kilometre. Their thickness frequently exceeds 46 m (150 ft). Knoll-reefs of this type, though of various ages, are found over the Central Lowland[8], in the Sligo-Leitrim-Fermanagh Uplands[9], and in the limestone synclines of the south-east.[10] The sheet form of the mudbank has little topographic expression and is therefore of less geomorphic significance than the knoll-reef.

Glacial deposits

During the Pleistocene, probably every part of the limestone outcrop was glaciated at one stage or another. The dominant action of the ice on the limestone areas, which are mainly low lying, has been the deposition of drift sheets and in consequence the burial of more ancient karsts. On the uplands, local relief has been subdued by drift infilling of depressions, and pavements have been initiated by the scouring of rock surfaces. Subterranean karst systems have been choked with drift and the groundwater circulation has thus been seriously impaired.

Crevices in the uppermost limestones usually contain injected boulder clay, but further underground the deposits are glacifluvial. Despite the humid climate and ceaseless flushing by streams, all but the most modern caves usually contain *in situ* glacifluvial sediments, occurring either as complete passage-fills or, where streams have been more active, as subterranean river terraces. The deposits are most commonly thick banks of laminated silt and clay, as in the Main Chamber of Poll an Ionian Cave in co. Clare, but may also take the form of repeated series of laminated silts with interbedded, current-bedded sands, as in the North-west Inlet Passage of Reyfad Pot, co. Fermanagh. Since the glacifluvial deposits of many caves known to the writer never show signs of undue deformation, beyond that accounted for by stream undercutting and slumping, it is likely they were laid down during the retreat stages of the last glaciation.

CONTEMPORARY SOLUTION PROCESSES

Limestone solution and transportation are the main karstic processes in any limestone area. All investigations of limestone corrosion have recognized the importance of dissolved carbon dioxide in increasing the solvent capacity of water by forming carbonic acid (H_2CO_3), and it is also generally accepted that the high concentration of this gas commonly found in natural waters is derived principally from organically produced carbon dioxide of the soil zone.

Other naturally produced acids have also been considered partly responsible for the high solubility of limestones, particularly organic or humic acids[11] and in the present context where bog drainage is important these organic solvents may be especially significant, although Gorham[12] and Hutchinson[13] attribute the acidity of bog-water to sulphuric and not to organic acids.

Measurements of absolute rates of solution in Ireland

The first measurement of limestone solution in Ireland was made by Kilroe[14] in 1907, who calculated corrosion in the Shannon basin as equivalent to a land surface lowering of 1 ft in 12,000 years (0.025 mm per year). A more recent estimate for the same river, although apparently dependent on very little more evidence, was offered by Corbel[15], who suggested a rate of 0.03 mm per year. But work by the writer, based on 23 monthly samples from Killaloe, indicates that a figure of 0.053 mm per year may be a more accurate assessment of solution in the basin. Other estimates of limestone corrosion in Ireland are presented in Table 1.

Investigations[16] into the spatial distribution of solution and calcareous deposition in the Fergus basin, a tributary of the Shannon, have shown that streams from Namurian shales and flagstones are usually aggressive towards limestone and that much solution is accomplished when the limestone outcrop is reached, as indicated by the numerous closed depressions, swallets and caves that mark the geological boundary. A similar morphological role was determined for streams draining the Old Red Sandstone. However, the corrosive activity of streams from entirely limestone catchments was found to be in contrast with both the above. In calcareous systems, the streamway is a mainline of solute transport, not a locus of corrosion; the solution takes place as rainwater percolates through the rock, that is, before it ever reaches the river.

In an analysis of the vertical distribution of solution, roughly 25 per cent of the total corrosion achieved in the Fergus basin was calculated to take place on the very surface of the limestone; a theoretical figure that accords very well with measurements of limestone pedestal heights beneath erratics (Plate VII). The latter indicate surface lowering of approximately 15 cm (6 in) since the last glaciation. The importance of solution in the superficial zone is further emphasized by results from caves that suggest that more than 80 per cent of total solution by percolating water may sometimes be accomplished in the uppermost 7–8 m (25 ft) of limestone.

Sampling has shown the hardness of water passing out of the Fergus and Shannon basins to change relatively little throughout the year, and in the case of the Shannon at Killaloe, the

TABLE I

Estimated absolute rates of limestone solution in Ireland

No.	Locality	Solution rate per year	Net rate in mm/1000 years or m³/yr/km²	Author	
1	Shannon basin above Limerick	1 ft/12,000 years	25	Kilroe (1907,	80)
2	Shannon basin above Limerick	0.030 mm	30	Corbel (1957,	345)
3	Ballintra, co. Donegal	0.014 mm	14	,, ,,	355
4	North-east of Sligo	0.040 mm	40	,, ,,	355
5	Keishcorran, co. Sligo	0.030 mm	30	,, ,,	355
6	Cuilcagh, co. Fermanagh	0.050 mm	50	,, ,,	355
7	East Central Lowland	0.010 mm	10	,, ,,	345
8	North Burren, co. Clare	0.080 mm	80	,, ,,	371
9	Central Burren	0.120 mm	120	,, ,,	371
10	Southern Burren	0.100 mm	100	,, ,,	371
11	South of Ennis	0.080 mm	80	,, ,,	376
12	Shannon estuary	0.040 mm	40	,, ,,	375
13	Cork syncline	0.050 mm	50	,, ,,	358
14	Killarney region	0.100 mm	100	,, ,,	379
15	River Fergus basin, co. Clare (initial estimate)	0.051 mm	51	Williams (1963, 440)	
16	River Fergus (detailed estimate)	0.051 mm	51	,, (1968, 14)	
17	Shannon basin above Killaloe	0.053 mm	53	,, (this chapter)	

percentage variation in total hardness ($CaCO_3 + MgCO_3$) is only 3.7. In both rivers a high positive correlation, significant at the 99 per cent level, is found between solute transport and discharge (Fig. 7.3), and four to five times more dissolved limestone is evacuated from the catchments during the period of maximum flow in winter than in summer.

KARSTIC LANDSCAPES IN IRELAND

The information now available on solution permits us to go a stage further in the interpretation of Irish limestone landforms than would be possible from morphological evidence alone. For the purpose of an analysis of the evolution of the landscape, it is convenient to subdivide the karsts encountered into upland and lowland types. This is a basic division, for strong morphological contrasts exist in the landscapes thus defined.

LOWLAND KARSTS

More than three-quarters of the limestone area of Ireland falls within this category, which embraces the extensive Central Lowland and the limestone synclines of the south (Fig. 7.1).

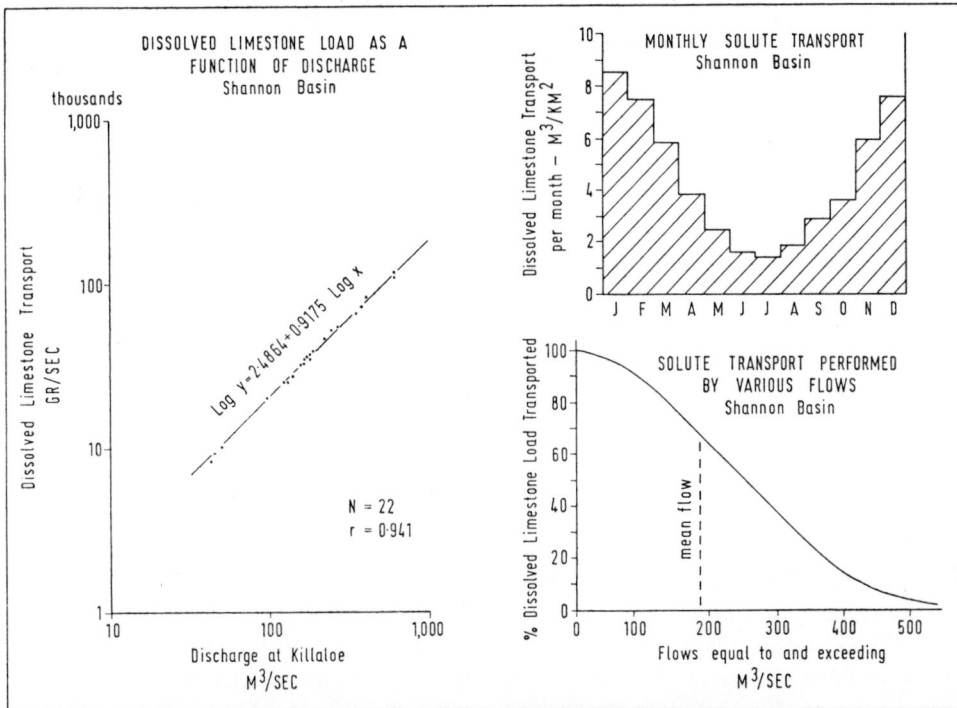

Fig. 7.3   River Shannon solute: discharge relations

The unifying characteristics of the lowland karsts are their low altitude and relief, and their gentle slopes. The surface of the Central Lowland rises gradually inland mostly to between 60 and 120 m (200 and 400 ft) and the level of the southern synclines seldom exceeds 120 m (400 ft). Only where the limestones are particularly impure, as in the festoon chert locality of Derravaragh, co. Westmeath, or where resistant reef facies are especially prominent does the terrain rise above the general low level, and even then by no more than 100 m (330 ft). Over wide areas slopes are less than 3 degrees and commonly less than 1 degree and only glacial deposits and the resistant facies noted diversify the limestone relief.

The Central Lowland

The flatness of the Central Lowland renders it one of the most monotonous parts of Ireland. Yet the very flatness, with slopes of less than 0.1 degree in some places, is one of its most significant geomorphic attributes. The limestones are generally mantled with thick glacial drift and peat bog and most karstic forms are buried. The area is thus a good example of 'covered karst'. The modern aspect is not of a karstic landscape, but of a plain of glacial deposition. This impression is purely superficial, for while the glacial epochs have greatly influenced the detailed topography, the overall bedrock relief is an unevenly planed surface stretching nearly 200 km (125 miles) east to west. This is manifestly not attributable to glaciation, and is clearly older than the Pleistocene deposits that mantle it. In fact the Lowland appears in places to be very ancient, judging by the early to mid-Tertiary deposits that lie on it at Ballymacadam[17], co. Tipperary. The writer considers the Central Lowland to represent the culmination of a very long period, perhaps 40 million years, of essentially karstic denudation. Normal fluvial action has also been important, particularly in the later stages when the area was reduced to low relief and surface drainage resumed, although some allogenic streams, rising on sandstone inliers and shale outcrops, may have functioned for a very long time. However, it seems unlikely that streams developed on sediments overlying the limestones[18] could have maintained their surface courses permanently, because of the disrupting influence of karst drainage.

It is improbable that marine planation can be invoked to account for the Central Lowland since no marine deposits exist above the 7.6 m (25 ft) interglacial raised beach except those associated with late- and post-glacial isostatic recovery on the north-east and north coasts. Miller[19] and Orme[20] postulated sea-levels to at least 213 m (700 ft) in southern Ireland, but field mapping has revealed no marine sediments, and the benchlands and breaks of slope on which the morphological arguments rest are open to several interpretations. Farrington's[21] subaerial explanation of surfaces in the same general locality is much less demanding on the facts.

The strongest points in favour of a subaerial, dominantly solution origin for most of the Central Lowland are, firstly, that relatively non-soluble rocks usually rise abruptly above the low-lying limestone surface, the change of slope often coinciding exactly with the geological boundary; secondly, that even where there is not a sharp break of slope at the geological contact, the surface on the adjoining non-limestone rocks never extends far at the level or gradient of the neighbouring limestone plain; and, thirdly, wherever limestone exists under a humid climate, chemical corrosion is always important and generally more significant than other forms of erosion.

The controlling Tertiary base-level seems to have been close to the present sea-level, judging from the low altitudes of the Central Lowland and the synclinal lowland karsts of the south. But a slight complication occurs. In the east, the rivers Boyne, Liffey, Suir, and Nore are incised into the Lowland in their middle and lower courses, whereas no comparable incision has taken place in the rivers draining limestone to the west (Fig. 7.1). This indicates that slight uplift has occurred in the east since the formation of the Central Lowland, which in the west slopes gently ($<$ 1 degree) to the sea but in the east terminates at roughly 30 m (100 ft) on the coast. The incision of the valleys dates at least from the Pleistocene, as Farrington[22] has shown in the case of the Liffey, but could be earlier. Corbel[23] suggested that the Liffey gorge was entrenched in the Pliocene as a consequence of earth movements that commenced in the Miocene. This may well be correct, but specific evidence is lacking.

While in some places the incised rivers are destroying the Lowland surface, elsewhere it is extending, though not entirely by solution. At several localities round the margins of the Lowland, the surface is almost exactly coincident with the very summit of the limestone

VII   Limestone pedestal with protecting erratic cap-rock at 1,137 ft (347 m) east of Leean Mountain, co. Leitrim

VIII   Post-glacial pitting of limestone pavement beside Lough Mask near the exit of the Cong canal, co. Mayo

IX   Limestone erratics on limestone pavement west of Lough Bunny, co. Clare

X   A limestone hill flanked by glacial drift in the 'Doons' area of Sligo–Leitrim north of Lough Gill

where it remains unconformably buried beneath Upper Carboniferous shales. At these sites the Lowland is enlarging as the shales are stripped back; thus structural and exhumed surface elements are produced. Such situations are found in the Fethard and Mullinahone areas of east Tipperary, and west of Ennis and Newcastle West in counties Clare and Limerick. In eastern Meath, especially near Duleek, a similar stripping of shales is taking place, but an erosional knoll topography is being revealed, reminiscent of the pre-Namurian relief described in parts of Yorkshire and Derbyshire by Hudson.[24]

If the Central Lowland was largely in being by the late Miocene, that is about seven million years ago, it is difficult to evaluate the role of solution since that time, particularly as allowance must be made for karstic processes changing as the climate deteriorated from sub-tropical in the mid-Tertiary to temperate and glacial in the Pleistocene.[25] If corrosion progressed at the present rate, more than 305 m (1,000 ft) of limestone could be removed in seven million years, but since this would utterly destroy the surface, this strongly suggests that solution in the late Tertiary was either slower than at present or operated differently. If a residual clay covered the surface, as seems probable in view of red clays found sealed beneath glacial drift in Wexford[26] and in limestone cavities in quarries near Drogheda, then post-Miocene solution would have been inhibited beneath the clay, but would have continued at the margins of the Lowland. The surface would therefore not have been appreciably lowered but would have extended by lateral solution planation, a well-known tropical and sub-tropical karstic process.[27] Once uplift took place in the east, the clay layer would have been breached along main valleys and local vertical corrosion would have ensued, but in the stable west of Ireland, lateral solution planation probably continued until the practically impermeable clay cover was destroyed by glacial erosion.

During the Pleistocene erosion stripped the Lowland of its residual clay, and glacio-eustatic falls in sea-level permitted short term rejuvenation of subterranean circulations. Underground systems such as the river Gort and Coole Cave date from this phase.[28] However, the deposition of glacial drift re-clogged joints in the limestone, and groundwater movement in the Lowland is still sluggish. Yet the heterogeneous glacial materials behave quite differently from impermeable residual clays, for percolation is rapid through areas of gravelly drift and everywhere the deposits are liable to solution.

Solution lakes

Certain features now present in the Central Lowland are of considerable interest and merit some discussion. The origin of the numerous lakes is especially controversial. Most of the many small lakes are simply situated in depressions in glacial drift or in ice-scoured rock hollows, but several of the largest lakes—which individually may occupy tens of square kilometres—are located in broad, limestone basins of debatable age and origin. Included here are loughs Ree, Sheelin, Derravaragh, Owel, Ennell, and others (Fig. 7.1). Sited mainly in limestone but lapping against non-calcareous rocks are loughs Derg, Corrib, Mask, Conn, Erne and Leane to name only the largest. The lake basins named have been attributed mainly to limestone solution and so were termed 'solution lakes'.[29] They have been regarded as such for nearly a hundred years, although Hull did point out that in some cases (e.g.

Lough Gill) glaciation contributed to their origin. Charlesworth[30] has since stressed that point. Nevertheless, the solution idea retained popular appeal, and more may have been claimed for chemical activity than is warranted. It is thus time for the solution hypothesis to be examined.

Doubt was first cast on the role of solution in the origin of some limestone lakes when carbonate deposition was found to be taking place in certain loughs of the Fergus basin.[31] A study of corrosion in the Shannon system has similarly cast doubt on the universal tenability of the solution lake hypothesis. In general, the water of the river Shannon becomes harder with distance from its source, but the river gains in hardness largely by the concentration of salts from its hardwater tributaries rather than by the direct solution of its bed. However, some post-glacial solution is indicated by undercut 'mushroom rocks' near the shores of Lough Ree.

Loughs Conn and Mask have also been examined, although measurements are at present too few to be conclusive. Nevertheless, indications are that aggressive streams flowing into these lakes from the non-carbonate mountains to the west may effect some corrosion before mixing with the super-saturated water of limestone streams from the east (Plate VIII).

Thus, processes in the limestone basin lakes are varied, but details cannot be elaborated here. While it is quite clear that calcium carbonate deposition is proceeding in some cases, it is possible that both solution and deposition occur simultaneously in different places in some loughs. The solutional origin of limestone lakes in Ireland therefore cannot be accepted uncritically.

Turloughs

Another characteristic phenomenon of the Central Lowland and one reported from nowhere else in the world is the turlough (from Irish, *Tuar Loch,* meaning dry lake). They were defined by Praeger[32] as "grassy depressions in the surface, sometimes small, sometimes extending over many acres, which during wet weather fill with water through subterranean passages in the rock, and empty by the same means". To this it is necessary to add that some turloughs also fill by surface streams. Martel, the celebrated French speleologist, briefly discussed them and implied a similarity to karst poljes.[33] He noted that turloughs apparently repeat exactly the periodic inundation experienced by poljes in the Slovenian Karst, but close examination shows that there the resemblance ends.

Karst poljes are essentially corrosional features with flat, planed, rock floors, frequently veneered with alluvium. They possess internal drainage and are usually not smaller than 1 km² (0.386 sq miles), and some cover tens of square kilometres. Turloughs are closed basins, seldom greater than 1 km² (0.386 sq miles) in area with internal drainage. Their basin form may be a consequence of a hollow in limestone, but is usually referable to irregularities in glacial drift. Turloughs are often no more than basins in till overlying limestone, and they do not possess planed rock floors. The only karstic attribute common to all turloughs is subterranean drainage, otherwise they are just as much glacial features. They are best classified therefore as glacio-karstic landforms.[34]

Turloughs may be subdivided according to their hydrological behaviour. The most numerous are the lowland turloughs which flood each winter with the annual upward oscillation of groundwater level. They do not necessarily dry out completely each summer, for they are sensitive to the short term balance of relatively dry or wet years. Such turloughs are particularly frequent in southern and eastern Galway, but occur on nearly every lime-stone lowland. Equally distinctive but less widespread are the upland turloughs. These flood whenever there is a spell of particularly heavy rain; the flooding mechanism being associated not with a rising regional watertable but with a local backing up of water in subterranean conduits that cannot cope with above average runoff. Most upland turloughs are found on the Burren Plateau, county Clare, where good examples are Lough Aleenaun, and Kilcorney turlough.[35]

Hums

To close the discussion on lowland karsts, a few points must be made concerning hums. There is misunderstanding of their accepted origin, and erroneous identification of the landforms themselves.[36] Hums are named after the feature near the settlement of Hum in Popovo Polje, Yugoslavia.[37] They are residual, conical hills remaining after corrosive planation of surrounding limestone, and karstic collapse is not considered important in their evolution. The hillocks of the Cork and Central Lowlands identified by Corbel[38] as hums and Kegel respectively are often nothing more than topographic expressions of knoll-reefs, as he partly realized. Since the reef forms would appear by differential erosion regardless of climate, no climato-morphological conclusions based on their occurrence are tenable.

UPLAND KARSTS

The upland karsts of Ireland are developed on the plateaux of Carboniferous rocks not yet consumed by the expansion of the lowlands. The largest group of limestone plateaux is in the north-west in counties Sligo, Leitrim and Fermanagh, where the Benbulbin Range, Dartry Mts., and Marble Arch Upland are the most well known karstic localities (Fig. 7.1). Covering a smaller total area, but more thoroughly studied, are the Burren Hills of co. Clare. Least important and the subject of very little investigation is the Stradbally Upland of the northern Castlecomer Plateau in co. Laois.

The landscapes of the uplands are more obviously karstic than those of the lowlands. Disappearing streams, caves, closed depressions, and resurgences are numerous, although glaciation has also produced features on the limestone that are not purely karstic, but glacio-karstic, such as upland turloughs and limestone pavements.[39] The main characteristics and contrasts of the upland karsts will be illustrated by descriptions of the Burren and Marble Arch Uplands of Clare and Fermanagh respectively (Plates IX and X).

The Burren

It is interesting and significant to note the similarity of meaning of 'Burren', derived from *boireann,* the Irish for a rocky place, and 'Karst', from *krs,* the Serbo-Croatian for a rock or stone, or *kras,* the Slovenian word for a bleak, waterless place. The barrenness and rockiness that so often mark karstic areas in Europe are, however, not the natural state, as modern palaeobotanical studies have shown. Most karstic regions were once forested, even if thinly, but their dryness and relatively sparse tree cover made them favoured for early settlements. Clearing, overgrazing, and soil erosion ensued, resulting in the desolate terrain that is now so often associated with limestone districts.

The geomorphology of the Burren district has been examined by Corbel, Sweeting, Williams, Smith and Nicholson and Farrington.[40] The evolution of the caves has been energetically studied by the University of Bristol Spelaeological Society since 1952, many valuable articles appearing in their *Proceedings,* by Coleman and Dunnington[41], and others. A list of references, complete to 1964, relevant to the speleology and geomorphology of the Burren is given by Coleman.[42]

The desolate, rocky upland of the Burren is confined by Galway Bay to the north and west, by the shale and flagstone hills of west Clare to the south, and by an appendage of the Central Lowland—the Gort Plain—to the east (Fig. 7.4). Except to the south where the limestones dip south-south-west at 1–5 degrees beneath shale hills, the Burren is bounded by bold scarps, with slopes up to 25 degrees and a relief sometimes exceeding 300 m (1,000 ft). At Black Head, the most north-westerly part of the Burren, the scarp descends directly into the sea. Summits on the plateau average about 334 m (1,100 ft); the two highest points being Slieve Elva (345 m, 1,134 ft) in the western Burren and Slieve Carran (327 m, 1,073 ft) in the east. Slieve Elva is developed on a tongue of shales and flagstones that still overlies the limestones, but Slieve Carran is on a limestone prominence only very recently exhumed from beneath the Namurian cover. In fact, the Burren summit is essentially a structural surface, convincing evidence for which can be derived from a comparison of structural contours, extrapolated from the base of patches of Namurian sediments overlying the Upper Limestones, with the generalized contours of the present plateau surface. This well preserved summit surface suggests only recent karstification of the Burren; an implication supported by the poorly organized groundwater system, even allowing for partial clogging by glacial drift. Caves act as independent drainage lines, flooding to different levels after heavy rain; upland turloughs inundate at varying frequencies from place to place; all risings exhibit considerable fluctuations according to prevailing weather, and are not sustained by a large groundwater body. Sections in quarries show that fissures are generally not opened to a great depth, and it seems that although rain passes quickly underground, it seldom penetrates deeper than 30–60 m (100–200 ft) before running off laterally in many small channels. Borings confirm the massive waterless nature of the limestones below 60 or 70 m (200 or 230 ft), and even where water has been struck in the Burren, never more than the requirements of a few farms has been obtained. This contrasts markedly with the copious water supply normally found in the limestones of the Central Lowland.

Supporting evidence of the geological modernity of the Burren karst may be obtained by comparing its landforms with those of other karsts. Such comparisons could be misleading because of different environments, but the divergences of magnitude of the karst features of, say, Yugoslavia and the Burren are so enormous that the utter 'youth' of the Burren is unmistakable. Evidence from present rates of corrosion also indicates that even the

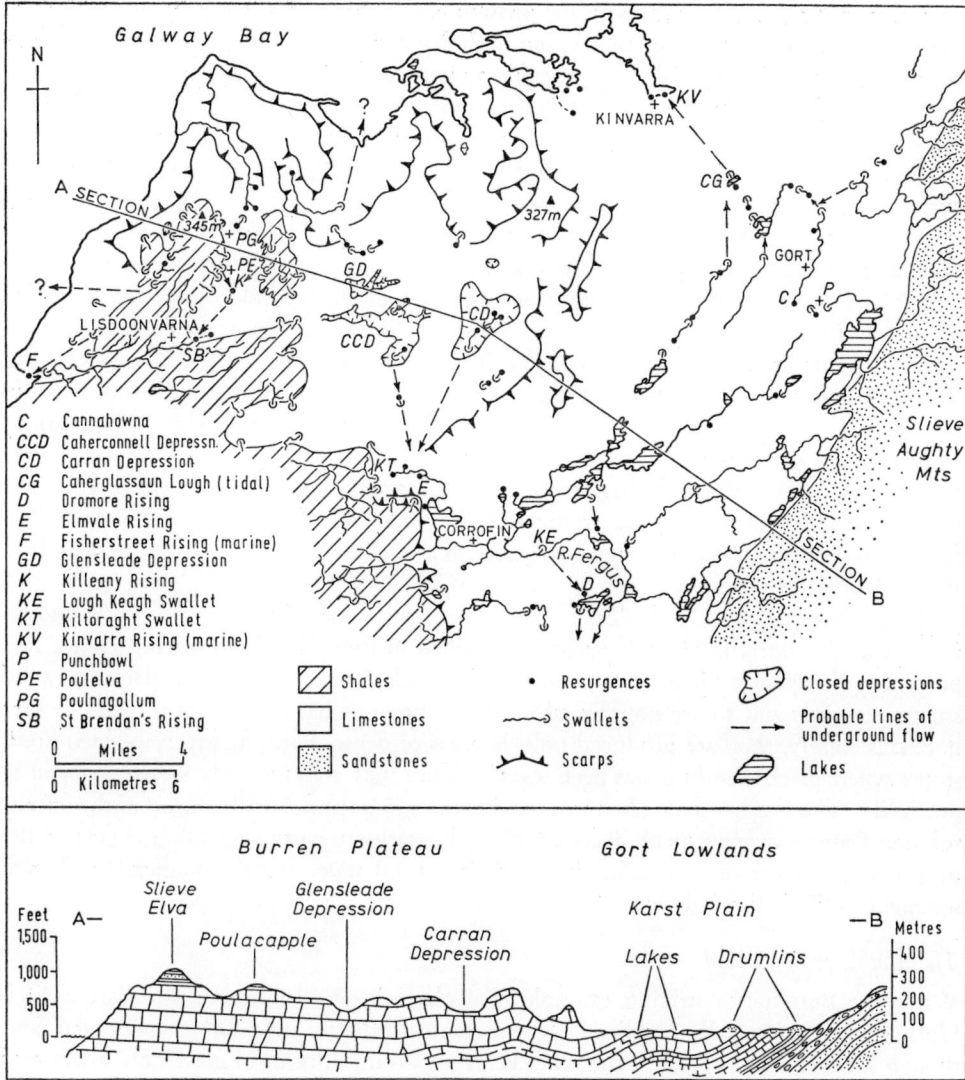

Galway Bay

N

KV
KINVARRA

CG

327m

GORT

C P

A SECTION
345m +PG
+PE
K
GD
CD
LISDOONVARNA
SB
CCD

Slieve
Aughty
Mts

F

KT
E
CORROFIN
KE
R.Fergus
D

SECTION
B

C   Cannahowna
CCD   Caherconnell Depressn.
CD   Carran Depression
CG   Caherglassaun Lough (tidal)
D   Dromore Rising
E   Elmvale Rising
F   Fisherstreet Rising (marine)
GD   Glensleade Depression
K   Killeany Rising
KE   Lough Keagh Swallet
KT   Kiltoraght Swallet
KV   Kinvarra Rising (marine)
P   Punchbowl
PE   Poulelva
PG   Poulnagollum
SB   St Brendan's Rising

Miles 0 4
Kilometres 0 6

Shales   · Resurgences   Closed depressions
Limestones   Swallets   Probable lines of underground flow
Sandstones   Scarps   Lakes

Burren Plateau   Gort Lowlands

Feet   A—   Slieve   Glensleade   Karst Plain   —B Metres
1,500   Elva   Depression   400
                     Poulacapple   Carran   Lakes   Drumlins   300
1,000-   Depression   200
500-   100
0-   0

Fig. 7.4 The Burren and Gort lowland

largest Burren basins such as the Carran and Caherconnell depressions could be produced well within three million years. These depressions probably started as swallow holes in the late Pliocene when the shale cover was first breached, but grew by coalescence of neighbouring basins. The depressions remained active so long as acidic surface streams from the shales drained into them, but became relatively fossilized as a result of successive glaciations which scraped off the surrounding weathered shales and hence removed the main source of corrosive water. Simultaneous with the growth of the depressions was the enlargement of the embryonic groundwater network, but both depressions and subterranean conduits later became choked with glacial drift. Present activity is slowly removing glacifluvial silts from some of the older caves such as Poll an Ionian[43] and the Cave of the Wild Horses[44], but those without streams will remain silt-filled indefinitely.

At the modern shale edge in the west and south Burren, contemporary processes are creating a whole new suite of caves, such as the Cullaun Series[45], and are extending pre-existing ones, like Poulnagollum[46] and Faunarooska.[47] Around the shale and flagstone hills of Slieve Elva, Poulacapple, and Knockauns Mountain near Lisdoonvarna are found upwards of twenty active caves, comprising roughly 56 km (35 miles) of surveyed underground galleries. Typically, the caves trend southwards, down dip, in meandering vadose passages. Their gradient is normally slight, like the dip, and vertical drops or pitches are few. The underground drainage of the eastern side of Slieve Elva and most of western Poulacapple is to the Aille river via St Brendan's Well near Lisdoonvarna (Fig. 7.4), as confirmed by a number of fluorescein dye tests by the Bristol University Spelaeological Society[48], but the ultimate resurgence points of drainage from western Slieve Elva and Knockauns are unknown and are presumed to be beneath sea-level. The subterranean flow from Carran in the Central Burren is southwards to the Fergus river as also determined by a Bristol University dye-test.

In addition to caves and closed depressions, limestone pavements are well known features of the Burren. These have been described in some detail elsewhere[49], but a few points need emphasis. Firstly, pavements are as much the consequence of glaciation as of karstic processes and so are not typical karstic features, as has often been implied in text books. Secondly, they are produced only in areas of dense, pure, massively bedded limestones where glacial scouring has been severe. Hence they are extremely well developed in north Clare and south Galway, but are rare elsewhere in Ireland. Finally, many of the micro-solution features on pavements were dissolved beneath a former vegetation cover; so the present open aspect of pavements is not their natural state, as palynological[50] and cave sediment studies[51] also indicate.

The Marble Arch Upland

While the Burren is a striking example of a glacio-karstic landscape, the Marble Arch Upland is more typically karstic. Pavements and turloughs are poorly represented, and though boulder clay is present, the relief bears no strong imprint of glaciation, a fact that may relate to the position of the upland near the country's major iceshed during the last glaciation.[52] The Marble Arch Upland is a triangular limestone shelf located on the north side of the Cuilcagh ridge (667 m, 2,188 ft) in county Fermanagh (Fig. 7.5). To the south the shelf is limited by the rising flank of the Cuilcagh massif, composed of Upper Carboniferous shales and flagstones, and in the west the faulted bench merges into low hills of the same formations. To the north-east it is dramatically terminated by an imposing scarp overlooking the Enniskillen lowlands. The geology of the neighbourhood has been examined by the Geological Survey[53], and in more detail by Padget[54], who investigated the

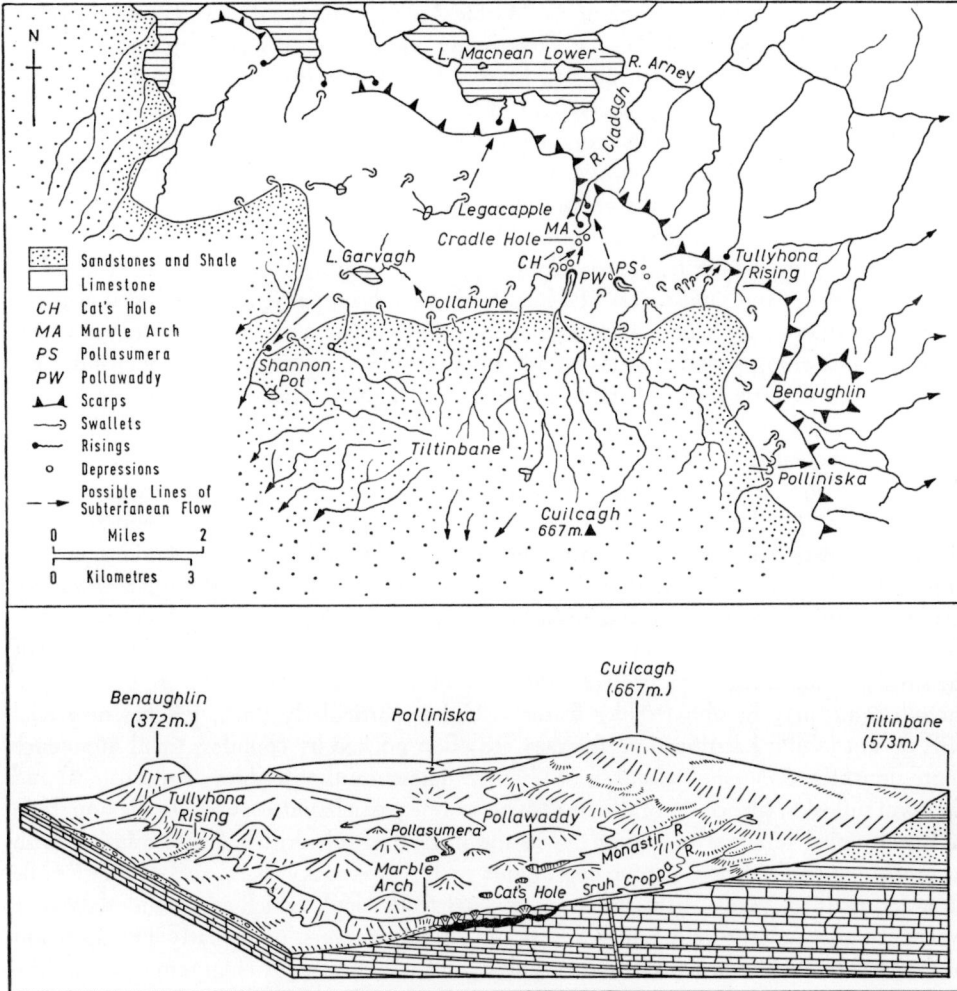

Fig. 7.5 The Marble Arch upland

Upper Carboniferous stratigraphy of Cuilcagh. Although no detailed accounts of the limestones are available, the character of the succession bears some resemblance to the Dartry Limestones of co. Leitrim.[55] The limestones are generally massive and well-bedded near Marble Arch Cave, but at the eastern end of the bench become extremely cherty and thin bedded in their upper part. Knoll-reefs are widely developed near the northern scarp edge where they often form prominent hills. Everywhere the tectonic dip is slight. A few igneous dykes traverse the limestones, but they have little topographic expression, and their influence on the karst hydrology is undetermined.

Geomorphological knowledge of the Marble Arch Upland, and indeed of all the other upland karsts in this part of Ireland, is exceedingly poor, which is surprising since the karst is amongst the finest in the British Isles. Marble Arch Cave, itself incompletely explored, is the largest penetrable resurgence system in Ireland, and the impressive Monastir (Polla-waddy) blind valley would not look out of place in the classical Karst. There are unfortunately no large closed depressions to complete the picture, but a variety of doline types is displayed. The main work of interest to the geomorphologist is by Martel[56], and concerns mainly the caves. His ideas were later closely followed by Corbel.[57]

Like all the upland karsts, the Marble Arch Upland commenced as a surface stripped of its cover of shales and sandstones. The limestones have been particularly denuded near the plateau's northern edge where no vestige of the original structural surface is left, and where knoll-reef hills rising 50–70 m (160–230 ft) above the plateau now dominate the landscape. The knolls show little sign of karstification beyond slightly widened fissures, because the massively jointed reef limestones with steep depositional dips shed water rather than absorb it. As a consequence, the topographic lows between adjoining knolls are lined with small closed depressions which develop there as a response to locally increased vertical drainage and corrosion. The larger features of the district such as the Cladagh gorge and Monastir blind valley date from at least the last interglacial, as glacial drift rests *in situ* in them. By implication the intervening Marble Arch cave system is of similar age, although preliminary results of solution studies show that it is still developing. The limestone bench must pre-date the landforms that are cut into it, and therefore is at least mid-Pleistocene in age. Many of the smaller swallets and depressions located in boulder clay over limestone are post-glacial, though some may lie above older features. Unless particularly thick, patches of glacial drift do not inhibit karstification, for they are often pocked by countless small subsidence depressions, the *Schwemmlanddolinen* of Cvijić.[58] These are the product of mechanical and chemical suffosion (processes of downwashing of fine particles into cavities in the limestone and corrosional removal of carbonates in the drift) and sub-drift bedrock solution with accompanying subsidence. Larger depressions with steep, rocky walls, such as the Cradle Hole [80 m (87.5 yards) diameter by 33 m (108 feet) deep], which are found above the courses of the underground Sruh Croppa and Monastir rivers, particularly just upstream of the Marble Arch resurgence, are the result of collapse induced by enlargement of cavities in the limestone (Fig. 7.5).

Solution in the locality appears very active judging from the twenty samples collected so far. Water sinking in the swallets of the plateau was found to be aggressive with total hardnesses commonly less than 40 p.p.m.; although at Pollasumera concentrations were higher (80 p.p.m.) as a consequence of the relatively long stream course across limestone. Most surprising and very important was the invariable aggressiveness of water rising at Marble Arch (40–70 p.p.m., pH 7–8) which had passed right through the limestone; a fact which emphasizes the role of streams in deep solution. The twin cascades rising of the Cladagh gorge, however, was considerably harder at 124 p.p.m., though apparently barely saturated.

The subterranean passages show a complete transformation along the Marble Arch

Upland from west to east, from completely waterlogged channels in the vicinity of Shannon Pot, through large relatively open, low gradient caves of the centre, to narrow, deep, jagged potholes in the east near Benaughlin and Polliniska. This considerable change in subterranean character is mainly attributable to relief increasing eastwards, accompanied by a corresponding deepening of the vadose zone and steepening of the hydraulic gradient, but in detail is also partly due to the lithological transition from massive, pure limestone in the west to cherty, thin bedded rocks in the east. In addition to the morphological variation in the underground systems, there is a complete reversal of drainage from a south-west flow round Shannon Pot to a north-east direction near Tullyhona rising (Fig. 7.5).

The karst hydrology of the Upland is of considerable interest, for the divide between the Shannon and Erne basins passes through the district. Yet little is known of the drainage in detail. The link between Pollawaddy (Monastir river), Cradle Hole and Marble Arch rising was confirmed by a fluorescein dye test by Brodrick[59], but no other connections have been proved, although on speleological grounds the Sruh Croppa River seems likely to join the Monastir upstream of Cradle Hole. Other likely lines of flow are indicated in figure 7.5. The Shannon Pot rising is probably sustained by water from Lough Garvagh, 2.41 km (1.5 miles) north-east of the pot, as Wilkinson and Cruise proposed, and that lake is in turn fed by streams from Tiltinbane Mountain, including perhaps subterranean water from Pollahune.

DISCUSSION

Scientific interest in Irish caves was shown from at least the first half of last century yet the limestone scenery inspired little comment. Various suggestions were proffered by officers of the Geological Survey on the origins of the topography, but its special nature was not appreciated. Had the elementary principles of limestone hydrology been understood, the theories of Jukes[60] and Hull[61] on the evolution of Irish drainage might well have been quite different. The considerable progress in the scientific study of limestone landforms in Europe since the mid-nineteenth century made absolutely no impression on Irish earth scientists, and even Martel's visit in 1895 seems to have had little effect on their thinking. Martel was the first to recognize the karstic nature of much of the country, and his ideas form the foundation of karstic studies in Ireland:

"les calcaires carbonifères d'Irland possèdent bien . . . . des cavernes et une circulation d'eau souterraine exactement disposées comme celle des Causses et du Karst".[62]

While research on caves has continued, especially through the efforts of Coleman since 1933, and the University of Bristol since 1952, no fundamental advances in the appreciation of Irish karst appeared until Corbel's investigations in the 1950's. Most important was his recognition, even if for partly incorrect reasons, of the influence of early and mid-Tertiary tropical weathering on the limestone scenery and his discussion of the evolution of the Central Lowland. While his work on Ireland is fraught with innumerable inaccuracies, most of which seem to stem from over-hasty judgments and superficial knowledge of the terrain, his study provides the first countrywide survey of Irish karst and is the source of many provocative and stimulating ideas.

ACKNOWLEDGEMENTS

The author is grateful to Mr T. Finch of the Soil Survey of Ireland, for collection of some water samples, and to Professor J. N. Jennings of the Australian National University for valuable criticism of the manuscript.

REFERENCES

1 I. M. Simpson, The Lower Carboniferous stratigraphy of the Omagh syncline, Northern Ireland, *Quart. J. Geol. Soc., London,* 110 (1953), 391–408; T. N. George and D. H. Oswald, The Carboniferous rocks of the Donegal syncline, *Quart. J. Geol. Soc., London,* 113 (1957), 137–79

2 D. H. Oswald, The Carboniferous rocks between the Ox Mts. and Donegal Bay, *Quart. J. Geol. Soc., London,* 111 (1955), 167–86

3 J. A. Douglas, Carboniferous limestone of county Clare, *Quart. J. Geol. Soc., London,* 65 (1909), 538–86

4 R. G. S. Hudson and H. E. Philcox, The Lower Carboniferous stratigraphy of the Buttevant area, Co. Cork, *Proc. Roy. Irish Acad.,* 64 B (1965), 65–79

5 W. E. Nevill, *Geology and Ireland,* (Dublin, 1963)

6 J. S. Turner, Upper Devonian and Lower Carboniferous of the Cork district, *Proc. Geol. Ass.,* 50 (1939), 319–23

7 A. Lees, The Waulsortian 'reefs' of Eire, *J. Geol.,* 69 (1961), 101–9; "The structure and origin of the Waulsortian (Lower Carboniferous) 'reefs' of west-central Eire", *Phil. Trans. Roy. Soc., London,* series B, No. 740, 247 (1964), 483–531

8 W. E. Nevill, The Carboniferous knoll-reefs of east-central Ireland, *Proc. Roy. Irish Acad.,* 59 B (1958), 239–303

9 D. H. Oswald, *op. cit.,* W. Schwarzacher, Petrology and structure of some Lower Carboniferous reefs in north-west Ireland, *Am. Ass. Petrol. Geol. Bull.,* 45 (1961), 1481–1503

10 L. B. Smyth, et al., The geology of south-east Ireland, together with parts of Limerick, Clare and Galway, *Proc. Geol. Ass.,* 50 (1939), 287–351

11 G. W. Fetzer, Humic acids and true organic acids as solvents of minerals, *Econ. Geol.,* 41 (1946), 47–56; A. N. Murray and W. W. Love, Action of organic acids upon limestones, *Am. Ass. Petrol. Geol. Bull.,* 13 (1929), 1467–76; W. D. Keller and A. F. Frederickson, The role of plants and colloidal acids in the mechanism of weathering, *Am. J. Sci.,* 250 (1952), 594–608

12 E. Gorham, Free acid in British soils, *Nature,* 181 (1958), 106

13 G. E. Hutchinson, *Limnology,* (New York, 1957)

14 J. R. Kilroe, The river Shannon; its present course and geological history, *Proc. Roy. Irish Acad.,* 26 B (1907), 74–96

15 J. Corbel, Les karsts du nord-ouest de l'Europe, *Mém. Docum. Inst. Etude rhodan, Lyon,* 12 (1957)

16 P. W. Williams, An initial estimate of the speed of limestone solution in county Clare, *Irish Geography,* 4 (1963), 432–41; An evaluation of the rate and distribution of limestone solution and deposition in the river Fergus basin, western Ireland, *Australian National University, Res. Sch. Pacific Studies, Dept. Geography Pub.* G/5 (1968), 1–40

17 W. A. Watts, A Tertiary deposit in county Tipperary, *Sci. Proc. Roy. Dublin Soc.,* N.S., 27 (1957), 309–11

18 J. B. Jukes, On the mode of formation of some of the river-valleys in the south of Ireland, *Quart. J. Geol. Soc., London,* 18 (1862), 378–403; E. Hull, *Physical Geology and Geography of Ireland,* (London, 1878)

19 A. A. Miller, River development in southern Ireland, *Proc. Roy. Irish Acad.,* 45 B (1939), 321–54

20 A. R. Orme, Planation surfaces in the Drum Hills, county Waterford, *Irish Geography,* 5 (1964), 48–72

21 A. Farrington, The south Ireland peneplane, *Irish Geography*, 2 (1953), 211–217

22 A. Farrington, The pre-glacial topography of the Liffey basin, *Proc. Roy. Irish Acad.*, 38 B (1929), 148–170

23 J. Corbel, op. cit.

24 R. G. S. Hudson, The pre-Numurian topography of Derbyshire and Yorkshire, *Trans. Leeds Geol. Ass.*, 5 (1932), 49–64

25 M. Schwarzbach, *Climates of the Past*, (London, 1963)

26 M. J. Gardiner and P. Ryan, Relic soil on limestone in Ireland, *Irish J. Agric. Res.*, 1 (1962), 181–88

27 J. Roglić, Les surfaces de corrosion dans le karst Dinarique, *Proc. Int. Geog. Un. Washington*, 1952, 366–69; Korrosive Ebenen im Dinarischen Karst, *Erdkunde*, 8 (1954), 113–4; H. Lehmann, Der Tropische Kegelkarst auf den Grossen Antillen, *Erdkunde*, 8 (1954), 130–9; K. Kayser, Karstrandebene und Poljeboden, *Erdkunde*, 9 (1955), 60–64; A. Gerstenhauer, Der tropische Kegelkarst in Tabasco (Mexico), *Zeit. für Geomorph.*, Suppl. 2 (1960), 22–48

28 P. W. Williams and J. C. Coleman, Coole cave, Co. Galway, *Proc. Un. Bristol Spel. Soc.*, 10 (1965), 299–304

29 E. Hull, op. cit.

30 J. K. Charlesworth, The bathymetry and origin of the larger lakes of Ireland, *Proc. Roy. Irish Acad.*, 63 B (1963), 61–9

31 P. W. Williams, op. cit. (1964, 1968)

32 R. L. Praeger, The flora of turloughs; a preliminary note, *Proc. Roy. Irish Acad.*, 41 B (1932), 37–45

33 E. A. Martel, British caves and speleology, *Geog. J.*, 10 (1897), 500–11

34 P. W. Williams, Aspects of the limestone physiography of parts of counties Clare and Galway, western Ireland, (Unpubl. PhD thesis, Univ. Cambridge, 1964)

35 J. C. Coleman, Flooding in the Lisdoonvarna area, Co. Clare, *Irish Spel.*, 1 (1966), 2, 32

36 W. E. Nevill, (1963), op. cit.

37 J. Roglić, (1952), op. cit.

38 J. Corbel, op cit.; Les phénomènes karstiques dans la region de Cork (Irlande du Sud), *Norois*, 2 (1954), 129–40

39 P. W. Williams, Limestone pavements: with special reference to western Ireland, *Trans. Inst. Brit. Geog.*, 40 (1966), 155–72

40 J. Corbel, Une région karstique d'Irlande: le Burren, *Rev. Géog. Lyon*, 27 (1952), 21–33; M. M. Sweeting, The enclosed depression of Carran, county Clare, *Irish Geography*, 2 (1953), 218–24; The landforms of north-west county Clare, Ireland, *Trans. Inst. Brit. Geog.*, 21 (1955), 33–49; D. I. Smith and F. H. Nicholson, A study of limestone solution in north-west county Clare, Eire, *Proc. Un. Bristol Spel. Soc.*, 10 (1964), 119–38;
A. Farrington, The last glaciation in the Burren, Co. Clare, *Proc. Roy. Irish Acad.*, 64 B (1965), 33–9
P. W. Williams, (1963, 1964, 1966, 1968), op. cit.

41 J. C. Coleman and N. J. Dunnington, The Pollnagollum cave, Co. Clare, *Proc. Roy. Irish Acad.*, 50 B (1944), 105–32

42 J. C. Coleman, *The Caves of Ireland*, (Tralee, 1965)

43 B. R. Collingridge, Poll an Ionian, *Proc. Un. Bristol Spel. Soc.*, 8 (1960), 135–37

44 R. F. Wilson, The Cave of the Wild Horses, Co. Clare, *Irish Spel.*, 1 (1965), 6–9;
F. K. Hanna, The Cave of the Wild Horses, Kilcorney, County Clare, Ireland, *Proc. Un. Bristol Spel. Soc.*, 11 (1968), 287–291

45 P. R. Acke, The Cullaun Series of caves, *Proc. Un. Bristol Spel. Soc.*, 7 (1954), 7–22

46 B. R. Collingridge, Poulnagollum—Poulelva caves, *Proc. Un. Bristol Spel. Soc.*, 9 (1962), 212–271

47 T. R. Shaw and O. C. Lloyd, Faunarooska cave, Co. Clare, Eire, *Proc. Un. Bristol Spel. Soc.*, 8 (1959), 186–194

48 C. D. Ollier and E. K. Tratman, The geomorphology of the caves of north-west Clare, Ireland, *Proc. Un. Bristol Spel. Soc.*, 7 (1956), 138–57

49 P. W. Williams, (1966), op. cit.
50 W. A. Watts, Late-glacial pollen zones in western Ireland, *Irish Geography*, 4 (1963), 367–76
51 P. W. Williams and R. B. G. Williams, The deposits of Ballymihil cave, Co. Clare, with particular reference to non-marine mollusca, *Proc. Un. Bristol Spel. Soc.*, 11 (1966), 71–82
52 F. M. Synge and N. Stephens, The Quaternary period in Ireland—an assessment, 1960, *Irish Geography*, 4 (1963), 121–130
53 S. B. Wilkinson and R. J. Cruise, *Explanatory memoir to accompany sheet 56 of the map of the Geological Survey of Ireland*, (1886)
54 P. Padget, The stratigraphy of Cuilcagh, Ireland, *Geol. Mag.*, 90 (1953), 17–26
55 D. H. Oswald, op. cit.
56 E. A. Martel, *Irlande et Cavernes Anglaises*, (Paris, 1897)
57 J. Corbel, (1957), op. cit.
58 J. Cvijić, Das Karstphänomen, *Geog. Abh. her. Penck*, 5 (1893), 3, 217–330
59 H. Brodrick, The Marble Arch caves, Co. Fermanagh, *Proc. Roy. Irish Acad.*, 27 B (1909), 183–92
60 J. B. Jukes, op. cit.
61 E. Hull, op. cit.
62 E. A. Martel, (1897), op. cit., 48

Postscript: Since going to Press the University of Bristol Spelaeological Society has published a book on the caves of the area: *The Caves of North-West Clare, Ireland*, ed. E. K. Tratman (Newton Abbot, 1969)

VIII

THE COASTLINE OF IRELAND

N. Stephens

Ireland has a coastline of over 3,000 km (2,000 miles) with a great variety of scenery which reflects the many different rock types present, from Pre-Cambrian to Holocene. There is a fundamental difference in geomorphology between different segments of coastline, for example, between the rugged Atlantic coast and the mainly drift-clad Irish Sea coast. It is the purpose of this essay to describe some of the more important geomorphological features and to comment upon the evolution of the coastline.

The main structural trends which affect the general plan of the coastline are shown in figure 8.1.[1] These structural features, and the morphology of the coastline which has resulted from the interaction between various geomorphological processes and the geological make-up of the island, will be described, beginning in the north-west in co. Donegal and considering first the Atlantic coast.

THE ATLANTIC COAST

The co. Donegal coast

The greater part of co. Donegal consists of Pre-Cambrian Dalradian rocks with a marked north-east to south-west strike, while a considerable number of granite masses have been intruded into the basement complex, which is also traversed by many Tertiary dykes trending north-west to south-east. The eastern edge of the Dalradian basement complex overlooking Lough Foyle is a fault-line scarp, which may extend north-eastwards off-shore. Possible north-west to south-east trending faults have been shown to occur north-west of Malin Head, and between the north coast of Inishowen and Inishtrahull Island, where there is a marked bathymetric depression in the sea floor.[2] It is possible that a major Tertiary fault zone extends north-west to south-east on the sea-floor and is reflected in the coastal trend between Malin Head and Inishowen Head, while intersecting the Lough Foyle fault beyond the mouth of the lough. It is perhaps significant that in spite of the pronounced Caledonian trend and the variety of rock outcrops in north Inishowen, this high cliffed coastline has a relatively simple outline and lacks the intricate crenulations which might be expected. To a limited extent this is accounted for by the presence of quantities of older drifts plugging some of the coastal valleys, and of sand dunes continuing the general line of the coast at Culdaff. Several other major north-east to south-west faults closely control

Vertical cliffs >100 ft high (31m)

Stepped cliffs   Bevelled cliffs } Rock Cliffs

Low rocky coast with off-shore reefs

Cliffs in drifts   Drumlin coasts

Ice erosion trough valleys   C Corries

Predominantly marine/fluvial deposition

Predominantly sand dunes

P   Extensive organic deposits (peat) form shoreline

Large landslips (slumped blocks)

N

Malin Hd

Lough Swilly

Bengore Hd

L. Foyle Syncline

Fair Hd

NORTH CHANNEL

Bloody Foreland

North-west

Antrim

Faulted Trough

Caledonian

Bann

Plateau

Gweebarra Bay

Granite

Highlands

Trough

Belfast Lough

BELFAST

Donegal Syncline

Lagan Valley

E. Down

Ards Pen.

Donegal Bay

Strangford L.

Lowlands

Broad Haven

Sligo Bay

Sligo Syncline

Mourne-Carlingford Tertiary Igneous Massifs

Dundrum Bay

Benwee Hd

Killala Bay

Mullet Pen.

N. Mayo Mountains and Plateaux

Ballina Syncline

Ox Mts

Carlingford Lough

Dundalk

Achill I.

Clew Bay Syncline

CENTRAL

IRISH

Clew Bay

S. Mayo Mts

Drogheda

Killary Harbour

Slyne Hd

CONNEMARA

Bertraghboy Bay

Galway Granite

LOWLAND

DUBLIN

GALWAY

SEA

Galway Bay

Aran Is

Burren Plateau

Wicklow

Hags Hd

Cliffs of Moher

Mutton I.

Liscannor Bay

Wicklow Hd

Shannon

Mountains

LIMERICK

Loop Hd

Lowlands

Kerry Hd

Cahore Pt

Dingle Pen.

South-east Lowlands

Dingle Pen.

Thrust Front

Dungarvan

WEXFORD

Dingle Bay

Armorican

WATERFORD

Carnsore Pt

South-west

Armorican Folding

Zone of Cleavage

CORK

Highlands

Ballycotton Bay

Bantry Bay

Cape Clear

Major synclinal axis

Major anticlinal axis

Fault zones

Possible fault zones

0   Miles   40

0   Kilometres   60

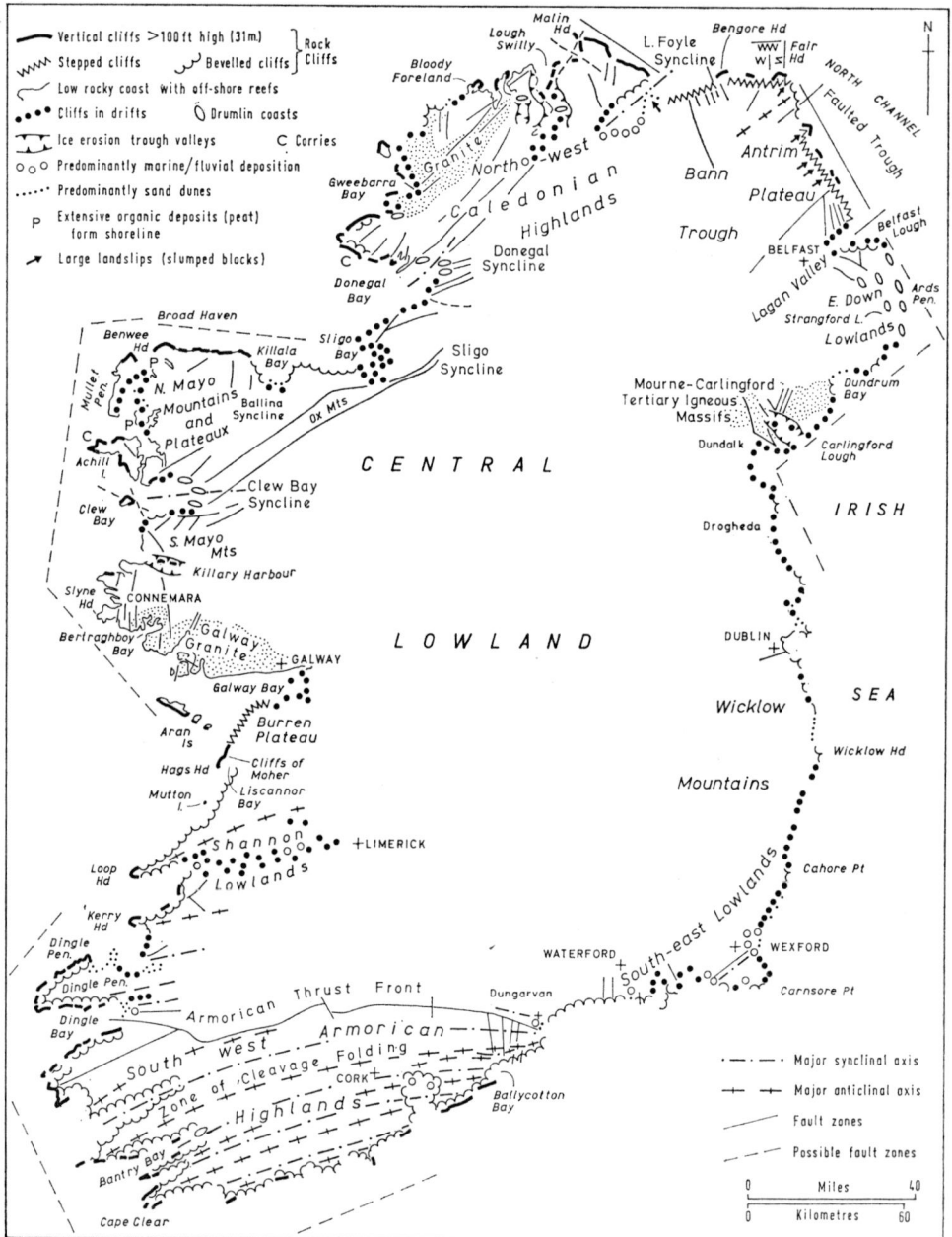

Fig. 8.1   The coastline of Ireland: some structural elements and morphological features

P Submerged peat deposits
   Submerged forest tree deposits } Post-glacial

180 Buried channels in rock

     Possible buried channels in rock

     Elevated rock platform, sometimes with ancient beach deposits

(map of Ireland with numerous coastal place-names and features)

KINTYRE

Malin Hd Inishtrahull Inishowen Hd Rathlin I.
Fanad Hd INISHOWEN Benbane Hd
Tory I. Horn Hd L. Swilly Portrush Fair Hd Red Bay Garron Pt
Bloody Foreland Mulroy Bay L. Foyle Carnlough
THE ROSSES LONDONDERRY
Aran I. ULSTER
Larne
Loughros Bay Island Magee Belfast L.
Ardara Roddans Port
Sl.-League BELFAST Helens Bay Ards Pen.
Muckros Hd Rossnowlagh Strangford
Donegal Bay LECALE Killough
Benwee Hd Killala Bay Sligo Bay Ballyconnell Dundrum Bay
Belmullet ERRIS Dundalk Carlingford L.
Blacksod Bay Dundalk Bay
Achill I. Mulrany Dunany Hd
Clew Bay CONNACHT Drogheda
Emlagh Pt MURRISK Balbriggan
Rinvyle Pt Killary Harbour Skerries
CONNEMARA Lambay I.
Slyne Hd Roundstone Ireland's Eye
Bertraghboy Bay DUBLIN Howth Hd Dublin Bay
Kilkieran Bay GALWAY Dalkey I.
Aran Is Galway Bay Bray Hd
Inishmore Black Hd BURREN Greystones
Cliffs of Moher LEINSTER Wicklow Wicklow Hd
Hags Hd Brittas Bay
Scattery I. Arklow Hd
Loop Hd River Shannon LIMERICK Cahore Pt
Kerry Hd Foynes Screen Hills
MUNSTER WEXFORD
Gt Blasket I. Newtown Fethard
Slea Hd Dingle Bay Dungarvan Ballyheigh Lough Carnsore Pt
Youghal Tramore Bay Lady I. Lake
CORK Garryvoe Waterford Harbour Tacumshin Lake
Kenmare River Ballycotton Bay
Howe Strand
Bantry Bay Courtmacsherry Bay
Cape Clear

NORTH CHANNEL

A — Maximum limit of ice sheets during the last glaciation
C — Drumlin re-advance limit
.58 — Late-glacial marine limit in northern Ireland (British O.D.)
20 — Isobases for the highest post-glacial shoreline
     Coastline without remnants of late- and post-glacial shorelines

Miles 0 ___ 40
Kilometres 0 ___ 60

Fig. 8.2   The coastline of Ireland: some Pleistocene and Holocene features

the orientation of a number of through valleys in west Donegal, but only in a very restricted sense do they influence the coastal trend or morphology.

Between Malin Head and Bloody Foreland there are few high cliffs and the coast consists of drowned inlets of various sizes, such as Lough Swilly, Mulroy Bay and Sheephaven, many of which are obstructed at their seaward ends by glacial drifts and long spits of shingle and sand. Massive storm shingle beaches occur where Atlantic waves have free access to this exposed coast and some of the finest examples of these occur at Rockstown and near the Bloody Foreland. Glacial drifts have undoubtedly provided, in part at least, the materials from which shingle ridges have been constructed, which rise in places 6 to 8 m (20 to 25 ft) above H.W.M.S.T.

Ice erosion forms are not conspicuous on the coast although granites forming The Rosses have been scoured and form an erratic-strewn surface sloping gently seawards. The interior mountains contain corries and transfluent and diffluent valleys, but large parts of Inishowen and the Slieve League Peninsula were untouched by last glaciation ice.[3] Such coasts display striking differences from those where fresh drumlins, kames and copious outwash gravel are found, for where older drift is thin or absent the coastal slopes are characterised by periglacial forms, shattered rock, polygons and buttresses and tors. Also, in north Inishowen and north Fanad, outside the Drumlin End Moraine, the highest late-glacial beaches in Ireland are found, in some places banked against an even more ancient cliff notch. The latter may represent the northern equivalent of the pre-glacial cliff (shoreline) and platform well known in eastern and southern Ireland as well as less conspicuously at other sites along the western coast (Fig. 8.2).

Prominent cliffs exceeding 136 m (450 ft) occur in north Inishowen between Inishowen Head and Culdaff, in Lough Swilly, where ice-erosion has accompanied over-steepening, at Horn Head 183 m (600 ft, on quartzite), on Aran Island, where west-facing cliffs reach 162 m (535 ft), below the summit of Slieve Tooey above Loughros Bay (greater than 183 m or 600 ft), and the finest, Slieve League (600 m or 1,900 ft) (Fig. 8.3, Plate XI). This mountain has been sculptured into corries, one or more of which may have been partially cut away by the sea on the south-west side to produce vertical cliffs 91 to 183 m high (300 to 600 ft) and scree-clad slopes extending from the sea cliffs to the summit 600 m (1,972 ft). Further west on the steep scree slopes, 6 to 12 m (20 to 40 ft) high buttresses of fissile quartzite stand out as relic forms indicating severe periglacial denudation of the coastal slope. The sea cliffs post-date the formation of the sub-aerial slopes, and probably also certain of the corries, which suggests that at least parts of the present cliffs are of post-glacial age. Between Bloody Foreland and Loughros Bay inlets of the coastline largely ignore the Caledonian structural trend, and where granites are exposed to the sea high cliffs are generally absent.

The north-east to south-west aligned Donegal syncline, although masked by countless drumlins (many of them linked by spits enclosing saltmarsh), is a prominent structural feature directly reflected in the geological strike and trend of numerous headlands such as Muckros Head, St John's Point and Doorin Point (Fig. 8.3). By coincidence the orientation of the drumlins is also approximately north-east to south-west, thus giving to this segment

XI The sea cliffs and scree-clad bevelled slopes of Slieve League, co. Donegal

XII Old Head of Kinsale, co. Cork

Photo by Aerofilms Ltd.

XIII The coast near Blackwater, co. Wexford, where the kame-kettle moraine of the Screen hills is being eroded by the sea.

XIV The cliff profile in glacio-fluvial sands and gravels immediately to the right of the camera position in Plate XIII

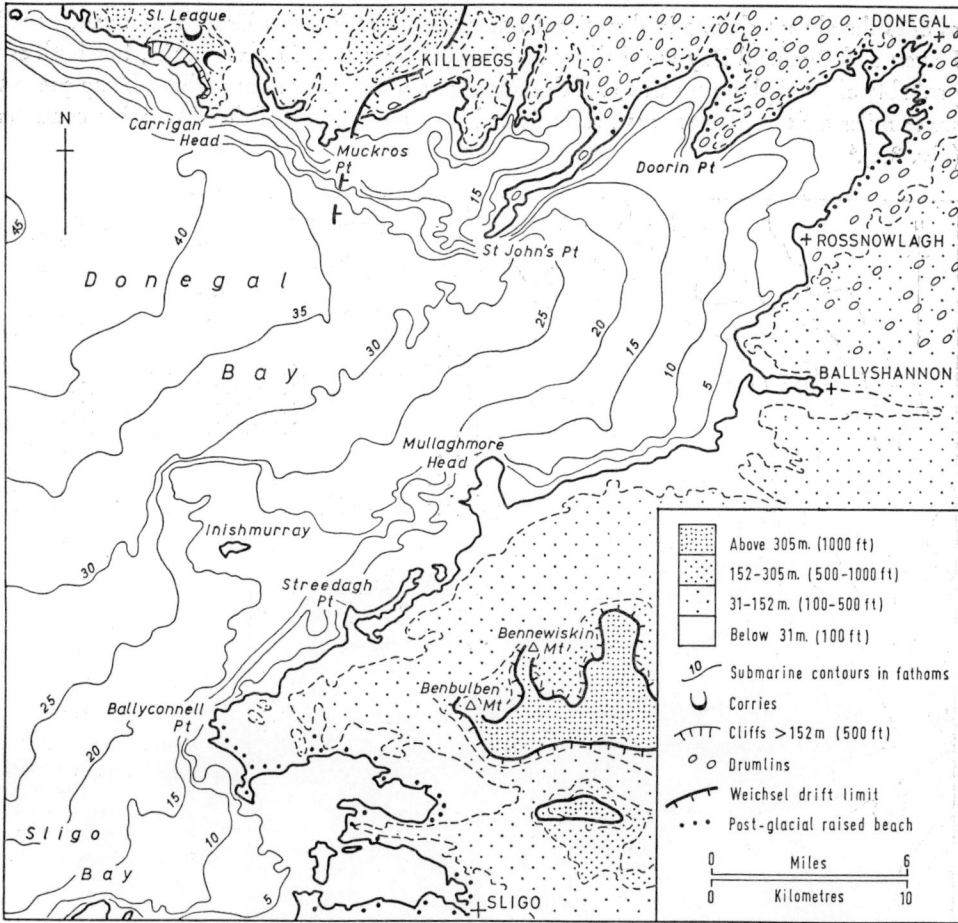

Fig. 8.3 Some features of the coastal geomorphology of Donegal Bay and Sligo Bay

of coast between Muckros Head and Ballyshannon a distinctively orientated morphology of low rocky headlands and drumlin hills.

The west Connacht coast

The three counties of Mayo, Sligo and Galway comprise the western part of Connacht, where the north-east to south-west structural trends change abruptly to mainly east to west. Between Sligo Bay and Broad Haven the coast has the same general trend (slightly north of west to slightly south of east), and the north coast of Galway Bay, formed largely of Connemara granite, and schist, also trends east to west. The nearness of deep water to the coastline west of Killala Bay suggests the presence of faults controlling the coastal trend,

K

as does the abrupt change in direction to north-south as Benwee Head is rounded. Broad Haven and Blacksod Bay are shallow and bordered by cliffs in glacial drift, but both are probably aligned along north to south fault-zones, a similar feature perhaps being present some miles off the Mullet coast, as indicated by close spacing of the submarine contours (Fig. 8.4).[4]

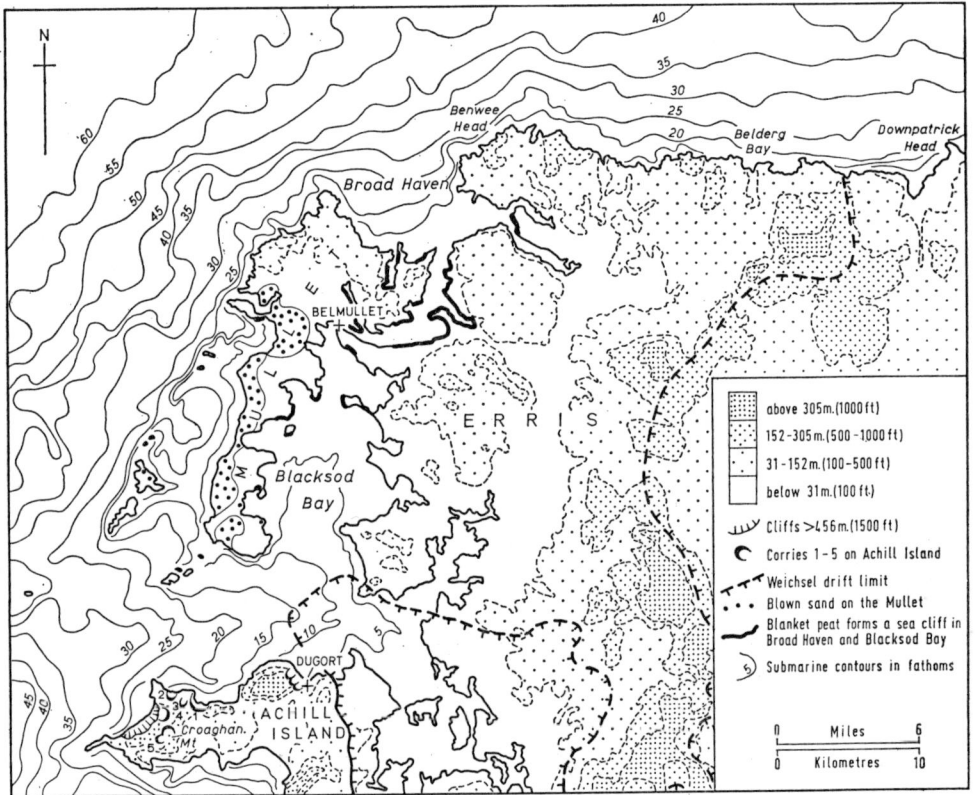

Fig. 8.4 Some features of the coastal geomorphology of north-west co. Mayo. Achill Island corries: 1—Lough Nakeeroge East. 2—Lough Nakeeroge West. 3—Bunnafreeva East. 4—Bunnafreeva West. 5—Lough Acorrymore

Most of the west Connacht coastline consists of pre-Carboniferous rock, with Caledonian affinities, and lacks any really high cliffs. Exceptions are found west of Killala Bay between Downpatrick Head and Belderg, where almost horizontal Carboniferous strata outcrop in vertical cliffs, sometimes with pronounced overhangs. Further west, between Belderg and Broad Haven, near vertical cliffs developed in schist and gneiss, reach 260 m (800 ft) in height, and the regional slope is southwards, away from the coast. The cliff tops are in places mantled with solifluction rubble (head), which can have been derived only from slopes which existed seawards of the present cliff edge, an indication that considerable coast erosion has occurred in the recent past.

The Mullet Peninsula consists of a series of low rocky islands and reefs of granite and metamorphic rocks, joined by plugs of older drift, together with spits, tombolos, and blown sand (Fig. 8.4). Low, freshly eroded cliffs in drift indicate continued retreat of the coast, while the presence of several peat bogs in Broad Haven, with their margins now awash at periods of high water, shows this to be a constantly changing coast. These blanket peats, with cliffs 1 to 2 m (3 to 7 ft) high, like those similarly submerged at high water north of Mulrany, are undoubtedly post-glacial features now being exposed for the first time to wave attack. Whether this has been brought about by a continued rise of sea level against a stable coast where there are only very doubtful traces of late- and post-glacial raised beaches, or by the breaching of old drift plugs or other coastal barriers, is not known. But there is no doubt that further considerable erosion of the drifts and the peats may be expected here.

Achill Island and the Corraun Peninsula possess a high, mountainous coastline where cliffs frequently exceed 305 m (1,000 ft) in height (Fig. 8.4). Croaghan mountain attains 680 m (2,192 ft); to the north-east a ridge some 3.2 km (2 miles) long is scarred by five corries, and for 2.4 km (1.5 miles) a north-west facing precipice falls 456 m (1,500 ft) to the sea. The lowest corries in Ireland are found on Achill[5], in one of which, Nakeeroge East, the rock floor descends below present-day sea level, and for a short distance the sea cuts into the corrie block moraine and the underlying Erris till. Other corries scar the coastal slope above Dugort. Above the sheer cliffs of Achill Head and Menawn, south of Keel Bay, are solifluction-trimmed sub-aerial slopes, which extend south-eastwards until dead-ice moraine and drumlins marking the western limit of Weichsel ice are encountered at the southern tip of Achill Island.[6] Some of the high ground of western Connacht stood as nunataks during the Weichsel glaciation, and so did a large area below 61 m (200 ft) between Emlagh Point and Killary Harbour. There is a remarkable contrast between this low coast, where cliffs in the older drift rarely exceed 6 m (20 ft) in height, and the densely clustered drumlins of younger drift in Clew Bay and the coast between Newport and Westport. The Clew Bay syncline contains Carboniferous strata and this drowned, fault-guided trough is choked with drumlins trending east to west. Many of them have been eroded and modified in shape by the sea, and cliffs 15 to 33 m (50 to 100 ft) high have been cut in those hills of drift which are exposed to Atlantic waves. Very considerable erosion of the drumlins is still in progress in Clew Bay, and in all probabliity the drumlins formerly extended 16 m (10 miles) further seaward, for they can be seen on the south-west coast of the Corraun peninsula and near Roonah Quay in north-west Murrisk. Although protected to some extent by Clare Island, Clew Bay is subjected to the powerful Atlantic swell and the rate of change of coastal outline can be measured accurately as spits and tombolos form and reform among the drumlin islands.[7] Moreover, the rate of change is demonstrably much greater than in Strangford Lough (Fig. 8.6) on the Irish Sea coast, thus emphasising the greater power of the larger Atlantic waves backed by several thousand kilometres of fetch.

The west Connemara schist and granite country contains many north-south faults, again perhaps reflecting the dominant trend of the structures which have brought about the pronounced north-south alignment of the west coast, and the orientation of the steep submarine slope less than 16 km (10 miles) off coast. This north-south trend appears to change to north-west to south-east as Slyne Head is reached, and the closely spaced submarine contours turn towards the north-western end of Inishmore, the largest of the Aran Islands.

Killary Harbour which trends north-west to south-east for part of its length, is a drowned fault-guided valley. It has been subsequently modified by ice erosion, being over-deepened to a depth of 24 m (78 ft) below present sea level, but with a shallow threshold at its mouth.

South-west Connemara was covered by streams of ice moving west and south-west during the Weichsel glaciation. South of Killary Harbour the cliffs seldom exceed 91 m (300 ft) and glacial till (sometimes as drumlins) overlying rock surfaces forms the coastal cliffs as far as Ballyconneely Bay. The north coast of Galway Bay is a low, lake strewn, and peat covered erosion surface, lacking both high rock cliffs and deep, eroded drift sections, but roches moutonnées are encountered frequently. The crenulate plan of the coast between Roundstone and Costelloe[8] can be related to the marine invasion of the lowered portions of granitic intrusions, where jointing may contribute some control to the minor features of coastal relief. The almost circular plan of Bertraghboy Bay corresponds with the drowned portion of a granite intrusion. The granite surface of negligible available relief rises gradually northwards towards the mountains, but southwards it disappears below Galway Bay, where a major dislocation may separate it from Carboniferous country to the south. Opinion differs as to whether or not granite continues southwards below the Carboniferous, but the abruptness of the geological break and the sharpness of east-west trend of the coast suggest that the present coastline may lie near the southern margin of the granite.[9]

The Clare–Limerick coast

Galway Bay lacks the many drumlins which characterise Clew Bay, and only low drift mounds mantle Carboniferous bedrock, where the Central Plain of Ireland reaches the sea. Carboniferous Limestone strata of north co. Clare project into the Atlantic as the Aran Islands The limestones, with shale partings, are tilted north-east and the highest cliffs (usually vertical and with prominent overhangs) face south-west into the full force of Atlantic waves, and exceed 61 m (200 ft) in height. On Inishmore the great dry-stone fort of Dun Aengus stands poised on the edge of a 91 m (300 ft) vertical cliff; the fort is semi-circular in plan, and it is possible that marine erosion has been responsible for reducing significantly the original area within its walls in the last 1,000 years.[10]

To the south of the Burren limestone plateau the most conspicuous cliffs consist of grits, flagstones and shales. The Cliffs of Moher extend for 8 km (5 miles) and achieve a height of between 121 m and 202 m (400 and 668 ft), and generally fall sheer to the sea from the edge of a low plateau, where the regional slope is sometimes inland away from the cliff top. Occasional sea stacks show how joint planes and lithological divisions permit erosion to continue and there is no sign of a coastal bevel of any size leading to the cliff edge. In other words, the present cliffs are 'young', in the sense that head deposits and hillwash which mantled the coastal plateau have flowed eastwards, from slopes now lost to the Atlantic, since Weichsel ice swept across this area. While the trend of the coastline from Black Head to Loop Head is roughly north-east to south-west, the highest of the Moher cliffs face due west. A major watershed extending from the Burren to Hags Head has been breached by the sea at Liscannor Bay, and older drift and solifluction debris appear in pockets along the bevelled cliffs on this coast, well exposed by wave erosion. Mutton Island is a plug of Weichsel drift preserved by a rock outcrop, but it is being reduced in size.

The Shannon lowland trends east-north-east to west-south-west, aligned along a series of faults and synclinal and anticlinal axes, the latter represented in the prominent headlands of Loop Head and Kerry Head. The estuary is generally shallow and bounded by low cliffs of drift, while a large tidal range causes the constant exposure and submergence of sand and mud banks. Scattery Island marks the south-western position of the limiting (end) moraine of the Weichsel glaciation, where it crosses the Shannon estuary.[12]

The south-west coast of co. Kerry and co. Cork

Although the Dingle peninsula lies just north of the Armorican Thrust Front, it may be included in the area to be described. The general east-west trend of anticlinal (Old Red Sandstone) and synclinal (Carboniferous Limestone) axes curve to east-north-east to west-south-west as the west coast is approached, and some north-south faults are also found (Fig. 8.1). The rias of the Kenmare River, Bantry Bay and Dunmanus Bay widen and deepen seawards (Fig. 8.5) as does the pitch of the fold structures. The coincidence of major geological structures and relief is close, although variation in dip of the strata can influence slope angles, and the marked asymmetry of the Sheep Head and Mizen Head peninsulas is reflected in steeper and higher north-west facing cliffs (Fig. 8.5). The cliffs are bevelled but the degree of undercutting of older sub-aerial slopes varies from place to place.

The headlands at the western extremities of the peninsulas have all been blunted by marine erosion; steep cliffs below bevelled coastal slopes testify to continued encroachment by the sea. Stacks and larger islands are numerous, many of them elongated west-south-west to east-north-east, approximately parallel with the geological strike (Fig. 8.5). The waves are quarrying slices of rock many metres thick along the strike, and aided by the jointing and other weaknesses of the rock, are bringing about the collapse of segments of cliff. The absence of remnants of the early Pleistocene rock platform from the majority of headlands is an indication of the extent to which recession has occurred, for the platform occurs within a number of bays and estuaries. In south-west co. Cork and co. Kerry many small streams have rapids or waterfalls, representing knick-points where they enter the sea, and rejuvenation by uplift is thought to have occurred before the last rise of post-glacial sea-level. This may indicate isostatic adjustment in this heavily glaciated area, where at a few points post-glacial raised beaches have also been recorded (Fig. 8.2)[11]; rapid coast erosion may account for some hanging stream profiles.

Some 16 km (10 miles) off-shore the submarine contours crowd together and trend north-west to south-east; a similar direction can be obtained by joining together the extremities of the three southern peninsulas, and the Blasket Islands off the Dingle peninsula.

It is possible that this north-west to south-east trend represents a return to Tertiary structures which appear to have influenced the overall shape of much of the Irish Sea, as well as the peninsula of Devon and Cornwall.[13] A sharp change in the line of the coast at Cape Clear matches that of the submarine contours, but by the longitude of Cork city the latter are more widely spaced and sedimentary features become more important.[14]

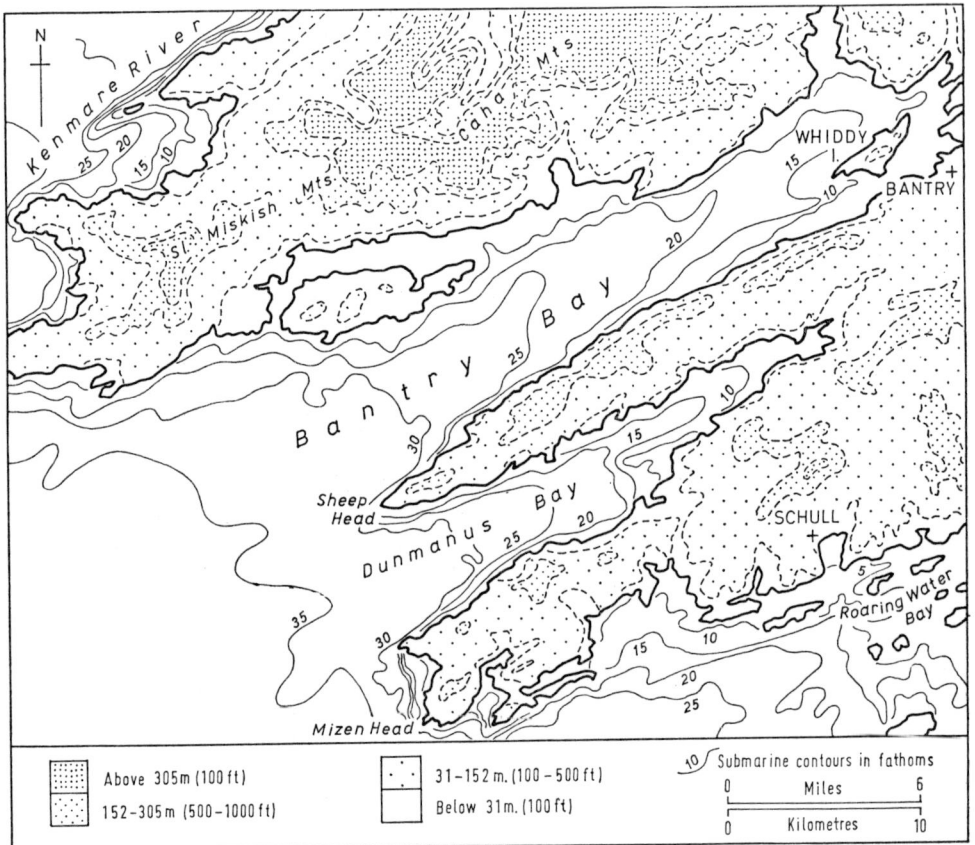

Fig. 8.5   South-west Ireland: an example of rias in the Armorican province

These wide, drowned valleys sometimes contain remarkable spits, such as those in Dingle Bay, and the Kenmare River.[15] In Bantry Bay a deep, buried channel has been discovered below the glacial drift forming the drumlins, of which Whiddy Island is an example. Such buried, sub-drift channels are well known in Ireland (Fig. 8.2) as in other parts of the British Isles; the best known in the south are those along the River Lee[16] above and below Cork city, and in the estuary of the River Blackwater above Youghal.[17]

THE SOUTH COAST

Between Cape Clear and Dungarvan the coast is still crenulate and many harbour entrances represent rias which cut across both the geological strike and topographical grain of the country. East of Kinsale a low 60 to 120 m (200 to 400 ft), undulating plateau rises away from the bevelled cliffs (Plate XII). There are patches of old wave-cut rock platforms and raised beaches, and glacial drifts of various ages occur on the coastal slope. Few sections in drift exceed 3 m (10 ft), except in Ballycotton Bay, where post-glacial erosion has been particularly severe.[18]

Between Dungarvan and the granite headland of Carnsore Point at the south-eastern tip of Ireland the regional geological strike is east-north-east to west-south-west, while the cliffs trend between north-north-east to south-south-west and east-south-east to west-north-west. The 61 m (200 ft) contour rarely reaches the coast and cliffs are much less conspicuous than further west. There is a low coastline of small headlands and broad bays, and fine spits have developed in Tramore Bay. The spits enclosing Tacumshin Lake, Lady's Island Lake, and Ballyteige Lough result from longshore drift from east to west, but face the direction from which dominant waves approach from the Atlantic (south-south-west and south-west).

Between Fethard and Carnsore Point much of the coastline is composed of glacial drifts and head deposits, in which rapid erosion is occurring, and as a consequence there is copious material for the construction of sand dunes as well as the large spits mentioned above. Where rock does appear it is often in the form of low headlands and wave-cut platforms.[19]

Although drift-covered, the coastal zone is remarkable for its lack of strong fresh relief. Only a few isolated kames break the subdued topography which may still be regarded as older drift terrain, in great contrast to the coast immediately north of Wexford. Carnsore Point is a low, drift-covered granite headland. The drifts are being cut back to reveal an irregular rock platform, with a discontinuous cover of large joint blocks. On the platform itself micro relief is controlled by differential weathering and jointing.

THE IRISH SEA COAST

The Irish Sea consists of a series of sedimentary basins separated by horst-like structures. In broad outline the form of the Irish Sea coasts are closely related to Caledonian, Hercynian and Tertiary structural trends. It has been suggested that Bouguer anomaly maps of th southern Irish Sea may indicate the presence of faulted boundaries to the enclosing land masses, and at least one enclosed sedimentary basin trending north-east to south-west. The same trend is reflected in the alignment of the Isle of Man (a horst block?), and the south-west to north-east trend of the Irish coast between the mouth of Strangford Lough and Dundalk Bay. Much of the solid geology of the floor of the Irish Sea is undoubtedly concealed beneath copious Pleistocene deposits—also found along parts of the west coast. These are responsible for masking some of the steep submarine slopes which are found around the Irish coasts, as indicated in figure 8.1. The North Channel seems to represent a convincing example of a rift-like structure, reflecting Hercynian and Tertiary trend lines orientated north-west to south-east.

The south-east coast of co. Wexford

North of Wexford Harbour the coast almost as far as Cahore Point is dominated by cliffs of hummocky drift, forming the eastern edge of the Screen Hills. Considerable erosion of this fresh drift topography is shown by the sheer cliffs, sometimes exceeding 20 m (65 ft) in height, field hedges and roads which hang at the cliff edge, and the presence off-shore of large deposits of sand and gravel (Plates XIII and XIV). At low water considerable banks are exposed, which are elongated north-south, presumably as a result of movement and scour by tidal currents.

The glacial drifts are not everywhere being eroded. Relic cliffs (not elevated) are in places masked by modern sand dunes, so that in the space of a few hundred metres erosion is replaced by deposition, and consolidation is observed to be taking place as marram grass and sea couch grass take root. This kind of shifting equilibrium, of cliff retreat, and progradation by accumulation of blown sand, is quite common along the east coast of Ireland between Carnsore Point and Belfast Lough, where glacial drifts are frequently exposed to wave attack. In contrast to the west coast of Ireland[20], where beach profiles are generally steeper, and where a great deal more glacial drift has been removed by wave action, the east coast beach profiles are frequently of the ridge and runnel type, and constructive waves act for longer periods. While considerable volumes of sand may be set in motion by wave action below high water mark (as in small pocket bays such as Helen's Bay, and Dundrum Bay, both in co. Down), there is likely to be an excess of sand available above high water mark of neap tides for dune construction. This is not a continuous process, as observations in Dundrum Bay have shown, for occasional winter storms from an easterly direction are capable of altering the beach profiles and removing parts of the young fore-dunes; removal may or may not be complete depending upon the volumes of sand involved.

The east coast

Parts of the coast of counties Wicklow and Wexford between Wicklow Head and Cahore Point are characterised by the presence of what G. L. Davies has termed a series of "platforms developed in boulder clay", extending from 16 m (50 ft) to 40 m (130 ft).[21] Nowhere else in Ireland have such features been described, for Davies considers the areas of platform he has mapped to differ from the usual undulating country of the older drifts. Moreover, there is a sharp contrast with the coast south of Cahore Point where fresh morainic topography is intersected by the present cliff line. Whatever may be the origin of the platforms, whether marine, sub-aerial, or sub-glacial deposition of till, the resulting landscape has the appearance of a low plateau sloping gently seawards, to end in cliffs of drift up to 16 m (50 ft) high, or in low rocky headlands. In spite of considerable progradation of the coast and protection of the degraded drift cliffs by sand dunes, for example in Brittas Bay, there remains a precarious balance between loss and gain of land along this coast.

Arklow Head, Wicklow Head, Bray Head, Dalkey Island (and headland), and Howth peninsula are the largest rocky projections which break the smooth outline of the east coast as far north as Dublin Bay. Glacial drifts are present everywhere except on the most exposed parts of the headlands, where bevelled cliffs may be seen. Considerable progradation of the coastline has occurred between Wicklow and Greystones, while immediately north of Greystones, and along Killiney beach, the coastal railway has had to be moved inland during the last hundred years as a result of continued incursions by the sea into cliffs of glacial drift and artificial sea walls. It is likely that Dalkey Island, Ireland's Eye and Lambay Island were formerly connected to the mainland by drift deposits, but only Howth remains joined by a tombolo, which in part at least is a post-glacial raised beach, the gravels of which contain Neolithic artefacts.[22]

The rivers flowing to the east coast, the Liffey, Tolka and Boyne, plunge into rock gorges for the last few miles of their courses, perhaps due to tilting of the Central Lowland 'surface', but rocky cliffs are inconspicuous, and it is glacial drifts, and more recent spits and sand dune formations, which dominate coastal landforms as far north as Carlingford Lough.

The north-south trend of the east coast north of Dublin Bay cuts across the regional strike of Silurian and Carboniferous strata, which form inconspicuous low headlands, generally drift-clad. The only new element to distinguish this segment of coastline from that south of Dublin is the presence of elevated, degraded shorelines of late-and post-glacial age cut in drifts. At places, such as Benhead, Balbriggan, Dunany Head, and near Rathcor and Templetown in the Carlingford Peninsula, subsequent erosion has cut back the drifts probably eliminating traces of the post-glacial raised beaches. Elsewhere, between Howth and Rush, at Laytown and Benhead, at Termonfeckin, and in places near Dundalk, shingle bars (inactive) and dunes protect the 'dead' cliffs cut in glacial drift.

The north-east coast of co. Down and co. Antrim

The North Channel is known from geophysical investigations to be aligned along north-west to south-east trending faults, and most of the structural dislocations which affect the coastline are late-Tertiary in age.[23] Systems of intersecting faults trending north-west to south-east and north-east to south-west control the alignment of some of the major features of the coastline north of Belfast Lough, such as Island Magee, Larne Lough, Garron Point and some of the glens of Antrim. The arrangement of the submarine contours (Fig. 8.7) suggests that slices of the edge of the basalt plateau have subsided seawards as a result of Tertiary faulting.[24] Moreover, the sharply defined edges of the Palaeozoic basement of co. Down also suggests fault control and the north-west to south-east fault system may continue south-eastwards off the Ards Peninsula (Fig. 8.1). The sharp change in direction of the coastline at the entrance to Strangford Lough suggests that Caledonian alignments may define the edge of the Palaeozoic basement in south-east co. Down, with perhaps a return to a north-west to south-east aligned structural control south of Dundalk Bay. Carlingford Lough is an over-deepened, ice-scoured depression, aligned by north-west to south-east faults within the Mourne-Carlingford Tertiary igneous complex; it has a shallow entrance where outcrops of Carboniferous limestone obstruct the channel.

Other possible fault-zones are shown in figure 8.1, where an explanation is required of particular topographical features, such as the entrance to Strangford Lough, which cuts across the north-east to south-west axis of the highest rock outcrops (91 to 123 m or 300 to 400 ft) in south-east co. Down. It seems likely that Strangford Lough is, at least at its northern end, a fault guided basin, because of the considerable thickness of Triassic sediments preserved in a depression in the Palaeozoic basement. But much of the bedrock is obscured

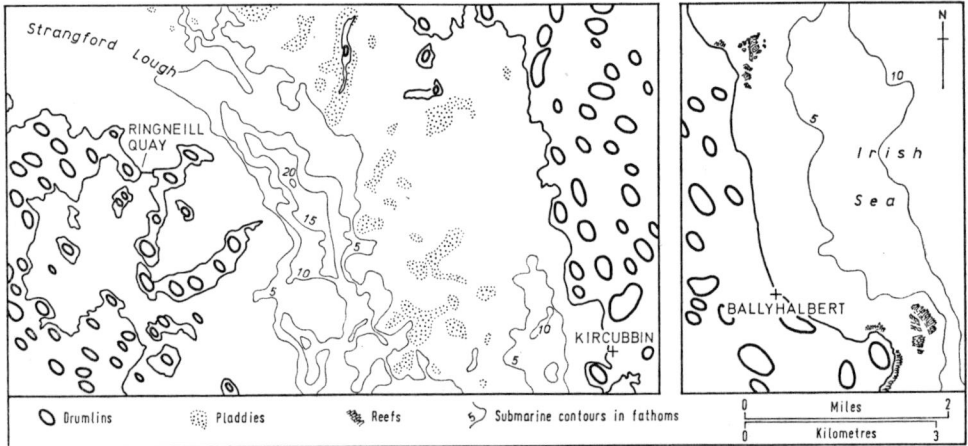

Fig. 8.6 A portion of Strangford Lough and the Irish Sea coast of the Ards Peninsula, co. Down: an example of a drumlin coastline, where 'pladdies' represent the sites of drumlins of which only piles of pebbles and boulders remain, usually exposed at low tide.

by a mantle of glacial drifts, including countless drumlins (Fig. 8.6, Plate XV), and further detailed geophysical investigations are necessary before these tentative suggestions can be substantiated or modified. If the glacial drifts were removed it seems likely that much of the coastal lowland of east co. Down would revert to an archipelago of rocky islands, rock platforms and reefs. Strangford Lough would be linked with Dundrum Bay to form part of a much larger shallow, island-strewn, salt water area, which would represent the submerged edge of the Palaeozoic basement, a basement which may have been tilted slightly east or south-east by Tertiary tectonic activity.

The sharp, and impressive stepped outline of the co. Antrim coastline has resulted from faulting, from Irish ice scouring along the east coast in a south-south-east to north-north-west direction, and from subsequent enormous landslips when ice pressure against the plateau edge was eventually reduced.[25] Thus most of the coastal landforms are no older than the maximum of the Weichsel glaciation, which is tentatively placed at about 20-25,000 years B.P., although of course influenced by earlier events such as Tertiary faulting.

The north coast of co. Antrim and co. Londonderry

The north coast of co. Antrim is also dominated by faulting along east to west and north to south, or north-west to south-east directions, and by the presence of numerous volcanic vents, which are at present intersected in many places by almost sheer cliffs with 'stepped' profiles.[26] The outline of Rathlin Island is almost certainly controlled by intersecting faults, while depressions in the sea floor to the north and south of the island probably result from scouring by ice which overswept Fair Head during the Last Glaciation (Fig. 8.7, Plate XVI).

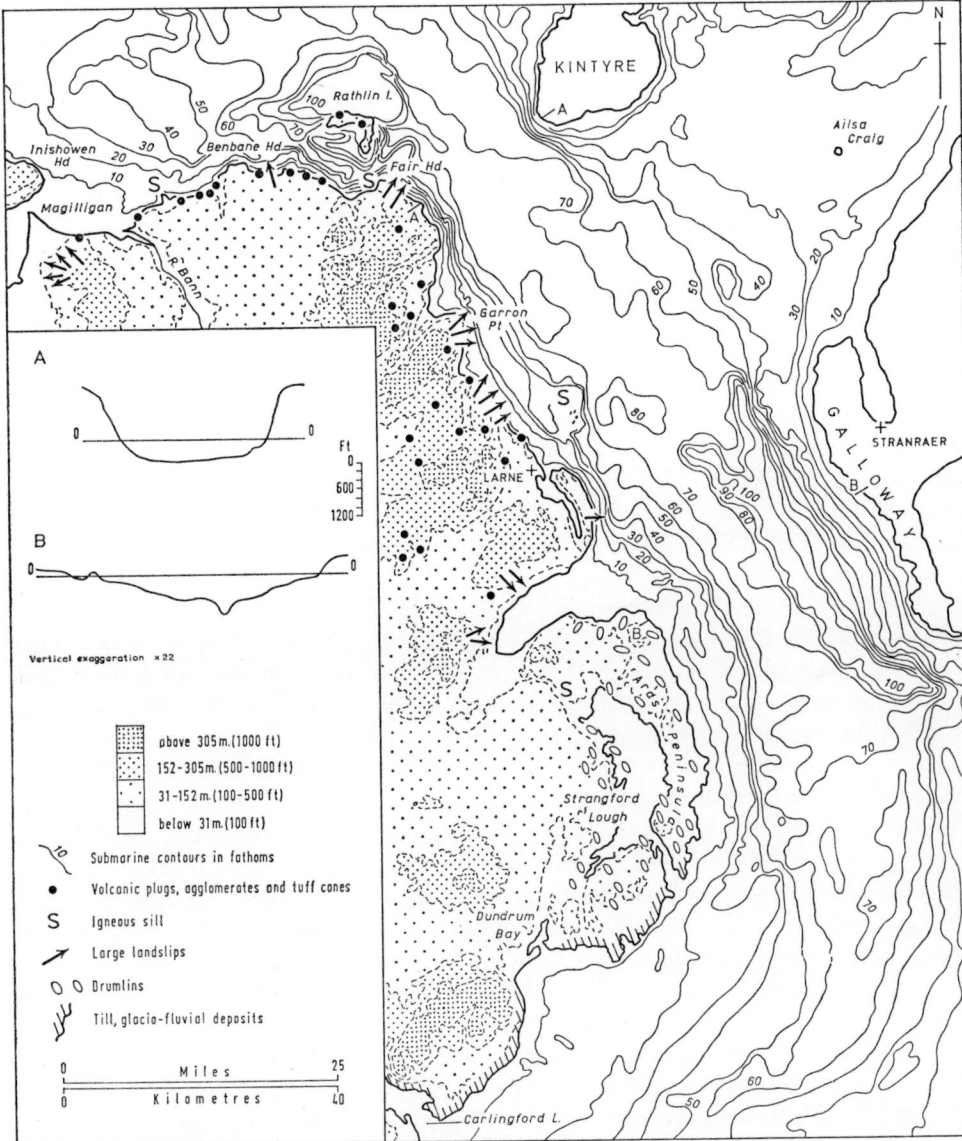

Fig. 8.7   Some features of the coastal geomorphology of north-east Ireland: the two cross-sections (inset) illustrate the presence of steep submarine slopes and the great depth of water encountered in the North Channel.

The basalt plateau edge, which forms the cliffline, is lower along the north coast (160 to 190 m or 500 to 600 ft at Bengore Head) than on the east coast (Garron Point, 310 m or 1,000 ft), but everywhere stepped profiles reflect the outcrop of lava flows making up the plateau, as well as the underlying chalk. Only in the extreme north-east, where Palaeozoic and Pre-Cambrian rocks outcrop, are stepped profiles replaced by bevelled profiles. Composite mudflows affect those parts of the coastal slope where large landslips have displaced Liassic clays, chalk and basalt, and elsewhere rock falls and debris flows have contributed to a general recession of the plateau edge. It should be noted that for long distances between Larne and Cushendall the Antrim coast road, which is sited upon one or more raised beach terraces, together with related sea walls, effectively insulate the actual cliff line from present day wave attack.[27]

Lough Foyle occupies a depression aligned by a north-east to south-west synclinal axis, which is defined by a major fault on its north-western side, against the Pre-Cambrian basement of Inishowen. The basalt plateau edge reaches the coast for only a short distance between Castlerock and Downhill, and the impressive landslips of Binevenagh overlook Magilligan foreland. This is a large complex spit, with extensive dunes, which almost closes the entrance to the lough and marks the site where morainic or outwash gravels exceed 50 m (165 ft) in thickness to form a basement for the spit. Much of the south-east coastline of the lough is protected by seawalls, where land reclamation has taken place, although some 1,200 acres have been lost to the sea near Muff because of the lack of maintenance of sea walls.

PLEISTOCENE FEATURES IN COASTAL MORPHOLOGY

The events of the Pleistocene period are so important that it is necessary to consider them further. Certain elements of coastal morphology have resulted directly from eustatic movements of sea level and isostatic movements of the land mass during this period (Fig. 8.2).[28] Although they cannot be given an absolute date the buried rock channels and wave-cut rock platforms are likely to be the oldest morphological features. Undoubtedly more buried channels exist than those shown in figure 8.2, but these will become known only in the future when deep borings for harbour works, off-shore investigations, and further removal of glacial drifts reveal the channel systems. Because most of them occur at the mouths or in the lower reaches of existing rivers, they are generally regarded as being fluvial in origin, perhaps eroded when withdrawals of the sea occurred during glacial periods. In some cases, however, deep gouging of bedrock in coastal situations has resulted from glacial erosion, for example in Lough Swilly, Carlingford Lough, and probably also in Strangford Lough.

Wave-cut rock platforms are well known to range in height from below present high water mark to cliff notches some 3 to 9 m (10 to 30 ft) above the present day limit of wave activity. They have been described by many authors, but efforts to explain the manner and speed in which they were cut, and also their age, have yielded few positive results. By their very presence they testify to the efficiency of wave action in a storm wave environment, but their full extent is not known because of the extensive cover of drifts and other superficial deposits. For example, the lowest of the relic wave-cut platforms exposed in post-glacial time at Garryvoe, co. Cork, exceeds 365 m (1,200 ft) in width, and in places exceeds 1.6 km (1 mile) in width where it is combined with higher elements of the same rock platform. In contrast, at the foot of some of the highest cliffs in Ireland, at Slea Head in co. Kerry, the Cliffs of Moher in co. Clare, near Keel on Achill Island, and below Slieve League in co. Donegal, rock platforms are almost non-existent at or above high water mark. On the east coast of Ireland rock platforms may reach a width of 16 to 60 m (50 to 200 ft) on the basalts, chalk and Keuper marl in co. Antrim. Inside Belfast Lough and southwards along the co. Down coast, remnants of platforms at several different levels emerge from beneath the drumlins, or are preserved on a succession of rocky reefs and islets for up to 1.6 km (1 mile) off-shore.[29]

Only in the south of Ireland (Fig. 8.2) have beaches been recorded in contact with one or more of the rock platforms, but doubt has been cast upon the contemporaneity of these beaches with the formation of the platforms on account of the included erratics. If these erratics have been derived from older tills or from ice-rafted material, then it is quite possible that the platforms pre-date the beaches by considerable periods of time.[30]

There is still considerable controversy about the age of the subdrift beaches of southern Ireland, just as there is concerning those in other parts of western Britain. These beaches have been traditionally assigned a Hoxnian age in Ireland, mainly because they occur below tills regarded as Saale in age, and sometimes, as at Newtown, co. Waterford, in close association with Hoxnian peat-muds. The absence of undoubted Eemian raised beaches is puzzling, and it may well be that further research will succeed in isolating Eemian from Hoxnian beaches in Ireland as Mitchell and Orme have claimed for the Scilly Isles, and John and others for south-west England and Wales.[31]

Late-glacial shorelines have been mapped and heighted, and their relative age is indicated by contemporaneity with the limit of the drumlins in north-west Donegal[32] and south-east Down.[33] In both localities end moraines and outwash gravels set a limit to ice advance on the one hand, and to marine transgression on the other. At Roddans Port, co. Down, a marine transgression across the isostatically depressed land mass has been dated as earlier than, or occurring in Pollen Zone I, at least 12,000 years B.P.[34] Shorelines associated with this late-glacial transgression normally notch the drifts, but at Malin Head and Fanad Head in north-west Donegal, massive shingle bars and washing limits sometimes coincide with an old cliffline in bedrock, in front of which an elevated rock platform is present. The age of the old cliff and platform is unknown but it could be a retrimmed portion of a pre-glacial feature.[35]

Elevated beaches without a shell fauna have been recorded at a few other places, such as in Broad Haven near Belmullet, on the Corraun Peninsula, and at Emlagh Point just south of Clew Bay, but it is uncertain if these represent late-glacial shorelines (Fig. 8.2). Beach deposits and washing limits have not been mapped on any other sections of coastline, and because of their distinctive nature north of a line from Bloody Foreland to Dundalk it must be concluded that this part of the island was deeply depressed isostatically, whereas to the south the rising sea was unable to submerge the land in pre-Flandrian times.

Isobases for the highest post-glacial beach known in northern and eastern Ireland are drawn in figure 8.2. While it is known that the highest beach is not everywhere of the same age between Rathlin Island and Dublin, and between Fair Head and Bloody Foreland these isobases give a measure of the post-glacial tilting during the last 10,000 years. But neither late-glacial nor post-glacial raised beaches enable us to calculate the total isostatic recovery of different parts of the island since the maximum of the last glaciation.[36]

The precise location of elevated post-glacial beaches in other parts of Ireland is not yet known with certainty, although fragments of raised beach have been recorded in Bantry Bay, on the southern shores of the Shannon estuary (rather more doubtful as raised beaches), in Galway Bay[37] and in Clew Bay. But by far the greater part of the coast south of a line from Dublin to Sligo lacks elevated post-glacial beaches. Here post-glacial time has been marked by transgression and erosion of drifts, elimination of drumlins, stripping of old rock platforms, and the submergence of the coastal zone.

Many coastal peat deposits in the British Isles have been described briefly by Godwin[38] and Steers[39], and the most important Irish examples are shown in figure 8.2. These peats, peaty muds, and submerged forests, often consisting of a few dozen stumps of trees apparently in the position of growth, are known from many sites. Most deposits occur between high water mark of spring tides and −16 m (50 ft). The submerged forests and peat beds are believed to be mainly of post-glacial age, even though a more detailed investigation of their pollen content and C-14 age range is required. What they do indicate is a progressive submergence of the coastal zone in the last 20,000 years. Systematic investigation of these submerged peats is long overdue because it is important to establish their age and if possible, their relationship to earlier late-Pleistocene sea levels.

CONCLUSION

In the future the overall shape of the island will depend in large measure upon the behaviour of world sea level and the relative tectonic stability of the various geomorphological units which make it up. In 1911 the net gain of land over erosion was estimated at 2,720 ha (6,721 acres), and it is likely to be more now because of reclamation at the chief ports.[40] While natural accretion and reclamation will continue to add land to the island there will still continue to be some spectacular losses, especially where glacial drifts are exposed to the sea. It is estimated that on the Irish Sea coast, and along the south coast of Ireland, cliffs composed of drift and head deposits may have been retreating at rates exceeding 3 m (10 ft) per century in post-glacial times. On the more exposed western coasts it is likely that the rate of loss has been far greater, as shown by the elimination of countless drumlins in Donegal Bay and Clew Bay, and the absence of post-glacial raised beaches between Rossnowlagh and Ballyconnell, co. Sligo.

There has been little scientific investigation of the rate of erosion of rock cliffs, but limited observations suggest that on basalts and limestones the rate may have exceeded 1.5 m (5 ft) per thousand years in post-glacial times. This would be sufficient to account for the width of those modern rock platforms which have been measured. However, it is important to stress that some cliffs are probably 'false', in the sense that wave action has not been the prime agent in their formation. Former watersheds and fault-line scarps have undoubtedly been intersected at the coast, and thus the dating of a particular segment of cliffline in rock may be difficult. It is also clear that over long stretches of coastline, for example, along the coast of co. Cork and co. Waterford, the cliffs are not modern but are places where the drifts have been removed and a relic cliff re-exposed to wave action during the last 6,000 to 7,000 years.

Finally, we should note that in Ireland as elsewhere, human activity constitutes a formidable geomorphological process, on the one hand initiating reclamation and the building of sea walls and harbour works, but on the other responsible for the removal of huge quantities of beach sand, shingle and seaweed from beaches every year. The Royal Commission commented upon this last factor in 1911, and it is still true that beach and cliff stability is being impaired in many places because of a general lack of understanding of the dynamic character of the coastal zone. It will be the task of geomorphologists for many years to come to provide much of the basic information necessary to understand the processes and factors involved in the evolution of the Irish coastline.

REFERENCES

1 J. K. Charlesworth, *Historical geology of Ireland*, (1963)
   W. E. Nevill, *Geology and Ireland*, (1963)
   J. R. Kilroe, *A description of the soil geology of Ireland*, (1907)
   H. I. S. Thirlway, Measurements of gravity in Ireland; gravimeter observations between Dublin, Sligo, Galway and Cork, *Dublin Inst. Adv. Studies, Geophys. Mem.*, 2, Part 2 (1951), 1–26
   J. B. Whittow, The structure of the southern Irish Sea area, *Adv. Science*, 56 (1958), 381–85
   A. Guilcher, Les surfaces d'erosion fossiles exhumées dans le nord de l'Irlande, *Ann. de Geog.*, 66 (1957), 289–309
   A. Reffay, Problèmes morphologiques dans la péninsule due sud-ouest du Donegal, *Rev. Géog. Alpine*, 2 (1966), 287–312
2 R. P. Riddihough, Magnetic surveys off the north coast of Ireland, *Proc. Roy. Irish Acad.*, 66 B (1968), 27–41
3 N. Stephens and F. M. Synge, Late-Pleistocene shorelines and drift limits in north Donegal, *Proc. Roy. Irish Acad.*, 64 B (1965), 131–53
   F. M. Synge and N. Stephens, The Quaternary period in Ireland—an assessment, 1960, *Irish Geography*, 4 (1960), 121–30
4 The submarine contours shown in figures 8.3, 8.4, 8.5, 8.6 and 8.7 have been interpreted from published Admiralty Charts, and further coastal information has been obtained from the *Irish Coast Pilot*, (London, 1954)
5 A. Farrington, Local Pleistocene glaciation and the level of the snow line of Croaghaun Mountain in Achill Island, co. Mayo, Ireland, *J. Glaciology*, 2 (1953), 262–67
6 F. M. Synge, The glaciation of west Mayo, *Irish Geography*, 5 (1968), 372–86
7 A. Guilcher, Morphologie de la Baie de Clew (Comté de Mayo, Irlande), *Bull. Ass. Géog. Français*, 303–4, (1962), 53–65
8 A. Guilcher and C. A. M. King, Spits, tombolos and tidal marshes in Connemara and West Kerry, Ireland, *Proc. Roy. Irish Acad.*, 61 B (1961), 283–338
9 D. McKie and K. Burke, The geology of the islands of south Connemara, *Geol. Mag.*, 92 (1955), 487–98

10 E. E. Evans, *Prehistoric and Early Christian Ireland, a guide,* (1966), 118–21

11 R. H. Bryant, The 'pre-glacial' raised beach in south-west Ireland, *Irish Geography,* 5 (1966), 188–203

A. Farrington, A note on the correlation of the Kerry-Cork glaciations with those of the rest of Ireland, *Irish Geography,* 3 (1954), 47–53

A. Farrington, Types of rejuvenated valleys found in Ireland, *Irish Geography,* 4 (1960), 117–20

12 T. Finch and F. M. Synge, The drifts and soils of west Clare and the adjoining parts of counties Kerry and Limerick, *Irish Geography,* 5 (1966), 161–72

13 W. R. Dearman, Wrench-faulting in Cornwall and south Devon, *Proc. Geol. Ass.,* 74 (1963), 265–87

D. J. Shearman, On Tertiary fault movements in north Devonshire, *Proc. Geol. Ass.,* 78 (1967), 555–66

14 A. H. Stride, North-east trending ridges of the Celtic Sea, *Proc. Ussher Soc.,* 1, Part 2 (1963), 62–3

N. H. Kenyon, Undescribed sand bodies of weak tidal current areas in the Celtic Sea, *Proc. Ussher Soc.,* 1, Part 6 (1967), 287–88

15 A. Guilcher and C. A. M. King, (1961), op. cit.

A. Guilcher, Drumlin and spit structures in the Kenmare River, *Irish Geography,* 5 (1965), 7–19

16 A. Farrington, The Lee basin; Part One; Glaciation, *Proc. Roy. Irish Acad.,* 60 B (1959), 135–66

17 A. R. Orme, Quarternary changes of sea-level in Ireland, *Trans. Inst. Brit. Geog.,* 39 (1966), 127–40

18 A. Farrington, The early-glacial raised beach in co. Cork, *Sci. Proc. Roy. Dublin Soc.,* Ser. A, 2 (1966), 197–219

19 G. F. Mitchell, Summer field meeting in Wales and Ireland, *Proc. Geol. Ass.,* 73 (1962), 197–213

F. M. Synge, A correlation between the drifts of south-east Ireland and those of west Wales, *Irish Geography,* 4 (1963), 360–66

F. M. Synge, Some problems concerned with the glacial succession in south-east Ireland, *Irish Geography,* 5 (1964), 73–82

20 C. A. M. King, Some observations on the beaches of the west coast of co. Donegal, *Irish Geography,* 5 (1965), 40–50

21 G. L. Davies, Platforms developed in the boulder clay of the coastal margins of counties Wicklow and Wexford, *Irish Geography,* 4 (1960), 107–16

S. Martin, Raised beaches and their relation to glacial drifts on the east coast of Ireland, *Irish Geography,* 1 (1955), 87–93

22 G. F. Mitchell, An early kitchen-midden at Sutton, co. Dublin, *J. Roy. Soc. Antiq. Ireland,* 86 (1956), 1–26

N. Stephens and F. M. Synge, The Quaternary deposits at Sutton, co. Dublin, *Proc. Roy. Irish Acad.,* 59 B (1958), 19–27

A. Farrington, Raised beaches near Dublin, *Irish Nat. Jour.,* 4 (1933), 211–12

23 W. B. Wright, An Analysis of the Palaeozoic floor of north-east Ireland, *Sci. Proc. Roy. Dublin Soc.,* 15 (1919), 629–50

A. H. Cook and J. Murphy, Measurements of gravity in Ireland; gravity survey of Ireland north of a line Sligo-Dundalk, *Dublin Inst. Adv. Studies, Geophys. Mem.,* 2, Part 4 (1952), 1–36

M. H. P. Bott, The deep structure of the northern Irish Sea—a problem of crustal dynamics, 179–201 in W. F. Whittard and R. Bradshaw eds., *Submarine Geology and Geophysics* (1965)

W. Bullerwell, The gravity map of Northern Ireland, *Irish Nat. Jour.,* 13, No. 10, (1961), 255–57

H. I. S. Thirlway, (1951), op. cit.

T. N. George, The stratigraphical evolution of the Midland Valley, *Trans. Geol. Soc. Glasgow,* 24 (1960), 32–107

24 N. Stephens, The evolution of the coastline of north-east Ireland, *Adv. Science,* 56 (1958), 389–91

N. Stephens, Geomorphological Studies in Ireland and western Britain, with special reference to the Pleistocene period; (Unpublished PhD thesis, The Queen's University of Belfast, 1966)

Photo by Aerofilms Ltd.

XV Drumlins along the western shores of Strangford Lough, near Ardmillan and White Rock, co. Down

Photo by Aerofilms Ltd.

XVI The cliffs of Fair Head (dolerite sill with columnar jointing), Murlough Bay
(landslips), and the bevelled cliffs extending southwards to Torr Head

25 N. Stephens, (1958, 1966), op. cit.
    A. R. Hill and D. B. Prior, Directions of ice movement in north-east Ireland, *Proc. Roy. Irish Acad.,*
    66 B (1968), 71–84
26 N. Stephens, Geology and physiography, in L. Symons ed., *Land Utilisation in Northern Ireland,*
    (1963), 59–74
    N. Stephens, (1958), op. cit.
27 D. B. Prior, N. Stephens and D. R. Archer, Composite mudflows on the Antrim coast of north-east
    Ireland, *Geogr. Annaler,* 50 A (1968), 65–78
28 A. Farrington and N. Stephens, The Pleistocene geomorphology of Ireland, in J. A. Steers ed.,
    Field Studies in the British Isles, (1964), 446–61
29 N. Stephens and F. M. Synge, Pleistocene shorelines in G. H. Dury ed., *Essays in Geomorphology,*
    (1966), 1–51. N. Stephens, Some observations on the 'Interglacial' platform and early post-glacial
    raised beach on the east coast of Ireland, *Proc. Roy. Irish Acad.,* 58 B (1957), 129–49
30 W. B. Wright and H. B. Muff, The pre-glacial raised beach of the south coast of Ireland, *Sci. Proc.*
    Roy. Dublin Soc., 10 (1904), 250–324
    A. Farrington, (1966), op. cit.
    G. F. Mitchell, (1962), op. cit.
    N. Stephens and F. M. Synge, (1966), op. cit.
31 G. F. Mitchell and A. R. Orme, The Pleistocene deposits of the Isles of Scilly, *Quart. Jour. Geol. Soc.*
    London, 123 (1965), 59–92
    B. S. John, Age of raised beach deposits of south-western Britain, *Nature,* 218 (1968), 665–67
32 N. Stephens and F. M. Synge, (1965), op. cit.
33 N. Stephens, Late-glacial sea-levels in north-east Ireland, *Irish Geography,* 4 (1963), 345–59
    N. Stephens, Late-glacial and post-glacial shorelines in Ireland and south-west Scotland, *Means of*
    Correlation of Quaternary Successions, 8 (VII INQUA Congress, 1968), 437–56
34 M. E. S. Morrison and N. Stephens, A submerged late-Quaternary deposit at Roddans Port on
    the north-east coast of Ireland, *Phil. Trans. Roy. Soc. London,* 249 (1965), 221–55
35 N. Stephens and F. M. Synge, (1965), op. cit.
36 F. M. Synge and N. Stephens, Late- and post-glacial shorelines and ice-limits in Argyll and north-
    east Ulster, *Trans. Inst. Brit. Geog.,* 39 (1966), 101–25
    D. B. Prior, Late-glacial and post-glacial shorelines in north-east Antrim, *Irish Geography,* 5 (1966),
    173–87
    A. Farrington, The level of the ocean in glacial and late-glacial times, *Proc. Roy. Irish Acad.,* 50 B
    (1945), 237–43
    G. F. Mitchell, Morainic ridges on the floor of the Irish Sea, *Irish Geography,* 4 (1963), 335–44
37 A. Farrington, Raised beaches in Galway Bay, *Irish Nat. Jour.,* 14 (1963), 216–17
38 H. Godwin, Coastal peat beds of the British Isles and the North Sea, *J. Ecology,* 31 (1943), 199–247
39 J. A. Steers, *The coastline of England and Wales,* (1946)
40 *Royal Commission Reports on Coast Erosion and Afforestation,* (3 Vols., London, 1911)

L

IX

RURAL SETTLEMENT IN IRELAND

R. H. Buchanan

Few themes in Irish geography are more closely identified with Estyn Evans than rural settlement. Its study has been his special interest, his chief contribution the identification of distinctive settlement forms such as the clachan, and their interpretation with reference to an evolving folkculture in which continuity of tradition is the outstanding feature. For Evans the formative years of this culture lie in the neolithic, which saw the first major modifications of the Irish landscape by man. Immigration and cultural diffusion brought many subsequent changes, but the indigenous culture absorbed new traits without radical change. During the first millennium A.D. new culture patterns did emerge, and were reflected in settlement changes; but older folkways persisted, surviving even the English colonisations of historic times.

The sequence of cultural development in Ireland was well established by the nineteen-twenties, but there had been little research on material folkculture or on the history of landscape evolution and settlement. This work began in the thirties when Evans published his first study of rural settlement[1] and important papers were also published in archaeology by his colleague Oliver Davies[2], and in ethnology by the late Ake Campbell.[3] From the pioneer work of this decade has stemmed all subsequent research on the evolution of Irish rural settlement which forms the subject of this essay.

The first farmers

The neolithic colonists who came to Ireland towards the end of the 4th millennium B.C. found a thickly wooded environment which had been little affected by the economy of their mesolithic predecessors. As farmers whose principal tool was the polished stone axe, the newcomers sought light well-drained soils, more easily cleared of timber than the low-land woods of oak and hazel, elm and alder. They found such areas mainly on the hill margins, where slopes provided seasonal grazing for the cattle which formed the mainstay of their economy. Pigs, sheep and goats were also kept, and wheat and barley grown in small quantities by shifting cultivation. It seems that this mode of living did not necessarily involve a frequent change of settlement, for temporary shelters might be erected on fishing expeditions[4] or while working on distant cultivation plots[5]. Certainly lengthy occupation is indicated in some places by the erection of permanent field enclosures[6], and by the continued use of large communal tombs in favoured localities.[7]

Few settlements of this period have been discovered, but that at Lough Gur, co. Limerick[8], revealed a small farm community which must have been typical of the Irish neolithic. It consisted of at least twelve houses, forming a loose cluster of dwellings, each placed at some distance from its neighbour. The houses were both round and rectangular in plan, each built on a light framework of upright timbers with walls of wattle or sods built on a stone foundation. The most elaborate, a rectangular house some 17 by 32 feet, had narrow internal aisles formed by the arrangement of its roof supports in a style similar to that of neolithic houses in northern Europe.[9] Lough Gur suggests a socially homogeneous community, co-operating in forest clearance and farming, and representing a form of settlement which recurs frequently in Irish history.

It is likely that farm clusters such as Lough Gur continued as the predominant form of settlement in bronze age times, for although this was a period of cultural innovation as well as of technical development, there is little evidence of fundamental changes in farming. The new bronze axe, made by specialist smiths, helped to extend clearances in virgin forest[10], and it is possible that more intensive land use and permanent cultivation followed from the introduction of the ard-plough.[11] But farming was still based more on cattle than on crop, although sheep became increasingly important towards the end of the period. Lough Gur itself was occupied until the middle bronze age, but few other farm sites are known, apart from the earliest phase of occupation on the Cathedral Hill, Downpatrick, co. Down.[12]

A new settlement form, the crannog, does appear, although at two sites its development was foreshadowed during the neolithic.[13] The few excavated bronze age crannogs show little sign of permanent occupation, suggesting that they were used either for defence or as seasonal camp grounds[14], perhaps by communities whose clustered farm settlements have yet to be found. It is possible, however, that the isolated, single farmstead appeared in Ireland at this time[15], although bronze age dates claimed for the raths at Cush, co. Limerick and the cashel at Carrigillihy, co. Cork have been disputed.[16] Other houses of this period are broadly similar in plan and construction to those of the neolithic[17], but Carrigillihy differs in that its walls were built with a rubble core faced with courses of dry stone. The house itself was enclosed with a circular, dry-stone wall, similar to the cashels of the first millennium A.D.

Celts and early Christians

The arrival of Celtic-speaking immigrants during the last quarter of the first millennium B.C. led to the development of a new pattern of culture, based on an iron technology and with economic and social institutions very different in character from those of Ireland's neighbours who came under Roman occupation. Economic growth was made possible by the introduction of the iron axe and the heavy coulter plough[18], which enabled the farmer both to clear the oakwoods and to cultivate the lowland soils. New crops were introduced, such as spelt, rye and especially oats[19], providing the basis for an expansion in arable farming which seems to have been encouraged by the early monastic communities.[20] Settled agriculture, sometimes in enclosed fields, is indicated by the literary sources[21], but cattle rearing dominated the economy, providing both a source of food and an index of wealth among the free classes of a strongly hierarchical society.[22] These included nobles, professional men and farmers, each class linked to the others by a complicated system of customary obligations and recognizing a nominal affinity of kinship through membership of a tribal group.[23] Beneath the freemen in status was a servile class, descendants perhaps of the indigenous farmers of prehistoric times who became the bondsmen of the first iron age colonists.

The scale of economic and social change is reflected in settlement by the advent of the hill fort and the single farmstead. Unlike England and Wales[24], few hill forts were built in Ireland by the immigrant chiefs, although that at Downpatrick, co. Down, first occupied c. 300 B.C., was defended by an elaborate timber-laced rampart in the continental Hallstatt style.[25] By early Christian times, most of the Irish hill forts seem to have lost their military function, although in the west, great stone fortresses continued to be built, such as the Grianan, co. Donegal, and Staigue in co. Kerry.[26] Like the promontory forts of the western coastlands, these belong mainly to the second half of the first millennium A.D. A similar defensive role was provided by the many crannogs built throughout this period. Some were quite small structures, but others had strong defences, such as the royal crannog at Lagore in co. Meath.[27]

These settlements symbolised the introduction of a new political authority, but the appearance of the single farmstead was as great an innovation in economic and social life. In Ireland it took the form of the rath or ringfort, a circular enclosure of between 60 and 110 feet in diameter, formed by one or more earthen banks and an external fosse; in stony areas the bank was replaced by a dry-stone wall, and the structure is known as a cashel. Some of the ring-forts were built during the pre-Roman iron age, but the majority belong to the period between the fifth and tenth centuries.[28] This dating raises a problem, for if the single farmstead was introduced by iron age colonists, as was the case in Britain, unenclosed dwellings must have been familiar elements in the pattern of Irish settlement for several centuries before the rath became common. So far there is no evidence to support or refute this suggestion, although on two excavated sites, farmsteads either unenclosed or with low surrounding banks were found to have preceded the construction of a rath.[29] Similar farmsteads may have co-existed with the raths in later centuries, associated perhaps with the many souterrains—underground chambers often found in raths and used for food storage and as refuges—which are found isolated in open country.

The rath, however, must be regarded as the typical, single-family farmstead of the first millennium A.D. owned by a free farmer who held his land mainly in severalty and perhaps in enclosed fields, with rights of common grazing.[30] The rath or cashel was his farmstead, occasionally roofed right over, more often containing free-standing outbuildings and a dwelling house, built in timber frame construction with walls of turf or wattle-and-daub, and roofed with thatch or shingles.[31] The majority of buildings were probably round, but rectangular dwellings were also common. Some contain two apartments, but no excavated site has yet revealed anything as elaborate as the aisled hall which the literature associates with royal residences such as Tara. Yet houses were now more elaborate, some with porches and clerestories[32], for iron tools meant higher standards of craftsmanship in joinery and the use of heavier timbers. That this resulted in the development of genuine architectural styles is shown in the early stone churches, whose design and structure is based on wooden proto-types.[33] Generally stone was used only where timber was scarce, as in the circular beehive *clochans* of the Dingle peninsula in co. Kerry, whose corbelled roofs hark back to a megalithic tradition of building in stone. But in response to Norse raids during the ninth century, stone came to be the preferred material, reaching its finest expression in native architecture in the graceful round towers, built as belfries and strong rooms for the monasteries.

Hill-forts, raths and cashels all represent a departure from the tradition of clustered farmsteads which seems to have been the norm during prehistoric times. Only a few house clusters can be dated archaeologically to the first millennium A.D., and the single farmstead seems to predominate. Yet there is circumstantial evidence to suggest that farm clusters may have survived in areas of light soil originally colonised by neolithic and bronze age farmers. Throughout Ireland, raths are proportionately fewer in such districts, and are most dense in lowland areas first cleared for farming during the early Christian period.[34] Some corroboration for this thesis is provided in the late Sean MacAirt's interpretation of the word *baile* (anglicised *bally*), which in the dark age literature refers to a specific type of settlement. Its form is unknown, but MacAirt believed the word was of pre-Goidelic origin, and might refer to the settlements of bronze age farmers. Where *baile* was a common element in place-names, he suggested that the pre-Celtic population could have remained on the land following the iron-age colonisation, though depressed to bond status.[35] Proudfoot tested this view in co. Down, and was able to show that raths were least common in areas where *baile* was strongly represented in place-names, and where there was evidence for a large and stable population during the first millennium A.D.[36] The suggestion here is that the farm population was living mainly in clustered settlements, as was certainly the case some centuries later.[37]

Archaeology cannot yet provide evidence for the existence of clustered settlement during this period, but at two sites, the relative disposition of a cashel and a cluster of stone huts suggests the dwelling of a free farmer with his attendant bondsmen.[38] In addition, the excavation of a rath at Duneight, co. Down, revealed traces of an unenclosed settlement nearby, which might be the *baile* of Duneight, burnt in 1010 according to the *Annals of Ulster*.[39] The available data permits no firm conclusion, but it seems reasonable to suggest that the unenclosed farm cluster was a significant element in the pattern of Irish settlement during the first millennium A.D., its form similar to the grouping of monks' cells in contemporary monastic communities.

The Anglo-Normans

Towards the end of the twelfth century, Ireland received the first major group of immigrants in more than a thousand years. The Anglo-Normans under Strongbow came as colonists, unlike their Norse predecessors who had been content to establish small trading ports on favoured anchorages. In Ireland the spread of Norman rule depended largely on the enterprise of individual barons, yet by the mid-thirteenth century they had gained control over nearly two-thirds of the country. Only in Ulster and parts of the west and south-west did native chiefly families remain in firm control of their ancestral lands, later to exploit the political rivalries which developed among the conquerors. Gradually in the frontier lands, Norman families were assimilated to Irish ways, and their political ascendancy was eroded steadily during the fourteenth and fifteenth centuries. By Tudor times it remained effective only in the Leinster Pale around Dublin.

From the twelfth to the sixteenth century, Ireland was thus divided into two main culture regions. Native institutions, developed during the previous millennium, remained dominant in the north and west, though influenced by intrusive elements from Norman districts; while in the eastern lands of Munster and Leinster, the Irish formed a substratum among the colonists[40], and were profoundly affected by the introduction of the manorial system. Its organisation reflected the complexity of a colonial society, embracing both the lands granted to Norman free tenants and burgesses, and those occupied by native tenants: the *firmarii,* who held by lease on a fixed term, and the *betaghs* who were of servile status.[41] The land itself was worked both in common fields and in farms held in severalty, the majority of farmers following a three course rotation except perhaps for the betaghs; their land was held on a joint tenancy and was separate from that of other social groups.[42] Under the manorial system, agricultural productivity seems to have improved steadily, but the main emphasis was still on livestock, with hides and wool forming the staple exports in an expanding trade with Britain.[43]

At the time of the Norman invasion, scattered single farmsteads and dwelling clusters were the two main forms of settlement, but the beginnings of urban life were foreshadowed in Norse ports such as Dublin and Waterford, and at some of the major monastic centres such as Armagh.[44] The major change in native settlement was the gradual abandonment of raths and crannogs, although some continued to be occupied until the close of the sixteenth century.[45] Little is known about the farmhouses which succeeded them on open sites, except that the round form was no longer used, although the structural transition to the rectangular house was marked by an oval, hip-roofed style, quite common in the late sixteenth century.[46] Most houses were built on a timber frame, probably with cruck construction, and walls were of clay and wattle or turf, on stone footings. Stone was used for more substantial houses, as in the pair excavated at Caherguillamore in co. Limerick.[47] They were built probably in the fourteenth century, their two-room, rectangular plan, with central hearth and single entrance closely resembling eighteenth century houses in the same district. So far there is no archaeological evidence for the existence of clustered settlement, although on manorial lands, the betaghs had their own settlement, designated *baile.* It is likely that these were house clusters in the same settlement tradition as the bond settlements of the first millennium A.D.[48]

In most parts of the country this settlement pattern survived throughout the mediaeval period, but in manorial districts new forms were superimposed. The most spectacular was the lord's residence which fulfilled both domestic and military functions. The earthen mottes built during the first phase of occupation, were not greatly different in appearance from the large multivallate raths, but the great stone castles, built between 1180 and 1310 on strategic sites such as Trim and Carlow, were imposing structures of unprecedented size.[49]

Less pretentious were the hall dwellings, exemplified in excavated sites such as Clough and Lismahon in co. Down[50], which must have formed the typical dwellings of minor land-owners and the principal free tenants during the thirteenth and fourteenth centuries. Usually they had farmyards attached, as at Cloncurry, co. Kildare[51], sometimes with an extensive range of outbuildings arranged formally around a courtyard[52]—a style which may well have been influenced by that of the monastic granges. But by the early fifteenth century, increasing military pressure from the native Irish made necessary a more easily defended residence. The tower house was the result, an elegant stone structure some three to four storeys high, which for the next two centuries formed the principle style of house built by the Anglo-Norman gentry[53], and of those native chiefs who adopted Norman styles within their own territories.[54]

More important for Ireland's economic development were the towns, sponsored by individual lords and granted borough status mainly to attract English settlers with the prospect of holding land on favourable leases.[55] Many such settlements were founded during the thirteenth century in the manorial districts, and although a significant number never developed, the remainder became small market centres often with craft industries such as pottery and metal-working.[56] The most prosperous were either the centres of large manors, such as New Ross in co. Wexford[57], or ports like Ardglass in co. Down, well situated to engage in the growing trade with England and Wales. Such settlements were frequently walled by the fourteenth century, their merchants building tower houses for additional protection and thus giving a characteristic townscape to the mediaeval borough, whose lesser citizens lived in single storied dwellings.[58] With these developments in urban life, Ireland began slowly to forsake its insular, Celtic heritage for a world in which commercial interests were becoming dominant.

Planters and landowners

The men responsible for effecting this change were a new generation of English immigrants who came to Ireland during the late sixteenth and seventeenth centuries. They included soldiers, civil servants, adventurers and farmers, and their colonisation took place under the plantations organised first by the Tudors, in Leix and Offaly and later in Munster, and then by James I in Ulster. All three schemes aimed to subdue Ireland by military action backed by colonisation, and in the case of Ulster these objectives were largely accomplished. But it was not until the end of the seventeenth century that the ascendancy of the new-comers was confirmed, by the granting of estates confiscated from Irish landowners following the uprising of 1641 and the Williamite wars of 1690. By the end of the century less than one-fifth of Ireland was retained by native owners, and this proportion was further reduced after 1695 under the penal laws.

Unlike their predecessors, the new landlords were primarily interested in their estates as a source of income, for they had acquired the land either in lieu of army gratuities or as a business speculation. Under the more peaceful conditions of the eighteenth century, some began to invest capital in schemes for land improvement, in urban development and road building. Others took little interest in their estates, but whether active improver or negligent absentee, the landowner was the chief influence in the wholesale reshaping of Irish landscape and settlement which took place during the eighteenth and early nineteenth centuries.

Two further factors helped to shape changes in settlement during this period. One was the growth in population, from an estimated 2.2 million in 1687 to about 4.4 million in 1788[59], with a further dramatic increase to 8.2 million at the 1841 census. The second was the development of commercial agriculture, forced on the Irish farmer by the steady increase in land values and rent during the eighteenth century. Dependence on the English market meant that until 1750 the emphasis was placed on cattle, but later in the century tillage became more important, and high grain prices prevailed until after the Napoleonic wars. Adjustment to these changing market conditions meant a profound reorganisation in an agriculture previously geared to subsistence needs, a transition made all the more difficult by mounting pressure of population on land resources.

The effect of these changes on settlement must be viewed in terms of the regional contrasts which were apparent by the end of the mediaeval period. For example, the manorial districts of Leinster and Munster already contained many large farms which were able to profit from the expanding livestock trade. Here single farmsteads were probably the most important elements in the pattern of settlement by the early eighteenth century, although in many districts there must have been house clusters formerly associated with betagh tenants. In contrast, Ulster, the province least affected by the Norman conquest, had been systematically colonised under the Jacobean Plantation with consequent changes in its pattern of settlement during the seventeenth century. Most important was the imposition of a framework of small towns and villages throughout the planted counties, in which the colonists were intended to live for their mutual defence. Despite the destruction of the 1641 rebellion, most of these settlements developed as planned, but an early complaint was that the farmers "lie not in townrids together as they were appointed, but lie scattered, up and down upon their proportions".[60] As a result, scattered, single farmsteads were predominant by the end of the seventeenth century in those parts of Ulster most strongly settled by the planters. Only in mountainous districts of the west, from Donegal in the north to Kerry and Cork in the south, did an older settlement pattern persist throughout the seventeenth century. Traditional folkways survived especially in Connacht, where many dispossessed Irish landowners from other parts of the country were forced to settle. Settlement changes during the eighteenth and early nineteenth centuries varied in each of these regions, but throughout the country the effect was broadly similar. This can be summarised as first the gradual disappearance of the farm clusters, earlier in the east than in the west; a great increase in the number of single farmsteads, with growing disparity of scale between the dwellings of rich and poor; and the development of market towns and smaller service centres.

In the eighteenth century the farm cluster, which Evans and later writers have termed *clachan,* was associated with the rundale system of partnership farming in common fields. This was based on the continuous cropping of an infield, mainly in oats, sometimes augmented by shifting cultivation of an outfield.[61] Common grazing was found on hill land, which sometimes involved a seasonal movement to distant pasture known as booleying.[62]

At present little is known in detail of the distribution of clachans in Ireland at the beginning of the eighteenth century, but the causes of their disappearance have been outlined by McCourt and other workers.[63]

In east Leinster and Munster for example, farm consolidation and enclosure leading to the break-up of rundale and the elimination of clachans, were undertaken by landowners intent on developing large grazing farms. This process began in the second half of the seventeenth century, often with the enclosure of land which had provided common grazing for rundale farmers.[64] Their eviction was made easier under a tenant law of 1695 which made Irish customary tenure equivalent to tenancy at will, and through the operation of the penal laws enacted a little later. Remission of tithes on pasture in 1735 made grazing even more profitable, with results described by Viscount Taafe: "The sculoag race (i.e. the peasant farmers) . . . who in my time cultivated the lands everywhere till . . . some rich grazier took their lands over their heads . . . has been broken and dispersed in every quarter and we have nothing in lieu but . . . the cottagers".[65] In areas unsuited to commercial grazing, rundale often survived until later in the century, when the emphasis shifted to tillage. Market demand favoured wheat and barley, cereals whose cropping was ill-suited to traditional rundale practice and which thus hastened the reorganisation of the common fields into holdings in severalty. Sometimes this was undertaken by landlords, sometimes by the farmers themselves; but the result was the gradual disappearance of the clachans and their replacement by single farmsteads, each placed on its own holding.[66]

In western districts meantime, clachans not only survived but actually grew in number and in size. For example, four to eight dwellings was an average size in the early eighteenth century; but by the first decade of the nineteenth, clachans in co. Donegal averaged thirty dwellings, rising as high as 120 to 200 in co. Clare.[67] The chief reason for this increase was rising population, which in the rundale system was accommodated by subdivision of holdings in the customary practice of gavelkind inheritance.[68] Towards the end of the century pressure of population was so great that even farms formerly held in severalty might become rundale holdings in this way, the new generation of joint tenants building their houses alongside the original dwelling to become clachans.[69] The same process sometimes took place on individual intakes by squatters on marginal land, though sometimes too late in the Famine decades for clachans to grow before population dropped abruptly after 1845–47.[70]

Initially subdivision was countenanced by most landowners, many of whom left the conduct of their affairs to middlemen whose chief concern was to extract the maximum rent from a numerous tenantry. But extreme fragmentation of holdings led to destitution, and even before the 1837 Poor Law made landowners financially liable for the support of their pauper tenants, attempts were being made to reform the rundale system. Two methods of consolidation were used. In one, holdings were laid out in squared fields, the clachans dissolved and new farmsteads built, each on its own holding. In the other, farms were planned in long strips, running for example, from valley bottom to hill margin, with houses forming a loosely woven ribbon of settlement on a road which ran along the valley sides.[71]

The break-up of clachans during the second half of the eighteenth century contributed to the great increase in single dwellings, especially in the east as the dispossessed farmers either gained new tenancies in compact holdings or were reduced to the status of labourers following eviction. But rising population under a tillage economy was also responsible for the new phase of building activity. Arable farming could support more people in smaller holdings than could livestock rearing, besides providing seasonal work for labourers. In addition to subdivision by the farmers themselves, subletting was also widely practised, both by the landowners when leases fell in, and by large graziers. In the words of a contemporary, they "kept the best of the land . . . and let the verges round at enormous rents to the poor tenants . . . the land is let at double the value".[72] Smaller plots were also rented at will to cottiers, who in large farm districts might account for more than half the population.[73] Of all sections of the rural community they suffered most in the post-1815 agricultural depression and during the Famine years when the small farmers also suffered increasing destitution. Only in the north-east were conditions slightly improved by the ancillary employment available in hand spinning and weaving for the domestic linen industry.

For much of the eighteenth century, the housing of the small farmers and cottiers showed little change from that of earlier periods. Stone was still rarely used except in upland and coastal districts, and the cruck frame dwelling, its walls "of hurdles plaister'd with cow dung and clay" must have been common.[74] As heavy timber became scarce it gave way to the couple-truss, mud walled house which was the norm by the early nineteenth century. Most houses were now of rectangular rather than oval form, although a majority probably retained the hip style roof. A rectangular house of early seventeenth century date, excavated at Lough Gur, co. Limerick[75], was probably typical of its period, although its central hearth and single entrance door belong to a house tradition—the jamb-wall type—normally associated with eastern districts, to which it may have been introduced from England in mediaeval times.[76] In the west, the most common type was probably the byre-dwelling, in which family and livestock shared the house.[77] In plan and construction these houses were little different from their earlier predecessors, their stark simplicity reflecting the economic conditions of the majority of the rural population during the eighteenth century. Few had surplus cash to invest in building, nor security of tenure to encourage better housing, and with the exception of the north, they obtained no compensation for any improvements made to the property if they were evicted. Indeed with increasing poverty towards the end of the century, housing conditions deteriorated further, with more than one-third of all Irish houses consisting of a single room by the 1840's.[78]

Yet some people profited from the growth of the rural economy and invested in more substantial buildings; these were the privileged tenants of the new landowners and their middlemen, the big graziers of Munster and Leinster, and the minor gentry among the northern planters. This last group introduced the box-frame timber house to Ireland, but after the 1641 rebellion, they saw the wisdom of building stone houses more capable of defence.[79] By the end of the seventeenth century, the stone house seems to have been the hallmark of this rural middle class, both north and south, often in the form of a two-storied thatched house, one room wide and with one apartment on each floor.[80] Later the Georgian villa became the dominant style, a scaled-down version of the landlord's mansion.

For the landlord, the great phase of building was between 1720 and 1800, when magnificent houses were built throughout the country, a symbol of the wealth and power attained by the new generation of Anglo-Irish gentry.[81] Their ancestors, preoccupied with the need for defence, had often been content to adapt existing tower houses, and it was not until after the Restoration that a more domestic style of architecture began to appear.[82] Castletown House, co. Kildare, begun in 1720, was among the first of the new Georgian mansions which during the eighteenth century formed a significant new element in the pattern of Irish settlement, their sheer size dominating a landscape then largely devoid of woodland. Their gardens and plantations took time to mature, and it was not until the latter half of the century that woodland finally screened the "big house" from the surrounding countryside, its social distance emphasised by high walls which enclosed demesnes of up to a thousand acres.

The country house itself was the residential focus of an extensive settlement complex, which included a home farm and frequently, an extra-mural village for demesne workers and servants.[83] With such nucleated settlements were associated market towns, by far the most important innovation in settlement during the seventeenth and early eighteenth centuries. The earliest were established under the Tudor and Jacobean Plantations,[84] their location in Munster, Ulster and the west midlands extending inland the pattern of urban settlements first developed under the Anglo-Normans.

Morphologically, many of the seventeenth-century planned towns were distinguished by central squares or 'diamonds', formed by the crossing of the two main streets, and with a centrally located market house and church. Few completely new towns were created during the eighteenth century, except in parts of the west[85], but the urban pattern was further developed by small service centres built by individual landowners. Population growth in existing settlements was often accommodated in a planned grid of broad streets and squares[86], and landlords frequently sought to control the standard of housing by special provisions in leases.[87] New civic buildings might include a courthouse, almshouse and perhaps a school and infirmary, as well as a new or enlarged church. The latter was usually of the established church, for the towns remained strong centres of English influence, their merchants, shopkeepers and craftsmen mainly Protestant. Yet few towns lacked a straggle of one-storied cottages, the homes of "the meer Irish", on their outskirts. Visually these struck a discordant note in what were otherwise carefully planned settlements, with a striking similarity in design and layout, made possible only in an age when the landlord was firmly in control.[88]

Civil servants and councillors

The great surge of building which characterised the eighteenth and early nineteenth centuries ceased abruptly with the Great Famine of 1845–47. Within four years the population had dropped by 2 million from its record high of 8.2 million in 1841, and its decline continued until the 1930's, levelling off around the 4 million mark and increasing only slightly to 4.4 million in 1966. Small farmers, labourers and craftsmen have all contributed to the emigration which has been endemic for more than a century. For example, the number of holdings has dropped by 47 per cent since 1841, while farms over 30 acres now amount to 48 per cent of the total compared with 7 per cent in 1841. Today rural depopulation continues, for the slight increase in population represents a growth in urban areas, mainly centred on Dublin and Belfast but including the larger country towns.

The past century has also seen the disappearance of the landlord as a formative influence on rural life and settlement. The tragedy of the Famine brought to light the appalling mismanagement which existed on many estates, although it was not until the last decades of the nineteenth century that ownership of land was finally transferred from the landlord to the farmer with the passage of various land acts. In settlement this transition was accompanied by the demise of the 'big house', hastened sometimes by incendiarism during 'the Troubles', or simply through neglect by owners whose income was now drastically reduced. Those that survive today are frequently institutions, housing schools and convents, hotels or government departments. Only the smaller houses are likely to remain in the hands of their original owners, or more likely, have been bought by wealthy newcomers.

With the disappearance of the landlord, the state began to assume many of the development functions formerly exercised on the best managed estates. One of the earliest government agencies was the Congested Districts Board, founded in 1891 to encourage the economic development of the poorest areas of the western seaboard, its powers passing to the Land Commission in 1923. In 1883 the Poor Law Guardians were authorised to build cottages for rent to agricultural labourers, a responsibility which passed to Rural District Councils following their organisation in the Local Government Act of 1898.[89] Since then the provision of housing for rent has been a statutory obligation of local authorities both in Northern Ireland and in the Republic, while state subsidies are paid for houses of specified size built by private developers, and special grants are available for improvements to farm dwellings.

The scale of government investment in rural housing, roads and public utilities has increased steadily during the last sixty years, but its direct influence on settlement has followed mainly from the planning legislation enacted during the last few decades. Only in the west was earlier settlement change directed by government through the Congested Districts Board, which continued the work of farm consolidation begun by improving landlords. Since 1891 the Board and the Land Commission have steadily replaced clachans with single farmsteads, and have even resettled some of their former occupants on new holdings, developed on demesnes bought by the Commission in eastern counties.[90] As a result the clachan has virtually disappeared as an element in Irish settlement, for continuing depopulation has led to the abandonment of many which survived the improving activities of landlord and government official.[91]

The single farmstead has also been affected by the general contraction in rural settlement. The ruins of deserted farm dwellings are most visible on the margins of modern farmland, and along remote roads and laneways. Yet these represent only the more substantial houses, abandoned by small farmers during the past century, for the poorest dwelling—the single room mud house, usually vanished without trace. In 1841 these numbered some 40 per cent of all rural housing, yet by 1911 this proportion had dropped to 1 per cent.[92] Meantime, the standard of the remaining farmhouses has improved enormously, spurred on by the land acts, especially the Wyndham Act of 1902, which finally gave the farmers security of ownership. 'American money', sent home by emigrants, often helped to modernise dwellings, by the addition of a second storey, roofed in blue slate instead of thatch, and with grey cement plaster replacing the traditional whitewash. Red brick and pebble-dash became standard finishes after World War I, but the influence of suburban house styles was not pronounced until the increase in building after 1945.

Far more numerous than the new farmhouses are the dwellings built by local authorities, especially during the last twenty years. Those built earlier in the century were mainly single-storied cottages, each standing on an acre of ground and dispersed along country roads. But since World War II, councils have tended to group their houses in clusters of six to twelve dwellings, mainly to save on costs of providing water, sewerage and power. Like the earlier single houses, the new clusters are mostly located in open countryside, notably in the north where each Rural District councillor expects his share of the council's housing to be sited in his own constituency.[93] The result is that council housing is often inconveniently situated for its occupants, far from shops, schools and services, and from the towns where the country dweller is now most likely to find employment.

Country towns have also suffered from the effects of rural depopulation, for most were created by landlords to serve the needs of a population now less than half its former size. Comparatively few have managed to attract manufacturing industry, and most new employment is provided through the expansion in services and in the functions of state and local government, in administrative offices, schools and hospitals.[94] These are mainly located in the larger centres, which have their quota of new housing, built along the main entries to the town. But whether large or small, the centres of many Irish towns are dominated by old buildings, public and private, whose drabness signifies the approaching end of their useful life. Renewal is necessary, but it is most likely to come only to those settlements within commuter range of growth centres selected in the processes of regional planning, or those whose locations have a special potential for recreation and tourism.

Many of these different phases of settlement survive as relict features in the present landscape. Traces of the homes of neolithic and bronze age farmers have long since disappeared, unlike their tombs, but the raths of the first millennium A.D. may be counted in their hundreds in every Irish county. More impressive visually are the castles of the Normans and the Planters, and the Georgian mansions which are most common in the rich lands of the Munster or Leinster plains, with their small, grey towns. Yet the past lingers in less obvious features too, in the alignment of roads and fields, or the design and construction of farmhouses and buildings. Often their secrets are known only to the country people themselves, in their folklore and tradition. Estyn Evans was one of the first of his generation of scholars to recognise the value of this tradition in a country whose social and economic history is poorly represented in official documents. The material he gathered around the fireside and in the fields he related to the findings of archaeology and conventional history. In this way he has made a unique contribution to the knowledge of Ireland's past, and in particular, to the history of its settlement.

REFERENCES

1 E. E. Evans, Belfast Naturalists' Field Club Survey of Antiquities; megaliths and raths, *Irish Nat. Jour.*, 5 (1935), 242–252, and Some survivals of the Irish openfield system, *Geography*, 24 (1939), 24–36

2 Summarised in O. Davies, A summary of the archaeology of Ulster, *Ulster J. Arch.*, 3rd series, 11 (1948), 1–41 and 12 (1949), 43–76

3 A. Campbell, Notes on the Irish house, *Folkliv*, 1 (1937), 207–34 and 2 (1938), 73–96

4 A. E. P. Collins, Excavations in the sandhills at Dundrum, co. Down, 1950–51, *Ulster J. Arch.*, 3rd series, 15 (1952), 2–26

5 G. D. Liversage, A neolithic site at Townleyhall, co. Louth, *J. Roy. Soc. Antiq. Ireland*, 90 (1960), 49–60

6 V. B. Proudfoot, Ancient Irish field systems, *Adv. Science*, 56 (1958), 369

7 E. E. Evans, Prehistoric geography, in J. W. Watson and J. B. Sissons, eds., *The British Isles*, (1964), 184

8 S. P. O'Ríordáin, Lough Gur excavations; Neolithic and Bronze Age houses on Knockadoon, *Proc. Roy. Irish Acad.*, 56 C (1954), 297–459

9 ibid., 304–5

10 G. F. Mitchell, Littleton Bog, Tipperary; an Irish agricultural record, *J. Roy. Soc. Antiq. Ireland*, 95 (1965), 127
E. E. Evans, The prehistoric and historic background, in L. J. Symons, ed., *Land utilisation in Northern Ireland*, (1963), 26

11 J. O'Loan, A history of early Irish farming, *Dept. of Agriculture Journal*, 60 (1963), 137

12 V. B. Proudfoot, Excavations at Cathedral Hill, Downpatrick, co. Down, 1954, *Ulster J. Arch.*, 3rd series, 19 (1956), 57–72

13 O. Davies, *Island MacHugh* (1950)
E. E. Evans, *Prehistoric and Early Christian Ireland; a guide*, (1966), 191–2

14 S. P. O'Ríordáin and A. T. Lucas, Excavation of a small crannog at Rathjordan, co. Cork, *North Munster Antiq. J.*, 5 (1946–47), 68

15 S. P. O'Ríordáin, Excavations at Cush, co. Limerick, *Proc. Roy. Irish Acad.*, 45 C (1940), 83–181
M. J. O'Kelly, An early Bronze Age ring-fort at Carrigillihy, co. Cork, *J. Cork Hist. & Arch Soc.*, 56 (1951), 69–86

16 V. B. Proudfoot, The economy of the Irish rath, *Medieval Archaeology*, 5 (1961), 99
E. E. Evans, (1966), op. cit., 77 and 143

17 for example, E. M. Fahy, A stone circle, hut and dolmen at Bohanagh, co. Cork, *J. Cork Hist. & Arch. Soc.*, 66 (1961), 93–104
A. J. Pollock and D. M. Waterman, A. Bronze Age habitation site at Downpatrick, *Ulster J. Arch.*, 3rd series, 27 (1964), 31–57

18 E. E. Evans, The Atlantic ends of Europe, *Adv. Science*, 58 (1958), 8

19 E. E. Evans, (1964), op. cit., 189

20 M. V. Duignan, Irish agriculture in early historic times, *J. Roy. Soc. Antiq. Ireland*, 74 (1944), 145

21 J. O'Loan, Land reclamation down the years, *Dept. of Agriculture Journal*, 55 (1959), 6–7

22 A. T. Lucas, Cattle in ancient and medieval Irish society, *O'Connell School Union Record*, 1935–7, (1958), unpaginated. V. B. Proudfoot, (1961), op. cit., 109–11

23 D. A. Binchy, Secular institutions, in M. Dillon ed., *Early Irish society*, (1954), 54 and 57

24 E. E. Evans, (1964), op. cit., 190

25 V. B. Proudfoot, (1956), op. cit., 71

26 M. and L. de Paor, *Early Christian Ireland*, (1961), 86

27 H. O'N. Hencken, Lagore crannog: an Irish royal residence of the seventh to tenth centuries, A.D., *Proc. Roy. Irish Acad.*, 53 C (1950–1), 1–247

28 V. B. Proudfoot, (1961), op. cit., 97–107

29 E. M. Jope, ed., *An archaeological survey of County Down*, (1966), 166. A second excavated site is at Coshquin, co. Londonderry (information from D. McCourt in advance of publication)

30 R. H. Buchanan, Field systems of Ireland, in A. R. H. Baker and R. A. Butlin eds., *Studies of field systems in the British Isles*, (forthcoming)

31 V. B. Proudfoot, (1961), op. cit., 101–4

32 for example, D. M. Waterman, The excavation of a house and souterrain at White Fort, Dromaroad, Co. Down, *Ulster J. Arch.*, 3rd series, 19 (1956), 73–86

33 H. G. Leask, *Irish churches and monastic buildings*, (3 vols.), 1 (1955), 43–8

34 D. McCourt, The rundale system in Ireland, (Unpublished PhD thesis, Queen's University, Belfast, 1950), 303–10
E. E. Evans, Ireland and Atlantic Europe, *Geographische Zeitschrift*, 52 (1964), 237

35 S. MacAirt, County Armagh, toponymy and history, *Proc. Irish Catholic Historians*, (1955), 1–5

36 V. B. Proudfoot, Clachans in Ireland, *Gwerin*, 2 (1959), 113–4

37 R. H. Buchanan, The barony of Lecale, co. Down, (Unpublished PhD thesis, Queen's University, Belfast, 1958), 109–23

38 O. Davies, Excavations at Lissachiggel, *J. Co. Louth Arch. Soc.*, 9 (1939–40), 209–43
O. Davies, The Twomile Stone, a prehistoric community in County Donegal, *J. Roy. Soc. Antiq. Ireland*, 72 (1942), 98–105

39 D. M. Waterman, Excavations at Duneight, co. Down, *Ulster J. Arch.*, 3rd series, 26 (1963), 55–78

40 J. Otway-Ruthven, The native Irish and English law in medieval Ireland, *Irish Historical Studies*, 7 (1951), 7
J. Otway-Ruthven, The character of Norman settlement in Ireland, *Historical Studies*, 5 (1965), 75–84

41 J. Otway-Ruthven, The organisation of Anglo-Irish agriculture in the middle ages, *J. Roy. Soc. Antiq. Ireland*, 81 (1951), 1–13

42 R. H. Buchanan, (forthcoming), op. cit.

43 E. M. Jope ed., (1966), op. cit., 107

44 G. Camblin, *The town in Ulster*, (1951), 6–7

45 E. E. Evans, (1966), op. cit., 28

46 G. A. Hayes-McCoy, *Ulster and other Irish maps c. 1600*, (1964), 2–12

47 S. P. O'Ríordáin and J. Hunt, Medieval dwellings at Caherguillamore, co. Limerick, *J. Roy. Soc. Antiq. Ireland*, 72 (1942), 37–63

48 R. H. Buchanan (forthcoming), op. cit.

49 H. G. Leask, *Irish castles and castellated houses*, (1944), 30–34 and 47–49

50 D. M. Waterman, Excavations at Clough castle, co. Down, *Ulster J. Arch.*, 3rd series 17 (1954), 103–63
D. M. Waterman, Excavations at Lismahon, co. Down, *Medieval Archaeology*, 3 (1959), 139–76

51 J. O'Loan, The manor of Cloncurry, co. Kildare, *Dept. of Agriculture Journal*, 58 (1962), 1–23

52 E. St J. Brooks, Fourteenth century monastic estates in Meath, *J. Roy. Soc. Antiq. Ireland*, 83 (1953), 143–4

53 H. G. Leask, (1944), op. cit., 75–92

54 for example in E. M. Jope, ed. (1966), op. cit., 196, and E. M. Jope, Harry Avery's Castle, Newtownstewart, co. Tyrone, *Ulster J. Arch.*, 3rd series, 13 (1950), 81–92

55 J. Otway-Ruthven, (1951), op. cit., 1, and (1965), op. cit., 79

56 E. M. Jope, ed., (1966), op. cit., 186

57 J. F. Lydon, The medieval English colony (c. 1300–c. 1400), in T. W. Moody and F. X. Martin, eds., *The course of Irish history*, (1967), 148

58 for example, E. M. Jope and W. A. Seaby, A new document in the Public Record Office; defensive houses in medieval towns, *Ulster J. Arch.*, 3rd series, 22 (1959), 119–22

59 K. H. Connell, *The population of Ireland, 1750–1845*, (1950), 25

60 C. Maxwell, *Irish history from contemporary sources*, (1923), 291
61 D. McCourt, Infield and outfield in Ireland, *Ec. Hist. Rev.*, 2nd series, 7 (1954), 369–76
62 J. M. Graham, Transhumance in Ireland, *Adv. Science*, 10 (1953), 74–79
63 D. McCourt, (1950), op. cit., 238–79
   D. McCourt, The rundale system in Donegal, its distribution and decline, *Donegal Annual*, 3 (1955), 47–57
   R. H. Buchanan, (1958), op. cit., 89–179
   J. H. Johnson, The disappearance of clachans from co. Derry in the nineteenth century, *Irish Geography*, 4 (1963), 404–14
64 I. Leister, *Das Werden der Agrarlandschaft in der Grafschaft Tipperary (Irland)*, (Marburg, 1963), 121
65 N. Taafe, *Oberservations on affairs in Ireland*, (1766), 12
66 I. Leister, (1963), op. cit., 254
   R. H. Buchanan, (1958), op. cit., 89–179
67 D. McCourt, (1950), op. cit., 91–2
   J. McParlan, *Statistical survey of the county of Donegal*, (1802), 64
   W. Shaw Mason, *Parochial survey: a statistical or parochial survey of Ireland*, 1 (1814), 485
68 R. H. Buchanan, (forthcoming), op. cit.
69 D. McCourt, (1950), op. cit., 40–4 and 180
70 P. Flatrès, *Géographie rurale de quatres contrées Celtiques*, (Rennes, 1957), 292
71 D. McCourt, (1955), op. cit., 52–6
72 *The Devon Digest*, (1847), 414
73 J. A. Edwards, The landless in mid-nineteenth century county Louth, *J. Co. Louth Arch. Soc.*, 16 (1966), 103–110
74 John Dunton's letters, in E. Machysaght, *Irish life in the seventeenth century*, 2nd ed., (1950), 358
75 S. P. O'Ríordáin, and C. Ó Danachair, Lough Gur excavations; Site J. Knockadoon, *J. Roy. Soc. Antiq. Ireland*, 77 (1947), 39–52
76 C. Ó Danachair, Three house types, *Ulster Folklife*, 2 (1956), 22–26
77 C. Ó Danachair, The combined byre-and-dwelling in Ireland, *Folk Life*, 2 (1964), 58–75
78 C. Ó Danachair, Some primitive structures used as dwellings, *J. Roy. Soc. Antiq. Ireland*, 75 (1945), 204–212
   C. Ó Danachair, The bothán Scóir, in E. Rynne ed., *North Munster Studies*, (1967), 489–98
79 E. M. Jope, ed., (1966), op. cit., 256
80 C. Ó Danachair, Some notes on traditional house types in County Kildare, *J. Co. Kildare Arch. Soc.*, 14 (1966–7), 243–46
81 *The Georgian Society records of eighteenth century domestic architecture and decoration in Ireland*, 5 (1913), 10–12
82 E. M. Jope, Moyry, Charlemont, Castleraw and Richhill; fortification to architecture in the north of Ireland 1570–1700, *Ulster J. Arch.*, 3rd series, 23 (1960), 97–123
   D. M. Waterman, Some Irish seventeenth-century houses and their architectural ancestry, in E. M. Jope, ed., *Studies in building history*, (1961), 251–74
83 P. Flatrès, (1957), op. cit., 283
84 R. A. Butlin, Urban genesis in Ireland, 1556–1641, in R. W. Steele and R. Lawton, eds., *Liverpool Essays in Geography*, (1968), 211–26
85 for example, T. Jones Hughes, Landlordism in the Mullet of Mayo, *Irish Geography*, 4 (1959), 16–34
86 for example, The Knight of Glin, Georgian Limerick, *Quart. Bull. Irish Georgian Soc.*, 3 (1960), 35
87 G. Camblin, (1951), op. cit., 91
88 T. Jones Hughes, Society and settlement in nineteenth-century Ireland, *Irish Geography*, 5 (1965), 85–6 and 92
89 J. Collins, *Local government*, (1963), 104

Photo by J. K. St. Joseph, Cambridge University Collection, Copyright reserved

XVII   Newtown Jerpoint, co. Kilkenny. Streets and enclosures of medieval town showing as earthworks in field with trees

XVIII   Ballyduagh, co. Tipperary. Earthworks of a medieval settlement?

Photo by J. K. St. Joseph, Cambridge University Collection, Copyright reserved

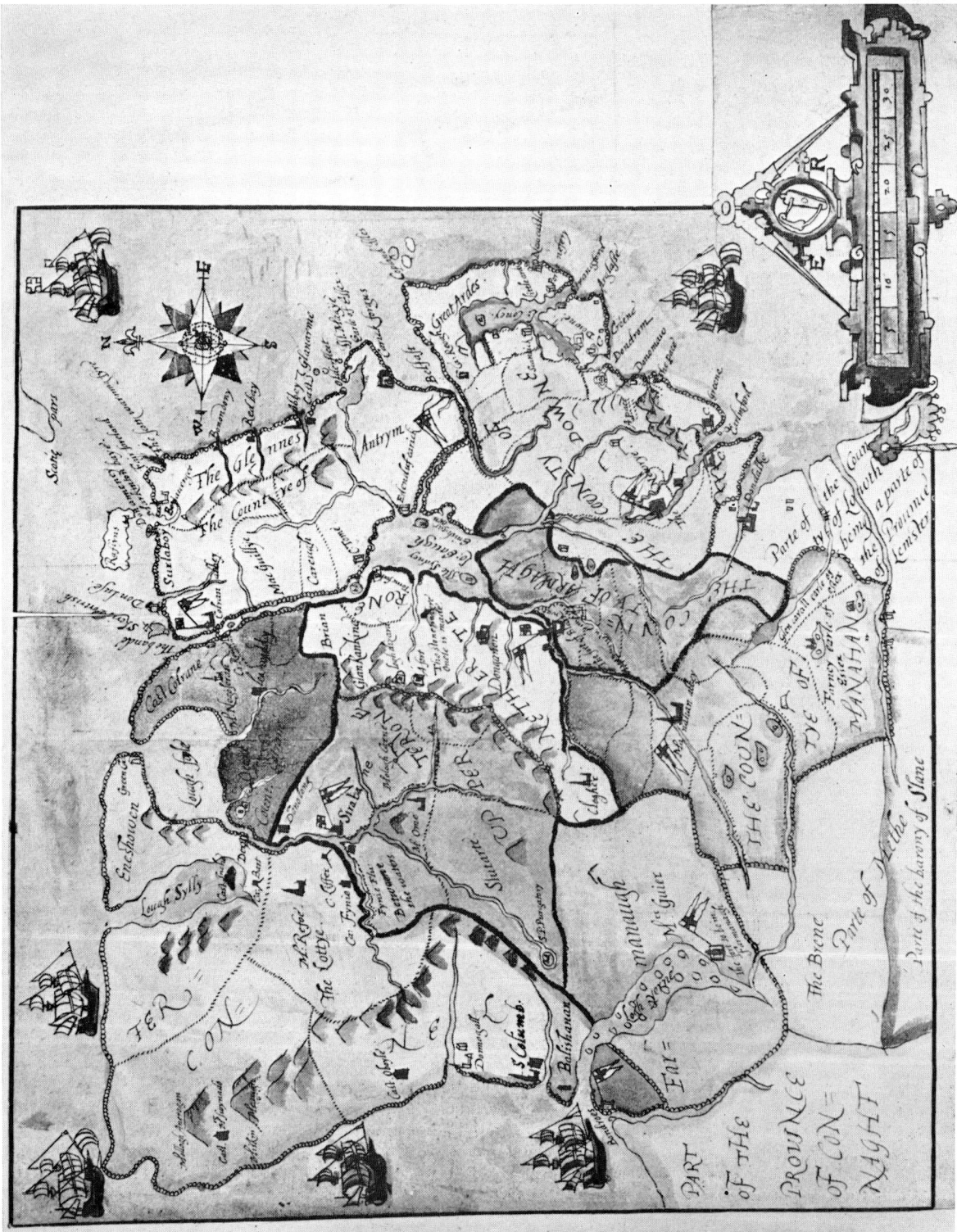

XIX   Francis Jobson's plan of 1598 for basing troops at Coleraine, Strabane and the Blackwater (2,000 men each) and at Belfast, Newry, Monaghan

90 B. O. Binns, *The consolidation of fragmented agricultural holdings*, (Washington, 1950), 72–75

91 R. H. Buchanan, Rural change in an Irish townland, 1890–1955, *Adv. Science*, 56 (1958), 291–300

V. B. Proudfoot, and T. D. Vaughan, Changes in settlement and population in Northern Ireland, 1835–60, *Ulster Folklife*, 5 (1959), 20–6

J. H. Johnson, Partnership and clachans in mid-nineteenth century Londonderry, *Ulster Folklife*, 9 (1963), 20–9

B. S. MacAodha, Clachán settlement in Iar-Connacht, *Irish Geography*, 5 (1965), 20–28

92 C. Ó Danachair, Change in the Irish landscape, *Ulster Folklife*, 8 (1962), 67

93 M. N. Hayes, Some aspects of local government in Northern Ireland, in E. Rhodes, *Public administration in Northern Ireland* (n.d.), 85

94 T. Jones Hughes, The origin and growth of towns in Ireland, *University Review*, 2 (1959), 13

X

MOATED SITES AND DESERTED BOROUGHS AND VILLAGES; TWO NEGLECTED ASPECTS OF ANGLO-NORMAN SETTLEMENT IN IRELAND

R. E. Glasscock

With the notable exception of Otway-Ruthven's studies, there has been little investigation into the nature of Anglo-Norman settlement since 1920 when Goddard Orpen completed his four-volume work on *Ireland under the Normans*.[1] The only really substantial work on the relict features of the Anglo-Norman period is that by Leask on the castles, churches and monastic houses.[2] There has been no general study of the mottes, and we still lack, fifty years after Orpen, a comprehensive list of Norman manors (with place-name identifications), and of those places where there is recorded mention of burgesses.

Two aspects of Anglo-Norman settlement which have received hardly any attention are moated residences, and manorial boroughs and villages. Their now-deserted sites have great potential for historical and archaeological enquiry and are of major importance to the historical geographer in seeking to reconstruct the geography of medieval Ireland. In this country the archaeological investigation of such settlements is relatively more important than in England because of the dearth of documentary evidence for the medieval period. Yet, despite their vital importance, not one medieval moated site or deserted settlement is yet in state charge, nor is either type recognised as a class of national monument. While we are not as yet experiencing the alarming disappearance of field monuments due to ploughing, as in England[3], government grants in this country for farm improvement encourage all too easily the destruction of sites, usually because their importance is not appreciated. Moated sites and settlements are particularly vulnerable as, being for the most part earthworks, they are easily removed by modern machinery.

This chapter outlines the first stages of a research programme currently being undertaken on these two types of settlement, dealing firstly, with moated sites, and secondly, with deserted boroughs and villages.

MOATED SITES

When preparing his map of the 'high motes', as he called them, Orpen made passing reference to another type of earthwork consisting of a rectangular platform, sometimes raised a few feet above the surrounding land, and surrounded by ditches and ramparts.[4] He noted them in counties Mayo, Galway and Roscommon and thought them to be of Norman origin although later than the mottes. Westropp, in his paper of 1901 also noted this type under the heading of 'rectilinear forts'[5]; he believed them to be found in every Irish county but that they were most common in Leinster, especially counties Wexford and Kilkenny (where they are in fact even more numerous than he thought).

There has been little follow-up to these references to this kind of earthwork. The only study is that by Hadden for Wexford[6] in which he points out that the rectangular earthworks of that county are of two kinds. The first, of which there are very few, is the heavily fortified type which he aptly calls 'ramparted forts' such as the great rectangular enclosure at Kilmokea parish probably the *caput baroniae* of Hervey de Montemorisco, and the hill-top fort at Ballyraine near Arklow, co. Wicklow. Hadden assigns this type to the first thirty years of Norman occupation and thinks that the building of such fortifications had ceased by about 1200.[7] The second kind of earthwork, and by far the more common, is the smaller, rectangular moated platform. In Wexford these invariably measure about 180 by 120 feet and are surrounded by a water-filled moat, the upcast of which has either been spread upon the platform to raise it above the surrounding land or has been used to make a bank around the edge of the platform. Such banks have an average height of 3 feet, although some are raised higher at the corners. In a few examples the moat upcast has been thrown outwards to form a bank outside the moat. On most moated sites there is a path across the moat at one point where cattle make use of what are presumed to be the original entrances. Hadden observes that in co. Wexford nearly all moated platforms are found on low, wet ground.

It should be stressed, however, that while the majority of moated sites in co. Wexford exhibit these general characteristics no two are the same and there is considerable variation in detail.[8] The majority are rectangular and some are almost perfect squares, for example Mylerspark and Clavass, and one, Garryrichard, is round. Sometimes the moat is still 30 feet wide as at Garryntinodagh, more often about 15 feet, while others, now silted up, are easily jumped across, and appear never to have been a real obstacle. Although they are generally in low-lying areas, some are situated on well-drained slopes, for example Ballymore, and it is a job to see how the moat was ever kept full of water. On many sites the banks are built up at the corners, but at Mylerspark the corners project, presumably to take some kind of corner-turret. The same feature may be seen on two of the corners of the moated site at Talbotstown, co. Wicklow, a particularly impressive example where the inner bank of the moat has a stone revetment and where there is a low stone wall around the enclosure. While some moated platforms are quite flat, others are irregular with a hint of stonework beneath. At some there are traces of outworks, as at Kilmagoura, co. Cork, and Ballynanty, co. Limerick.

These differences are stressed to show that the label 'moated site' is a blanket term which is used for a wide variety of square and rectangular earthworks in much the same way as the term 'souterrain' is used for so many types of underground structures. Moated sites are, however, unquestionably settlement sites; none that I have recorded in the field is likely to have been built merely as a cattle enclosure or for other purposes, such as some in England appear to have been.

Hadden and Jeffery's work in Wexford prompted me to widen the net in an attempt to establish the number and location of rectangular earthworks in the country as a whole. As a preliminary to field survey, and without air photo coverage, the best way of doing this was to examine the first edition of the Ordnance Survey Six Inch maps, compiled for the whole country around 1840, and on which the field monuments of the country are particularly well recorded and represented. Working from map evidence only has, however, certain disadvantages. Firstly, it is evident that only some of the rectangular earthworks are of the moated type. Sometimes a bank and ditch merely isolate a rectangular enclosure; such sites resemble more closely a 'rectangular rath' and the term 'moated site' is a misnomer. It is not possible to make a clear distinction of these types from map evidence alone and the breakdown of rectangular earthworks into these two types awaits field survey. Secondly, a few moated sites known to exist are not shown; for example, the very fine square, moated platform with a wide water-filled moat in the townland of Shandrum, co. Cork. Thirdly, so many sites marked on the maps are irregular in shape; some are represented as rectangular with rounded corners, others are irregular in plan but have two parallel sides. The maps of co. Tipperary, for example, are full of awkward sites which makes the preliminary recording and counting of rectangular earthworks very subjective.

Bearing these drawbacks in mind, a preliminary survey compiled from map evidence alone shows about 750 rectangular sites in the country (Fig. 10.1). Only a handful of these are in Ulster and Connacht; no county in these two provinces has more than half a dozen examples except Roscommon with 13 and Galway with 35, and it must have been this group that originally attracted Orpen's attention. Most of the sites, as Westropp thought, are in Leinster and Munster, with high numbers in counties Tipperary, about 200, Cork 100, and Wexford 80. Westmeath, Kilkenny, and Limerick have about 40 each, Clare 30, and Laois, Offaly, Wicklow and Waterford about 20 each. The resulting map is merely a preliminary to further enquiry—nothing more. At this stage the significance of the distribution is not known and it will only be established when the sites have been verified in the field and their characteristics recorded and studied in the physical and historical context of their local areas. However, it may be said that the distribution, with its marked concentration in the south and east is certainly an Anglo-Norman one, and as such it points to a twelfth to fourteenth century origin for these sites. There is however no proof that those in the west are related to those in the east; they may be of a different period, and Irish not Norman.

When and why were the moated sites constructed? As Emery has shown, there are between 3,000 and 4,000 moated sites in England.[9] Although these occur widely, certain counties have far more than others, and there are large numbers in the east-coast counties from Yorkshire down to Suffolk and Essex, both of which have over 500. The majority seem to be moated homesteads dating to the period between the twelfth and fourteenth centuries with a concentration between about 1250 and 1320.[10] In Ireland there are at most only about a fifth of this number and even in areas where they are common they are never as thick on the ground as in Suffolk or Essex. In Ireland the maximum density, calculated on the basis of a Six Inch sheet covering 24 sq miles, is 1 site to every 2 to 2½ sq miles. This density is found in parts of co. Wexford, especially around Enniscorthy, in co. Westmeath

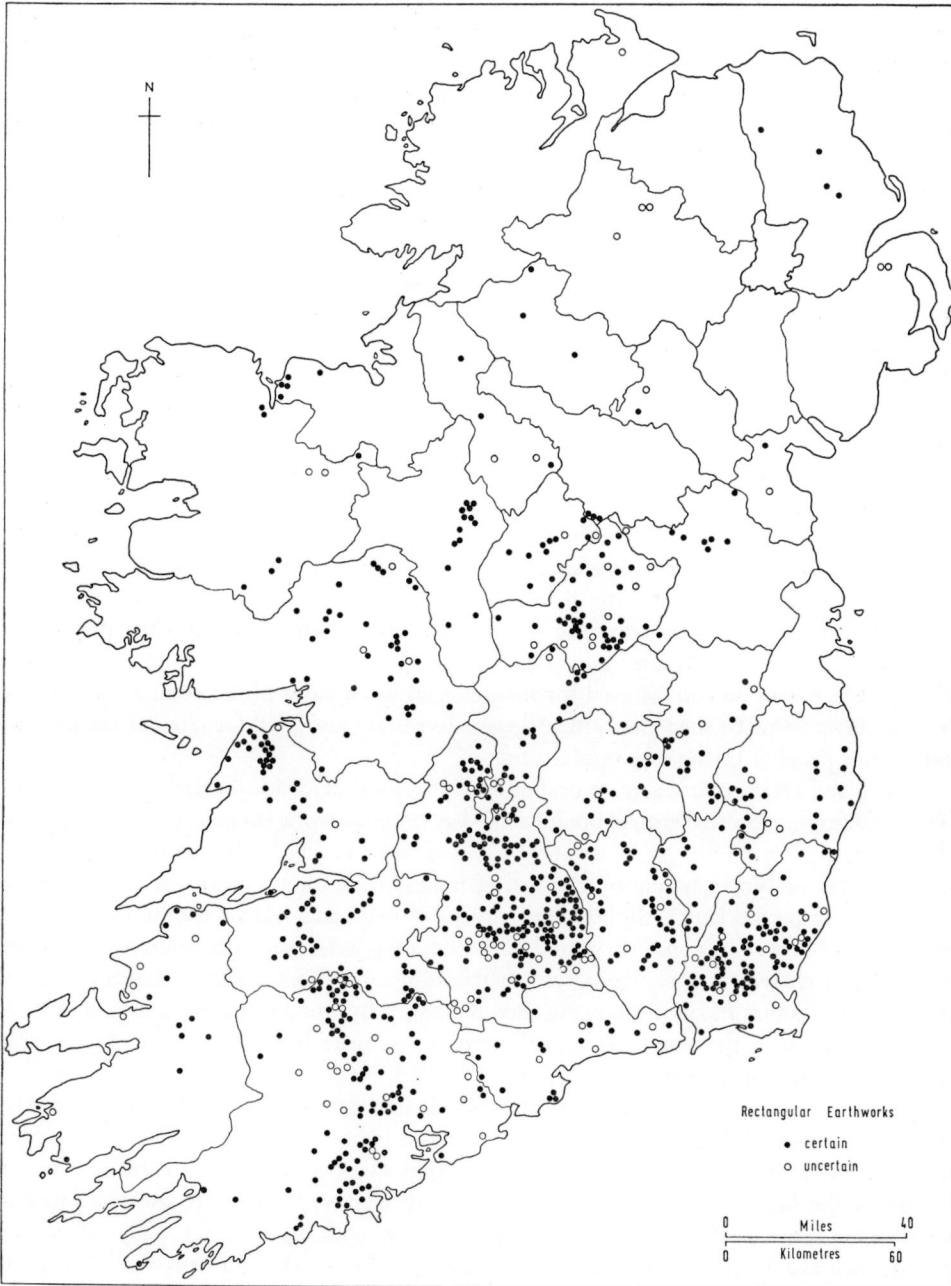

Fig. 10.1   Rectangular earthworks shown on the First Edition of the **Ordnance Survey Six Inch** Map, circa 1840.

where just south of Mullingar they are interspersed among, and almost indistinguishable from, irregular shaped raths, and in parts of co. Tipperary especially around Cashel and the Ballingarry-Grangemockler area along the co. Kilkenny border. This shows that, as in England, moated sites are often localized within counties and must clearly be explained in terms of particular sets of physical and/or social conditions.

In Ireland it would be misleading to describe moated sites by the rather tranquil term 'homestead'. Nor is Hadden's term 'grange' very satisfactory, for in modern usage this is apt to suggest a monastic origin for all these sites (which undoubtedly is true for some, for example, The Raheen in Kilpoole Upper, co. Wicklow).[11] The majority were defended residences of Anglo-Norman tenants and centres of local control and administration. Hadden has argued this convincingly in accounting for the distribution in co. Wexford, where the moated sites are concentrated in the Anglo-Norman baronies of Ballaghkeen and Bantry which bordered the Kavanagh country in the north of the county. The location of these sites as defended residences in border country may explain why there are so few within the Pale. Their use as fortifications throughout the medieval period is suggested by the continued use of the term 'castle' to describe a number of examples, especially in the east, such as Clondaw, co. Wexford, where the moated site is described as 'site of castle' on the Six Inch map[12], Ballynagran, co. Wicklow described as 'Macdermot's castle'[13], and Castlewarren, co. Kilkenny, where 'site of Castle Warren' is marked together with structures inside the enclosure.[14] In the west the sites usually carry Irish names, and the prefixes *lis* (Irish, *lios*—a fort or enclosure) and *caher* (Irish, *cathair*—a fort) are common. The term *raheen* (Irish, *ráithín*—a fort) is used for moated sites in all parts of the country and sometimes gives its name to the townland. All these terms are also used for circular earthworks and are not peculiar to the rectangular sites.

In England there is now a great deal of archaeological evidence for dating these sites to the twelfth to fourteenth century, but in Ireland as yet little work has been done. The period 1250–1320, the time of greatest moat-building activity in England, was the time of the intensification of Norman rule over much of Ireland. It is likely, however, that the main moat-building period here is slightly later, say 1280–1350, and was a response to increasing pressure on the Normans once their hold on the country weakened. The interesting account in the Bigod records of the digging and barricading of a moated site at Balliconnor, co. Wexford shows that moats were being used in 1283.[15] In broad terms we may assign their building and use to the thirteenth and fourteenth centuries but there is probably a great range in the dates of their desertion.

Nor is it easy to explain the plans of moated sites, for although some are square the majority are rectangular. Is this simply a devolution of the motte-and-bailey form where the motte is omitted, or is the rectangular moated site a poorer man's earth-and-wood version of the keepless castles of the late thirteenth century? There are distinct parallels between the moated sites and the almost-square castles with high curtain walls and corner towers, such as Liscarroll, in north co. Cork. Rectangularity, the emphasis on the corners, the position of the entrance midway along one side, are features common to both types. The difference is one of scale and the substitution of moat and palisade for curtain walls of stone. In Ireland there is no doubt that the primary purpose of the moat was fortification, and that all its other uses as for example a source of water supply, were ancillary. The theory that in England climatic deterioration may have encouraged moat-building[16] has no supporting evidence in Ireland.

Defended residences, using the moat as the main means of protection had to be sited in localities where the moat could be effective, that is, in places where the water table was near the surface or where a stream could be diverted as a feeder. Thus we have the curious paradox of defended residences being situated in low-lying areas not well suited for defence. In addition to this physical determinant of location it is likely that the defended residences represent in any case the secondary infilling of pieces of border country by Norman over-lordship and thus it would be the less attractive, poorly drained areas which would be settled at this stage. Local studies should be able to establish the locational relationship between moated sites and stone castles, and between moated sites and tower houses. Did tower houses replace moated houses in some areas, and if so why? Did moat building go out of fashion in favour of building higher in stone? Were the two types contemporaneous in the same areas or were they mutually exclusive? In purely numerical terms there is a striking similarity between the counties with most moated sites and those with most tower houses[17], but the local chronological relationship between the two types remains to be studied.

The answers to the problems of moated sites will come from historical and archaeological enquiry: the classification of sites on the basis of field survey alone is not enough. So far, the only major excavation of a moated site has been that at Kilmagoura, co. Cork where a 'rescue' dig was conducted in 1967 preceding the levelling of the site for farm improvement. Before excavation Kilmagoura had a strong resemblance to a 'non-ramparted square fort' as described by Hadden in Wexford. In this case, however, the moated site occupied the corner of a once-larger enclosure of which little trace remained.[18] The moated platform, which was raised 2 feet above the surrounding land measured 195 by 144 feet (60 by 44 m) and was surrounded by a water-filled moat fed by the diversion of a stream. The upcast of the moat had been thrown inwards to form a bank, which had raised corners.

From excavations the following points emerged. The platform had been deliberately raised with upcast from the moat and possibly also with soil taken from the surrounding area. Although there were no surface indications the enclosure had stone foundations for a building, around which were covered drains, showing the need for further drainage despite the elevation of the platform. A palisade ran around the inner slope of the bank, not as was expected, along the top of it. Although the bank was built up at the corners no structures of any kind were revealed there, and it may be that the characteristic heightening at the corners of these sites is due in the first place to the extra amount of upcast thrown inwards as the moat was dug around a right-angle. Below the modern cattle path into the enclosure were the foundation timbers of a wooden bridge across the moat, with square uprights tenoned with tightening wedges into morticed sleeper beams.

The excavation at Kilmagoura pin-pointed some of the archaeological problems and potentials of moated sites. On the one hand, building and occupation of the site could not be dated owing to a lack of datable small finds and the complete absence of pottery—a drawback common to most small medieval sites in Ireland. On the other hand, the water-logged moats have great possibilities for the preservation of timber; at Kilmagoura days of toil in deep, black mud were made fully worth-while by the discovery *in situ* of the bridge into the enclosure. The excavation underlined the difficulty of determining whether earlier structures preceded the construction of the moat. To answer this the whole of the raised enclosure must be stripped down to the old turf level; if time prevents this, as it did at Kilmagoura, sections have to be used instead and these are very unsatisfactory for the detection of flimsy timber structures. In sections at Kilmagoura signs of burning at the old turf level were interpreted as the remnants of fires made during the clearing and digging of the moat, but without complete stripping one cannot be absolutely sure that there were not earlier structures.

Such are some of the historical and archaeological problems raised by moated sites, and attention is now turned to some associated problems of nucleated settlements.

DESERTED BOROUGHS AND VILLAGES

Deserted settlements (Fig. 10.2) are not only of interest in themselves but, like moated sites, they are the means whereby archaeology may make a considerable contribution to our knowledge of medieval settlement in Ireland. Such sites have the advantage that they are unencumbered by later settlement; early structures have not been destroyed and total excavation is often possible. This is not usually so in 'living' settlements where the foundations of recent buildings have destroyed the traces of earlier ones.

We know of no very large Anglo-Norman town that was subsequently completely deserted and therefore their study has to combine historical investigation with urban archaeology—with all its attendant difficulties.[19] Only in Dublin, with the clearance of old property in the central area has the opportunity for excavation been taken and a start made. We have, however, nothing on the scale of Biddle's investigations of early Winchester, and a strong case could be made for modelling the investigation of other towns, such as Cork, Limerick, Galway, Drogheda and New Ross, on these lines. Being realistic, however, it is unlikely that a great spate of urban archaeology in Ireland is imminent. It is for this reason that attention is directed towards deserted settlements, not only for their archaeological potential, but because they present smaller practical and financial problems than excavation within built-up areas.

Deserted boroughs

A good starting point is the very place at which the Anglo-Normans landed and set up one of their first corporate towns, Bannow, co. Wexford. In 1307 there were about 160 burgages here.[20] Until the middle of the seventeenth century streets and houses could still be seen[21] but before 1700 the remains of the town were overwhelmed by drifting sand and now only a ruined church remains.[22] Although its desertion is relatively late Bannow is the only site of its kind and should the sands ever recede or be removed it could be the Skara Brae of medieval Irish towns.

Fig. 10.2 Deserted Anglo–Norman settlements

Four miles north of Bannow at the head of the bay are the ruins of the nearby Anglo-Norman port of Clonmines, its harbour silted up and the town abandoned before the end of the seventeenth century. As a medieval borough it went on, nevertheless, sending members to parliament until the Act of Union. The ruins here, comprising four small castles and three churches, are as a group among the most impressive in the country. Although we have no figure of the exact number of burgesses here in the thirteenth century, the ruins suggest that it was an important place in the fourteenth and fifteenth. The town is said to have occupied 20 acres[23], which probably extended over the ploughed fields on the west side which show traces of occupation. The site is of interest not only for the architecture of its ruins, but because it is a fine example of a medieval town where only the stone elements survive; all the houses of timber and clay have disappeared.

A similar site is that of the borough of Kilbixy, co. Westmeath where again the fabric of the town has been stripped away leaving only the stone buildings as reminders of its former existence.[24] The town was one of the borough towns of Meath in the fifteenth century and was deserted, for reasons unknown, by the late seventeenth.

Another late desertion is the town of Newtown Jerpoint, co. Kilkenny (Plate XVII) which was situated on the opposite side of the Little Arrigle river to the Cistercian abbey of Jerpoint. The town was founded about 1200 (*Nova villa de Jeriponte*)—a true medieval plantation—and was probably deserted in the late seventeenth century[25]; its life-span was much the same as Bannow and Clonmines. Now only the church of St Nicholas remains, but there was still enough of the town to be seen in 1839 for the Ordnance surveyors to make a plan of the streets and houses.[26] Sometime later in the nineteenth century an improving farmer gathered together the stone foundations of the houses into heaps which have remained and now obscure the sites of the houses as shown on the Ordnance Survey plan. Nevertheless, many house foundations—presumably of the seventeenth century but with medieval predecessors beneath—are still visible in their accompanying burgage plots. Their plans leave only slight surface traces but irregularities such as these may be seen on the ground at other deserted sites. Newtown Jerpoint is an extremely important site for future large scale excavation.

Two other sites where there may have been sizeable Norman boroughs are at Athassel, co. Tipperary, and Rindown, co. Roscommon. At Athassel only the magnificent ruin of the large Augustinian priory of St Edmund remains. A town founded by William de Burgo at the end of the twelfth century is said to have been burned twice, in 1319 and again in 1329[27], and signs of the site in the form of crop-marks are visible from the air in the cut-off loop of the river[28], although it is hard to discern anything on the ground. If the town was in fact destroyed finally in the early fourteenth century Athassel is one of the few places where we have a fairly definite date of desertion, a factor of immense value in archaeological excavation. Moreover, in a town adjacent to such a wealthy monastic house datable imported pottery must surely be found.

At Rindown there is a tradition of a thirteenth-century town occupying the small peninsula that juts out into Lough Ree.[29] The remains on the site are of considerable interest; at the south end of the peninsula is an early thirteenth century castle with a medieval nave-

and-chancel church nearby. North of these, across the neck of the peninsula is a huge fortified wall with a central gate and towers, presumably to protect the town on the landward side. Between the wall and the castle, a distance of a quarter of a mile, there is no sign of any town! The fields are large, flat and regular; the only suspicious signs are some curious heaps of stones, reminiscent of those at Newtown Jerpoint, which lie roughly along the axis of the site between the gate of the town wall and the castle. They could be the cleared remnants of foundations. There is no evidence of the size of the town in the middle ages and in terms of archaeological investigation Rindown is less important than either Newtown Jerpoint or Athassel.

A Norman town that is not deserted but is only a shadow of its former self is Bunratty, co. Clare. The town had 226 burgages in 1287[30], which leads Russell to rank it the fourth or fifth biggest town in Anglo-Norman Ireland.[31] A fortification surrounded the town, remnants of which remain and have already been described by Westropp.[32] Many houses were already ruinous by the early fourteenth century[33] and the town never regained its importance. By the early nineteenth century it was very small; the first edition of the Six Inch map, surveyed 1840, shows the castle with its adjacent fair green, a very small village, and a ruined church 1,000 yards to the west in the demesne.

Deserted rural-boroughs

The term 'deserted rural-boroughs' is used here to denote those settlements, since deserted, where there is some documentary reference to burgages or burgesses, but which were probably primarily agricultural in function and never true towns.[34] One of the best examples of this type is Kilmaclenine, co. Cork, founded as a borough by the bishop of Cloyne *circa* 1238.[35] The site was kindly shown to me in 1967 by Mr C. J. F. McCarthy of Cork. The borough had 27 burgesses in the middle of the fourteenth century[36], yet there is no sign of the settlement either on the ground or from the air.[37] There is a seventeenth-century house at Kilmaclenine but all that remains of the medieval settlement is the curtain wall of a rectangular castle perched on an outcrop high above green fields, and the ruined church 300 yards away. Was the medieval borough in the space between?

Kilmaclenine typifies the problem of these deserted Anglo-Norman sites. Of these settlements only the stone buildings remain, usually the castle and the church. For a few, such as this one, we have evidence of its existence and size at one point in time, and we may infer that being a burgage settlement it was in fact nucleated. The logical extension is therefore to question whether many of the places where a ruined castle and a medieval church stand a few hundred yards apart—and there are hundreds of them in the south and east of the country—are in fact deserted Norman nucleated borough or village settlements for which we have no documentary evidence. Or are we to believe that churches and castles stood in isolation? Where were the retainers and the parishioners? Why do castle and church invariably stand apart in this way? At this early stage of the field survey of such sites it already seems certain that many Anglo-Norman nucleated manorial settlements are represented in the present landscape by the relict features of castle and church, and that these rural-boroughs and villages were far more common than has hitherto been thought.

Some other examples may strengthen this argument. For Glenogra, co. Limerick an extent of 1298 shows that the manor had about 120 burgesses.[38] (The usual burgage rent was one shilling *per annum* and the burgesses rendered 119 sh. 6d.) At Glenogra now are a ruined castle and church, and the Six Inch map marks a fair green, a sure indicator of its former importance as a central place. There is no sign of where 120 burgesses, their families, and the rest of the population lived. The fields to the south of the church have no earth-works, although there are some surface irregularities. Moyaliff, co. Tipperary is a similar example of a place where only the castle, incorporated in the grounds of a later house, and the church survive. There is no clue on the ground as to where the 62 burgesses of 1305[39] could have lived. This rural-borough may have been deserted in the fourteenth century as it was already going downhill in 1338.[40] The ruined church stands on its own in demesne land; not even the eye of faith could conjure up the earthworks of a borough!

There are other rural-boroughs where it must be presumed that the settlement was in the vicinity of the castle and/or the church. For example, Ardscull, co. Kildare was a sizeable borough of 160 burgesses in 1282.[41] Here only the fine motte remains, forcing the Athy-Naas road to skirt around its base. At Greencastle, co. Down a strategic settlement of the Anglo-Normans at the mouth of Carlingford Lough, the borough was already in decline by 1333[42]; again, its exact site is not known although it is presumed to be in the vicinity of the stone castle or the motte, or along the shore beneath the present village. The 'New town of Leix' was another borough which had fallen on bad times before 1340—in common with many others.[43] The number of burgesses had dropped from 127 in 1283 to only 40 in 1324.[44] Its fortunes tend to mirror those of the Anglo-Normans generally after about 1310. The most likely site of the 'New town of Leix' is at Dunamase where the Ordnance surveyors of 1839 marked 'site of ancient village' half a mile west of the Rock of Dunamase where the castle stands.[45] On the ground the field is bumpy and there are signs of disturbance but no structures can be identified.

These examples are of rural-boroughs where complete desertion has taken place at some point in time for reasons unknown. There are far more Norman rural-boroughs that have not been deserted but are only a remnant of their former size having only a few houses. Following the terminology of English deserted medieval villages these might be termed 'shrunken rural-boroughs'. As they offer similar possibilities for historical and archaeological investigation to those of the complete desertions, a number of examples are included here. Odagh, co. Kilkenny had 110 burgages in 1307[46] and is now little more than the castle and church. In co. Tipperary, at Ardmayle where burgesses are mentioned in 1338[47], only a few houses remain, and Lisronagh must be much smaller than it was in 1333 when it had nearly 50 burgesses.[48] Of the rural boroughs of medieval Kildare[49], Ardree, Dunfierth, Dunmanoge, Glassely and Tipper are all now very small. In co. Wicklow there is no sign of the rural-borough of Ballinacloch, and Donaghmore which had almost failed by 1303[50], has kept going but is very small.

While many more boroughs could be mentioned only three others are selected here. They all had over one hundred occupants in 1306 but their exact sites are not known. The first is 'Castle Fothered' (?Castlemore, co. Carlow) which had 79 burgages and 29 cottagers in 1307[51] and of which Orpen observed "there is now no town or village there".[52] The other two are in co. Wexford; Carrick on Slaney had 112 burgages in 1307, three of which were waste in 1324 when the castle was *vacuum et fractum* with a ruined hall and chapel.[53] Also in 1307 there seem to have been about 110 burgesses in the 'town of the Island'[54], now no longer an island and part of Kilmokea parish. It is doubtful whether the borough ever occupied the circular earthwork of Kilmokea as has been suggested.[55]

Deserted sites other than boroughs

For all the places already mentioned there is some documentary evidence, however slight, for their existence in the medieval period, and the presence of burgesses. The sequence of study has been, first, documents and written sources and, second, field survey. But there are other sites with visible earthworks whose origins are as yet unknown. The paradox is that few documented sites have earthworks and that known earthworks have no documents! Such undocumented sites have been discovered in three ways, from maps, from field survey and from air photography.

The Ordnance surveyors seldom missed obvious earthworks. We have noted already their plan of Newtown Jerpoint and their notes on old settlements such as Kilbixy and Dunamase. The surveyors in co. Tipperary, for example, noted several settlement sites, sometimes even attempting a plan of the earthworks. The best of these is that of Kiltinan[56], a very extensive site with a recognisable ground plan. On the ground there are boundary banks and intersecting streets and although no house sites may be seen they must surely have been along the street frontages. Needless to say there is an adjacent medieval church and castle, and the site is probably that of a late-deserted medieval village where the houses were of wood and clay; the site is reminiscent of some deserted villages in the English midlands where the ground-plan is clear but where no house foundations are visible, for example Burston, Buckinghamshire.[57] At Baptistgrange the surveyors also recorded 'site of old village' adjacent to the ruined castle and church[58], although here the earthworks are very confused and no structures can be identified. The same is true of the 'site of Piperstown village'.[59] At other sites, for example, Mortlestown[60] and Ballynahinch[61] earthworks are shown. Similar settlement sites have been discovered from the maps of other counties, such as Croghan, in Cannakill townland, co. Offaly[62] and Moonhall in co. Kilkenny.[63] One of the finest fields of earthworks in the country is that shown as 'site of old town of Granard' at Granardkill, co. Longford.[64]

From current field survey another group of sites with earthworks has been located. A field at Newtown, co. Kilkenny has a fine hollow-way running from the ruined medieval church to the King's river. There is a castle nearby and everything suggests that this is a deserted settlement of the Anglo-Norman manor of Erlestown.[65] In co. Tipperary, Kilconnell has a fine set of earthworks with a hollow-way near the castle and the site of the church, and similarly there is a field of earthworks around the church of Galbooly. If no historical evidence is forthcoming only archaeological excavation is likely to tell us more about these sites, all of which are likely to be Anglo-Norman manorial villages. Excavation has already brought to notice the medieval settlements at Caherguillamore, co. Limerick—

one of the few sites where medieval peasant houses have been excavated[66]—and Liathmore-Mochoemog, co. Tipperary.[67]

The third means of discovery is air photography for which the reconnaissance surveys of Dr J. K. S. St Joseph in Ireland since 1963 have been of inestimable value. Not only has he photographed many of the settlement sites mentioned above but he has discovered several new sites with earthworks, for example, Donaghmore, co. Tipperary, Ballyduagh, co. Tipperary (Plate XVIII), Stonecarthy, co. Kilkenny[68], and in co. Kildare, Feighcullen, Flemingstown and Kilmoney.[69] These last sites await inspection on the ground as do many others where air photography has given a valuable lead. It should be stressed that air photography has an especially valuable role to play in medieval studies in Ireland where documentary evidence for settlements is harder to come by than in England.[70]

ACKNOWLEDGEMENT

I would like to thank Miss Kathleen White and Mr David Owen for their help in the preparation of the map of rectangular earthworks.

GRID REFERENCES TO PLACES MENTIONED

Grid references are to the Irish National Grid, preceded by the sub-zone letter. The most convenient maps for locating these places are the Irish Ordnance Survey $\frac{1}{2}$ inch to 1 mile (1:126,720) series, the sheet number of which is given before the reference, i.e. sheet 23, sub-zone T, grid ref. 077298.

In moated sites section

Ballymore	23, T 077298	Garryntinodagh	23, T 065333
Ballynagran	16, T 273913	Kilmagoura	21, R 467213
Ballynanty	17, R 608384	Kilmokea	23, S 692164
Ballyraine	19, T 225741	Kilpoole Upper	16, T c.328897
Castlewarren	19, S 596617	Mylerspark	23, S 767233
Clavass	23, S 982441	Shandrum	21, R 494212
Clondaw	23, T 052424	Talbotstown	16, S 919873
Garryrichard	23, S 848197		

In deserted boroughs and villages section

Ardmayle	18, S 058457	Baptistgrange	18, S 210301
Ardree	16, S 687925	Bunratty	17, R 453608
Ardscull	16, S 726977	Caherguillamore	17, R 612397
Athassel	18, S 011365	Carrick on Slaney	23, T 016235
Ballinacloch	16, T 278920	'Castle Fothered'	19, S 831730
Ballyduagh	18, S 115380	Clonmines	23, S 843129
Ballynahinch	18, S 036405	Croghan	15, N 472330
Bannow	23, S 823072	Donaghmore, Tip.	18, S 187288

In deserted boroughs and villages section—*contd.*

Donaghmore, Wick.	16, S 923941	Kilmoney	16, N 704197
Dunamase	16, S 523980	Kiltinan	18, S 230319
Dunfierth	16, N 777381	Liathmore-Mochoemog	18, S 225577
Dunmanoge	19, S 729831	Lisronagh	18, S 201295
Feighcullen	16, N 728208	Moonhall	19, S 593565
Flemingstown	16, N 893147	Moyaliff	18, S 042560
Galbooly	18, S 162556	Newtown (Earls)	18, S 463438
Glassely	16, S 756982	Newtown Jerpoint	19, S 570403
Glenogra	17, R 595149	Odagh	18, S 457623
Granardkill	12, N 322803	Piperstown	15, M 952037
Greencastle	9, J 247114	Rindown	12, N 004541
Kilbixy	12, N 322615	Stonecarthy	19, S 522414
Kilconnell	18, S 138395	Tipper	16, N 918185
Kilmaclenine	21, R 505062	'town of the Island'	23, S c.687163

REFERENCES

1 G. H. Orpen, *Ireland under the Normans, 1169–1333,* 4 vols. (1911–20). Reprinted, Oxford University Press, 1968
2 H. G. Leask, *Irish castles and castellated houses,* (revised ed. 1951); and, *Irish churches and monastic buildings,* 3 vols., (1955, 1958 and 1960)
3 See discussion in, How can we preserve our past?, *Current Archaeology,* No. 14 (May 1969), 70–72
4 G. H. Orpen, *Ireland under the Normans 1169–1216,* II (1911), 343–4
5 T. J. Westropp, The ancient forts of Ireland, *Trans. Roy. Irish Acad.,* 31 (1896–1901), 702–3
6 G. Hadden, Some earthworks in co. Wexford, *J. Cork Hist. & Arch. Soc.,* 69 (1964), 118–22
7 Ibid., 120
8 I should like to record my thanks to Dr George Hadden and Mr W. H. Jeffery for showing me some of the Wexford sites, in company with Professor E. Estyn Evans in 1968, and for giving so freely of their knowledge.
9 F. V. Emery, Moated settlements in England, *Geography,* 47 (1962), 387–8
10 Ibid., 383–4
11 Liam Price, *The place-names of co. Wicklow,* VII (1967), 435
12 Wexford Six Inch sheet 20. All references to the Six Inch map are to the first edition.
13 Wicklow, Six Inch sheet 31
14 Kilkenny, Six Inch sheet 15
15 G. Hadden, (1964), op. cit., 121
16 Discussed in D. G. Hurst and J. G. Hurst, Excavation of two moated sites: Milton, Hampshire and Ashwell, Hertfordshire, *J. Arch. Ass.,* 30 (1957), 83–6
17 Compare Fig. 10.1 with the map of Irish tower houses in P. Smith and P. Hayes, Llyseurgain and the tower, *Pbns. Flintshire Hist. Soc.,* 22 (1965–66), 1–8
18 R. E. Glasscock, Interim note on the excavation of this site in *Med. Arch.,* 12 (1968), 196–7
19 Currently under discussion in *Antiquity,* No. 166 (June 1968) 109–16 and No. 169 (March 1969), 42–3.
   See also papers in J. G. N. Renaud ed., *Rotterdam Papers: a contribution to medieval archaeology,* (1969)
20 G. H. Orpen, (1920), op. cit., III, 88
21 P. H. Hore, *History of the town and county of Wexford,* 6 vols., (1900–11). (Duncannon etc., 459–61)
22 For description see, Samuel Lewis, *A topographical dictionary of Ireland,* (1837), 1, 183–4

23 P. H. Hore, (1900–11), op. cit., (Tintern, Rosegarland, and Clonmines, 217)
24 Westmeath, Six Inch sheet 11
25 W. J. Pilsworth, Newtown Jerpoint, *Old Kilkenny Rev.*, 10 (1958), 31–5
26 Ibid. Pilsworth reproduces an enlarged version of the original plan on Kilkenny, Six Inch sheet 28
27 Samuel Lewis, (1837), op. cit., I, 81. The original reference is not known to me.
28 St Joseph, air photographs, ATA 52–6 (1967) (National Museum, Dublin)
29 See, for example, Lord Killanin and M. V. Duignan eds., *Shell Guide to Ireland,* 2nd ed. (1967), 346.
   See also G. H. Orpen's note on Rindown in, Athlone castle: its early history, with notes on some
   neighbouring castles, *J. Roy. Soc. Antiq. Ireland,* 37 (1907), 274–5
30 G. H. Orpen, (1920), op. cit., IV, 76
31 J. C. Russell, Late-thirteenth-century Ireland as a region, *Demography,* 3 (1966), 508
32 T. J. Westropp, on Bunratty in *J. Roy. Soc. Antiq. Ireland,* 47 (1917), 14–15, and plan
33 Ibid.
34 A concept developed by Otway-Ruthven in her papers, The organisation of Anglo-Irish agriculture
   in the middle ages, *J. Roy. Soc. Antiq. Ireland,* 81 (1951), 1–13, and The character of Norman
   settlement in Ireland, *Historical Studies,* 5 (1965), 75–84
   The term 'deserted Norman rural-borough', is defined and its use discussed with examples in
   R. E. Glasscock, Deserted villages in Ireland, in J. G. Hurst and M. W. Beresford, eds., *Studies in
   deserted villages,* (forthcoming)
35 A. J. Otway-Ruthven, (1968), op. cit., 117
36 Ibid.
37 St Joseph, air photographs ATD 5–8 (1967) (National Museum, Dublin)
38 *Cal. Docs. Ireland, 1293–1301,* 255. See also Rev. J. Begley, *The diocese of Limerick, ancient and
   medieval,* (1906), 165–6
39 Newport B. White, ed., *The Red Book of Ormond,* (1932), 64–6, and A. J. Otway-Ruthven, (1965),
   op. cit., 81
40 Ibid.
41 *Cal. Inquisitions Post Mortem, II,* 251
42 The Archaeological Survey of Northern Ireland, E. M. Jope, ed., *An archaeological survey of co.
   Down,* (1966), 103 and 106–7
43 A. J. Otway-Ruthven, (1968), op. cit., 252
44 A. J. Otway-Ruthven, The medieval county of Kildare, *Irish Historical Studies,* 11 (1959), 184
45 Queen's Co., Six Inch, sheet 11
46 G. H. Orpen, (1920), op. cit., III, 86–7
47 *Cal. Inquisitions Post Mortem, VIII,* 119
48 A. J. Otway-Ruthven, (1965), op. cit., 81–2, and E. Curtis, Rental of the manor of Lisronagh,
   Proc. Roy. Irish Acad., 43 C (1935–37), 41–76
49 See A. J. Otway-Ruthven, (1959), op. cit., 181–99 and map
50 *The Red Book of Ormond,* op. cit., 19, and A. J. Otway-Ruthven, (1959), op. cit., 183
51 *Cal. Justiciary Rolls Ireland, 1305–07,* 346
52 G. H. Orpen, (1920), op. cit., III, 82
53 Ibid., 87
54 *Cal. Justiciary Rolls Ireland, 1305–7,* 349 and G. H. Orpen, (1920), op. cit., III, 83–4
55 *Shell Guide to Ireland,* 2nd ed. (1967), 136
56 Tipperary, Six Inch sheet 70
57 M. W. Beresford and J. K. St Joseph, *Medieval England: an aerial survey,* (1958), 115–6
58 Tipperary, Six Inch sheet 77
59 Tipperary, Six Inch sheet 4
60 Tipperary, Six Inch sheet 19
61 Tipperary, Six Inch sheet 60

Photo by J. K. St. Joseph, Cambridge University Collection, Copyright reserved

XX Old field patterns underlying present-day fields two miles south-east of Oldcastle, co. Meath

XXI Part of the lands of Newcastle, co. Dublin, 1768. (National Library of Ireland)

62 King's Co. Six Inch sheet 10

63 Kilkenny, Six Inch sheet 20

64 Longford, Six Inch sheet 10. Discussed in R. E. Glasscock, op. cit., forthcoming. An air photo of this site is published in *Undergraduate studies in Science,* (Queen's University, Belfast, 1968), 52

65 G. D. Burtchaell, The manor of Erley, or Erlestown, county Kilkenny, *J. Roy. Soc. Antiq. Ireland,* 36 (1906), 154–65

66 Seán P. Ó'Ríordáin and John Hunt, Medieval dwellings at Caherguillamore, co. Limerick, *J. Roy. Soc. Antiq. Ireland,* 72, Pt. II (1942), 37–63

67 H. G. Leask and R. A. S. Macalister, Liathmore-Mochoemog (Leigh), county Tipperary, *Proc Roy. Irish Acad.,* 51 C (1945–48), 1–14. Currently under further excavation by R. E. Glasscock See interim note in 1968 annual report of The Deserted Medieval Village Research Group.

68 St Joseph, air photographs, AIF 19 (1963); AIE 7 and 16 (1963); and AIF 43 (1963), respectively (National Museum, Dublin)

69 St Joseph, air photographs, ATA 31 and 32 (1967); ATA 69 (1967) and ATA 65, 66 and 67 (1967) respectively. (National Museum, Dublin)

70 Discussed at more length in R. E. Glasscock, op. cit., forthcoming.

N

XI

GEOGRAPHY AND GOVERNMENT IN ELIZABETHAN IRELAND

J. H. Andrews

Ireland presented a cheerless picture to the Elizabethans, under-improved, under-populated (except perhaps for the mountains) and under-exploited. The country was divided among a confusingly large number of territorial rulers, great and small, who offered varying degrees of disrespect to the monarchy that had claimed their allegiance since the reign of Henry VIII. Over wide areas, their strongholds provided the chief focal points in a landscape that was bleakly deficient in towns and villages, and where the 'mere' Irishman was an elusive and barbarous figure with an apparent lack of locational roots that reduced the epithet 'Tartarian' almost to the level of an Elizabethan cliché. Economic assets in these Irish heart-lands consisted principally of livestock, more mobile than any force that could be sent to seize them; houses were flimsy, squalid, and so easily rebuilt that burning them down could never constitute much of a punishment; and though most of the country's churches lay in ruins, religious beliefs retained their medieval shape. It was the last point, especially, that compelled the attention of a Protestant queen: unless brought to submission, Ireland presented an easy and tempting prize to her Catholic enemies on the continent.

This danger fluctuated in intensity with the shifting patterns of both Irish and European politics, and English activity fluctuated in proportion. Elizabeth was notoriously loath to lay out money and man-power except under urgent pressure, and then she usually did too little, too late, to achieve a lasting solution. The interest of her reign, however, lies not so much in what was done as in what was written, for in consequence of the businesslike habits of the queen's principal adviser, Lord Burghley, there survives an excellent collection of documents (including many maps) to illustrate the forty-year period in which, without ever crossing the channel themselves, he and his sovereign shared the preoccupations of their government in Dublin. For the first time in the course of Irish history, the modern student can hear the decision-makers speaking for themselves; and among them the geographer will find a number of useful witnesses, ranging from the more large-minded and articulate of the queen's deputies, like Sir Henry Sidney (1566–71, 1575–78) and Sir John Perrot (1583–88), through the secretarial class of whom Edmund Spenser is the best-known representative, to private petitioners and memorialists whose panaceas were perhaps more concerned with demonstrating their authors' diligence and loyalty than with actually influencing the course of events. Much of this writing can be related, either by its contents or its archival situation, to one or other of the crises with which the whole period was closely punctuated. But there are many items which cannot be so easily placed in sequence and it is these, whether or not they really mark a higher level of deliberation and detachment, that make it necessary to distinguish the government's sources of geographical knowledge from the various uses to which that knowledge was put.

On the macrogeographical plane Ireland was tolerably well documented. From early in the sixteenth century a succession of treatises and memoranda had summarised its history and enumerated its administrative divisions, its corporate towns and its leading families. Minor territorial detail was less easily encompassed. As E. Estyn Evans has pointed out, the 'Tartarian' view of Celtic society was contradicted by the close network of 'ploughlands', 'balliboes' and other permanent land divisions, most of them considerably smaller than a typical English parish, among which the greater portion of the island was partitioned. So far as crown property was concerned, there should have been some record of these units in the office of the surveyor-general, established in 1549; but the Elizabethans never attempted the kind of nationwide inventory that followed the Norman occupation of England and that was to follow the Cromwellian reconquest of Ireland. Total numbers of ploughlands were sometimes quoted for provinces and counties, but seldom with much conviction. Perrot, for instance, who as lord deputy should have had access to the best information, was apologetic about the meagreness of his data on this point,[1] and many of the statistics on the same subject given in Spenser's *View of Ireland* are obviously no more than the roughest of estimates.

As for the contents of individual parcels, words like 'ploughland' and 'ballibo' suggest an origin as units of economic input or output rather than by any process of admeasurement on the ground. It is interesting in this connection that when the Earl of Essex was asked in 1574 to report the acreage of his proposed colony in Clandeboye the only figure he could supply (or at any rate the only one he thought the government could understand) was that the territory was capable of feeding 100,000 cattle.[2] Such vagueness was understandable in Ulster, where the English imprint had always been weak, but even in a 'civil' county like Kilkenny it could be admitted, in 1592, that "the quantity or number of acres . . . are . . . not certainly known because said ploughlands or horsemen's beds were (as we understand) made in the beginning by view and estimation and not according to the quantity or number of acres".[3] Ploughlands were often thought of as fixed in size (120 acres, excluding bog and mountain, was a common reckoning) but this was unsatisfactory even as a generalisation, for while an acre could safely be defined as 160 perches, the Irish or 'plantation' perch had not yet been stabilised at its modern value of twenty-one feet. At Cork, for instance, the perch marked out on the city wall was twenty-nine feet long, but even in Munster this standard did not command unanimous assent.[4] The fact was that Ireland had no community of professional surveyors to lay down national standards of linear or areal mensuration.

Clearly, then, any government programme involving small parcels of land was likely to have to depend on local reckonings as obtained from local documents or from local hearsay. The problem of small-scale regional cartography was less intractable and indeed the later sixteenth century may be ranked as one of the most productive periods in the history of the map of Ireland. A secretary of state, contemporaries were told, must have "the book of Ortelius's maps, a book of the maps of England . . . a good description of the realm of Ireland . . . and if any other plots or maps come to his hands, let them be kept safely".[5] Though couched in the form of advice, this was no more than what the queen's chief minister had already tried to do. The version of Ireland which Abraham Ortelius had copied from Mercator's map of 1564 was certainly worth noting in its day as an improvement on anything previously published, but it is clear from the corrections which Burghley made to his own copy (now in the National Library, Dublin) that he was conscious of its inadequacy, especially outside the better-known areas of the south-east. His requests for new maps were a continuing source of trouble for the royal officials in Dublin, who seem seldom to have initiated mapping projects of their own or even to have made a regular practice of keeping duplicates of the maps they sent to London.[6] Draftsmen and colourists were as scarce in Ireland as surveyors, and private students or patrons of cartography were scarcer still: the bias of local scholarship was non-geographical (nobody is known to have challenged Edmund Campion's statement that Ireland is shaped like an egg), and Burghley had to get most of his maps from English officials, some as presentation copies, others commissioned at considerable expense. In spite of these difficulties he built up a remarkable if heterogeneous collection.[7]

Although it was usual to send cartographers to London to give a *viva voce* explanation of their work, most of them followed stylistic conventions that had now become international. The symbols applied to coasts, rivers, woods, mountains, settlements and major territorial boundaries (roads seldom appear) were all of a kind familiar to English map-readers, except that in Ireland, where parochial organisation was weak, the red-painted buildings which marked parish centres in England were generally used to indicate castles or abbeys. Perhaps the most distinctively Irish feature of these maps, however, was the prominence given to the names of territorial lords, and the many such names added in Burghley's own hand show that one of the chief uses of his collection was as a geographical index to the government's friends and enemies.

Conjecture played its part in every map of Ireland, but the element of genuine observation increased throughout the period. As the history of Saxton's English atlas suggests, chorographic surveys could be made with surprising speed by one man filling in sketched detail around a network of angular measurements of towers and hill-tops. Not that Ireland was mapped as rapidly as England, for its field-workers suffered more from bad weather, from a general lack of amenities, and from expressions of antagonism by the local population. A greater source of delay was the piecemeal, *ad hoc* fashion in which the map-makers were put to work. Thus Robert Lythe's survey of 1567–70 was not meant to extend outside the province of Ulster, where a map was necessary to help with the settlement that followed the rebellion of Shane O'Neill, and it seems to have been only through Sidney's unusual perspicuity that this able cartographer remained, after he had failed in the north, to map the south of Ireland instead.[8] In the same way, Francis Jobson's more successful visit to eastern and central Ulster in 1590 may be seen as a belated sequel to the division of Tyrone three years earlier, and the mapping of Connacht by the John Brownes, uncle and nephew, grew partly out of threats from Scotland and Spain and partly out of the rebellion of the Mayo Burkes. The great northern war of Elizabeth's last decade brought new demands for maps of central and western Ulster which were met by John Thomas's survey of Lough Erne in 1594 and, some nine years later, by Richard Bartlett's excellent *Generalle description* of the whole province.

Bartlett, beheaded by the natives before finishing Donegal, died in the knowledge that he had reached the last frontier of Irish regional cartography. Small-scale map-making had kept pace, for the most part, with the demand for maps, but the whole process had been lacking in co-ordination and continuity. Lythe got back to England as soon as he could: he never attempted to complete his survey or to revise it in the light of other men's work. The Brownes, a 'new English' family who had already acquired strong local interests in Mayo, appear to have confined themselves to their own province.[9] Jobson, although he aspired to a professional career in Ireland as a cartographer, was surprisingly ill-informed about the achievements of his predecessors. Thomas's map, as a contemporary collector noted on the back of it, gave an 'altogether false' picture of certain well-frequented areas that the author did not happen to have surveyed himself.

To judge from what Burghley is known to have written about maps and from what he wrote on them, his instinct was to preserve everything that came in (irrespective of merit), to meet each new crisis by asking for a new map of the area concerned, and in resolving the crisis to consult a wide selection of the maps already in his possession. In these circumstances he would have been well advised to make special arrangements for safeguarding maps (always a temptation to the 'borrower') and for collating and in some way editing their geographical contents; but in London, as in Dublin, there was no central cartographic establishment to which such a task could be referred. This point was underlined by the governor of Connacht when he warned that Browne's map of the province was in danger of being lost unless it was committed to print. His advice was ignored, perhaps for reasons of security, perhaps because of the high cost of engraving, and sure enough the map disappeared into a private collection before any other cartographer could make use of it.[10] Burghley's apparent indifference to the process of compiling maps is defensible on scholarly grounds, for compilation introduces new kinds of error. But his collecting habits, like his custom of ordering his maps on a province-by-province basis, were also symptomatic of an essentially compartmentalised approach to Irish problems in general and it is interesting that synthetic cartography, as practised by Norden and others, did not revive until the end of Elizabeth's reign, when the conquest of Ireland could plausibly be regarded as all but complete.

The history of sixteenth-century map-making, like the contents of the maps themselves, exemplifies the distinction within Ireland between the wild north-west, unwelcoming to cartographer and administrator alike, and the more highly anglicised and civilised south-east. This regional dichotomy, which some modern scholars have seen as analogous to the highland and lowland zones of English historical geography, did not escape the notice of sixteenth-century commentators. Sir James Croft, in 1552, had divided the country by a line from Galway through Lough Ree and the head of Lough Erne to Carrickfergus[11], and another version, marking off the south-west as well as the north-west, appears on a rough map of Ireland (P.R.O., London, M.P.F. 72) which is assigned to the first year of Elizabeth's reign. Many contemporaries, no doubt, would have expressed the difference in terms of groups of counties. But this was not so much a mere hypostatisation of administrative territories as a regional concept with a life of its own. As such it owed some of its vitality to, and was indeed at times indistinguishable from, the idea of the English Pale, a notion which, having lost its old meaning of a country embanked against marauders, had itself now begun to show affinities with the concept of a moving 'colonial' frontier.

For however and wherever they might have defined the pale, most Englishmen believed that the queen's policy should be to increase its size, "abating cost behind" (as one writer optimistically put it) "as she shall bestow it forward".[12] Thus in 1577 Sir William Gerrard proposed making Irish countries into counties and so "by little and little to stretch the pale further".[13] Essex rashly claimed to be advancing the pale to the Ulster Blackwater when he established a fort on that river in 1573.[14] And seventeen years later, Sir George Carew expressed the hope that as a result of the distribution of lands currently being organised in county Monaghan, "the pale will be so much enlarged, that from henceforth Maguire's country and Tyrone are like to be the Irish border".[15] In these three statements, three kinds of locational policy may be distinguished, each involving more complex geographical ideas than the last and making more demands on geographical technique. Firstly there were suggestions for extending the network of administrative areas inherited from the middle ages. When rebellion showed this policy to have been ineffective, it gave way to preoccupations about the placing of forts, garrisons and patrols. And when a purely military regime began to seem intolerably expensive, attention shifted to the idea of self-sufficient civil colonies. This progression was not so much a single orderly sequence of events as a cycle of ideas that repeated itself obsessively without ever being fully translated into fact. As ideas, the three topics were to some degree inextricable: local government reform was linked with the making of new towns, and civil plantations would probably need to be protected by soldiers. In practice, however, this interdependence was never properly appreciated, and to that extent it is historically defensible, as well as convenient for purposes of exposition, to give separate treatment to the three themes of administrative geography, military geography and colonial geography.

The administrative utility of the county unit was becoming increasingly clear to sixteenth-century Englishmen in their own country, so it is not surprising to find that the process of turning Ireland into 'shire ground', begun in earlier reigns, was given statutory backing by the Dublin parliament in 1569 and then put into effect by degrees until the whole island had been at least theoretically brought into the system. 'Superimposed' boundaries, in the modern political geographer's sense, were not in themselves alien to contemporary modes of thought, as can be seen from the attempt in 1573 to delimit Essex's new domain by a straight line from Belfast to the nearest point of Lough Neagh.[16] But it was probably clear to most administrators that Ireland's cartographic foundations were too weak to carry new-fangled territorial structures of this kind; at any rate the usual practice when altering administrative 'divisions was to select a 'natural bound' (a term applied to the Shannon in 1601[17]), as was done with the River Barrow between King's and Queen's counties, and with the Suck between Galway and Roscommon. The representation of drainage systems on contemporary maps was generally good enough to play its part on these occasions, and when Burghley suggested using the Blackwater to separate Turlough O'Neill from the Baron of Dungannon he seems to have been thinking cartographically rather than verbally, for he forgot the river's name and had to leave a blank space in his notes.[18]

The simplest and most common practice, however, was to evade the issue of boundary demarcation by defining new territories entirely in terms of old ones, so that the only knowledge required was of the names of the countries abutting on to a given country, augmented perhaps by the kind of roughly estimated figures of length and breadth which seem to have been available even for territories that had not yet been mapped in detail. In such circumstances cartography could be dispensed with, and in fact there are few surviving maps that are known to have been drawn especially for the purpose of forming new administrative divisions. An important example of this labour-saving approach was the choice of the historic province in 1569 as a framework for the kind of regional government that already existed in Wales. By the same principle, as Perrot noticed when shiring Ulster in 1585, some Irish countries were comparable in size with the counties of England and could therefore be adopted without alteration. Perrot made a point of remarking that the smallest of his new counties was nowhere less than twenty-four miles across.[19] Otherwise there seems to be no record of any concept of optimal or limiting size, only a feeling that certain counties were too large (Cork, Tyrone and Down were mentioned at various times in this connection), and others too small, like Kerry and Desmond, which on one occasion it was proposed to unite as the county of 'Maine'. If ready-made divisions failed to present themselves, as happened in Sidney's shiring of Connacht, the normal practice (though nowhere explicitly described as such) was to form new units by the addition, or subtraction, of the minimum number of pre-existing constituents, so that a province would be altered by transferring one or more whole counties, and a county by transferring the next smallest unit, namely the barony or its equivalent. These principles, though geographically unsophisticated, were as a rule sufficient to prevent the kind of medieval-style fragmentation that still disfigured the administrative map of much of the English Pale.

Geographical caution was also desirable when choosing sites for the gaols and sessions houses that were an essential part of the county system. The best location was of course a town, preferably a walled town; or, in the purely rural counties of the north and west, the chief residence of the principal Irish lord. To symbolise the change from personal government to the concept of the central place, a number of territories were named or renamed after their proposed new county seats, so that O'Rourke's country became Leitrim and MacMahon's country Monaghan, while other suggested county names included 'Carrickfergus', 'Ferns', 'Limavady', 'Omagh' and 'Enniskillen'.[20] The same thing happened at the next lowest level of the territorial hierarchy in 1561 when native districts in King's County, caconymous to English eyes and ears, were grouped into baronies with names like Warrenstown and Coolestown.

Apart from the question of technical convenience, this pouring of new administrative wine into old territorial bottles might have been expected to serve a useful political purpose by neutralising the regional loyalties of the Irish people. Such hopes were ill-founded, and administrative machinery proved useless without a population that was already loyal. Nowhere was this more apparent than in Ulster, where Perrot's county of Tyrone could be criticised as too large to be ruled as a unit and too small to support a sheriff.[21] It was an irresoluble paradox, and within a short time Perrot's work had been engulfed in a wave of insurrection.

In war as well as peace the principle of locational conservatism had an obvious part to play, for in every theatre of operations there were medieval castles or prehistoric forts suitable for improvement by the Elizabethan military engineer. The chief exceptions were on the coast, where the threatened presence of well-armed and well-organised naval forces from the continent introduced a new factor into the strategic geography of Ireland. What was described (in a navigational sense) as 'the coast of peril', fronting the Irish Sea, might be expected to remain immune, but the vulnerability of the southern harbours from Waterford to the Shannon had become obvious before any attempts had actually been made on them. It was plainly impossible to fortify and garrison every harbour on a coast where good harbours were reckoned to be no more than five miles apart. Attention had to be confined to the principal seaports, and here the problem was to command the lower harbours instead of, or as well as, to improve the mural defences of the towns themselves. Robert Lythe, Francis Jobson and the better-known English experts Edmund York and Paul Ivy were among those involved in the mapping and designing of Irish harbour defences. As the queen herself observed, it was a controversial subject ("one day places are described to be of importance to be fortified, and another day they are held merely inutile") but at least one basic and long-lived doctrine was agreed on as early as 1578 when the same kind of promontory situation was simultaneously chosen at Duncannon in Waterford harbour, at Corkbeg in Cork harbour, and at "a certain neck of the land beside Kinsale which is in manner of an isthmus or peninsula".[22]

Although much time and money went into the making of large-scale plans of individual forts, there was a sense in which coastal protection could be conceived one-dimensionally, and based on non-cartographic surveys drawn up in the manner of a seaman's rutter. Away from the coast, this kind of linear thinking was hazardous. When Essex wrote of extending the Pale to the Blackwater he did not say what was going to happen to the rest of the periphery of the Pale, and it was perhaps ominous that he was unable to meet Burghley's request for a map to illustrate his scheme. As a point on the line from Armagh to Dungannon the Blackwater fort made sense; in a larger geographical context it had little meaning, though this did not become clear until an English army was defeated in trying to relieve it. A more advanced strategic concept was to place a number of garrisons at 'passes' and river crossings so as to enclose the enemy's territory in a polygon, followed up perhaps, as in Mountjoy's successful Ulster campaign of 1601–3, by networking the whole area with roughly equidistant strongpoints. Jobson's plan for Ulster, illustrated as it was by a reduced version of his own map (Plate XIX), is of special interest in the present connection, but his was only one of a long series of projects in which the importance of such places as Newry, Belfast, Coleraine and (later) Lifford, Ballyshannon and Enniskillen was repeatedly affirmed. Other authorities, such as Raleigh and Pelham at the time of the Desmond rebellion, recommended treating Munster in the same way, or even 'walling in' the whole country, as Perrot proposed to do in 1584 with his curious project for seven towns, seven bridges and seven castles.

In the heat of an Elizabethan campaign, maps were probably of limited importance. The Irish are not known to have used them (except for the ones they captured or stole to pass on to their Spanish allies[23]) and the English armies in the field may be supposed to have depended on guides for most of their topographical intelligence: otherwise we should expect to hear of commanders being misled by faulty maps. But when a policy of encirclement was under discussion between Dublin and London, whether before or after the enemy had actually been engaged, some kind of two-dimensional diagram was a necessary visual aid; and the chief use of small-scale maps to the lord deputy's administration, to judge from such records as are available, was in persuading a reluctant queen and council to plant their garrisons more thickly.

The making of regional maps and fort plans never seriously strained the government's technical and administrative competence. But the planning of wholesale colonisation brought the state into a cartographic field, and indeed many other fields, that had previously been reserved for private enterprise. Of course there was nothing, in theory, to prevent an individual landowner from settling an immigrant colony on his estate, but without official support few of them made much effort to do so. There were powerful motives for giving this support, however. A large 'new English' community in Ireland would provide the authorities with an oasis of peace and security, a reserve of military man-power, and a specimen society on which with luck the Irish might be tempted to model themselves. Since it was patently impracticable to fill the whole country with Englishmen or to empty it of Irishmen, these new communities needed to be planned within some kind of regional framework. Yet not even the most theoretically minded of the government's advisers seems seriously to have thought of integrating a number of separate civil colonies into a single national plan. As a matter of practical politics, in any case, planting had to be confined to areas of recently-suppressed rebellion, for most Elizabethan statesmen, unlike their successors, accepted that some colourable moral justification was needed before an existing landowner could be coerced or dispossessed. In these circumstances it is all the more remarkable that from both the theoretical and the actual colonial schemes a fairly clear regional pattern emerges. The Leix-Offaly plantation marked an interest in the borders of the pale that was to recur in the early seventeenth century. Otherwise the most favoured areas were the eastern margins of Ulster from Monaghan round to the lower Bann, and the coastlands of Munster from the Blackwater to the Blaskets. In both cases a new colony would benefit from access by sea to English markets and sources of supply; and in both cases it would act as a bulwark against a possible invader—the Scots in Ulster (more effective planters, throughout the sixteenth century, than the English) and the French or Spaniards in Munster.

Within the limits of any large region selected for planting, it was not difficult to theorise about the kind of sub-district that ought to be reserved for English settlement. According to a project of 1585 for peopling the lands escheated as a result of the Desmond rebellion in Munster, the best qualifications were "fertility of the soil . . . natural defences. . . good neighbourhood either of the sea or great rivers or cities or people living in obedience".[24] It was expecting too much, however, that natural defences and fertility of soil should coincide: on the contrary, the arable lowlands would be the very areas most exposed to the Irish enemy, while the places that resisted the attacker would probably resist the settler as well. It was true that bogs could be drained—a somewhat academic proposition in sixteenth-century Ireland, though not wholly ignored; and it was true that forest clearance would serve an economic as well as a strategic purpose if, as in one Munster proposal, the wood was consumed in industries like charcoal, pottery and brick-making.[25] But the hills would always remain as refuges for the disorderly: "mountain soil is apt to bring forth such fruit" was Gerrard's 'environmentalistic' judgment on the area south of Dublin. Gerrard was drawing chiefly on his own experience as vice-president of Wales, but Irish history could have supplied him with plenty of examples, as witness Spenser's comment that in the middle ages it had been the areas "near unto any mountains or Irish deserts" that had first been displanted and lost. Spenser's Ireneaus thought that there were enough broad and fertile valleys between the mountains for English husbandry to prosper, but this was essentially a Munsterman's view and even there it was to prove oversanguine, as his creator's experience among the displanted was soon to testify. In fact, uncertainty about whether to settle the uplands or the lowlands continued to find expression in the plantation literature of the early seventeenth century without ever being properly resolved.

As well as their physical setting, the spatial organisation of the proposed colonies was the subject of much discussion. Some schemes were urban in emphasis, others rural, but a leading motif in many of them was the concept of centre and hinterland. It was most explicitly stated, perhaps, in Sir Thomas Smith's plan for the Ards peninsula, with its erudite references to classical precedent[26], and worked out in most detail in relation to the Munster scheme in 1585. In Munster the basic division was to be the 'seignory', conceived as a square of about $4\frac{1}{4}$ miles dimension that was to serve as both manor and parish for a carefully adjusted cross-section of rural society. In one version (Fig. 11.1) the 32 houses nearest the centre of the square were to be occupied by a wheelwright, a smith, a tailor, a shoemaker, a carpenter, a miller, a thatcher, an inn-keeper and a parish clerk as well as by labourers and gardeners; and the surrounding farms were to be graded in six sizes ranging from 1,000 acres to 78 acres, with a settlement pattern that struck an ingenious compromise between nucleation and dispersal, keeping each farmhouse on its own land without an excessive length of road. A square block of nine seignories would constitute a hundred or wapentake in which the central village would be raised to the status of a market town with 96 families instead of the usual 32, and a wider occupational range including clothiers, tuckers, weavers and masons. Here was an Elizabethan version of the hierarchy of central places.

It was in Munster, too, that plantation theories were put to their most searching test.[27]

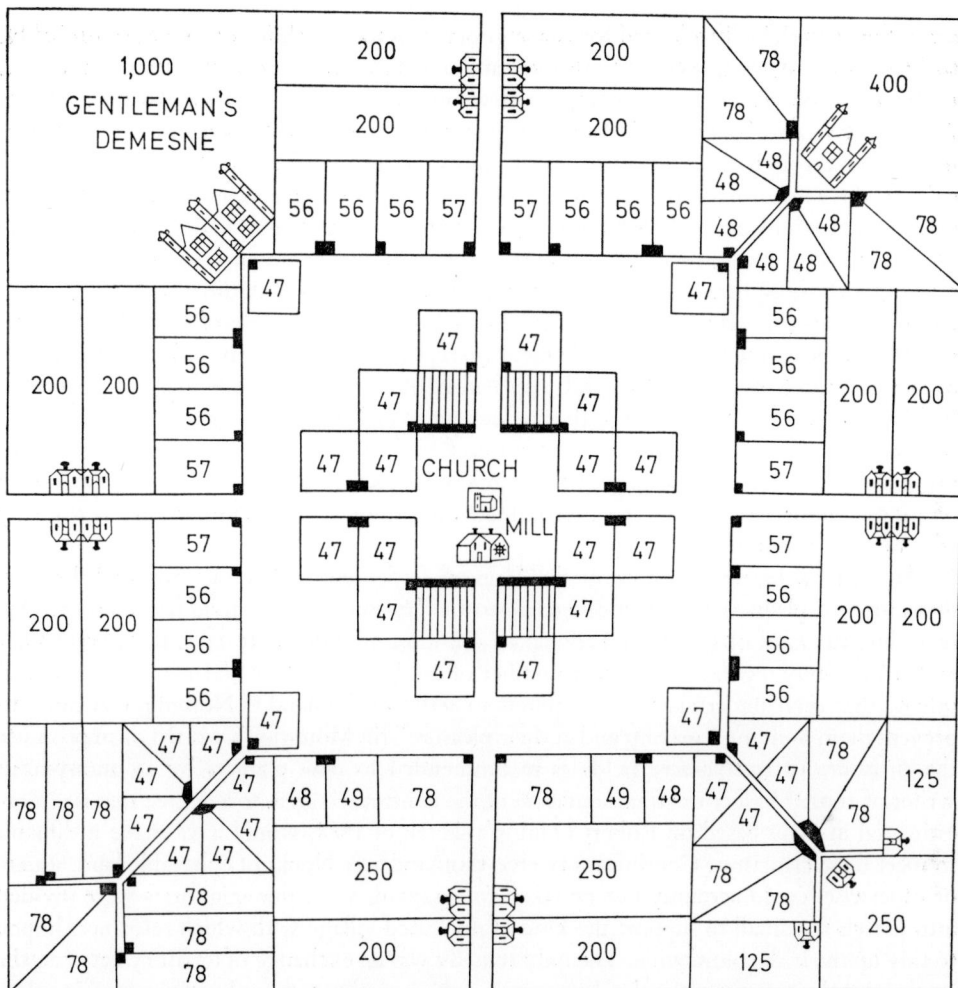

Fig. 11.1 Proposed lay-out of a Munster seignory of 12,000 acres, 1586 (PRO, M.P.F. 305), showing roads, houses and farm boundaries. The smallest holdings, those of the thirty-two cottagers, are of $5\frac{1}{2}$ acres each; the acreages of the larger holdings are shown by figures. Holdings of 47–57 acres were to be brought up to an equivalent of 78 acres by allotments in the 1,692 acres of arable which surround the central block of 47-acre tenements, or of grazing rights in the 184 acres of common pasture which occupy the square between the two rows of cottages. Eight acres, presumably of glebe land, are unaccounted for.

Many of the reasons for the ensuing debacle lay outside the regional planner's terms of reference: the shortage of man-power, for instance, and the effects of the uprising of 1598. But there was one source of failure with strongly geographical overtones, and that was the excessive burden laid on the shoulders of the individual 'undertaker'. Twelve thousand acres, the size originally adopted for the seignory, was too much for one man; so probably, to begin with at least, were the six thousand and four thousand acre sizes from which, under a revised version of the plan, the newcomers were allowed to make their choice. An equally serious fault was the lack of any attempt to mediate between government and undertaker through the kind of regional authority that might have helped provide the colony with a much-needed infrastructure of roads, towns and garrisons. A reformed county organisation could have played a useful role here; but nothing was done to reduce the unwieldy size of Cork, or to bring the western peninsulas more effectively into the shire system, or to adjust those county boundaries, such as the Cork-Waterford boundary, which cut across the regional groupings of the new seignories. This failure of overall vision was reflected in the cartography of the scheme. In earlier discussions of Leix and Offaly and even of the ill-fated Ards, a good general map had been recognised as essential, whatever else had been neglected. But although the fundamentals of Munster geography had been well depicted by Robert Lythe, the government preferred to block out its ideas on diagrams of pre-Lythian crudity and the project was already four years old before Jobson, apparently on his own initiative, showed the approximate disposition of the seignories on a reasonably accurate small-scale map.

At the local level the feature of the Munster settlement that most impressed the next generation of planners was its indifference to the lay-out of the individual seignory. Disregarding the kind of detailed locational advice illustrated in figure 11.1, the government ended by simply regulating the total number of English freeholders, farmers, cottagers and others, that each undertaker was required to settle on his land.[28] Nothing was done to prevent them building "sparsim and at their pleasure" (in Mountjoy's words) or to promote the enclosure of twelve-acre fields as recommended to new planters by an anonymous writer of 1601.[29] In fact the fragmentation of the confiscated area, to a degree that is underestimated in maps based on Robert Dunlop's sketch of 1888, would have made it difficult to meet these criticisms. Continuous twelve-thousand acre blocks of cultivable land, square or otherwise, could certainly not be taken for granted, and some seignories were divided into parcels too small to support the kind of nucleated village with which reformers hoped to tidy up the Irish countryside. The only remedy was an exchange of territory between the crown and the non-forfeiting landowners, but this expedient, though suggested more than once, would have meant adding to a quantity of survey work that was already proving insupportable.

For it was here, in translating the ploughlands taken from the Irish into the acres promised to the English, that the plantation encountered its most specifically geographical or at any rate geometrical problem.[30] A rough preliminary survey of the confiscated area was made in 1585, but it was not until late in the following year, with the weather already deteriorating, that the appointed measurers (among them the ubiquitous Jobson) took the field. According to the plantation commissioners, five or six surveyors would be needed to map the 580,000 forfeited acres in a year; the actual number recruited was four, and only two of these were left by Christmas 1586. A possible solution, suggested by the home government, was to abandon the "exact sort of working by the line" with which the survey had begun and to continue "in a more speedy and superficial sort by the eye or by the instrument, by persons skilful therein to be sent from hence". But men of skill were not so easily enticed across the channel. As a pre-plantation Munster resident, Jobson was a special case; so was his fellow measurer Arthur Robins, who happened to be an undertaker himself. But it was hard to see why an Englishman with no other stake in Ireland should be attracted by 3s 4d a day (the kind of sum the government had in mind) when according to Robins he could earn three times as much for doing the same work at home. In England, moreover, estate surveyors could expect assistance and hospitality from both lord and tenant; in Munster all the problems of Irish map-making would be aggravated as they sought the help of hostile monoglot Gaelic speakers to identify the half-forgotten mearings of a depopulated and over-grown countryside. Understandably, no new surveyors arrived. Jobson, at any rate, seems to have continued with his "exact sort" (a boundary traverse, presumably), using a wire line of four perches with the results "justly by the said measure plotted upon the instrument" at a scale of forty perches to the inch. "Plotted upon the instrument" might be taken to suggest a plane table. But whatever the instrument was, its rapid, "superficial", use is mentioned only once more, and then in a context that shows it to have been exceptional: this was when part of county Limerick proved to be "so full of large and thick underwoods, that the measurers with the line were not able to pass through them so that by the help of sundry stations truly measured with the line, the rest was accomplished by the instrument".

The only other ways of hastening the survey were either crude estimation or a sampling technique in which by measuring two or three ploughlands in each district an average value could be applied to the others. Accordingly in 1587 the undertakers were given the choice of accepting an estimated or extrapolated figure at once or waiting until it was possible to make a full admeasurement. This solution brought its own difficulties. One advantage of maps, as Robins pointed out, was to show how the land might "most aptest be laid out into seignories". Without them, the new estates would be in danger of becoming unnecessarily intermixed. Another problem, in the absence of any order for the preserving and inspecting of field notes and protractions, was to distinguish estimates from genuine surveys. Some of Robins's 'measurements' were suspiciously low, suspiciously round-numbered, and sus-piciously prompt; and as an undertaker, who had accepted hospitality from other under-takers, he was not well placed to answer criticism on this score. Jobson too was exposed to temptation in so far as he hoped for future patronage as a private surveyor; but although he did in fact secure employment in this capacity (thereby staking a claim to be regarded as the father of the Irish estate map) there is no positive ground for doubting his good faith.

These delays and disagreements naturally held up the progress of the plantation. Some undertakers had to wait so long for their lands that they lost heart and went home. Others were deterred from dividing and enclosing by continued uncertainty about acreages and boundaries. All tended to grow jealously obsessed with mere quantity of land, though in fact there was probably no planter without more than he could manage. Meanwhile the original owners, regaining confidence, were coming forward to question the undertakers' titles and dispute their mearings, and the old stewards or 'sergeants', who might have helped settle the latter, were beginning to die off. It was easy enough to press for lands to be measured again (one planter was still demanding a resurvey in 1613) but, as a government official asked, which surveyor does one believe when surveyors disagree?

In Ireland generally, as in Munster, the Elizabethans learned much but achieved little, and we must qualify the idea (sometimes encountered in modern writings) of a new spatial pattern imposed by the Tudors with un-Celtic rationality and an un-Celtic willingness to spend. What the record shows is a series of locational exercises strung out along the border-line between theory and practice without penetrating very far on either side. That these problems were inter-related and that their solution called for similar abilities is shown by the many appearances of a man like Francis Jobson. And the failure of the authorities to grasp this point may perhaps be illustrated by Jobson's embittering struggles for adequate status and remuneration, and particularly by his unsuccessful attempt to obtain a permanent appointment as official 'plotter and measurer'.[31] He was not the last cartographer to seek such a position, but for another two centuries Irish governments preferrred to deal with geographical questions sketchily and one by one. Under James I, for instance, anomalies of county geography were reviewed more searchingly than before, but maps of nineteenth-century exactitude were needed before the problems of administrative boundary-making could be tackled at the root. Military geography was institutionalised in Ireland by the creation of the office of overseer of fortifications in 1612: the sequel was a number of plans of individual strongpoints, but it was not until 1785 that the whole kingdom was embraced by Charles Vallancey in a single military map. In the field of settlement geography the last Elizabethan surveyor-general, Williams Parsons, took a significant step forward by making a collection of plantation maps, but it needed another cartographic failure, in Ulster, to re-educate the authorities in the importance of exact and properly organised admeasurement. When instrumental operations began again in Leinster and Connacht several features of the Munster system were re-introduced and sure enough the name of Francis Jobson (junior?) appears in 1615 among the plantation measurers in Longford.[32] Apart from the intrinsic interest of their own efforts, then, the Elizabethans are notable for the precedents they set. But it was only in the hey-day of the Ordnance Survey in the 1830s and 1840s that the three strands of development referred to in this chapter—administrative, military and cadastral—were woven into the fabric of an effective all-purpose institute of applied geography.

REFERENCES

1 *The government of Ireland under Sir John Perrot* (1626), sig. d.
2 PRO, State papers, Ireland, Elizabeth (cited below as SP 63) 45/37 (Notes addressed to the Earl of Essex concerning Ulster, 29 March 1574) and 45/67 I (Essex's reply, 15 April)
3 A book of the ploughlands otherwise called horsemen's beds in the county of Kilkenny, 1592: *Calendar of Ormonde deeds,* (Irish MSS Commission), 5 (1941), 165
4 Report on the Earl of Desmond's lands, 1584: Lambeth palace, Carew MS 627, f. 93
5 Quoted in Conyers Read, *Mr Secretary Walsingham and the policy of Queen Elizabeth,* I (1925), 428–9
6 For an example see Lord deputy to Burghley, 20 July 1593: *Calendar of State Papers, Ireland* (cited below as *CSPI*), 1592–96, 130

7 For official maps of this period see R. Dunlop, Sixteenth century maps of Ireland, *Eng. Hist. Rev.* 20 (1905), 309–37, and G. A. Hayes-McCoy, *Ulster and other Irish maps, c. 1600* (1964)

8 J. H. Andrews, The Irish surveys of Robert Lythe, *Imago Mundi,* 19 (1965), 22–31

9 Robert Southwell referred in 1684 to documents (now apparently lost) relating to Browne's survey of Ireland (*Calendar of Ormonde MSS* (Hist. MSS Commission), N.S., 7 (1912), 263), but this reference, unsupported as it is by others, may be due to a misapprehension of the scope of the Connacht survey.

10 Sir Richard Bingham to Burghley, 8 February 1591: SP 63/157/12. George Bingham to Burghley, 25 October 1592: ibid, 167/11. Dunlop, art. cit., 315

11 Quoted in Dean G. White, The reign of Edward VI in Ireland: some political, social and economic aspects, *Irish Historical Studies,* 14 (1965), 206

12 Notes and propositions for the reformation of Ireland, by Edmund Tremayne [? 1571]: SP 63/32/66

13 Gerrard to Walsingham, 8 February 1577: ibid, 57/18

14 Quoted in R. Dunlop, Sixteenth century schemes for the plantation of Ulster, *Scottish Hist. Rev.* 22 (1924–25), 206

15 Carew to Sir Thomas Heneage, 9 December 1590: *Calendar of Carew MSS, 1589–1600,* 45

16 Queen to lord deputy, 28 September 1573: *CSPI, 1601–3 (addenda),* 589

17 Some reasons to induce the not altering of the county of Clare . . . from the province of Connaught to Munster [1601]: Carew MS 614, f. 127

18 Memorial by Burghley on the government of Ireland, 20 April 1574: SP 63/45/77

19 Perrot to privy council, 7 September 1585: printed in *Analecta Hibernica,* 22 (1943), 27

20 A plot for Ulster to be made shire ground [1592]: SP 63/167/64. Fiants, Elizabeth, No. 5027 (18 August 1587): *Sixteenth report,* deputy keeper of the public records of Ireland (1884), 34

21 Earl of Tyrone to privy council, 5 November 1593: *CSPI, 1592–96,* 172

22 Privy council to lord deputy, 31 May 1578: SP 63/60/69

23 Advertisements delivered by James Jans, 10 July 1591: ibid, 159/9. Deposition of Jordan Roche, 19 November 1602: *CSPI, 1601–3,* 529

24 Project for the transporting of English colonies into Ireland, 1585: BM, Harleian MS 1877, f. 50

25 Short notes to be considered upon for the reducing and settling of Munster, 1584: *Calendar of Carew MSS, 1575–88,* 396

26 D. B. Quinn, Sir Thomas Smith (1513–1577) and the beginnings of English colonial theory, *Proc. Amer. Phil. Soc.* 89 (1945), 543–60

27 Idem, The Munster plantation: problems and opportunities, *J. Cork. Hist. & Arch. Soc.* 71 (1966), 19–40;
R. Dunlop, The plantation of Munster, 1584–89, *Eng. Hist. Rev.* 3 (1888), 250–69

28 Articles concerning Her Majesty's offers for disposing her lands in Munster, 1 March 1586: SP 63/123/2

29 Quoted in F. M. Jones, *Mountjoy, 1563–1606, the last Elizabethan deputy* (1958), 191. For enclosures, see A discourse of Ireland [1601]: *CSPI, 1601–3,* 252–3

30 The following account of the Munster surveys is based on maps and documents in the Irish state papers and elsewhere for which it is hoped to provide full citations in a study now being planned.

31 Jobson to Burghley, 23 June 1592: SP 63/165/17

32 Treasurer at war's accounts, Ireland, 1615–16: PRO, E.351/272

XII

RURAL SOCIETY IN CONNACHT 1600—1640

Jean M. Graham

Recent work on Ireland in the seventeenth century has paid little attention to the way of life of the majority of its inhabitants. Historians have tended to avoid agrarian history, historical geographers to avoid the century. The aim of this essay is to examine what detailed material is available in the Connacht records of the period, and from it to reconstruct a picture of rural society. Any Gaelic characteristics which appear will give a strong hint of the pattern and practices of rural society during the preceding centuries; any new trends will indicate the form of development until the great famine of 1845–7. For at the roots of rural society are the families who farm the land, who modify their agricultural methods and their social institutions only gradually, and who remain throughout history, contributing to it a strong element of continuity.

The most important source of material is the detailed land survey of Connacht (the counties of Galway, Mayo, Roscommon, Sligo and Leitrim) made during 1636–7, under Sir Thomas Wentworth, later the Earl of Strafford, much of which has been preserved in the Books of Survey and Distribution.[1] Other detailed, although less comprehensive, documents exist for the same area in the same period.[2] From a geographical point of view, all these records suffer from a preoccupation with ownership, but it is nevertheless possible to trace in them something of the pattern of rural society and many of the conditions affecting it. Connacht is of particular interest in that rural society there had remained Gaelic until the sixteenth century.[3] Even then, the changes introduced by the English government under the Tudors, Elizabeth in particular, took some time to have effect. Consequently, much in rural life that was of Gaelic origin persisted well into the following century. The years 1600–40 were a period of peace and relative prosperity during which, for the majority of farming people, changes were the result of economic influences. With the rebellion of 1641, and the succeeding eleven years of war, external forces were released which swept away many of the surviving Gaelic institutions and introduced new trends. The first detailed topographical surveys of Connacht were thus made at a time of great change in rural society, producing a wealth of documentary material for the later part of this vital period in western Ireland.

Within so large an area as Connacht uniformity obviously was not complete. There are, on the one hand, marked physical contrasts. Particularly significant is the contrast between

XXII   Belfast: the new dry dock

XXIII   A Bellferry container ship and modern handling machinery at Waterford

Photo by Lensmen, Dublin

BELL VICTOR

Photo by *B.K.S. (Technical Services Ltd.), Dublin*

XXIV   The urban/rural fringe at Santry, north Dublin (north lies to the right-hand edge of the air photograph)

the extensive drumlin covered, limestone lowlands, which occupy much of the centre and east, and the peripheral fringe of lowlands round the great mountain ranges and bog-covered plains of the west. The former are attractive, fertile lands with a long history of close settlement and of conflict between land-owning families; the latter are areas of isolation, of culture survivals, of poverty of resources. On the other hand, the influence of Anglo-Norman settlers varied within Connacht. They had secured ownership of much of the land in Galway and Mayo, and had large estates in other counties, but most had become thoroughly gaelicized. Some of the major families retained their connections with England, but on their extensive lands the life of the people must have been indistinguishable from that on the estates of the great Irish lords. Once English ideas of feudal tenure and primo-geniture had been accepted by the Connacht lords in the sixteenth century, the relationship between lord and follower, which was a basic feature of Gaelic society, could not persist. The criterion of status had changed—from numbers of followers who owed loyalty to size of estates owned. Without the responsibilities which the old social order had imposed upon them, the Irish lords recognised the same advantage in owning large estates as did the wealthy merchants and new English planters. All were acquiring land as a source of income. They were equally responsible for the subsequent changes in the economic position of other groups of the population.

A study of the records shows that every land was named, and that most can be traced in the names of modern townlands. It also shows that each land was recorded as a unit—quarter, trine, cartron or gneeve. It is clear that Strafford's surveyors superimposed acreage measurements on these units, and that, since the latter were based on the farming value of the land and not on its area, there was no uniform scale of equivalence. The records indicate not only a division of quarters and trines into cartrons and gneeves (1 quarter=4 cartrons= 6 gneeves), all with individual place-names and separate map reference numbers, but also further fractional subdivisions, sometimes named and numbered. We must conclude that all such land-units were distinct and capable of separate demarcation, though the smallest can only have been localities within a land-unit. The names quarter (Irish *ceathramha*, anglicized *carrow*, a quarter) and trine (Irish *trian*, anglicized *trine* or *treen*, a third) suggest that they had their origin in a larger unit. Such a unit had commonly survived into the seventeenth century in Connacht, where it was still widely recognised and named. Com-posed of three trines or four quarters, it was a township (Irish *baile*, anglicized *bally*), in the historical sense of a rural settlement with all the necessary types of land for a self-contained economy. *Bally*, *carrow* and *treen* are common elements in place-names, as also is *leah* or *le* (Irish, *leath*, a half) as a prefix attached to *bally* or *carrow*. Such townships varied in size according to land quality, but especially according to the amount of infertile ground in the area. The three townships comprising Kilcummin parish, to the west of Killala Bay, co. Mayo, had 326, 307 and 278 profitable Irish acres[4] respectively[5], but their total acreages were recorded as 336, 535 and 1,117 Irish acres as, further from the coast, they included more rough ground. In the records, townships and their subdivisions can be traced so frequently, and in such diverse areas, that they must have been universal in Connacht at some time before the seventeenth century. They were always composed of a small area of relatively

O

fertile ground, a larger area of less fertile land, and, wherever the natural environment included great areas of mountain or bog, each township adjacent to it claimed that part which was in their immediate vicinity. Subdivision of the fertile lands of a township into quarters and trines as population increased, as inheritances were divided, and as land became more intensively used, naturally led to the division of the township's mountain, bog and woodland. This had often caused the separation of pasture lands from the lowland settlements to which they belonged, a feature frequently seen in the seventeenth-century records. The further gradual subdivision of land-units into named subsidiary parts under the natural development processes resulting from Irish inheritance customs ended with the substitution of primogeniture for partible inheritance and the replacement of many Irish landowners by English ones. The peculiar anomalies in the size of present-day townlands reflect this artificial break in traditional land-unit development, and the fossilization of a variety of old Irish land units as townlands.

At first sight the Books of Survey and Distribution seem to be full of details concerning land use as Strafford's surveyors saw it in 1636–37. Closer investigation reveals serious deficiences. For a number of baronies neither land use nor numbers are entered, the maps to which the plot numbers refer have been lost, and acreages of mountain and bog must have been only very roughly estimated. The most serious limitation, however, is the result of the estimation of arable and good pasture together, rendering it impossible to determine how important and how widespread cultivation was. John Browne, whilst Sheriff of Mayo, wrote to Walsingham in 1585[6] that little corn was grown in the west of the county where the people lived mainly on the milk of their livestock; but in the east plenty was grown— even of a part of Kilmaine barony, recently waste, he said, "the ploughs dig in every part". Sir Philip Sidney commented in 1572 that the Earl of Clanrickard's land was well tilled, and O'Shaughnessy was reputed to have had fourteen score reapers working on his demesne at harvest time about the middle of the sixteenth century.[7] Some land seems to have been tilled wherever the phrase "arable" was used in the surveys, and we can conclude that there was some tillage in each township though not in every constituent quarter. In a particularly barren area of west Galway the entry is "Som Arrable digged with Spades". Although writing in 1684, O'Flaherty says of the same area, it is "so craggy and full of stones, and so destitute of deep mold, that in very few spots of it a plow can goe; yet the tenants, by digging, manure it so well, that they have corn for themselves, their landlords, and the market".[8] Oats were commonly used to supplement winter pasturage, and oatmeal foods were in everyday use for human consumption, especially during the winter months, whilst barley and wheat were also grown on the better lands. The surveyors' purpose, however, was to distinguish and measure profitable land irrespective of its use.

Woodland was surveyed separately because of its potential profitability, but even this could not always be clearly delimited on the ground. There was a grading from oak woods, through hazel woods, to heathy ground with some shrubs, all used as pasturage. In the west the acreages involved were small, but to the east, in Sligo, Roscommon and Leitrim, woodland was more widespread. The survey of Sligo distinguished between "firewood" and "tymberwood", a distinction of greater interest to would-be landowners than to those

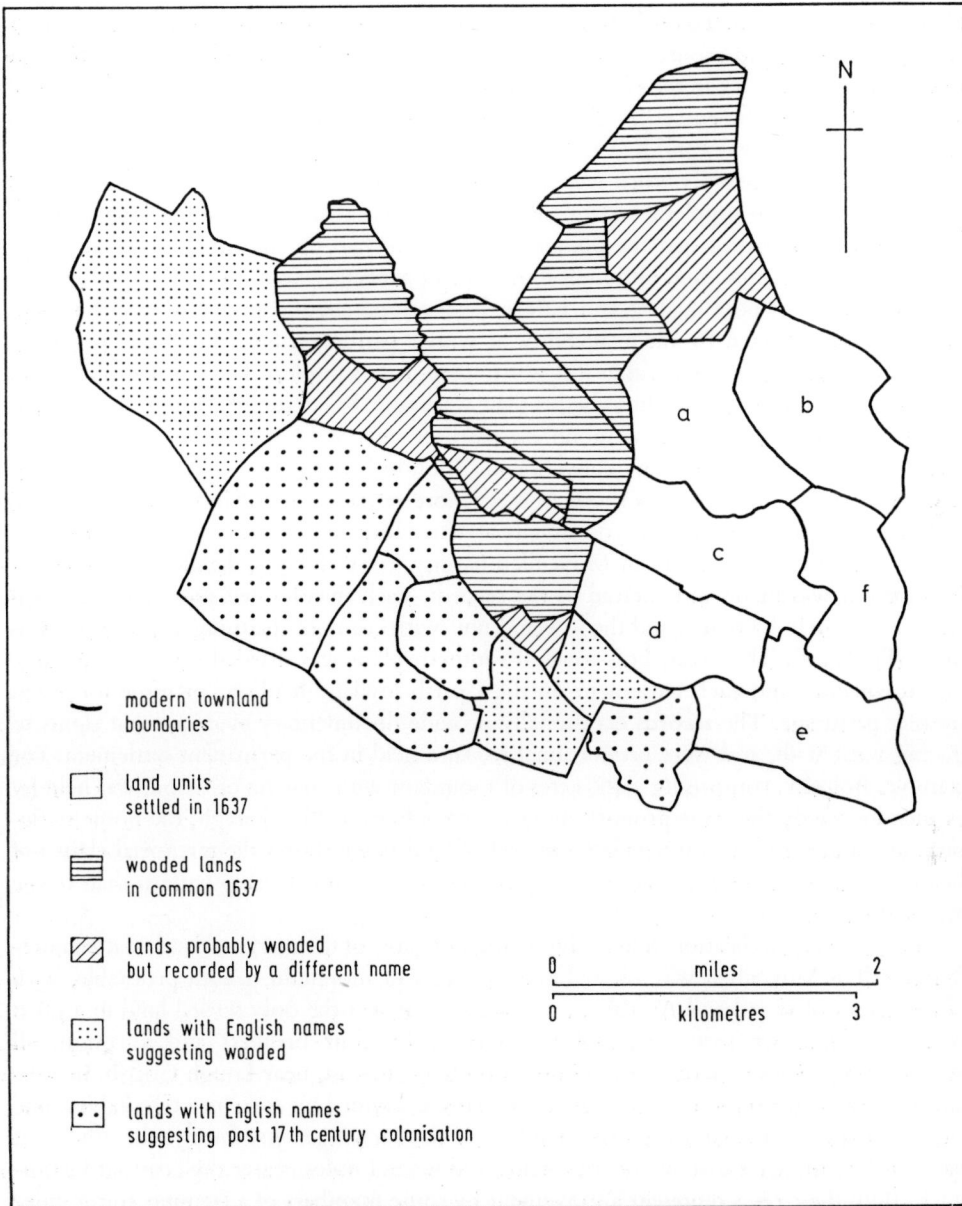

Fig. 12.1   Part of Killian parish, Killian barony, co. Galway, showing woodland land units common
to adjacent settled lands in 1637, and outer ring of later English place-names.
a—Lissarogy 1/2 qr; b—Cregganegrogy 1/2 qr; c—Ballynecorra 1 qr; d—Carrowroe 1 qr;
e—Lissegellevane 1 c; f—Blenegousse 1/2 qr.

who occupied the land. To the latter, woodland offered a supplementary source of pasturage for cattle and pigs, and a source of fuel, and as such it was divided and used by the settlements adjacent to it (Fig. 12.1). In the same way small bogs useful as summer pasture were common to nearby lands, as the entry "A Bogg in Comon between Clunibirne, Lisnarigh, Ballinboher, Tonlagee, Boyana and Killerna which doe claime their severall parts, containing 250 acres"[9] indicates. Where livestock were an important element in farming, all marginal land represented potential supplementary pasture and had been claimed by some township.

It was in this respect that the poorer western areas had the advantage over the more fertile eastern lowlands. But, although thousands of acres in extent, the rough pasture was seasonal and of very poor quality, and, before the development of commercial stock farming, its usage was restricted by the availability of winter pasturage. Such mountain pasturage frequently appears in the records as if it was unused, for example, "The Curlews mountain being Course and long heath little better than wast . . . 1885 acres".[10] More often we find references to common usage of mountain pastures such as "Great Mountain pasture in comon to the 4 qrs of Balleshanevohye", and "Mountain in Comon to Ye Severall Lands of Crospatricke". Other entries show an even more restricted use than these suggest, and it becomes obvious that the surveyors usually attached little importance to the careful survey of such unprofitable land. But in Moycullen barony, co. Galway, a detailed assessment of the situation was made and entered in the records. Each uncolonised mountain land was entered separately by name, and the lowland unit with common pasturage rights on it was noted (Fig. 12.2). The great, bog-covered southern plain was divided into named parts, now townlands, and each settlement on the Corrib lowland held one or more for use as summer pasturage. The records occasionally provide documentary evidence that rights to grazing went with, and were proportional to, land held in the permanent settlement. For example, Bolosky, comprising 2,460 acres of mountain with 29 acres of wood, was held by six men in exactly the same proportions as their holdings in Myaskeragh, the home settlement nine miles away.[11] So detailed a record of land usage shows the territorial claims of the occupying farmers were more closely related to the old township pattern than to the estates of landowners.

In 1637 there is indication of new colonisation of some of the marginal lands. Littermore-O-Donnell in Moycullen was assessed as 2,840 acres of mountain, 1/20th profitable, with "Two peeces of wood and Arrable . . . 17 acres".[12] It was the only settled land in a great expanse of summer pasturage, and was farmed by four brothers and a cousin, all McDonnoghs, whose relatives owned lands to the north-east, near Lough Corrib. In Ross parish, Galway, the mountain land called Brenan was divided by 1619 into two halves: one half was owned and occupied by six members of the McKiggan Joy family, the other half was still the summer pasturage of Joys who lived several miles nearer the coast, at Cloghbrack. Both these cases represent a movement by some members of a farming community to colonise a part of their mountain pastures. Other references in the records point to a recent extension of settlement into marginal lands—"pasturable woods with some spotts of Arable", "very Rocky pasture with Som Arrable digged with Spades" and "Course heathy Mountain with about 3 or 4 acres of Arrable diged". Opportunities for colonisation

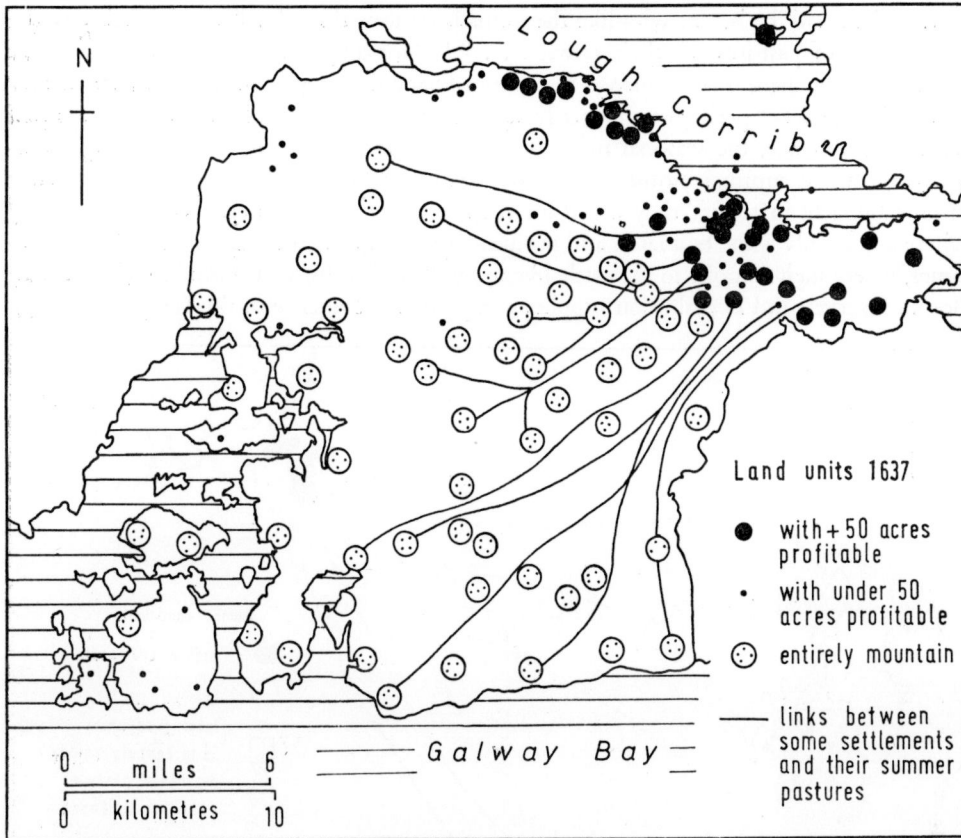

Fig. 12.2   The territory of Gnó Mór, Moycullen barony, co. Galway, showing settled lands and their mountain pastures in 1637.

by assarting obviously varied, but they were present even in the fertile lands of the east. Connacht was fully, but not densely, settled in the seventeenth century. Each township still contained marginal lands—wood, heath and mountain valley—capable of more intensive use. The period between the Elizabethan wars and the Confederate war was a time of slow expansion on to the more attractive of these.

Many contemporary writers noted the amount of milk products ("whitemeates") consumed by the ordinary Irish people. Dairy cattle had a vital role in the farming of Connacht, as in much of Ireland at this time. Occasionally contemporary accounts supply details of pastoral practices, but some have confused interpretation such as Spenser's "I will then begine to Counte there Customes . . . of the which there is one use amongst them to kepe theire Cattell and to lyve them selves the moste parte of the yeare in Bollies, pasturing upon the mountaine and waste wilde places, and removinge still to freshe land as they have depastured the former dayes, . . . "[13], and Fynes Moryson— "I trust no man expects among these gallants any beds, . . . who like the nomads remove their dwellings according to the commodity of pastures for their cows, . . . ".[14] Nomadic peoples have no permanent settlement, but there is no evidence that the ordinary farming population of Ireland ever lacked them, except perhaps temporarily as a result of war. Nomadism has been confused with transhumance, the seasonal movement of livestock from permanent farming settlements to distant summer pastures. Roderick O'Flaherty accurately described the practice in Iar-Connacht in 1684: "they dwell for the most part next the borders of the countrey where commonly is the best land, and in summer time they drive their cattle to the mountaines, where such as looke to the cattle live in small cabbins for that season".[15] The Galway Book of Survey and Distribution supplies corroborative evidence of this (Figs. 12.2, 12.3).

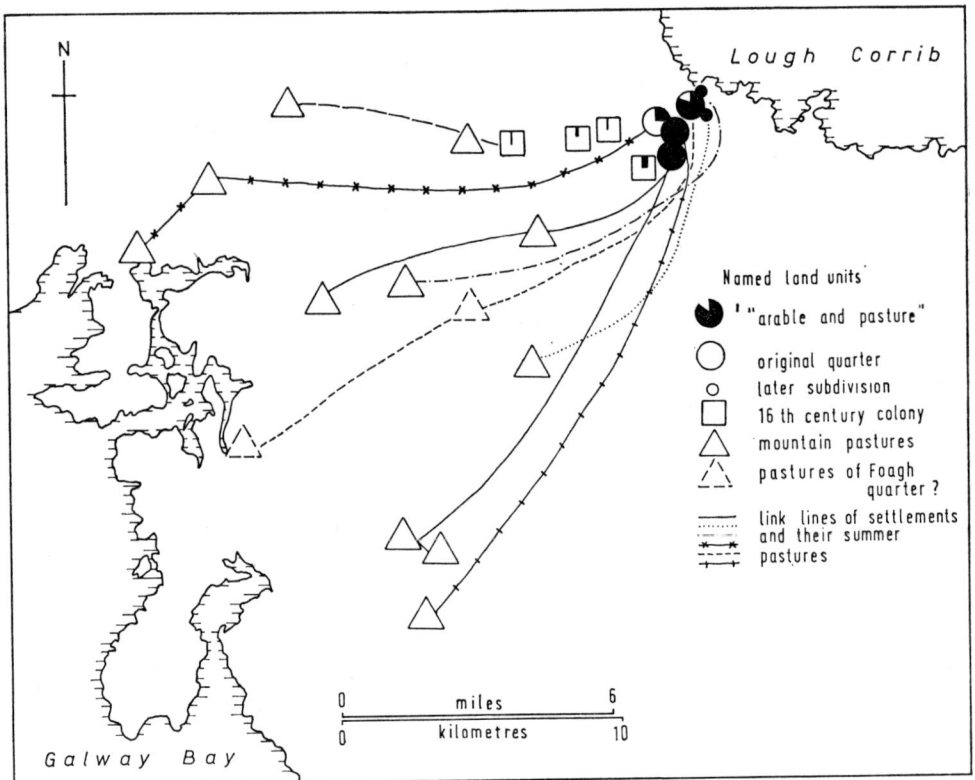

Fig. 12.3 Diagram of Foagh township, Moycullen barony, co. Galway, 1637, showing permanent settlements, recent colonies on marginal land and summer pasture lands.

The same records show, with less detail, that a similar arrangement existed wherever there was an excess of rough pasturage. Details of the Irish form of transhumance, in Irish "buailteachas", anglicized to booleying, can be gained from Achill Island and other remote areas in which the practice continued, and from the descriptions of later travellers.[16]

Temporary huts were erected or repaired annually at the *buaile* or milking place on the summer pastures. The dairy cattle from a farming settlement were taken there traditionally on 1st May, were looked after during the summer by girls from the farms, and were returned at the end of October when the harvest was in. Goats, sheep and dry cattle were also moved to summer pastures but, unless reared for milking, these were not in the charge of the dairy maids. Under certain conditions such a form of pastoralism was necessary. Dairy cattle cannot be moved over long distances each day. Thus, where summer pastures were several miles distant from the home farms, it was not practicable for the cattle to move, nor for the dairy maids to travel daily. In such cases booleying developed. But where summer pasturage was not distant, the dairy cows could be herded and milked without the need for transhumance. This must have been the situation in many fertile districts of central and eastern Connacht even before the seventeenth century.

Removal of livestock from the vicinity of the tilled land during the cropping season was necessary because of the unenclosed nature of the cultivated ground. "And, because their fields be open and unclosed, one neighbour encroacheth upon the other's metes and bounds, and likewise endanger one another by their cattle" could be said in 1623.[17] The same writer could also say "Where wood is plentiful they hedge in all their corn with stakes and bushes and pull them down in winter and burn them, and the next year make up new hedges with bushes and the like". Such temporary fences were never proof against livestock however, which would also require herding to be kept out of the corn field. Enclosure was uncommon enough to be remarked upon in the seventeenth century. In Sligo, for example, William Browne of Kilvarnet had, before the rebellion, "great store of inclosures there lately made by him quicksetted".[18] There is so little information about tillage that it is difficult to decide whether references are always to land cultivated in common, or sometimes to the tilled ground of farms held in severalty. But Dominick ffrench, when he purchased half a cartron of land in Ballykinknava township, gained with it a "moiety of the garden-plot called Garrydahie, parcel of the field"[19], which must be a reference to a small common field. The right to a share in common pasturage is an indication of some communal farming. The fact that it was proportional to farmed land does not necessarily mean that cultivation itself was in common. Communal usage of rough pasture, woodland and bog is not incompatible with dispersed farms within the community, particularly where livestock rearing is the dominant element in agriculture. Other evidence would suggest that small common fields and separate tilled plots, defined by balks or banks, and sometimes with temporary fences, existed side by side in the seventeenth century.

Stinting of common lowland pasture was probably universal. This provided winter pasturage which, in Connacht, was more restricted in extent than summer pasturage, and thus required limitation of the stock using it. The stint in Ireland was always based on a full-grown cow, which was one unit, a *collop* (Irish, *colpa*) or, in parts of Sligo and Mayo with Ulster influence, a *sum(m)* (Scottish, *soum*). The collop represented the amount of grass a fullgrown beast would require during a season. In the nineteenth century in western Mayo, mountain pasturages were always assessed in terms of their summ capacity, and in Sligo in the 1635-36 survey all land units were given a rating of the number of cows they would graze. The term *"cow's grass"* as a measure of land was still in common use in the last century. A scale of equivalents for other livestock was another feature of later stinting which it seems certain must always have existed. One scale was 1 collop=1 full-grown cow =3 year-old stirks=8 sheep=8 goats=20 geese, but local variations existed later and probably had always done so.

The mode of settlement in Connacht was of no more interest to Strafford's surveyors than was agriculture. In the Patent Rolls, however, mention is sometimes made of groups of cottages. On the lands granted to the Earl of Clanrickard in the manor of Castletowne there were 40 cottages in eight different places, and the lands attached to his manor of Loughrea lay in various towns "and other hamlets". Both the words "town" and "hamlet" in these records are ambiguous, sometimes being used for a small grouped settlement, sometimes being used in the sense of "township". Thus the "Town of Bealaleege" contained "a thatched castle and six cottages with small gardens", whilst Walter Bourke was granted "The manor, castle, town and lands of Mohine, with the hamlets of Lecarrow and Lismohine, containing 1 quarter". Luke Gernon writing in 1620 of nearby Limerick, said "In every village is a castle, and a church, but both in ruyne. The baser cottages are built of underwood, called wattle, and covered some w͡th thatch and some w͡th green sedge, of a round forme and w͡thout chimneys, and to my imaginac͡on resemble so many hives of bees, about a country farme".[20] There are references in the Tipperary Civil Survey to thatched houses as distinct from such cabins, and in the Strafford surveys to stone houses as distinct from castles with bawns. The scattered comments that do occur suggest that clustered near the castle or stone house of a substantial landowner was a hamlet of cabins, beyond which were cultivated plots in a small open field. But they also indicate hamlets of tenants' cottages on rented lands, small hamlets of kinsmen on joint farms, and a scattering of dispersed, thatched farm houses, the dwellings of prosperous freeholders. The pardons granted to Irishmen in Connacht by James I mention gentlemen, yeomen, husbandmen and labourers, but it seems more likely that these categories were defined in terms of locally accepted social status rather than in the more concrete terms of ownership, agricultural practice and settlement. By 1672 Sir William Petty could write "6 of 8 of all the Irish live in a brutish nasty Condition, as in Cabins, with neither Chimney, Door, Stairs nor Window . . . ".[21]

The purpose of the seventeenth-century surveys, which was to assess the land of Connacht for confiscation prior to a plantation, led to an emphasis on the record of ownership. But by that time the majority of the rural population were tenants. Under the Composition of Connacht in 1585[22] the more important Irish and Old English lords surrendered their lands and received them back as grants from the Crown. In doing so they frequently acquired as personal demesnes family lands to which they were not entitled under Gaelic law. Nevertheless it is clear that at this time a large part of Connacht was owned by freeholders in small estates. In the Patent Rolls there are still long lists of freeholders, owning a few named lands each or holding shares in one or two lands, and recognising themselves socially as "gentlemen" or as "yeomen". The trend towards the concentration of land ownership in the hands of a comparatively few individuals which began after 1585, rapidly accelerated after 1620. The main causes were economic, but the confiscation of all estates under 60 acres in the plantation of co. Leitrim abruptly completed the change there. Morogh O'Flaherty of Ballynahinch barony, head of the main family in that district of Galway, was, as early as 1590, advancing mortgages and buying up the lands of many of the small proprietors[23], and in 1618 legally acquired the lands of some of his yeoman farmers.[24] Before he died he owned most of the barony.[25] In 1619 Kilvegonta half quarter, estimated in 1637 to be 42 acres of arable and pasture, was owned and occupied by eleven male members of the O'Dunena family. They owned no other land, though they must also have had common grazing, so that Kilvegonta must have supported them and their families as a joint farm. In 1637 it was owned by a local Irish landowner William Shawnussy. Yet there can be no doubt that the O'Dunena family still farmed it, in the same way as before, but as tenants. From 1585 on the Irish lords, great and small, were building up personal estates on the English pattern. They were joined by wealthy merchants and by newcomers to Connacht, Irish and English, looking for property to buy and incomes to be gained from investment in land.

Any evidence of land still owned by freeholders is of much greater interest in a study of rural society. For some of these men inhabited and farmed the estates they owned and, in the absence of information about tenants, provide the only available details concerning occupation of the land. Most owned individual farms, named subdivisions of a land unit within their family lands, and shared common pasturage. The five cartrons of Crannagh (now a townland of 407 statute acres) for example, each separately named and equally assessed by the surveyors as 28 profitable and 5 unprofitable acres, were owned by five men, four of them O'Heynes.[26] Some individuals owned two to four pieces of land, usually within one township, whilst others owned fractional shares in several scattered lands. In such cases the lands may have been pasturage, easily used by the owner or owners although separated from the home farm or farms. In other cases they included tillage, and may have been let to a tenant or tenants, the rent then going to the single owner or being shared by the several owners. Very few of this class of proprietor owned more than this, and those who did were the heads of families, and thus intermediate between the freeholders generally and the larger land-owners. There remain a few instances in the 1636–37 records of joint ownership, where a number of kinsmen held fractional shares, not always equal, in one or two small pieces of land. These represented estates too small to be subdivided into separate farms, and were usually in the poorer lands and in lands where assarting was difficult. Much more common in Galway and Mayo than in Sligo and Roscommon, they were to be found among families both of Irish descent and of Anglo-Norman origin. A typical example was the sharing by five O'Connors of the ¼ cartron of Carrowconougher, one having 5 acres, the others 3 acres each.[27] The greater number of jointly owned small estates in 1619 than in 1637 is an indication of the rate of depression of this group of poor farmer-owners into tenancy. A similar change must have affected other freeholders at earlier periods in history, especially as a result of the territorial conquests both of Irish lords and of Anglo-Norman barons. They remained as the occupiers of the land, they continued to farm it according to their old agricultural methods, and they formed the bulk of the population.

That ownership of estates should have become fragmented, and small estates become

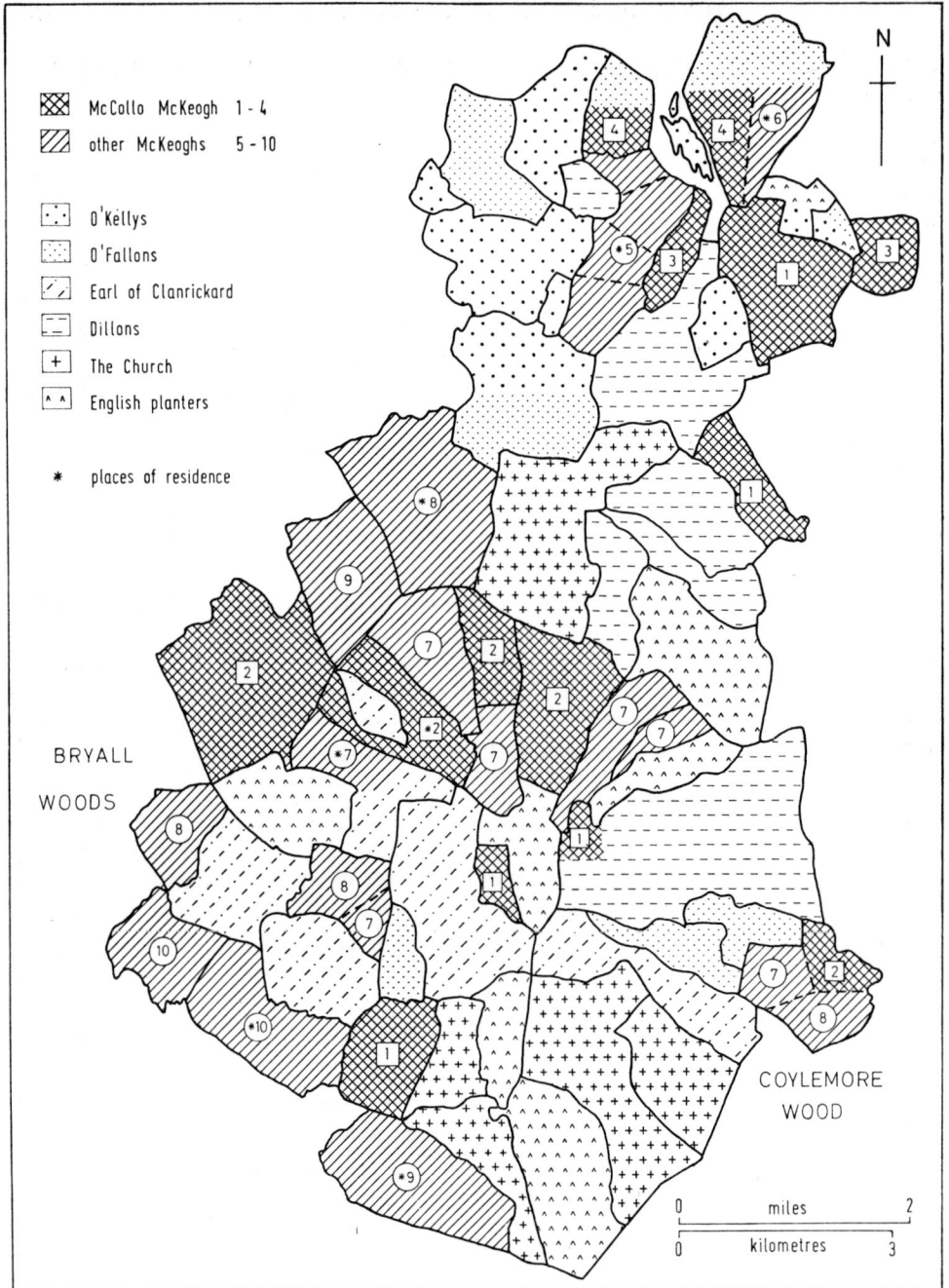

Fig. 12.4 Map of a part of Athlone barony, co. Roscommon, showing the landowners 1636–7. The modern townlands in each case correspond in name to a seventeenth century land unit. Where subdivisions existed which cannot be traced, the ownership shading is not intended to indicate the exact location of the estate. McKeoghs: 1—Edmond mc Collo, 2—Donogh mc Collo, 3—Rory mc Collo, 4—William mc Collo, 5—Teige mc Redmond, 6—Donell mc Don, 7—William mc Laughlin, 8—Donogh mc Connor, 9—Teige mc Donogh, 10—Rory mc Teige.

joint farms, was a result of the continued practice of partible inheritance. Among the Irish it was always the law to divide an inheritance equally between sons, thus providing each with land to farm. There is no evidence that families were generally large, or that estates had been excessively subdivided because of large numbers of co-heirs. On large estates division was in terms of whole land units, quarters or cartrons (Fig. 12.4), and even on many relatively small estates the lands of any individual were separate and named localities. The acceptance of feudal tenure and primogeniture by the Connacht lords did not affect the freeholders, and even after gavelkind (as it was called by the English, after a similar custom in Kent) had been officially abolished by law early in the seventeenth century, it continued in practice. The wealthy could buy up land to provide new estates for their younger sons, but the ordinary farming freeholder continued to provide farms for his sons by subdivision of his own land. It is clear that in areas where all waste land was improvable and pasture land was greatly in excess of tilled ground, it had always been possible to expand the farmed land to meet the needs of increased population, by incorporating small areas of waste ground and converting it into improved land. Within the family lands of a kinship group this must have been possible by agreement, and with mutual benefit, in that the land of any individual who died without direct heirs was re-inherited by less closely related members of the family group. In tenant communities it must have been equally possible by agreement with the lord.

Among Irish freeholders it had been the practice in the early sixteenth century to regard the land as owned by the kinship group, with individuals having continued use of separate pieces, while leaving the family as a whole the right to re-inherit under certain conditions, and to prevent family land from being alienated. There are many indications that during the century such family rights were decreasing and that individuals were gaining sole possession and control over their inherited share. This did not affect the continuation of gavelkind inheritance, and in some cases it led to a new cycle of fractionalisation on small estates and to the re-development of joint-farms. A number of instances of co-heirs jointly owning one or two small pieces of land, holding equal or unequal fraction shares in them, which appear in the 1636–37 records, can be traced back to a single holding one, two or three generations earlier (Fig. 12.5). The newly developing trends to individual ownership within family lands (including the pastures) and to the sale of land (again including pasture land) to outside interests, prevented assarting as a means of bringing such farms back to an economic level. Their owners frequently relinquished their title to the land under the economic pressures of the period. As tenants, they had to continue to divide the land they farmed between their sons, in order to provide each with a means of livelihood. In doing so, they added to the number of joint-tenancies with cultivation in a rundale open field, and stinted shares in a common pasturage.[28]

One feature of partible inheritance among more substantial freeholders which persisted longer than any other, was the joint ownership of the family castle and the land which supported it. Maintenance of a share in it represented the right to partake in kinship affairs, including inheritance. But it was an anachronism in the 1630s and, although often noted in the Strafford Inquisition of Mayo, the tendency to allot shares in terms of specific rooms,

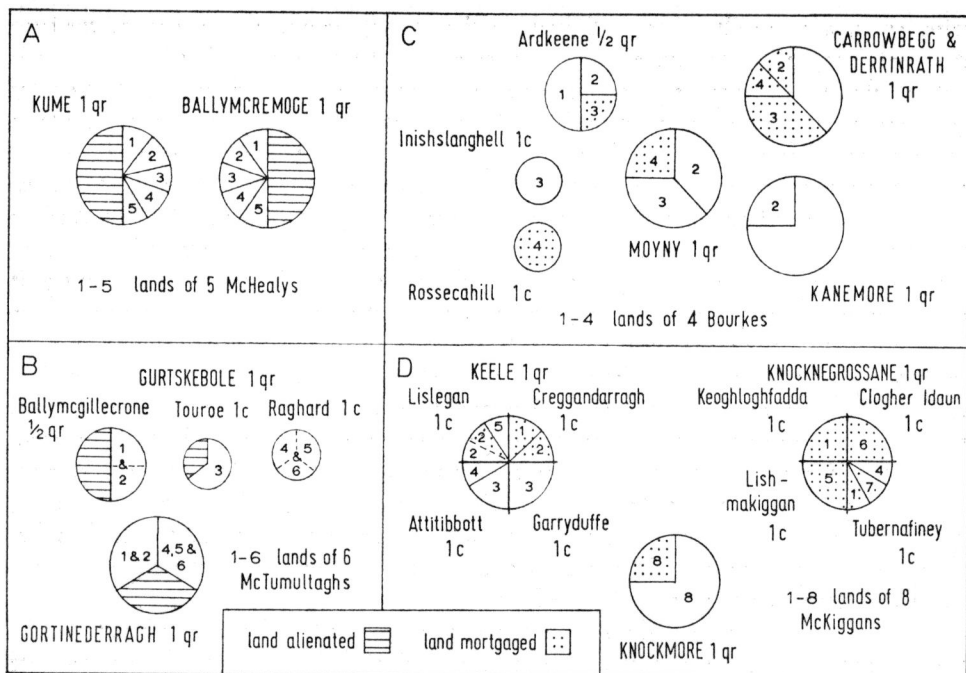

Fig. 12.5 Diagrams showing renewed partible inheritance and mortgaging and sale of family lands on small estates in co. Mayo, 1635–7. A—McHealy lands, Tirawley barony; B—McTumultagh lands, Tirawley barony; C—The lands of 4 Bourkes, Burrishoole barony; D—McKiggan lands, Carra barony

and to sell and mortgage them, indicates the decline in the significance of such rights. Of the six shares in the McDonnell castle, bawn and town of Aghlehard, Stephen Lynch, a Galway merchant, had, by 1635, bought two and held mortgages on three. In 1629 Ogh and Nehemias McBrehowne sold "¼ part of the castle of Lecarrow, together with all the houses, rooms, garden-plots and parks, and a share of the commons of the town and lands of Lecarrow". Richard oge Bourck of Moyly in 1635 mortgaged "the middle room of the castle of Moyly, with a share of the seller, bawn and barbican thereof".[29]

Various economic pressures were encouraging the breakdown of traditional Irish society at this time. Towards the close of Elizabeth's reign the Irish coinage was debased, and for some decades afterwards there was a shortage of money and a distrust of the new coinage. Prices and rents rose sharply. By the sixteenth century the change to a cash economy had made considerable headway. In 1585 the services and dues exacted by the Irish lords from their freeholders were officially commuted to an annual cash payment. But even before that time rents from tenants on the estates of both Irish and Old English lords were paid partly or wholly in money. In 1584 Roger O'Flaherty of Moycullen claimed that he had lost, over a period of ten years, rents from his estates and property from his demesne valued at £2,947 and 400 cows.[30] Of the 37 quarters of land in the estate of Farrell O'Gara in Coolavin barony in Sligo in 1635, he kept one as his demesne and let the others to tenants for an annual income of £397.[31] Yet there were still many instances of produce and services being involved in both the rents from tenants and in the chiefries paid by freeholders. In co. Sligo, for example, Lecarowmoneygalta ½ quarter was 'set' to tenants for 2 fatt muttons, 4 meddars of butter, 8 meddars of meale, 10 workmen (i.e. 10 days work), and 10 horses a night (i.e. 10 horses to be stabled for one night).[32] In Mayo, among the chief rents due to Viscount Bourck was "a chiefrie of £3, a beef, 40 quarts of butter, a basin of meale and a basin of malt" annually from the ½ quarter of Keillkish.[33]

Shortage of money, rising costs, increased individual ownership of land with sole right of disposal, and new restrictions on assarting, combined to initiate widespread development of mortgage and sale amongst those most vulnerable to economic pressures, the freeholders. Those with several lands mortgaged or sold all but one farm (Fig. 12.5), those with fractional shares raised money on these. Whole townships passed from freeholding families to investors, sometimes acquired piecemeal over several years. Dominick ffrench, between 1627 and 1632, purchased the lands of Ballykinknava township in this way from eleven owners.[34] In other cases individual cartrons, or even fractional shares in cartrons, passed into the hands of the new landowners. By 1635 sixteen out of twenty-five O'Malys, whose hereditary territory was in Murrisk barony, Mayo, had mortgaged some of their land. In 1629 seven members of the McBrehowne family held land in each of the three quarters comprising Ballinambrehowne. Before 1635 three had mortgaged land and four had sold some; eight outsiders then had an interest in the family lands. This change in the ownership of farms and small estates was not entirely from freeholder to investor. There was also rearrangement of holdings within the community, some increasing their land and consolidating their farms, others becoming labourers. Edmond O'Cloghussy built up a farm for himself by advancing mortgages to two persons in 1622 and 1623 totalling £42 18. 4., 12 cows and 2 milch cows. John, Tibbott, William and Richard McGibbon, who jointly owned one and a half of the two cartrons of Clondacon, advanced mortgages for the remaining half cartron to John and Tibbott McPhilbin in 1620 and 1627 respectively.[35] Had the drastic changes in ownership, made after the rebellion, not taken place, this trend would have resulted in a class of prosperous small farmer-owners in Connacht. In the event these farmers also became tenants. The payments involved in most of these transactions were in pounds sterling, and the amounts paid depended on the quality of the land, and probably on the individuals involved. But among farmers stock were also sometimes used, in particular cattle of specified type—milch cows, barren cows, beef cows, and two-year-old cows.

Most of the new landowners were buying up the land as a source of income, derived from the rents of tenants. Many of them let the lands to their former owners, who in a few years had paid in rents more than they had received in purchase price or mortgage. In addition they were now exposed to increases in rent. Among the larger landowners, both Irish and English, the practice of leasing land to a middleman, who in turn sub-let to tenants—at a profit—had begun before 1635.[36] Another new trend in agriculture, the leasing of pasturages to stock farmers for commercial sheep or cattle farming had also made its appearance.[37] Although there is no evidence that, at this time, tenants were displaced to allow this development, there can be no doubt that it meant a serious curtailment of the pasture grounds available to them. The agricultural economy of the tenantry depended on the use of common pasturage which they rented from the landlord with their farms. But the number of animals kept by tenants certainly declined as a result of their decreased prosperity, so that their need for extensive pasturages would not be as great. The interest of the new landlords in the woodland for commercial timber equally restricted pasturage in those areas of Connacht which were still well wooded. The economy of Connacht was assuming a new appearance; trends which persisted until the nineteenth century had already become established.

The period 1600–1640 was thus one of transition for rural society in Connacht. The people remained, but conditions affecting them underwent irreversible changes. The majority were farmers, either freeholders or tenants, and during this period many of the former sold or mortgaged their land and joined the tenantry. The land confiscations after the 1641–52 war completed this change. Thereafter there were two main groups in rural society: the large landowners, increasingly English or Anglo-Irish and Protestant, and the tenantry. The gap between them widened continuously. The new trends established before 1635 towards commercial stock farming, exploitation of the land resources, and absenteeism on the part of the landlords, with middlemen and bailiffs controlling their estates, became increasingly more important after 1652. The majority of the population, whether tenants of long standing or of recent conversion, continued to farm the land under more difficult economic conditions. Agriculture among these people underwent no great changes until the potato became increasingly important as a subsistence crop for the poorest farmers. Some rented individual farms, others held joint tenancies. Continued subdivision of rented land, to accommodate increases in population, in some cases caused single holdings to be converted into joint tenancies. In others it eventually resulted in the large hamlets and the complicated morcellation of open field in rundale which, in the poorer parts of Connacht, was a marked feature of the nineteenth century. The increased pressure of population during the succeeding centuries also caused expansion into marginal lands, and the colonisation, in hamlets and dispersed farms, of lands which had once been summer pasturages. The tenants continued to practice mixed farming, less dominated by livestock now. In the mountainous west many joint-tenancies included both a lowland townland and a mountain townland, and, in a few places, the people continued to practice transhumance in spite of reduced livestock numbers and reduced pasturages. It was amongst this farming population that traces of pre-seventeenth century Gaelic institutions and customs survived. For these were the people who had inherited and inhabited Connacht for many centuries, the people who represented continuity in rural society.

REFERENCES

1 *Books of Survey and Distribution,* (B.S.D.). (MSS. 20 vols. in P.R.O.I., Dublin) Published for some counties by Irish MSS. Comm.
R. C. Simington, ed., Vol. I (1949), *Co. Roscommon*
R. C. Simington, ed., Vol. 2 (1956), *Co. Mayo*
B. Mac Giolla Choille, ed., Vol. 3 (1962), *Co. Galway*
Sligo Survey, Harleian MSS. 2048, (microfilm, Nat. Lib. Ireland)
2 W. O'Sullivan, ed., *The Strafford Inquisition of County Mayo,* (Irish MSS. Comm., 1958)
Cal. Pat. Rolls Ireland
Chancery and Exchequer Inquisitions, (P.R.O.I., Dublin. MSS. RC 4/14, 9/14; R.I.A., MSS. 14 D/4–7)
3 G. A. Hayes-McCoy, Gaelic society in Ireland in the late sixteenth century, *Historical Studies,* 4 (1963), 45–61
4 All measurements in the records were in Irish or 'Plantation' measure of 21 feet to a pole, instead of the English 16½ feet. All areas were also underestimated.
5 *Mayo, B.S.D.,* 188
6 M. J. Blake, A map of part of the county of Mayo in 1584, *J. Galway Arch. Hist. Soc.,* 5 (1907–8), 146
7 *Cal. Pat. Rolls Ireland,* 13 Jas. 1, 301
8 Roderic O'Flaherty, *A chorographical description of West or H-Iar Connaught,* (1684) ed. James Hardiman (1846), 56
9 *Rosc. B.S.D.,* 34
10 ibid., 141
11 *Galway B.S.D.,* 58 and 62
12 ibid., 65
13 Edmund Spenser, *A view of the present state of Ireland* (1596), ed. W. L. Renwick (1934), 64
14 Fynes Moryson, The description of Ireland, in C. L. Falkiner, *Illustrations of Irish history and topography,* (1904), Pt. 2, 1 A, 231
15 Roderic O'Flaherty, op. cit., 16
16 J. M. Graham, Transhumance in Ireland, *Adv. Science,* 37 (1953) 74–9
17 Sir Henry Bourgchier, *Advertisements for Ireland,* (1623), ed. G. O'Brien, R.S.A.I., extra vol. (1923), 33
18 W. G. Wood-Martin, *History of Sligo,* (1889), Vol. 2, App. B., 199
19 *The Strafford Inquisition of County Mayo,* op. cit., 107
20 Luke Gernon, A discourse of Ireland, (1620), in C. L. Falkiner, op. cit., Pt. 2, 3, 355
21 Sir William Petty, The political anatomy of Ireland, (1672), in C. H. Hull, *The economic writings of Sir William Petty,* (1899), 1, 156
22 A. M. Freeman, ed., *The Compossicion Booke of Conought,* (Irish MSS. Comm., 1936)
23 R.I.A., MSS. 4 A. 34
24 *Cal. Pat. Rolls. Ireland,* 15 Jas. 1, 349
25 Chancery Inquis. 1626 (Copy, P.R.O.I., Dublin, MS. RC 5/29)
26 *Galway B.S.D.,* 250–1
27 ibid., 231
28 D. McCourt, The rundale system in Donegal, *J. Donegal Hist. Soc.,* 3 (1954), 47–60
29 *The Strafford Inquisition of County Mayo,* op. cit., 109 and 62
30 J. Hardiman, (1846), op. cit., App. 387–9
31 W. G. Wood-Martin, op. cit., Vol. 1, App. D., 402–5
32 ibid., Vol. 2, App. A., 141–2
33 *The Strafford Inquisition of County Mayo,* op. cit., 40
34 ibid., 106–8

35 ibid., 7 and 11
36 W. G. Wood-Martin, op. cit., Vol. 2, App. A, 179–80
37 ibid., 183

XIII

THE ORIGIN OF ENCLOSURES IN EASTERN IRELAND

F. H. A. Aalen

In northern and western Ireland, where the decline of rundale organisation in the late eighteenth and nineteenth centuries has been actively studied, the nature and recency of enclosure is relatively well-known. There has, however, been little investigation of the origin of enclosures in eastern Ireland, most writers regarding them as of lengthy but unspecified age.[1] It is the primary aim of this essay to show that the eastern enclosure pattern, although older on the whole than that of the west, is nevertheless of comparatively recent origin, and to illustrate some of the main processes involved in its formation. The documentary evidence does not always permit definitive generalisations, but taken as a whole it strongly suggests that the main part of the enclosure pattern originated in the eighteenth century. Enclosure had however been occurring piecemeal from the late-medieval period, and the late-seventeenth century probably saw some quickening of the process before the unprecedented rate of spread in the eighteenth century.

The term 'enclosures' presents considerable problems of definition and has been used in a variety of senses. It is here taken to mean the division of farmed land into small units or fields, surrounded by substantial boundaries, continuous and permanent. The main purpose of enclosures is to check the movement of livestock. Enclosed farmland was distinct from open-field systems where the intermixed holdings were defined only by 'balks' or 'mearings', which seem to have taken the form of either unploughed strips, low mounds, or stones placed at intervals. The boundaries of enclosed fields can be constructed in many ways. In Ireland they are commonly made by piling up stones and sods to form a bank. (These banks are called 'ditches' by the Irish countryman, but this is a confusing usage and in this essay the Irish 'ditch' is called a bank and the term ditch is used in the English sense to describe a sunken feature and not a raised one.) Where hedges exist they are usually grown on top of the banks. Field boundaries themselves are often referred to as enclosures and this additional usage seems acceptable and useful.

Eastern Ireland is here taken to mean the province of Leinster, with special reference to the contiguous counties of Louth, Meath, Westmeath, Dublin, Kildare, Offaly, Laois and Wicklow, in the north of the province. With the main exception of co. Wicklow this northern area is low lying and physically well endowed, the rateable valuation of the land is higher than elsewhere in Ireland, the farms larger and the rural population density low. A distinguishing feature of the rural landscape is the predominance of large regular shaped fields ('vastes enclos reguliers')[2] averaging perhaps 3.25–4 ha (8–10 acres), which is large by Irish standards. Also, in this area the impress of medieval feudal organisation on the landscape is more discernible than in any other part of Ireland, although the major elements of the rural scene are residual from the time when the estate-system reached its peak in the eighteenth and early-nineteenth centuries.

Over wide areas of eastern Ireland the enclosure pattern must be of relatively recent establishment because the land has only been reclaimed from moor, bog and forest since the late-seventeenth and early-eighteenth centuries. For example, large portions of Laois and Offaly, counties which today are almost completely reclaimed and enclosed in medium and large-sized fields, were still well-wooded at the time of their Plantation in the late-sixteenth century. These woods are shown on a contemporary map[3], and in a survey by Walter Cowley[4] (the King's Surveyor), which preceded the Plantation in these parts, they are referred to as "great woods" shared in common by several communities. Cowley's survey makes no reference to enclosures; "mearys and boundes" are usually formed by streams, roads, lanes, ditches or woods. Until the closing decades of the seventeenth century, most visitors to Ireland, applying standards derived from the English landscape, regarded the country as comparatively well wooded.[5] Of particular relevance to the extent of woodland in eastern Ireland is the following comment written by Gerard Boate[6] in the middle of the seventeenth century:

> Yet notwithstanding the great destruction of the woods in Ireland . . . there are still sundry great woods remaining . . . The County of Wicklow, King's County and Queen's County are throughout full of woods, some whereof are many miles long and broad.

In co. Wicklow the most extensive woods were located in the south-west, in the barony of Shillelagh. Although some remnants of these woods were still surviving in the early-eighteenth century[7], the process of deforestation was then almost complete and the reclaimed land already partially enclosed.[8] It was still being stipulated in eighteenth-century leases granted to tenants in Queen's county (Laois) that several areas of woodland should be cut, burnt and destroyed to clear the land for the plough.[9] Arthur Young, an intrepid and painstaking observer of agricultural developments at first hand in several countries, is a key witness to the importance and extent of enclosure formation in the late-eighteenth century. He emphasises that at this period enclosures were creeping up formerly bare hill-slopes in many places in Ireland, while wasteland and commons were being actively enclosed.[10] At Kilfaine in co. Kilkenny he writes "they are beginning to cultivate the mountains, the inclosures creep up the sides gradually", and in Ravensdale, in north co. Louth, Young was "pleased to see the inclosures creeping high up the sides of the mountains stony as they are". The vast scale and thoroughness of these eighteenth century enclosure projects, which often involved the establishment *ab initio* of the essentials of the present-day field patterns, is illustrated forcibly by Young's account of developments on the estate of Baron Forster at Cullen in co. Meath. Forsters' estate was some 2,000 ha (approximately

5,000 acres) which little over 20 years before had been waste sheep-walk covered with heath, furze and fen. The improvements here were the greatest that even Young had ever seen. The land was wet, and at the outset extensive drainage and liming operations were necessary. He reported that "the whole tract was inclosed in fields of about 10 acres each with ditches 7 feet wide and 6 deep at 1s a perch, the banks planted with quick and forest trees. Of these fences 70,000 perches were done." As part of the improvements roads were also made, new farmhouses built and a colony of French and English protestants settled on the land. The improvements at Cullen were of course outstanding, but there were many others that were impressive and extensive. Young relates that Lord Bective of Headfort, near Kells in co. Meath, had enclosed his land with walling, and some 4,000 ha (approximately 10,000 acres) of bog and rough land in co. Cavan had been drained and improved by the Bective family, and the dry rocky land divided with walls.

Besides the considerable areas, referred to above, where reclamation and enclosure were roughly simultaneous and recent, there are unquestionably portions of the east which have been continuously settled and farmed from the medieval period and earlier. From the late Bronze Age down to the beginning of the medieval period the outstanding settlement form throughout Ireland was the rath or 'ring-fort'. These circular earthworks (which exceed 30,000 in number) are the sites of dispersed farmsteads and some examples suggest their association with limited areas of small squarish fields. This assumption that the raths and the juxtaposed enclosures were contemporary is consistent with the prevailing view of the raths as 'einzelhöfe' from which was practised farming of a mixed (arable-livestock) character.[11] The alleged co-existence with the rath settlements of a primitive form of open-field cultivation, associated with an inferior stratum of rural society, remains an interesting but unproven possibility. The only evidence for fields is in the immediate vicinity of the raths, and there is thus no reason to suppose that extensive areas of landscape were enclosed. Moreover, it is difficult to demonstrate any continuity of these ancient field patterns down to the present day. The famous excavations of O'Riordain at Cush in co. Limerick[12] are of particular importance in discussions of landscape continuity, as they appeared to show that enclosures with low banks of stone and sod, identical with those existing widely in the present landscape, were associated with the raths. But, as Evans has pointed out, this may not be an illustration of absolute continuity but rather "a case of similar needs in different periods producing similar results".[13] The extent of enclosure in the Irish landscape may well have varied considerably from one major historical period to another depending on the changing balance between agricultural and pastoral influences. Thus if, as proposed here, a new system of enclosure was introduced after the medieval openfield systems declined, it could be a case of a lengthy history repeating itself, with the important qualification that the area of land covered by prehistoric enclosures was not remotely comparable with the area covered by enclosures at the present day.

Recent aerial photographs have shown in a number of restricted localities that older field outlines, probably dating from the rath period, underlie the present-day enclosures. In eastern Ireland the most striking examples lie to the south-east of Oldcastle in co. Meath, on the flanks of the Loughcrew hills.[14] In all cases the underlying field pattern is one of small, irregular block fields (on average not exceeding 0.5 ha), while the present day fields are larger in area, more rectangular and even-shaped (Plate XX), and their boundaries cut across the older pattern. There is thus no suggestion of an evolution from one pattern to the other; nor is there any clear indication whether the present-day fields are the immediate successors of the older pattern, or whether the latter had been abandoned for many centuries before the present day pattern was laid down.

Little attention has been paid by geographers to the medieval Irish landscape, probably because of the total lack of terriers and detailed map material from the Middle Ages. However, recent studies by historians of surviving medieval charters and deeds do permit a tentative description of the broad outlines of the rural settlement and economy of the Anglo-Norman colony which was established in Ireland in the late-twelfth century.[15] This colony was largely rural in character and not, as conventionally thought, exclusively urban or aristocratic. Considerable bodies of Welsh, English and Fleming peasantry were settled in southern and eastern Ireland, from co. Kerry to co. Louth, with outposts in the baronies of Lecale and Ards in south-eastern Ulster. Manorial organisation was also introduced.[16] Most important for this discussion, it is now reasonably clear that village settlements with open-fields and large regular strip-holdings, worked sometimes on a two- or three-field system, were of fundamental importance in the rural economy. This being the case, we have no reason to envisage that enclosures were numerous in the medieval period and no additional evidence is available as yet to suggest their existence on any appreciable scale. On most demesnes the land of the manorial lord was a compact unit, quite separate from the lands of other socio-economic groups: this separation may have entailed some form of enclosure but it was probably by sunken ditches. There are, moreover, cases where the lord's land always lay in the open-fields, as at Swords, co. Dublin[17], and Dromiskin, co. Louth[18], and was never separated or consolidated. Although the term 'manor' occurs in old Anglo-Irish documents it does not always imply an estate worked after the medieval village pattern found in lowland England; it is clear that taken as a whole the economic and social structure of eastern Ireland in the medieval period was more comparable to 'Lowland Britain' than to 'Highland Britain'. The common assertion that villages, as distinct from mere clachans, have never been a feature of the Irish landscape is thus misleading.

The native Irish population was in many areas embraced within the manorial framework, and the servile tenants (betaghs) who were present on most manorial estates were, at least in the early phases of Anglo-Norman settlement, almost exclusively Irish. Normally this servile element occupied a separate portion of the manorial land which may have been cultivated on a native open-field system, more fluid, irregular and limited in area than that introduced by the Anglo-Normans. With this native open-field system there was probably associated a nucleated pattern of settlement comprising mere clusters of farmsteads some of which have survived into the present century as clachans. The Anglo-Norman village on the other hand, especially in northern Leinster, might contain tower houses and a medieval church, and sometimes served as a parochial centre. The decline of the Anglo-Norman colony, following an Irish revival at the end of the thirteenth century, must have meant the degeneration if not the disappearance of many villages, and consequently in some regions it is either difficult or impossible at the present day to determine whether the nucleated settlements are of native or medieval colonial provenance. This is especially true in certain areas peripheral to the Pale, such as Wicklow, Westmeath and north Louth, but also in north Kilkenny and the district of Lecale, co. Down.

The manner in which the medieval landscape of arable open-fields and adjacent commons was transformed into the modern landscape of enclosed fields and predominantly scattered farms has been little explored. But enclosure in most parts of Britain was characteristically a continuing process with phases of intensive activity following periods of gradual evolution, and such an interpretation seems consistent with the available evidence for eastern Ireland.

There is evidence that engrossing of strips, and perhaps also the occasional erection of enclosures, had been occurring in places since the late-medieval period, at which time there are frequent references to 'imparking', and to 'crofts' and 'parks' located among the 'acres' and 'stangs' which are the open-field strips.[19] But before the middle part of the seventeenth century there is no suggestion that the process of engrossing was anything other than a piecemeal operation involving the occasional transfer of strips between individual land holders. However, the cumulative results were considerable and where maps can be found which show strip-holdings (none of these are earlier than the mid-seventeenth century) the pattern of holdings is clearly a modified form of the medieval arrangement, comprising a mixture of rectangular, irregular, and long narrow fields representing bundles of strips (Fig. 13.1). In the royal manor of Crumlin, co. Dublin, a deed of 1468[20] shows that some enclosed areas (referred to as 'crofts' and 'parks') already existed among the open-fields, and in the seventeenth century a number of arable strips were parcelled out among Cromwellian planters, presumably to form compact holdings.[21] But a large part of the village lands of Crumlin were still in open-field in the eighteenth century as bills for the consolidation and enclosure of the parish were presented in 1735 and again in 1751 to enable "the several proprietors of the Lands in the Parish of Crumlin . . . to exchange several intermixed lands lying in the said Parish and for dividing and inclosing several parcels of Common thereunto amongst the several proprietors of the land".[22] The correspondence of Robert Molesworth (1656–1725), a noted agricultural improver, gives us further insight into this process of strip engrossing at Philipstown, co. Offaly, and Swords, co. Dublin.[23] His comments show that piecemeal consolidation was continuing in the eighteenth century and the process was, in some cases at least, not wholly legitimate:

"There is nothing which requires more careful inspection than these scattered estates of ours about Swords. Of all our estate it is the place where we have been most wronged. In Phillipston, indeed, they may scrable pieces among them that I may lose my rent, but I can scarce loose any property there, because almost all is my own. But in Swords, where there are many properties, Archbishop's land, my land, Taylor's land, Church, Oeconomy lands, Peppards lands, and some no man's land or concealed lands, there is such stealing, chopping and changing that everyone of us have lost something at last to my cousin Taylor who, by residing in the town, and knowing nicely all the parcels and secrets of these lands, finds a way to make all these stolen and concealed parcels to centre in him, either by taking them in lease himself and then paring and ploughing up the mears . . . "

Fig. 13.1 A Typical field pattern in Eastern Ireland. Rectangular fields defined by hedged banks and ditches. Brannanstown, co. Meath. O.S. Sheet 25.

B Part of the fields of Ballymore-Eustace, co. Kildare, in the mid 17th century (Down Survey). The scattered holdings of three tenants are shown.

C Present day field pattern at Rathcoole, co. Dublin, resulting largely from the enclosing of old open-field strips. There is a noticeable contrast between the narrow fields on the old arable area and the broader fields on the old Commons (Coolmine). O.S. Sheet 21.

D Fields near Drogheda, co. Louth. The ditched boundary of the old town-fields is shown by the pecked line. (From Air Corps aerial photograph 307 V/1608).

(The scale of the drawings made from O.S. maps and aerial photograph is six inches to represent one mile)

The old nucleated settlements, whether of Anglo-Norman or native provenance, with their arable open-fields and commons, remained an important ingredient of the eastern landscape until the late-seventeenth and early-eighteenth centuries. At that period, despite modification and rationalisation of the arable areas by piecemeal engrossing of strips over several preceding centuries, there is plentiful evidence that 'intermixed holdings' or open-field holdings still existed in many parts of eastern Ireland (Fig. 13.2).[24] Indeed a number of exceptional, large villages in north-east Leinster, especially on the great estates of the Archbishops of Dublin (e.g. Tallaght, Rathcoole, Swords) and Armagh (e.g. Dromiskin, Termonfeckin), retained their open-field organisation until the late-eighteenth century and even the nineteenth century. As late as 1825 the medieval strip-fields survived in great number around the villages of Rathcoole, Dalkey and Saggart, although in the case of Rathcoole comparison with a map of 1780 shows that consolidation had been proceeding and the complexity of the strip pattern had been considerably reduced.[25] In these cases it was primarily the conservative institutional framework, characteristic of ecclesiastical estates, which served to retain traditional rural structures. However, analogous survivals occurred in areas of poor physical endowment. Open-field organisation, presumptively of rundale provenance, was long retained in the glens and on the isolated upland fringes of the Wicklow mountains[26]: in Glencullen until the present century, and until the late-nineteenth century on the Hillsborough estates in west Wicklow.[27] Similar late survivals could be found in the remote mountainous peninsula of Cooley in north Louth.[28]

The piecemeal engrossing of strips on old open-field areas does not seem to have given rise to many enclosures. Growth of an extensive pattern of enclosed fields, as previously stated, did not commence until the latter half of the seventeenth century, from which time enclosure schemes were undertaken in a more comprehensive manner, within the framework of estate organisation and government policies. Perhaps the most persuasive evidence for the relative recency of the enclosure pattern in eastern Ireland can be derived from the accounts of travellers, topographers, and agricultural improvers. Henry Wallop wrote in 1585 that "At this present in verie few places of Ireland have they any enclosures".[29] *The Advertisements for Ireland* published in 1623 state: "Their fields lie open and unenclosed. Where wood is plentiful they hedge in all their corn with stakes and bushes and pull them down in the winter and burn them". In 1641 there was a move in the Irish Parliament to draw up a bill "for the mearing and bounding and inclosing of lands".[30] No legislation appears to have followed, but clearly the subject was in the air at the time and there must have been a current need for enclosures. An anonymous writer at the end of the seventeenth century states that "enclosures are very rare amongst them, and those no better than a midwife's toothless gums".[31] A contemporary illustration of the battle of the Boyne (1690) shows a landscape of open arable land without any enclosures.[32] References in the Molyneux papers (c. 1680)[33] suggest that large areas of farmed land were still open or 'champain' country. For example, Sir Henry Piers in his detailed description of co. Westmeath notes the absence of hedges and fences "a defect which we cannot hope in our days to find how to be remedied unless our proprietors become inhabitants also". Piers, like the previously quoted *Advertisements for Ireland,* states that Irish farmers would erect only slight

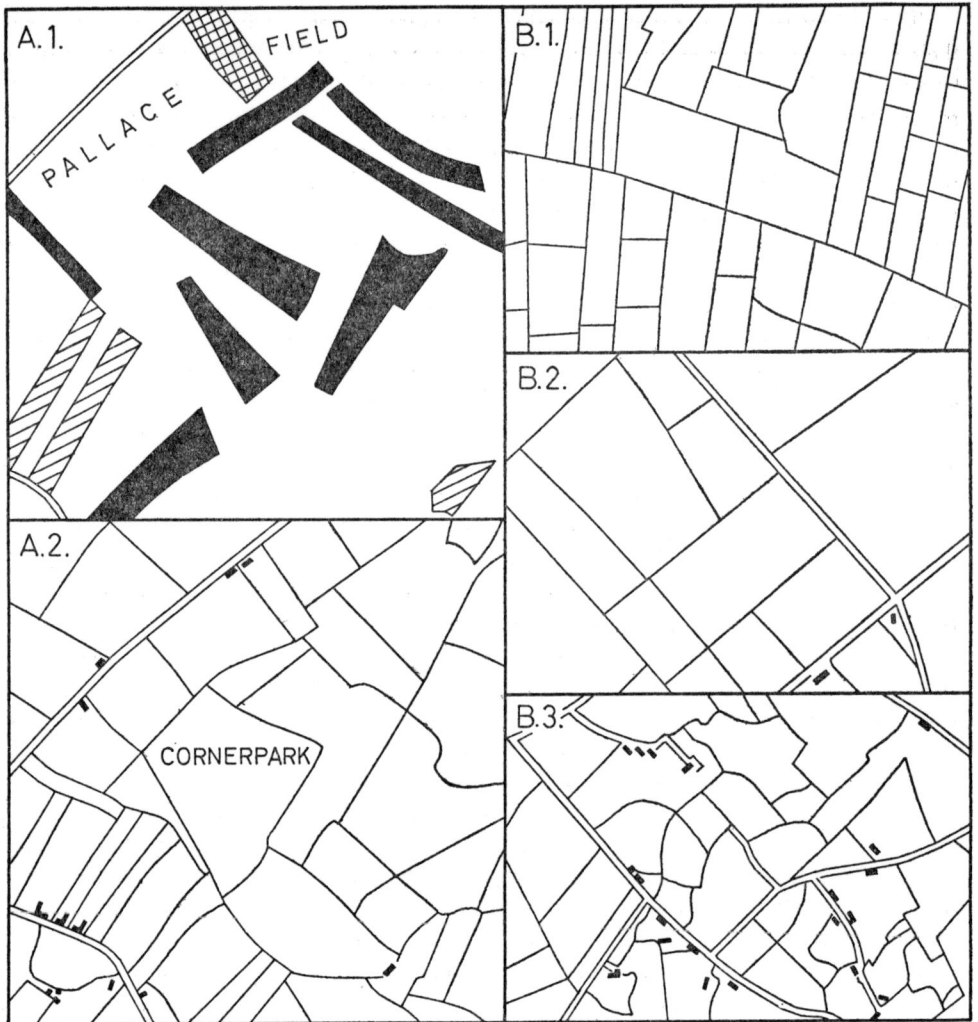

Fig. 13.2 A1 Scattered strip holdings at Newcastle, co. Dublin, in 1765. The holdings of three tenants
are shown in the 'Pallace Field'.

A2   The same locality today. O.S. Sheet 21.

B1   'Striped' fields on Garristown Commons, co. Dublin. Enclosed by Act of Parliament in 1803.

B2   Regular rectangular fields on Dromiskin Commons, co. Louth. Enclosed by Act of Parliament
in 1801.

B3   Broadleas Commons, Ballymore-Eustace, co. Kildare. Irregular enclosures associated with
19th century squatter encroachments.

(The scale of each drawing is six inches to represent one mile)

temporary fencing of the open arable areas in summer. However, the same manuscript contains references to the well-hedged and fenced landscape in the Wexford baronies of Bargy and Forth, an important reminder of the possible regional variety of enclosure conditions. In his tours of 1709 Thos. Molyneux[34] describes the Irish landscape as open and unenclosed, with the arable only fenced temporarily. However, he points out that around the large towns, such as Limerick, there was some enclosure. The rural environs of Dublin were probably enclosed well before the end of the seventeenth century. John Stevens, writing of the winter stay of the troops of James II in Dublin before the battle of the Boyne, says that they cut down all the trees and hedges in the fields around the city for fuel.[35]

Taking the previous evidence as a whole it does strongly support the idea that very few enclosures existed, except in limited areas, down to the close of the seventeenth century. This was so because of the continued existence of open-field agriculture around the medieval villages, and the generally backward character of farming. There were in many areas no fixed field boundaries and during periodic intakes the crops were protected by temporary or purely seasonal fencing.

The late-seventeenth and especially the eighteenth century saw far-reaching changes in the rural landscape of eastern Ireland. These changes involved not only the large scale spread of enclosures but also developments in the basic patterns of settlement. The changes were in the long term an implication of fundamental alterations in the political structure of the country and of land ownership. The seventeenth century saw the final reduction of all Ireland to English authority and as a result of the Cromwellian Confiscations and Williamite Land Settlements a new ruling class, mainly Protestant and of English origin, was introduced, and intended to be the mainstay of English authority in Ireland. Their wealth was based on landed estate. Almost the whole country was divided into large compact estates, on to which, especially in the east, the landlords frequently introduced privileged tenantry from Britain, who were established on new compact holdings.

The eclipse of the old village communities must have been closely bound up with the economic and social demise of the 'old English', which was one of the major results of the Cromwellian conquest. As the descendants of the original settlers in the Anglo-Norman colony the 'old English' had substantial landed interests in eastern Ireland and were probably still the backbone of the old village communities. They provided a focus of resistance to Cromwell and not unnaturally they suffered heavily in the subsequent land transfers. The formation of new compact holdings to accommodate Cromwellian settlers at the expense of open-field village lands is nicely illustrated by a surviving map of the manor of Drumcashel in co. Louth, made in 1655, within a year of the manor's transfer to the new Cromwellian owners.[36] In 1640 the manor belonged to John Roth, outlawed for participation in the 1641 rebellion. After confiscation the bulk of the manor was divided between two of Cromwell's officers, who received compact portions of 140 ha (approximately 350 acres) and 83 ha (approximately 207 acres) respectively. The remainder of the manor (some 80 ha or 200 acres) is clearly shown to be lying in open-field strips. A concentration of six houses and what appears to be the remains of a motte are shown near the centre of the manor and presumably represent the original medieval village. Where the open-fields once lay there are today large square fields; the motte remains but the village has completely disintegrated.

Although many new compact holdings were being established in the latter half of the seventeenth century there was in most places very little actual enclosure. The boundaries of individual farms and townlands may increasingly have been fenced and ditched, but the general impression is still of an open landscape with portions of the land used periodically for cultivation and grazing. Thus while many acres of the east were described by contemporary writers as open or 'champain' land, perhaps this need not always imply the prevalence of open-field systems *sensu stricto*. Comparable developments occurred in Ulster. In co. Armagh, for example, there is evidence that following the establishment of the new planters the townlands were the primary units of enclosure. The townlands were subsequently subdivided and the outbounds of the farms ditched and quickset. In the early-eighteenth century pasture land was fenced off from meadow and arable land, while the great hedgerows are the product of the landlord enclosure policy of the mid-eighteenth century.[37]

In eastern Ireland the progressive subdivision of large areas into the patchwork of enclosures of the present day can be reconstructed in some places by reference to eighteenth-century estate maps. The Kildare Estate Maps of John Rocque show that in 1758 ditches and hedgerows were rare in the two manors of Castledermot and Graney, except along townland boundaries; and almost one third (540 ha or 1,350 acres) of the area lay in eight large fields, all of them exceeding 40 ha (100 acres) in extent. By the early-nineteenth century these had been subdivided by a combination of ditches and hedgerows into the regular pattern of medium to small enclosures still existing today, with an average field size of around two ha (five acres).[38] A similar picture emerges in the Glen of Imaal in co. Wicklow where at the beginning of the nineteenth century the degenerate farming was attributed to "the total want of regular inclosures".[39] This situation had been partially remedied by the time of the first Ordnance Survey maps in the 1840's and comparison with the second edition shows that by the end of the century there had been further subdivision of the land into regular orderly fields.

Two contrasting patterns of field development thus seem to emerge, one involving the gradual engrossing of old open-field strips, or, in effect, the formation of larger units from smaller, and another involving progressive subdivision of large open units. It is natural to associate the latter form of development more with previously under-utilised areas, such as commons, and reclaimed heath and bog, than with the traditional arable areas around ancient villages. But there was almost certainly a third mode of field origin where the fieldscape was created *ab initio* in a more or less complete form over an extensive area of country. It is this type of wholesale enclosing to which Arthur Young seems to be referring in the passages quoted earlier and to which the Statistical Surveys, undertaken at the initiative of the Royal Dublin Society in the early-nineteenth century, make frequent references.

The defining and demarcating of property boundaries, following the establishment of the Ascendancy landlordry and the new planter class, led to the first important steps in the formation of a close pattern of fixed enclosures in the countryside. But the results were slight in comparison to the enclosure movement which affected the country as a result of the agrarian revolution in the eighteenth and early-nineteenth centuries. Especially in the latter half of the eighteenth century the ideas of 'agricultural improvement' and the 'new husbandry' were gaining momentum in Ireland, as throughout Britain, and improvement was invariably coupled with enclosure. The new estate structure with its autocratic landlords provided the framework within which radical changes in rural economy could be effectively and rapidly carried out, while the growth of a commercialised economy and the expansion of demand for cattle conditioned the pattern of 'improvement', emphasising in particular the conversion of land to pasture. The new enclosures were primarily designed to provide a large number of small fields to suit the new forms of livestock husbandry made possible by improved pasture and the use of hay and roots for winter fodder. Hedged fields provided shelter for the livestock and effectively checked their movements, thus making it possible to rotate production with maximum flexibility on each farm. It was emphasised by the improvers that enclosure provided an opportunity to drain the land along the field boundaries, so that ditching and hedging were considered to be complementary operations.

In eastern Ireland, and especially on the best agricultural land, the characteristic field boundary is a very substantial feature comprising a deep wide trench and a bank of stone and sods with a hedgerow planted on it. Such features were a hallmark of avant garde improvers. Arthur Young describes in detail their construction in a number of places in counties Dublin, Meath, Louth and Kildare. He relates that a Colonel Marlay of Celbridge, co. Kildare, "practised husbandry with great success . . . his fences excellent, his ditches 5 by 6 and 7 by 6; the banks well made and planted with quicks". He describes similar features on the land of Mr Clements at Killadoon, "he has been very attentive to bring his farm into neat order respecting fences, throwing down and levelling old banks, making new ditches, double ones six feet wide and five deep, with a large bank between for planting, more effectually than ever I saw in England". The same features had been established on reclaimed heathland at Grange Geath near Drogheda where, Young states, "the fences about new inclosed pieces, and those made in general by gentlemen, are ditches six feet deep, seven feet wide . . . with two rows of quick in the bank . . . ".

There is no doubt that the spirit of 'improvement' was making itself very widely felt in Ireland in the eighteenth century, and eastern Ireland was ahead of the rest of the country both in the timing and quality of agricultural innovation. The eastern areas were not only among the most favoured from a physical standpoint, it was here also that the estate system was most firmly entrenched. J. Bush wrote in 1769[40] that "the province of Leinster and the middle parts of the kingdom in general are the best cultivated and the most generally improved". This view is corroborated by Vallencey's *Royal Map of Ireland* (1795)[41] which shows 'improved land' by conventional fields defined by hedgerows, and the extent of land so covered corresponds generally with that stated by Bush.

The relatively short period during which the main enclosure movements occurred, the autocratic character of estate organisation combined with the scientific approach implicit in the 'new husbandry', and the relatively level terrain, explain the essentially uniform character of the enclosure pattern now existing over the bulk of eastern Ireland (Fig. 13.2). More complex and interesting field plans can be identified around some of the old villages and are a legacy of a long gradual evolution previously described. The old arable land in the immediate vicinity of the large villages of the Pale seems to have been peculiarly resistant to thorough-going engrossment and sometimes the only result of the improver movement was the erection of hedgerows along the old mearings which divided the strip holdings. Such a process produced the remarkable linear fields of Rathcoole (Fig. 13.1). Around other medieval villages, however, there are the regular planned fields apparently dating from the improvement and no existing signs of an evolved field pattern, for example Maynooth, co. Kildare, and Whitestown, co. Louth. In some of these instances old maps do show that the present field patterns have only recently replaced strip fields. In figure 13.2 a portion of the fields of Newcastle (originally a royal manor in co. Dublin) as they exist today is compared with the same area as shown on a map of 1765.[42] The latter map (Plate XXI) may well have been made to facilitate the enclosure of the remaining open-fields. It is of particular importance in the study of eastern field-systems because it distinguishes and names three major areas around the village (the Pallace Field, Augh Mullin, Shiskeen Commons) which may well be the fundamental divisions of a three-field system. The enclosure movements of the 'improvement' thus did in some cases embrace old arable open-field tracts, involving not only the erection of hedgerows but the introduction of completely new field outlines. C. Varlo (1776) provides further evidence of this.[43] His opposition to the enclosure of open-fields by expanding graziers in England was based on his experience of the same phenomenon in Ireland. In the case of most villages there is a mixture including both the evolved field shapes and regular field outlines of more recent establishment, for example, Crumlin, Swords, Rathcoole, Garristown, and Ballymore-Eustace. The field patterns near Drogheda are instructive, for within the area of the old town-fields, which is still partly bounded by a deep ditch, the dominant field shape is elongated, with the slight curvature diagnostic of medieval plough strips. Outside the ditch there is an abrupt transition to regular block-type fields associated with the period of improvement (Fig. 13.1).

The study of deserted villages which has proved so fruitful and interesting in England has not been pursued in eastern Ireland, although it seems very likely that some villages have disappeared and in a number of cases their dissolution may well be associated with the spread of enclosures. The example of Drumcashel in co. Louth has been cited earlier. Lord Taaffe, writing in 1765[44], complains that he had seen the removal of many villages and their arable lands owing to enclosures for grazing. The increasing coverage of the countryside by high quality aerial photographs holds out exciting possibilities of tracing deserted villages. By 1968 over 40 sites in Ireland had been provisionally classified by St Joseph as deserted villages. There is a concentration in co. Tipperary but almost half of the remainder lie in eastern Ireland. Some of the sites may be clachans or even large farmsteads; only detailed archaeological investigations can confirm their true character and perhaps their date. Some old villages now exist in a very vestigial form. They have in some instances been reduced to merely a farm or two adjacent to a ruined medieval church or castle, for example, Kilteel and Rathmore in co. Kildare, Salterstown in co. Louth and Esker in co. Dublin, while in other cases they had become by the nineteenth century simply the residence of agricultural labourers, for example, Rathcor, co. Louth. Other old settlements were improved and remodelled in the eighteenth century to emerge as typical estate towns with primarily commercial rather than agricultural functions, for example, Maynooth and Ballymore-Eustace in co. Kildare, and Donard, co. Wicklow.

At the beginning of the eighteenth century the commons were still an important element in the rural landscape of eastern Ireland. The existence of such open and unimproved areas was felt by many to be inconsistent with the prevailing spirit of agricultural improvement, and the pressure of an increasing rural population, together with the decay of borough and manorial organisation, encouraged encroachment upon the commons both by landlord enclosure schemes and squatter settlements. The Tudor foundation of Philipstown, co. Offaly, for example, had some 140 ha (350 acres) of commons attached to the corporation, but "after the purchase of the borough by Lord Belvidere (in the middle of the eighteenth century) the neighbouring landlords, as the freemen and burgesses who held the lots died off, encroached upon the commons until merely one acre remained".[45] The commons of Gaskinstown, co. Meath, were open until 1832 but in the two succeeding years they were "entirely enclosed by poor persons in lots of one half to four or five acres".[46] At Swords, co. Dublin, the commons of 48 ha (120 acres) were preserved intact until 1800 but "subsequently strangers settled upon them and enclosed so that . . . about 20 perches only are now unenclosed".[47]

Numerous Acts of Parliament were passed in association with enclosure projects, especially those on commons. In the case of co. Dublin, for example, they provide a close chronological record of the progress of commons enclosure schemes, the bulk of which occurred in the first three decades of the nineteenth century and involved over 1,620 ha (4,050 acres). Enclosure of a common by Act of Parliament or on the private initiative of a landlord was often a single comprehensive project and the resulting field pattern is generally regular and geometrical, the fields being either very long, narrow and straight as at Garristown, co. Dublin, enclosed in 1803, or squarish as at Dromiskin, co. Louth, enclosed in 1801. On the other hand commons which were encroached upon by illegal squatter settlements can often be distinguished from surrounding townlands today by their close pattern of smallholdings and small irregular enclosures, representing uncoordinated and piecemeal enterprise as at Ballymore-Eustace (Fig. 13.2).

The enclosing of the commons was the last major phase in eradicating the medieval legacies in the Irish landscape. By the time of the first Ordnance Survey mapping of Ireland in the 1830's, at a scale of six inches to one mile, the essentials of the present day enclosure pattern of eastern Ireland had been established. However, the Ordnance Survey maps record the end product of a century and a half of very substantial change.

REFERENCES

1 G. O'Brien, *The economic history of Ireland in the eighteenth century*, (1918), 81, 133; A. Campbell, Irish fields and houses, *Bealoideas*, 5 (1935), 57–74; J. O'Loan, in Recent research on Irish rural settlement, ed. R. H. Buchanan, Belfast (1963), (Unpublished).

2 P. Flatrès, *Géographie rurale de quatre contrées Celtiques*, (1957), Chapter 8

3 A mappe of Leax and Ophaley, c. 1565 (British Museum, Cotton MS., Augustus 1, ii, 40).

4 E. Curtis, The survey of Offaly in 1550, *Hermathena*, 45 (1930), 312–52

5 J. H. Andrews, Notes on the historical geography of the Irish iron industry, *Irish Geography*, 3, No. 3 (1956), 139–49

6 Gerard Boate, *Ireland's Naturall History*, (London, 1652)

7 George Hibbard, *Survey and Book of Maps of the Coppices and Scrub Woods In the Kingdom of Ireland belonging to the Right Honourable the Earl of Malton*, (1743)

8 *Molands Survey, 1728* (Documents 7 and 8 are in the Fitzwilliam Estate Office at Coolatin Park, Co. Wicklow)

9 J. O'Hanlon and E. O'Leary, *History of the Queen's County*, 1 (1907), 7

10 Arthur Young, *A tour in Ireland in the years 1776, 1777 and 1778*, (1780)

11 V. B. Proudfoot, The economy of the Irish rath, *Medieval Archaeology*, 5 (1961), 94–122

12 S. P. O'Riordain, Excavations at Cush, Co. Limerick, 1934 and 1935, *Proc. Roy. Irish Acad.*, 45 C (1940), 83

13 F. H. A. Aalen, Enclosures in eastern Ireland, *Irish Geography*, 5, No. 2 (1965), 29–39

14 National Museum of Ireland. Reference collections of prints of aerial photographs taken by Dr J. K. St Joseph, Director in Aerial Photography, University of Cambridge. Photos No. AHN 38, 48–52

15 A. J. Otway-Ruthven, The organisation of Anglo-Irish agriculture in the middle ages, *J. Roy. Soc. Antiq. Ireland*, 81 (1951), 1–13

16 A. J. Otway-Ruthven, *A history of medieval Ireland*, (1968). The Marquess of Lansdowne, An early rental of the Lord of Lixnaw, *Proc. Roy. Irish Acad.*, 40 C (1931–32), 1–18

17 J. Gilbart Smyly, Old deeds in the library of Trinity College, V, *Hermathena*, 71 (1948), 45–6. *Curia Dominae Reginae Eliz. de Esker et Cromling* (Marsh's Library, Dublin, Loftus (MS).

18 J. B. Leslie, Extracts from rent rolls of the See of Armagh, 1703, *J. Co. Louth Arch. Soc.*, 9 (1938), 89

19 A. J. Otway-Ruthven, (1951), op. cit., 2–6

20 ibid., 5.

21 J. D'Alton, *The History of the County of Dublin*, (1838), 698

22 *The Journals of the House of Commons of the Kingdom of Ireland*, 1751–52, 16 December 1751

23 *Report on Manuscripts in various collections, VIII*, Historical Manuscripts Commission (Wood, Clements, Unwin), (1913), 261

24 *J. Co. Louth Arch. Soc.*, 12 (1951), 158 (Poghenstowne, Co. Louth, 1715, '43 acres commonly known as Lord Carlingford's acres intermixt in said lands'); *J. Co. Louth Arch. Soc.*, 9 (1938), 89. (Dromiskin, Co. Louth, 1703. 'near 200 acres of the above townland which belong to several freeholders who are possest thereof and that they lye intermixt with Lord Primat's land')
Molyneux Papers, Trinity College Dublin MS (Westmeath c. 1780)
Patent Rolls, James 1, 1607, 330 ('the walls of a chapel and 80 ridges of land nigh the Gan near Carlingford'); Woods, Clements, Unwin, op. cit., (Swords and Philipstown, 1712)

25 *Longfield Maps*, Co. Dublin, 2, Nos. 76, 79, 80, 89 and 3, No. 77 (National Library of Ireland)

26 R. Frazer, *General view of the County Wicklow*, (1801), 81.

27 Jno. Longfield, *A survey of the manor of Blessington, 1806*, Map 7, (Downshire Estate Papers, N.I.P.R.O., Belfast).

28 F. H. A. Aalen, Some historical aspects of landscape and rural life in Omeath, Co. Louth, *Irish Geography*, 4, No. 4 (1962), 256–78

29 Henry Wallop to Lord Burghley, *State Papers, Ireland,* 120/9
30 *The Journals of the House of Commons of the Kingdom of Ireland,* 1641, 1, 5, 7 July
31 Anon. *A brief character of Ireland,* (1692)
32 Reproduced in E. MacLysaght, *Irish life in the seventeenth century,* (1950), 115
33 *Molyneux Papers,* op. cit.
34 ibid., 4, 16, 17
35 C. Maxwell, *The stranger in Ireland,* (1954), 110
36 J. O'Loan, Land reclamation in Dromiskin, Co. Louth, *Dept. of Agriculture Journal,* 54 (1957–58), 7
37 W. H. Crawford, The woodlands of the manor of Brownlow's—Derry, North Armagh, in the seventeenth and eighteenth centuries, *Ulster Folklife,* 10 (1964), 57–64
38 A. A. Horner, Aspects of the historical geography of parts of the Duke of Leinster's estates in Co. Kildare, c. 1750–1850, (unpublished BA dissertation, Dept. of Geography, Trinity College, Dublin, 1968)
39 R. Frazer, op. cit., 86
40 J. Bush, *Hibernia Curiosa,* (1769), 137
41 C. Vallencey, *The Royal Map of Ireland,* (1795). MS Ordnance Survey Office, Dublin
42 A map of part of the lands of Newcastle, etc., by Pat Roe, 1765. (National Library of Ireland)
43 C. Varlo, *A new system of husbandry,* (1772)
44 N. Taafe, *Observations on affairs of Ireland,* (1776), 12
45 Parliamentary Reports, *Corporations, Ireland, 1835,* 27, 241
46 ibid., 173
47 ibid., 239

XIV

THE TWO 'IRELANDS' AT THE BEGINNING OF THE NINETEENTH CENTURY

J. H. Johnson

In their study of the history of Guinness's brewery, P. Lynch and J. Vaizey suggested that Ireland fell into two economic regions at the end of the eighteenth century.[1] Three-quarters of the population lived under a largely subsistence and rural economy, without the money to purchase commercial products and, in any case, without the organization to distribute these goods. The rest of the country possessed what they called a 'maritime' economy, based on cash transactions and linked to Britain by "ties of trade and credit and by a constant traffic in people".[2]

Lynch and Vaizey described this latter system as occupying an eastern coastal strip, stretching from Belfast to Cork, with outliers in the towns of Limerick and Galway: figure 14.1 reflects this situation, with the Irish export trade (largely to Great Britain) being channelled through east and south coast ports. Fingers of 'maritime' Ireland also penetrated from Dublin into the midlands of Ireland, stretching along the recently constructed Royal and Grand canals. In their view this system continued into the nineteenth century, with the limits of the area dominated by a cash economy being slowly pushed back during the early decades of the century, but with no large inroads being made into the traditional subsistence system until after the Great Famine.

Such a generalization may serve as a convenient framework for the study of some aspects of the history of a brewery, but this simple theory requires elaboration and refinement before it can form a useful frame of reference for an examination of some of the other geographical features of early nineteenth century Ireland. For example, even if the idea of two 'Irelands' can be fully accepted—and this is a matter which must be debated—the towns of Sligo and Londonderry have to be added to the outliers of maritime Ireland, and it is also clear that at this time many rural areas away from a narrow east-coast strip already possessed elements of a commercial economy.

Yet, on its face value, the idea has an immediate appeal for those interested in the historical geography of Ireland, since studies of modern conditions suggest that many geographical changes are often connected with the replacement of a subsistence economy by one based on cash transactions. Agricultural practices, settlement patterns and the rural labour force are all sensitive to this change. When a cash economy becomes established a

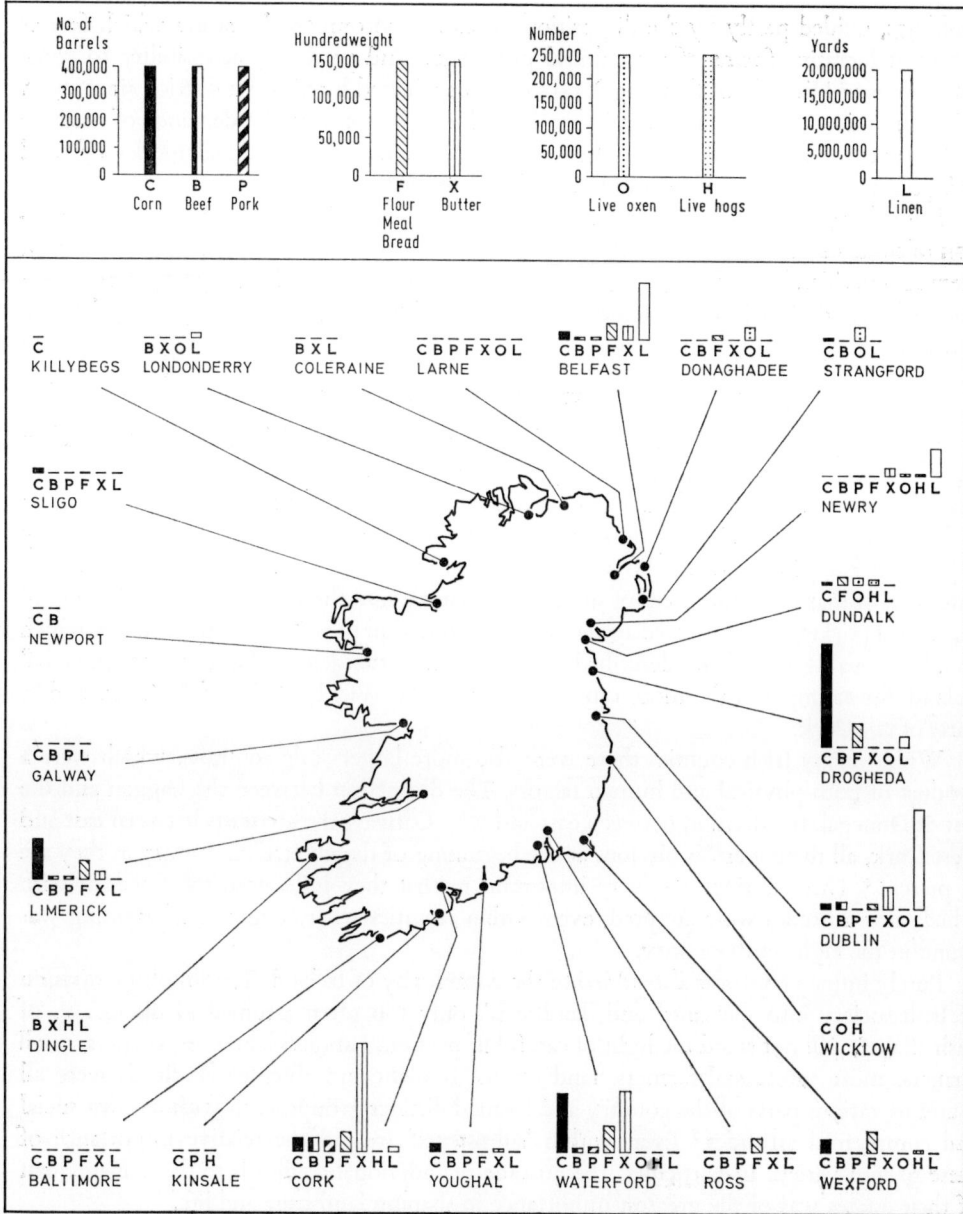

Fig. 14.1   Ireland, exports 1791

farmer begins to count the cost of his labour and he is more willing to alter long-established social values. He is likely to reappraise the use of his land and the location of his farm

Q

buildings, guided partly by the disposition of those environmental features which favour the most lucrative forms of agricultural production and partly by accessibility to communications.[3] His scale of thinking is no longer dominated by his own district, since, with this economic change, a farmer is increasingly likely to consider the demands of national and international markets. He is also encouraged to reassess traditional modes of rural living, in terms of the economics of agricultural production.

But although the division of Ireland into two economic regions provides a neat explanation of some of the features of Irish geography at the beginning of the nineteenth century, there are considerable difficulties in applying this idea in practice. This essay briefly considers some of these difficulties and attempts to reappraise the nature of the two 'Irelands' at this period.

THE COMPLEXITIES OF THE IRISH SCENE

One important difficulty springs simply from the complexity of the Irish scene, which is partly derived from its underlying physical geography. In particular, uplands provide extensive areas close to the limits of cultivation in widely scattered parts of the country; and, as a result of local population pressures, at the beginning of the nineteenth century cultivation had often pushed above the economic limits of cropping, thus leading to the extension of many separate areas of subsistence farming into these marginal lands.[4] Many of these local pockets of subsistence agriculture were found in those parts of the country which could reasonably have been described as being within the general limits of 'commercial' Ireland, for example in the more remote valleys of the Wicklows, in the Mournes and in parts of co. Cork.

Within many Irish counties there were also more larger-scale contrasts, which were a product of both physical and human factors. The distinction between the Laggan and the rest of Donegal, the division between east and west Galway, the contrasts between east and west Cork, all these were as obvious at the beginning of the nineteenth century as they are at present.[5] These distinctions were important in that they influenced the freedom with which new attitudes were adopted, even within counties where commercial farming was found in the eighteenth century.

Purely human contrasts also added to the complexity of Ireland. The simplistic division of Irish society into 'peasants' and 'landlords', only too often assumed in discussions of Irish affairs[6], will not stand the light of careful inspection. Landless labourers, cottiers, small farmers, more substantial farmers, land agents, resident and absentee landlords were all found in various parts of the country and formed distinct groups, each with its own social and commercial attitudes.[7] Even within 'subsistence' Ireland the relative importance of these groups varied. In particular, the attitude of individual landlords to the management of their estates was of the greatest importance in shaping landscape and life.

T. Jones Hughes has argued that the valuations given to agricultural land in the mid-nineteenth century provide a general indication of the distribution of the areas remodelled by landlords at this time.[8] Interestingly enough, the results of his analysis of this source tie in neatly with the suggestions of Lynch and Vaizey, although there is plenty of evidence to show that individual landlords were improving their estates in the more remote parts of the country; presumably the improving activities of landlords must have been most common where a clear financial return was probable (Fig. 14.2). Rural areas valued at over £1 per acre in the 1850's were highly restricted to land within easy reach of important ports; and even areas with valuations over 10 shillings per acre did not extend far beyond the counties along the southern and eastern coasts of Ireland. It was within these areas that, in Jones Hughes' view, landlords had succeeded in establishing the basis of commercial farming by the middle of the century.

Nevertheless there are problems in drawing such a specific conclusion from a map of this kind. Some of the factors which shaped this distribution were independent of the activity of landlords, since the valuation stressed the intrinsic capacity of a holding to produce for the market. Measured by almost any standard, physically poorer agricultural land was much more common in the western counties; and location away from the east coast markets for agricultural produce increased transport costs and lowered the rent-paying ability and valuation of holdings in western Ireland, even if landlords had been active in promoting change and commercial life had been established.

However, there were certain features of this higher-valued region which gave it distinctiveness. Jones Hughes has suggested that agriculture in this area was orientated towards either the cultivation of wheat and barley for sale or the fattening of cattle for export and the Dublin markets. He has claimed that in this region there was a greater proportion of resident proprietors, a greater diversity of life in villages and towns (which were themselves in the creation of landlords), and that this was also the area where the Irish language had disappeared. Here, too, there were a number of substantial tenants and a market-orientated economy.[9] In short, although the precise limits provided by these various criteria did not coincide, particularly in the north-east where industrial changes in the Lagan valley were a greater stimulus to change than landlordism, there was a 'heartland' in southern and eastern Ireland which accords well with Lynch and Vaizey's 'maritime' Ireland.

There is also evidence that demographic changes had taken place in this same area. In particular, much of the recent controversy about the age of marriage in pre-Famine Ireland[10] can be resolved if allowance is made for regional variations in the pattern of marriage. Literary evidence suggests that the amount of celibacy and the age of marriage was highest in south-eastern Ireland, and an analysis of the 1841 census returns confirms this suggestion.[11] For example, the proportion of married men was lowest in the rural areas to the west and south of Dublin, and the proportion of women of fertile age who were married was also lowest in this same general region. It is reasonable to follow K. H. Connell's suggestion, based on conditions later in the nineteenth century, that this change in marriage owed much to the increased commercialism of rural life, which had come earlier to this part of Ireland.[12] There is also evidence that the age of marriage was increasing in the early decades of the nineteenth century, but it is important to notice that this evidence of change was not confined to the south and the east.[13]

Indeed, it is when attention is turned to the rest of Ireland that the idea of the two 'Irelands' is more difficult to sustain, largely for two related reasons. One is the degree to

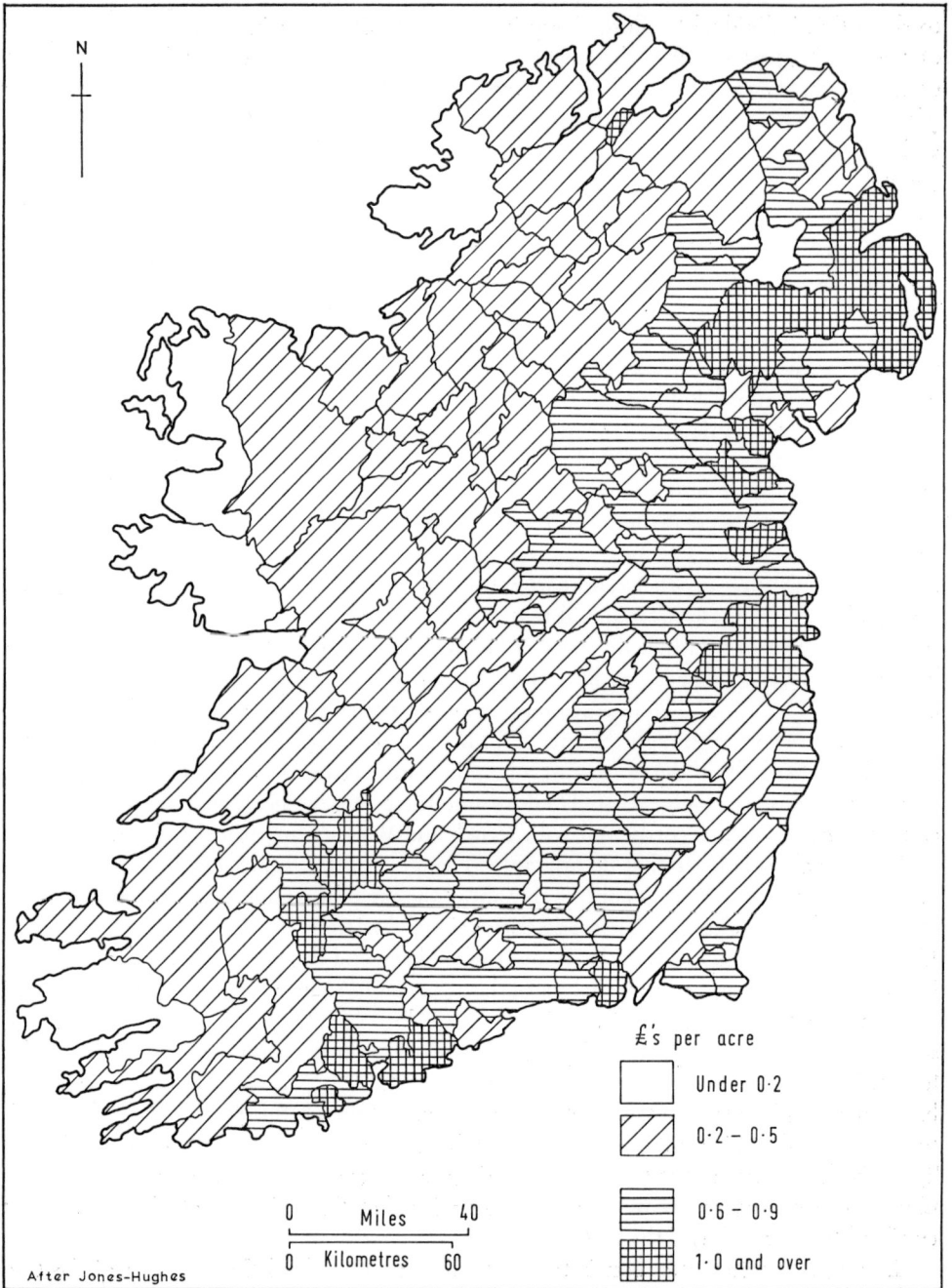

£'s per acre

Under 0·2

0·2 – 0·5

0·6 – 0·9

1·0 and over

0   Miles   40

0   Kilometres   60

After Jones-Hughes

Fig. 14.2   Valuation of rural areas, circa. 1850 (after Jones-Hughes)

which change was already taking place in so-called 'subsistence' Ireland. The other is the degree to which commercial transactions had already entered into the economy of those parts of Ireland which were located away from the east and south coast.

One indication of the rising level of commercial activity in rural Ireland is the return of rent from property. Rent from rural property formed the staple source of income for the great majority of the large land-owning families in Ireland; and these incomes were increasing rapidly in the second half of the eighteenth century.[14] Some of this increase was occurring on estates in 'maritime' Ireland and may have had a different effect on geographical change here than in other areas. The Fitzwilliam estates, to cite but one example of many, were located in counties Wicklow, Wexford and Kildare. The return from rents on these estates increased by 86 per cent between 1746 and 1783, and by nearly 90 per cent from 1783 to 1815.[15] The upward movement of rent does not necessarily imply an improvement in the financial position of tenants, but the rise in prices during the Napoleonic wars was likely to have its most direct influence on those parts of Ireland which were accessible to the English market, and there is some evidence that many tenants in these areas maintained their economic position or even improved it, in spite of the parallel increase in rents.[16] It also seems likely that agricultural improvements were more commonly undertaken, which were designed to maintain rents on a more permanent basis.

On the other hand the degree of economic change in the more remote parts of Ireland is commonly underestimated. The Enniskillen estates in co. Fermanagh produced a rent of £981 in 1738 and £3,807 in 1780, an increase of 288 per cent. This change took place in spite of the fact that Beaufort could describe the county as being in "a rude state" in the last decade of the eighteenth century.[17] Similarly, the Kenmare estates in co. Kerry and co. Limerick had a gross rental of about £3,000 in 1747, about £12,000 in 1796 and £21,658 in 1814; and the rent from the Cloncurry estate in co. Limerick increased by 205 per cent between 1775 and 1818. Admittedly, in the areas of greater agricultural difficulty the increase was less dramatic, but it was still present. The Dillon estate in co. Galway showed an increase in gross rental of 51 per cent between 1767 and 1780, and the Cremorne estate in co. Monaghan one of 54 per cent between 1790 and 1808.[18]

SOURCES OF MONEY IN 'SUBSISTENCE' IRELAND

In spite of the evidence of rural valuations, one source of cash in the rural economy of 'subsistence' Ireland was farming itself. The movement of cattle from the western to the eastern counties of Ireland, which is a dominant feature of modern agriculture, was already a well established practice at the beginning of the nineteenth century. In co. Tyrone, for example, there were 159 cattle fairs each year; and from August to the beginning of November "a much larger and better sort [of cattle]" was brought for sale from other parts of Ireland.[19] In this same county wethers were "brought from the West by jobbers..." and sold to butchers.[20] Beaufort described how the upland areas of co. Leitrim at the end of the eighteenth century were far from unprofitable, "for, producing abundance of coarse grass, they annually pour forth immense droves of young cattle"; and in co. Fermanagh large herds of young cattle were being reared for sale.[21] Income was not just derived from livestock. Even in co. Mayo, which McParlan described in 1801 as being "the remotest part of Ireland from intercourse with the interior of the kingdom and the capital . . . "[22], barley was sold locally and the export of oats had been considerable for the last few years "even to Dublin and England".[23]

Such activity was restricted to a relatively few farms in co. Mayo; and it may be argued that most of the small farmers, who dominated the agriculture of the north and west of Ireland, were largely, if not entirely, concerned with providing local subsistence. But it should not be thought that farming was the only source of cash in the rural economy. At least two other activities spread commercial practices deep into 'subsistence' Ireland.

One of these additional contacts with a money economy was the domestic linen industry, which in one way or another influenced most of the small farm belt in the north of Ireland. Machinery was successfully applied to the spinning of flax only in the second quarter of the nineteenth century. As a result, except for the bleaching process which developed as a specialized trade during the eighteenth century, the domestic industry remained unchanged in the early 1800's. Indeed, the power loom did not exert any great influence until after 1850, although after the 1820's the profitable sector of the domestic industry became increasingly concentrated in and around the Lagan valley.[24]

Some impression of the area in which linen weaving brought commercial returns at the end of the eighteenth century is given by the distribution of brown linen markets, where unbleached linen was sold by weaver-farmers to specialist bleachers in much the same manner as an agricultural product (Fig. 14.3). Much of Ulster was influenced by this business, but the commercial production of linen was largely confined to the north of Ireland long before the nineteenth century. Indeed, only in north-east Ireland did the linen industry develop a fully commercial system, with drapers, weavers and spinners meeting at public markets; but weaving was also of some importance in counties Donegal, Cavan and Monaghan[25], although in these areas the production of yarn made a greater financial return.[26]

In the weaving areas the domestic linen industry had penetrated deeply into a rural life that could not in any sense be described as possessing a self-contained subsistence economy. In 1801, although very little grain was sold at markets in co. Tyrone, flax seed was sold in the spring, not only in market towns, "but even in small villages", yielding profits of up to 40 per cent to retailers.[27] At markets in co. Tyrone, too, the poorest in the community were buying coarse stockings and blankets, which had been made in Connacht[28], again hardly suggesting a completely subsistence economy. In co. Londonderry at the beginning of the nineteenth century much of the flax seed used by farmers was imported from Europe and North America, and even at this period flax itself was being imported from overseas and yarn from co. Donegal. Unbleached linens from co. Londonderry were being exported to Liverpool and other destinations, and bleached linen cloths were being sold in Dublin and also shipped direct to Liverpool.[29] Contacts of this kind were typical throughout the area where the domestic weaving industry was well established; and this region was at its most extensive at the beginning of the nineteenth century.

The effects of the domestic industry, however, were not solely limited to this area. Flax

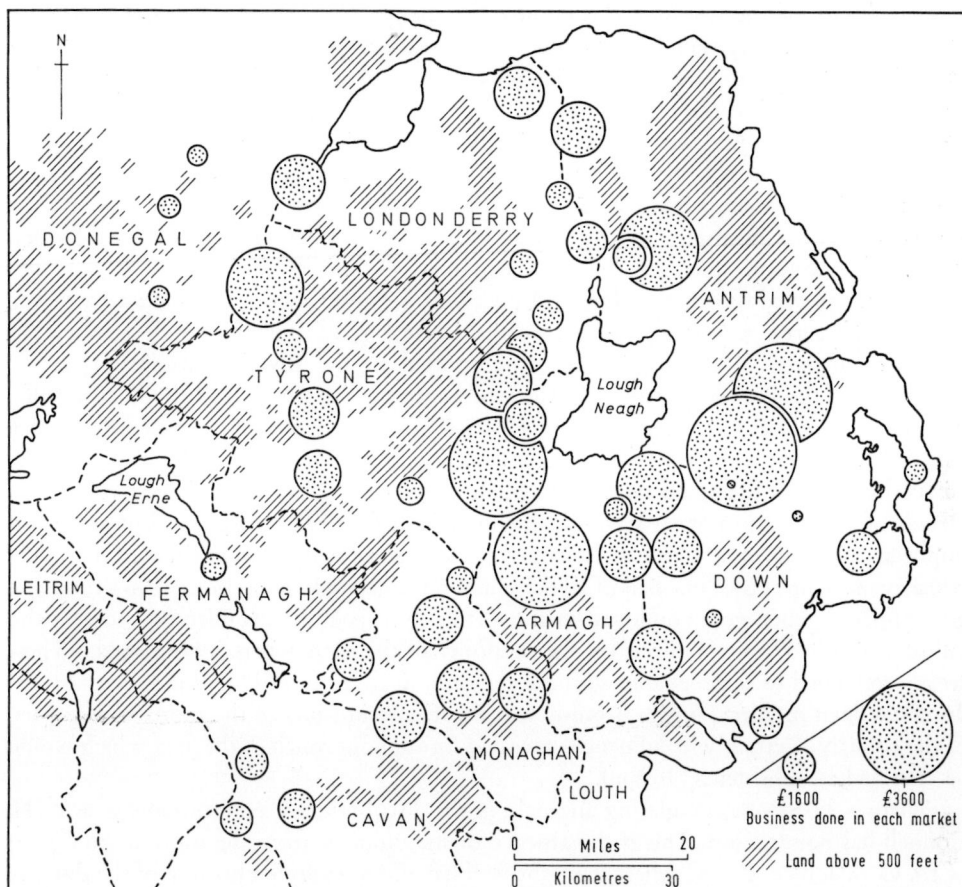

Fig. 14.3   Brown linen markets, 1816

was grown in Connacht and the north midlands, and yarn was spun into thread in these areas.[30] In co. Mayo, for example, large quantities of linen thread and yarn were sold at the Ballina market; and a few landlords had been attempting to introduce linen weaving.[31] Thread was brought into north-east Ireland from areas like these, as well as from Scotland, where steam-driven mills were operating at the beginning of the nineteenth century. Like the fattening of cattle in eastern Ireland, the linen industry also spread its influence into the western counties of Ireland (or, at least, those north of co. Galway). Admittedly these influences were strongest in the most accessible and prosperous parts of these western counties, but at least these areas had very real direct contacts with commercial Ireland, and indirectly with Britain.

The illicit distillation of whiskey was an additional stimulus to the introduction of a cash economy into the more remote parts of Ireland. The manufacture of poteen had been a normal part of the subsistence economy for many centuries, but K. H. Connell has shown that at the beginning of the nineteenth century poteen-making reached its period of greatest importance as a commercial activity.[32] In 1815 the duty on whiskey reached 6s 1½d per gallon, and the manufacture of illegal spirit flourished, necessarily in the more remote parts of Ireland. There is no doubt that by this time the manufacture and sale of poteen was a regular commercial activity, since there were regular markets where poteen was sold and the materials for its manufacture bought. Farmers in co. Antrim and co. Londonderry, for example, were growing barley for distillers in Donegal, and farmers in co. Clare were producing barley for Connemara distillers.[33]

Poteen was sold throughout Ireland by various nefarious means, but the area where it was manufactured was quite distinct at the beginning of the nineteenth century. K. Danaher's analysis of the parish reports submitted to the Royal Commission on the Condition of the Poorer Classes in Ireland shows that in the mid 1830's the illicit distiller was active mainly in Connacht and west Ulster (Fig. 14.4); and with the exception of that part of co. Antrim and co. Down immediately accessible from Belfast, this area coincides fairly closely with the small farm belt which dominated the north and west of Ireland. Details of the trade in poteen are difficult to uncover, for obvious reasons; but at least its importance for the area where it flourished is clear, since it has been estimated that illicit whiskey made up at least one half of all the spirit consumed in Ireland. More than a thousand government agents were employed in the 1830's to impede its manufacture, so that this industry also had indirect effects on the economy of the areas where it flourished.[34] These areas overlapped to some extent with the region influenced directly and indirectly by the domestic linen industry, but in detail it was also found in some of the more remote parts of the country. Certainly its influence extended throughout much of the area which would be classified as 'subsistence' Ireland.

There is, however, one glaring anomaly in the distribution of poteen making, as K. H. Connell has pointed out. This is the absence of the industry from the more remote parts of co. Cork and co. Kerry, where it might well have been expected because of the distance of these areas from the eyes of the law. Connell quotes the explanation of Alexander Nimmo, who suggested that within range of Cork city butter was a marketable product, comparable with poteen in its value for weight and without the risks of illegality.[35] The argument is not conclusive, since the production of butter may have penetrated some of the more remote areas because of the lack of a cash income from poteen making. What is important in this context is the manner in which butter from co. Kerry was conveyed up to 70 miles to the Cork market, for its eventual export to Britain. It seems likely that at least some of this butter must have come from within the area which would be classified as forming part of 'subsistence' Ireland.

POPULATION MOVEMENTS IN 'SUBSISTENCE' IRELAND

One of the most important distinctions made between 'maritime' and 'subsistence' Ireland was in the nature of population movements, one region with a self-contained

N

● Prevalent illicit distillation

□ Occasional illicit distillation

0   Miles   50

0   Kilometres   80

After Danaher

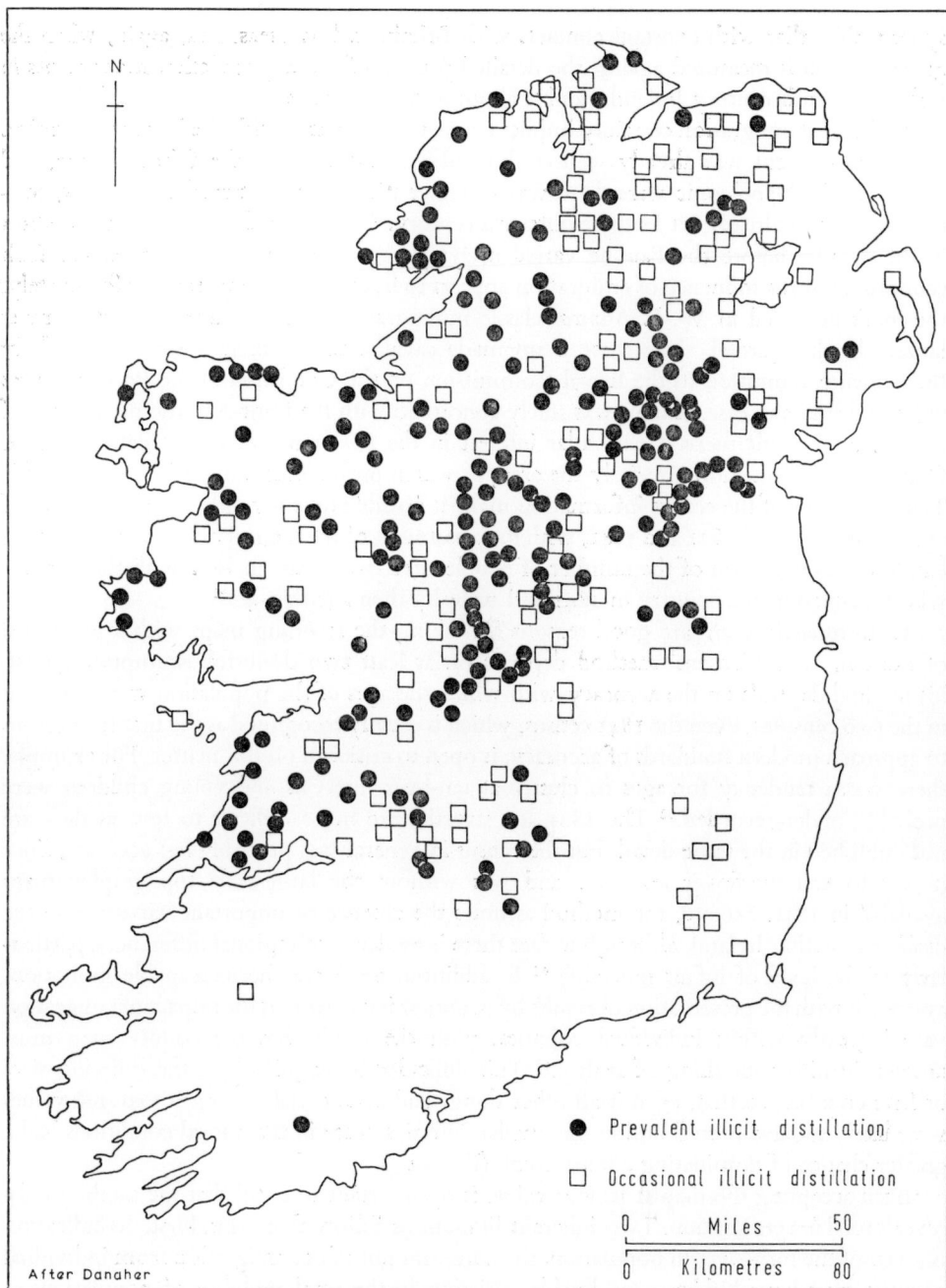

Fig. 14.4   Illicit distillation, 1826 (after Danahar)

system, the other with constant contacts with Britain and overseas. But, again, when the generalization is measured against the detailed pattern of actual population movements in early nineteenth-century Ireland, doubts about its validity arise.

Permanent emigration certainly implies contact with areas outside the local community. Such a movement was already well established in Ireland before the Great Famine, and following the Napoleonic wars there was a greater stimulus to outward movement, continuing a trend already set in the eighteenth century.[36] The annual amount of emigration in the decades before the Famine varied in sympathy with the vicissitudes of the Irish economy, but the influence of emigration appears to have been widespread. Unfortunately, the maps provided in W. F. Adams' classic monograph on pre-Famine emigration must largely be disregarded, since these maps made cavalier use of their sources, particularly the evidence submitted to the Royal Commission on the Condition of the Poorer Classes in Ireland.[37] In any case, Adams was solely concerned with the trans-Atlantic movement of people. As a result there is particular interest in the recent use of census data by S. H. Cousens to delimit more precisely the areas in which pre-Famine emigration was found.[38] The limitations of the census information make it possible to study only the distribution of emigration between 1821 and 1841, with the assessment of the intensity of emigration being based on a comparison of the number of people aged 0–20 years in 1821 with the number who remained in the country in 1841 and were by then aged 20–40.[39]

Unfortunately there are good reasons for taking the resulting maps with a great deal of caution, since Cousens' method depends on at least two doubtful assumptions. First, his method depends on the accuracy with which the ages of the population were returned in the two censuses; even the 1841 census, which is usually recognised as the first Irish census to approach modern standards of accuracy, is open to criticism on this matter. For example, there was a tendency for ages to cluster at ten-year intervals and young children were probably under-recorded.[40] The 1821 age statistics are more difficult to test, as they are not published in the same detail, but the census in general was probably less accurate, since it was backed by fewer resources and was without the large-scale topographic maps available in 1841. Second, the method assumes the absence of important variations in the death rate within Ireland, although in fact there is evidence of regional differences, particularly in the level of infant mortality.[41] In addition, there are the inescapable limitations associated with the presentation of results by counties: it is clear that the impact of emigration varied greatly within individual counties, with the result that the county map must necessarily hide something of reality.[42] This difficulty is magnified by the differing sizes of Irish counties, so that, even if all other things had been equal, the most extreme values were likely to have been found in the smaller counties, since in them local conditions had a greater chance of dominating county totals (Fig. 14.5).

Even accepting the map at its face value, it is important to recall that the method only reveals total net emigration. Two inherent limitations follow from this. First, no indication is given of the turn-over in population, the same amount of net emigration from individual counties may have hidden considerable variation in the total mobility of population, as inward movement could have replaced some of those who left; for example, it is likely

N

?

?

After Cousens

Per cent

0 – 2·4

2·5 – 4·9

5·0 – 7·4

7·5 – 9·9

12·0

| 0 | Miles | 40 |
| 0 | Kilometres | 60 |

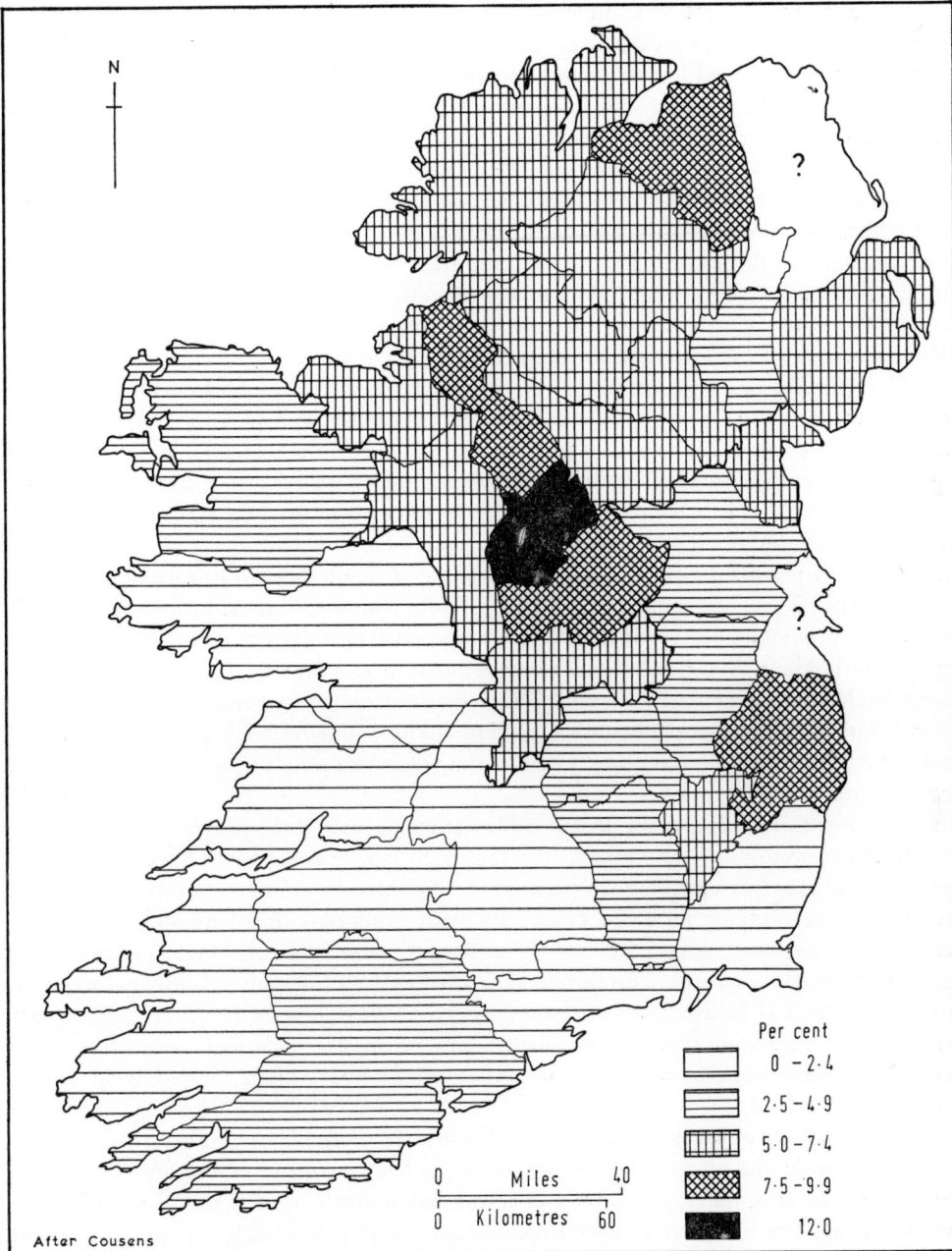

Fig. 14.5   Ireland, emigration 1821–41 (after Cousens)

that the absolute emigration from some of the eastern counties dominated by Belfast and Dublin was considerably greater than the net figures would suggest. Second, the method records areas which had lost population to destinations elsewhere within the British Isles as well as to North America, thus presenting further difficulties in interpretation, since the movement to these various destinations probably involved different social groups and motives for moving.[43]

Nevertheless, figure 14.5, which is based on Cousens' calculations, will stand at least one relevant conclusion. Counties which experienced net outward movement of population were widespread throughout Ireland; and the areas where the movement was particularly important covered contrasting economic regions. As well as being found in co. Down and co. Louth, which clearly formed part of 'commercial' Ireland as defined by Lynch and Vaizey, emigration was particularly important in much of north-west Ireland.

The transatlantic emigrants were often small farmers, many of whom were noticing a contraction in the domestic linen industry in the 1830s[44], and were at least sufficiently absorbed in a commercial economy to be aware of the benefits that such an economy can bring and the opportunities available elsewhere. Indeed, there was a long tradition of emigration in the north of Ireland, particularly among the Presbyterian small farmers— a tradition which created social attitudes which were favourably disposed towards emigration and also provided practical help in the form of remittances from relatives who had already crossed the Atlantic.[45] Information as well as money flowed in from America[46]; and the Ulster system of Tenant Right allowed the small farmer to raise a capital sum by the sale of his holding. As a result it can be argued that these emigrants came from areas with considerable outside contacts. Certainly they were not the poorest in the community, and detailed study shows that the majority of them did not come from the poorest agricultural areas.[47] At the same time it is quite clear that they were not simply drawn from a restricted coastal strip in eastern Ireland.

Movement to Great Britain demanded fewer resources and the people who went were certainly less well-off. S. H. Cousens has suggested that seasonal harvest work in Britain played some part in encouraging permanent migration.[48] Certainly temporary harvest migration was bringing increased familiarity with conditions elsewhere and, later in the century at least, there was a tendency for seasonal harvesters to take semi-permanent and permanent work in Britain. This would certainly explain the high level of net emigration in counties such as Leitrim, Roscommon and Sligo, where literary evidence suggests that transatlantic emigration was less prevalent.[49] But no matter what their destination, these emigrants came from areas with powerful external links, often located deep within 'subsistence' Ireland.

The prevalence of harvest migration is, of course, relevant in its own right. In the 1830's, the first date in the nineteenth century when the source regions of this movement can be precisely located, the migrants were concentrated in north-western and western Ireland, with Galway, Mayo, Leitrim, Sligo, Roscommon and Donegal being the most important counties involved.[50] Within this area there were some internal contrasts (Fig. 14.6). In particular, in parts of north-west co. Mayo the movement was unimportant because these

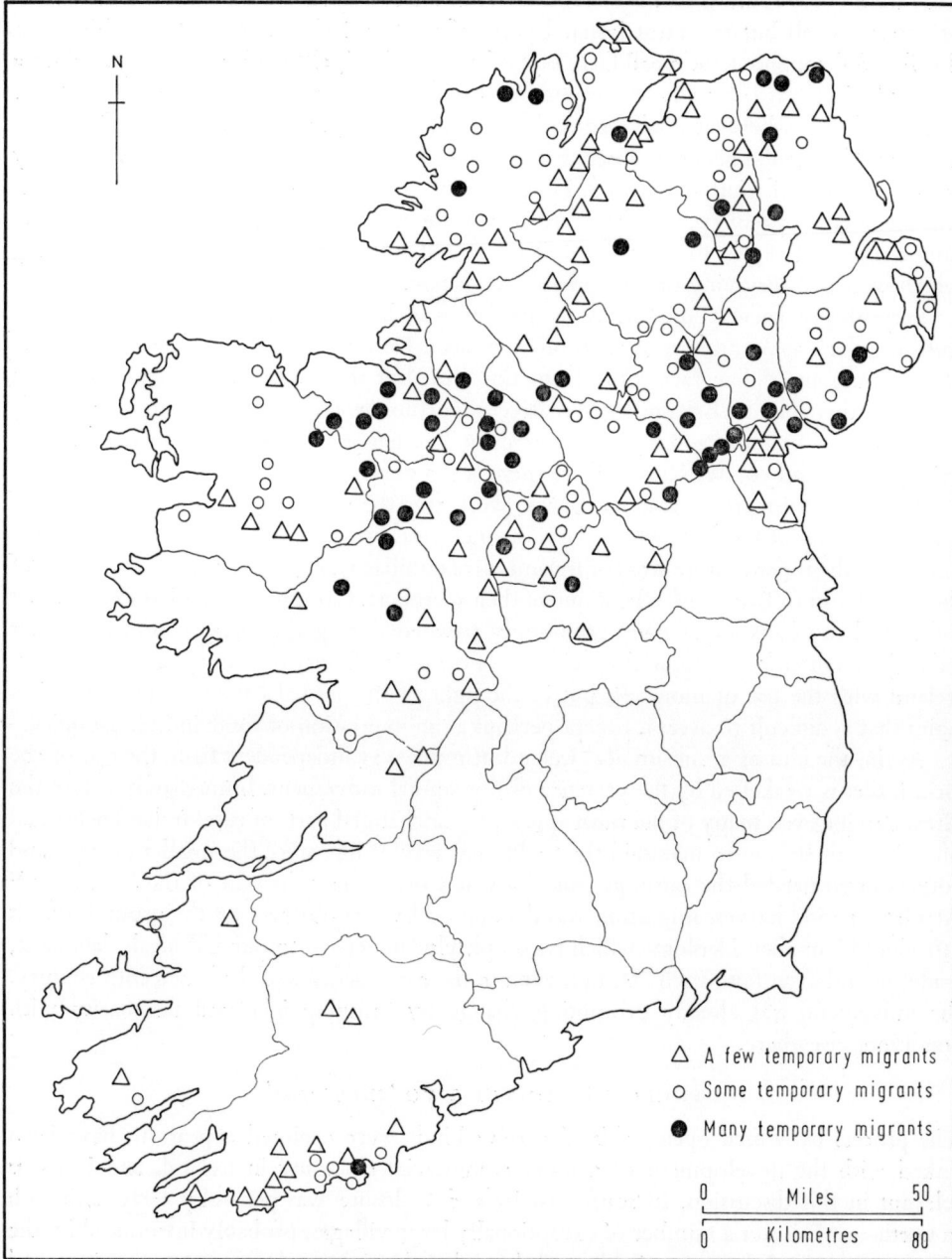

△ A few temporary migrants
○ Some temporary migrants
● Many temporary migrants

0   Miles   50

0   Kilometres   80

Fig. 14.6   Harvest migrants to Britain, 1834

areas were "very retiring and very remote"[51]; but harvest migration could be said to have penetrated to all but the most isolated parts of western Ireland. Harvest migration was also found throughout the small farm belt of north Ireland, although when measured on a county basis it was relatively less important than further west. In fact, the movement was well established wherever small farmers lived on restricted resources away from alternative urban employment—hence its absence in rural areas around the Lagan valley. The densely populated areas of south-eastern co. Londonderry, the fringes of the Mourne mountains, and the north coast of co. Antrim were among the areas from which the movement was important in the 1830's. In other words it was found in those pockets of subsistence farming which were still surviving or were unable to change.

Surprisingly, harvest migration to Britain was largely absent from south-western Ireland, which again appears as an anomalous area. Here the explanation seems to be that harvest migrants did in fact come from this area, but they went to destinations within Ireland, rather than to Britain.[52] Alternative opportunities lay closer to hand, for example in the Golden Vale of co. Limerick, where the hay harvest demanded extra hands, or in east co. Cork and co. Wexford, where there was a commercial grain harvest to save.

The cash return from seasonal harvest work was the single most important source of money in many of the areas where the movement was present. As a result even the poorest families in the more remote areas of Ireland were familiar with the use of money because of the annual visit to Britain of at least one of their members. Campbell Foster has claimed that in co. Galway bank notes were commonly pawned during the Great Famine, and this example has often been repeated as evidence of the unfamiliarity of many people in western Ireland with the use of money[53]; but in the light of the annual harvest migration it is a point that is difficult to accept, except perhaps as an expression of some individual quirk.

Again, the idea of a 'subsistence' Ireland in some way independent from the rest of the British Isles is weakened by the presence of this annual movement. Immediately before the Great Famine even many of the most apparently unchanged parts of rural Ireland depended on links with Britain to maintain the traditional way of life, since the smaller farmers and cottiers often needed the earnings from harvest work to pay the rent of their holdings.[54] At a later period harvest migration was denounced by one observer on the grounds that it introduced "an alien ideology which is completely subversive to our old ideals, language, tradition and even faith itself"[55]; but, even in the early decades of the nineteenth century, the movement was already promoting change by bringing increased familiarity with conditions elsewhere.

ENCLOSURE IN THE TWO 'IRELANDS'

The process by which open fields of various kinds were enclosed appears to have been linked with the development of a more commercial economy in Ireland, and hence is relevant in this discussion. In south-east Ireland enclosure was generally early, although in north-east Leinster a number of exceptionally large villages, probably introduced by the Normans, retained their open fields until the end of the eighteenth century, and in marginal lands evidence of early, more informal types of settlement linger on even later.[56] The earliest enclosures were made around the most prosperous towns: much of the country-side around Dublin, for example, was enclosed by the end of the seventeenth century. F. H. A. Aalen has suggested that the growth of a commercial economy and the expansion of a demand for cattle were important factors in extending enclosure in this region, so that, as a result, most of Leinster was enclosed by 1800.[57] The growth of eighteenth-century Dublin to reach 170,000 people about 1800, and thus form the second largest city in the British Empire, must have directly encouraged rural change, although it can hardly have had the same profound influence as eighteenth-century London, which had a population of 900,000 by this time.[58]

Away from the south-east the position was much more complex. D. McCourt and P. Flatrès have both shown that clusters of farm-buildings were widespread in the 1830's, and these 'clachans' were found both in the most remote parts of the west and in some areas of eastern Ireland.[59] Sometimes these clusters merely represented relics of past conditions, but where they still represented functioning groups of farms they were often associated with open fields, which bore a family resemblance to the Scottish infield-outfield system. In fact, clachans and single farmhouses, with compact holdings around them, coexisted in most regions of Ireland.[60] Even in areas such as co. Down, where commercial farming was well established, the two settlement types were found. Indeed there is some evidence that, in part of co. Down at least, clachans were often occupied by largely subsistence cultivators, while other farmers in larger, isolated holdings, were much more closely involved in commercial production.[61]

The process of enclosure and the extension of commercial farming were not always inevitably linked. A landlord might well consider that the rent-paying ability of his tenants would be increased by enclosure, but it did not necessarily follow that the economic forces were present which would lead inescapably to the introduction of commercial farming. Even so, the removal of traditional field systems and settlement forms at least indicated the presence of strong forces encouraging social, if not economic change, whether the new way of life was willingly accepted by the tenants themselves or imposed by landlords for a variety of motives, sometimes selfish, sometimes paternalistic.[62]

If enclosure is taken as such an index, the evidence of change was widespread at the beginning of the nineteenth century. In co. Limerick, where a transition between 'maritime' and 'commercial' Ireland might be expected, enclosure was well advanced. For example, in topographically suitable areas there was already evidence in 1824 of 'ladder' farms, that is, rectangular holdings with the fields of individual farms arranged in a line up and down slope, giving evidence of the activity of landlords in rationalizing earlier field systems.[63] The limited map evidence suggests that certain farmers were expanding the size of their holdings, commonly on land which was better suited for commercial farming, while in the same townlands the more poorly drained areas were being subdivided and sublet.[64] Maps of the estate of Lord Cloncurry, drawn in 1814, show a number of substantial farms, but also reveal that cottiers were living on some of these holdings, as well as the principal tenants themselves.[65] In short, the map evidence suggests that changes had already taken place in co. Limerick, that there was social diversity within small areas and, probably, that there was associated variation in the degree to which individual families were concerned with commercial farming. In Londonderry, which was a county also undergoing change at the beginning of the nineteenth century, estate maps again give an indication of recent enclosure, particularly in the north of the county at this time.[66] In the south-east of the county the varied interest of individual landlords in their estates could already be picked out, since here enclosure was partly underway but at the same time traditional field systems and settlement types still commonly survived.[67]

Eastern co. Galway exhibited the same kind of diversity even within the lands held by one landlord. On the Blake estates, for example, the situation varied from townland to townland.[68] In 1806, 125 acres of tillage ground in Ballyheal were located around a large clachan, with no other settlement being present in the townland. On the other hand, in Ballycahallane, near Gort, there were both compact holdings and farms held by a number of joint-tenants, who lived in clachans.[69] In east co. Galway, too, some of the farm clusters had a more formal plan, with houses arranged along a main street, as for example in Killtullagh.[70] This was an area where at least some landlords were active in the management of their estates during the late eighteenth century, and the fact that informally-planned clachans and compact holdings with isolated farmsteads coexisted with the 'street' villages and dominated the settlement types on neighbouring estates suggests that later replanning by some landlords must have had some influence in producing this regionally-distinctive plan.

In the agriculturally marginal and congested areas of west co. Galway the scope for agricultural change of any kind was much more restricted, but again landlords were active at the beginning of the nineteenth century. One local landowner was encouraging the growth of Roundstone and another had created the town of Clifden. In 1815 Clifden contained one house, but by 1840 there were 400 buildings, including an hotel; in 1814 the town and a large tract of adjoining country yielded no revenue at all, but by 1835 it was producing £7,000.[71] Hence even in this remote and unpromising area money was entering more firmly into the economy.

Much work will be required before these necessarily local observations can be rendered into any kind of general statement, but what is quite clear is that changes were being made in the landscape of many parts of Ireland, other than those in the eastern and southern zone of predominantly commercial agriculture.

CONCLUSION

A simple division of early nineteenth century Ireland into two contrasting economic regions is an attractive concept, but it is an idea which requires considerable qualification. Certainly there were major contrasts between eastern Ireland and the west, reflecting different styles of life, which were closely linked with the spread of more commercial attitudes; but no simple index seems adequate to define these general regions. The importance of commercial farming, the disappearance of the Irish language, the activity of landlords in shaping the landscape may all be advanced as diagnostic features of 'maritime' Ireland, but close examination shows that the limits of these various phenomena were vague and the correlation between them far from complete.

Nor was each of the two regions identical throughout its own area, even if their limits could be satisfactorily established. The small farming belt of the north-west, the area influenced indirectly by the linen industry, the districts producing poteen, the source areas of the harvest migrants, and the remote pockets where traditional life continued completely unchanged, all lay within 'subsistence' Ireland and did not coincide, although some of them overlapped. Similarly, within 'maritime' Ireland the cattle-fattening region, the wheat and barley-growing areas, the dairying areas of the south-west and the commercial heartland of the domestic linen weaving industry all represented differing conditions, which responded in a variety of ways to changing economic circumstances.

In addition, the two 'Irelands' were far from separate economically, since many of the commercial activities of the east had contributions from elsewhere in the country. The linen industry and the production of cattle depended to some extent on links with subsistence Ireland, harvest migrants provided services to the farmers of the east as well as crossing to Britain, and poteen was sold throughout Ireland. Indeed, the prevalence of some of these activities may be taken as an indication that change was taking place within 'subsistence' Ireland.

For this reason it cannot be claimed that a stable situation existed in the decades before the Great Famine. The wind of change was blowing most strongly and consistently in the south-east. There were distant corners of Ireland where little if any alteration was found in traditional ways of life, although even in the more remote areas there were patches here and there where new features were being introduced into rural life. There were also considerable 'grey' areas where commercial influences were widespread, but much less clearly dominant than in the south-east. These changes had not yet produced the dramatic depopulation which was to characterize rural Ireland in the second half of the nineteenth century, but already society in most parts of Ireland was being prepared for what was to come.

REFERENCES

1 P. Lynch and J. Vaizey, *Guinness's Brewery in the Irish Economy, 1759–1876* (Cambridge, 1960), 9–17
2 Ibid., 9
3 See, for example, R. G. Ward's discussion of this process in Cash cropping and the Fijian village, *Geog. J.,* 130 (1964), 484–500
4 K. H. Connell, The colonization of the waste land in Ireland, 1780–1845, *Ec. Hist. Rev.,* 2nd series, 3 (1950–51), 44–71; see also the regional descriptions in T. W. Freeman, *Pre-Famine Ireland: a study in historical geography* (Manchester, 1957)
5 See espec. Freeman, (1957), op. cit., 296–9, 258–68, 230–41
6 e.g. see C. Woodham-Smith, *The Great Hunger: Ireland, 1845–9* (London, 1962), 20–9
7 For a contemporary statement see, J. K. Trimmer, *A Brief Inquiry into . . . Agriculture in the Southern Part of Ireland . . .* (London, 1809), 12–19
8 T. Jones Hughes, Society and settlement in nineteenth century Ireland, *Irish Geography,* 5, No. 2 (1965), 79–96. espec. 81–3
9 Ibid., 87–8

R

10 J. Lee, Marriage and population in pre-famine Ireland, *Ec. Hist. Rev.*, 2nd series, 21 (1968), 283–95;
M. Drake, Marriage and population growth in Ireland, 1750–1845, *Ec. Hist. Rev.*, 2nd series, 16
(1963), 311; K. H. Connell, *The Population of Ireland, 1750–1845* (Oxford, 1950), see espec. chap. 2,
27–46

11 J. H. Johnson, Marriage and fertility in nineteenth century Londonderry, *J. Stat. and Soc. Inquiry
Soc. of Ireland*, 21 (1957–8), 99–117, espec. figs. 4 and 5, 112–3

12 K. H. Connell, Peasant marriage in Ireland: its structure and development since the Famine, *Ec.
Hist. Rev.*, 2nd series, 14 (1961–62), 502–23

13 J. Lee, (1968), op. cit., 291

14 D. Large, The wealth of the greater Irish landowners, 1750–1815, *Irish Historical Studies*, 15 (1966),
21–47, espec. 27–8

15 Ibid., appendix, 46–7

16 Ibid., 31

17 D. A. Beaufort, *Memoir of a Map of Ireland* (London, 1792), 33

18 D. Large, (1966), op. cit., 46–7

19 J. McEvoy, *Statistical Survey of the County of Tyrone 1801 and 1802* (Dublin, 1802), 61

20 Ibid.

21 D. A. Beaufort, (1792), op. cit., 70, 33

22 J. McParlan, *Statistical Survey of the County of Mayo . . . 1801* (Dublin, 1802), iv

23 Ibid., 23, referring to the Barony of Tyrawley

24 E. R. R. Green, *The Lagan Valley, 1800–50: a local history of the Industrial Revolution* (London, 1949),
chap. 3, 57–94: C. Gill, *The Rise of the Irish Linen Industry* (Oxford, 1925), 2, 315–34

25 C. Gill, (1925), op. cit., 21; For a map of the distribution of linen weaving and flax cultivation
towards the end of the eighteenth century see I. Leister, Landwirtschaft und agraräumliche Gliederung Irlands zur Zeit A. Young's, *Zeit. für Agrargeschichte und Agrarsoziologie*, 10 (1962), 9–44,
map 4, 21

26 *Minutes of the Trustees of the Linen and Hempen Manufacturers of Ireland . . .* (Dublin, 1817), 61

27 J. McEvoy, (1802), op. cit., 53

28 Ibid., 89

29 G. V. Sampson, *A Memoir . . . of the county of Londonderry, Ireland* (London, 1814), 246–7

30 C. Gill, (1925), op. cit., 25

31 J. McParlan, (1802), op. cit., 27

32 K. H. Connell, Illicit distillation: an Irish peasant industry, in T. D. Williams, ed., *Historical Studies*,
3 (1961), 58–91

33 Ibid., 67; J. H. Johnson, Agriculture in county Derry at the beginning of the nineteenth century,
Studia Hibernica, 4 (1969), 96

34 Connell, (1961), op. cit., 91

35 Ibid., 78, 80–1

36 W. F. Adams, *Ireland and the Irish Emigration to the New World from 1815 to the Famine,* (New Haven,
1932)

37 Ibid., Map 2, opposite p. 158

38 S. H. Cousens, The regional variation in emigration from Ireland between 1821 and 1841, *Trans.
Inst. Brit. Geog.*, 37 (1965), 15–30

39 Ibid., 19

40 J. H. Johnson, (1957–8), op. cit., 101; J. Lee, (1968), op. cit., 287–91; J. Drake, (1963), op. cit., 109

41 A point made by S. H. Cousens himself in The restriction of population growth in pre-famine
Ireland, *Proc. Roy. Irish Acad.*, 64 C (1966), 91, and fig. 2, 90

42 See for instance the detailed study in J. H. Johnson, Population movements in county Derry during
a pre-famine year, *Proc. Roy. Irish Acad.*, 60 C (1959), 141–62

43 Ibid., 152–4, 159

44 W. F. Adams, (1932), op. cit., 170–2
45 Ibid., 181
46 A. Schrier, *Ireland and the American Emigration, 1850–1900* (Minneapolis, 1958), 18–42, discusses this influence at a later period. See also B. MacAodha, Letters from America, *Ulster Folklife*, 3 (1957), 64–9
47 J. H. Johnson, (1959), op. cit., 146–9
48 S. H. Cousens, (1965), op. cit., 24
49 See, for example, parish reports in Ordnance Survey Memoirs, although they are less complete for this area (MS deposited in Library of Royal Irish Academy, Dublin)
50 J. H. Johnson, Harvest migration from nineteenth century Ireland, *Trans. Inst. Brit. Geog.*, 41 (1967), 97–112
51 *Condition of the Poorer Classes . . .* , (1835), op. cit., evidence of Capt. Ireland for Kilkommen and Kilmore, and evidence of Rev. M. Kelly for Kilkommen West, Appendix A (Supplement), 25
52 J. H. Johnson, (1967), op. cit., 102–3
53 T. C. Foster, *Letters on the Condition of the People of Ireland,* (London, 1846), 314; C. Woodham Smith, (1962), op. cit., 82
54 J. H. Johnson, (1967), op. cit., espec. 99
55 Irish Folklore Commission, MS 1245, 526, referring to North Erris
56 J. Otway-Ruthven, The origin of Anglo-Irish agriculture in the middle ages, *J. Roy. Soc. Antiq. Ireland*, 81 (1951), 1–13; F. H. A. Aalen, Transhumance in the Wicklow Mountains, *Ulster Folklife*, 10 (1964), 65–72
57 F. H. A. Aalen, Enclosures in eastern Ireland, *Irish Geography*, 5, No. 2 (1965), 30–36, espec. 32
58 c.f. E. A. Wrigley, A simple model of London's importance in changing English society and economy, 1650–1750, *Past and Present*, No. 37 (July, 1967), 44–70
59 D. McCourt, The rundale system in Ireland, (unpublished PhD thesis, Queen's University, Belfast, 1950);
P. Flatrès, *Géographie rurale de quatre contrées Celtiques,* (Rennes, 1957), separate folding map: "les villages d'Irlande vers 1840"
60 D. McCourt, Infield and outfield in Ireland, *Ec. Hist. Rev.*, 2nd series, 7 (1955), 369–76, espec. 376
61 R. H. Buchanan, J. H. Johnson and V. B. Proudfoot, Excavations at Murphystown, Co. Down . . . 1957 and 1958, *Ulster J. Arch.*, 22 (1959), 132
62 For an example of paternalism see O. Robinson, The London Companies as progressive landlords in nineteenth-century Ireland, *Ec. Hist. Rev.*, 2nd series, 15 (1962), 103–18
63 National Library of Ireland, Longfields Maps, 21 F 40 (7–13)
64 Ibid., e.g. maps 7 and 10
65 Ibid., map 12
66 Ibid., map 13; J. H. Johnson, Partnership and clachans in mid-nineteenth century Londonderry, *Ulster Folklife*, 9 (1963), Fig. 5, 25
67 D. McCourt, Traditions of rundale in and around the Sperrin mountains, *Ulster J. Arch.*, 16 (1953) 69–84
68 National Library of Ireland, Maps and descriptive matter on Blake estates, 21 F 74 (1–26)
69 Ibid., maps 5 and 6
70 Ibid., map 11; for photograph see Flatrès, (1957), op. cit., plate IV
71 Mr and Mrs C. S. Hall, *Ireland: its scenery, character etc* (3 vols., London, 1841), vol. 3, 484

XV

TOWN AND BAILE IN IRISH PLACE-NAMES
T. Jones Hughes

In Ireland the vast majority of the names of places are of Celtic origin and they have survived in such large numbers, in spite of the virtual disappearance of Irish as a spoken language over the greater part of the country, because they are mainly the names not of settlements, but of land units known as townlands. Such names acquired legal title at an early date and came to be specifically recorded over many centuries in the large-scale maps and ledger books that accompanied the great land transfers that have been such a prominent and notorious feature of Irish history. These land surveys culminated in the Ordnance Survey townland maps on a scale of six inches to the mile, the first edition of which was completed for the whole island c. 1840. Scholars such as John O'Donovan and Eugene O'Curry were responsible for providing the Survey with the anglicised forms of Irish place-names and it is these anglicised forms which have been in general use ever since. It is fortunate that their names and territorial limits were accurately represented on large-scale maps at a time when townlands would be expected to have the greatest meaning in the day-to-day lives of the majority of the rural population. This is important because many of the names of administrative units employed in nineteenth-century Ireland, especially those of baronies and parishes, were bestowed by aliens largely for their own purposes and they never gained local recognition. The two Talbotstown baronies in west co. Wicklow would probably be typical of such unrecognised entities. This is rarely true of the townland. In the absence of separate names for individual homesteads in the countryside, other than the names of the families that lived in them, the townland units became the sole means of distinguishing between small areas locally, and as such their layouts have been familiar to the countryman over many centuries. Apart from that of the provinces and certain counties the townland net is in fact the only surviving administrative framework in Ireland with a continuous history of development going back to medieval times if not earlier, and the confused pattern of land holding and working which prevailed in the nineteenth century served to enhance rather than diminish the importance of the townland as the basic territorial division.

Townlands were created at various times and for a variety of purposes. In the east and south of the country the majority appear to have crystallised as territorial divisions in the middle ages, and over much of Leinster the network was designed for the reallocation of land among alien settlers mainly in the thirteenth and fourteenth centuries. There is no doubt however that some of the units now familiar to us are late accretions which came into being as part of the effort made by the Ordnance surveyors to devise a network of small administrative divisions for the whole country. It was probably at this time that the four townlands called simply 'Suburbs of Cork' came into being and that streets on the outskirts of expanding Dublin, such as Conyngham Road (St James's parish), acquired townland status. With the same aim in mind the surveyors proceeded to give English names, some of which were not necessarily translations from the Irish, to uninhabited offshore islands and lake islands in Connacht and elsewhere and some of these too came to be recognised as townlands. Today townland and neighbourhood consciousness is most evident in those extensive areas of the country where small-scale family farming prevails, particularly in counties such as Armagh, Cavan and Clare. In this respect it is important to recall that the general outline of the townland framework, as we know it, originated in very different economic and social circumstances and that it was virtually completed for the whole country by the beginning of the seventeenth century, at a time when family farming was still in its infancy.

There are in all over 62,000 townlands, and their primary purpose is to distinguish between landed interests locally. Their names therefore usually refer to permanent, visible and easily identifiable features of the landscape. Such features may be divided into two groups. The first group consists of 'toponyms' or elements which refer to physical or natural features, usually of a topographic or botanical nature. The second group is concerned with 'cultural' items which are the product of human activity and these refer mainly to either land units or types of settlement. The following are the major name elements in each group:[1]

Toponyms
 (i) topographic features (14 per cent, 9,000).
 druim, 'ridge'; *cnoc*, 'hill'; *corr*, 'hill'; *cúil*, 'corner, angle'; *tulach*, 'mound'; *gleann*, 'glen'; *carraig*, 'rock, rocky place'; *árd*, 'height'; *mullach*, 'summit, height'.
 (ii) botanical features (7 per cent, 4,500).
 cluain, 'field cleared in a bog or forest, meadow'; *doire*, 'oakwood'; *currach, corrach*, 'marsh, moor'; *móin*, 'bog'; *eanach*, 'marsh'; *garrán*, 'shrubbery'; *muine*, 'shrubbery'.

Cultural elements
 (i) land units (19 per cent, 12,000).
 baile, 'place, land, farm'; *town*; *gort*, 'field'; *ceathramha*, 'quarter'; *achadh*, 'field'; *páirc*, 'field, demesne'; *field*; *ceapach*, 'tillage plot'; *garrdha*, 'garden, cultivated plot'.
 (ii) items of settlement (7 per cent, 4,500).
 cill, 'church'; *lios*, 'enclosure', ring fort'; *ráth*, 'fort'; *dún*, 'fort'; *cathair*, 'stone fort'.

One third of the total number of townland names in Ireland therefore contain elements which refer either to major types of land units or to prominent topographic features. Another quarter of the total are concerned with the most obvious of botanical features or with certain types of settlement which were characteristic of early Ireland. An analysis of the major elements, by groups, therefore serves to remind us of the very limited range of items, both toponymic and cultural, that are referred to in Irish place-names. In particular we notice that they tell us little about the social and economic conditions which prevailed locally at the time when they were bestowed. We find few references, for example, to crops and livestock or to patterns of land occupation. Names which refer specifically to social groups, such as Ballynamought (Bantry barony[2], Cork), 'place of the poor people', or Ballinlaban (Moycashel barony, Westmeath), 'place of the labourer', are very rare. So also are references to any kind of institution within the settlement pattern, other than churches, forts, castles and corn mills and it is only in the immediate vicinity of Dublin, for example, that we find mention of the existence of inns in medieval Ireland. Thus there is a Buckandhounds in Clondalkin parish and a Butchersarms in St James's parish, both in Uppercross barony. Place-names therefore throw little light on the origin and development of forms of early settlement. This is as we would expect, bearing in mind that we are dealing with the names of land units.

When the distribution of representative elements from both the typonomic and cultural groups are plotted on maps they are sometimes found to be mutually exclusive. This is especially true of those which are widely diffused throughout the island; these we shall refer to as the ubiquitous elements. Other name elements, both toponymic and cultural, recur locally in large numbers and these may display strong regional associations and our main concern is to identify and attempt to interpret some of these place-name regions. Ireland possesses several advantages from the point of view of the study of early regionalism. It is a small and compact island on the edge of a continent and it has considerable internal uniformity in terms of topography, climate and early conditions of plant life. In the occupied parts the main obstacles to movement are the wet lands but these are rarely continuous over widespread areas. Its insular and peripheral character had ensured that over long periods in its early history it had remained aloof from external influence and the constant repetition of the same place-name elements throughout the country testify to the exclusiveness of early Celtic culture. A cursory examination of Irish name elements will however reveal that this exclusiveness was rudely challenged and greatly modified as a result of the Anglo-Norman invasion of the late twelfth and thirteenth centuries, especially as the invaders brought with them ideas concerning the organisation and management of area which were radically different from those of the native. The present-day range and variety of name elements in Ireland are largely a product of the interaction of the two cultures in the middle ages. From this point of view it may be possible to recognise three general areas of influence: a zone of durable Norman rural occupation, discontinuous peripheral regions which were out of the reach of the invading culture and, in the third place, a broad but fragmented division where the native way of life was in varying degrees influenced by the presence of the stranger.

THE TOWN ZONE

About 14 per cent (8,800) of the total number of townland names in Ireland are English names. The majority of these may be referred to as being 'old English' names in that they originated in medieval times. Among the most common recurring elements are *castle, court, farm, field, grange, grove, hall, hill, land, mill, park, town* and *wood*. Of these by far the most important numerically is the suffix *town* (with a total of 2,684) followed by *park* (403), *hill* (327) and *field* (217). Some English name elements are particularly interesting because of their very restricted occurrence; these include *acre, close, heath, lots, moor* and *stang*. Very few old English name elements in Ireland are toponyms. The most numerous of these are *hill* and *wood*. The bulk of English names refer either to types of enclosure or to particular items of settlement. There are also 'new English' place-names in Ireland. In origin these are related mainly to the sixteenth and seventeenth-century land settlements and to the early years of estate organisation. The new names are even more restricted in their range but they are more widely and indiscriminately dispersed over the whole island. The new English elements include *brook, dale, lawn, lodge, mount* and *ville*. Our main concern is with the older names of medieval origin.

The suffix *town* stands out not only numerically but also in terms of its distinctive territorial distribution (Fig. 15.1). It appears in 31 per cent of the total number of English townland names in Ireland and no other name element, Irish or English, has such a widespread, compact and continuous distribution and such sharply defined limits. Over a large part of north Leinster this single element dominates over all the other name elements to such an extent that we feel justified in referring to this area of dominance as the '*town* zone'. It will be seen that this zone embraces most of north co. Dublin, the whole of Meath apart from its northern and western extremities as well as the whole of Louth with the exception of the Cooley peninsula. The *town* zone also extends into the eastern half of co. Westmeath and into east Kildare. Away from this area the suffix *town* is a dominant element in place-names only in the baronies of Bargy and Forth in south-east co. Wexford, and here the density of *town* names is as high if not higher than anywhere in north Leinster. Within the *town* zone the highest totals of the name element per barony occur in Forth (Wexford), 105 (total names 409); Ardee (Louth), 62 (198); Bargy (Wexford), (235), and Ratoath (Meath) (129) with 57 each, and Duleek Upper (Meath), 52 (108). Outside the areas of high incidence *town* is prominent only in a few southern counties such as Kilkenny, south Tipperary and east Limerick. It is almost entirely absent from Ulster, Connacht and west Munster.

The *town* zone in north Leinster, both in terms of its shape and territorial extent, clearly belongs to the level boulder-clay plains and the name element disappears as these clay plains degenerate westwards, in Westmeath and Kildare, to the wet lands of central Ireland. To the north the limit appears to be sharply set against the southern edge of the drumlin belt in Ulster. In the mid-nineteenth century, and to a lesser extent today, this same area of Leinster represented the most continuous expanse of large-scale farming in the country, with exceptionally low population densities and correspondingly high valuations per unit area. Dunshaughlin parish (Ratoath barony) in the heart of the *town* zone in south-east Meath, for example, had an area in 1851 of 5,300 acres, was valued at £5,100 and had a population (excluding the town of Dunshaughlin) of 745. Such an agrarian structure may have had its roots in medieval times when the townland names were first bestowed. The *town* zone may thus represent that part of Ireland which experienced the most durable impact of Anglo-Norman colonisation and settlement and there is a close relationship between its location and extent and the Pale as this has been depicted by historians. The

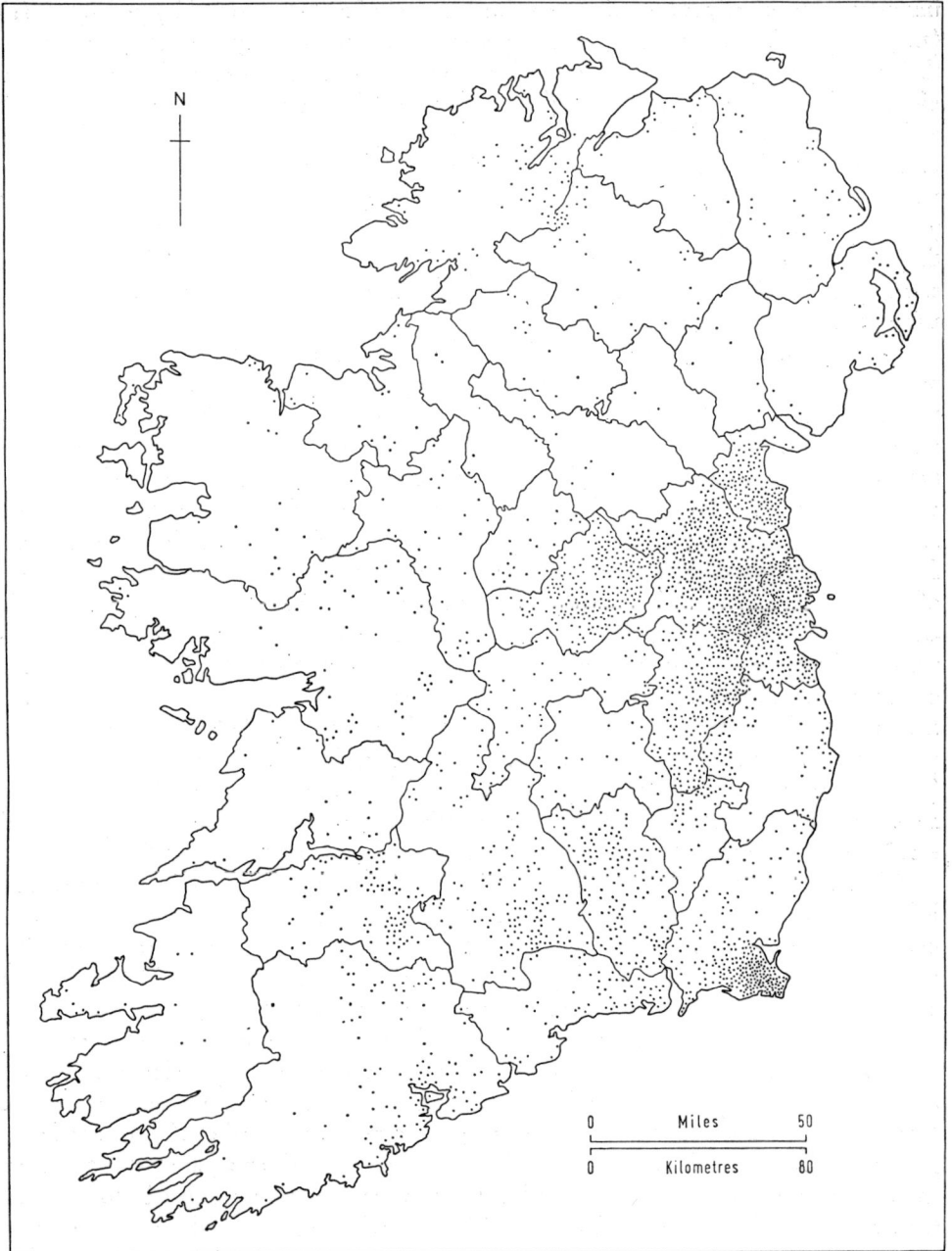

Fig. 15.1 *Town* as a suffix

highest densities of the name element occur immediately to the north and north-west of the capital, astride the Dublin-Meath-Kildare borders. This is the core of the *town* zone and it includes the baronies of Balrothery West, Castleknock and Nethercross in north co. Dublin; Dunboyne, Ratoath, Skreen and Deece Upper and Lower in co. Meath, and North Salt in north-east co. Kildare. Certain parishes within this group of baronies, such as Castleknock (Castleknock barony), Clonalvy (Duleek Upper), Dunboyne (Dunboyne), Lusk (Balrothery East) and Stamullin (Duleek Upper), have over 40 per cent of their total names incorporating the element *town*. Today this core area survives as that part of Ireland with the lowest population density (under 50 per square mile). The parishes are compact around strong centrally-situated villages or small towns bearing the same names, and their early churches are sometimes dedicated or rededicated to continental or biblical rather than to Celtic saints. Such villages, especially if they were manorial centres, as in the case of Swords (Nethercross) or Newcastle Lyons (Newcastle), must have acted as powerful anglicising influences from an early date. In these parishes too townland boundaries give the impression that they have been laid out systematically and the townland divisions are among the smallest in the country. In Castleknock parish, (9,303 ha: 21,000 acres), for example, their average size is 95 ha (214 acres), as compared with around 177 ha (400 acres) for Ireland as a whole.

The thoroughness of the Norman settlement of north Leinster is impressive when it is recalled that in the Dark Ages the Meath province had emerged as the metropolitan area of Celtic Ireland. In terms of place-names the displacement was so complete that only a few of the Irish elements that are prominent in other parts of the island have survived here and the majority of these are toponyms. One of the more prominent of the cultural elements is *ráth;* 20 per cent (232) of the total for the entire country are in the five counties of Dublin, Kildare, Louth, Meath and Westmeath. *Ráth* appears to have survived partly because it was employed by the invaders as if it was synonymous with their *town* and in this connection it is sometimes found in combination with a Norman personal name and this cannot be said of any other prominent Irish name element in any part of the country. Thus we find names such as Raheenarosita or Rochestown in Bantry barony (Wexford) and Baggotrath in Dublin barony. Another Irish cultural element which is prominent in north Leinster is *cill.* Whilst *ráth* is more numerous in Leinster than in any other province, *cill* is one of the finest examples of an ubiquitous element in the sense that it is evenly and widely distributed throughout most of the island. *Cill* is hardly ever found compounded with an English element and we would look in vain, for example, for any place with the name Kiltown. Even Churchtown is rare and translations such as Brideschurch (a parish in Naas barony, co. Kildare) are very few.

Other vestigial Irish name elements in north Leinster are the toponyms which commonly refer to landscape items belonging to the marginal land. The most prominent of these are *cluain* and *cnoc. Cluain* refers especially to the extensive meadows and ill-drained bottom lands which are important features of the clay plains. Like *cill, cluain* is an ubiquitous element among Irish names but unlike *cill* it has strong regional associations. It is especially numerous in east Connacht and in north Leinster it is most common along the wetter western fringe in counties Meath, Westmeath, Offaly and Kildare. A few of the recurring Irish toponyms such as *cluain, currach, inis* and *cnoc* were accepted early into the English terminology of eastern Ireland and *cnoc,* for instance, combines indiscriminately with both Irish and English elements in the baronies of Bargy and Forth (Wexford). By and large, however, it is true to say that some of the most familiar of Irish toponyms, such as *carraig, cuil, doire, moin* and *tulach,* are scarce in north Leinster.

The bulk of the *town* names are clearly of medieval origin and this is indicated in north Leinster by the fact that the element *town,* unlike some of the other prominent English suffixes, such as, for example, *field,* is rarely compounded with anything other than personal names and the majority of these are of Norman families. Moreover, Norman personal names are rarely found in conjunction with any other name element. Occasionally, towards the edge of the zone, *town* may combine with Irish personal names as, for example, in Mahonstown (Kells Upper, co. Meath and Fartullagh, co. Westmeath), but this is unusual. The element *town* in conjunction with a personal name was thus a term used by the coloniser with specific reference to land appropriation and reallocation. In this respect there is a surprisingly wide range of personal names in use, especially in the core area of the zone. In the parish of Lusk (Balrothery East, co. Dublin), out of a total of 81 townlands, 31 have the suffix *town* and among these there are at least 26 different personal names. In the core area we also find a tendency for some personal names to repeat themselves extensively. Thus out of a total of 45 Johnstowns in Ireland eight are in Meath and seven in co. Dublin. Other repeating personal names include Brown, Thomas, Harris and James. Towards the edge of the *town* zone and especially in the direction of regions noted for the recurrence of a limited range of Irish elements we find that even Irish toponyms combine with Norman personal names, for example, Carrickbaggot (Ferrard, Louth), Cavanrobert (Ardee, Louth), Clashwilliam (Gowran, Kilkenny), Mullaghdillon (Slane Upper, Meath) and Tullaghanstown (Navan Upper, Meath). Such names usually belong to the areas which were regaelicised in the late fourteenth and in the fifteenth century. The majority of the medieval Norman family names have long disappeared from north Leinster; they are commemorated only in the names of townlands. Their former presence in such large numbers does mean however that we learn very little from place-names about the economic and social organisation of their newly acquired lands by the Normans in this important area. Away from north Leinster and south-east Wexford the *town* element is significant only in parts of counties Kilkenny, Waterford, Tipperary and Limerick. In these counties the tendency is for the element to combine less and less with personal names. Instead compounds such as Newtown, Castletown and Milltown are numerous. In co. Limerick, for example, one half of the total of *town* townlands (87) are without personal names. The castle and the mill, together with the church, were integral parts of the nucleated settlements which were established, usually as parish centres, by the Normans in those regions where they never succeeded in acquiring a dominant foothold as farmers. In such areas it was not a question of the generous allocation of land among new colonists but the retention of a precarious foothold in the vicinity of small village and town centres.

If a comparison is made between the distribution of the element *town* and the distribution

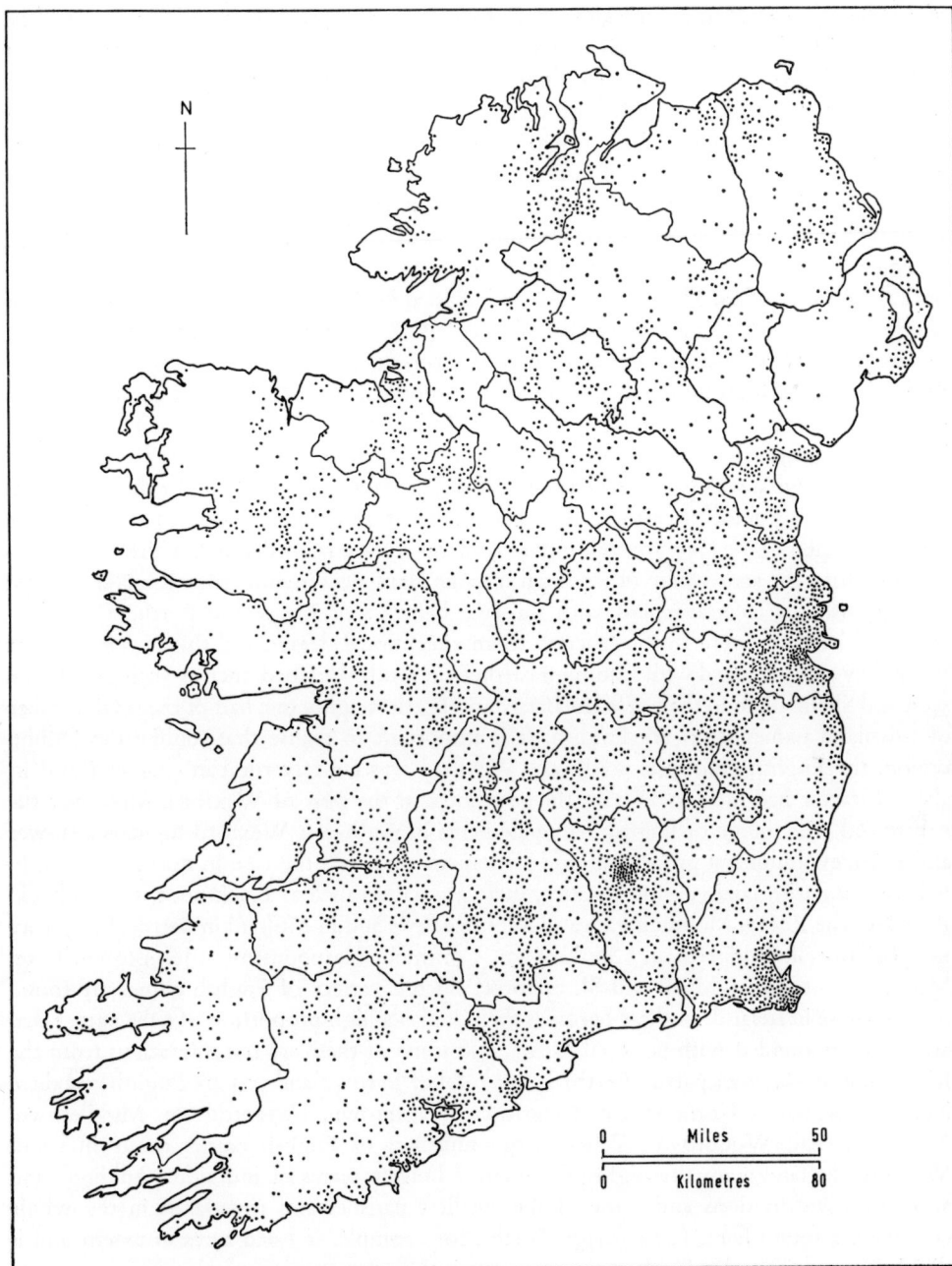

Fig. 15.2   Townlands with English names, excluding those with the suffix *town*

of all the other English name elements in Ireland (Fig. 15.2), it is found that among the other English elements north Leinster does not emerge as a distinctive territory. In other words within the *town* zone this one element is so predominant that it excludes not only the most ordinary of Irish elements, both cultural and toponymic, but in addition most other English elements as well. High densities of *town* in association with the high incidence of other English elements are found in three areas only and these are therefore the areas with the greatest diversity of English names in the country as a whole. The first such highly anglicised area occurs in north co. Dublin, immediately to the north of the city, in the baronies of Castleknock, Coolock and Nethercross. The small barony of Dunboyne, in the adjacent part of co. Meath, may also be included in this area. Some parishes in north co. Dublin were almost completely anglicised in terms of townland names at a very early date. In the parish of Swords (Nethercross barony), for example, out of a total of 54 names, 42 are English and 29 possess the suffix *town*. A comparison of figures 15.1 and 15.2 also shows that an area with a high incidence of English names, other than *town* names, is found in the immediate vicinity of the capital. Many of these are the new English names of mansions and villas set up around Dublin in the late seventeenth and during the eighteenth century. In the second place there is a strong admixture of other English name elements in the extension of the *town* zone along the Kildare-Wicklow borderland. Thirdly in south-east Wexford the area where other English name elements are numerous coincides almost exactly with the *town* area and with the two baronies of Bargy and Forth. These two Wexford baronies were thus anglicised to an exceptional degree and this is very evident when they are compared with adjoining baronies in south Wexford, such as Shelburne to the west and Shelmaliere to the north. In Bargy and Forth roughly one half of the total number of townland names (634) are English. It is important to realise that, unlike the Dublin region, the English colony in south co. Wexford was entirely rural in character and its alien character had little to do with the proximity of the port of Wexford. Moreover the nature and wide range of English name elements in south-east Wexford suggests a slower and more evolutionary process of land settlement than was the case in north Leinster. In Kilmannan parish (Bargy), for instance, there are names such as Blackmoor, Glenbullock, Knock of the Rocks, Mountaingate and Wetmeadows and in Mulrankin parish (Bargy) we find Brideswell, Bridgetown, Churchtown, Common, Harpoonstown, Johnstown, Lake, Moor, Mountcross, Oldhall and Sheephouse. Such a variety of English names are found nowhere else in Ireland. In these baronies there is also a high proportion of *town* names that are not compounded with personal names, and some of these are transliterations from the Irish. Thus in Mayglass parish (Forth) with a total of 38 townlands, 25 are English and these include Braestown, Cornerstown, Crosstown, Damptown, Haggardtown, Middletown, Moortown and Woodtown. Where large numbers of English names occur in south Wexford the land is usually highly fragmented both in terms of individual holdings and administrative divisions and some of the smallest parishes and townlands in the whole country are found here. Carn parish (Forth), for example, is 1,960 acres in extent and is divided into 40 townlands whose average area is thus 50 acres.

A further comparison between figures 15.1 and 15.2 will indicate that the other English name elements are flung far and wide over the whole country and regional concentrations are not prominent. It has already been suggested that the diffusion of English names in this way is partly due to the fact that many of them are 'new English' and were introduced by the more influential landowners with the estate system of land management. By far the most conspicuous is the impact of the Butler or Ormonde family on the fertile and attractive plains of north-central Kilkenny, and Kilkenny city itself must have been a very powerful centre making for innovation in south Leinster. On a more restricted scale many of the English names in south and east co. Kildare were on the lands of the Duke of Leinster and the estates of the Duke of Devonshire left a similar impression in the valley of the Blackwater in co. Waterford. Individual towns also acquired anglicised rural surroundings but these were usually very confined. Prominent among these are diocesan centres such as Cashel or Trim. South coast ports such as New Ross, Youghal and Kinsale had aureoles of townlands with English names from the medieval period. Thus the 5,000-acre St Mary's parish of New Ross was divided into 39 townlands and 14 of these were under 50 acres in extent; 30 townlands had English names and at least 10 appear to have originated as burghal lands. By and large, however, the impact in this way, of the old-established port towns of the east and south coast was surprisingly slight even in the case of large centres such as Waterford, Cork and Limerick, Finally, figure 15.2 shows that large parts of Ireland appear to have been little influenced by the English intrusion. Even the coastlands of south Leinster and of Munster remained doggedly Irish in nomenclature. In Ulster the plantations came too late to affect the names of the smaller administrative divisions, and counties such as Londonderry and Down are almost completely devoid of English townland names. It is important to bear in mind this limited territorial impact of early English influence.

THE HYBRID AREAS

It is of course wrong to think that the English names of places in Ireland may be studied in isolation. One important consequence of the Norman invasion was the appearance of extensive hybrid areas where two cultures met, intermingled and struggled for supremacy. These sometimes took the form of strongholds of the native culture emerging on the edge of the invaders' area of influence and they were often the homelands or transferred homelands of powerful Irish families. They included the lands of McMurrough Kavanagh in co. Wexford, O More in Laois, O Reilly on the Meath-Cavan border, O Conor in north co. Kerry and O Maddan and O Kelly in east co. Galway. In east Clare, north Tipperary and east Limerick, in particular, such lands came to be pin-pointed in the landscape by the presence of large numbers of castles and tower houses. There appears to be a certain correlation between the distribution of these hybrid areas and the use of the element *baile* in place-names to refer to units of land holding and working (Fig. 15.3). For the country as a whole *baile* is by far the most numerous element in Irish names and it is also the most varied and flexible in its usage, in that it combines with the greatest range of elements. This is not the place to examine the nature of *baile* compounds. Our particular interest is in the fact that the Irish *baile* and the English *town* appear to be employed in very similar

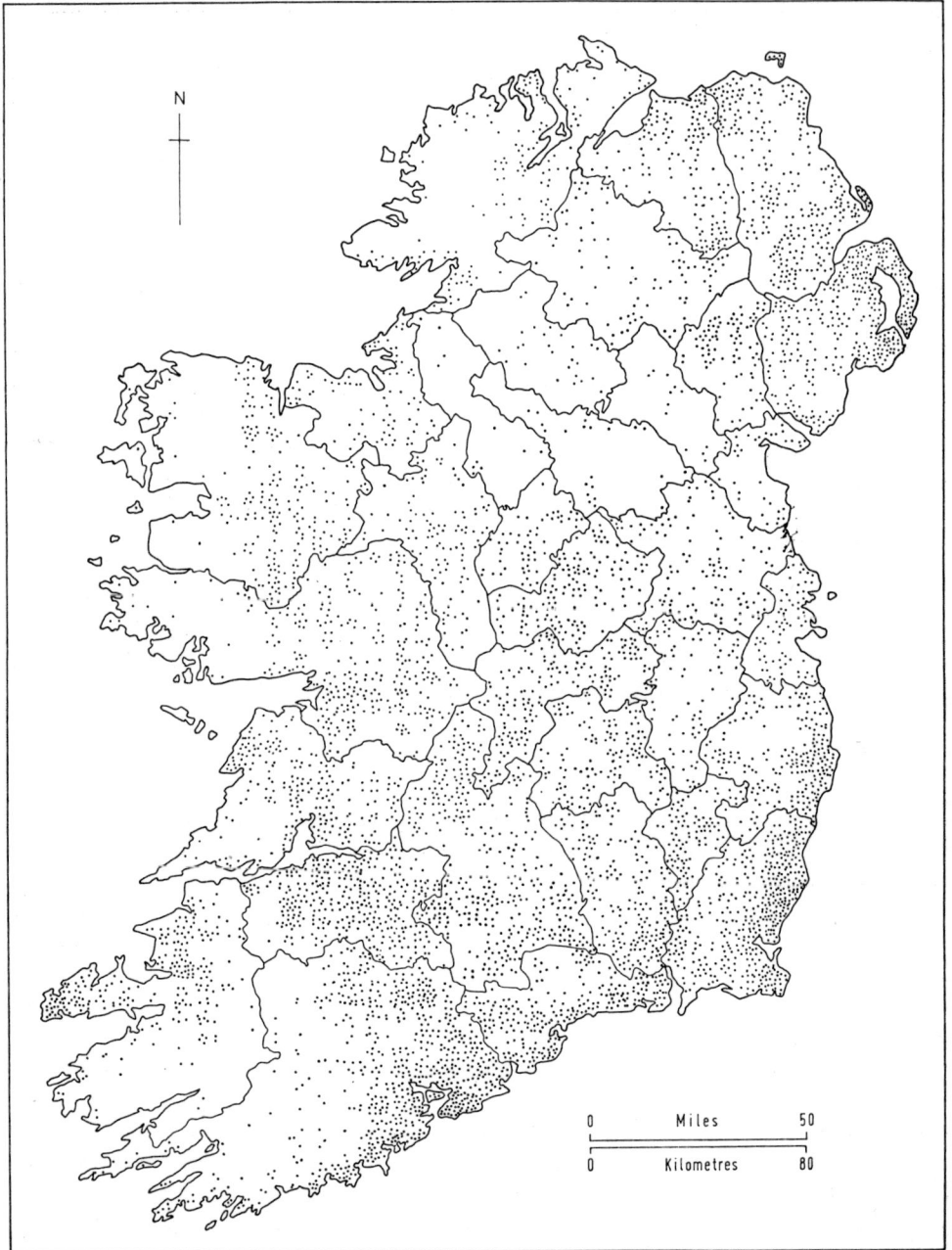

Fig. 15.3   *Baile* as a prefix and suffix

circumstances and that in the broad transitional areas of influence of the two cultures the elements are interchangeable. Two places named after the English family of Boden, for example, are called respectively Bodenstown in the lowlands of the Liffey valley in Naas barony, north co. Kildare, and Ballyboden on the slopes of the adjoining hills in Rathdown barony, co. Dublin. Complementary terms of this kind, with their own peculiar regional associations, are common in place-names. The settlement elements *ráth* and *lios,* for example, are interchangeable in co. Offaly where the dominant areas of the two forms meet. In a similar way *ceathramha* and *cartron* are found alongside each other among the names of land units in east co. Galway and in co. Roscommon, and *cartron* is of Norman origin. There is therefore a tendency for the density of *baile* names to increase along certain sections of the rim of the *town* zone as, for example, in Rathconrath barony in co. Westmeath and *baile* names also appear to provide a projection of the *town* zone in the direction of the lower Barrow valley in co. Carlow. In the foothill country along the Carlow-Wicklow border and especially in Rathvilly barony, which had experienced the waxing and waning of the two cultures, *baile* names are generally placed upslope of the *town* names.

In addition to being by far the most numerous element encountered in Irish place-names *baile* is also remarkable for its ubiquitousness. It occurs in substantial numbers in almost every county but like *town* it also displays strong regional preferences. It is, for example, especially characteristic of the broad coastlands and the peninsular areas in the east and south of the island. This may be significant as there is little evidence that coastlands were particularly attractive as areas of principal settlement in Celtic Ireland. Few, if any, of the main administrative centres, secular or ecclesiastical, for example, were placed in coastal locations. Prominent among the peninsular areas of *baile* settlement were Ards, Lecale and Dufferin in east co. Down, Bargy and Forth in co. Wexford, the Déise in co. Waterford, Imokilly in south-east co. Cork and the western extremity of Corkaguiny in co. Kerry. The largest and most continuous belt of *baile* names occurs, however, in a wide stretch of coastland extending southwards from Wicklow Head in the direction of Wexford Harbour and the most typical section of this *baile* coastland is to be seen in the barony of Ballaghkeen in north-east co. Wexford. *Baile* names are also prominent along routeways which follow the major river valleys in some of the southern counties as, for example, in the valleys of the Barrow, Suir and Blackwater. East Munster emerges as a particularly strong *baile* area especially co. Limerick and east co. Cork. In certain parts of the south there is a generous admixture of *baile* and *town* names, such as in the baronies of Ida in south-east co. Kilkenny, Gaultiere in east co. Waterford, Iffa and Offa East in south co. Tipperary and Smallcounty and Coshlea in east co. Limerick. These are therefore the more obvious hybrid areas in the southern counties. Again south-east co. Wexford is in an anomalous position in that it is only here that we find very high densities of both *baile* and *town* names. This may suggest the presence in Bargy and Forth of a truly mixed community in medieval times because apart from these two baronies the *baile* element is notably absent from the *town* zone.

Few recurring Irish name elements are found to compound freely with personal names and those that do usually refer to specific types of settlement, such as *caher, dún,* or *lios.*

Baile, on the other hand, like its English counterpart, combines indiscriminately with an enormous range of Irish personal names and within the hybrid areas *baile* is also found in association with Norman personal names to a far greater extent than *town* is ever found in combination with Irish personal names. This is especially true of east Munster and typical of such townland names would be the following which refer to the Norman-Welsh family of Carew: Ballincarroonig (Imokilly barony, co. Cork) and Ballincarroona (Coshlea and Smallcounty baronies, co. Limerick). One of the main purposes of the townland in the *baile* areas therefore was to distinguish between rights to land on a family or kin basis. It is of course not the only Irish name element to serve this purpose. Towards the north and west of the island its place is taken by other name elements which also refer to divisions of land. *Gort* serves the same purpose in hill country in both Munster and Ulster as, for example, on the flanks of the Keeper Mountains in north co. Tipperary, on the eastern slopes of the Slieve Gallion-Slievemore upland in east co. Tyrone and also among the hills of the Cavan-Fermanagh borderland. On the extensive calcarious pastoral lowlands of east Connacht, where Anglo-Norman landowners and tenants intermingled with their Irish counterparts, the romance element *park* or *páirc* is often substituted for *baile* and *town* in both languages, especially in the baronies of Athenry, Clare and Dunkellin in east co. Galway. In counties Roscommon, Sligo, east Mayo, and to a lesser extent in east Galway, the three elements *baile, ceathramha* and *cartron* are most numerous in the same areas. In sharp contrast to *baile,* however, western elements such as *ceathramha* and *cartron* are, for the most part, found in combination with a simple and restricted range of compounds and they are hardly ever seen in association with personal names. Indeed unlike *baile* they frequently stand on their own. Out of a total of 706 *ceathramha* names, 60 are Carrowkeel, another 60 are Carrowmore (20 of these are in co. Mayo) and 50 are Carrowreagh. This extraordinary repetition of the same compounds in conjunction with terms employed in western areas to refer to units of land may suggest that the townland framework in the western counties, as we know it, was systematically imposed over extensive areas, perhaps as late as the seventeenth century.

PERIPHERAL REGIONS

An important feature common to both the *town* and *baile* areas is the absence of conspicuous concentrations of recurring toponyms. In Ireland such place-name regions are, for the most part, relegated to peripheral situations, especially towards the north and the west of the island. They are found especially as part of the harsh Atlantic world of stone, moorland and bog that has developed in a wet and windy climate and the townland names of such areas help to convey to us the initial impressions these western environments left on the minds of their first literate Irish colonisers. They were among the last parts of the island to be permanently settled and extensive sections of west Ulster, west Connacht and west Munster have never known any form of human habitation. Among the recurring toponyms which show strong regional associations in the west and north of the island are *carraig, corr, cuil, cuileann, doire, druim, inis, mullach* and *tullach*. An example of a toponymic region is provided by the *druim* country in counties Fermanagh, Cavan, Monaghan and south Leitrim (Fig. 15.4). These four counties contain 41 per cent (900) of the total number of *druim* names for

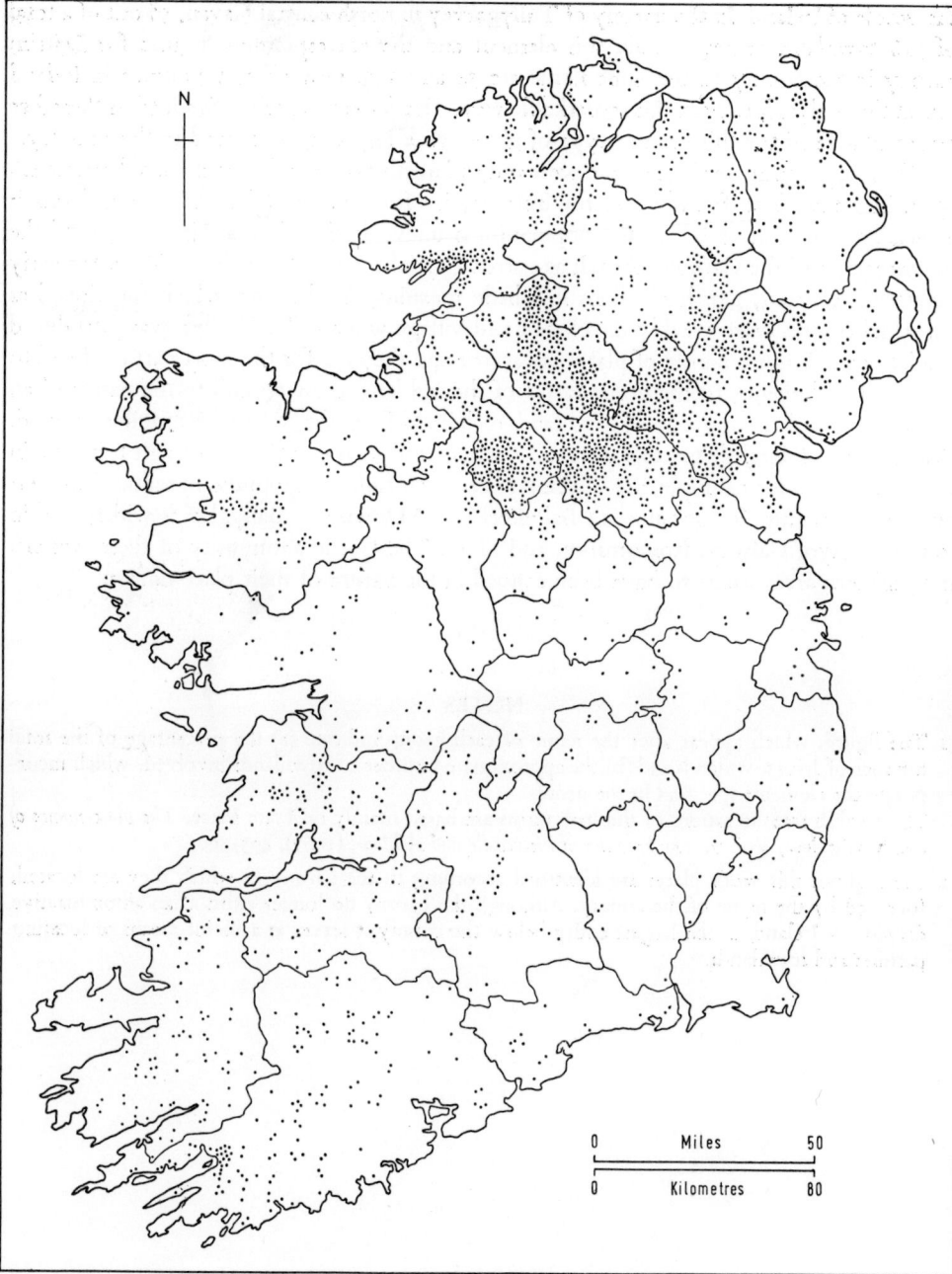

Fig. 15.4 *Druim* as a prefix and suffix

the whole of Ireland. In the barony of Tullygarvey in north central Cavan, 56 out of a total of 318 townland names contain this element and the corresponding figures for Leitrim barony in the county of the same name are 54 and 353. Few other toponyms in Ireland repeat themselves locally in this remarkable way. The *druim* zone of south Ulster is therefore representative of the third major type of place-name region encountered in this country.

These toponymic regions of the west and the north possess other and related characteristics. The townland framework, for instance, is often coarse and ineffective and this is especially true of areas where the population is unevenly distributed. Similarly, until the re-emergence of the Catholic church as a strong social force in the countryside in the early nineteenth century, parish divisions had little meaning. Settlements which functioned as parochial centres were weakly developed and village and small-town life was introduced at a late date. English names of places are scarce and they are for the most part confined to nucleated settlements, to the home farms of the old landed estates and to the names of an occasional townland or group of townlands reclaimed from the waste in the modern period. The handful of English townland names encountered in the extensive Iveagh territory in west co. Down, for example, are of this nature. Even *baile* compounds are reduced to their simplest. There are, for instance, 14 Ballykeel in co. Down and Ballyglass is widespread in counties Mayo, Galway, Roscommon and Sligo. The Gaelic anonymity of these western and northern areas seems to have been echoed in the nature of their place-names.

NOTES

1 The figures which appear after the name of each group indicate (a) the percentage of the total number of Irish townlands and (b) the approximate number of townlands involved, which incorporate the elements specified in the group
The English transliterations of the Irish terms are based mainly on Liam Price, *The place-names of county Wicklow*, Vol. 7, *The baronies of Newcastle and Arklow*, (1967), 495–506

2 Throughout this work places are identified according to the barony in which they are located, followed by the name of the county. Although the barony no longer exists as an administrative division in Ireland, as the largest entity below the county it serves as a useful means of locating parishes and townlands.

XVI

RURAL LAND UTILISATION IN IRELAND

L. Symons

Life in Ireland has always been closely dependent on the land, and farming an activity with which a high proportion of the people have been intimately associated. Even in the more industrialised north, most townsfolk are only a generation or two away from the land and few do not have relations or friends still in farming.

The produce of the land plays a much larger role in the economy of Ireland than in that of Great Britain. Even after the development of manufacturing industry in the past half-century, about one-quarter of the gross national income of the Republic of Ireland is derived from agriculture and forestry, and no less than three-fifths of the Republic's export income is earned by agricultural products. One in three of the working population is employed on the land. In Northern Ireland the relative importance of agriculture and forestry is less, but even so one in five of the gainfully employed work in the fields and forests.

The traveller in Ireland could be forgiven for assuming that agriculture would be even more important to the island than figures suggest. Essentially, the countryside is still a rural one, crops and pasture accounting for nearly 5 million ha (12 million acres) in the Republic and about 840,000 ha (2 million acres) in Northern Ireland. To these totals must be added, to obtain the total agricultural area, the rough grazings of the hills and mountains, and some at least of the peat bogs of the lowlands.

What is also apparent to the discerning traveller, and is borne out by the statistics, is that the agricultural industry in Ireland is still based on a large number of small farms, many of which have not shared fully in the growth of prosperity that has been characteristic of most of Great Britain, and indeed of Western Europe, since 1945. The state of the rural economy has been a subject for concern in Ireland since the beginning of modern times and this is still true today. In particular, there is some justification for accusing the agricultural industry in general of being wasteful in its employment of land and labour.

Throughout Ireland there has been a very considerable effort by government bodies and private individuals to deal with structural and technical problems in agriculture during the post-war period and particularly during the past decade. At the same time reafforestation has been pursued actively, mainly by the respective government bodies entrusted with the task north and south of the border. In spite of all efforts, however, farmers and foresters find themselves still in a rather insecure position, with a great deal of uncertainty as to what policies to adopt or to advocate in the immediate future.

This feeling of insecurity is to some extent inseparable from employment in primary production from the land, where, to the hazards of adverse weather and the constant threat of disease in plants and livestock, are added fluctuations in supply and demand conditions, all of which are reflected in price instability of a kind virtually unknown in manufacturing industry. Adding further to this normal state of uncertainty is, however, the question of British and Irish entry into the European Economic Community, which has been a live issue for about a decade and, at the time of writing, seems no nearer solution than it was at the beginning of the campaign for membership. This is a matter in which the situation may change from day to day and it would not be appropriate to comment at length in an essay of this nature, which, prepared a year before it is expected to appear in print, is more satisfactorily written in reflective than in forecasting terms. It is, however, essential in any estimate of the present position of an industry, and when commenting on its performance in the past, to take cognizance of special factors making for uncertainty and delays in decisions.

Notwithstanding the present uncertainties, the position of the farmer today is vastly better than it was in 1938. Government support and guaranteed markets have been established and maintained in the United Kingdom for most farm enterprises, while a large measure of state support has also been introduced in the Republic of Ireland.

In 1938 Ireland was still suffering from the aftermath of the world economic depression. Although agricultural prices had picked up after the disastrous collapse that had followed the end of the first World War and the manipulation of currencies, governments remained reluctant to commit themselves to subsidies, guaranteed prices for agricultural produce, or even planned purchasing schemes. Farms which had been allowed to revert to pasture remained in what could be called grass only euphemistically, the cover being commonly a mixture of rank and wild grasses with buttercups, daisies, ragwort and other useless and even poisonous vegetation. Farm buildings and fences suffered from lack of maintenance, field drains were choked, and livestock of nondescript breeds showed poor performances in liveweight gain, milk yields or other indices, the recording of which was, in any case, little practised.

Concern with the state of the land, and the lack of knowledge which existed about its use, stimulated geographers in Britain to launch the first nation-wide land utilisation survey undertaken in any country of the world. The use of every field in Great Britain was recorded and published in a series of land-use sheets on the scale of one inch to one mile.[1] Ireland was not included in this survey but the preparation of similar maps for the six northern counties was undertaken shortly afterwards by the Geographical Association of Northern Ireland. Learning from the experience of the Land Utilisation Survey of Great Britain, the survey of Northern Ireland incorporated a number of improvements and the field sheets completed in 1939 were probably the best record of land use made on a common basis for any complete political unit up to that time.[2] No similar survey was undertaken, or has since been made, in the Republic of Ireland, but the Northern Ireland maps remain valuable both as historical documents, showing the position over a large area of the country just before the outbreak of war, and as the basis for present-day comparison and planning.

The war resulted in great changes in the Irish landscape. Northern Ireland, as a constituent part of the United Kingdom, was involved directly in hostilities for the whole period of the war, and its agricultural industry came under controls similar to those employed to secure sharp increases in production in Great Britain. Stimulation of agriculture took the form of economic benefits such as guaranteed purchases and prices for many commodities, and a wide extension of subsidies, the first of which had been introduced for ploughing-up old grassland just before the outbreak of war. The Republic of Ireland, though remaining politically neutral, experienced economic advantages from the assured markets now offered by beleaguered Britain and a consequent rise in prices. In both parts of Ireland, as in Britain, the acreage under the plough was greatly expanded, and numbers of livestock also increased steadily.

After the war, the United Kingdom continued to maintain its agricultural industry at a high level by means of a continuation of guaranteed prices and subsidies, to which were added numerous schemes for improvement of farms and their equipment by means of capital grants. Such extensive subsidisation of agriculture could only be made by a country in which the agricultural sector was relatively a small part of the total economy, since the resources to be so employed had to be earned by other sectors and diverted through taxation.

Thus, the agricultural industry in Northern Ireland was, in general, able to pull ahead, economically and technically, of its counterpart in the Republic. At the same time, in spite of a relatively buoyant demand and government support, even Ulster farms remained at a disadvantage compared with those in most parts of Britain. The facts of geography dictated that, compared with British suppliers of the same markets, all Irish farmers would remain at some disadvantage because of the need to ship produce to Britain, with all the consequent delays and high freight and handling costs. There was, and is, therefore, some grading down of profitability from British farms through to those of Northern Ireland and then to those of the Republic. Farmers in the Republic continue to derive some indirect benefits from British guaranteed prices and subsidies, such as high prices for store cattle, which may still qualify for government payments if they are fattened in Northern Ireland. There has been some closing of former gaps in prices between the two parts of Ireland in recent years and the Free Trade Agreement now in force between the two countries is expected to increase this tendency.

Changes since 1938

We may now turn to consider some of the salient changes in rural land use that have occurred between 1938 and the present period. 1938 was chosen for comparison as it was the last 'normal' year before the war, and also the central year of the main mapping programme of the Land Utilisation Survey of Northern Ireland (1937–39). For the year to represent 'the present', 1967 is accepted as being the last year for which statistics are available at the time of writing.

The official figures for the main categories of crops and livestock in 1938 and 1967 have been plotted on a semi-logarithmic scale and joined by trend lines, neglecting all fluctuations, to provide a simple comparison of the changes in thirty years in Northern Ireland and the Republic of Ireland (Fig. 16.1).

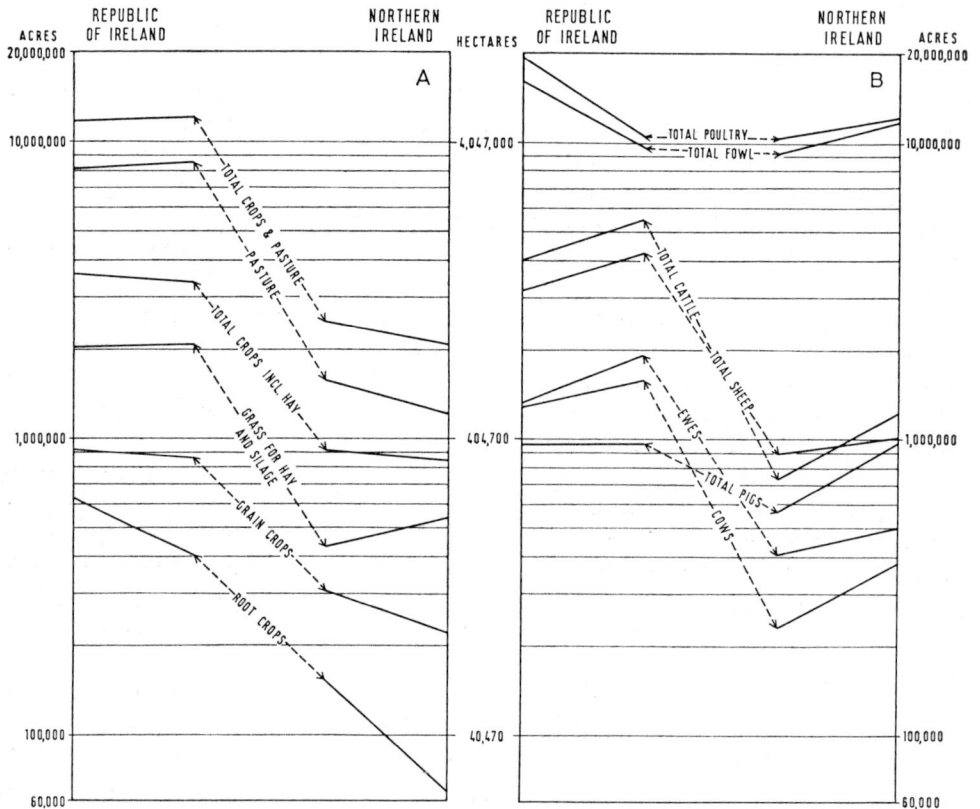

Fig. 16.1   Northern Ireland:
(A)   Changes in crops and pasture, 1938–67
(B)   Changes in livestock, 1938–67

It is seen that the pace of change has been faster in Northern Ireland than in the Republic. In the latter, the total area of crops and grass is little changed but a higher proportion of the total is now under grass. Most of the decrease in the ploughed area is accounted for by the smaller area of root crops, with a slight accompanying decrease in the area of grain crops. In the smaller area of Northern Ireland the proportionate decrease in the cropped area has been greater, with the greatest relative decrease in root crops, but with a significant decrease also in grain crops. In both areas, the fall in the root crop is explained mainly by the decreasing area devoted to potatoes, with turnips and mangolds also sharply down. In grains, the decrease in cultivation of oats has been partly offset by the increase in barley.

Whereas, in the Republic, the area reported as mown for hay has increased only slightly, grass for mowing in Northern Ireland has increased substantially. This statistical change conceals a more fundamental change in grassland management, the hay area having changed but little, whereas about a fifth of the mown grass is now used for silage. In Northern Ireland, the area of pasture (other than rough grazing) has diminished but in the Republic there has been an increase in this form of land cover.

One other major change in the crops which is not apparent from these statistics is the disappearance of flax from the Irish landscape. In 1938 there were over 8,000 ha (20,000 acres) of flax in Northern Ireland and some 1,600 ha (3,900 acres) in the Republic. This crop is now to be seen only in experimental fields under the supervision of institutions which are trying to encourage renewed attention to the crop. Meanwhile, the linen mills, meet their requirements, much diminished with the growth of chemical fibres, by imports.

At first sight this may appear to be a depressing picture of diminution of farming activity but land cover and production figures fortunately show different trends. Livestock products dominate agricultural output in Ireland and on the agricultural areas, little changed in total, many more livestock are now carried (Fig. 16.1). Cattle numbers have increased substantially in both the Republic and Northern Ireland, and there have been noteworthy increases in sheep in the Republic and in pigs in Northern Ireland, with smaller increases in sheep in the north and pigs in the south.

To obtain an overall picture of the increase in livestock numbers it is necessary to convert the figures for the different classes to livestock units based on feed or other common requirements. Table 1 shows the results of conversion by commonly accepted factors. The increase in the case of Northern Ireland is seen to be 44 per cent of the 1938 figure, while the Republic's livestock have increased by about half this percentage. The increase in Northern Ireland's cattle numbers is particularly striking, though it must be remembered that store cattle from the Republic contribute to these numbers.

Poultry have declined in numbers in the Republic, but horses constitute the only major class of livestock to decrease in both areas. Horses were used largely for draught and transport purposes and were not therefore in the same class as other livestock from which food for human beings is the object of production. Futhermore, if the produce of the land is being used for feeding draught horses it cannot be used for agricultural end-products so that in evaluating the numbers of livestock units horses may be omitted. If this be done the increase in agriculturally productive livestock supported (i.e. livestock excluding horses) is seen to be greater than the figures quoted above. In the case of Northern Ireland it is as high as 57 per cent, or two per cent per annum, while the increase in the Republic is 33 per cent or just over one per cent per annum.

Not only have numbers of livestock increased, but there has also been marked improvement in yields of milk per cow, killing-out percentages of fat cattle, wool yields and other indices. Increased yields of crops have made possible this increase in livestock production without much diversion of production from crops for human consumption. The reduction in the areas devoted to potatoes has been the main expression of the latter. On the other hand, the switch from oats, grown mainly for horses, to fodder barley has reduced the need

TABLE I

Livestock Units, Ireland

	Conversion Factor	Northern Ireland		Republic of Ireland	
		1938	1967	1938	1967
Bulls	1	4,600	6,500	24,900	13,900
Cows	1	229,300	381,000	1,281,800	1,567,900
Heifers	1	30,100	48,600	64,000	177,500
Cattle >2 years	1	85,000	172,400	729,700	1,140,700
Cattle 1–2	2/3	127,000	200,000	621,200	900,000
Cattle <1 yr	1/3	64,000	108,700	341,300	445,600
Total cattle		540,000	917,200	3,062,900	4,245,600
Rams	1/10	1,300	1,800	4,900	5,800
Ewes	1/5	80,200	100,300	264,300	387,400
Other sheep	1/15	32,000	35,000	121,400	150,000
Total sheep		113,500	137,100	390,600	543,200
Boars	$\frac{1}{4}$	400	1,100	500	700
Sows	$\frac{1}{2}$	29,000	51,000	48,400	55,200
Other pigs	1/7	72,000	124,000	123,000	124,600
Total pigs		101,400	176,100	171,900	180,500
Poultry	1/100	102,000	119,400	196,300	106,000
Horses	1	80,000	2,600	442,000	142,700
Total		936,900	1,352,400	4,263,700	5,218,000
Increase			415,500 (44%)		954,300 (22%)
Total excl. horses		856,900	1,349,800	3,821,700	5,075,300
Increase			492,900 (57%)		1,253,600 (33%)

Sixth report upon the agricultural statistics of Northern Ireland, 1930 to 1953, Cmd. 371, Belfast, (1957); *Seventh report . . . 1952–1961,* Cmd. 508 Belfast, (1967); *Statistical abstract, 1939,* Dublin, (1939); and official returns of agricultural statistics, 1967.

for potatoes for fodder. Imports of feeding-stuffs have, however, been increased and recently these have formed about 25 per cent of total feed costs in both Northern Ireland and the Republic, but the total feed costs in the latter have been lower.[3] This is largely because of the reliance on pasture in the south. There has been a substantial increase in the quantities of other inputs employed, especially of fertilisers and lime, and much more machinery and equipment of all kinds has been brought into use.

The cost of the changes

The changes since 1938, as shown by rising production graphs, seem complimentary to the farmers of Ireland, especially to those of Northern Ireland. Much more produce is being derived from a smaller area of land than in 1938, by about half the former labour force. The decrease in the cropped area has been offset by more intensive use of land, especially sown grass, for which the climatic conditions are well suited, and which is practicable with a reduced labour force.

While noting the magnitude of the gains, it is necessary, however, also to take account of the costs involved. An analysis of the position in both Northern Ireland and the Republic, (where statistics are not strictly comparable), would be beyond the scope of this essay, but it may be noted that in Northern Ireland the average annual gross value of agricultural products, adjusted for changes in value of stocks, for the three production years 1964–65 to 1966–67 was £118 million[4], including the value of deficiency payments received by farmers. Production grants, such as the subsidies paid on hill cattle, hill sheep, calves, fertilisers, lime and the ploughing of grassland, totalling about £10 million, raised farmers' receipts to an average of £128.3 million. Total input was calculated at an average of £101 million, leaving the net income of farming averaging less than £28 million. To arrive at the income available in farm households, the estimated value of family labour, counted as an input, must be added in again, and this gives an average for the three years of £37 million.

A ratio of 1:1.17 between input and output is not particularly impressive, but what is more disturbing is that the net income, including the value of family labour, of £37 million contains not only £10.4 million production grants, but also an average for the three years of £15.1 million in price subsidies (deficiency payments) and £2.5 million in capital grants, making a total in subsidies and grants of £28 million.[5] Thus subsidies and grants are equal to three-quarters of the net income arising on farms, and these subventions do not include the concealed subsidy afforded by the exemption of agricultural land from local government rating. In short, subsidisation of various kinds alone makes possible the continuation of farming in Northern Ireland as a remunerative occupation.

Such a situation must give rise to disquiet. There are two main alternatives: one is to allow prices to rise, curbing imports, which is the solution adopted in the E.E.C.; the other is to reduce subsidies progressively, forcing farmers to seek greater efficiency or to leave the land. To those who prefer to see food available at moderate prices, reaping the benefit of produce available cheaply from overseas, the first solution is both socially repugnant and economically insupportable. It is also, however, economically unsound to continue to subsidise butter production in Ireland, for example, when the world's most efficient producer, New Zealand, can undersell even the subsidised product and has unused production capacity.

The subsidisation of the Republic's much larger agricultural industry is at a more moderate level, amounting in 1965–66 to £32 million for roughly comparable purposes, including subsidies and grants, and excluding expenditure on education, research, technical services, relief of land annuities and rates. Subsidisation has, however, been rising rapidly, the provisional figure for 1967–68 being £46 million. There has been a particularly rapid rise in subsidies on butter and other milk products, from £8 million in 1964–65 to £13.8 million in 1966–67 and a provisional figure of £19.3 million for 1967–68.[6]

Butter poses the most difficult and delicate question in agricultural marketing in the British Isles, the problem being worsened by dumping by European countries which over produce and yet maintain high prices at home, so discouraging consumption. Unless Britain closes her doors to these non-traditional suppliers who make no effort to restrict their dumping, only higher prices, high subsidies, or greater efficiency, can enable the British and Irish producers to remain in business. To the writer, a tightening of quotas to non-traditional, high-cost suppliers, guilty of dumping, together with an increase in allocations to efficient low-cost suppliers, and some progressive reduction in subsidies, seems to be the fairest and most promising combination of measures to attack this and similar problems.

The farming industry naturally denies that it is inefficient, and it is true that there are many efficient farms in all parts of the British Isles, but farming is characterised by structural inefficiency arising largely from the multiplicity of small units, and this is particularly true of Ireland.

The problem of farm size

In both the Republic and Northern Ireland the present century has seen a considerable amount of consolidation of farms, with a corresponding increase in average and modal size of units. Table 2 shows the changes in numbers of holdings by size groups from 1938 to 1967, in the case of Northern Ireland, and to 1965 in the case of the Republic of Ireland.

There has been considerable progress in getting rid of small holdings, those under about 12 ha (30 acres). In all larger-size groups there is now a slightly higher percentage of farms than there was in 1938, but the figures quoted are of total farm size and many of the larger farms contain substantial areas of rough grazing of low value. In fact, of the 66,338 holdings enumerated in Northern Ireland in 1967, 54,404 (82 per cent) had less than 20.2 ha (50 acres) of crops and grass.

The picture is improved by taking into account the fact that some holdings are worked jointly, and the 1967 census indicated that in Northern Ireland there were about 40,100 farm businesses which could utilise more than 50 standard man-days labour per farm. Of these, however, fewer than 22,000 required more than 200 man-days and only 16,441 needed more than 275 man-days.[7] In Great Britain it is accepted that 275 man-days (employment for one man for 5½ days per week for 50 weeks of the year) represents a satisfactory division between part-time and full-time farming. This division was found by the Ministry of Agriculture for Northern Ireland to be unrealistic, for while many farms in Northern Ireland theoretically required less than 275 man-days per year, they provided the sole form of earnings for the farmer, so that in this sense they were not part-time farms. Furthermore, the adoption of the standard of 275 man-days would have meant that only 16,441 farms, or about 41 per cent of farm businesses in Northern Ireland, would have been classed as full-time. The more modest level of 200 man-days was chosen as an arbitrary division between 'full-time' and 'part-time and sub-viable' units for Northern Ireland.

TABLE 2

Number of holdings of over 1 acre by size groups (based on total area)
Northern Ireland & Republic of Ireland 1938 and 1965/1967

Size group ha (acres)	Northern Ireland				Republic of Ireland			
	1938		1967		1938		1965	
	Number	% of total	Number	% of total	Number	% of total	Number	% of total
0.4 and under 2.02 (1 and under 5)	10,142	11.2	3,670	5.5	27,756	8.4	23,052	8.1
2.02 and under 4.05 (5 and under 10)	12,301	13.6	6,950	10.5	33,717	10.3	22,871	8.1
4.05 and under 6.07 (10 and under 15)	10,871	12.0	7,165	10.8	34,145	10.4	22,033	7.7
6.07 and under 12.14 (15 and under 30)	24,017	26.6	16,328	24.6	90,663	27.7	68,769	24.3
12.14 and under 20.24 (30 and under 50)	16,108	17.9	14,499	21.9	62,290	19.2	61,238	21.6
20.24 and under 40.47 (50 and under 100)	12,530	13.9	12,980	19.6	49,670	15.2	55,197	19.5
40.47 and under 80.94 (100 and under 200)	3,330	3.7	3,744	5.6	20,920	6.4	23,325	8.3
Over 80.94 (Over 200)	958	1.1	1,002	1.5	7,430	2.3	6,971	2.5
Total over .04 ha (1 acre)	90,257	100.0	66,338	100.0	326,591	100.0	283,456	100.0

This was a justifiable division but it has the unfortunate result of masking the seriousness of the economic weakness of farming in Northern Ireland. The Ministry of Agriculture is, in effect, saying, hopefully, that a farmer in Northern Ireland need consider his farm as sub-viable only if it occupies him for less than four days per week. Many farmers, of course, put in more than this time on a holding which would not require so much work if it were equipped to the standard normal in Britain, and this is part of the reasoning by the Ministry for regarding such a farm as full-time, but, again, it conceals the technical lag on farms in Northern Ireland compared with those in Britain.

Between the levels of 200 and 275 man-days, there are about 5,400 units in Northern Ireland, almost one-eighth of the total. The inclusion of these as 'full-time', as long as this term also conveys the impression that it means economic viability, must tend to detract from the urgency with which the situation is viewed, not perhaps in the Ministry of Agriculture, but possibly in other official circles, and certainly in the view of the public. To the writer it seems that only the farms requiring 275 man-days offer any real hope of long-term economic operation and that those between 200 and 275 man-day requirements should be classed as 'marginal'. The term 'marginal' implies that the farmer would normally have difficulty in maintaining an income equal to that of a farm labourer's wage plus an approp-riate return on capital invested. The 'sub-viable' farms would normally provide a net income less than the minimum farm wage, averaging probably not more than £300 per year.[8]

The distribution of the non-viable and marginal farms clearly illustrates the deterioration of economic conditions in the west and south of the province and in the upland areas. The percentage of farms utilising, or capable of utilising, 50–199 man-days is plotted in figure 16.2 for rural districts in Northern Ireland. Between one-third and one-half of all farm businesses fall into this category in most eastern and northern districts. When the percentage of farm businesses requiring 200–274 man-days is added in and all farms classi-fiable as either non-viable or marginal (50–275 man-days inclusive) are plotted, the pattern is similar (Fig. 16.2). The relatively disadvantageous position in the west and south is now emphasised, with some rural districts in co. Fermanagh and south Armagh having over 70 per cent of farms in this category. Over half of the farms are so classed throughout the central areas and the parts of counties Londonderry and Antrim which have a substantial hill area within the Rural District boundaries.

Data comparable with that for Northern Ireland are not available for farms in the Republic of Ireland, but in the National Farm Survey carried out there between 1955 and 1958 farms were classified by income groups. It was found that the annual family farm income, averaged over the three years of the survey, was below £400 for 52.8 per cent of the holdings.[9]

It is known, of course, that the problem of prevalence of farms of inadequate size is worse in the western counties of the Republic of Ireland than in the eastern areas. The average area of crops and grass per farm in many western rural districts is under 8.1 ha (20 acres), compared with over 20.2 ha (50 acres) in eastern areas, with the central areas in an intermediate position.[10] In terms of farm size, as well as spatially, Northern Ireland approxi-mates also to an intermediate average. As long as Ireland has so many non-viable holdings its agriculture is bound to be adversely affected in competition with other producers, and the subsidies and grants paid to it must be largely dissipated over holdings which offer little promise of ever being economic. That the position in Ireland is worse than elsewhere in the British Isles may be judged from comparison with Great Britain. Holdings of over 40.5 ha (100 acres) crops and grass form about one-quarter of all British farms, whereas only about one-seventeenth of the farms in the Republic of Ireland and one-thirtieth of those in Northern Ireland exceed this comparatively satisfactory size.

Economic production of crops and commodities such as milk and butter is to no small

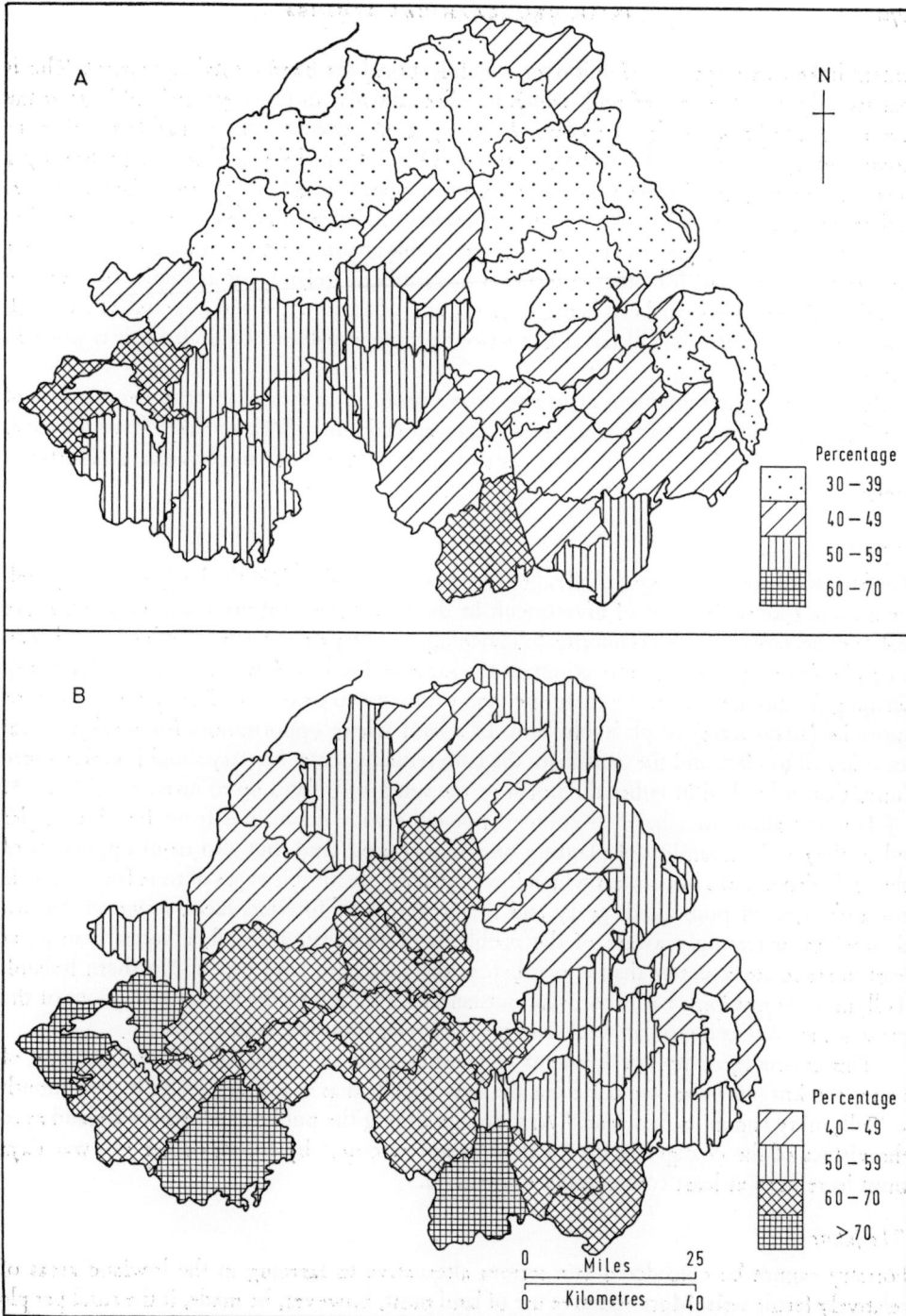

Fig. 16.2 Northern Ireland: Non-viable and marginal farms
(A) Percentage of farm businesses non-viable or part-time (50–199 man-days)
(B) Percentage of farm businesses non-viable (part-time) or marginal (50–274 man-days)
The blank areas within Northern Ireland represent Lower Lough Erne, Lough Neagh and Belfast
County Borough.

extent linked with the size of unit over which is spread the fixed capital equipment. This is particularly so in the case of milk which is collected daily. In Northern Ireland in 1967 the average herd size was only 11.5 cows. As many as 76 per cent of herds had fewer than 15 cows and 53 per cent had fewer than 10 cows.[11] This can be placed in perspective by a recent statement, that "there is no place on a dairy farm for a herd of fewer than 25 cows, unless the farm is being run as a part-time business . . . herds of 40–50 cows are regarded as about the minimum size to aim for if a reasonable income is to be obtained".[12] Similar figures can be quoted for other enterprises in Northern Ireland, for example, the average number of beef cows per herd being only 6.3 and of sows 5.1. If the dispersal of livestock over large numbers of small farms is a serious problem in Northern Ireland, it is worse in the Republic.[13]

The hilly and mountainous areas also pose a problem of special severity because few of the farms which lack a sufficient area to carry an economic flock of sheep have adequate crops and pasture for diversification, as shown in a study of sample areas in Northern Ireland.[14]

Forestry

Forestry is, of course, a major challenger for use of hill land and, in the long term, may well be a more economic form of investment. In the meantime, reafforestation employs more men per hectare than does economic hill farming. Forestry operations utilise about one man to 16 ha (40 acres) of plantations, much the same as lowland farming, whereas hill sheep farming should need no more than one man to some 600 ewes, which may require 800 or more ha (2,000 acres) of plantable land. In a land where opportunities for work in rural areas are all too few and the drift from the land remains acute, forestry should receive more funds than it has had in either the north or the south of Ireland up to now.

Forestry authorities have to contend not only with opposition from farming circles when they seek expansion of planting on sheep-rearing land, but also from opponents of the dark, dense ranks of conifers which form the only practicable types of trees for economic reafforestation of podsolised, peaty and rocky soils. The foresters have, however, shown themselves increasingly aware of the problems of amenity, and public access is now, at least in some areas, better than it was before the change in land use. In Northern Ireland, Tollymore Forest Park has become an outstanding addition to the tourist attractions of the province as well as a regular week-end place of relaxation for local people.

This encouraged the development of another park at Gortin Glen Forest. In spite of being 129 km (80 miles) from Belfast the new park had as many visitors in its first month as Tollymore had in its first year.[15] Any doubts among the public of Northern Ireland as to the virtues of the changes in the rural landscape wrought by forestry since pre-war days must have been at least considerably diminished.

The future

Forestry cannot be considered as a serious alternative to farming in the lowland areas of relatively fertile soils. More effective use of land must, however, be made, if the rural people are to enjoy anything like the social benefits that are available to townsfolk, and if the drift from the land is to be halted or even kept to the level which will leave in the rural areas a justifiable percentage of the more intelligent young people born there. It is no longer sufficient to excuse inadequate housing and low income on the grounds that farming is a way of life in which personal satisfactions outweigh economic and social disadvantages. They may do up to a point, and more so perhaps for older people, but they will not count sufficiently with the young, ambitious and competent.

Any substantial increase in subsidies or protective measures beyond their present level must surely be avoided. Greater efficiency must be sought and it would seem that this must lie in much higher levels of mechanisation, including more imaginative utilisation of electricity. With this must go more sophisticated farm planning and knowledge of the economics of the farm and each of its constituent enterprises. Overheads must be spread over larger areas of crops, larger herds and flocks, and greater output. To achieve this, only three ways seem to be open. One involves a greater appreciation of the possibilities offered by the physical environment leading to a reduction of costs such as that achieved in New Zealand.[16] The second necessitates further amalgamation of farms to achieve more economic working without major technical changes. In fact, some blending of these must be expected and the current trend is in the direction of continuing amalgamation of farms with slight improvements in utilisation of soil and local climatic conditions. The third way is in the direction of factory farming.

Factory farming, such as intensive livestock raising, involving stall feeding and zero grazing, conflicts with almost all the ideals of the countryman while its products appeal less to the average housewife, if she can recognise them, because they have not been produced under natural conditions. Factory farming is, however, spreading rapidly, and its champions include, not only, as might be expected, the directors and chairmen of state and collective farms in the communist countries, but business men in Western Europe and North America. Pig rearing on one factory farm in Germany involves a throughput of 200,000 pigs annually, in which each pig is fed nine times per day with measured rations for just 90 seconds, but is kept always hungry for maximum fodder utilisation. This can be matched by an Italian farm which produces 50,000 calves a year, muzzling the young calves between feeding-times to prevent them satisfying themselves with their straw bedding. (These were examples from Germany and Italy in 1968). When more business men see the profits to be made in this kind of farming, it will spread at tremendous speed and the ordinary farmer will be unable to compete with the prices at which these industrial enterprises will make contracts with the suppliers of supermarket chains.

Unless farming on traditional lines can become much more efficient, the changes that will occur in the next thirty years will make those of 1938 to 1967 appear insignificant. In 1968, Ford Tractor Operations of England published a filmstrip and commentary which attempted to look forward to agriculture in A.D. 2000. This envisaged some changes which might appear unrealistic at first glance but are not without a basis of scientific prediction. Even if their picture of the remote control of hovercraft cultivating the soil to a perfect tilth by ultrasonic waves is not realised, massive investment in entirely new forms of machinery, accounting and computing, and plant and animal breeding, are almost certain. Again, it is unlikely that the 12-hectare, 15-cow farm will have any place in this pattern. If the farmer as we know him today, and as we knew him in 1938, is to survive, he will have to accept more sweeping changes in the structure of farming than he has yet appeared willing to do.

It was suggested in 1967 that in Northern Ireland in 1971 there might be about 32,000 farming units of which 18,000 would be full-time farm businesses, farming an average of 34.4 ha (85 acres) compared with 25.5 ha (63 acres) in 1966.[17] The present writer feels that if this position is not reached, the future for private farming will be bleak in Northern Ireland. In particular, attention should be directed to eliminating the very small units by their amalgamation. The percentage of farm businesses operating with less than 12 ha (30 acres) 30 livestock units, or needing fewer than 275 man-days, will give a better indication of the size of the remaining problem than the average farm size and performance, which is unduly weighted by a relatively small number of large, profitable farms.

It has been shown that the amalgamation of farm land in Northern Ireland can take place only within the confines of the inheritance mechanism and limited marketings of agricultural holdings.[18] The position would appear to be broadly similar in the Republic of Ireland, but there appears to be some prospect of government action to reduce the prevalence of conacre letting.[19] With conacre letting, in the view of the present writer, the evils of inadequate long-term care of the land consequent upon temporary occupation offset any advantages of flexibility such as have been claimed for the system.[20] The time may well have come for a freeing of the restriction of letting land on a long-term basis which was a nineteenth-century solution to the problem of absentee-ownership. Today, the conditions have changed and legislation must change to permit a far greater degree of flexibility in land occupation to deal with present-day problems. In spite of generous government assistance schemes to help with modernisation and amalgamation of farms, it can be said in 1968, as thirty years earlier, that the pattern of farm businesses in Ireland is dominated by small and often unprofitable holdings. In spite of marked increases in carrying capacity, in terms of livestock numbers and of output per unit area in crops, the rate of change is insufficient to cope with present-day economic needs. Only by greater structural and technical changes in the future will farming in Ireland be made into an industry capable of yielding products to consumers at competitive prices and simultaneously yielding adequate rewards to the farming population.

REFERENCES

1 L. D. Stamp, *The Land of Britain, its use and misuse,* (1948, 3rd ed., 1962)

2 L. Symons, ed., *Land use in Northern Ireland,* (1963), contains information on the history of the survey as well as summarising its results.

3 E. A. Attwood, Agricultural developments in Ireland, north and south, *J. Stat. and Soc. Inquiry Soc. of Ireland,* 21, part 5, (1966–67), 9–34

4 *Farming in Northern Ireland, statistical review June 1966–May 1967,* Ministry of Agriculture, Belfast, table 1, 14–15

5 Ibid., table 2, 16

6 *Current budget tables, 1968,* Dublin, (1968), table 5, 44. See also comments in discussion on paper by E. A. Attwood, op. cit., 27, 28–9, 31

7 *Statistical review, June 1966–May 1967,* op. cit., table 11a, 28

8 D. J. Alexander, Northern Ireland farming today—some facts and figures, *The green mountaineer,* Greenmount Agricultural College, (1968), 10–18

9 National Farm Survey, 1955/56–1957/58, final report, Dublin

10 This and other distributions have been mapped by D. A. Gillmor, The agricultural regions of the Republic of Ireland, *Irish Geography,* 5, no. 4 (1967), 245–261

11 *Statistical review June 1966–May 1967,* op. cit., 40

12 K. Dexter and D. Barber, *Farming for profits* (2nd edition, 1967) 136

13 E. A. Attwood, op. cit., Table VIII, 22

14 L. Symons, Farm size as a basis for indication of profitability in hill farms, an example from Kintyre and Northern Ireland, *Irish Geography,* 5, no. 5 (1968), 408–27

15 C. S. Kilpatrick, Northern Ireland's forest parks, *Town and Country Planning,* 36, 3 (1968), 164–69

16 L. Symons, The pastoral economy of New Zealand and some comparisons with Ireland, *J. Stat. and Soc. Inquiry Soc. of Ireland,* 20, part 4, (1960–1), 94–131. More recent prices are given in the regular statistical publications issued by the respective governments. Output costs, prices and incomes for Ireland are quoted by E. A. Attwood, op. cit.

17 D. J. Alexander, op. cit., 18

18 D. J. Alexander, Farm land mobility and adjustments in farming in Northern Ireland, *J. Stat. and Soc. Inquiry Soc. of Ireland,* 21, part 3 (1964–5), 1–14

19 M. O'Morain, Paper to Agricultural Science Association, published in the *Report of the Land Commissioners, 1961–62,* Pr. 7040, Stationery Office, Dublin, 1963, quoted by E. A. Attwood, op. cit.

20 H. J. Shemilt, Adjustments in family farming in the Northern Ireland economy, *J. of Agricultural Economics,* 16, no. 1, (1964), 53–67

The author wishes to acknowledge the co-operation of the Ministry of Agriculture for Northern Ireland and the Central Statistics Office, Dublin, in supplying statistical material. The author is solely responsible for the opinions expressed.

T

XVII

A MULTIVARIATE MODEL OF THE SPACING OF URBAN CENTRES IN THE IRISH REPUBLIC

P. N. O'Farrell

The majority of urban studies in Ireland have been idiographic in their methodology: detailed, largely qualitative, unique case studies of towns viewed as individual morphological and functional entities.[1] Such work has provided data on specific urban centres at a given moment in time and in the case of certain historical studies has yielded some information on change through time. Much of this urban research, including that of planning consultants[2], has been characterised by the *a priori* nature and variety of techniques employed with the result that data collected at one point, even if in a generic form, was seldom comparable with data gathered elsewhere—thus rendering inter-area comparison somewhat difficult. We have little understanding of the processes which influence many aspects of the functional structure, organisation, internal differentiation, size, spacing and distribution of towns in Ireland. The recognition of empirical regularities requires a contrasting methodological orientation with an emphasis upon a nomothetic approach to facilitate discovery of any inherent order in the urban system and to permit identification, analysis and explanation of deviations from an expanding body of theory. This chapter attempts to explain the spatial distribution of urban centres in Ireland by isolating and measuring the influence of some of the various factors which affect it; to establish how many exogenous variables influence the pattern of variation, and to determine whether they are interrelated or orthogonal. It is necessary to establish which variables are the most important in explaining the distributional pattern and to measure any spatial variation in the relative importance of these variables. It is probable that a few variables exert the most influence upon the dependent variable and these may be regarded as 'first order' independent variables[3], but it is also desirable to assess to what degree they explain the variation in the dependent variable and to examine the pattern of the unexplained variation.

No model has been developed which will universally account for the spatial patterns of urban centres; this is largely due to the inadequacy of existing theory, the lack of objective empirical research, and the spatial variation in the influence of different exogenous variables. It is therefore proposed to place this present investigation within the framework of Christaller's theoretical model which was derived to explain the size, number and distribution of central places.[4] The form of this classic theory, together with its assumptions, has already been discussed by several authors and no detailed account of it will be included here.[5] Christaller's partial equilibrium system of central places, supported exclusively by tertiary economic activity, are regularly distributed over an isotropic resource, transportation and income surface serving evenly distributed, rational consumers with identical consumption functions. Order and vertical organisation are introduced into the system by assuming that groups of key functions have similar threshold values which, together with the postulate that high order places perform all the functions of low order places plus a group of functions differentiating them from these lower order centres, result in a hierarchical class system of centres with each class possessing specific groups of central functions. Christaller's derivation, that each functional class is characterised by a discrete population level of its centres, was derived from additional empirical information.[6] An optimum spatial pattern for a K-3 network, without excess profits, can only be achieved for functions whose market areas are equal to one-third, one-ninth, one twenty-seventh, and so on, of the size of the highest order function.[7] As all central places on a specific tier of the hierarchy perform identical highest order functions it follows that market area sizes for the highest order goods are equal and all distances between neighbouring places on the same hierarchical level are constant. It will be necessary to refer again to the spatial elements of the Christaller model when formulating hypotheses to explain the distribution of urban centres in Ireland.

The form of the input data

The empirical findings are divided into two discrete sections: (i) the development of a multivariate model to explain the pattern of spacing of the thirty-one centres with a population of greater than 5,000; and (ii) the building of a similar model to describe the spatial distribution of the ninety-eight centres in the Irish Republic with a population of more than 1,500 (Fig. 17.1).[8]

The straight-line distance in miles from a specific centre to its nearest neighbour of the same or larger population was used in this study as a measure of the location of a central place in relation to other places.[9] As Thomas and others have done, it is reasonable to use the distance to nearest neighbour of the same size, or, whenever a centre of higher population is located closer to another centre than its nearest neighbour of the same size, to use distance to the larger centre.[10] This is also consistent with one of Christaller's principal postulates which states that each higher order central place performs all the functions of lower order central places. Assuming that consumers are highly rational and are interested in minimising travel costs, the distance between a given centre and its nearest neighbour of equal or greater population is a meaningful statistic. Implicit in this methodology is the assumption of a positive relationship between the population size of a town and the number and complexity of tertiary goods and services offered in it. A recent study by O'Farrell[11] has demonstrated that there is a correlation coefficient of 0.945 between population size and centrality of centres in co. Tipperary. Also, as many urban centres have a manufacturing component to their economic base a manufacturing employment variable will be incorporated into the analysis in order to extract the effect of this variable upon the spatial pattern.

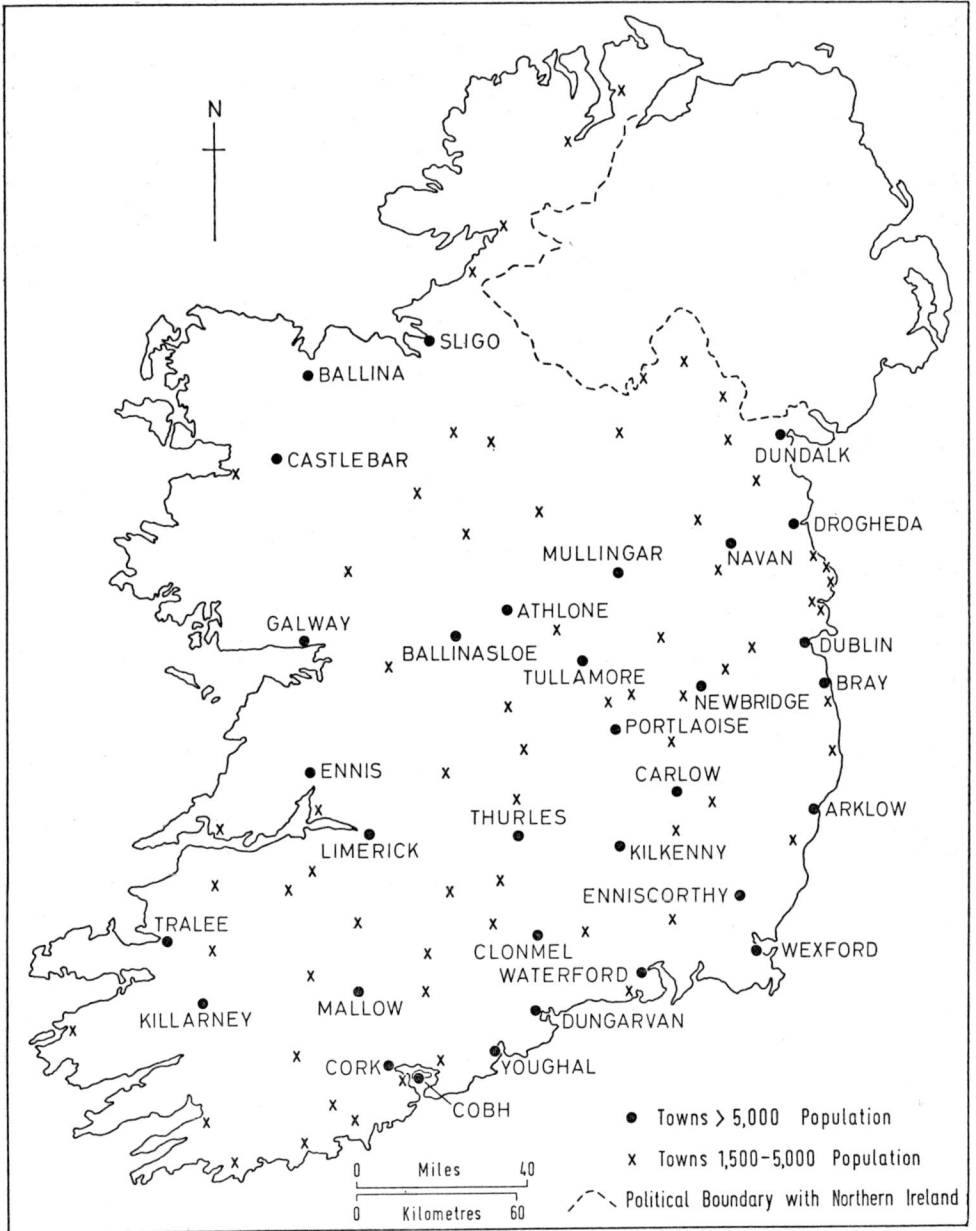

17.1   The distribution of urban centres in the Republic of Ireland

Since the publication of Christaller's work the majority of studies concerned with the spacing of central places have continually emphasised the existence of discrete population-size groups and average distances.[12] However, Thomas has shown that empirical evidence exists to demonstrate that population-sizes of central places are in general unimodally distributed.[13] Adequate testing of Christaller's formulations calls for an explanation of spatial patterns. It also requires that spacing be regarded as a continuous variable. In Christaller's theoretical landscape, with an isotropic income surface and rational consumers, population size accounts for the total variation in spacing but when tested against reality certain of the assumptions must be relaxed and other factors must be incorporated into an explanatory model. Also, if distance is expressed as a continuous variable, the generality imposed on an observation by adopting a taxonomic system is avoided and the precision of each individual measurement is retained. King and Vuicich used multiple correlation and regression methods for their analysis of the relationships between the spacing of places in the United States and selected physical, social and economic factors.[14]

It is proposed to attempt to explain the spatial distribution of urban centres in Ireland by examining the relationship between the endogenous variable, distance to the nearest neighbour of equal or larger population size[15] and a number of exogenous variables: distance to metropolitan centres of over 100,000 population, population size, population density, percentage employment in manufacturing industry, income density, population change. The use of simple and stepwise multiple regression and correlation analysis will permit consideration of the influences, either independently or simultaneously, of the exogenous variables. In the first stage the linear relation between the endogenous variable and each exogenous variable is examined separately; succeeding stages of the analytical procedure involve the addition of other independent variables with the object of improving the overall level of explanation.

Formulation and testing of hypotheses

In formulating the hypotheses relating to the degree of association between the dependent variable, distance (y), and the independent variables, it should be emphasised that one variable, population size (X_1) is derived from the theoretical model of Christaller. The other exogenous variables are introduced by relaxing certain assumptions of the theoretical model, or otherwise are those which intuitively appear to be most relevant. Firstly, within the constraints set by the assumptions of the central place model, the distance between two towns of the same population size should be a function of the population of the two towns. It may therefore be hypothesised that there is a positive relationship between the distance separating a given centre from its nearest neighbour of the same or greater population and the population of the given centre. The theoretical rationale supporting the first hypothesis has already been outlined in the introduction.

Secondly, by relaxing Christaller's assumption of an isotropic population density surface, it is hypothesised that density of population[16] (X_2) will be inversely associated with distance. Areas of greater population density will generate, other things being equal, a larger demand per unit area for tertiary goods and services than those of lower density, and thus the distance separating a town of population 'p' from its nearest neighbour of equal or larger size should be less in a region of high population density than the distance separating a town of equal population from its nearest neighbour in an area of lower population density.

The theoretical model postulates an isotropic income surface whereas in reality a differentiated surface exists. Therefore it may be postulated that where income densities are high the distance between a centre and its nearest neighbour of equal or larger population should be less, *ceteris paribus,* than the distance separating a centre of the same population from its nearest neighbour in an area of lower income density. Hence the relationship postulated between distance and income density (X_4) is an inverse one. The income data, at the county level of aggregation, represents the findings of Attwood and Geary[17] for 1960 and was quantified as Personal Income[18] minus the Value of Subsistence Production[19], all expressed as a per acre ratio (Table 1). For this data, which was initially transformed to income per head at county level, resultants were obtained as follows: the county level data of incomes per head were assumed to exist uniformly throughout the county; in the case of centres located in different counties the value for each county that lay on the straight line between two nearest neighbours was multiplied by the fraction of the straight line distance that lay within the county; and the products were then summed to provide the resultants; the resultant was then multiplied by the population density between the two centres to yield the income density variable.

Fourthly, in this analysis population size is being used as a surrogate for centrality on the assumption that there is a high positive correlation between these variables. Towns have been considered as nodes of tertiary economic activity within the framework of the central place model; but in reality many places have a manufacturing component to their economic base and population will not be an adequate surrogate for centrality. It is therefore necessary to introduce a manufacturing variable, for manufacturing units support a residential population which in turn provides revenue for retail and service establishments in a town. But the retail and service provision has a lower support population, other things being equal, than in a market centre of equal population size with no manufacturing industry.[20] This is because the residential population resulting from the presence of manufacturing is not matched by the residents of a corresponding rural area. Thus where the percentage of manufacturing population is high, one expects urban centres to be more closely spaced. The manufacturing variable was operationally defined as the percentage of the employed population engaged in manufacturing industry (X_3) in each centre for 1961[21], and the relationship postulated with distance is an inverse one.

Central place theory is a static spatial model of tertiary economic activity and a population change variable (X_5) will now be incorporated in order to introduce a dynamic element into the analysis. Percentage population change[22] between 1956 and 1966 was employed as the exogenous variable. The direction of change was negative in over two-thirds of the cases and it is thus hypothesised that two nearest neighbours will now be, *ceteris paribus,* too closely spaced; the relationship postulated is an inverse one. It was necessary to transform the values from negative to positive by lateral conversion to permit logarithmic transformation, and the postulated relationship with distance also becomes positive. This hypothesis

TABLE I

Input data for towns of greater than 5,000 population

	Distance (Y)	Population 1961 (X₁)	Population density per square mile (X₂)	Percentage employed in manufacturing industry (X₃)	Income density per acre (X₄)	Percentage population change 1956–66 (X₅)
Cork	136	125,283	76	42	25.5	+ 5.7
Limerick	54	58,082	83	38	25.0	+ 0.5
Waterford	64	29,842	79	40	24.1	+ 0.5
Galway	45	26,295	48	35	11.8	− 4.6
Dundalk	44	21,678	132	50	46.2	+10.7
Drogheda	20	17,908	102	50	27.8	+ 0.4
Bray	11	13,668	480	41	172.4	+12.6
Sligo	68	13,424	59	35	14.5	− 7.3
Wexford	28	12,744	73	40	21.6	− 4.9
Kilkenny	28	12,030	66	38	21.5	− 5.7
Tralee	53	11,976	78	39	21.7	− 3.8
Clonmel	26	11,457	69	36	22.8	− 1.3
Athlone	46	10,744	53	38	13.0	− 6.7
Carlow	18	9,765	46	42	14.9	− 4.0
Ennis	19	9,181	75	36	17.5	− 4.6
Mullingar	26	7,943	41	27	12.2	− 2.3
Thurles	23	6,949	42	36	13.3	− 5.6
Killarney	17	6,877	63	31	15.6	− 7.6
Tullamore	19	6,874	53	46	15.5	− 1.4
Cobh	8	6,726	279	43	83.4	+ 0.9
Enniscorthy	12	6,279	67	35	18.4	− 4.4
Ballina	31	6,084	29	36	6.3	−14.4
Arklow	26	6,083	51	52	14.0	− 4.5
Navan	14	5,907	62	49	20.3	+ 0.8
Portlaoise	23	5,873	50	35	14.7	− 2.8
Mallow	19	5,845	92	39	27.5	+ 0.9
Ballinasloe	13	5,828	52	36	12.1	−11.7
Castlebar	17	5,629	62	31	12.8	−13.2
Dungarvan	11	5,380	33	40	10.9	− 1.3
Youghal	13	5,221	56	50	14.5	− 1.3
Newbridge	23	5,161	114	49	40.8	+11.6

rests upon the assumption that readjustment in the functional structure of a central place in areas of population decline results in a reduction in the number of central functions and functional units and consequently in the number of employees in tertiary activity. Thus in time the size of the town is gradually reduced; it is postulated that there is a time-lag between the feedback of reduced demand (because of population decline) into the system and functional and demographic adjustment within the nodes of the system.

Finally, population size is likely to prove an inadequate surrogate for centrality in the case of centres which lie within commuting distance of the two cities, Dublin and Cork. It is postulated that these dormitory towns have a higher percentage of their working population employed outside their urban areas. It is believed that this factor, combined with proximity to high order metropolitan centres, has resulted in a higher population than might be predicted from the range of tertiary goods and services offered in them. Berry[23] has produced empirical evidence from the suburbs of Seattle to support this type of hypothesis. Distance from the city centre (Dublin or Cork) is used as an operational variable for commuting and the relationship postulated with the dependent variable is positive.

Testing of hypotheses: towns over 5,000 population

The hypotheses considered in the earlier part of the chapter were tested initially by means of simple correlation and regression analysis; the regression of the endogenous variable, distance, was considered on each exogenous variable without reference to the effects of other exogenous variables. There is clearly a symmetrical relationship between distance and population size, but as the objective is to explain a spatial pattern it is logical to define distance as the endogenous variable although no direction of causality is implied. A linear product moment correlation model was employed to test the degree of association between distance and population size and yielded a correlation coefficient of 0.868. However, two important assumptions of the regression model which required to be satisfied were: (i) that the errors in the 'y' data be normally distributed with the means of the distribution located along a line, and (ii) that the variances of the errors be constant. Transformations of the variables were tested and the most normal and homoscedastic transformation functions were common logarithms of both variables. After double-log transformation the correlation coefficient was 0.759 with the regression of distance on population size having the form:

$$\text{Log } Y = -1.185 + 0.642 \text{ Log } X_1 \qquad (1)$$

In the case of all correlation and regression analyses carried out a number of transformations, such as semi-log, double-log and reciprocals have been tested for homoscedasticity and normality of error distribution and the transformation with the greatest degree of error normality and the most homogeneous variance has been used in all cases.

The initial stage of the analysis incorporated the regression of the first three exogenous variables, population size (X_1), population density (X_2) and percentage employed in manufacturing industry (X_3) on the endogenous variable, distance. The results of this analysis are summarised in Table 2 which reveals that the strongest correlation is between distance and population size, $r_{yx_1 \cdot x_2 x_3} = .829$, thus demonstrating that population size accounts for more than half of the variation in the dependent variable. It also reveals that, as stated in the hypothesis, there is an inverse relationship between distance and percentage employed in manufacturing industry, but the degree of correlation is very low ($r^2_{yx_3 \cdot x_1 x_2} = -.00005$), and is not significant at the .01 level, indicating that this variable may be regarded as redundant. It should be emphasised that data for Dublin city is not included in the analysis, for, being the largest centre, it has no nearest neighbour of equal or larger population. Also a degree of multicollinearity between the other two exogenous variables population size and population density ($r_{x_1x_2 \cdot yx_3} = .527$) is shown in Table 2. This demonstrates that when distance and percentage employed in manufacturing industry are held constant there is a degree of interdependence between population size and population density. This has the undesirable effect of inflating the value of the multiple correlation coefficient and also makes it difficult to interpret the partial correlation coefficients which indicate, in the case of orthogonal variables, the precise contribution of each of these variables to the overall level of explanation.

TABLE 2

The correlation of Y on X_1, X_2 and X_3 for towns over 5,000 population (n = 31) Variables
(Log of all variables are used)

Dependent variables: Y = Distance
Independent variables: X_1 = Population size
                         X_2 = Population density
                         X_3 = Per cent in manufacturing

Zero-order correlation matrix   First order partial correlation
                                              coefficients

	X_1	X_2	X_3
Y	.759	—.180*	—.068*
X_1		.213*	.056*
X_2			.311*

$r_{yx_1 \cdot x_2} = .829$ $r_{yx_3 \cdot x_2} = —.013*$
$r_{yx_1 \cdot x_3} = .766$ $r_{x_1x_2 \cdot y} = .546$
$r_{yx_2 \cdot x_1} = —.536$ $r_{x_1x_2 \cdot x_3} = .206*$
$r_{yx_2 \cdot x_3} = —.167*$ $r_{x_1x_3 \cdot x_2} = —.011*$
$r_{yx_3 \cdot x_1} = —.170*$ $r_{x_2x_3 \cdot x_1} = .307*$

Second order partial correlation coefficients

$r_{yx_1 \cdot x_2x_3} = .829$ $r^2 = .688$ $R_{y \cdot x_1x_2x_3} = .835$
$r_{yx_2 \cdot x_1x_3} = —.516$ $r^2 = .267$
$r_{yx_3 \cdot x_1x_2} = —.007*$ $r^2 = .00005$ $R^2_{y \cdot x_1x_2x_3} = .698$
$r_{x_1x_2 \cdot yx_3} = .527$ $r^2 = .278$
$r_{x_1x_3 \cdot yx_2} = —.0004*$ $r^2 = .0000002$
$r_{x_2x_3 \cdot yx_1} = .259*$ $r^2 = .067$

*Not significant at the .05 level

The study proceeded firstly by eliminating the percentage employed in manufacturing industry variable, and secondly by relaxing the homoscedastic assumption and testing various transformations of the population size and population density variables. This did not reduce the degree of multicollinearity and so income density (X_4) was incorporated. This variable, although functionally related to the population density variable, $r^2 = .762$, introduces an important additional element into the model, namely the concept of purchasing power per unit area. Thus the marked spatial variation in income levels throughout the Republic of Ireland[24] is accounted for; there was a correlation of —0.277 between distance and income density, confirming the original hypothesis.

A dynamic factor, population change, was also introduced into the model. As postulated there is a positive relationship between distance and population change, but the degree of correlation is very low ($r = 0.047$) and is not significant at the .01 level. This variable may therefore be eliminated from any subsequent analysis.

The exogenous variables X_1 and X_4 together account for 70 per cent of the variation in the dependent variable (Table 3). The distinct contributions of each of the variables to the explained variation cannot be determined precisely because a degree of interdependence exists between the population size and income density variables ($r_{x_1 x_4 \cdot y} = .171$). The values of the partial correlation coefficients, indicating the statistical relationship between two variables with another variable held constant, are only a totally accurate measure of the contribution of each exogenous variable to the explained variation when the variables are orthogonal. This is a situation seldom if ever present in the mix of factors associated with

TABLE 3

The correlation of Y on X_1 and X_4 for all towns of over 5,000 population (n = 31)

Variables (Log of all variables are used except for Income Density)
Dependent variable: Y = Distance
Independent variable: X_1 = Population size
                          X_4 = Income density

Zero order correlation coefficients		Partial correlation coefficients	
$r_{yx_1} = .759$	$r^2 = .576$	$r_{yx_1 \cdot x_4} = .827$	$r^2 = .684$
$r_{yx_4} = -.277^\star$	$r^2 = .077$	$r_{yx_4 \cdot x_1} = -.559$	$r^2 = .312$
$r_{x_1 x_4} = .111^\star$	$r^2 = .012$	$r_{x_1 x_4 \cdot y} = .414$	$r^2 = .171$

$$R_{y.x_1 x_4} = .842$$
$$R_{y.x_1 x_4} = .708$$

Regression equations

$$\text{Log } Y = -1.185 + 0.642 \text{ Log } X_1 \tag{2}$$
$$\text{Log } Y = -1.237 + 0.677 \text{ Log } X_1 -0.004 \ X_4 \tag{3}$$

$\star$Not significant at the .01 level.

the majority of geographical problems. However, from an examination of the multiple coefficient of determination and the partial correlation coefficients in Table 3 one may conclude that population size accounts for approximately half the variation in the endogenous variable and income density explains approximately 10 per cent of the variation.

The pattern of residuals from equations (2) and (3) were not particularly meaningful

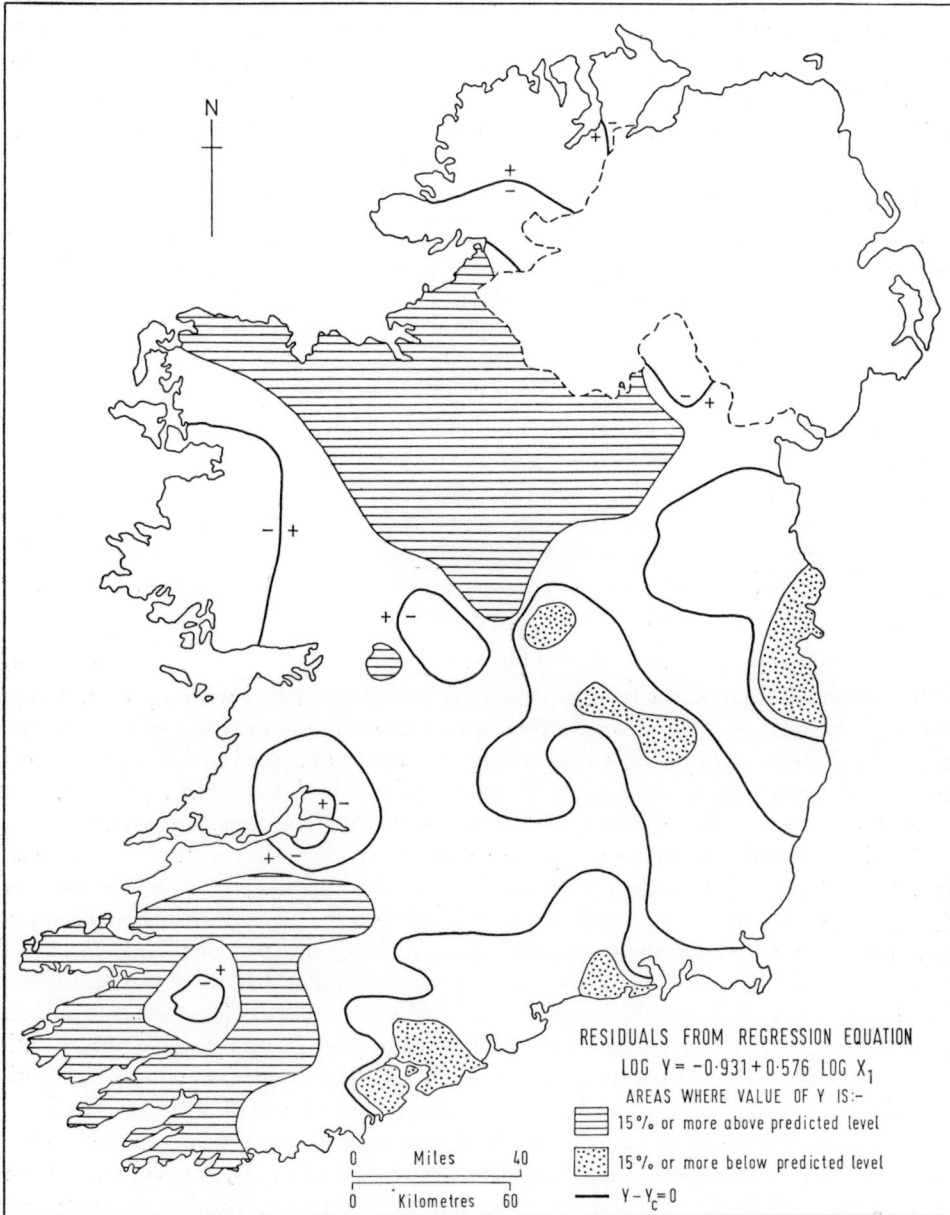

RESIDUALS FROM REGRESSION EQUATION
LOG Y = −0·931 + 0·576 LOG X₁
AREAS WHERE VALUE OF Y IS:−
15% or more above predicted level
15% or more below predicted level
Y − Yc = 0

17.2   Isarithmic residual surface after regression of Y on X₁

for there were only thirty-one central places over the whole country and thus systematic variations could not be identified. There appeared to be a tendency for positive residuals to be more common in the west of the country and for negative deviations to be concentrated along the east and south-east coasts. The mapping of residual surfaces from the second stage of the analysis will enable systematic variations to be determined with more certainty.

Testing of hypotheses: all towns greater than 1,500 population

For the second stage of the experiment the scope of the inquiry was expanded to include all towns in the country with a population of greater than 1,500. This resulted in the inclusion of sixty-seven centres with populations in the range 1,500 to 5,000 in addition to the thirty-one towns of larger than 5,000 population. The percentage employed in manu-facturing industry variable was excluded from the analysis as this data is not available for towns in the population range 1,500 to 5,000; but the commuting variable was incorporated to give a total of five exogenous variables. The population density variable again manifested a high degree of multicollinearity with population size and it was excluded. The analysis proceeded by considering the form of the functional relationship between distance and population size. Logarithmic functions were again used as input data for the regression model to insure greater homoscedasticity and normality of errors, notwithstanding a higher correlation when both variables were expressed as linear functions. The coefficient of correlation was 0.713 and the relationship took the form

$$\text{Log } Y = -0.931 + 0.576 \text{ Log } X_1 \tag{4}$$

The mapping of residuals from equation (4) provides a means whereby relationships among phenomena may be viewed in their spatial dimension in the form of an isarithmic map. Actual distances (Y) do not correspond to distances (Y_c) predicted from the model since linear correlation is not perfect. Therefore, when absolute residuals ($Y - Y_c$) are mapped one obtains a map showing the performance of the regression equation.[25]

Absolute residuals have either a negative **sign** (in cases where the equation overestimates the value of Y) or a positive sign (in cases where the equation underestimates the value of Y). Figure 17.2 illustrates graphically the spatial variations in the performance of equation (4) in describing the endogenous variable because it shows that part of the magnitude of the variable which is associated with exogenous variables other than those included in the model. The form of the residual surface generated from equation (4) displays a distinct regional variation (Fig. 17.2). The western half of the country forms a positive surface with two high ridges in the north-west and south-west; the surface slopes away to the east with a number of negative basins, notably around Dublin, Cork and Waterford. The large positive anomaly ridge in the north-west (deviating by more than 15 per cent from the predicted level) forms a zone of approximately 4,000 square miles, 88.5 km (55 miles) wide from Ballina to Ballyshannon and stretching 96.6 km (60 miles) inland to the south-east to include the counties of Sligo, Leitrim, Cavan, Longford, and Roscommon. The second positive anomaly ridge includes most of co. Kerry, part of west co. Cork and part of south co. Limerick. These two areas are characterised by low population densities, low incomes

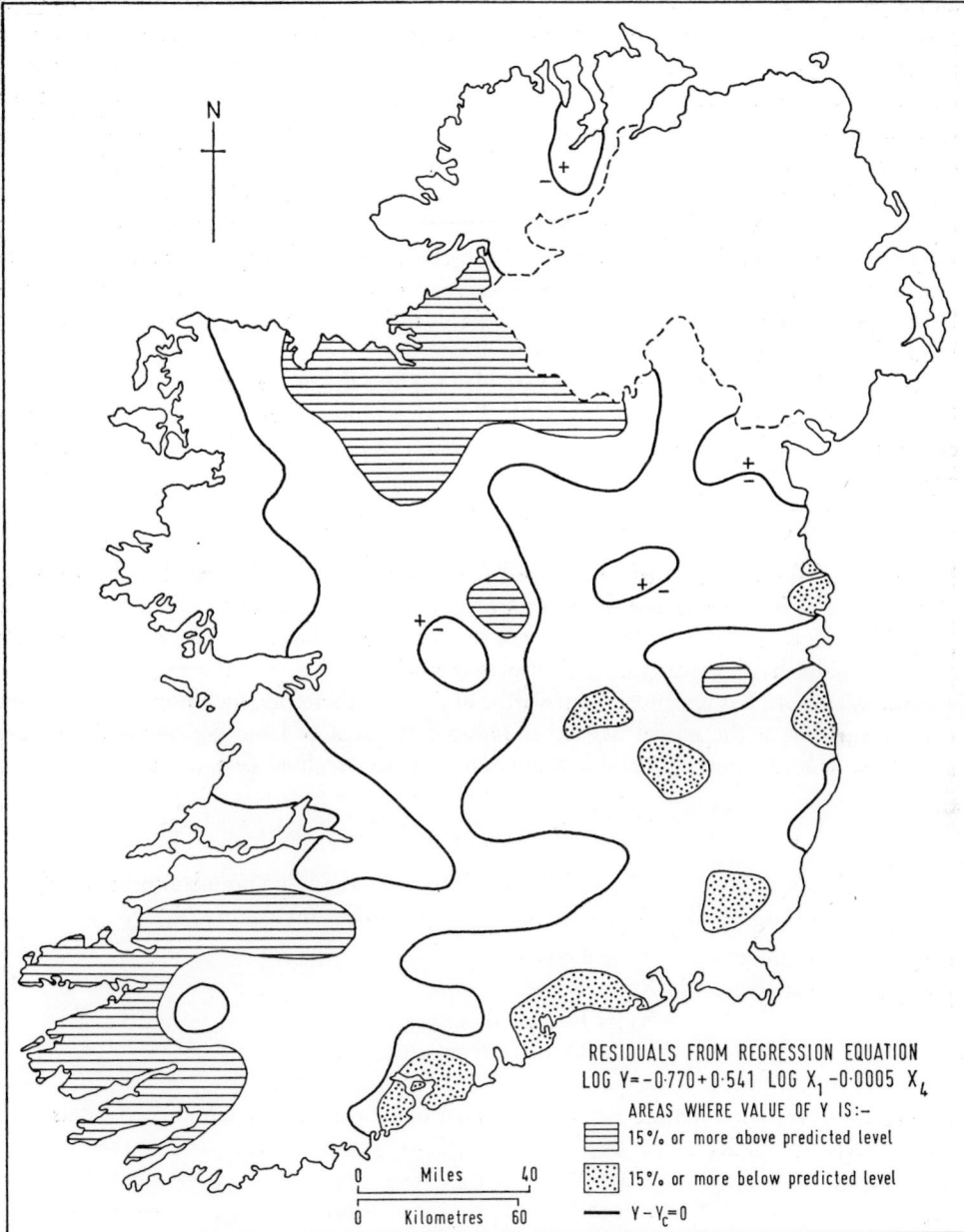

RESIDUALS FROM REGRESSION EQUATION
LOG Y = -0·770 + 0·541 LOG X_1 - 0·0005 X_4
AREAS WHERE VALUE OF Y IS:-

15% or more above predicted level

15% or more below predicted level

$Y - Y_c = 0$

17.3 Isarithmic residual surface after regression of Y on X_1, and X_4

and high population loss. Consequently, urban centres in these areas are, relative to their predicted values from equation (4), too far from their nearest neighbours of equal or larger population. It seems logical to select new variables which show a similar spatial pattern to the residual values. Addition of exogenous variables into the model which account for income density, population change and commuting should improve the overall level of explanation and reduce the extent of the 'unexplained' areas. The two largest negative anomaly 'lows' indicated in figure 17.2 are, firstly, a zone around Cork city including the towns of Passage West, Cobh and Middleton, and secondly, an area within commuting range of Dublin and including Skerries, Rush, Swords, Malahide, Bray and Greystones-Delgany. These negative anomaly zones—where towns are too close to their nearest neighbour—are located in areas of highest population density, of greatest purchasing power per head of population and of largest population gain.

Introduction of the income density variable (X_4) into the model results, as hypothesised, in an inverse functional relationship with distance yielding a zero order correlation coefficient of —0.383 (Table 4). Addition of variable X_4 produces the multiple regression equation

$$\text{Log } Y = -0.770 + 0.541 \text{ Log } X_1 - 0.0005 \ X_4 \qquad (5)$$

The form of the residual surface mapped from equation (5) is indicated in figure 17.3. Comparison of figure 17.2 and figure 17.3 reveals that the areal extent of the two positive 'highs' in the west of the country has been considerably reduced, the large negative basin around Dublin has been fragmented into two small troughs, and the extent of the low around Waterford has expanded westwards. In general, therefore, inclusion of the income density variable in the model has either reduced the area of large positive and negative anomalies or broken up high and low zones into small, localised deviations.

TABLE 4

Correlation of Y on X_1, X_4 and X_6 for all towns over 1,500 population (n = 98)
Variables (Log of all variables are used, except for Income density X_4)

Dependent variable: Y = Distance
Independent variables: X_1 = Population size
                           X_4 = Income density
                           X_6 = Distance from city

Zero order correlation matrix

	X_1	X_4	X_6
Y	.713	—.383	.422
X_1		—.158*	.135*
X_4			—.286

First order partial correlation coefficients

$r_{yx_1 \cdot x_4} = .716$ $r_{x_1 x_4 \cdot y} = .178$*

$r_{yx_1 \cdot x_6} = .731$ $r_{x_1 x_4 \cdot x_6} = —.116$*

$r_{yx_4 \cdot x_1} = —.391$ $r_{x_1 x_6 \cdot y} = —.262$

$r_{yx_4 \cdot x_6} = —.263$ $r_{x_1 x_6 \cdot x_4} = .081$*

$r_{yx_6 \cdot x_1} = .470$ $r_{x_4 x_6 \cdot y} = —.267$

$r_{yx_6 \cdot x_4} = .323$ $r_{x_4 x_6 \cdot x_1} = —.372$

Second order partial correlation coefficients

$r_{yx_1 \cdot x_4 x_6} = .731$ $\quad r^2 = .534$

$r_{yx_4 \cdot x_1 x_6} = -.264$ $\quad r^2 = .069$ $\qquad R_{y.x_1 x_4 x_6} = .802$

$r_{yx_6 \cdot x_1 x_4} = .380$ $\quad r^2 = .144$

$r_{x_1 x_4 \cdot yx_6} = .116^\star$ $\quad r^2 = .014$ $\qquad R^2_{y.x_1 x_4 x_6} = .644$

$r_{x_1 x_6 \cdot yx_4} = -.226^\star$ $\quad r^2 = .051$

$r_{x_4 x_6 \cdot yx_1} = -.232^\star$ $\quad r^2 = .054$

Regression equations

$$\text{Log } Y = -0.9307 + 0.576 \ \text{Log } X_1 \tag{4}$$

$$\text{Log } Y = -0.770 + 0.5410 \ \text{Log } X_1 - 0.0005 \ X_4 \tag{5}$$

$$\text{Log } Y = -1.1577 + 0.5247 \ \text{Log } X_1 - 0.0003 \ X_4 + 0.2660 \ \text{Log } X_6 \tag{6}$$

*Not significant at the .01 level

Finally, the distance from city variable (X_6) was introduced into the model, and, as postulated, manifested a positive statistical relationship with the dependent variable $(r = 0.422)$. Inclusion of this exogenous variable yielded the multiple regression equation

$$\text{Log } Y = -1.158 + 0.525 \ \text{Log } X_1 - 0.0003 \ X_4 + 0.266 \ \text{Log } X_6 \tag{6}$$

and a multiple correlation coefficient of $R_{y.x_1 x_4 x_6} = .802$. Table 4 shows that the three exogenous variables, population size, income density, and distance from city, explain approximately 64 per cent of the variation in the dependent variable. Examination of the second order partial correlation coefficients indicates that although the variables are not orthogonal the degree of multicollinearity is low. Population size accounts for about half of the total variation in the dependent variable; distance to city approximately 10 per cent and income density 6 per cent.

Examination of the form of the residual surface (Fig. 17.4) from equation (6), after the inclusion of all three variables, shows that the large area of positive residuals in the north-west has shrunk to a small elliptical 'high' about 48 km by 24 km (30 miles by 15 miles) along the major and minor axes respectively. The other large positive high in the south-west has been bisected into two smaller units. The negative residual troughs, which occur principally in the east and south of the country have been reduced in their areal extent with the inclusion of the commuting variable. The negative anomaly zones, other than those around the major cities, are less stable in location and extent than the positive ones. The largest positive anomaly zones in the north-west and south-west of the country are areas where factors other than those included in this analysis are operating. Subsequent work on the problem of explaining the spatial pattern of urban centres should commence with a consideration of these two areas.

CONCLUSION

Operating within the conceptual framework of the central place model, hypotheses to describe and explain the spacing of urban centres in Ireland have been formulated and tested both for towns over 5,000 population and for all centres larger than 1,500. A regression

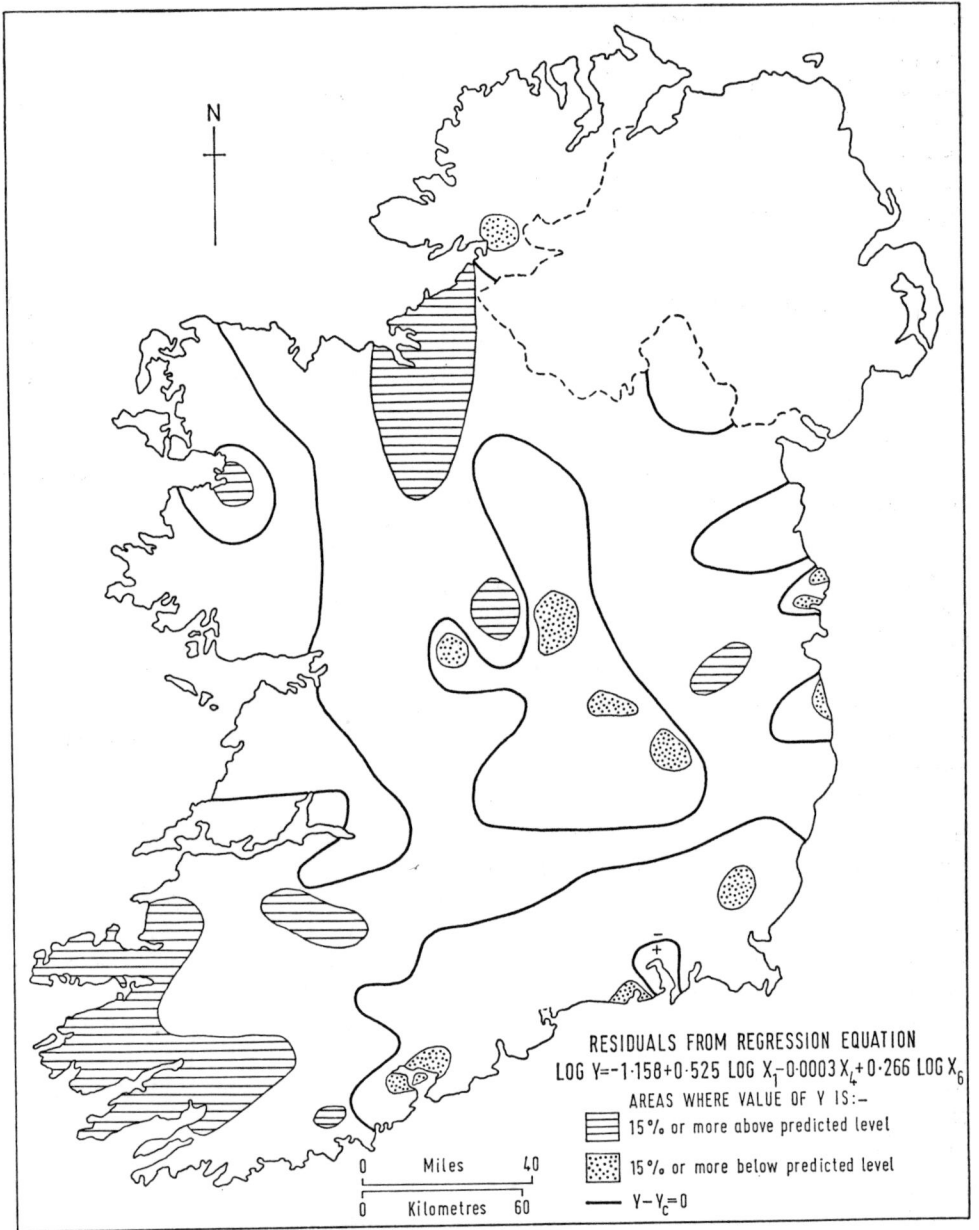

17.4 Isarithmic residual surface after regression of Y on X_1, X_4 and X_6

model was developed to analyse the relationship between the spatial pattern of central places and six exogenous variables. Using multiple regression techniques three variables, percentage employed in manufacturing industry, population change and population density were eliminated from the analysis: the first two because their correlations with the endogenous variable were low and not significant at the .05 and .01 level, and the latter because of an intolerable level of multicollinearity with the population size variable. The equation

$$\text{Log } Y = -1.158 + 0.525 \text{ Log } X_1 - 0.0003 \, X_4 + 0.266 \text{ Log } X_6$$

may be taken as a reasonably accurate description of the spatial distribution of towns in Ireland in that it accounts for approximately two-thirds of the total variation. These findings may be compared with those of King[26] who explained 25 per cent of the variation in spacing for a sample of 200 towns in the United States. This study has also confirmed that size of centre, accounting for half of the total variation, is universally the most important factor influencing the spatial pattern. Despite the assumptions of the theory this conclusion agrees in broad terms with Christaller's model, where population size is the sole explanatory variable. Thomas[27] explained 60 per cent of spatial variation in Iowa, a state approximately equal in size to Ireland, by population size and O'Farrell[28], employing the same exogenous variable, accounted for 75 per cent of the total variation in spacing in co. Tipperary.

The fact that almost one-third of the variation remains unexplained shows that the spacing of urban centres, like other geographical phenomena, is the result of complex interrelationships between many variables. The results must be supplemented by an acknowledgement that stochastic and historical factors other than population change may account for a proportion of the unexplained variation.

In conclusion, by isolating and quantifying the influence of a mix of factors on the spatial distribution of towns in Ireland, this study has produced some findings at a national level which could prove of value to regional planning authorities concerned with rationalising the urban system in Ireland about pre-existing nodes. It is also hoped that the essay will be viewed as a small contribution both to the essential task of identifying the processes influencing the spatial aspects of the urban system in Ireland, at the inter- and intra-urban level, and towards the derivation of general laws concerning those spatial elements.

REFERENCES

1 Examples of such studies include, *inter alia:* T. W. Freeman, The town and district of Carrick-on-Shannon, co. Leitrim, *Irish Geography,* 2, No. 1 (1949), 1–19; and The town and district of Roscommon, *Irish Geography,* 2, No. 2 (1950), 64–76

2 N. Lichfield and Associates, *Report and Advisory Outline Plan for the Limerick Region,* (Dublin, 1966)

3 W. C. Krumbein, The sorting out of geological variables illustrated by regression analysis of factors controlling beach firmness, *J. Sedimentary Petrology,* 29, No. 4 (Dec. 1959), 575–87

4 W. Christaller, *Central Places in Southern Germany,* translated by C. W. Baskin, (New Jersey, 1966), from *Die Zentralen Orte in Suddeutschland,* (Jena, 1933)

5 See for example, B. J. L. Berry and A. Pred, *Central Place Studies: A bibliography of theory and applications,* (Philadelphia Regional Science Research Institute, 1961); E. von Böventer, Towards a united theory of spatial economic structure, *Papers Regional Science Ass.,* 10 (1962), 163–91; and B. J. L. Berry, *Geography of market centres and retail distribution,* (New Jersey, 1967)

U

6 E. von Böventer, (1962), op. cit., 169

7 ibid.

8 All population values are from the *Census of population of Ireland, 1966,* and include the 'environs' of urban districts, municipal boroughs and county boroughs.

9 It was shown, for a sample of towns, that there was a high correlation between straight line distance and road distance. Also nearest neighbours outside the study area in Northern Ireland were included where appropriate.

10 E. N. Thomas, The stability of the distance population-size-relationship for Iowa from 1900–50, *Proceedings of the I.G.U. Symposium in Urban Geography, Lund 1960,* (Royal University of Lund, 1962), 21

11 P. N. O'Farrell, A multivariate analysis of the spacing of central places in county Tipperary, *Irish Geography,* 5, No. 5 (1968), 428–39

12 See for example, J. E. Brush, The hierarchy of central places in south-western Wisconsin, *Geographical Review,* 43 (1953), 380–402 A. Lösch, *Die Räumliche Ordnung der Wirtschaft,*(Jena, 1944), translated by W. H. Woglom and W. F. Stolper as *The Economics of Location,* (New Haven, 1954), and J. E. Brush and H. E. Bracey, Rural service centres in southwestern Wisconsin and southern England, *Geog. Rev.,* 45 (1955), 559–69

13 E. N. Thomas, Toward an expanded central place model, *Geog. Rev.,* 51 (1961), 400–11

14 L. J. King, A multivariate analysis of the spacing of urban settlements in the United States, *Ann. Ass. Amer. Geogr.,* 51 (1961), 222–33; and G. Vuicich, An analysis of the spacing of small towns in Iowa, (unpublished PhD thesis, Department of Geography, State University of Iowa, 1960)

15 This variable is hereinafter simply referred to as 'distance'.

16 Population density was measured as the mean density of the aggregate of District Electoral Divisions lying along a straight line between a given centre and its nearest neighbour of equal or larger population.

17 E. A. Attwood and R. C. Geary, Irish county incomes in 1960, *The Economic Research Institute, Paper,* No. 16 (Dublin, 1963)

18 ibid., Table II, Column 6, p. 11

19 ibid., Table 3, Column 12, p. 12

20 For a discussion on problems of data preparation see A. H. Robinson, J. B. Lindberg, L. W. Brinkman, A correlation and regression analysis applied to rural farm population densities in the Great Plains, *Ann. Ass. Amer. Geogr.,* 51 (1961), 211–21

21 *Census of population of Ireland, 1961,* Vol. 3, Occupations, Table 6A

22 Population change was quantified as the mean percentage change, 1956–66, of the aggregate of District Electoral Divisions lying along a straight line between a given centre and its nearest neighbour of equal or greater population.

23 B. J. L. Berry, (1967), op. cit., 35

24 E. A. Attwood and R. C. Geary, op. cit.

25 E. N. Thomas, Maps of residuals from regressions: their characteristics and uses in geographic research, (State University of Iowa, Department of Geography, Report 2, 1960)

26 L. J. King, (1961), op. cit.

27 E. N. Thomas, (1962), op. cit., 27

28 P. N. O'Farrell, (1968), op. cit.

· XVIII

TOWNS AND PLANNING IN IRELAND
Jean Forbes

The word 'planning' is used in so many contexts, that explanatory prefix words, for example, 'economic', are often appended to clarify the sense in which the term is used. In this paper I use the word to mean planning for the *spatial* distribution of population and resources. This is an operation which may be carried out at three levels of scale: national, regional and local. These levels vary both in the precision with which their functions are defined, and in the strength of the statutory powers which each may have. However, the notion of three levels is readily understood and it serves as a framework within which to discuss a nation's planning system.

Broadly speaking one may suggest that planning at the national level is concerned with policy decisions about the scale of investment in, and the role of, each of the nation's component regions. The objective is to ensure that these regions, in aggregate, constitute a prosperous and efficient nation. The regional planner receives the policy decisions from the national level and proceeds to design a settlement and communications pattern for his region, which will maximize the functional efficiency of the region and enable it to play its part in national development. The local planner occupies a key position. It is he who gears down the strategy of the regional planner into detailed land allocations on statutory development plans. It is he who, through the operation of the statutory machinery, causes slums to be demolished or new houses to be built.

In Ireland, the political division complicates the thinking about the three levels of spatial planning. Two different versions of the three level system are in operation. (The local levels are similar in both and may be disregarded for the moment.)

In the Republic, the system is similar to that which holds in Britain. National policies and the general overseeing of regional strategies are managed by the central government or its agencies, or by consultants whom it retains. The full development of regional level machinery is inhibited as it is in Britain, by the lack of elected regional assemblies. It is open to discussion whether or not this inhibition of the development of the middle tier of the institutional structure, has had any repercussions on the quality of the regional planning which has been done hitherto.

In Northern Ireland a unique planning situation exists. There is an elected legislature for an area which, politically, is only a region within the United Kingdom. Planning powers are devolved from the British government to this local legislature, which enacts its own planning laws separately. As a result, the Northern Ireland government planners are, simultaneously, national planners and regional planners for the same territory. This tele-scoping of national and regional roles leaves Northern Ireland planners in an unusually isolated position. On the one hand their territory is rarely included in a British level national over-view of spatial planning policy. This is not merely because the institutional structure is not suitable for doing otherwise, in view of the devolution of powers and separation of the legal measures. It is made virtually inevitable by the presence of the Irish Sea which renders redundant any need to co-ordinate the regional strategy of Northern Ireland with the strategies of neighbouring regions across the sea. On the other hand Northern Ireland cannot be included in an all-Ireland 'national' over view of planning strategy. Indeed it will be obvious that no such 'national' view can exist *officially* while the political division of Ireland lasts. There is no sound reason why such a strategy should not evolve at technical level given increased technical co-operation. In the meantime, Northern Ireland planners must operate within a uniquely closed planning system.

This is the institutional structure within which Irish planners work to-day and within which their planning methodology has developed. It is interesting to study the responses to Ireland's particular set of planning problems and to observe the similarity of treatment throughout the island, political divisions notwithstanding. In this chapter it is proposed to concentrate upon the regional and national levels of planning in Ireland, focusing in particular upon the adaptations of the 'growth centre' idea in recently published regional plans. Later, some comment will be made upon the future implications of this idea for the time when technical co-operation renders possible co-ordinated strategy making on an all-Ireland basis, knitting together the component regional strategies.

All Ireland's planning problems are connected back to the two-sided core problem— slow industrial growth and population decline. Ireland lacked the raw materials of coal and iron ore upon which the first Industrial Revolution was based. The nineteenth-century industrial development of the north-east was on a small scale by British standards. As a result Ireland has a weak tradition of industrially based urban development and a com-paratively unskilled labour force. The vigorous attempts to win modern industrial develop-ments, supported by generous grants from both Irish governments, are achieving results, but not fast enough to offset the factors which continue to create unemployment. Modern industry is highly automated and this cuts down the numbers of jobs created per firm to quite a low level.

These new job opportunities are attempting to offset the numerically large decline in jobs in agriculture and, in the north-east, jobs lost through closure of obsolete industrial concerns. This latter obsolescence is complemented by its attendant planning problem— deterioration of the fabric of the towns which grew up to serve the needs of nineteenth-century industry.

The idea of growth centres

Ireland's peripheral and insular location in relation to Britain and Europe is an additional handicap to attracting new industrial developments. The planner in Ireland is therefore forced into a very narrow decision space. He must accurately place his limited capital in locations which will be of maximum value in attracting modern industrialists in sufficient number to generate the economic growth which is essential to the provision of better opportunities for more of Ireland's people.

In similar circumstances, Scottish planners have developed the idea of growth centres. This might be described as investing in a few towns which are most likely to succeed. By concentrating investment one can give each of the selected towns a substantial boost towards the, as yet undefined, threshold of self perpetuating growth. Irish planners have adopted this idea, and various applications of it have been manifested in the three major regional plans produced during the 1960's for the Belfast, Limerick and Dublin regions.

It is clear that the success of growth centre policy depends upon two things: firstly, the number of centres selected (since this affects the share of investment which may be allocated to each), and secondly, the locations (towns) chosen. A choice of too many growth towns may fragment the booster effect and thus fail to achieve the economies of scale which are attractive to industrialists. A choice of even a few towns in the wrong location would be equally wasteful.

In the exercise of choice it is desirable that the national planner, and then later the regional planner, should understand the existing central place system. The selection of growth centres is an intervention in what might be described as the free market situation within which the existing central place system has developed. The planner is now setting out deliberately to accentuate the importance of some towns and thus, relatively, to depress others. The implications of his choice will have wide social repercussions. He has a duty to consider the aggregate 'best interest' of the whole community and he will be better guided towards an optimum choice if he has a feeling for the inherited system, which he is now proposing to control.

Academic studies of the Irish central place system were not available to guide the makers of the three regional plans which have been produced during the 1960's. Each team of planning consultants worked its way towards an evaluation of the intra-regional system with which each was concerned. The three efforts are not strictly comparable and therefore cannot be taken as contributing to a true all-Ireland view of the Irish central place system, a synoptic study of which remains to be done. A sketchy preliminary view of the system will be presented in the latter part of this paper. In the meantime, it is appropriate to review the three regional plans, as they give three varying examples of growth centre planning in action (Fig. 18.1).

Regional plans of the 1960's

The first illustration of the growth centre idea in Ireland came in the Matthew plan for the Belfast region, published in 1964.[1] The region for study was, fortunately, not defined precisely in the remit and this left the research team free to study the city of Belfast in three contexts: first as the core of a rather untidy Greater Belfast; second as the major focal point of a 40 km (24.8 miles) radius commuter region; third as the principal city (and politically the capital city) of Northern Ireland.

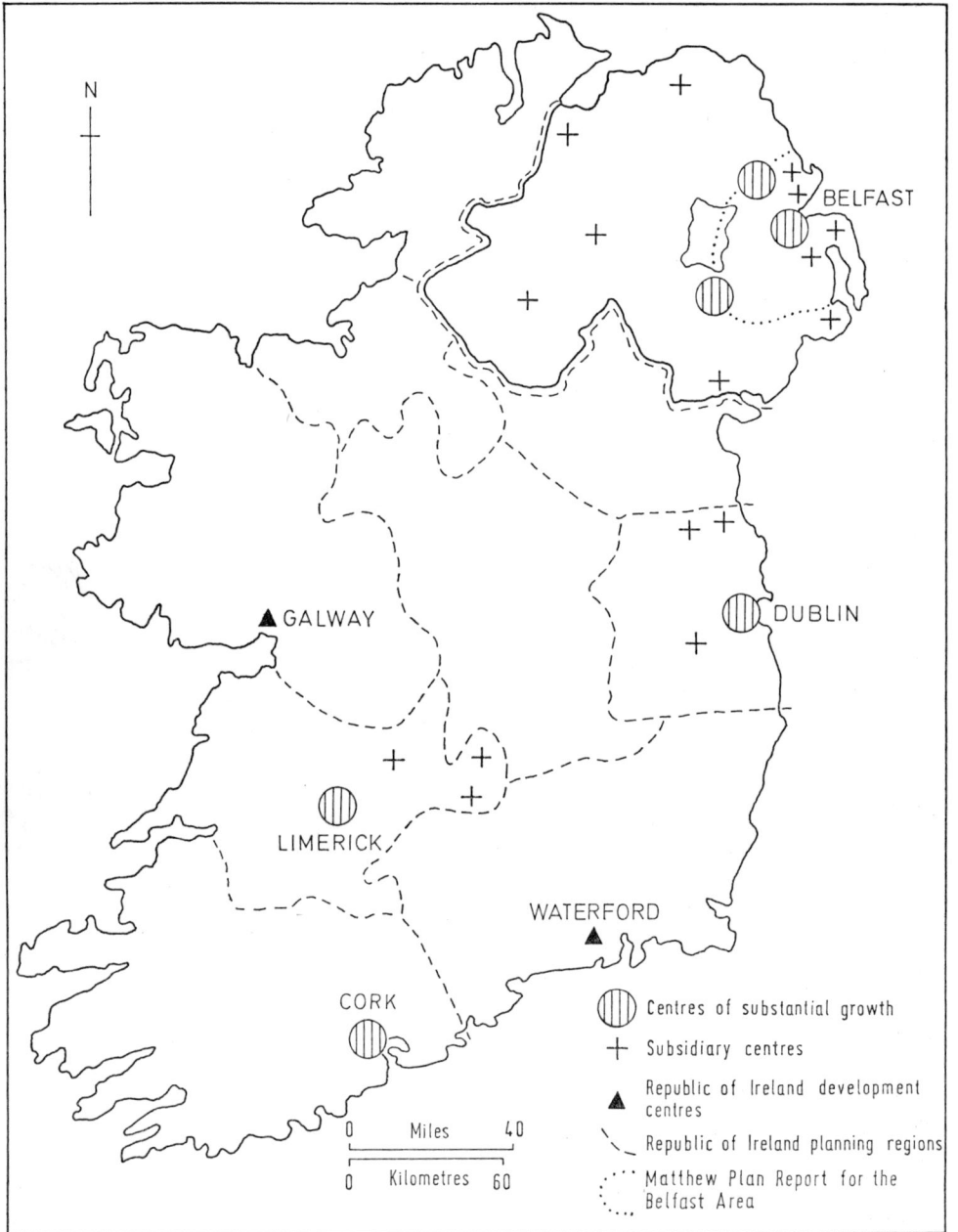

N

BELFAST

GALWAY

DUBLIN

LIMERICK

WATERFORD

CORK

◉ Centres of substantial growth
+ Subsidiary centres
▲ Republic of Ireland development centres
╱ Republic of Ireland planning regions
⋯ Matthew Plan Report for the Belfast Area

0   Miles   40
0   Kilometres   60

Fig. 18.1 Planning regions and growth centres in Ireland, 1968

The problems of the Northern Ireland level region were discerned as problems of intra-regional imbalance. It was felt that the internal migration which focuses upon Belfast and the Lagan Valley was drawing population from the western counties at a rate which diminished steadily their ability to support a reasonable standard of economic growth. The migration into the Belfast commuter region and into the central urban area was contributing to rising traffic congestion there. Over and above these problems, it was evident that physical obsolescence in the city itself would necessitate a full-scale urban renewal operation. This could be counted on to raise the further problem of overspill of displaced population—a potential centrifugal movement of population running against the tide of the centripetal rural to urban migration.

The Matthew Plan sought to use this latter stream of potential migration to create conditions which might help to intercept the former. It argued that by selecting one or two towns for major development, it might be possible to attract industrialists interested in the advantages of a large centre. If the towns were selected at locations which were within commuting distance of Belfast, overspill families might be willing to go to them. Furthermore, if the towns were selected in positions which straddled the lines of migration towards Belfast then it was likely that the centripetal migration could be intercepted.

The Plan indicated that Portadown and Lurgan, which are 6 km (4 miles) apart, had the necessary locational attributes and had, in addition, a substantial combined population of over 30,000 to provide a basis for growth. This development was given priority over the next most likely contender, Ballymena. Subsequent plans have been prepared for the substantial expansion of Portadown-Lurgan, and of Ballymena and its neighbour Antrim. In addition, the Matthew Plan selected other, although minor, growth towns within the commuter region, some, such as Bangor and Newtownards being sufficiently close to Belfast to be regarded almost as outer suburbs. Beyond the commuter region it recommended that investment be concentrated into Coleraine, Londonderry, Omagh, Enniskillen, Dungannon and Newry.

In order to accelerate the growth of the selected towns the plan proposed the containment of the Belfast urban area[2] by means of a stop-line. Argument has raged subsequently over this component of the plan. Taken by itself it could conceivably be described as a potential deterrent to industrialists, who, it is said, might not come to Northern Ireland at all if they are to be denied sites in the immediate vicinity of the city. This case is not yet proved, and it must be pointed out that in any case potential expansion of Belfast is restricted by topography. There is little time-distance difference between a site in the now far-flung suburbs and a site in one of the inner growth towns such as Newtownards or Carrickfergus. The problem is one of balancing risks. On the one hand there is a risk of repelling the industrialist whose range of locations may be so small as virtually to tie him to the large city. On the other hand, any breaches of the stop-line may jeopardize the efforts to divert new industry to the growth centres.

A weakness in the planning machinery has, however, undermined part of the Matthew design. There is no formal organization for resettling overspill population. If any families have moved out of Belfast they have had to arrange the transfer entirely on their own. This is a serious defect and will inhibit speedy build up of the major growth centres. The success of the Glasgow overspill operation offers an example of what can be achieved given an efficient Overspill Section in the parent city's Housing Department.

The Matthew Plan must be judged in the context of its time. Its greatest contribution may be seen, in future, to have been its ground-breaking function rather than its planning proposals as such. It was produced in an atmosphere which was decidedly anti-planning, and in a community intensely suspicious of change. The Matthew Plan provoked a vigorous public debate which still continues, and this has served to bring planning to public notice in Northern Ireland.

Application of the growth centre policy has followed in the Republic of Ireland, subsequent to the publication there of the *Second programme for economic expansion* in 1964.[3] A number of towns were indicated as potential growth centres, over and above Dublin and Cork which are sufficiently large and flourishing not to require special investment. The other towns were Limerick (and Shannon), Galway and Waterford. The Republic has been divided into nine planning regions, most of which have thriving regional towns to serve as focal points (Fig. 18.1). An amenity plan for one of the regions, Donegal, has been published[4], and so have two full scale regional plans, one for the Limerick Region by Lichfield[5] and one for the Dublin region by Wright.[6] At the time of writing, plans for the other seven regions are being prepared by Buchanan & Partners.

In the Limerick region there is an unusual component in the basis for growth. "Among the factors that have had a considerable effect on the growth at Shannon and in the District and Region, is the requirement that trans-Atlantic aircraft landing in the Republic should do so at Shannon."[7] This requirement is the result of a decision by the government to forestall the possible redundancy of the airport, which is no longer required as a refuelling stop on the Atlantic crossing.

Lichfield reiterates the choice which all Irish planners have to face at all levels " . . . granted that Ireland has only limited resources, should they be invested in trying to raise

TABLE I

Towns	Population		
	1961	1966	1968 Target
Limerick and Ennis	60,000	65,000	95,000
Nenagh	4,000	5,000	6,000
Roscrae	3,000	4,000	4,000
Thurles	6,000	7,000	9,000

Source: *Census of Population* 1961 and 1966 and Lichfield (figures rounded to the nearest thousand)

the level in the less developed areas or in pushing ahead the developed areas as fast as possible so as to create new wealth from which the aid to the poorer areas can come?" Within the region, he faced the choice between investing in one growth centre or in a range of several centres. The final choice was to declare the Limerick-Ennis-Shannon triangle as the Central Growth Area and have Nenagh, Roscrae and Thurles as subsidiary centres.

One of the problems in Irish planners' attempts to implement the growth centre idea, is to find population concentrations of sufficient size for the economies of scale to begin to operate early in the growth period. The combination and articulation of the Limerick-Ennis-Shannon group of towns is clear good sense in a region with few large towns.

The other published regional plan is that for the Dublin region. Its starting assumption was that the government's policy to stimulate growth in the other growth centres such as Limerick will work in the long term and that the Dublin region's share of the Republic's economic activity will remain as of 1961. The calculated population growth expected is still large since the city and county already contain 794,000 people (1966). The problem facing Wright was to produce a strategy for the accommodation of the expected population. In this respect his exercise had to move along the same chain of reasoning as did Matthew's. However, in this region there are very few other large independent towns of say 15,000 persons, around which overall growth could be crystallized, as it could be in the Belfast region.

Wright's solution to the Dublin problem was to accept that continued physical growth of 'Metropolitan Dublin' was not merely desirable but in this context virtually inevitable, and that the correct procedure would be to design accordingly. Four subsidiary outlying growth centres of varying significance were discerned at Drogheda, Naas/Newbridge, Arklow and Navan.

TABLE 2

	Population		
	1961	1966	Targets 1985
Dublin City and County	718,000	794,000	+ 1 million
Drogheda	17,000	18,000	35,000
Naas/Newbridge	10,000	11,000	20,000
Arklow	5,000	6,000	10,000
Navan	5,000	6,000	10,000

(figures rounded to the nearest thousand)
Source: Wright p. 157 and p. 199

The expansion of the metropolitan area itself should, it is suggested, be accommodated in a massive westward extension. This would consist, not of a single slab of development but rather of several westward reaching 'fingers', the road pattern being designed to articulate the 'hand and fingers'.

The regional plans just described (Fig. 18.1) illustrate the application of the growth centre idea in three very different regional contexts. In geographical terms, each has proposed a manipulation of the intra-regional central place system in an attempt to maximize attractiveness to incoming industrialists. It seems most likely that the policy will be further applied and adapted in the future. In the absence of a comprehensive central place study, the planning consultants have made their decisions internally to each region and have used various 'one-off' surveys as the factual foundation for their choices. Spatial planning in Ireland is thus, clearly, at a stage where geographical analysis of the existing central place system could be of great value. The critical questions which must be asked before growth centres are selected, have been stated already. They can be repeated in summary, that is, how many towns should be selected and in which locations are these most likely to succeed?

Ideally, an all-Ireland selection of the higher order growth centres should be made first. This would provide a series of major nodes around which meaningful functional regions could be organized. The further stage of selecting the support growth centres within each region could then follow. The selection processes which have operated hitherto, have not passed through this sequence of stages. Re-designs of intra-regional central place systems done in isolation, can make sense in the strictly regional context but nonsense in the 'national' context. It is entirely arguable that if one had a comprehensive macro study of the all-Ireland central place system upon which to base judgements, one might well balance the main Irish growth centres differently in relation to each other than do the present proposals. (The present proposals consist of an informal aggregation of the extant regional plans.) It might be said, in turn, that intra-regional balance would probably be viewed differently also.

It may seem rather academic to speculate like this, about any rebalancing of the system of growth centres, whether at national or regional level. When Buchanan & Partners publish their regional plans in 1969, all the land area of Ireland will be subject to policy proposals of one kind or another. In these circumstances, is any rebalancing at all likely? If it is not, then, clearly there is little point in continuing to argue the thesis of this chapter, which is that a macro study of the central place system is urgently needed.

Happily few regional plans are ever so rigid that modification is not possible and very few do not contain in their text, pleas that their findings and proposals be frequently reviewed. The debate is far from closed, and the geographer has opportunity to make a significant contribution. New knowledge will continue to be needed as regional and national strategies pass through the reviewing process—as they all must in due time.

The current changes in thinking about the whole nature of the planning process further emphasize the openness of the situation. Until now both statutory local and advisory regional plans have been rather static set pieces. They have consisted of a series of snapshots in time. The first snapshot is the survey section of the planning document, which portrays to-day's conditions and to-day's problems. The last snapshot portrays the planned-for conditions at the target date, perhaps 1990, when the proposals of the plan are expected to be visible on the ground. In between may be a series of intervening snapshots at staging dates, perhaps 1970 and 1980, to illustrate the build up of the planned city or region towards the 'winning post' at 1990.

The new kind of planning methodology will not deal in end-state plans but in broad policy guidelines about spatial strategy and scale of investment. The guide lines will be pointed towards certain future dates, to impart a sense of phasing to the plan's implementation. These dates are better thought of as mile posts rather than winning posts. The planning process will consist of steering the region (or nation) along the policy course yet at the same time being capable of adjusting the course in response to advancing knowledge. Indeed the time mile-posts and the policy goals may themselves be frequently re-set— something which may also necessitate course adjustments. This cybernetic view of the planning process relies heavily on the input of information, in the widest sense. The initial setting of goals and the plotting of courses require the input of formal knowledge. As the process moves through time there has to be continuous monitoring of how things are working out on the ground and a constant feedback of this information to the control system. This feedback, together with input of yet more formal knowledge from external research workers, is the basis for the course correction process. In this new kind of systemic planning there will be more scope than ever for the academic researcher to contribute. The new approach will have the flexibility to absorb new input at any time. The old end-state plans tend to be monolithic structures difficult to modify once the implementation stages have begun.

The door is continuously open for the incorporation of new ideas in the new style planning process. In these circumstances it is feasible to propose that studies of the all-Ireland central place system can begin on a crude level if necessary and gradually be refined. To be useful to Irish planners in selecting and then managing a system of growth centres, central place studies must meet two requirements. First the coverage must be all-Ireland. Secondly the study must be capable of speedy up-dating. Refinement of methodology is a requirement coming lower down the order of priorities. It is on this ordering of priorities that the mode of thought of the planner, on the one hand, differs markedly from that of the academic geographer on the other.

There is no ready made data bank for either planner or geographer to draw upon. Both are forced to choose between two strictly different alternatives: one option is to make a collection of rather primitive data in order to get out a rough but macro study of a large area quckly, leaving open the possibility for later refinement. The other option is to promote detailed field work and work out a careful and precise study of a territorially small area, leaving open the possibility for later territorial extension. The planner, who is driven always by pressure of time and the need for a synoptic view will opt for the macro but primitive. The geographer who is free from the importunities of the electorate, will opt for the micro but refined. Both kinds of work are essential in the long run. The planner must plan in the pursuit of social aims with whatever tools come to hand. He has no time for refinement in the early stages of his work. He looks to the academic for continuous development of methodology, and this can only be done on a micro scale for an area for which one can collect the detailed data.

As regards central place studies in Ireland, the same awful choice lies before anyone stepping into the field. The scholarly work of O'Farrell on the central place system of Tipperary is an outstanding example of the refinement option being developed.[8] His work is based on extremely detailed field work and sets out a method of assessing the degree centrality of a service centre of even the smallest order. The extension of the coverage of O'Farrell's work to the other 31 counties of Ireland, would provide an unshakeable foundation for all subsequent central place studies. To provide an all Ireland snapshot in time, at his degree of detail, would however involve an enormous number of research workers in the field at the same time (Sequential study county by county would not do). From the planner's point of view the prospect of up-dating such an all-Ireland study, even at infrequent intervals, would be staggering, in view of the field work involved. Yet up-dating capacity is essential to permit trend analysis. The very refinement of O'Farrell's work limits the practicability of extending it territorially and temporally, unless and until the data scene improves. If one had available a computerized register of all service establishments in Ireland, by size and grid referenced locations, then one could fully exploit the considerable methodological value of O'Farrell's work.

In the present conditions of data famine, the planner needs "something to be going on with" as regards a view of the central place system. This chapter is written from the planners' side of the fence. Its concluding section will explore the possibilities of the other option mentioned above, that is, the option for a speedy macro study capable of being easily up-dated and based on published data rather than on field work.

What follows is a preliminary rough and ready view of the Irish central place system. It does not seek to contradict or modify the refined work of any academic geographer and should not be compared with such work. This short study is like a child's crayon drawing waiting to grow up into mature art whenever the better data archives of the future allow the geographer's refined methodology to be combined with the planner's time scale and territorial scale for the better solution of planning problems.

The method of analysis used here is basically one of determining the centrality score or degree of significance of each central place in Ireland. The quantitative structure of the central place system as revealed by this method is then considered in comparison with the traditional rank/population size method. The centrality scores are examined in their actual spatial distribution and some interpretations of the urban geography of Ireland offered.

Determination of centrality score

The classic Christaller measure of centrality was a numerical expression of the degree to which a town served its surrounding region.[9] The measure used was the number of telephones which the town had in excess of what it might be expected to have in relation to the regional average of telephones per head. There are two stumbling blocks in the way of applying the Christaller measuring system. Firstly, the possession of telephones is no longer an indicator of only business communication and is therefore now a poor measure of central place functions. Secondly, in order to count the excess of telephones (or any other indicator) one has to define the region dependent on the town; this is not merely time consuming but raises the awkward problem of which of the innumerable possible regional boundaries one should use.

Smailes' use of qualitative indicators of central place significance, allowed him to discern a hierarchy of the towns in England and Wales.[10] His hierarchical levels were counted and labelled by means of a descriptive system of letters. The Smailes system is based on the view that the central place hierarchy is clearly stepped. It provides descriptive tests which allow one to classify towns into broad order groups, but it does not permit one to take the continuous function view of rank/size analysis and arrange the towns in a rank order list. To do the latter a numerical scoring system is needed like Christaller's centrality score, but one derived from modern indicators.

There is a multitude of functions which are readily recognized as central functions. Selection from this large range is bound to be subjective, but this need not invalidate a scoring system based upon a selection. Christaller himself selected one indicator (telephones) the use of which, at the time of study, he considered to be a valid reflection of central place significance. Any other selection should seek to be equally relevant.

The selection used in the present study is as follows:

> Banks
> Woolworth's shops   } representing commercial functions
> Newspapers
> Secondary schools
> Employment exchanges   } representing public service functions
> Principal post offices

Each of these is a fairly high order function admittedly. This will mean that the use of these indicators will fail to pick out the very small cross-roads central places. However, at an all-Ireland scale, and especially when one is interested in potential growth centres, such cross-roads settlements are of no significance whatever. The use of this level of functions also renders one relatively free of the problem of major inaccuracies which sometimes occur in directory sources. If a Woolworth's shop, or a bank, exists it will surely feature in the Telephone Directory. If a school is recognized by government, it will feature in government lists. Such sources are usually reliable. In this study the only non-government source relied on exclusively was the Newspaper Press Directory.

Lists were made of the occurrence of the selected functions in the towns of Ireland and the total number of establishments in each category determined. It was necessary to ignore the fact that there is a hierarchy of size within every single category, for example the branch of the Ulster Bank in Ballyconnell, co. Cavan, is a different size of establishment from the branch in Donegall Place in Belfast. It would take a very considerable time to determine size measurements and organize internal weighting systems within each category of establishment. It is acknowledged that in the absence of this a mere counting of establishments is somewhat crude. A certain necessary refinement was introduced to render weekly and daily newspapers into a comparable form. Daily papers were counted as being each equivalent to six weekly papers. This weighting was necessary to make this indicator work sensibly.

The totals for each category were then compared. The most commonly occurring function, was the bank. It was assigned the score of 1 point and all other scores were worked out to reflect the ratio between their respective totals and the bank total.

	Banks	Woolworths	Papers	Schools	Empl. Exch.	Principal Post Offices
Number	658	43	163	643	68	66
Points allocated	(1)	(15)	(4)	(1)	(10)	(10)

Each town in Ireland was then given a points score according to its tally of the selected central functions.

Example

Town	Banks	Woolworths	Papers	Schools	Empl. Exch.	Post Offices	
Athlone Co. Westmeath	3	0	1 weekly	5	1	1	
allocation of points	3	0	4	5	10	10	Total 32

Rank order listing of central places

Each central place (as here defined) now had a specific numerical description of its importance in relation to all the other central places. The rank order list was then drawn up on this points score basis. Table 3 lists the first fifteen names, for illustration.

The total number of central places identified by the points system was 342. Eleven of this number did not feature in the population census and were therefore omitted from any calculations involving comparisons of points scores and population leaving an effective total of 331 places. It is of interest to observe, even within the small scope of Table 3, that the points rank order is different from any ranking which might be done on the basis of population size. For example few people would expect to see the large sized Galway ranked twelfth or the small sized Armagh ranked sixth, in any list of Irish towns. Superficial examination of the complete list of points scores and population suggests that although the two ranking lists might differ in detail, as exemplified in Table 3, there is a broad underlying relationship between the two. A statistical comparison of the two sets of data was then made.

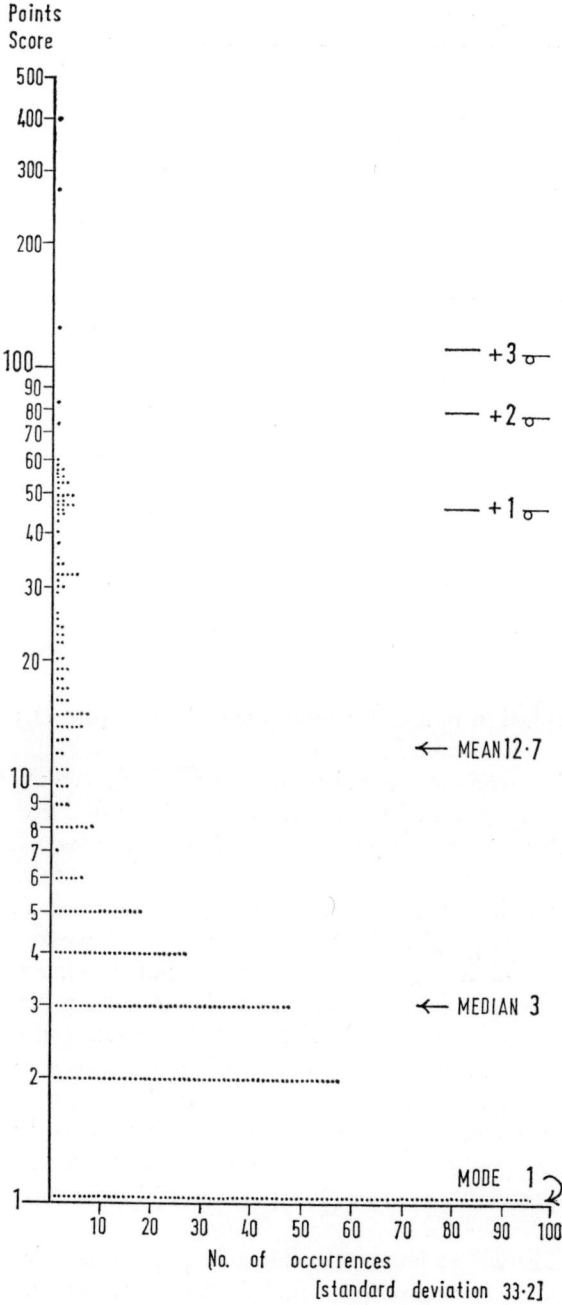

Fig. 18.2   Frequency distribution of points scores

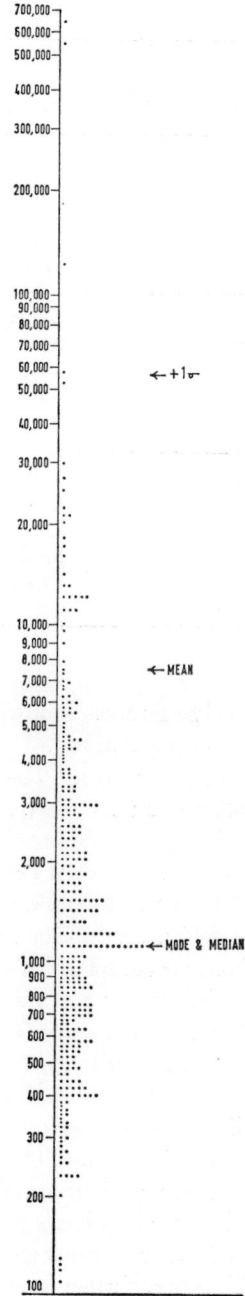

Fig. 18.3   Frequency distribution of populations of 'central places'

TABLE 3

Rank	Town	Points	1966 Population
1	Dublin	431	650,000*
2	Belfast	293	550,000*
3	Cork	126	122,146
4	Limerick	83	55,912
5	Londonderry	74	55,681
6	Armagh	60	11,000
7	Newry	59	12,214
8	Waterford	57	29,842
9	Ballymena	57	15,992
10	Dungannon	56	7,335
11	Enniskillen	55	7,154
12	Galway	55	24,597
13	Omagh	55	9,857
14	Strabane	54	8,813
15	Coleraine	53	13,578

*Estimates for built-up areas

The frequency distributions are graphed in figure 18.2 (points scores) and figure 18.3 (town populations).

The correlation co-efficient for points scores and populations is 0.92, which certainly indicates a relationship. However, this may give a greater impression of relationship than really exists because of the peculiarly skewed distribution of the population values which affects the Standard Deviation calculated therefrom. The presence of the two large centres of Belfast and Dublin tends to swamp the characteristics of the other town populations, all of which are smaller by more than 400,000 people. The Standard Deviation if worked from the complete list of towns is 48,600. Mean $+\sigma = 55,000$ which is a population exceeded by only 3 of the 331 towns. Thus 98.8 per cent of the values lie within σ of the mean. The correlation coefficient of 0.92 was produced from a calculation incorporating this Standard Deviation. A reworking of the calculations leaving out Belfast and Dublin gave a reduced correlation coefficient of 0.84. The relationship is still sufficiently evident to allow one to suggest that a points scoring system is at least as good a method of assessing the relative importance of towns as is straight population size. In so far as the points system can be up-dated, it is an obviously more practicable measure than population size measures which are hopelessly tied to census years.

In view of the discrepancies of detail between a points order list and a population order list, it may further be suggested that a points scoring system is probably more useful to the planner. A town's points score reflects not its size but its degree of importance as an urban service centre. It is the scale of services which attracts people to a town. Most people can very quickly assess the 'liveability" of a town through an assessment of the services. Few

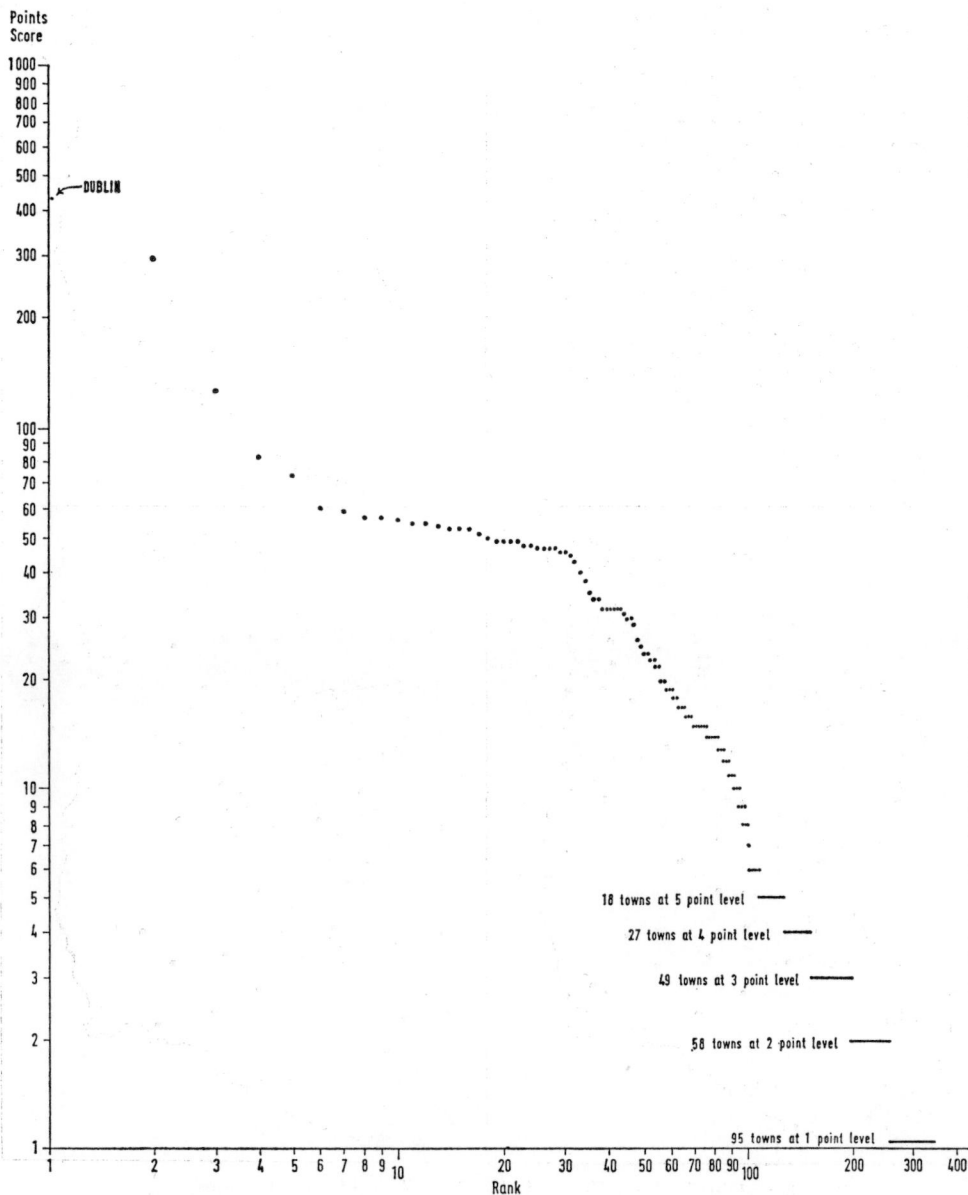

Points
Score

1000—
900—
800—
700—
600—
500—
400— ←—DUBLIN

300—

200—

100—
90—
80—
70—
60—
50—
40—
30—
20—
10—
9—
8—
7—
6—
5—   18 towns at 5 point level ——
4—   27 towns at 4 point level ——
3—   49 towns at 3 point level ———
2—   58 towns at 2 point level ——
1—   95 towns at 1 point level ——
   1   2   3   4 5 6 7 8 9 10   20   30   40 50 60 70 80 90 100   200   300 400
                              Rank

Fig. 18.4   Rank/Importance graph

X

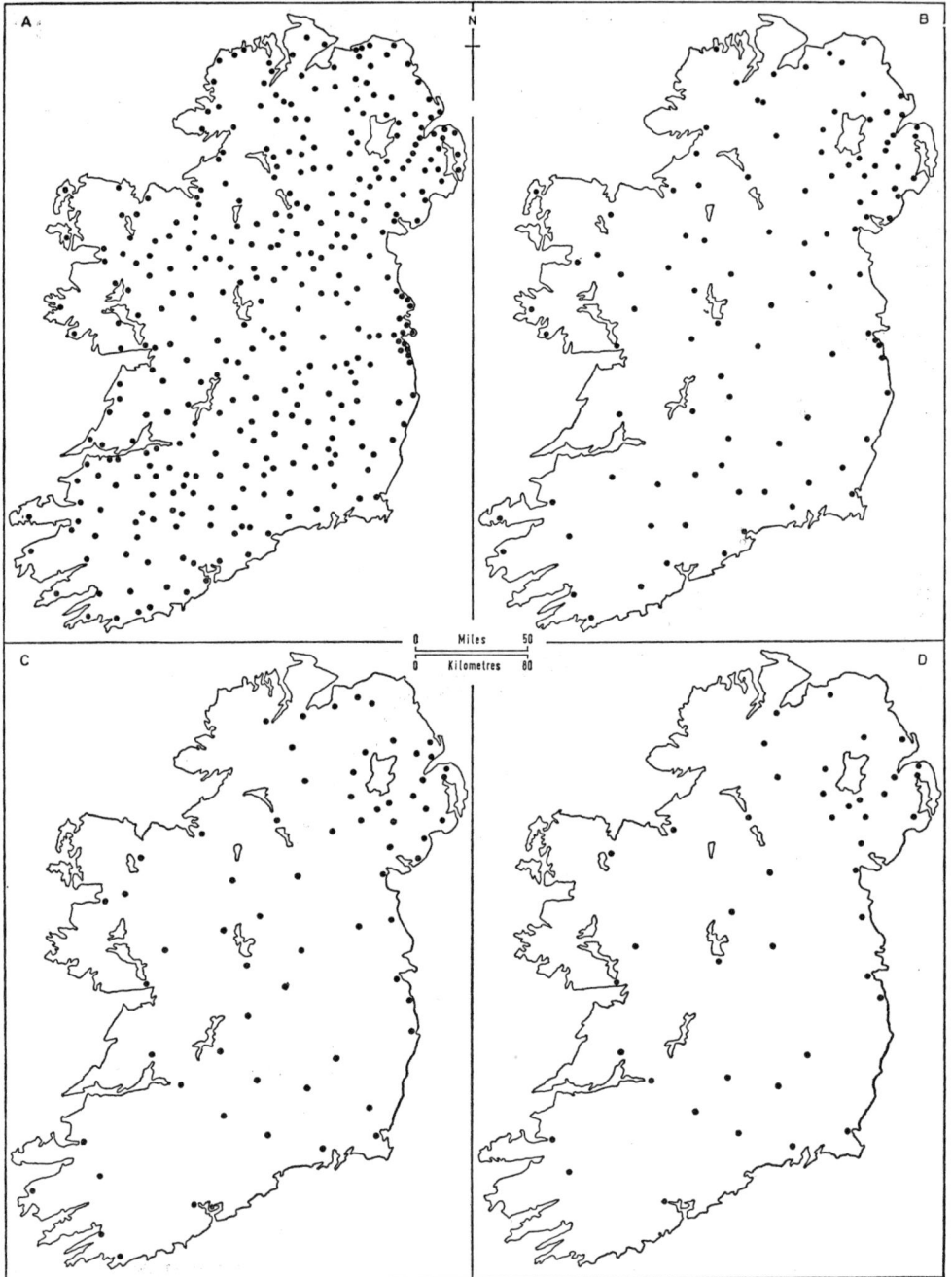

Fig. 18.5 Distribution of 'central places' of selected levels of importance.

A. Towns having a one point score and over
B. Towns with a five points score and over
C. Towns with a fifteen points score and over
D. Towns with a thirty points score and over

people are swayed in their choice of a place to live by sheer size alone. It is therefore highly relevant to a planner that he should know the scale and distribution of present urban facilities, as well as of urban populations, before he sets out to enhance the attractiveness of certain selected centres.

Points scoring systems are not new, but they have perhaps been rather neglected in central place studies made by planners. It is of interest to note that Wright's plan for Dublin assessed the significance of intra-regional central places on a points scoring system.

A summary of the rank/points score relationship of the Irish towns is given on the graph (Fig. 18.4). The long S-shaped curve, so frequently noted by scholars of rank/size distributions, is clearly evident. The graph has a slightly flattened top, Dublin being less dominant than the theoretically 'primate city' might have been expected to be.

Spatial distribution of centrality scores

The points scores can be thought of as spot heights from which one could construct a contoured map of the urban services surface in Ireland. It would be easy to make a three dimensional model of this surface, with pegs of appropriate heights set upon a base board with a map outline traced on it. Diagrams of this sort of surface can also be drawn by computer. For our purposes it is sufficient to imagine that, in the maps (Fig. 18.5), one is taking horizontal slices through the urban services terrain, which such a model might represent. The slices are taken at datum level (which is 1 point score), at 5 points level, at 15, 30, 45 and at 60 points levels. The choice of these main breaks was suggested by the rank/importance graph.

These 'slice' maps speak volumes about the configuration of the urban surface. At datum level (Fig. 18.5) there is an astonishing spatial regularity. This presumably reflects the relative lack of topographic constraints upon movement, as only the uninhabited mountainous areas in the cores of counties Donegal, Galway and Kerry make perceptible holes in the coverage. Progressing up the points scale, the pattern changes (Figs. 18.6). Gradually the coverage shrinks into the urban plateau of north-east Ulster, with only isolated peaks elsewhere in Ireland. The final map leaves only the big coastal cities showing.

This set of maps gives a rudimentary impression of the configuration of the urban services surface. The urban dominance of Ulster is demonstrated again, as it was in Table 3 which listed the fifteen top scoring Irish towns in rank order. Out of those fifteen towns ten are in Ulster. Reading the map sequence has, however, limitations. It does not pick out easily variations in the density of urban services coverage, except in areas of obvious concentration like Ulster. It might conceivably be more suitable to locate one's growth centre in an area where a number of medium order towns are found close together, rather than to crystallize new growth around a single free-standing city, even if it should be very big and important. It will be remembered that the Matthew proposals for the Belfast Region capitalized on the density of existing urban provision and infra-structure in the Lagan Valley.

A three-dimensional model would convey the visual impression of density by portraying

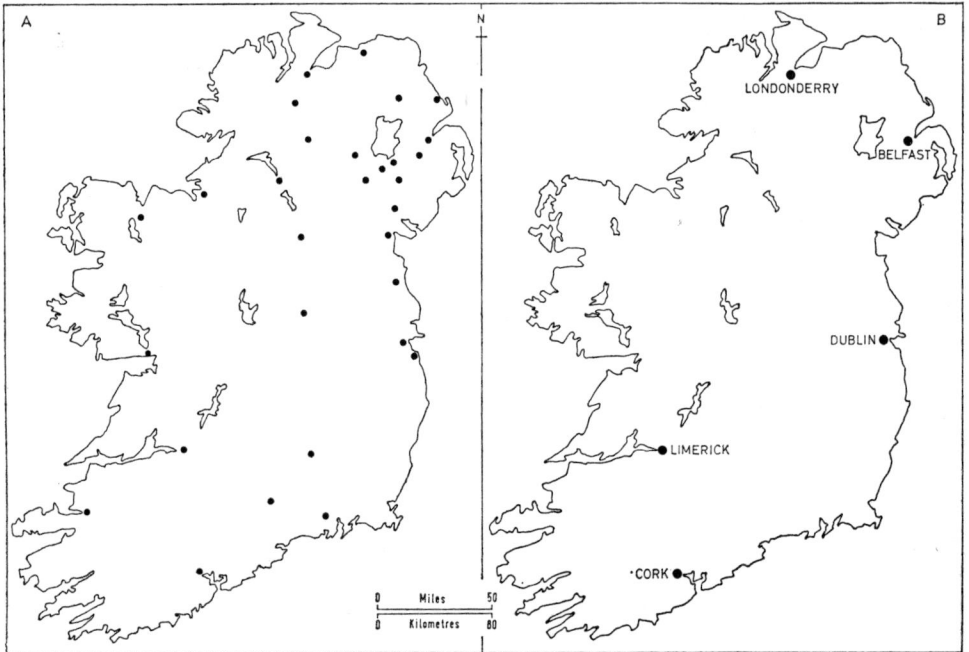

Fig. 18.6   Distribution of 'central places' of selected levels of importance.
E.   Towns with a forty-five points score and over
F.   Towns with a sixty points score and over

the heights and hollows in the urban services surface. Even that however has still not quantified this important characteristic. A certain quantification can be achieved using a version of a technique developed by Hägerstrand.[11] This expresses the phrase "density of coverage" in slightly different words. It seeks to produce a map of "accessibility to urban services". In the context of this central place study, the map (Fig. 18.7) was constructed as follows. Taking each town in turn one asks "what radius of circle is required to enclose 100 points?" The measurement is made and the required radius noted against the town. When all towns have been considered these radii values are used as spot heights and contours of accessibility are interpolated.

This last map is a two-dimensional representation of the surface configuration which one would appreciate visually on an urban terrain model. Thus it summarizes on one map the previous sequence of distribution maps. The map shows up some of the observations already made about the dominance of the north-east. It demonstrates again with great clarity that Belfast sits on an urban service plateau of supporting towns, while Dublin is an extraordinarily isolated giant. Among the new aspects of the central place coverage revealed is the presence of a substantial 'ridge' of medium density coverage in the prosperous farming area of North Munster.

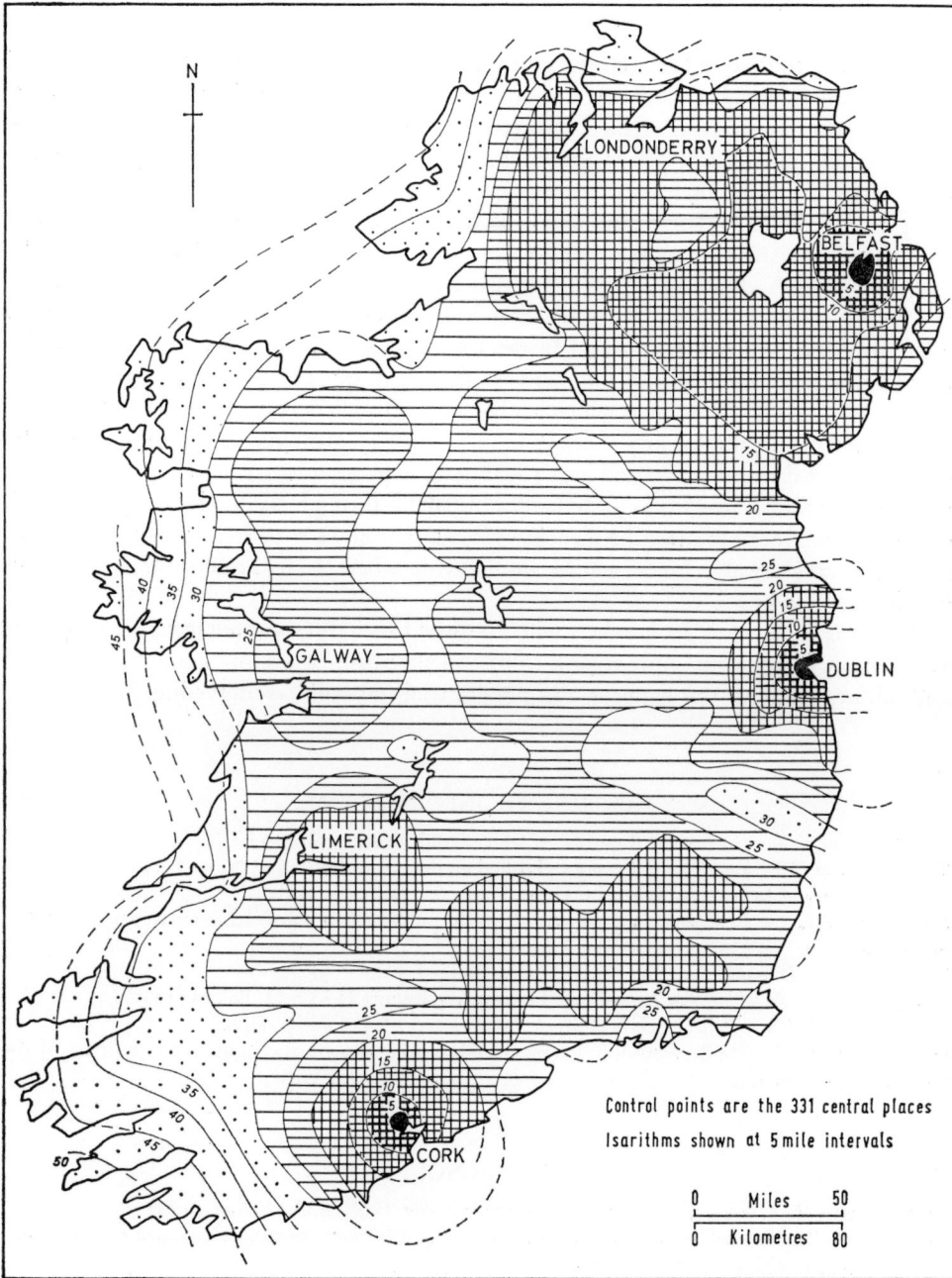

Control points are the 331 central places
Isarithms shown at 5 mile intervals

18.7 Radius of circle required to enclose one hundred points aggregate.

CONCLUSION

The theme of this paper has been the potential inter-relationship between geographer and planner. An attempt has been made to argue that the research methods of these two sets of people are the products of their respective circumstances and their research results are not so readily interchangeable as one might imagine. There is no logical reason why the geographer has to be useful to the planner. The geographer may see his obligations as being to contribute to the greater pool of knowledge. However, if he does seek a rapport with the planner then he must operate within the planner's time scale. This means that he must evolve methods of research which are capable of producing a first draft rapidly, which can be continuously refined thereafter, which gives results as up to date as possible *and* which is capable of being up-dated in the future. In short, the geographer working for planning purposes must bear in mind always the word 'speed'.

The brief central place study which has been described here is an exercise in testing what a geographer can produce in a short time on a topic of planning significance. It is to be hoped that the demonstration will prove of interest to geographers as well as to the planners who, for the foreseeable future in Ireland, must think through the implications of growth centre policy. Not only must the planner evaluate critically the all-Ireland balance of those growth centres already chosen, but he must decide when (or if) more centres are chosen, which they shall be.

Neither planners nor geographers will be satisfied with this short test exercise. However, by its very crudity it may provoke a riposte in the form of a more comprehensive and sophisticated study. If this happens, this present trial run will have served its purpose.

SOURCES OF INFORMATION

The Telephone Directories for the Republic of Ireland and Northern Ireland.
The Belfast and Northern Ireland Directory published annually by the Belfast News Letter.
Thoms Directory of Ireland, published by Hely, Thom of Dublin, periodically.
Post Offices in the United Kingdom and the Irish Republic published by the Postmaster General, London, periodically.
Newspaper Press Directory, London, Published annually.
Census of Population—Northern Ireland 1966 Preliminary Report H.M.S.O. Belfast (1967)
Census of Population of Ireland 1966 Volume I. Stationery Office, Dublin, (1967).
Lists of recognized secondary schools are produced periodically by the Education ministries of the two Irish governments.

REFERENCES

1 Sir Robert H. Matthew, *Belfast regional survey and plan,* (H.M.S.O., Belfast, 1964)
2 The term "Belfast urban area" refers to the continuously built-up area of city and surroundings, containing c. 500,000 people in 1961
3 *The second programme for economic expansion,* (S.O., Dublin, 1964)
4 *Planning for amenity and tourism,* An Foras Forbartha, (Dublin, 1966)

5 N. Lichfield, *The Limerick region,* (S.O., Dublin, 1967)

6 M. Wright, *The Dublin region,* (S.O., Dublin, 1967)

7 N. Lichfield, op. cit., 14

8 P. N. O'Farrell, A proposed methodological basis for the determination of the centrality and rank of central places, *Administration,* 16, No. 1 (1968), 17–32

9 W. Christaller, *Central Places in Southern Germany,* translated by C. W. Baskin, (New Jersey, 1966)

10 A. E. Smailes, The urban hierarchy in England and Wales, *Geography,* 29 (1944), 41–51

11 T. Hägerstrand, The geographer and the computer, *Trans. Inst. Brit. Geog.,* 42 (Dec. 1967), 1–19

Note: This chapter was written before the publication of *Regional Studies in Ireland* by Colin Buchanan and Partners, in association with Economic Consultants Ltd.

XIX

DECISION-MAKING AND THE FORMULATION OF REGIONAL DEVELOPMENT OBJECTIVES: THE CASE OF RURAL IRELAND

M. A. Poole

THE PROBLEM OF GOAL DEFINITION

The choice of planning objective, although only one stage—the initial one—in an entire sequence of operations culminating in the selection and implementation of a strategy for action, is clearly a critically important stage, and it is axiomatic that efficient planning requires a clear definition of goals, even if they are not necessarily made fully public. Yet it is equally self-evident that, especially with regard to regional planning, many governments have been markedly equivocal and ambiguous in the enunciation of their objectives.[1]

One of the reasons for such equivocation is, of course, the danger of possible detrimental political consequences which might follow from being too specific in the statement of objectives. However, the most fundamental reason for the frequently inadequate clarity of goal definition is the immense number of alternatives from which the choice of the specific objective to be implemented must be made. The problem of selecting a regional planning objective is thus a complex one, and the discussion of the problem in this chapter is based on the proposition that this complexity is best unravelled by viewing the selection-process, not as a single decision, but as a whole set of decisions. Thus the process of selecting a specific objective is not complete until all the individual decisions, representing the component elements of the set, have been made.

The decision-set may be divided into three distinct subsets, and, although they do not form an obvious sequence, the order in which they are discussed in the chapter is as follows:

The operationalisation of the welfare concept;

The width of spatial welfare disparities;

The choice of spatial units.

The entire decision-set is discussed with special reference to the Republic of Ireland, where, as in Northern Ireland, regional planning is now being attempted in a more coherent fashion than ever before in the country's history. The problems of rural areas have featured particularly strongly in the regional planning policies implemented by the government of the Republic of Ireland[2], and, therefore, the discussion of the choice of planning objectives is oriented specifically towards the design of policies for application to rural Ireland. The theme of the chapter is that, for such policies to be more rationally conceived in future, each of the individual decisions comprising an element of the decision-set will have to be made explicitly and systematically, for in no case can the optimum form of the decision be assumed or taken for granted without careful consideration being given to the problems involved.

CONFLICTING VIEWS ON THE PROBLEMS OF RURAL IRELAND

In addition to official government statements, there exists a voluminous literature, lay and clerical, academic and journalistic, on the social and economic problems of rural Ireland in general and of the western part of the country in particular. Even a cursory perusal of this literature soon reveals the wide range of alternative objectives which may be advocated, for the authors who have written on this subject differ profoundly in the particular policy objectives they emphasise, a divergence which follows principally from the wide divergence in their initial value-judgements. The critical importance of the goal-selection stage in the sequence of operations culminating in the choice of a planning strategy, is clearly revealed in this literature, because writers who differ in the objectives they advocate, almost invariably, in consequence, diverge in the policies they propose as solutions to the problems of rural Ireland, and they even disagree about the very identification of these problems.

This gulf of opinion may be illustrated by reference to the recently expressed views of two Irish writers, McDyer and McCarthy. McDyer argues that "the more people we can usefully and gainfully employ on the farms, the better for the nation as a whole", because "if our agricultural economy in the west continues to run down, and if our numbers diminish much further, they will soon not have the strength or the interest left to develop the spiritual and cultural resources of our people and offer to the world evidence of an individuality justifying our struggle for independence".[3]

McCarthy is rather less unequivocal, for he is careful not to commit himself explicitly to a specific policy objective or planning strategy; nevertheless, he does imply a preference for a positively planned policy of farm-acreage enlargement, and hence of a reduction in the number of farmers, the object of this policy being to raise the average farm income from its present low level. Thus he states that there are only two alternatives to such a policy. The first is the collapse of the social and economic structure of the west of Ireland, which would follow inevitably in the absence of strenuous government action, because the current unplanned process of depopulation is producing a "non-viable residual community"; while the second alternative is "social subsidization on an immense scale, which will both degrade the recipients, impose an appalling strain on the rest of the community and make economic progress in this country extremely difficult".[4]

Thus McCarthy is proposing a substantial reduction in the agricultural population, while McDyer, on the other hand, is advocating the maintenance of the current population level on the farms. To McCarthy, therefore, one of the critical problems is overpopulation, while McDyer, taking a diametrically opposite view, regards emigration as the basic problem. These differences of opinion on development strategy and problem identification follow largely from the difference in the relative emphasis given to each of the various social objectives which planning may have. In particular, planning "has both material and nonmaterial elements which together include all components making up a person's or society's state of well-being".[5] Of these two elements, McCarthy appears to give top priority to increasing people's material welfare, while McDyer places more emphasis on other aspects of welfare, especially the spiritual and cultural values of society.

THE OPERATIONALISATION OF THE WELFARE CONCEPT

Of the three decision-subsets specified, two are unique to regional planning: these are the width of spatial welfare disparities and the choice of spatial units. The other subset, however, relating to the operationalisation of the welfare concept, comprises decisions which have to be taken in national, as well as in regional, planning. Thus both national and sub-national planners are presumably guiding their policies towards the maximisation of the level of welfare of the people for whom their policies are designed, and, in consequence, all face the problem of having to operationalise this rather nebulous concept of the objective in terms of one or more variables amenable to observation, measurement and analysis.

The relevance to national planning of the problem of choosing operational variables to incorporate into the goal, together with the prominence given to national planning in the Irish Republic since the late 1950's, is responsible for the subset of decisions relating to the operationalisation of the welfare concept having been considered fairly extensively by Irish writers, both in official government publications and elsewhere.[6] Moreover, although the field of spatial planning is much less developed in Ireland than is national planning, the literature on the former field also includes much material on the problem of operationalising welfare. The extent of the conflict of opinion on this problem is well illustrated by the views of McDyer and McCarthy, quoted earlier, and Newman has vigorously attacked what he feels to be the excessive concentration of government policy on improving material welfare at the expense of his conception of non-material welfare.[7]

Because of all this attention which has been given to the subset of decisions relating to the operationalisation of the welfare concept, little space will be devoted to it in this chapter: instead, the discussion will concentrate on the other two subsets, the width of spatial welfare disparities and the choice of spatial units. In order to place the discussion of these last two subsets in its appropriate context, however, it is pertinent to quote the Irish government's statement of its three objectives for rural development in the Second Programme for Economic Expansion. These are, "first, to ensure the more intensive use of land within the limits set by market possibilities so that the maximum number of people can be retained in agriculture consistent with social and economic progress; second, to create viable family farm units in small farm areas with minimum disturbance of the population; and third, to ensure, as far as practicable, that those who leave agriculture have adequate employment opportunities in the other sectors of the economy".[8] This statement of objectives is repeated verbatim in the Third Programme, published in 1969.[9]

These objectives represent, in fact, strategies designed to achieve the fundamental objective of increasing national welfare, and it appears from this statement that each of the three variables, which, as Klaassen shows, are most commonly used as operational welfare indicators for regional planning purposes in Western Europe have been taken account of in designing the strategies: these variables are the unemployment rate, the net migration rate and the mean per capita income.[10] A strategy designed to maximise welfare, measured in terms of one of these variables, will rarely, however, succeed in maximising welfare measured in terms of any of the other variables.[11] This explains why each of the three strategies listed is hedged around with qualifications, but it cannot justify the excessive degree of imprecision present in the government statement: the decision on the operational-isation of the welfare concept not only should involve the choice of variables as welfare indicators, but it should also involve the assignment of relative priorities to each of these variables, a process which would succeed in removing much of the imprecision, allowing an explicit statement of a specific compromise between conflicting objectives.

THE WIDTH OF SPATIAL WELFARE DISPARITIES

Spatial disparities and the national welfare maximisation goal

These decisions on the operationalisation of the welfare concept form, however, only the first subset of decisions which must be made as part of the task of goal definition. The next problem is to decide whether the object of concern is simply to raise the average level of welfare in the sovereign state in question or whether the distribution of that welfare is to be regarded as important for its own sake. The notion of the desirability of a distribution of welfare in accordance with the principles of social justice is, of course, a familiar one, about which Marx, amongst others, has had something to say, but the concept of an equit-able distribution between regions, as opposed to a fair distribution among social classes, has achieved much less prominence until recently. Political realities, as well as social justice, may encourage a policy of reducing spatial welfare disparities, for unrest in poorer regions may pose a threat to national unity, as in parts of Latin America[12], or may at least lead to the election of opposition party candidates.

Whether the motive is social justice or political pragmatism, the reduction of spatial welfare disparities is a commonly expressed desire in Ireland, as elsewhere. The possible consequences of such a policy should, however, be at least understood and considered in the process of decision-making. As a prominent Irish economist has pointed out, "there are serious economic dangers in excessive regional or inter-sectional redistribution of wealth—economic dangers which are rarely stated explicitly enough and which can threaten the success of the whole process of raising the living standards of all our people".[13]

It was reasoning of this type which led Whitaker, in his report preceding the implemen-tation of the Irish Republic's First Programme for Economic Expansion, to point out that, if the objective was to maximise the growth in national income, then economic development should be concentrated in those parts of the country where there is most potential for growth.[14] Since, as in most other countries, such a policy would probably involve encouraging growth primarily in those regions which are already most highly developed and whose inhabitants enjoy the highest level of welfare in the country, the effect would be to widen spatial welfare disparities still further. Whitaker himself certainly assumed that most growth potential existed in the already prosperous areas, for he argued that development should be concentrated in the largest ports and urban centres, which, in practice, would mean those parts of the east and south which have the highest incomes and the lowest unemployment rates in the country and which suffer least from emigration.

On the other hand, a strategy directed towards the reduction, rather than the widening, of spatial disparities in material welfare may sometimes be necessary in order to achieve the maximisation of national welfare. Wilson has used three main arguments to justify this thesis.[15] Firstly, national economic output can be raised by directing development towards areas characterised by excessive underemployment of the actual or potential labour force. Secondly, although national output can be raised by reducing the unemployment rate anywhere, it will lead to inflation if this is done in all regions, including those with an already low rate, so development policy should discriminate in favour of regions with high rates of unemployment. Thirdly, excessive social costs may be incurred by further development in already congested regions.

Arguments of this type have been proposed in relation to Ireland: for example, Meagher has suggested that the problems of congestion in Dublin are sufficient to justify a limitation of further development there, though no quantitative evidence is provided.[16] Empirical evidence on this and other problems is essential in order to learn what spatial distribution would lead to the maximisation of over-all national welfare. Such information is necessary in order to allow a systematic decision to be made on the relative priority to be given to the mutually inconsistent objectives of maximising national welfare and removing spatial welfare disparities: the assignment of these relative priorities will help to determine the most desirable compromise between these two extreme objectives.

The reduction of spatial welfare disparities for its own sake.

The second of these two extreme objectives, the elimination of spatial disparities, is usually rejected as impracticable, but it is, nevertheless, exceedingly common in Ireland, as elsewhere, to view at least the reduction of regional welfare disparities as an objective of fundamental value for its own sake. Such a view, for example, inspired the operation both of the differential grants policy, dating from 1952, and of the pilot areas scheme for agricultural development, introduced in 1964; both of these policies were designed to give special assistance to the twelve less prosperous western and north-western counties of the Irish Republic.[17]

Moreover, the notion of regarding a reduction of regional welfare disparities as important for its own sake is fundamental to the views expressed by many writers on regional planning in Ireland. Thus Curtin has suggested that one of the major objectives of Irish planning is the achievement of "balanced regional development"[18], while Meagher has asserted that planning should be designed to avoid "seriously unbalanced population distribution, radical variations in levels of income and rates of growth at the regional level, with large areas declining despite the realization of national growth targets".[19]

Like many writers on planning, these authors invoke the physical analogy of balance to justify their case, though Fisher has discussed the ambiguities of this concept in some detail.[20] In the absence of explicit clarification, it will be assumed that the users of the concept regard it as identical to that of equality. However, the notion of equality, too, is, to quote Reiner, "a slippery concept"; as he stresses, "the general proposition that regions and their inhabitants should be treated equitably—widely voiced in development circles— most be rendered more specific". In particular, is the objective to remove spatial disparities in welfare and thus achieve equality of regional welfare distribution, or is the aim to achieve growth rates which are equal in all regions?[21] If the latter is the aim, it should, however, be remembered that, if two areas achieve equal percentage growth rates, the absolute welfare gap between the two will actually widen. Thus for example, the gross domestic product per head in the Republic of Ireland expressed at constant factor cost, rose by 32 per cent between 1958 and 1965 but by only 30 per cent in Northern Ireland; nevertheless, the gap widened in absolute terms, from £68 to £85.[22]

It may be questioned whether either a region's average level of welfare or its mean growth rate is the appropriate measure to build into a regional objective. It can be argued that an important objective should be to reduce the fluctuations in the level of welfare in a region[23]: such fluctuations are especially likely in regions with a narrowly based economy, such as that of co. Clare, with its heavy dependence on cattle: 49 per cent of the total income arising in the county is derived from cattle.[24] Moreover, it may be suggested that the nature of the distribution of a region's welfare amongst its inhabitants is critical[25]: the rates of unemployment and of migration are both indicators of welfare distribution, but they are very crude measures since they reduce the problem to a simple dichotomous variable.

However, the possibility of using more sophisticated distribution measures or of reducing welfare fluctuations, especially the former, is usually ignored in regional planning: it is normal to consider simply either a measure of central tendency, such as average income, or a percentage value, such as the unemployment rate or the net migration rate. Such a simplification may well be justifiable, provided that the planning objective does include an explicit statement on the width of the spatial disparities which will be tolerated: such vague, non-quantitative goals as the achievement of balanced regional development carry virtually zero information content and cannot provide a guideline for efficient and systematic planning.

THE CHOICE OF SPATIAL UNITS

The size of spatial units

The decision on the width of spatial welfare disparities to be aimed at in the programme for regional planning cannot, however, be divorced from decisions on the specific spatial and temporal context. Thus any statement on the width of spatial disparities to be tolerated or aimed at must be specific to a particular time-period. Clearly, long-term objectives can incorporate more ambitious goals, in terms, for example, of reducing regional disparities, than can short-term objectives; moreover, the relative priority given to the two objectives of increasing national welfare and reducing spatial disparities may well vary according to the time-span considered.

A much less frequently considered problem than the specification of the temporal context, however, is the choice of the set of regions whose welfare is being planned. The range of alternatives, from which this choice of region-set must be made, is very wide indeed, for there is an extremely broad continuum of aggregation-levels at which the spatial distribution of welfare could be considered: this continuum ranges from the micro-level of the individual household, the variation between which is necessarily spatial since each household occupies a unique location, to highly macro-levels, such as the difference between the average welfare levels of the west of Ireland and of the rest of the country.

From this continuum of possible aggregation-levels, a choice must be made of the size of each of the areas whose average level of welfare is to be regarded as relevant to the planning objective: for example, in the Irish Republic, is the relevant set of areas the nine planning regions, the twenty-six counties or the entire set of towns and parishes? Indeed, perhaps the policy objective should be formulated with reference to more than one aggregation-level. Not only might there thus be a hierarchy of spatial units, but the type of objective aimed at for one level might be fundamentally different from the type designated for another level: thus it might be intended to reduce disparities between large regions, but to accentuate the variation between subregions within such a large region by focusing development on a limited number of growth points.

Such a divergence of objective between different levels of spatial aggregation is made likely by the fact that, the smaller the region, the lower the probability that it contains anywhere with real development potential.[26] Moreover, the degree of spatial welfare variation may be expected to be greater at lower aggregation-levels, since the aggregation process itself filters out variation; therefore, if the intention is to reduce spatial disparities, it is likely to be harder to achieve this for a set of small regions.[27]

It is true that one of the assumptions underlying the Irish government's adoption in principle of a growth centre policy in 1965 was that the benefits will spill over into the surrounding larger region[28], but it is at least arguable that this overspill will be insufficient to induce a uniform level of welfare throughout the region surrounding the growth centre, unless the density of such centres is high and each surrounding region accordingly small.

Regardless of whether or not the planning objective is formulated with reference to a hierarchy of spatial aggregation-levels, the choice of region-set must be a conscious decision rather than an arbitrary one if the spatial welfare distribution aspect of regional planning is justifiable. After all, if the decision is arbitrary, this implies that it does not really matter what aggregation-level is selected, and this further implies that the objective of regional planning is not sufficiently important to justify a conscious decision.

Criticism must therefore be levelled at Meagher, who, writing about regional planning in Ireland, evades the problem of region-size by suggesting that it is impossible to be dogmatic and that, in any case, the ideal size will vary with the type of plan.[29] The second of these two points does not, of course, justify ignoring the problem of area-size: on the contrary, it suggests the need to select a hierarchy of region-sets. The first point, asserting the impossibility of being dogmatic, is true, but cannot justify ignoring the problem of deciding on a region-set: it simply means that this decision, like all the other decisions relating to the choice of planning objectives, depends on value-judgements.

The spatial units used to administer sub-national planning in the Irish Republic are the Local Authority areas (counties, county boroughs, municipal boroughs and urban districts), which were given responsibility for preparing development plans by the Local Government (Planning and Development) Act of 1963. In addition, plans have been prepared, at a higher level of spatial aggregation, for nine planning regions (Fig. 19.1), with the intention that the Minister for Local Government should use these as a basis for ensuring co-ordination between Local Authority plans.[30] However, it cannot be stressed too strongly that these sets of regions, which are used for organising such aspects of administration as the formulation and implementation of sub-national plans, should not automatically be used for the specification of such fundamental objectives as the reduction of spatial welfare disparities: the decision on the set or sets of areas in relation to which fundamental objectives are specified should be a completely different decision from that relating to the choice of the administrative regions used to implement the development strategy.

A further problem, which may be referred to very briefly, is that the choice of spatial units involves two decisions: these are the choice of size for the regions and the choice of specific boundaries. The latter is worth mentioning explicitly because of the possibility of a type of gerrymandering. As Leven rather cynically suggests, "an alternative way of eliminating a good bit of existing interregional differentials would be simply to redefine the boundaries of the regions we are comparing. If we would redefine Appalachia as a relatively narrow band extending a few hundred miles east and west instead of a few hundred miles north and south from West Virginia, it might turn out to be much less under-developed according to the resultant statistical comparisons".[31] Thus it needs to be borne in mind that three of the five Irish counties with the highest net emigration rates between 1961 and 1966 are the adjoining counties of Cavan, Leitrim and Longford[32], and that, if, even without a deliberate intention to gerrymander, these three were allocated to different regions, instead of being grouped together, then the apparent severity of spatial emigration disparities in Ireland would be significantly reduced.

The urban-rural dichotomy

The grouping of households into discrete, unfragmented regions, is however, not the only way to perform spatial aggregation. One alternative is to aggregate places on the basis of a classification into rural and urban areas, and, in formulating objectives for the planning of spatial welfare distribution, a decision must be made on whether or not to specify separate goals for rural and urban households. Above all, should an attempt be made to close the welfare gap between the rural areas and the towns?

None of the conventional methods of differentiating rural from urban areas, using such criteria as population density, settlement size and the degree of dependence on agriculture

Fig. 19.1   Counties and Planning Regions of the Republic of Ireland

employs a binary variable, however, so the concept of an urban–rural continuum is generally deemed preferable to that of a simple dichotomy. But even the validity of a continuum has been seriously questioned. The decline of the agricultural population in rural areas has reduced the relevance of this particular criterion, and, moreover, the increased mobility, both of people and of goods, has created economic and social links between rural and urban people, thus welding the two groups into a more integrated socio-economic system and reducing the cultural differences between urban and rural dwellers.[33] Nevertheless, Lupri, for example, has demonstrated that differences in fertility rates, family power structure and attitudes do exist between urban and rural dwellers in Europe, especially in the less economically advanced parts[34], and Newman has alluded to the continued survival of cultural differences between urban and rural areas in Ireland.[35]

Pahl has denied that the existence of these differences has any sociological relevance, however. In essence, Pahl appears to be suggesting that there may be a statistical relationship between the urban–rural variable and certain sociological variables, but that this relationship is not a directly causative one: therefore, neither the urban–rural dichotomy nor the alternative concept of a continuum is of much operational value in understanding the functioning of the social system. Pahl argues that, while the many suggested sociological criteria for distinguishing the urban from the rural may be useful for classifying people, they are useless for classifying whole communities because of the huge variation between different groups within what are physically urban or rural environments, especially in view of the existence of what he calls 'urban villages' and 'metropolitan villages' in, for example, England.[36] Little relevant research has been done in Ireland, but it is probable that some of Pahl's urban villages exist in the larger towns and that metropolitan villages have begun to develop around Dublin.

This debate on the urban–rural variable would appear to be highly relevant to the formulation of socio-economic planning objectives, for the extent to which urbanisation is to be encouraged or discouraged and the form which urbanisation is to take are critical problems, the decisions on which must be incorporated into those objectives. Thus Newman assumes both that there is a critical difference between rural culture and 'city-type' culture and that these cultural differences represent a causal relationship which will ensure that the preservation of the rural population will guarantee the preservation of a distinctive rural culture. He avoids the extreme "rural fundamentalist view that the only good life is the rural life", which, as Robock points out, "is widespread throughout the world"[37], by advocating that it is in the national interest for Ireland to contain major elements of both rural and urban culture, each of which has its own distinct advantages and disadvantages: appealing to the old physical analogy, Newman calls for a balance between rural and urban culture.[38]

It must therefore be decided what ratio of urban to rural dwellers is in the national interest, from the point of view of both the material and the non-material welfare of the country, in addition to having to decide whether to attempt to reduce the welfare disparity between rural and urban areas. Moreover, if a reference to the rural–urban variable is to be incorporated into the planning objective, then the problem of choosing a specific operational definition of the difference between the two types of environment must be tackled.

Y

CONCLUSION

Summary of the decision-set

It is clear that the design of a planning strategy for rural Ireland, like all regional planning policy formulation, is a complex problem involving many individual decisions, and it is useful at this point to summarise the most important of these decisions which have been discussed. Initially, it must be decided what operational variable or variables are to be incorporated into the fundamental objective of the plan, and, if more than one such variable is to be built in, the relative priority to be given to each variable must be decided upon. The regional planner must decide, too, whether priority is to be given to the achievement of a regional distribution of welfare such that average national welfare is maximised or to the achievement of some other pattern of spatial welfare distribution. If some other pattern is regarded as desirable, then this pattern must be specified, and this involves deciding how wide the spatial welfare disparities aimed at are to be for any given point in time, how large the relevant spatial units should be, where the boundaries of such units are to be, and whether or not rural and urban areas should be separated from each other in the specification of fundamental planning objectives.

It is essential that each of these decisions be made consciously, deliberately and systematically if socio-economic planning in rural Ireland is to avoid being inefficient. The concept of efficient planning implies both the choice of a strategy for action which is optimal for the achievement of a specific objective and also the choice of an objective which, as well as being realistic, is most closely linked to what is regarded as the relevant set of value-judgements. Thus is the decision-maker to base his choice of planning objective on what he feels the public actually wants, on what he feels the public should want or, as a compromise between these two, on what he feels the public might be persuaded to accept?

The political context

Perhaps the most potent force ensuring that what the public itself actually wants is taken into account when making planning decisions is that the decision-maker is a politician, dependent to a greater or lesser extent on public support, and thus responsive to public opinion. Thus the choice of a planning objective may be made either for the ideological reason that the implementation of this decision will represent a step towards a vision of the ideal society or for the personal reason that the decision-maker wishes to maintain and increase his own and his party's political power.

As an example of the ideological reason, a major guiding principle in Polish regional planning has been that "socialist society is an equalitarian one; therefore everybody, wherever he lives, should have the same opportunity for work, good living conditions and social advancement"[39], and, although the extent to which socialist principles should guide Irish regional planning may be debatable, this notion of social justice is certainly not unknown in Ireland. On the other hand, the same policy might be adopted, not for ideological reasons, but because an attempt to reduce regional welfare disparities may be deemed necessary to capture votes in regions with low levels of welfare.

Frequently, however, there is liable to be conflict between the policy which the professional regional planner and the politician might believe to be in the national interest and the strategy which the politician realises to be the best guarantee of political survival. In particular, the short-term goals, which are the goals most people are conscious of and which are therefore important for maintaining the politician in power, are liable to be in conflict with the long-term objectives which the planner believes to be most important for national welfare.[40] Again, the control of power may depend significantly on responding to certain sectional interests and pressure groups with more importance than their direct voting strength alone would indicate, and their views might not be in the national interest as perceived by, for example, the planner. Thus Brewis has criticised many local religious leaders in depressed areas of Canada for having been more often concerned about the reduction of their flock than about its low per capita incomes[41], and Leven has pointed out that, in an area of declining population, there is frequently more objection to depopulation from local traders with shrinking markets than from the people who actually migrate.[42]

Because of the strong possibility of conflict between the ideological and the personal reasons for choosing the planning objective, perhaps the most fundamental decision which needs to be made, is, in fact, on the assignment of relative priorities to these two types of reason: what specific compromise should the decision-maker select between the extremes of doing what he believes is best for the country and of doing what he feels is most likely to improve his political position? Only after this choice has been made can the decision-set, summarised previously, even begin to be considered, for, in rural Ireland, as elsewhere, the choice of planning objective cannot be realistically discussed out of its political context.

REFERENCES

1 Y. Oishi, Some theoretical problems of regional planning and regional analysis in Japan, *Papers Regional Science Ass.*, 16 (1966), 65–6
2 C. H. Murray, National and physical planning, *Administration*, 14 (1966), 293
3 J. McDyer, Employment on the land, *Christus Rex*, 19 (1965), 207–8
4 M. D. McCarthy, Some Irish population problems, *Studies*, 56 (1967), 245
5 M. D. Thomas, Resource and regional development—some comments, *Papers Regional Science Ass.*, 13 (1964), 201
6 Department of Finance, *Economic development* (Dublin, 1958): and, *Second programme for economic expansion*, Part II, (Dublin, 1964) T. K. Whitaker, Economic planning in Ireland, *Administration*, 14 (1966), 277–85
7 J. Newman, *New dimensions in regional planning: a case study of Ireland*, (Dublin, 1967), 112–13
8 Department of Finance, *Second programme*, (1964), op. cit., 102
9 Department of Finance, *Third programme: economic and social development 1969–72*, (Dublin, 1969), 168
10 L. H. Klaassen, *Area economic and social redevelopment: guidelines for programmes*, (Paris, 1965), 53–7
11 T. N. Brewis, Growth and the Canadian economy: the problem of regional disparities, in W. D Wood and R. S. Thoman eds., *Areas of economic stress in Canada*, (Kingston, Ontario, 1965), 111 C. L. Leven, Establishing goals for regional economic development, *J. Amer. Inst. Planners*, 30 (1964), 103
12 R. J. Meyer, Regional economics: a survey, *Amer. Ec. Rev.*, 53 (1963), 27

13 G. Fitzgerald, The economist and Catholic social doctrine, *Christus Rex,* 17 (1963), 272

14 Department of Finance, *Economic development* (1958), op. cit., 159–60

15 T. Wilson, Policies for regional development, *Univ. of Glasgow, Soc. and Economic Studies, Occ. papers,* No. 3 (Edinburgh, 1964), 3–11

16 G. A. Meagher, Planning and national development, *Administration,* 13 (1965), 250

17 D. A. Gillmor, Foreign participation in Irish manufacturing, *Irish Geography,* 5, No. 2 (1965), 97–8, and Department of Finance, *Second programme,* (1964), op. cit., 104–5

18 V. Curtin, Regional planning problems and possibilities in Ireland, in F. Rogerson and P. OhUiginn eds., *Planning in Ireland,* (Dublin, 1967), 50

19 G. A. Meagher, (1965), op. cit., 247

20 J. L. Fisher, Concepts in regional economic development, *Papers Regional Science Ass.,* 1 (1955), W11–W16

21 T. A. Reiner, Sub-national and national planning: decision criteria, *Papers Regional Science Ass.,* 14 (1965), 114

22 Central Statistics Office, *National income and expenditure 1965,* (Dublin, 1967) 15: An Roinn Slainte, *Tuarascail ar staidreamh beatha 1966,* (Dublin, 1968), 2: Govt. of N. Ireland, *Economic development in Northern Ireland,* (Belfast, 1964), 144: Govt. of N. Ireland: Economic Section, *Digest of Statistics,* 24 (1965), 4, and 30 (1968), 4, 98.

23 J. L. Fisher, (1955), op. cit., W8–W9

24 E. A. Attwood and R. C. Geary, *Irish county incomes in 1960,* The Economic Research Inst., Paper No. 16, (Dublin, 1963), 10, 12

25 T. A. Reiner, (1965), op. cit., 114

26 T. N. Brewis, (1965), op. cit., 105

27 T. A. Reiner, Organizing regional investment criteria, *Papers Regional Science Ass.,* 11 (1963), 68

28 Department of Finance, *Third Programme,* (1969), op. cit., 165

29 G. A. Meagher, (1965), op. cit., 253–4

30 Ibid., 248–9

31 C. L. Leven, A regionalist's view of public sector planning in a capitalist society, *Papers Regional Science Ass.,* 17 (1966), 11

32 Central Statistics Office, *Census of population of Ireland 1966,* (Dublin, 1967), 1, 5

33 G. P. Wibberley, Changes in the structure and functions of the rural community, *Sociologia Ruralis,* 1 (1961), 119–21

34 E. Lupri, The rural-urban variable reconsidered, *Sociologia Ruralis,* 7 (1967), 1–20

35 J. Newman, (1967), op. cit., 37–42

36 R. E. Pahl, The rural-urban continuum, *Sociologia Ruralis,* 6 (1966), 299–329

37 S. H. Robock, Strategies for regional economic development, *Papers Regional Science Ass.,* 17 (1966), 136

38 J. Newman, (1967), op. cit., 37–42

39 K. Dziewonski, Theoretical problems in the development of economic regions (with special emphasis on Poland), *Papers Regional Science Ass.,* 8 (1962), 45

40 S. H. Robock, (1966), op. cit., 131

41 T. N. Brewis, (1965), op. cit., 195

42 C. L. Leven, (1964), op. cit., 104

XX

IRISH PORTS: RECENT DEVELOPMENTS
N. C. Mitchel

The 1960's have seen both growth and diversification of trade passing through Irish ports. This welcome trend reflects the overall expansion of the economies both of the Republic and Northern Ireland. Such expansion has been influenced considerably by government economic and social policies, and by new shipping and cargo handling methods which have made this decade a time of revolutionary change in the traditionally conservative maritime realm. This essay assesses the impact of these developments on the 72 ports active in trade in present-day Ireland, just over two thirds of which are in the Republic, and on fishing and recreational ports which do not submit trade returns. Because the impact of change varies according to port size, a general classification of ports is deemed necessary.

Port size

It is well known that all methods of assessing port status have severe limitations.[1] In a recent study of New Zealand ports, Rimmer made a useful contribution towards solving the problem by establishing statistically the superiority of one criterion, namely cargo tonnage.[2] When applied to Irish ports, cargo tonnage shows a similar high correlation (about 0.90) with net registered tonnage—which is a measure of a ship's carrying capacity—and the number of ships visiting port per unit time. But the increasing amounts of bulky raw materials which pass through a single berth or jetty often make it misleading to use cargo tonnage as sole guide to port status. Unfortunately, none of the other accepted criteria for assessing port status offer satisfactory alternatives. Trade value figures cannot be used as up-to-date statistics for the ports of the Republic are not available after 1959. The new shipping and cargo handling techniques have made statistics of berthing accommodation virtually useless because a single unit load berth may have a through-put equal to six or more conventional berths, thus making large lengths of quay a poor measure of a port's importance. Morgan[3] maintains that for determining the relative importance of a port the net registered tonnage of shipping is a better guide than weight, or value of cargo, but it, too, has assumed new drawbacks in recent years. Ship capacity, for example, tends to be under-estimated because it is now common to carry unit loads, usually containers, as deck cargo, a development not provided for by this measurement. However, net tonnage remains a useful check on ports handling large amounts of bulky raw materials. In this respect an additional check is provided by the annual reports of the Docks and Harbour Authorities' Association which give details of members income earned from dues on vessels entering port. This information can help to decide rankings made suspect by reliance on cargo tonnage alone. Dublin, for example, the leading port in the Republic, earns on average four times as much revenue from dues based on ship tonnages than Cork, although its cargo tonnage was less in 1967 and only fractionally ahead of Cork's in 1968. Over 80 per cent of Cork's trade is made up of bulky raw materials, mostly oil and oil products.

On the basis of ranking by cargo tonnage, and using net tonnage, and the Association's annual reports as checks against over-weighting by bulky raw materials, the ports of Ireland may be conveniently classified into three groups. The first group consists of five large ports, Belfast, Dublin, Cork, Larne and Londonderry, all handling over one million tons of cargo and net tonnage of shipping annually. Belfast, Dublin and Cork, the three largest urban centres in Ireland, dominate this group. Belfast is the largest and the busiest port in Ireland and one of the major ports of the United Kingdom. In 1968 it handled 6.3 million tons of goods (metric equivalent, 1 ton = 1.016 tonnes), almost two-thirds of Northern Ireland's total trade.[4] Dublin and Cork each handled just over 5 million tons. The port of Cork, which includes not only the estuarine upper harbour with its city quays but the magnificent, deep-water lower harbour where Whitegate, Cobh, Haulbowline Island and Crosshaven all trade directly with the outer world, has experienced extremely rapid growth in recent years. Between 1957 and 1967 its trade increased by 4.7 million tons, largely the result of the establishment of Ireland's first oil refinery at Whitegate in the lower harbour in 1959. Larne and Londonderry have much smaller cargo tonnages than the other three, but in terms of value Larne's trade was almost two-thirds of Belfast's in 1968. Larne is also an example of recent rapid growth. In 1947 its trade, a mere 147,000 tons of goods, was that of a small port; in 1968 1.5 million tons passed through the port. The early use of new shipping and cargo handling techniques explains this success. Londonderry's trade was 1.3 million tons in 1968, much of it in the form of bulk raw materials for the industrial complex at Maydown and Coolkeeragh. The second group of ports may be called medium-sized. They range from Limerick with 678,000 tons of cargo in 1968 to Galway with 268,000 tons. Other ports within this group are Waterford (638,000), Drogheda (381,000), New Ross (373,000), and Newry (306,000). All these ports have over 150,000 net tons of shipping arrivals per annum. The third group is composed of 61 small ports of which 17 are in Northern Ireland. In terms of 1968 cargo tonnages the most important are Greenore (about 200,000), Dundalk (188,000) and Arklow (172,000) in the Republic, and Warrenpoint (224,000) and Carrickfergus (209,000) in Northern Ireland. But few small ports handle such substantial tonnages. 80 per cent of them handle less than 20,000 tons of cargo annually and 30 per cent less than 5,000 tons. Their trade is often intermittent with only a few visits each year from small coasters. Co. Donegal's 13 small ports, for example, together account for only 100,000 tons of cargo each year. All small ports had less than 150,000 net tons of shipping arrivals in 1968.

The size of present-day Irish ports bears a close relationship to location. Most large and medium-sized ports are found on the east and south coasts where they serve the main

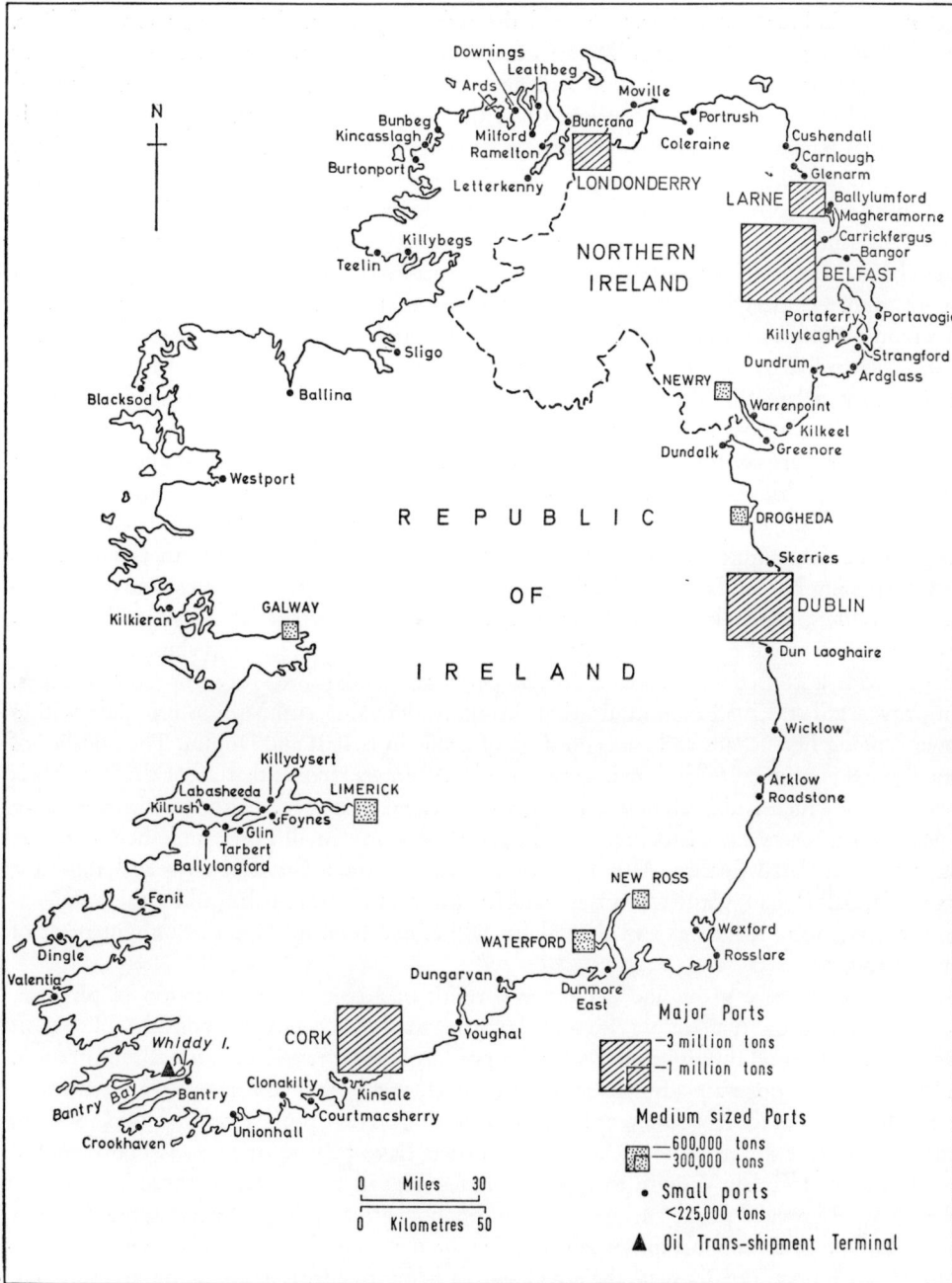

Fig. 20.1 Irish ports: a classification based upon cargo tonnage

urban and industrial concentrations and the richest agricultural parts of the island (Fig. 20.1). The east coast ports, and Waterford, are benefiting most from recent developments because of this favourable location and nearness to Great Britain, the main market and supplier of raw materials and tourists. Over the course of the last century their economic advantages have come to outweigh certain physical disadvantages of site of which silting was the most difficult to overcome. Dublin, for example, long had the reputation of being the most dangerous port to enter in the British Isles, a reputation lost only in the 1820's when measures were taken to confine the tidal stream and use its scouring effect to keep the channel open. In response to economic incentives, Parliamentary legislation for port works and technical innovations, such as the steam dredger, combined in the 1840's to overcome Belfast's problems of difficult entry through extensive areas of estuarine mud flats, known locally as 'slobland'. Practically all the modern port is built on this slobland and further reclamation for much needed port expansion is under way. The slobland, once a disadvantage, is now an important asset.

Small ports are common on all coasts. They prevail on the exposed west and north-west coasts which, although offering some excellent natural anchorages, lack the economic advantages of the east. Such ports were once more numerous than to-day. Their hey-day came in the late eighteenth and early nineteenth centuries when trade with Great Britain was increasing but land communications were still slow and tedious. The export of agricultural products, minerals and stone was then widespread. By the late nineteenth century many of these small ports were in decline. Steam had replaced sail, and ships had become larger with a consequent demand for deeper water and more space for port facilities. Improved rail and road communications brought increasing competition for trade within over-lapping hinterlands and concentration of traffic in Belfast and Dublin. The number of small ports continued to decline into the 1950's. Andrews records that 20 of the Republic's small ports which had been active in 1938 had ceased to trade by 1954.[5] However, since 1954 the prospects have become more hopeful for many small ports, and their numbers have not decreased further. Although some ceased to trade between 1954 and 1968, for example, Balbriggan, Castletown Bere and Baltimore, they were balanced by the rejuvenation of Greenore, Killybegs and Clonakilty which had been inactive throughout most of the 1950's.

Ports of any size grow and decline as a result of a complex inter-action of physical, historical and economic factors. Present-day growth also depends to a considerable extent on the initiative and foresight shown by the port authorities responsible for administration. The majority of ports are administered either by elected boards of harbour commissioners, usual in the case of the large ones, or by local authorities. Three ports, Howth, Dun Laoghaire and Dunmore East, are state-owned, while others have private owners. While it would be dangerous to relate growth to types of ownership, in general terms there is no doubt that privately owned ports, Larne and Greenore in particular, showed most appreciation at an early date of the opportunities afforded by the new shipping and cargo handling techniques. Such ports usually have the advantage of being free from trade union and shipping company pressures which enables them to adapt quickly to new developments. On the other hand, Dun Laoghaire, one of the state-owned ports in the Republic, has recently benefited from this status by having a new passenger and car terminal for tourist promotion built entirely at government expense. Such developments at other ports would depend to a substantial extent on a port authority's own capital resources. The opportunities for growth, which may or may not be taken by port authorities, stem largely from two main sources, namely the expansion of national economies and technological innovation. These recent developments merit analysis for the trends now apparent are likely to be intensified in the 1970's.

IMPACT OF ECONOMIC EXPANSION

In recent years both Northern Ireland and the Republic have attracted a wide range of new industries from overseas. Their governments have also encouraged the intensification of agriculture, sea fisheries and tourist development, while legislation in the Republic has helped the exploitation of its mineral resources. These developments have affected port activity but their impact on individual ports has varied, much depending on the size of port concerned. The development and diversification of port industries, for example, has affected mainly the large ports.

Port industry

While there has been a trend towards industrial diversification in recent years, new industries, for example, Du Pont's synthetic rubber and fibre plants at Londonderry, and the oil refineries at Cork and Belfast, perpetuate the more traditional port industries' demand for level land and access to deep water. Such sites often involve reclamation of land, an expensive undertaking usually the preserve of large ports. To dyke, reclaim and service an acre of estuarine mud may cost as much as £10,000. Rents for such scarce new land are high but the advantages of such locations are so obvious that there is keen competition for them from an ever-widening range of industry. Both Belfast and Dublin, as a matter of principle, allocate reclaimed land to industries which cannot locate economically elsewhere.

By preparing these new sites port authorities help national policies of industrial attraction. In return they receive some government help but on the whole the initiative for improvements rests with them. In the Republic the 25 ports scheduled under the Harbour Act of 1946 are eligible to receive government grants if improvements will help to attract new industries.[6] The government allocated £572,000 to them between 1964 and 1970, hardly an excessive amount.[7] Ports in Northern Ireland, in common with those in Great Britain, receive grants of up to 20 per cent of the total cost of approved developments. Both Irish governments make grants direct to port industries thereby stimulating port activity. Although the actual figures are not published government grants and loans to ports and industries in Northern Ireland are much more generous than those given in the Republic.

Grants and loans are also given to established industries for modernisation. Harland and Wolff's shipyard, for example, received substantial help in the form of a loan authorised by the U.K. government's Shipbuilding Industry Board for its new building dock. The Belfast Harbour Commissioners cooperated by giving the site for the dock, the largest in the world, when opened in 1969. They will now have to re-align the Musgrave channel so that at some future date a million ton super-tanker could be taken out to sea from the dock. The cost of this improvement will be charged to the shipyard or otherwise all port users would have to pay higher port dues. When improvements affect a number of port users, however, the port authorities are more likely to finance them. The Belfast Harbour Commissioners, for example, although receiving some government aid, were largely responsible for financing the port's new dry dock (Plate XXII) which can take ships of up to 200,000 tons. Only a large, relatively wealthy port authority could afford such heavy, initial capital expenditure. Most small and medium-sized ports lack the space, the capital and the services to attract such new facilities and industries. Exceptions include Galway and Waterford, for example, where industrial estates have been established recently as part of the government's growth centre policy.

Both governments have encouraged the use of greatly increased amounts of agricultural fertilisers in recent years. While fertiliser plants in large ports have stepped up their production some of the increase has benefited smaller ports such as Arklow and New Ross. Arklow was in decline in the early 1960's; in 1963 its imports were a mere 7,000 tons, but these had increased to 150,000 by 1967. This was the result of the establishment of the state-sponsored Nítrigin Éireann Teoranta's fertiliser plant near the port in 1964. A second plant was opened in 1968, and the growth of the port's trade may be expected to continue. A similar development of fertiliser production by a private company rejuvenated New Ross in the 1950's. It is the import of fertiliser raw materials such as potash and phosphate that has brought these substantial increases in cargo tonnages. Exports of fertilisers have virtually ceased since C.I.E., the state-sponsored transport company, introduced a special flat rate for fertiliser delivery by rail and road anywhere in the Republic.

Export of ore concentrates and road stone

Some of the smaller ports are benefiting considerably from increasing exports of ore concentrates and road stone. In 1965 Galway's exports barely reached 5,000 tons a year and its imports, chiefly coal and fertilisers, amounted to 56,000 tons. In an effort to regain trade, major port improvements were undertaken and their completion coincided with the opening in 1966 of the nearby lead-zinc mines at Tynagh, one of the largest developments of its kind in Western Europe, and by 1968 exports had risen to 200,000 tons. Foynes on the Shannon also exports lead-zinc concentrates which come by rail from Silvermines in co. Tipperary. The export of road stone to England and the continent, much of it for motorway construction, has literally put an east coast port on the map in recent years. Known locally as the Roadstone jetty, it is less than a mile south of Arklow but has its own port authority. It started operations in 1963 to export granite from the company's adjacent quarry and an oil distribution depot was established later. The jetty now handles a larger cargo tonnage and more shipping than Arklow.

Rationalisation of the fishing industry

The fishing industry, so long characterized by successive periods of prosperity and decline, is now in a buoyant mood. The extension seawards of national limits has reduced the former fierce competition from foreign trawlers, especially in the Irish Sea. Better marketing organisation is now encouraging the growth of local demand; previously fresh fish rarely reached the local markets. Fishermen's co-operatives allow western ports in particular to sell their fish more effectively. Ancillary industries such as the smoking, drying and freezing of fish, and the production of fish meal, have been encouraged and government loans and grants for bigger and better equipped boats are at a record level in both the Republic and Northern Ireland.

Until 1960 the catch was dominated by herring and whiting. Although these remain important, especially in the Republic, increased landings of hake, plaice, haddock, and, above all, of shellfish, have brought welcome diversification to the industry. The demand for *nephrops norvegicus,* the Norway lobster, or, to use its local name, the Dublin Bay prawn, grew rapidly after the merits of scampi were publicised on television in 1956. *Nephrops* is now the most valuable single species landed at ports in Northern Ireland. Worth £221,000 in 1967, its value far exceeded that of whiting (£89,000) and herring (£30,000).[8] One half of Northern Ireland's total catch and almost one-third of the Republic's are now accounted for by shellfish. The Republic anticipates a five-fold increase in the value of its shellfish landings within the next ten years. Lobsters, important commercially all along the rocky west coast since the early nineteenth century, crayfish, mussels, escallops, periwinkles and in recent years, crabs, are in popular demand, especially for continental use.

The expansion of fishing fleets and increased landings of fish have created demands for better port facilities, and in 1964 the government of the Republic accepted the recommendation of Swedish consultants that five ports should be selected for special development.[9] In order of importance these ports are Killybegs, Dunmore East, Howth, Galway, and Castletown Bere. They serve particular parts of the coast and specialise in different kinds of fish. Howth is a demersal port and Dunmore East a pelagic port, while the three west coast ports operate mixed fisheries. Major reconstruction of port facilities should be completed by 1970. Quays are being enlarged to lessen congestion and sites prepared for ancillary industries. In Northern Ireland there is the same trend for concentration of facilities at certain ports. The government has financed major harbour improvements at the two large fishing ports, Kilkeel and Portavogie. These ports, together with Ardglass, account for 95 per cent of landings.

In the Republic the development of the major ports does not necessarily mean that the smaller fishing ports, of which 24 have landings valued in excess of £10,000 per year (Fig. 20.2), will cease to operate. Shellfish can be caught just as efficiently from small boats as from large ones and thus extensive port facilities are not required. Also, the government has taken the advice of American consultants, who reported in 1964 that with relatively minor expenditure on small fishing ports the returns in some cases could be greater than from major development works, and that small ports should not be discouraged because of their size.[10] Social aims as well as economic ones are involved in this recommendation. Kilronan pier in Inishmore, the largest of the Aran Islands, was improved recently with these aims in mind. As a result, local fishermen can now berth their trawlers at the pier and

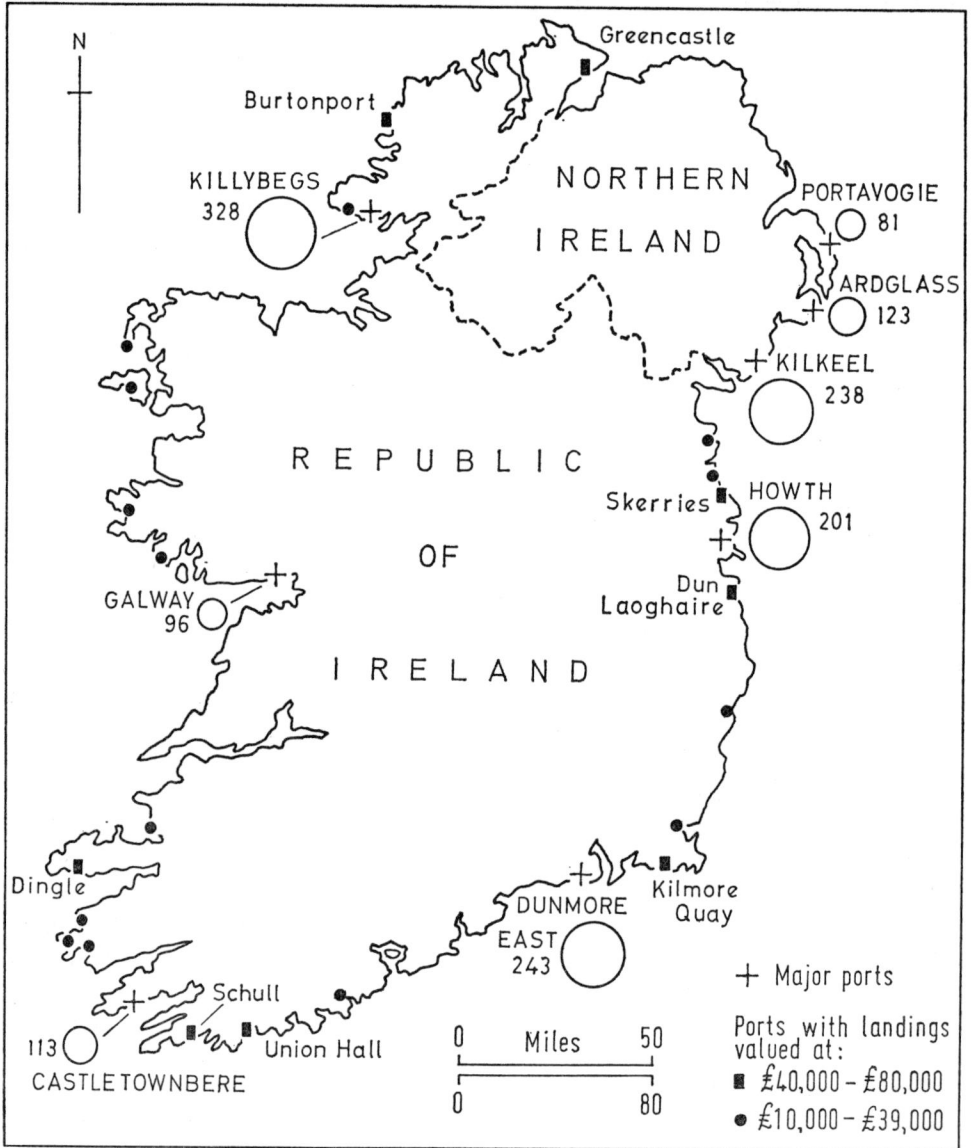

Fig. 20.2 Fishing ports: value of landings at major ports shown by proportional circles (figures indicating £'000's)

live at home after landing their catch at Galway. By making employment in fishing more attractive, emigration from the islands may be reduced.

Demands for recreation.

In recent years deep-sea fishing has become an important tourist attraction especially on the south coast where drowned estuaries near major fishing grounds provide shelter and attractive sites, such as Schull, Baltimore, Glandore, Courtmacsherry, Cobh, Kinsale and Youghal. Kinsale and Youghal, two of the oldest ports in Ireland, were both to the forefront of medieval trade and urban life but fell into decline with the change from sail to steam and the growing competition from Cork in the nineteenth century. Today Kinsale is the main yachting and deep-sea angling centre of the entire coast, its new hotels catering for an affluent clientele. Despite facilities for oil storage and new berthing accommodation, its future prosperity appears to be linked increasingly with recreation. Youghal's future looked bleak in the 1950's, but like Kinsale it is now a recreational port although on a more modest scale. Dun Laoghaire also adds recreation to its other functions, while annual fishing festivals are popular at west coast ports such as Westport and Killybegs.

IMPACT OF TECHNOLOGICAL INNOVATIONS

In the 1960's such trends as the introduction of unit loading and bulk transport in extremely large ships began to make an important impact on Irish port activity. Somewhat belatedly passenger traffic, too, changed its character with the introduction of car ferries on almost all the major Irish Sea routes.

Car ferries

Eight new car ferries have come into operation since 1965 as a result of the expansion of the tourist trade and the consequent demand for improved shipping services. These ships required new facilities including terminal buildings more in keeping with the aim of creating a good tourist image. Newly reclaimed land was made available by port authorities for Dublin's terminal, opened in 1968, and Cork's in 1969.

In 1968 passenger arrivals at Irish ports were still in excess of arrivals by air despite the dramatic increase in air travel during the preceding twenty years. Ports handled 1.3 million arrivals in that year, of which Northern Ireland's ports received just under half. Defining a tourist as a person with no ties of relationship or business in the country visited, sample surveys taken in 1967 show that 36 per cent of Northern Ireland's passenger traffic and 52 per cent of the Republic's was in this category.[11] In addition, 37 per cent of arrivals at Northern Ireland's ports and 35 per cent of the Republic's were described as "visiting friends and relatives"; 85 per cent of all the tourists came from Great Britain and one third of them (328,000 people) travelled with cars.[12] Car carryings into Northern Ireland have increased from 16,915 in 1960 to just over 70,000 in 1968, and in the Republic from 10,669 to 92,000 in the same period.[13] Car carryings to both parts of Ireland have doubled since 1964 when only one car ferry was in service.

The ferry ports which serve this growing passenger traffic are six in number (Fig. 20.3). In order of importance they are: Belfast, with services to Liverpool, Heysham,

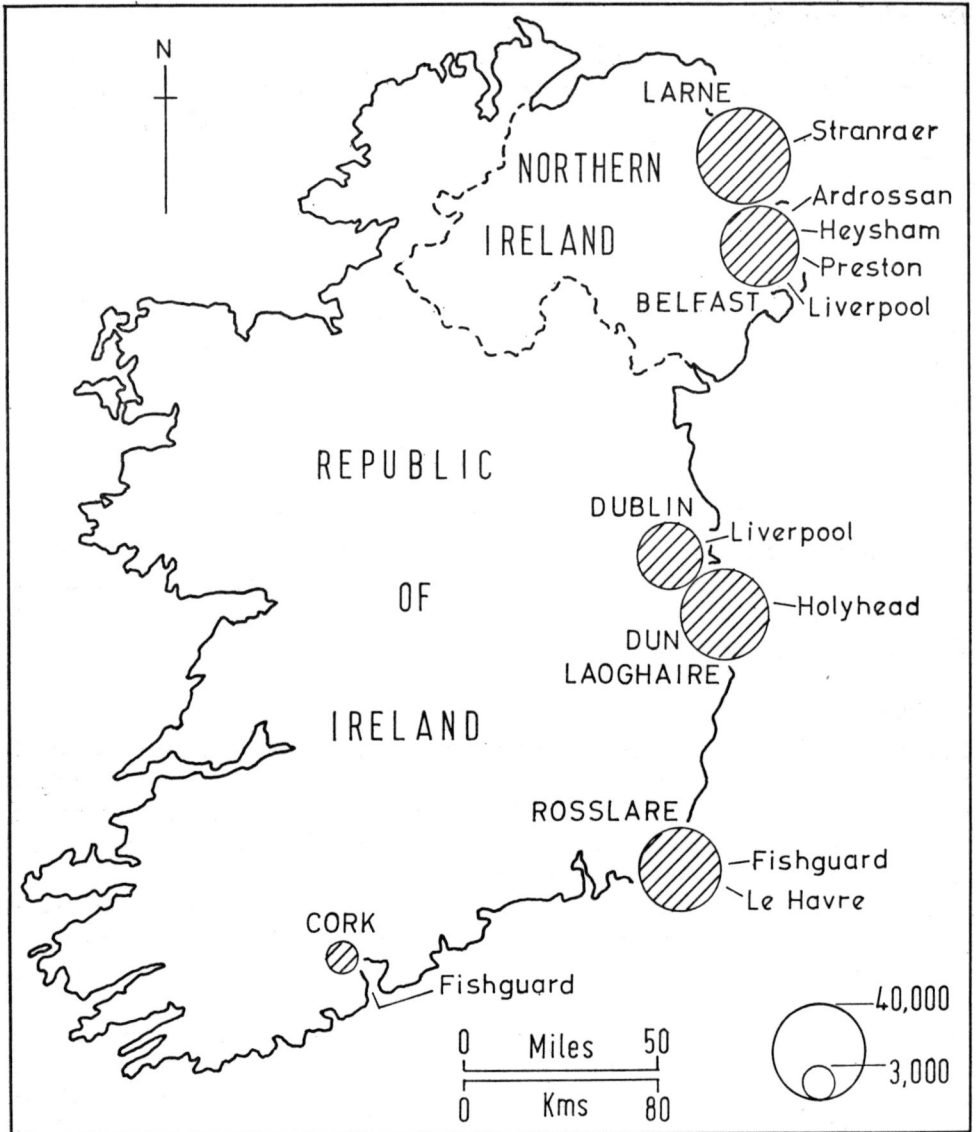

Fig. 20.3   Ferry ports: number of car arrivals in 1968

Ardrossan and Preston; Larne to Stranraer; Dun Laoghaire to Holyhead; Rosslare to Fishguard and Le Havre in France; Dublin to Liverpool and Cork to Swansea, a service which replaced the one to Fishguard in 1969. In 1969 the Belfast–Heysham route was the only one not served by a car ferry but one is scheduled for 1970. The Larne-Stranraer route carries more passengers and cars than any other single route. It is the shortest sea crossing and was the first to have a car ferry. Its share of Northern Ireland's passenger traffic increased from 17.6 per cent in 1960 to 37.6 per cent in 1967, while its share of total car arrivals now averages 60 per cent, about 42,000 cars per annum. All the Belfast routes have lost traffic since 1960. The Belfast–Heysham service had almost double Larne's share of passengers in 1960 but now averages nine per cent less and the Belfast–Glasgow service was discontinued in 1968. However, the new car ferries introduced to Liverpool in 1967 and to Ardrossan in 1968 are already regaining traffic at Larne's expense, although the latter still shows growth.

Taken as a whole the Republic's ferry ports received more tourists and more cars in 1968 than Northern Ireland's ports despite a smaller car-carrying capacity. This is a reflection both of the Republic's better tourist image and Northern Ireland's greater emphasis on industrialisation and commercial traffic which create demands for as much as one third of the total space available on the car ferries even at the height of the tourist season in summertime. The shortest sea crossings, from Dun Laoghaire to Holyhead and from Rosslare to Fishguard, are the busiest routes. When its new terminal and ferry come fully into operation daily crossings from Dun Laoghaire will equal Larne's in mid-1969. Three other new car ferries are due to operate in 1969, from Rosslare to Le Havre, from Dublin to Liverpool and from Cork to Swansea. They will help to boost the car-carrying capacity of the Republic's ferries above that of ferries operating to Northern Ireland. The Irish Tourist Board envisages as many as 150,000 car landings in 1970.[14] If this figure is attained, port authorities will have to consider further expansion of facilities.

Unit loads

Cargo traffic has also undergone considerable change in the 1960's. The adoption of unit loads has both aided the growth of national economies and stimulated port activity. The theory behind the unit load is simple, yet its implications are far-reaching and represent a change as great as the change from sail to steam. Traditional methods of loading and discharging cargo usually mean that on short sea crossings a ship spends more time in port than at sea and this is both costly and wasteful of time. If cargo is already packed when it reaches port a ship can be loaded and discharged faster. Cargo may arrive pre-packed in containers, large aluminium or steel boxes of standardised proportions, on flats on which bulky cargo is covered with a tarpaulin, or on detachable trailers. Demountable tanks are used for liquids. Small loads may be stacked on pallets. Pantechnicons, a type of large van, are popular with some firms. These unit loads may be lifted or driven aboard ships, which can be loaded and discharged in a matter of hours instead of days as was formerly the case. The latest type of container transporter crane in use in Ireland is theoretically capable of handling 600 tons of cargo per hour compared with between 25 and 75 tons by more conventional methods.[15] Unit loads lessen the risk of damage and pilfering and help to keep freight rates stable. The specialised container ship in which containers are stacked in cells or compartments is proving to be more economical to operate than the older drive-on/drive-off ships, but both types of ships require adequate dock space for stacking and sorting containers.

The development of unit load services involves substantial investment in ports and shipping. The Irish Sea shipping companies and the large ports were slow to take advantage of them. The introduction of such highly automated techniques was unpopular with port labour because the redundancy rate was high. Some port authorities already committed to developing new berthing and warehouse accommodation facilities were reluctant to provide entirely new facilities. Larne was the first Irish port to accept the challenge. A service to Preston began to operate in 1948 on which drive-on/drive-off ships were first used, each capable of carrying a hundred vehicles. Specialised container ships were introduced later on the Preston and Ardrossan services.

From the mid-1960's other ports followed Larne's example (Fig. 20.4). From Belfast daily services now operate to Heysham, Liverpool, Preston, in Lancashire, and to Ardrossan in Scotland, and there are less regular services to the continent and North America.

Fig. 20.4   Container ship routes and ports on the Irish Sea, with motorway links to other parts of Great Britain

Londonderry, Newry and Warrenpoint all have services to Lancashire ports. Accurate figures of cargo tonnages carried in unit loads are not available in every case because some operating companies do not wish to release them. However, it is probable that Belfast and Larne each handle about one million tons and the other three ports in Northern Ireland between 100,000 and 200,000 tons of unit load traffic each year. Warrenpoint's potential is thought to be considerable for with government assistance in the 1970's it may replace Newry, a port handicapped by an awkward canal connection with Carlingford Lough.

In the Republic the first port to introduce regular unit load services was Greenore. Services to Preston and Sharpness in the Bristol Channel began in 1960 and a direct weekly service to Rotterdam in 1968. Greenore handles up to 200,000 tons of unit load cargo each year. It is a spacious port and is attracting new industry.[16] Although somewhat isolated at the tip of the Carlingford peninsula, it has successfully withstood competition from ports which later introduced unit load services. Dublin is now the major unit load port in the Republic, and, with 843,000 tons of cargo transported in this way in 1968, is third in Ireland after Belfast and Larne. Its first regular service commenced to Preston in 1963. Others now operate to Liverpool and Weston Point (Cheshire) and there are continental and trans-Atlantic links. In the Republic, Waterford is second in importance to Dublin. It has shown the most rapid growth of any unit load port in recent years. In 1963 21,000 tons of goods went through the port in containers; in 1968 the figure had risen to 203,000 tons which was 32 per cent of the port's total cargo trade. Although 24 km (15 miles) from the sea, this port was chosen by Bellferry (Plate XXIII) for its container service to Bellport near Newport, Monmouthshire because of its excellent location serving the rich agricultural area of south-east Ireland. The Republic's cheese and much of its butter exports now pass through the port. The terminal operates one of the largest transporter cranes in Europe. It came into operation in late 1968 and should help to increase through-put. In 1968 the neighbouring port of New Ross, with two sailings a week to Newport, handled 65,000 tons of cargo in unit loads. The remaining unit load ports are Drogheda and Cork. Drogheda is a minor container port which handled 49,000 tons of goods on its Preston service in 1968. Cork lost its service to Liverpool in late 1968 when the state-sponsored British and Irish Line withdrew it in favour of concentrating its services on Dublin.

The example of Cork well illustrates certain trends in unit load development. Firstly, it shows that the time-distance factor operates in favour of east coast ports and Waterford. Although Galway and Limerick plan to develop unit load services to win back some of their general cargo trade, their prospects are hardly encouraging. Secondly, it shows that despite the social aims of state-sponsored companies, greater rationalisation of traffic seems inevitable in face of increasing competition. British Railways are planning to invest heavily in container ships and a new terminal at Holyhead to serve both Dublin and Belfast in the 1970's. The B & I Line feel obliged to counter this development with new terminals at Dublin and Liverpool. Cork had to be sacrificed although provision is to be made to bring freight from the south-west by rail to Dublin. However, private companies may be tempted to operate new services from Cork, a port determined to have its share of the new trade, especially when its new Tivoli terminal is opened in 1969.

z

In the long run the heavy capital investment in facilities in Dublin and Belfast by state-sponsored companies may have a depressing effect on the private companies operating from smaller ports. But at the moment ports such as Waterford, Greenore and Warrenpoint are increasing their traffic, and services are planned from even smaller east coast ports. Strangford, for example, a tiny port at the difficult entrance to Strangford Lough in Northern Ireland, is to have a service to Lancashire in 1969. The smaller ports have some important advantages over Dublin and Belfast; they are less congested, have much lower overheads with little expense involved in maintaining deep channels, and excessive labour forces. As a result they can often undercut freight rates charged by companies operating from the large ports. The shallow draft container ships in service on the Irish Sea routes can operate from them just as easily as from the large ports.

The unit load revolution throws great emphasis on good communications between ports and their hinterlands. There is little value in gaining time in port and losing it on congested roads. Narrow roads also prohibit the use of the largest containers. In Northern Ireland the government has indirectly encouraged unit load services to develop at Belfast and Larne by providing new motorways and dual carriage-ways to serve them, while the improvement of the road link between Newry and Warrenpoint is receiving high priority. But port hinterlands tend to be large for this type of traffic, and there is a growing amount of cross-border traffic. Larne, for example, takes Harp lager from the Guinness brewery in Dundalk and fish from Killybegs in co. Donegal, while Greenore obtains one third of its traffic from Northern Ireland.[17] Traffic gravitates to the port offering the best service for the particular commodity at the cheapest rate, despite Customs delays at the border between the two parts of Ireland.

The super-tankers

In September, 1968 the Japanese-built 'Universe Ireland', a super-tanker of 312,000 tons, and the largest ship in the world, inaugurated Western Europe's first major oil trans-shipment terminal when she unloaded her cargo at Whiddy Island at the head of Bantry Bay in south-west co. Cork. The terminal is operated by the Gulf Oil Corporation, the world's fourth largest oil company, which chose the site because of its deep water and shelter, and its relative remoteness from major shipping lanes.[18] The terminal has a capacity of one million tons of crude oil which is trans-shipped to smaller tankers of about 100,000 tons for delivery to Gulf Oil's refineries at Milford Haven in Wales, Gulfhavn in Denmark, Europoort in the Netherlands and Huleva in Spain. An additional five super-tankers, each of 312,000 tons, are to come into service to supply the terminal with oil from the Persian Gulf and Nigeria.

The Whiddy Island terminal demonstrates the economies of scale to be gained from conveying bulk cargoes in giant ships to remote deep water ports for trans-shipment to smaller tankers. In 1968 no established port in Western Europe could take a tanker of this size and thus Bantry Bay's natural advantages were in demand. However, the terminal's contribution to the Irish economy is a matter for argument as no port authority was constituted and thus no port dues are collected. It is perhaps a poor recompense for the potential threat of oil pollution but offsetting this to some extent is the undoubted tourist attraction of seeing the world's largest ships in such a fine natural setting.

THE FUTURE

The new cargo and passenger flows which have developed in recent years have accentuated the importance of port location on the east coast, and of large ports, while at the same time favouring the growth of some smaller ones. One can infer that the future will emphasize these tendencies. Port growth appears to be linked mostly to industrial development and the adoption of the new shipping and cargo handling techniques. Large ports have had a major share of new port industries which provide them with a significant proportion of their incomes. Industries are likely to increase in number and variety if national policies of industrial attraction continue to be successful and ports can provide sites for them. However, the two largest ports, Belfast and Dublin, although increasing their trade in the 1960's, have had a smaller percentage of total trade than was the case in the previous decade. Belfast's share, for example, was 70 per cent in 1950 but only 60 per cent in 1967.

The smaller shares of total trade of Belfast and Dublin may be attributed to the growth of other large ports, in particular Larne and Cork. But to some extent it may also be explained by the growth of some medium-sized and small ports which are either taking advantage of an east coast location to adopt unit load services or are benefiting from the location of one or more industries in or near them, or are handling bulk materials such as crude oil, ore concentrates and road stone. The growth of Warrenpoint, Greenore, Arklow and Foynes, for example, may be expected to continue so that they will soon become medium-sized according to the classification adopted in this essay. This change in status need not necessarily imply greatly increased port areas because the new cargo handling techniques do not require extensive facilities. Small ports engaged in fishing and recreation also appear to have good prospects and these activities may rejuvenate others now in an economic backwater. But it is difficult to be optimistic about the future prospects of small ports which maintain a traditional emphasis on trade in agricultural products and bulk materials such as coal. Many of them exist on the very margin of trading activity.

Both governments regard most ports as commercial undertakings which should be largely self-supporting. They must pay their way or decline. Only in the case of the major fishing ports is there anything resembling a national policy of port development. No counterpart to the recently proposed National Port Authority in Great Britain is as yet foreseen. However, despite their lack of direct control, the two Irish governments can affect port development in many ways. They may, for example, make grants and loans to port authorities or to industries within or near ports. Refusal to give such financial help may be used in a negative way to favour one port against another. The government in the Republic can work through its state-sponsored industrial and transport companies to encourage port development in what is considered to be the most useful manner. In Northern Ireland an Act of Parliament is required to change Belfast's structure of port charges and thus its revenue can be affected. The relationships between government and ports are complex and often subtle but are usually mutually beneficial. In the last analysis, however, the decision of any shipping company or trader to route traffic through a particular port depends largely on the facilities and efficiency of that port and, therefore, on the costs incurred.

In the future the role of the governments may become even more important. Already, studies by the Maritime Institute of Ireland, an independent body concerned with all aspects of port activity, indicates that the government of the Republic could best aid efficiency by encouraging the grouping of estuarine ports under one port authority, a development inherent in the plan for the development of ports in Great Britain. A Shannon Port Authority to include Limerick, Foynes, and small ports further down the estuary such as Tarbert and Kilrush is the kind of development envisaged.[19] The opposition Labour Party in the Dáil has also advocated something like the British plan which would entail the delimiting of port hinterlands, and, it is implied, the sharing of available traffic between ports. This is a reflection not only of a belief in national planning and control but of the strength of vested interests and local loyalties. It is arguable that such a development would increase efficiency but it illustrates the importance of assessing political factors as well as economic ones when considering port prospects.

At the moment one of the most difficult problems facing Irish ports is the time it takes to construct port and harbour works which are often very costly and have a long life. Operating decisions, which have to be taken well in advance, may well be out of date when implemented. Is, for example, Belfast's dry dock already too small, and will Whiddy Island's oil terminal be redundant if experiments in the trans-shipment of oil at sea are successful? It seems significant that Gulf Oil has taken only a 20-year lease on the terminal. In order to survive port authorities must at least try to keep pace with technological change. Some have already ear-marked sites for Hovercraft, while on the horizon are giant ocean-going container ships and barges from which containers can be trans-shipped for distribution to ports, both large and small. Cooperation between port authorities and government, shipping companies, industry and trade unions is essential if the large ports in particular, which handle most of the trade, are to cope successfully with the new demands which the 1970's will bring. Ireland's insular position and her close economic ties with Great Britain will continue to demand efficient and cheap transport services. These will only be possible if her ports are efficient.

REFERENCES

1 P. J. Rimmer, The problem of comparing and classifying seaports, *Professional Geographer,* 18, No. 2 (1966), 83–91
  J. Bird, *The major seaports of the United Kingdom,* (1963), 21
2 P. J. Rimmer, The changing status of New Zealand seaports, 1853–1960, *Ann. Ass. Amer. Geogr.,* 57 (1967), 88–100
3 F. W. Morgan, *Ports and harbours,* (2nd ed., 1958), 7
4 All trade statistics were provided by the Department of Transport and Power in Dublin, and the Ministry of Commerce in Belfast.

5 J. H. Andrews, The patterns of trade in Ireland's smaller seaports, *Irish Geography*, 4, No. 2 (1960), 97

6 *The second programme for economic expansion,* Part II, S.O., Dublin (1964), 225

7 Ibid.

8 Statistics provided by the Fisheries Division, Ministry of Agriculture, Belfast.

9 *Report on Improvement of Fishing Harbour Facilities,* S.O., Dublin, (1960)

10 *Recommendations for Improvement of the Sea Fisheries of Ireland,* S.O., Dublin (1964), 14

11 Statistics provided by Northern Ireland Tourist Board and Bord Fáilte Éireann.

12 Ibid.

13 Ibid.

14 *Bord Fáilte Éireann, report for 1968,* 12

15 Information provided by Mr G. W. Hollwey, Managing Director, George Bell Group, Dublin.

16 D. A. Gillmore, The survival of Greenore, a minor seaport, *Irish Geography*, 5, No. 4 (1967), 332

17 Ibid.

18 R. A. Butlin, The Bantry Bay crude oil terminal, *Irish Geography*, 5, No. 5 (1968), 484

19 Information provided by Dr J. de Courcy Ireland, Maritime Institute of Ireland, Dublin.

XXI

LAND DRAINAGE AND WATER USE IN IRELAND

R. Common

While there is abundant evidence to indicate that harmonious interrelationships have existed between society and water resources for a long period of time in Ireland[1] the scale of human intrusions into the hydrological cycle has increased significantly during the last 200 years. It therefore seems prudent to consider some of the results of changing and often competing demands for water so that future actions may profit from more recent experience.

The problem of elucidating the hydrological cycle in different parts of Ireland is complex, because of the regional variations in physiography and climate. Slightly more than three quarters of the land lies below 150 m (500 ft). Mountainous country occupies only a small area and it is thinly sprinkled about the central lowlands in west Connacht, west and south Ulster, south-east Leinster and south Munster. Catchment characteristics are not wholly determined by the distinctive patterns of hill and plain, as portions of river systems which originated in Tertiary times appear to have been preserved in some districts while elsewhere significant derangements to surface drainage stem from Quaternary events.[2] The presence or absence of glacial drifts is especially meaningful to those areas underlain by rocks of Lower Carboniferous age, for the succession of limestone, sandstone and shale has significant variations in porosity and permeability.

The climatic regime is a mild, oceanic one marked by frequent showers, high relative humidity and low annual ranges of temperature. It is only in those areas of high hills and low mountains, previously mentioned, that growing temperatures are limited to 5 or 6 months in the year. Here, too, the expectation of snow can lengthen to a month or six weeks compared to the week or fortnight periods of the interior lowlands. Most precipitation normally occurs in the period between late summer and early spring with considerable amounts falling in the western districts of counties Donegal, Mayo, Galway, Clare, Kerry and Cork. Average annual totals decrease towards east central Ireland but the reliability of rainfall occurrence diminishes to the south-east.[3] Consequently it is in the area lying between the mouths of the Boyne and the Blackwater that the susceptibility to slight soil moisture deficits in summer is most marked (Fig. 21.1).[4]

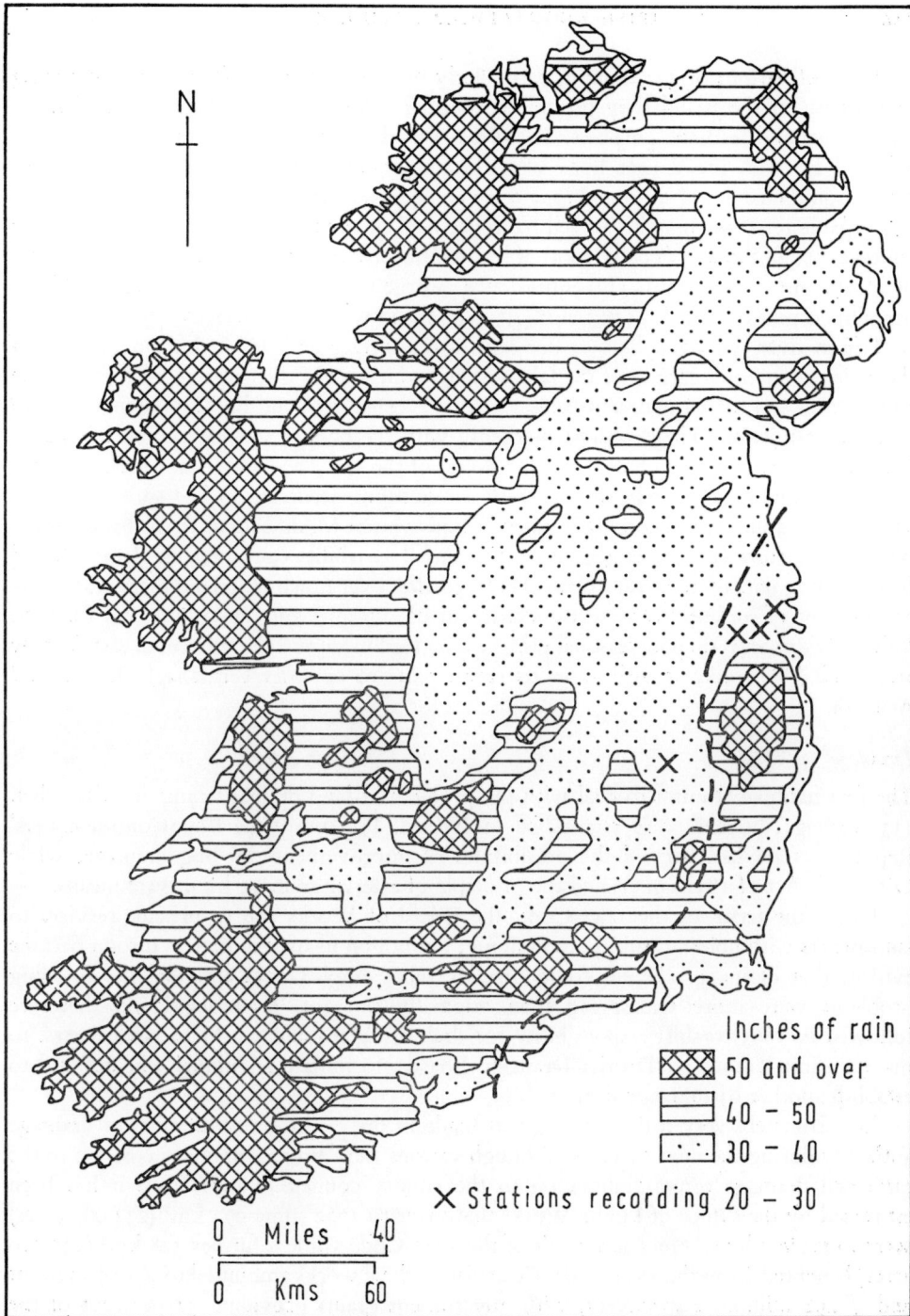

Fig. 21.1 Average annual precipitation (1916–50)

Inches of rain
50 and over
40 – 50
30 – 40
× Stations recording 20 – 30

0   Miles   40
0   Kms   60

N

Lakes of various origin abound, particularly in Connacht and Ulster, and in covering one fiftieth of the island they provide a considerable reservoir of water for utilitarian, recreational and aesthetic purposes. The other, less obvious, depository of surface water is afforded by widespread peat bogs which when drained or stripped produce dramatic hydrological changes of short and long term consequence. A measure of the importance of this organic reservoir may be judged from personal observations that the weight of water contained in 28,317 cm³ (a cubic foot) of brown, fibrous peat can be equivalent to a volume of 16,518 cm³ (1,008 cu in). This equivalence can rise to 17,698 cm³ (1,080 cu in) in black, humidified peat but reach 21,713 cm³ (1,325 cu in) in wet bog material.

Fifteen river systems collect 64 per cent of the surface drainage in Ireland and five of these also contain the largest of the lake systems which act as discharge regulators. All the trunk streams of these catchments possess gentle average gradients but display moderate to marked attenuation. They contrast markedly with the host of smaller catchments which form a peripheral zone within 32 km (20 miles) of the sea. The basic form of most surface discharge curves is relatively simple, with a minimum occurring in late spring or early summer and a maximum coming in early or mid-winter. Modifications to the basic regime by lake regulators, catchment geometry and rainfall variability can be readily demonstrated from existing data on the Irish streams.[5] Nevertheless over much of Ireland there is an over-endowment of surface water, to the detriment of enterprises in agriculture and forestry. Relatively dry areas do pose seasonal problems on Inishmore and the Burren, in east Galway and south Tipperary, as well as in restricted parts of counties Fermanagh, Down and Armagh.

Drainage

The first national attempt to deal with the problem of land drainage came in 1842 when 113 drainage districts were established in Ireland. Previously the Bog Commissioners' Report of 1809 had stressed the possibilities of improvements by bog drainage, while O'Farrell's Act of 1831 enunciated the principle of arterial drainage by private means.

Under the terms of the 1842 Code, the Board of Works was to provide services to landowners with holdings subject to flooding, but not on its own initiative. It soon became evident that drainage schemes could provide relief employment and that the flooding problems were more widespread than originally thought. Fresh legislation therefore followed in 1863 to shift responsibility for drainage plans and works to landowners, to maintain installations by District Drainage Boards, to initiate additional schemes and to establish another 63 drainage districts.

Unfortunately very little progress was made in the evolution of an efficient drainage authority during the next 61 years, although various Acts did pass drainage costs on to the rates and drainage responsibilities on to the county councils. Nevertheless it has been estimated by the Office of Public Works that prior to 1922 some 992 km² (244,000 acres) were improved by schemes as a result of the 1842 Code while a further 528 km² (130,000 acres) benefited from the 1863 Code. Costs for all these works amounted to £1.67 millions and £0.98 millions respectively, with government grants providing 52 per cent of the charges under the first code but only 5 per cent of the costs under the latter one.

With partition in 1921 the Ministry of Finance (N.I.) inherited the McMahon drainage scheme for the Lough Neagh area and by the terms of the 1929 Drainage Act (N.I.) it was authorized to undertake new works on both the loughside and the outflowing River Bann. Activity in the Lough Neagh area has been fairly continuous ever since and with the lowering of the lake level to 15.25 m (50 ft O.D.) in 1959 the combined effects of drainage now affect 601 km² (148,000 acres) directly.

Wartime conditions, and especially the need to increase productivity on the lowland farms, together with the findings of a provincial Drainage Commission were largely responsible for the Drainage Act of 1942. Under the previous 1925 Act responsibility for initiating and financing drainage schemes rested with owners, but the execution of work depended upon county councils. That these arrangements for sharing costs and responsibilities were too poorly defined was clearly demonstrated by the rapid improvement of 40.5 km² (10,000 acres) under this new Act. Direct state assistance affected five streams in Armagh, three in Down, two in Fermanagh, one in Antrim and one in Tyrone, at a cost of £200,000.

Further legislation followed in 1947 to establish a provincial Drainage Council and involved the Ministry of Agriculture, as well as the Ministry of Finance. Henceforth the former ministry was charged with the implementation of drainage schemes on main rivers while the state also accepted financial responsibilities, with local authorities, for a 20-year programme to provide adequate drainage facilities. Meanwhile the serious risk of flooding on the south side of Lough Foyle, and the need for an effective means of mitigating the recurrent flooding of central Fermanagh, demanded attention and remedial action.[6]

Nineteenth-century reclamations had added 14.3 km² (3,500 acres) to the area between the mouths of the Foyle and the Roe. By 1953, however, the gradual deterioration of defences necessitated a new act in order to undertake a ten-year programme of river and sea works costing £350,000. Mutual agreement with the Republic over the use and control of water in the Erne catchment was formally recognized in 1950. Hydro-electric generation at Ballyshannon along with more effective control of surface discharge rates and lake levels in Fermanagh were to be the outcome of this beneficial cross-border co-operation. Ten years later this successful precedent was to be followed by the Border Schemes Act, which permitted joint drainage works in catchments, such as that of the Flurry, which straddle the political boundary.

As the benefits of planned drainage works accrued it was inevitable that the urban authorities previously excluded from the schemes should seek eligibility for assistance from the provincial Government and their omission was rectified in 1957. Work on the main water courses also generated interest and concern for a correctly phased programme in the minor catchments. Although joint improvement schemes were possible on the smaller streams under the terms of the 1947 Act, a comprehensive programme was not possible until the 1964 Drainage Act (N.I.) had been approved.

For the first time this new act placed all the drainage functions into the charge of one ministry and it provided for more state involvement with the financing and implementation of drainage work. Thus apart from professional staff, the Drainage Division of the Ministry of Agriculture now employs 750 labourers and equipment worth £525,000 for its work over the Province. Since 1947, twenty years of effort have resulted in improvements to 264 km² (65,000 acres) of land and 80 per cent of the 1,822.5 km (1,132 miles) of main water courses, at a cost of £6 millions. Following the 1964 Act, some 4,830 km (3,000 miles) of minor streams are now expected to be improved at a rate of 322 km (200 miles) per year.

The particular drainage needs of some catchment areas, and the general problems arising from the needs of an agricultural society living in a damp environment, have stimulated actions in the Republic which echo those just described for Northern Ireland. On the other hand, the greater extent and diversity of the physical environment, and a different order of priorities in social and economic development, have produced certain differences.

In the Republic a number of special cases soon merited legislation. The state took responsibility for the Owenmore in 1926 and upon completion of the drainage works it then transferred this catchment to the care of the county authorities. A similar procedure took place over the Barrow, after 1927. Work on this particular river was distinctive for its pioneer qualities, since the catchment received comprehensive, rather than piecemeal, treatment with mechanical equipment. Costs in these two projects amounted to £618,000 but resulted in improvements to 23.4 km² (6,200 acres) in the Owenmore and 174.7 km² (43,000 acres) in the Barrow catchments.

The Shannon, with a catchment area covering 16 per cent of the Republic's surface, has provided flood and drainage problems which still await a comprehensive solution. Before drainage work attendant to the First Navigation Act of 1835 some 140.9 km² (34,700 acres) were subject to flooding but by 1866 this expectation had been reduced to about 101.4 km² (25,000 acres), in spite of the main preoccupation with navigation and water-borne traffic. Quite rightly, responsibility for the whole catchment now rests with the state and is shared by the Office of Public Works and the Electricity Supply Board. This arrangement followed upon the Shannon Electricity Act of 1925 and has already been responsible for considerable alterations to pre-existing river installations. Nevertheless 20.25 km² (5,000 acres) are still prone to flooding between Lough Allen and Lanesborough while another 9.5 km² (2,350 acres) are susceptible to inundation between Lanesborough and Athlone. From Athlone to Meelick low banks endanger 37.7 km² (9,260 acres), while downstream of Meelick another 11.2 km² (7,190 acres) are liable to flooding. The most recent 1961 Flood Report considered both a full relief scheme and a summer relief scheme. The former proposal involves capital expenditures that are unjustified in terms of derived benefits, whereas the latter scheme does offer worthwhile returns. Cheaper, partial works could benefit 1,422.2 km² (350,000 acres) and extra power potential would be made available, for a capital outlay of £18½ millions and annual charges on this capital expenditure of £1.4 millions.

It is of interest to note that a Drainage Commission was reporting on its findings in the Republic at the same time as its northern counterpart. By a consequential act, in 1945, the

Commissioners of Public Works in the Republic were empowered to prepare and undertake drainage schemes at state cost, but maintenance costs were to be drawn from county councils. A Central Drainage Authority and a hydrometric survey were officially established, although the installation of discharge and rainfall gauges had already begun in 1940 on an interim recommendation of the Drainage Commission.

Subsequently catchments have been classified by area and type so that priorities can be allocated for work on major, intermediate and minor scales. The pace of catchment work has quickened while its scope has widened in recent years and consequently the needs for costly equipment and for skilled as well as unskilled labour have grown. Field equipment has involved an investment of over £2 millions and about 2,000 men are normally employed on arterial drainage works alone.

Implementation of the 1945 Act began with work on the Brosna in 1948, but in the following year the Local Authorities (Works) Act extended the coverage of flood relief schemes and thus provided for a greater flexibility of arrangements. By 1959, 406.25 km² (100,000 acres) of agricultural land and 170.5 km² (42,000 acres) of bogland had been drained as the result of planned programmes, while work in progress involved another 345.3 km² (85,000 acres) of agricultural land and 93.6 km² (23,000 acres) of bogland. Eight years later target figures had risen still further, so that 1,251.1 km² (308,000 acres) of agricultural land and 353.6 km² (87,000 acres) of bogland have received, or will be subject to drainage improvement schemes in the near future. When it is recalled that, in 1940, the Drainage Council called for works on 2,381.6 km² to 2,588.2 km² (586,200 to 612,500 acres) some measure of the overall task and the rate of improvement may be judged.[7]

Paradoxically, many of the streams which were prone to flooding also encouraged the early development of inland navigation. But the effective promotion of an inland waterway system[8] belongs to the eighteenth century, when some determined individuals convincingly allied subjective terrain appraisals with over-optimistic economic forecasts. The fundamental weakness in the speculative development which ensued lay in building canals and improving streams that were to create trade rather than to cater for it. Even the joint navigation and drainage works, which became so fashionable during the nineteenth century, proved to be of only limited value. All these inland waterways showed a profit for only short periods of time and their services were usurped first by the railways and then by motor vehicles. Even the traffic demands of two wartime periods in this century could not arrest the spread of dereliction throughout the 1,347.6 km (837 miles) of this canal, lake and river system. Since 1945 the care and maintenance of these costly waterways have become the responsibility of both governments, but unfortunately they still remain under-used for drainage, supply and recreational purposes.

WATER SUPPLY

Provision of proper and adequate water supplies dates from the Public Health (Ireland) Act of 1878, but until the Second World War it was the larger towns and villages which profited most from piecemeal water supply and sewerage disposal arrangements. Despite modest rural expectations and demands, four small towns and 109 villages or hamlets in Northern Ireland still awaited a piped supply in 1943, and at about the same time (1946) a mere 8.6 per cent of the 423,189 private dwellings in the rural areas of the Republic had been provided with piped water.

In 1945 only Dublin, Cork, Dun Laoghaire and Limerick possessed comprehensive water systems within the Republic. Less than 10 per cent of households in the counties of Longford, Cavan, Leitrim, and Roscommon received piped water, and it was only in counties Dublin, Louth and Wicklow that more than one third of the householders enjoyed this amenity. By 1961 100 per cent water supply had been achieved in the 89 cities or towns with local government, and in 450 towns with populations exceeding 200 persons tap supplies were provided to over 90 per cent of the inhabitants. But the smaller settlements, with clusters of 20 or more occupied houses, could supply only 41.6 per cent of their potential consumers, while the truly rural dwellers remained self reliant. Sewerage facilities had been considerably improved by the same year and their provision tended to parallel the new supply systems.

In an effort to speed the rate and the extent of supply arrangements the government introduced a ten-year programme in 1958. A capital expenditure of £35 millions was proposed and subsidies to local authorities were henceforth increased, with a differential scale to the benefit of poorer or outlying areas. New schemes in the Gaeltacht, for example, qualified for cost loans of 60 per cent compared to 40 per cent in Dublin city. Loan repayment periods were also stretched to 50 years and county authorities were called upon to submit supply programmes to the Minister of Local Government. Such encouragement immediately boosted the total value of loans sanctioned and resulted in work on 31 new supply systems during 1960. By the end of the following year counties Dublin, Clare, Wexford and the South Riding of Tipperary were all committed to five- or ten-year comprehensive schemes costing £2, £0.8, £1.5 and £3.9 millions respectively. Interim programmes for three to five years had also been approved for the counties of Cork, Donegal, Leitrim, Westmeath and Wicklow at an estimated cost of £3.5 millions.

Meanwhile rising living standards and improved working conditions, the desire to increase agricultural productivity, and the growth of a tourist trade in rural districts created another insistent demand for water. The promotion of well and small water supply schemes with financial assistance, was one solution attempted by the government. A rural electricity scheme which would be eligible for financial aid and related to small water schemes was another inducement offered to the country folk. Once installed, a rural electricity supply was to be coupled with pumps and storage tanks to serve small clustered communities. Eventually the whole range of rural needs was recognized by the government who then offered assistance in supply schemes catering for individual, group or small village needs. As in Northern Ireland the cost of connecting individual houses to a water supply has varied considerably, from £212 to £520, while the subsequent price of water to these houses may range from 5½d to 34s 5d per 4,546 litres (1,000 gallons), depending upon local conditions. It seems likely therefore that the cost of a complete rural supply in the Republic will eventually inhibit the authorities concerned just as it has done in Northern Ireland.

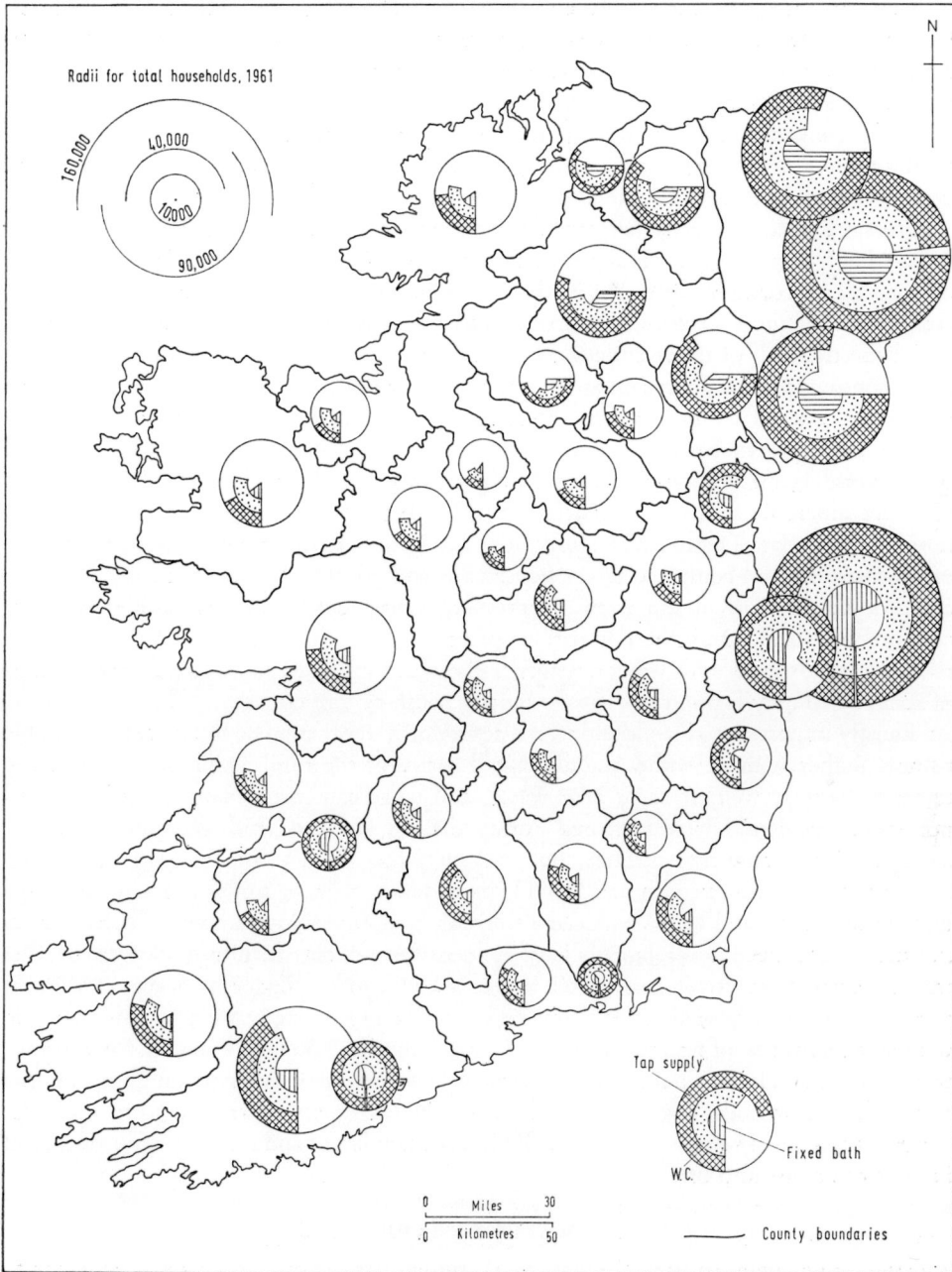

Fig. 21.2   Selected water facilities in Irish households, 1961

Government grants for supply and sewerage schemes in Northern Ireland followed legislation in 1945, and since then £21.6 millions have been contributed towards a total expenditure of £45¼ millions. A piped supply is now provided to 78 per cent of the total population and this high per capita investment has involved the laying of 4,830 km (3,000 miles) of trunk mains. Since 1945 the tendency for Joint Supply Boards to be established by the pooling of resources has been slow, but progress has been made at a time when rural water demands have been provided over wide areas.

Storage capacity has been increased by 22,730 mill litres (5,000 mill gallons) in Northern Ireland but it is still inadequate for existing demands in certain periods, as the dry summer of 1968 clearly demonstrated. As in the Republic, direct intake from a river or lake is common while most service reservoirs in water schemes have only a few day's storage.

The second half of the twentieth century has been characterized therefore by a rapidly rising consumption of water and an increased dependence upon public supplies from local authorities, assisted by government finance.[9] The rate of these developments has been swiftest in Northern Ireland, but inevitably the present supply deficiencies within the Republic will be made good as the recently approved water schemes mature. The availability of water amenities in Irish households in 1961 (Fig. 21.2) was greatest in the county boroughs of Belfast, Dublin, Waterford, Cork and Limerick, Although the western counties of Northern Ireland contained fewer households and poorer facilities than those found in counties Antrim, Down and Armagh, they still compared favourably with most other counties in Ireland. Only the populations of counties Louth, Dublin and Wicklow were relatively well served with water amenities. Elsewhere in the Republic the domestic wants of society had only begun to be satisfied in the south-eastern counties.

Equally important to the individual is a desire for water that is safe to use and pleasurable to taste (either with or without adulterants). Many of the rural dwellers still rely upon untreated spring, well, river or lake water, and so remain exposed to the risk of local pollution. These risks have increased during the last 20 years, with changing domestic, agricultural and industrial practice, but only in a few districts are they permanent and serious enough to cause concern. The widespread habit in the past of discharging sewerage into the sea, rivers and lakes produced a tolerable pollution. Now, however, recent urban growths or industrial developments have yielded waste discharges into the lower stretches of the Lagan, Roe, Foyle, Liffey and Boyne which can no longer be accepted without question. The quality of the raw water collected for piped supply varies considerably, as does the effectiveness of water treatment before distribution.[10] In most counties, for example, there is a marked lack of fluorides[11] in the water while the iron content is high in counties Donegal, Leitrim and Clare (Fig. 21.3). Since regional supply schemes tend to multiply, the quality of piped water should gradually improve, as larger and more effective treatment installations come into use.

WATER DEMAND

An attempt was made to assess the scale of the 1961 water demands, by counties and county boroughs, to provide perspectives on the supply problem (see Table 1). The year 1961 was

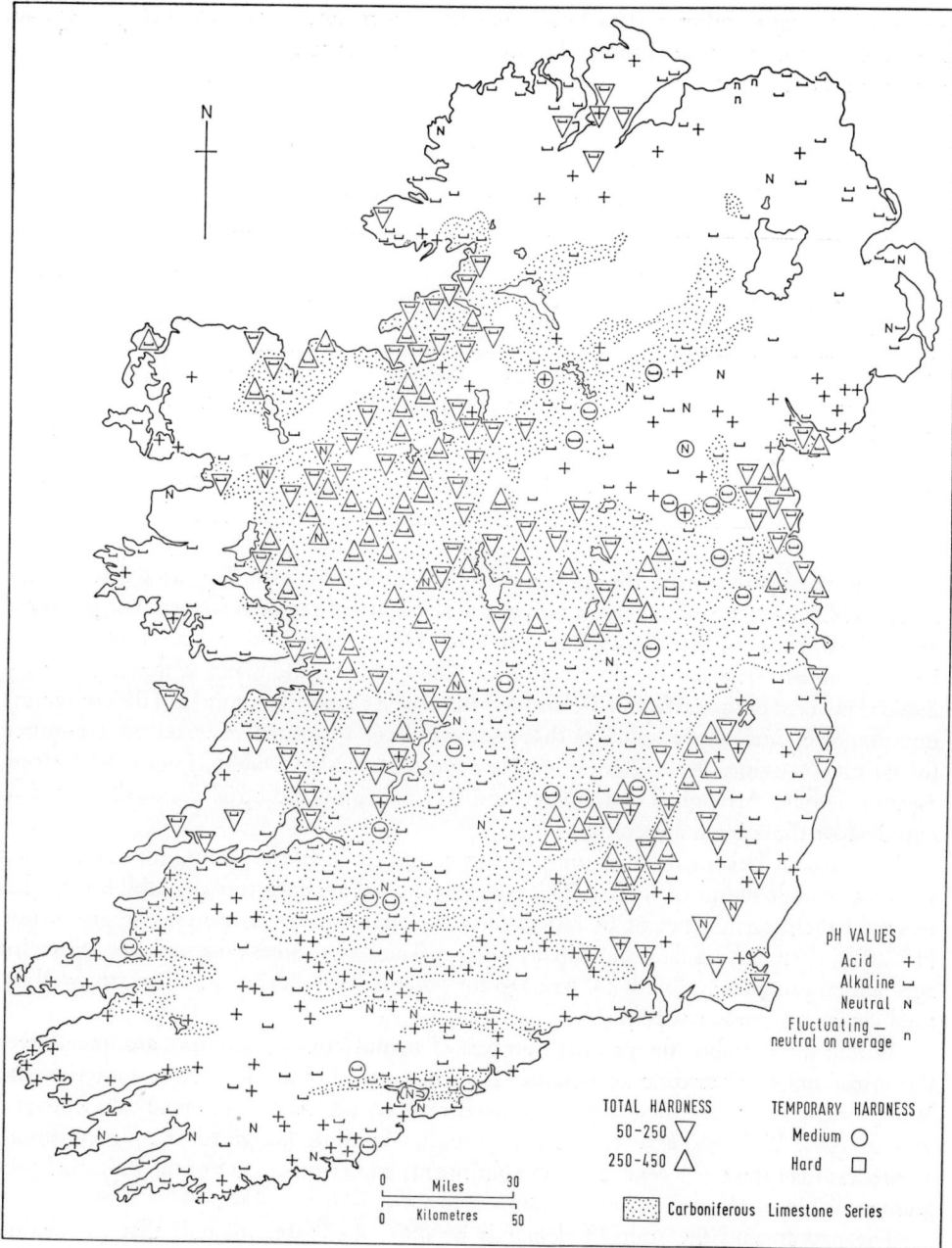

Fig. 21.3 Values of water hardness (pH) for selected settlement water supplies in Ireland, 1960–63

selected for comparability of data[12], and the partial estimates for industry included textiles, agricultural products, other food and drink enterprises, paper and paper products, mineral and chemical products.

TABLE I

The scale of water needs in 1961

Northern Ireland	Millions of litres	Millions of gallons	Republic of Ireland	Millions of litres	Millions of gallons
Domestic	70,960	15,606.20	Domestic	140,200	30,821.00
Agricultural	21,140	4,652.05	Agricultural	131,800	29,009.12
Basic Industrial	175,000	38,491.30	Basic Industrial	40,700	8,955.30
1961 Total Estimate	267,100	58,749.55	1961 Total Estimate	312,700	68,785.42

It will be apparent from the subsequent observations and from Fig. 21.4 that demand ranges widely over the island and involves a multiplicity of regional factors. The estimated demands from 1.4 million domestic consumers in Northern Ireland and 2.8 million in the Republic clearly reflected the distribution of households on the island at this time (1961). Since 64 per cent of the surface of Ireland was improved crop and pasture land the continuing importance of agriculture indicates that relatively large quantities of water were required for farming activities in most counties. However, in counties Dublin, Louth, Waterford, Antrim, Down, Armagh, Londonderry and Tyrone rising industrial demands tended to overshadow those from agriculture.

In Northern Ireland most of the population and the manufacturing industry is found within a 30-mile radius of Belfast. This concentration of manufacturing establishments has made for the pre-eminence of Belfast County Borough and co. Antrim in the production of textiles, chemical, mineral and paper products. These same areas rank with co. Down for agricultural products and with co. Armagh for other food and drink industries, to swell the total demand for water supplies.

Within the Republic the greatest numbers of manufacturing industries are spread over the urban and rural districts of counties Dublin, Cork, Louth, Tipperary, Limerick and Waterford; collectively these areas contained over 60 per cent of the establishments and jobs in 1961. Little industry is found in counties Leitrim, Longford and Roscommon, where less than three per cent of the establishments and two per cent of the industrial jobs were available.

The pattern and the scale of demands in 1961, therefore, suggests that population differences between Northern Ireland and the Republic were partially compensated for by the greater needs of manufacturing industry in the former area. Since noteworthy water-

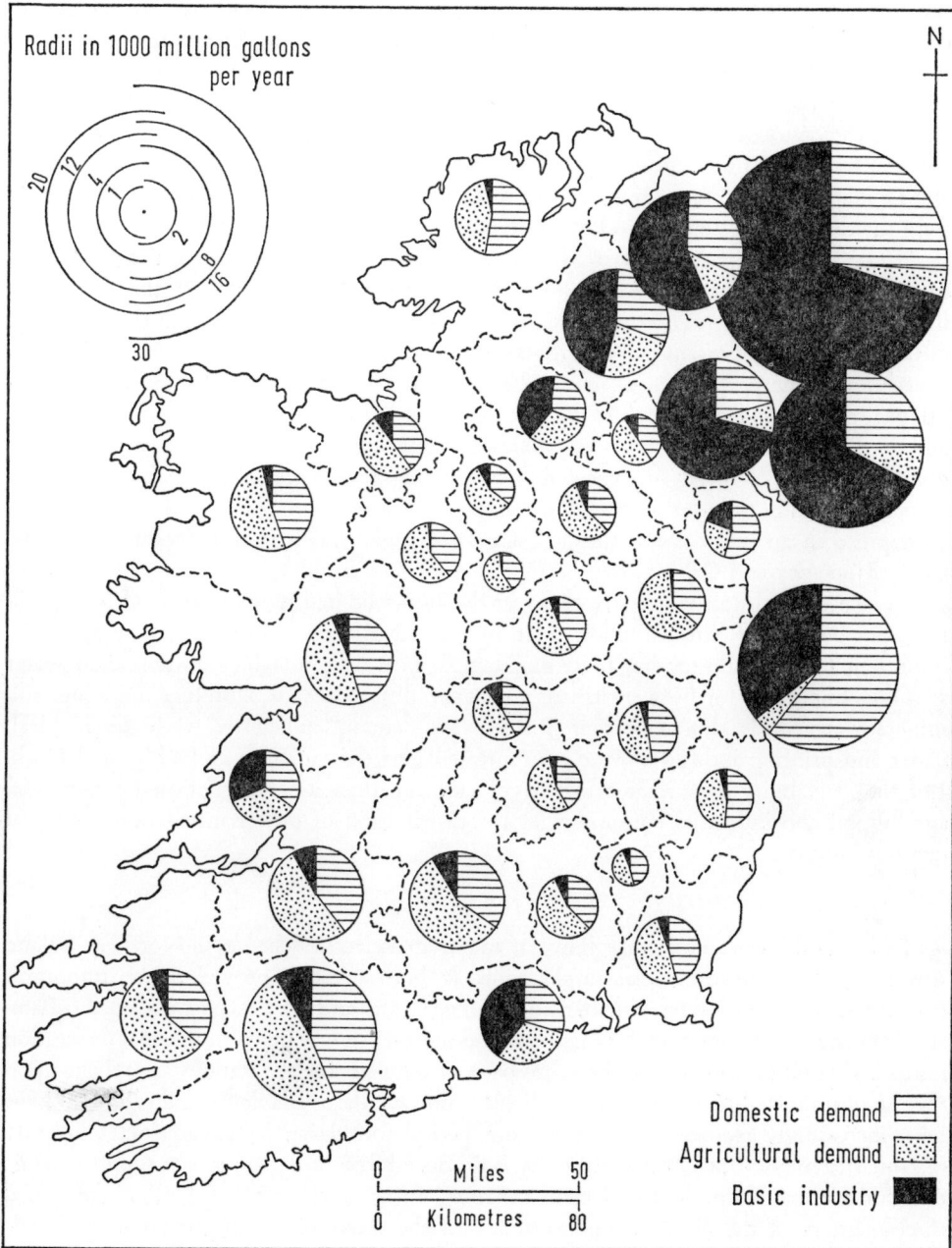

Fig. 21.4   Estimated water demands by county for 1961

using industries in Northern Ireland have already been considered elsewhere[13] the subsequent observations on estimates used in Fig. 21.4 will be confined to the Republic.

The woollen and worsted industry, a heavy consumer of water, showed a concentration in co. Cork but production in counties Dublin, Offaly, and Donegal was significant. By contrast the cotton, linen and rayon industries were strongly localized in north-east Leinster and at a few coastal sites elsewhere. Shirt making was virtually shared by counties Dublin and Donegal, but the concentration in a few factories of the former area contrasted sharply with the dispersed nature of production in the latter.

While numerous factories were distributed throughout 19 counties for the production of bacon, ham, and lard, only 15 counties had meat processing plants. On the other hand there was a marked concentration of activity within counties Tipperary, Cork and Kerry, in the nationally important dairy products industry.

Although the production of jam and marmalade was encouraged by the Finance Act of 1924, the canning of vegetables did not begin until after 1930. The commercial canning and bottling of fruit followed ten years later, but freezing and dehydration processing dates only from 1950. As might be expected fruit growing and its related processing enterprises all occupy land in the south-east of the country. The associated growing of sugar beet was widespread in 20 counties but the production of sugar was limited to counties Carlow, Cork, Tipperary and Galway.

At one time almost every townland in the Republic had its own water-driven grain mill, but because of rationalisation their numbers had been reduced to 23 by 1961. An important leather industry has been maintained, however, in which an abundant water supply is important for both treatment and waste disposal needs. Distilling, brewing, and mineral water production made their greatest water demands in Leinster, while the chemical, paper and printing industries were concentrated into the vicinities of Dublin and Cork. But the availability of surface water involves more than its consumption by domestic, agricultural and industrial consumers, as the distribution of power installations and peat deposits indicate.

WATER POWER

Earlier in this century the feasibility of two hydro-electric schemes in Northern Ireland was recognized but the social implications of both projects proved to be important deterrents. Estimated water potentials of 15 megawatts and 27.5 megawatts on the Bann and Mourne rivers were therefore ignored and preference was given to thermal generation instead. Coastal locations have therefore been developed, for the stations are reliant upon the use of imported fuels. In the Republic, by contrast, the available natural resources have been increasingly realized during the same period for electricity generation. Currently one-quarter to one-third of the electricity is produced from indigenous peat supplies, while two-fifths come from hydro-electric schemes. In 1925 the city of Dublin consumed three-quarters of the electricity generated, and the intention of the first hydro-electric scheme on the Shannon was to quadruple the supply of electricity quickly in order to serve all the larger settlements.[14] Two years later the Electricity Supply Board was established and this organisation has subsequently flourished to the point where it employs over 6,500 persons and provides services worth £25 millions annually. By 1961 almost all the worth- while hydro-electric generating potential had been realized and the installed capacity of 219 megawatts approximated to the minimum load. Five catchments are now harnessed but the average annual water inflows at the Shannon and Erne stations are respectively 40 and 20 times greater than at Gweedore, co. Donegal, on the Clady. Again, because of climatic conditions, the peak generation period for water turbines occurs in the winter, from November to February, yet the drier summer season, which reduces the surface discharges to the hydro-electric installations, paradoxically benefits harvest prospects for the air-dried peat fuel of the small thermal stations. Thus a carefully coordinated generating and transmission system has had to be evolved using Irish water and peat resources, together

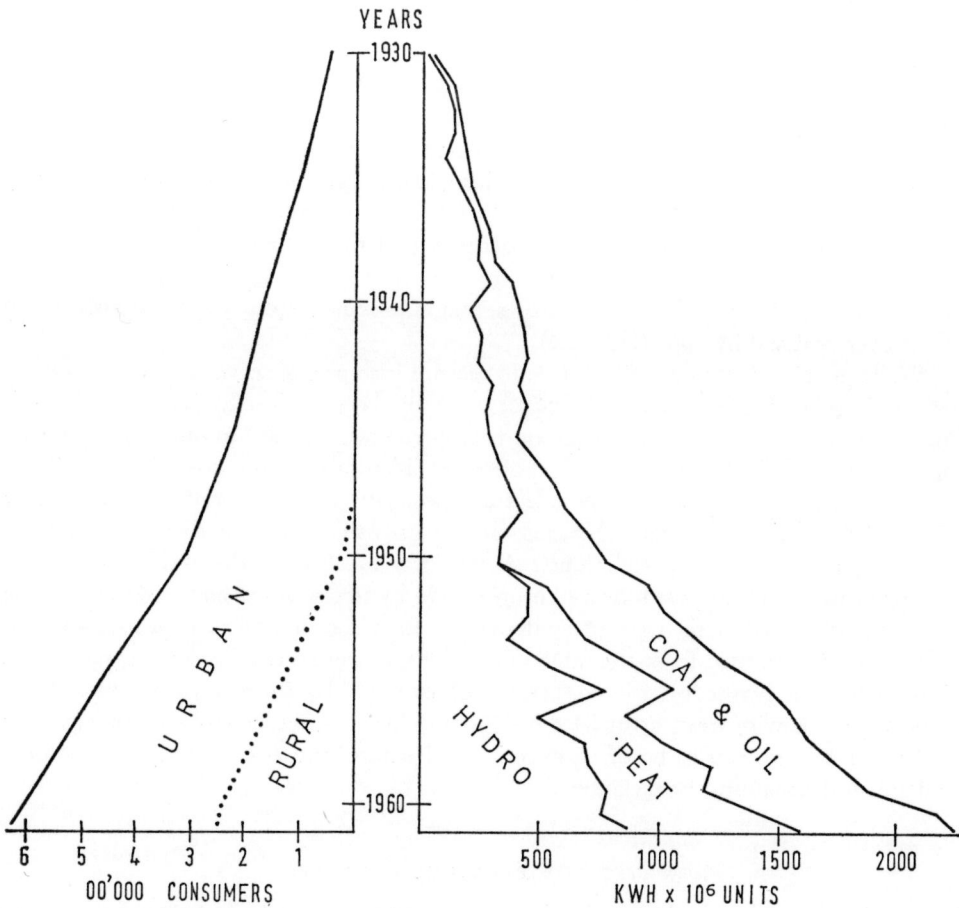

21.5   Generation and consumption of electricity in the Republic of Ireland

with imported supplies of coal and oil. As the location factors of the different types of generating station involved are distinctive, and the supplies of river water or dried peat fuel fluctuate annually, the generating programme must also be flexible enough to cope with operational requirements. In the near future the Turlough Hill pumped storage scheme within the Wicklow mountains, the exhaustion of peat fuel supplies, and the possibility of sharing nuclear power with Northern Ireland all indicate that further changes may be anticipated in supply arrangements (Fig. 21.5).

Recent estimates indicate that the resources of workable peat in Ireland have already been halved since 1814, but while 914 km² (225,000 acres) remain in the Republic there are only about 24.4 km² (6,000 acres) in Northern Ireland. In the former area Bord na Mona is capable of working through 730.6 km² (180,000 acres) by 1995, with their present methods, and by this date the remaining area in Ireland will probably have been stripped by other techniques, if recent rates of extraction are maintained. Despite the finite fuel resources Bord na Mona has grown, since 1946, to provide jobs for 5,000 to 6,000 employees, and after the Turf Development Act of 1950 it has also been able to provide housing for its own workers. It supplies more than one and a half million tons of machine-cut turf annually to the Portarlington, Lanesborough and Allenwood power stations in addition to about two million tons of milled peat yearly to the Ferbane and Rhode stations. Hand-won peat still provides for the needs of the small stations at Cahirciveen, Miltown-Malbay, Screeb and Gweedore, to swell the total installed capacity of peat fuelled stations to more than 200 megawatts. Increasingly Bord na Mona has cooperated with agricultural and forestry interests over land use problems, for their activities produced 1,015.5 km² (250,000 acres) of cut-over peatland by 1964 (Fig. 21.6).

While piecemeal attempts were made to reclaim Irish peat areas with limited resources before the Second World War subsequent work has been more effectively coordinated, financed and publicized. Forestry trials on peat were first necessary to discover the varied tolerances of suitable trees such as Lodgepole pine, Sitka spruce and Norwegian pine. Time was also needed to demonstrate the effect of phosphate dressings, or the significance of copper and molybdenum trace elements on tree growth, as well as to develop correct ploughing and preparatory techniques. A technical break-through in this work dates only from 1950, and this was followed immediately by tree planting on 190.8 km² (47,000 acres) of peatland within the western counties of the Republic, in the next 11 years. Northern Ireland has also profited from the same innovations, as can be readily demonstrated by a visit to either the Navar forest in co. Fermanagh or the Lislap forest in co. Tyrone. Meanwhile the work with trees, artificial dressings and crops on the cut-over or thin peat of lowland areas continues to be of an experimental nature, and consequently an extensive land area still remains to be reclaimed.[15]

WATER FOR PLEASURE PURPOSES

During the last one hundred years, the changing tastes and means of society have encouraged private and public investments for a widening range of pleasurable activities using rivers

N

LONDONDERRY

DONEGAL

BELFAST

SLIGO

LONGFORD

NAVAN

ATHLONE

GALWAY

DUBLIN

LIMERICK

KILKENNY

TRALEE

KILLARNEY

CORK

Peat moss	▲
Sod peat	●
Briquette	▥
Milled peat	▦
Peat-fired power station	◖
Hydro-electric power	✕
County boundaries	- - - - -

0   Miles   50

0   Kilometres   80

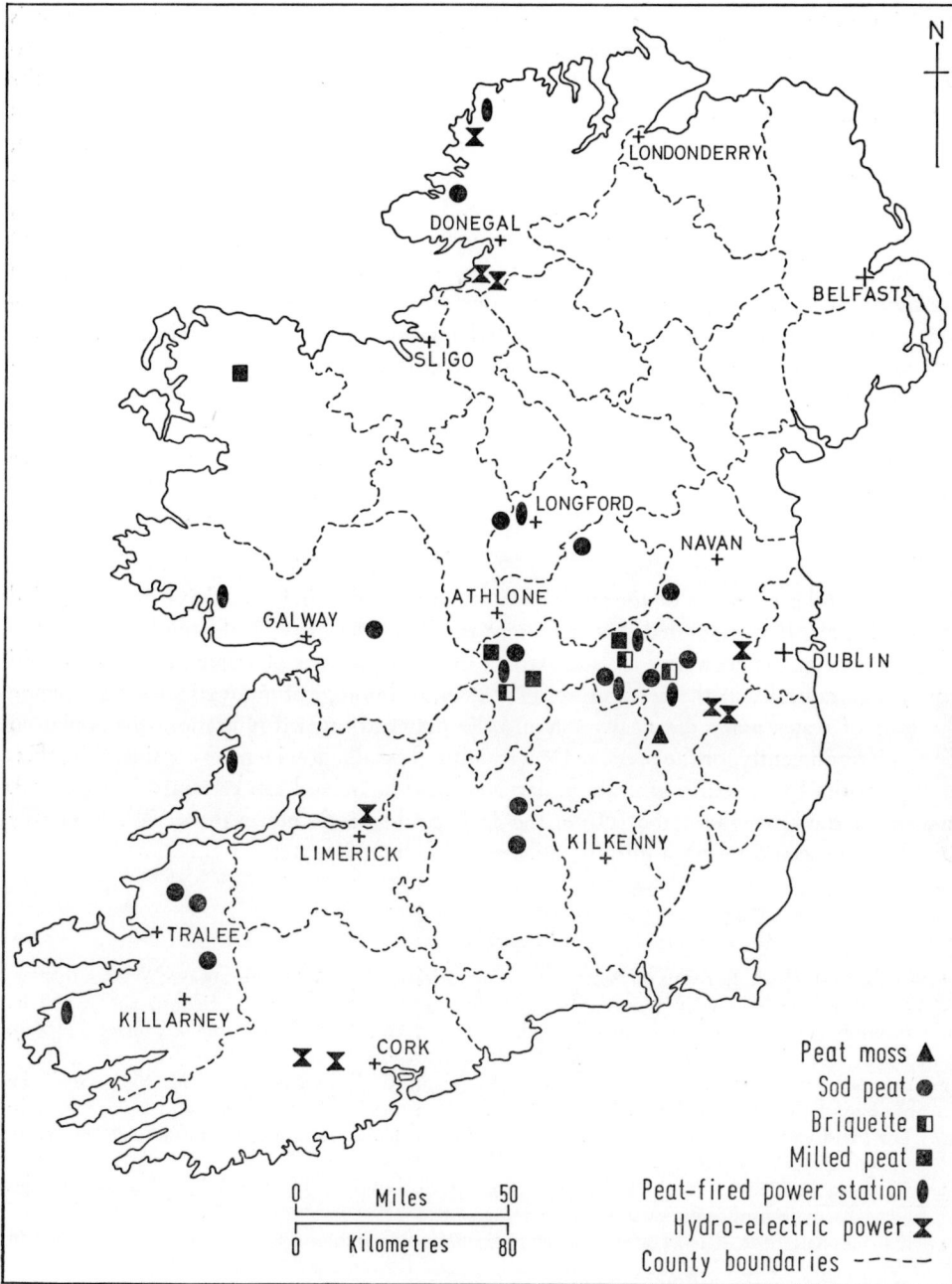

21.6 Fuel and power supplies in the Republic of Ireland, 1961

and lakes. In some catchment areas these new demands have already necessitated reappraisals on the potential uses of water and the formulation of multipurpose arrangements to satisfy many different users. Operating commitments of the hydro-electric schemes, for example, involve the interests of inland fisheries, as well as the problems of flooding and navigation of the Shannon. The sale of fish and the letting of fishing rights on the Shannon, Lee and Erne alone exceeded £20,000 in 1961, when the total value of all inland fisheries in the Republic amounted to about £1 million. The corresponding total value for salmon, trout and eels caught in Northern Ireland amounted to £308,000. When it is realized that a visitor now spends about £30 for hotel, transport, and incidentals to catch a salmon, then the significance of the fishing potential to tourism in Ireland becomes apparent. Furthermore, with 53 angling clubs in Northern Ireland and 173 in the Republic, the need for fishing waters to be cared for by conservators and commissioners is amply reinforced by the demand from resident anglers.[16] And yet the current incidence of trout disease and the public concern for the Lagan valley show that it will not be long before even wider policy decisions will be needed to protect those very waters and waterscapes which now prove to be so attractive.

CONCLUSION

Some scale and perspective on the availability and use of water in Ireland have been provided in this chapter. It is suggested that if present trends in the growth of population and the development of the economy are maintained then the patterns of water utilisation should not change radically in the near future. However, technological innovations could change the scale of water usage drastically. Should the present outward migration of population diminish significantly, or the pressure for agricultural production increase considerably, then new priorities for schemes to drain under-used land in Ireland can certainly be expected. Indeed, in thinking about the future, the Irish could profitably examine contemporary Dutch response and research into the utilisation of all fresh water.

REFERENCES

1 See, for example, E. E. Evans on boats and fishing in *Irish folk ways,* (1957), 233–52; W. S. Cordner, The cult of the holy well (Unpublished MA thesis, Queen's University, Belfast, 1953); and R. Common, Water and society in Ulster, in J. House ed., *Northern Geographical Essays,* (1966), 79–102

2 Tertiary river systems are considered by A. R. Orme, G. L. Davies, and F. M. Synge in "The physique of the south of Ireland", and Quaternary events by A. Farrington and N. Stephens in "The Pleistocene geomorphology of Ireland", both in J. A. Steers ed., *Field Studies in the British Isles,* (1964), 482–99 and 445–61

3 S. Gregory in Chapter 4 of J. W. Watson and J. B. Sissons eds., *The British Isles,* (1964), provides fuller information on regimes and regional variations.

4 M. J. Connaughton, *Global solar radiation, potential evapotranspiration and potential water deficit in Ireland,* being Tech. Note 31, Dept. of Transport and Power, Met. Service, Dublin (1967)

5 Thanks are due to Mr J. D. O'Donoghue of the Electricity Supply Board in Dublin for providing discharge data on several Irish rivers, upon which this generalisation is based.

6 N. Stephens and L. Symons, The Lough Erne drainage scheme, *Geography,* 41 (1956), 123–26

7 Further information on drainage problems is available in: *Agriculture in Northern Ireland,* 42 (4), 104–6; 42 (5), 148–51; 42 (6), 175–77, (H.M.S.O., Belfast 1967); also in *Oibre* 4 (1966) and 5 (1967), (Commission of Public Works, Dublin); and in *The river Shannon flood problem* (report, S.O., Dublin 1961).

8 Fuller details on the canals are available in, W. A. McCutcheon, The development and subsequent decline of the chief in land waterways and standard gauge railways of the north of Ireland, (Unpublished PhD thesis, Queen's University, Belfast, 1962), and, D. & C. Delaney, *The canals of the south of Ireland,* (1966).

9 For further information on water supply arrangements, see, for example, B. J. Tighe, Rural water supply in the Republic of Ireland, *J. Inst. Water Engineers,* 21 (1967), 479.
Also, *Report on the problems of water supply and sewerage in Northern Ireland,* (Cmd. 223, H.M.S.O., Belfast, 1944). and, *Statistical Abstract of Ireland,* (Pr. 5984, S.O. Dublin, 1961).

10 E. English, The treatment of Northern Ireland water supplies, *J. Inst. Water Engineers,* 14 (1960), 425–41

11 Health (Fluoridation of water supplies) Act 1960. Reports on the incidence of dental caries in school children, (S.O., Dublin, 1962–5)

12 The assistance and information given by Mr B. Tighe and the engineers of all the various water authorities in the Republic of Ireland on water supply and demand are gratefully acknowledged.

13 R. Common, Water resources in Northern Ireland, *J. British Waterworks Ass.,* 45, 387 (1963), 778

14 It was estimated that the Shannon would supply 150 million units, an amount worth comparing with the 932.4 million units actually produced by all the hydro-electric stations of the Republic in 1961

15 Report of Bord na Mona for the year ended 31st March (Dublin, 1962)
H. M. Fitzpatrick, ed., *The forests of Ireland,* (Bray, 1966).
Forestry research review 1957–64, (Forestry div., Dept. of Lands, Dublin, 1967)

16 Details of a Bord Failte (Irish Tourist Board) scheme for inland fisheries are provided in E. P. Kearney, Five-year fishery development plan, *Administration,* 9, 3 (1961), 215–23
See also: *Foyle Fisheries Commission, 10th Annual Report,* (H.M.S.O., Belfast, 1961); *Report of the Advisory Committee on Inland Fisheries in Northern Ireland,* (Cmd. 455, H.M.S.O., Belfast, 1963)

XXII

THE URBAN-RURAL FRINGE OF DUBLIN

J. P. Haughton

The physical site of Dublin has hitherto offered no effective barrier to urban expansion for, even in the east, the shallow waters of Dublin Bay have been easily reclaimed. Consequently, social and economic factors have been paramount in controlling the spread of the city and there has been a strong tendency towards a symmetrical growth around the centre with expansion along radiating lines of communication. This symmetry was evident in the eighteenth century with the building of the north and south circular roads approximately equidistant from the city centre. However, they enclosed much open land at the time of their construction and subsequent infilling was markedly asymmetrical with building concentrated in the north-east and south-east sectors as well as in the southern extension around the old settlement of Rathmines.

This same trend was continued in the nineteenth century but expansion was slow and by 1837 the built-up area was only beginning to extend beyond the circular roads.[1] By the end of the century suburban development had spread round the margin of the Bay and southwards towards the hills but, in the west, open land was still to be found within a mile of the centre of the city. There were a number of reasons for the persistence of this asymmetrical growth. On the positive side there was the building of two outports for Dublin, the first on the north of Howth Head, and then its rival at Dun Laoghaire on the south side of Dublin Bay which soon became the chief packet station for Holyhead. These towns drew improved communications in their respective directions and when Dun Laoghaire was linked to Dublin by rail in 1834 it was possible for business men to commute daily from there to the city. Howth had a rail connection in 1846 which served Clontarf, Raheny and Sutton but suburban development here was more limited and somewhat later than on the south side where the chief attraction was its proximity to the area of well-preserved Georgian housing which occupied the south-east sector of the city. This sector was continued outwards during the nineteenth century by high quality suburban terrace housing laid out in the Georgian tradition of wide streets and open spaces.

Other factors affecting growth included the Phoenix Park which formed a barrier to the west on the north side of the river Liffey, while eastwards from this a military barracks, mental hospital, prison and similar institutions discouraged residence in the north-west sector of the city. In the Liffey valley, westward growth was checked by the grounds of another military establishment and three hospitals, but the valley of its south bank tributary, the Camac, was lined by small industrial concerns for a distance of 4 km (2.5 miles) beyond the city boundary. It is not so easy to explain the lack of residential development to the south-west where there was plenty of suitable land close to the city but since the town grew only slowly throughout the nineteenth century, the south-eastern suburbs and the more accessible sites on the margin of the Bay doubtless met the needs of the relatively small group of business and professional men who could afford such accommodation. The great majority of the inhabitants of Dublin crowded into the decayed Georgian houses within the city.

When Dublin was provided with a tramway system it was designed mainly to serve existing centres of population but two lines were built westwards through open country. One of these followed the Liffey valley to Lucan (1883), and the other went south-west into the hills to link Terenure with Blessington and Poulaphuca (1888). Neither line stimulated much development partly because the trams were slow and inefficient, and because when they were first built, their termini were in the Dublin suburbs.

The twentieth century

The growth of Dublin in the present century has accelerated, especially since self-government in 1921, and the city has gradually regained its symmetrical outline. The population increased from 404,094 in 1926 to 650,153 for the enlarged metropolitan area in 1966. The net increase for the period 1961 to 1966 for this same area was 52,689 or 8.9 per cent.[2] This growth has been accompanied by a massive change in the distribution of population within the urban area. In general, the crowded central city areas have declined in numbers while the peripheral areas have shown a steady gain with the result that Dublin has gradually become a city of suburban dwellers. In 1926 the inner wards of the city contained 67 per cent of the population but by 1966 their share had fallen to 22 per cent. There has not been a comparable outward move of services. These have remained highly centralised although there is now some adjustment to the situation with the location of new industry and better shopping facilities on the urban fringe. Within the city itself there has been a steady shift of the centre of gravity eastwards from the site of the Norman town. This was strongly marked in the eighteenth century when the building of Carlisle (now O'Connell) Bridge created the great north-south route which is, today, the main shopping axis of the city. But the eastwards shift continues and has veered south-east towards the Ballsbridge area where new office blocks and a luxury hotel have recently been built. This eastward move stimulates further reclamation on this side of Dublin Bay where it is hoped to provide further space for industrial development.

Recent population change

The percentage change in population 1961 to 1966 for Dublin city and the contiguous townlands is shown in figure 22.1. The rate of change is arranged in roughly concentric zones each of which has a distinctive character and function. The central city wards lose population as slum property is cleared and in places office blocks replace former residences, but to the north-west and south-west of the central area losses are associated with the earlier suburban municipal housing. These areas, populated in the first instance by people from the city centre with preference given to those with large families, show a decrease because the children have grown up and moved elsewhere. Around this area of decrease is a broad zone of modest increase (1 to 10 per cent) in the older suburban areas. This increase is due partly to the infilling of the relatively few open spaces available for development but is primarily the result of the division of the older houses into flats and lodgings. It is in this zone that the newcomers to Dublin find their first accommodation, for such people are not eligible for

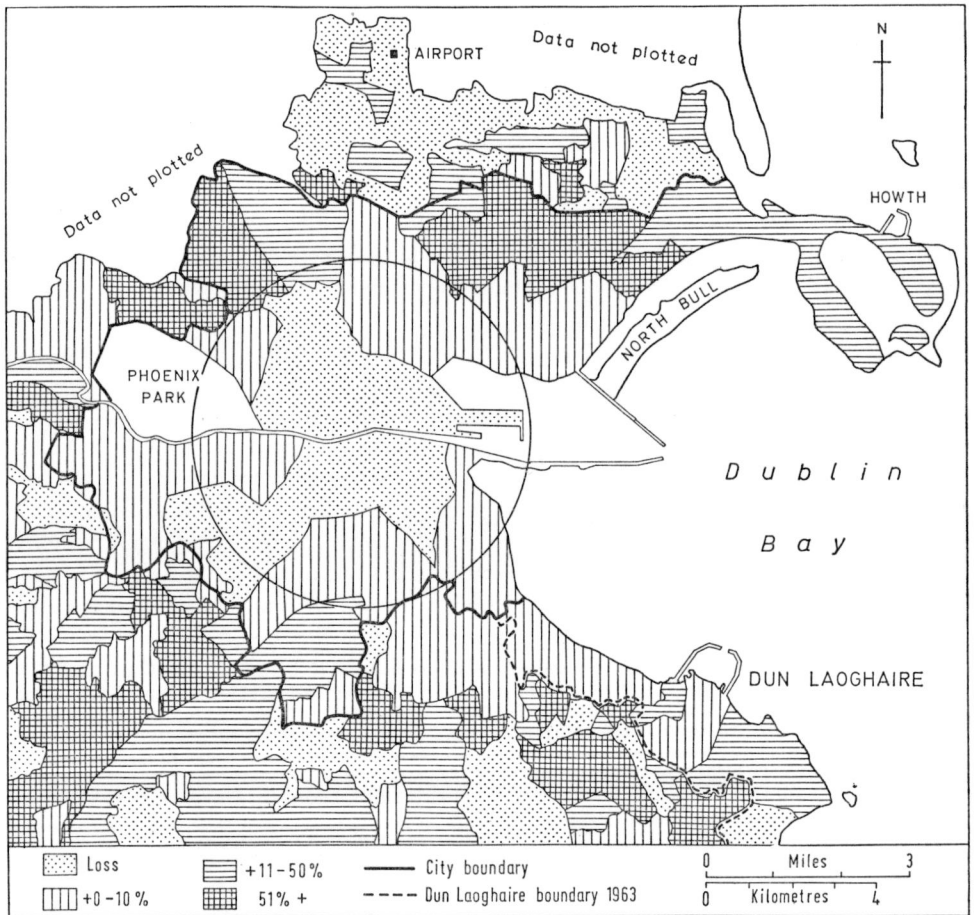

Fig. 22.1   Percentage change in population of Dublin and adjoining townlands 1961–66. The city boundary has been adjusted periodically to take in new building but further adjustments are clearly necessary in the south. The circle is drawn with a radius of 4 km (2.5 miles) from O'Connell Bridge.

Corporation housing and few can afford to purchase suburban houses when they first arrive in the city. Surrounding this zone is another of major population increase which reflects large scale current development. On the north it is largely the result of Corporation building. To the south-west along the Dodder valley there have been several large scale private development schemes; but much of this is farmland with a low density of population that has needed only a very few new houses to produce a large percentage change. East-wards from this, population change is more irregular and reflects small scale building schemes filling in empty spaces. An interesting feature is the pockets of decrease which in some cases at least are related to areas where redevelopment is imminent.

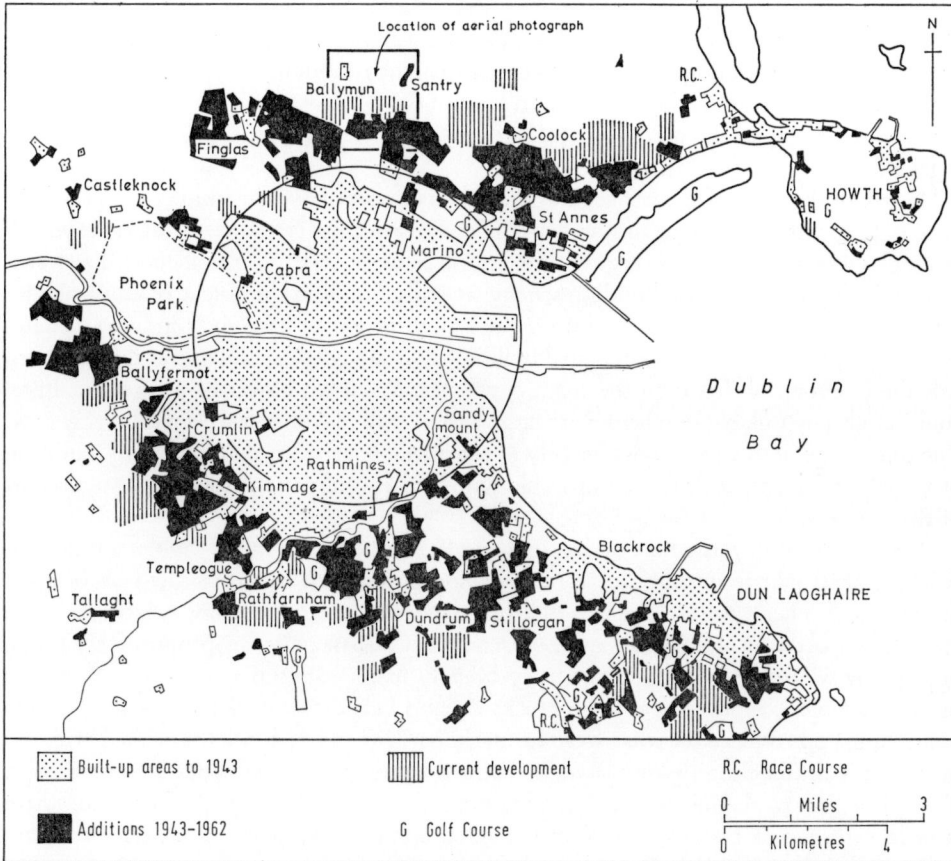

Fig. 22.2 Recent additions to the built-up area of Dublin. The fragmentary nature of building to the south and south-east is clear. On the north side the open belt about 4 km (2.5 miles) from the city centre and the large scale developments on its outer edge are notable features as also is the empty area north-west of Cabra along the Tolka river valley. The circle is drawn with a radius of 4 km (2.5 miles) from O'Connell Bridge.

This zone of rapid population change is by far the most significant feature of modern Dublin. It has widespread implications for the planning of the city as it is largely a migration of working population to the suburbs, which in turn leads to an extended journey to work and increased traffic congestion. It is also a development that shows little overall planning control and there is a serious encroachment on valuable agricultural land. The nature of this urban-rural fringe will now be examined.

THE URBAN-RURAL FRINGE

The fringe of Dublin where agricultural land interdigitates with suburban dwellings forms a band on the periphery of the city averaging about 2.5 km (1.5 miles) in width (Plate XXIV). Its extent is indicated in figure 22.2 which shows the areas built-up between 1943 and 1962 as well as current development. It has been, in part, an infilling and a rounding off, but there has been a widespread intake of farm land to the north-west and to the south-west so that the symmetry of the built-up area, lost in the nineteenth century, has gradually been regained.

North of the Liffey the inner edge of the belt is in places less than 3 km (1.9 miles) from the city centre. It reaches a maximum depth of more than 3 km (1.9 miles) around the village of Finglas where land has been set aside for industrial use as well as for residences. Eastwards from this a major municipal building scheme at Ballymun is in the course of construction. Other growth centres are Santry and Coolock both of which have their industrial estates and a mixture of private and municipal building. On the whole, throughout this northern belt the Corporation has been the main developer. Extensive blocks of open agricultural land have been available so schemes are large and overall planning has been relatively easy. The outer edge of this zone ends abruptly in a farmed countryside and there is no transition of very low density residences comparable with that existing to the south and south-west of the city.

South of the Liffey, the zone of development lies farthest from the city in the south-west. It is also at its narrowest here, for further extension has been halted by the lack of main drainage and other services. The belt widens eastwards towards the coast where the broad embayment between the Dublin and Dun Laoghaire urban centres is progressively filling up. On the whole the development here is different from that on the north side. With one or two notable exceptions few large blocks of land have been available and most of the building has taken place on what were formerly gardens and paddocks associated with old houses. It is almost entirely speculative and aimed at the middle and upper income groups. Though subject to planning control in relation to density of housing and other details there is little evidence of overall control in the relationship between one building estate and another; and the provision of services is left to the developer.

It is clear that this urban-rural belt is homogeneous neither in character nor in function. It contains five main elements one of which may be dominant in a particular area. These are firstly, municipal housing estates; secondly, private speculative buildings; thirdly, shopping centres; fourthly, industry; and fifthly, the remaining open spaces.

THE MUNICIPAL HOUSING

This is by far the most important element in the northern and south-western suburbs (Plate XXV). It is the result of an extensive rehousing programme initiated by Dublin Corporation in the nineteen twenties as part of the slum clearance programme for the city centre. Though many people have been rehoused in renovated houses or in new flats within the city, the primary problem of overcrowding was solved by removing the remainder into estates of two-storey cottage houses in the suburbs. The magnitude of this operation is indicated by the fact that up to March 1967, 37,173 cottage units had been built. The majority of these (65 per cent) are four-roomed houses though a significant number (15 per cent) have five rooms.

In the earlier schemes, proximity to the city was a major consideration as it was assumed that for a long time to come the inhabitants would continue to look towards the city for their work, social contacts and daily needs. Hence there was no attempt to create a self-sufficient community by building shops and factories though it was necessary to provide new churches and schools. The need for relatively large blocks of land so that there could be a fully planned layout limited the places near the city where such schemes could be located as also did the high price of land in some areas which forced the Corporation to use the less popular parts of the city where they were not in competition with the speculative builders.

Until the second World War it was not too difficult to find sufficient land for development reasonably close to the city but, since then, with the occupation of the more convenient sites and the upsurge of speculative building, it has been necessary to look for sites farther and farther out from the centre, and in some cases beyond the city boundary. Increasing distance from the city has created problems of communication and made it necessary to provide shopping facilities and other services on a scale that had not hitherto been contemplated.

Among the earlier schemes those at Marino and Cabra are typical. Both are on the north side within 2.5 km (1.5 miles) of the city centre and each was initially between 60 and 80 ha (150 and 200 acres) in extent. The Marino estate is roughly triangular in outline with a large circular open space in the centre from which the main streets radiate. There are 432 five-roomed houses in blocks of 4, 6 and 8 with gardens front and rear and each block differs in style from its neighbour. At Cabra the estate lies between converging railway lines. The focus here is a school and a church; the open spaces are more restricted and variety is provided by curved roads rather than by differences in house style. Initially this scheme had 641 four-roomed houses but subsequently extension to the west has added a further 2,254 units (Plate XXV). Somewhat similar development took place in Drimnagh and Crumlin to the south-west of the city. Here again the basic lay-out is radiating roads linked by circular ones but there is not absolute symmetry as the schemes were fitted into a pre-existing road system. Both these estates are more than 3 km (1.9 miles) from the city centre and at the time they were built this was considered to be the limit to which people would be prepared to move out from the downtown area.

When first constructed all these estates were monotonous and unattractive but with the painting of the woodwork in different colours and the growth of gardens they have improved greatly in appearance; and the Corporation policy of making some of the more valuable land fronting on the main roads available for private development has added some buildings of a more substantial nature. A few shops were provided but these were limited in number and variety.

In the post-war period increasing competition for land and the lack of further space close to the urban area has directed attention more and more to the periphery. Where possible, existing schemes were added to and there was rapid extension west of Kimmage and around the old village centre of Crumlin where one scheme consisted of 2,975 three-roomed houses. A major new development took place at Ballyfermot on the south side of the Liffey valley more than 5 km (3.1 miles) west of the city centre. This was socially and economically a more independent community than the earlier ones. Although the houses are the typical two-storey type, the layout is less formal than in some of the earlier schemes. More recently the Corporation has turned its attention to the northern fringes of the city where broad areas of farm land with a low density of population lie within 4 km (2.5 miles) of the city. This district is separated from the city proper by a number of institutions set in extensive grounds which form an almost continuous open belt from the Phoenix Park to Clontarf. These institutions were located here mainly in the late nineteenth century and undoubtedly delayed suburban development in this direction. The new building schemes represent a leap over this zone into an area where not even low density surburban housing had existed previously. The land is reasonably level, easy to drain and relatively cheap to develop. A major project has been completed around the village of Finglas where both shopping and industrial facilities already existed. Most of the houses here are the conventional two-storey four-roomed type. The layout is spacious and pleasing and the estates give way abruptly to farmed land at the the city boundary (Plate XXVI). It would seem that no immediate extension is contemplated here and Corporation activity is currently concerned with the completion of a major project within the same zone at Ballymun 2.5 km (1.5 miles) east of Finglas. This scheme, sponsored by the Minister of Local Government on behalf of Dublin Corporation is designed to supplement and speed up the Corporation large scale housing programme. It represents a complete break with tradition in the building of a variety of house types including several tall residential blocks. These are grouped round an area of 3 ha (about 8 acres) which has been reserved for a shopping centre where some 43 to 44 shops will face on to pedestrian precincts. There will also be two banks, two department stores, a police station, a health clinic and a large entertainment complex with a swimming pool and other amenities. Most of this is to be built by private developers but the area set aside would seem to be far too small to service a community which will shortly have 19,000 people residing within a radius of 1 km (0.6. miles) Already many of the houses are occupied but as yet no permanent shops or recreational facilities have been provided. Consequently there is no focus for community life and the inhabitants are developing patterns of shopping and social activities different from those envisaged. It remains to be seen if this new settlement can develop an identity of its own. Its proximity to Dublin ensures that its ties with the city will remain strong but its degree of independence will be related to the range and quality of retail facilities and social amenities provided. It is unfortunate that these were not phased in more closely with the occupation of the houses (Plate XXVII).

East of Ballymun, around the village of Coolock, there is more Corporation housing of conventional type although the houses are rather larger than elsewhere. Here again another centre has been planned incorporating about 25 shops, supermarkets, a swimming pool and other amenities. The building of this will be undertaken by a private developer in partnership with Dublin Corporation. It is very slow to get off the mark and, in the meantime, the inhabitants continue to look to the downtown area for other than their basic needs and are likely to continue to do so for some time to come.

Private speculative building

The speculative builder and land developer have long been active in the Dublin suburbs where they have provided the bulk of the residences for the middle and upper income groups. Their activities have not been confined to particular areas though in the pre-war period the borders of Dublin Bay and the southern suburbs were the favoured parts. Few of these earlier schemes were large; their distribution was discontinuous and the built-up areas were often surrounded by open fields.

In the post-war period such open spaces have been progressively filled up and land values have risen so steeply that the building is usually at the maximum permitted density. Many of these building sites are little more than the large gardens and paddocks of the older houses and there is often insufficient space to lay out an adequate road system. These roads are lined with identical semi-detached houses with gardens front and rear. The houses themselves are usually of sound construction with rather more accommodation than their counterparts in Great Britain but the overall effect is monotonous and uninspiring (Plate XXVIII). Moreover, with land costing as much as £5,000 per acre it is not surprising that the minimum provision is made for open spaces or other amenities. The few exceptions to this, such as the building of Dundrum Heights where there has been careful landscaping and the preservation of trees, are all the more striking because of their rarity. Apart from the cost of land, various planning bye-laws and grant regulations tend to tie the hand of the architect in laying out an estate, especially the rules relating to density of housing which prevent the clustering of dwellings at high density on part of a site in order to leave the rest of it open. Although speculative building is to be found in most Dublin suburbs it is currently active in the south and south-west but the area of greatest immediate potential lies to the north and west of the Phoenix Park where already there is some low density building around Castleknock. However, the Draft Development plan for the city of Dublin specifically states that no development will be allowed which will necessitate a large increase of traffic through the open areas of the Park and it will be the policy to preserve its open character westwards in the vicinity of Castleknock and the Liffey valley.[3] This would seem to be a serious limitation to building in this area but it is one difficult to assess.

Shopping centres

Urban spread has recently engulfed a number of old villages. On the north these include Finglas, Santry and Coolock; on the south, Dundrum, Rathfarnham and Templeogue and on the west, Palmerston and Castleknock. In none of these has there been a spectacular redevelopment. Small self-service stores have replaced the family grocers; branches of banks and dry cleaners have appeared but there has been no significant renewal of the shopping areas and only very limited extensions to them. Finglas, for example, which lies in one of the major development areas has some vacant shops and although sites are available no more shops are currently under construction. A number of factors contribute to this situation. In the first place the property in the villages is in small units and it is difficult for the developer to get possession of several of them at the same time so as to make development worth while. Moreover, under various landlord and tenant acts, anyone who is in occupation of business premises has a right to renewal of the lease, which makes it very hard for the owner to get possession of a site and inflates the price of the few that do become available. There are also parking problems which are not easily solved. Another problem is the small groups of residential shops that occur within the new estates. There are four such groups within 1.5 km (1 mile) of Finglas and each is composed of six to eight residential shops in a row with parking space in front. They supply primary needs and typically include a butcher, a post office with fancy goods, a chemist, a grocer, a fruiterer and a fish-and-chip shop. There may also be a turf accountant, a public house and a small self-service store. Many of these shops do not give the impression of being prosperous and some are for sale, but undoubtedly they take trade away from Finglas. If the older village centres are to develop they will have to offer a much more sophisticated range of goods than these local stores and as long as they fail to do this the inhabitants will continue to make periodic shopping trips into the centre of Dublin for other than their basic needs. In all, the Corporation has provided some 90 shops in new municipal residential areas while private enterprise has provided comparable facilities elsewhere. The new shopping centres at Ballymun and at Coolock have already been mentioned. These are to be on a very much grander scale than any yet envisaged but they are as yet only in the building stage and their impact is problematical.

On the south side of the city, development has mainly been in private hands and is of a different kind. The large self-service store with abundant parking space is typical. These are usually situated close to major road junctions and draw their motor-borne clientele from far distances, so there is intense competition among them. There is also one large departmental store on the outer fringe of this area which serves customers from the whole of south Dublin. However, the most significant development of all is the Stillorgan shopping centre which has parking space for 600 cars and contains 56 shops and three supermarkets. It is attractively laid out with pedestrian walks, restaurants and other amenities, and meets most of the needs of the relatively sophisticated middle and upper income groups who occupy south-eastern suburbia. This is the only comprehensive shopping centre outside the older urban cores.

XXV   Typical municipal housing in Cabra West

XXVI   New municipal housing in Finglas West

XXVII   Ballymun: multistorey residential blocks constructed by Dublin Corporation

XXVIII   Speculative development south of Dundrum, co. Dublin

Industry

Suburban Dublin has long had small industries associated with the river valleys but the growth of industrial estates is a recent phenomenon which has been stimulated by the difficulty of getting sites within the city, and facilitated by the ever-increasing use of road transport for the collection and distribution of raw materials and manufactured goods. It is also a move towards the new pools of labour on the municipal housing estates. Most of the industries involved are of recent introduction though a few of the old established city businesses have moved to the periphery. No single motive actuates the choice of site but location within industrial estates is favoured because of the provision of electricity and water and other facilities. Factory building, therefore, has taken place in well defined areas although the isolated plant does occur, an interesting case being the use of the upper floor above six shops as a clothing factory in a recent Corporation housing estate.

The two major concentrations of industry lie to the north-west and south-west of the city respectively. The former has grown up around the village of Finglas where the products are as diverse as transformers, steel containers, and toilet preparations. Here, as elsewhere, several private industrial estates compete with each other for custom. The other industrial zone is situated at the south-western exits from the city. There is, in this area, a long tradition of industry associated with the narrow Camac valley. Today, there is a paper mill, light engineering works and the manufacture of pharmaceutical goods and soft drinks. Apart from these two main areas there are factories around Santry in the north and Coolock in the north-east where some very attractive premises are concerned with food processing and printing. There is also a more scattered development in the south around Rathfarnham Dundrum and Kill o' the Grange.

Most of these industries draw their wage-earners from near at hand and only a few of the factories find it necessary to provide a canteen. The salaried workers, on the other hand, may live almost anywhere in the city suburbs and some of them travel long distances to work often passing right through the city on the way. This is partly due to the lack of suitable housing near some of the industrial estates. In this respect, Santry and Coolock are better off than elsewhere for they are well-balanced communities with a wide range of housing in their vicinity. During the period 1955 to 1967, 51 firms with foreign participation started production in the Dublin area. Of these 32 found sites in the urban-rural fringe, mainly on the industrial estates; 14 were located within the city and the remaining 5 were built in outlying urban centres.

The location of industries in the north-west and south-west industrial sectors poses problems for those who make much use of the port of Dublin, for their lorries have to traverse the heavily congested city roads. The need for feeder ring roads is widely recognised and they have high priority but as yet no such road has been completed.

The open spaces

It is clear from figure 22.2 that considerable open spaces exist between the developing fringe and the city proper. In view of the active development of the urban fringe and the abnor-

BB

mally high price of land it is clear that these open spaces are of primary importance and it is necessary to consider the extent to which they are available for development. On the north side this land is chiefly occupied by ecclesiastical institutions which include seminaries, schools, asylums and hospitals but there is also an extensive cemetery, the Glasnevin Botanic Gardens, and a golf course. All evidence so far suggests that the religious institutions are likely to resist the incursions of speculators but the sports fields and recreational areas not attached to these institutions are more vulnerable and the extensive land of the Albert Agricultural College has recently become available for development. Not far away from this, Artane Industrial School with its large farm has a decreasing number of boy boarders and it too may see big changes in the near future. Two other open spaces are important. To the east, on the coast, the grounds of St Anne's, formerly a private demesne, have been set aside as a public park. In the extreme west a broad embayment south of Finglas is traversed by the valley of the Tolka, and while some development is already taking place there it is the policy of the Corporation to keep the immediate vicinity of the river free from building.

To the south and south-west of Dublin many of the existing open spaces are paddocks associated with houses and small farms that have so far resisted the developer. Some of these are still privately owned but many have been bought by religious orders for schools and other purposes. There are also numerous sports fields including eight golf courses and a race course. Where the land is owned by the clubs and not just leased there is resistance to developers but where this is not the case these very desirable open spaces rapidly disappear as has recently happened to a golf course in Rathfarnham.

In general the number of open spaces available to the public in the urban-rural fringe is being reduced rather than increased. Apart from the green strip along the Dodder valley no adequate provision has been made for park areas or for public sports fields on the south side of the city. It is true that on the north side, St Anne's Park and the neighbouring Bull Island, with its sand dunes and broad beach, provide a unique recreational area for Dubliners, but in other areas planning has come too late and the opportunity for setting aside substantial areas of land for recreational purposes has already gone.

SUMMARY AND CONCLUSIONS

Over the past thirty years the development of Dublin has been largely on its perimeter. The nature of this growth has been dictated by social and economic considerations, for although the city has had the attention of town planners from the time of Abercrombie onwards (1914)[4], there is little evidence on the ground of their activities. The fact is that trained planners have been few and have remained powerless while the developers have been strong. The present draft plan for the city and county (1967)[5] which lays down general policy and guide lines with land use zoning can only be an interim measure, for it is largely a recognition of the present situation rather than a forward looking document. The City Planning Officer has admitted that he looks to peripheral expansion to cater for another five to ten years' growth.[6] In general, the land use has been influenced by the existing development on the townward side so that Corporation housing estates generate similar estates on their outer edge; and extensions to middle class suburbs continue to provide similar accommodation. Thus there has been a tendency towards social segregation in sectors. New shopping centres have neither been large enough nor comprehensive enough to reduce pressure on the central business district and this, combined with the relative lack of opportunities for work in the suburbs, results in increasing congestion on the roads leading into the city.

As the urban-rural fringe pushes outwards three important limiting factors come into play. The first of these is the Dublin mountains which already block extension to the south. The second is Dublin airport which restricts growth to the north, and the third is the slowing up of reclamation in Dublin Bay. The attention of the planners, therefore, has turned towards the west. A linear development is already evident (Fig. 22.2). This is the basis of the Myles Wright plan which envisages four new towns aligned east-west and separated by strips of open country to the west of the city.[7] This plan has its critics but a suggested alternative, the removal of the airport and growth northwards along the coast[8], cannot be taken very seriously if only because it would encroach upon Dublin's only market garden area which is concentrated in the Rush-Malahide area; the city is not surrounded by a market garden zone.

These schemes all lie in the future. The present reality is that there is a belt of development around Dublin which is greater in extent than the whole existing built-up area of the city. It is an area subject to strong economic pressure where planning decisions are challenged by the developers and where the only effective controls have been the presence or absence of water and main drainage. But even these will cease to be limiting when the new main drainage for the western sectors is completed. In the meantime much of old city centre in the vicinity of Christ Church Cathedral lies derelict and in urgent need of renewal. Imaginative planning here could bring this area back to life and its reconstruction could play an important part in reducing pressure on the perimeter. Such work must be the direct responsibility of the Corporation who own most of the property and, in any case, the speculative developers are only interested in building prestige office blocks in other parts of the city. It is a pity that the first pilot scheme for central area redevelopment (the Lichfield plan for 1964)[9] does not deal with the old city core but is concerned with the replacement of 31 ha (77 acres) of obsolescent property on the north side of the river. This is not likely to contribute much towards the solution of the major problems of housing, traffic congestion and continued extension of the suburbs into the surrounding countryside.

REFERENCES

1 Ordnance Survey of Ireland, 1:10,560, Dublin, Sheet 18 (first ed. 1837)
2 Vol. 1. *Census of population of Ireland 1966,* (Central Statistics Office, Dublin, 1967)
3 Mathew Macken and Michael O'Brien, Dublin City Development Plan, (1967), (draft), 44
4 P. Abercrombie, Sketch development plan of Dublin, (1939)
5 Mathew Macken and Michael O'Brien, op. cit., and Dublin County Development Plan, (1967), (draft)

BB*

6 Michael O'Brien, Planning in Dublin, *J. Town Planning Inst.*, 53, No. 7 (1967), 292
7 Myles Wright, *The Dublin Region—Advisory Regional Plan and Final Report*, (S.O., Dublin, 1966)
8 K. Madden, A coastal plan for Dublin; special planning supplement in *Build*, (Dublin, Sept. 1968)
9 Nathaniel Lichfield, City of Dublin Pilot Scheme of Central Area Redevelopment, (1964), unpublished

XXIII

SOCIAL SPACE IN THE BELFAST URBAN AREA

F. W. Boal

The classic work of Emrys Jones[1] has provided a more comprehensive urban geography of Belfast than is perhaps available for any other city of comparable size. This is an excellent foundation on which further study is being based. Much of his work used data obtained from the 1951 census of population, and most of the analysis was restricted to the County Borough of Belfast, However, since 1951 the population of the County Borough has declined by over 44,000, while the built-up area outside the city had, at the 1966 census, a population of 161,000, or about 29 per cent of the total population of the whole urban area. On these grounds alone a further analysis seems justified. In addition, there is now a greater range of data available for the whole of the urban area, derived from the 1966 Census of Population, from the Belfast Area Travel Survey, and from various planning surveys. Finally, the availability of computers makes it possible to use new techniques for analysis of the data.

Urban social geography in general has been heavily orientated towards the description of the areal distribution of a range of socio-economic characteristics. This is in line with the social area analyses of sociologists such as Shefky and Bell.[2] However, the spatial aspects of interaction between areas has received little attention except in transportation studies and investigations of shopping patterns. Because of the system nature of urban complexes it would appear that social area analysis can be improved by a study of interaction both within and between such areas. The present study then, will consist of two principal parts: first an analysis of the whole urban area leading to its subdivision into a series of broad socio-economic regions, and second, an analysis of some aspects of interaction within the broader context established in the first part of the study.

Urban area analysis

Urban areas have been characterized in terms of a number of gradients. E. W. Burgess suggests a positive gradient outwards from the city centre in terms of class—working class in the inner areas grading through to the highest income groups on the periphery.[3] Colin Clark, and subsequent workers, have demonstrated the existence of a general negative

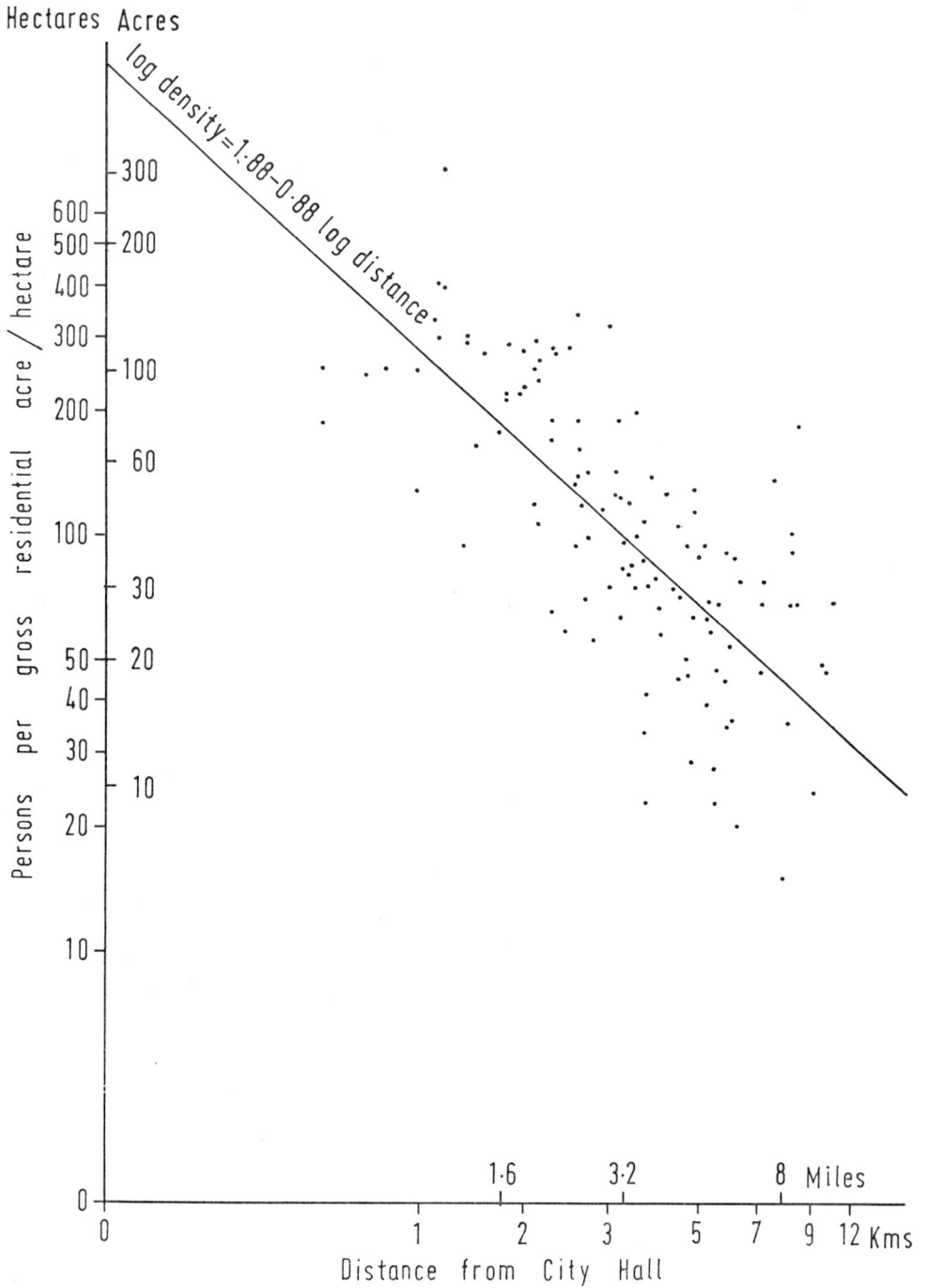

Fig. 23.1 The relationship between the population density of 119 census zones and their distance from the City Hall (1966)

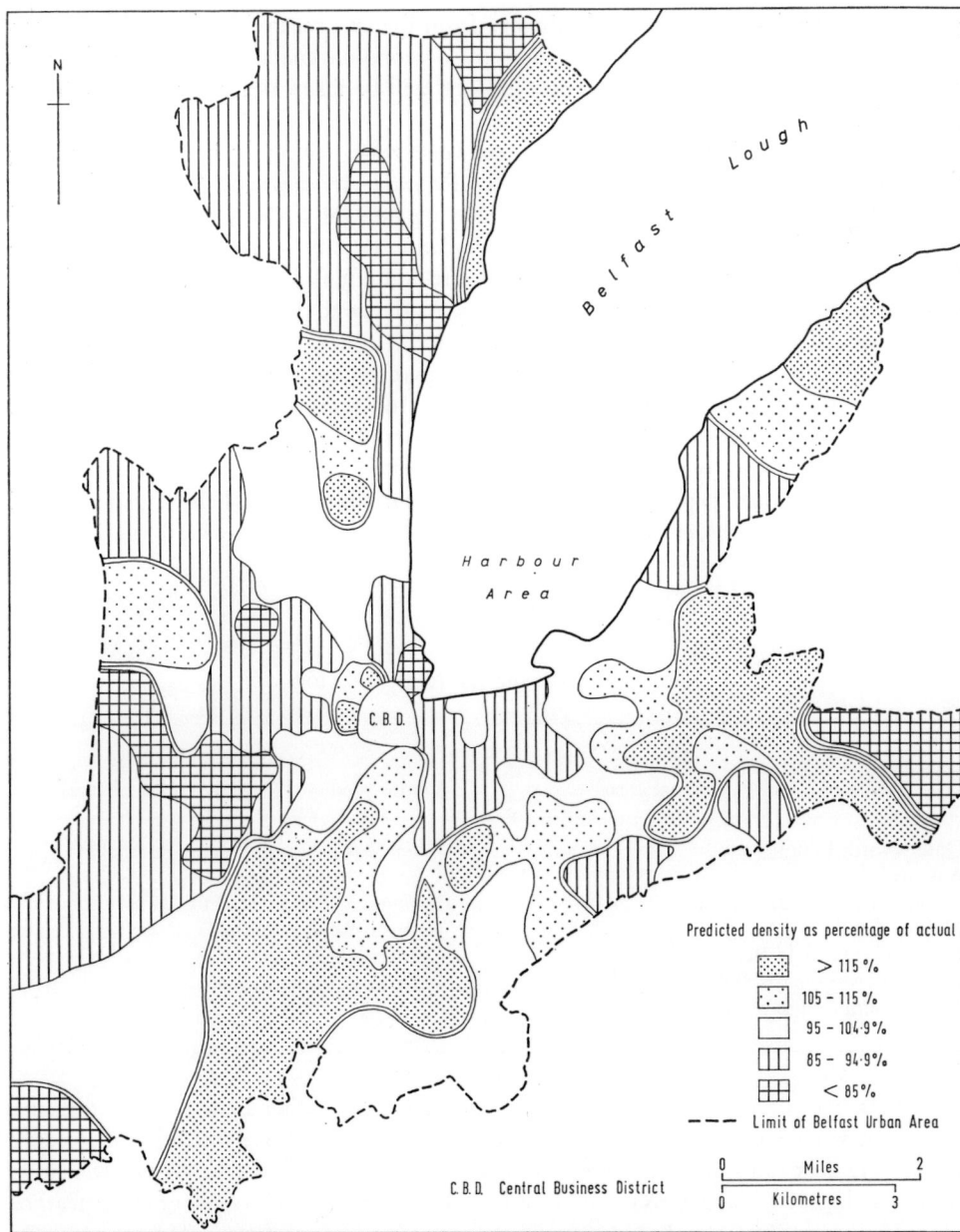

Fig. 23.2 Belfast: residuals from regression of density against distance from the city centre. The regression equation used to obtain residuals was log gross residential density (persons per acre) = 1.88—0.88 log distance (miles). For locations named in text see figure 23.5

gradient of population density with distance from the city centre.[4] Both sets of gradients indicate a concentric arrangement of various socio-economic characteristics focused on the central business district. These concentric models will be taken as a point of departure in this study.

The gross population density for 119 Census data zones within the Belfast area, ranging from 0.6 km (0.35 mile) to 10.5 km (6.54 miles) from the city centre (City Hall) is shown in figure 23.1. The data has been plotted on double log axes and a least squares regression line fitted which is based on the equation, log population density = 1.88 —0.88 log distance (where density is persons per gross residential acre and distance is in tenths of a mile). The negative form of the density gradient is obvious. At the same time it is clear that individual data zones differ considerably from the general trend. These deviations from the regular "model" density surface can be computed and mapped in terms of residuals from the regression (Fig. 23.2). The spatial distribution of the residuals displays a well defined pattern and can be described in terms of thirteen sectors forming an alternating series in which density is either over- or under-predicted. Where density is over-predicted, actual densities are less than expected from the model, and conversely where under-predicted actual densities are higher than expected. The two sets of sectors are indicated in Table 1.

TABLE I

Positive and negative residual sectors

Over predicted (positive residual areas)	Under predicted (negative residual areas)
Outer North Lough Shore	Inner North Lough Shore—Rathcoole
Antrim Road	Crumlin Road—Ligoniel
Ballygomartin Road (weak)	Springfield Road—Falls Road
Malone Road	Ormeau Road (weak)
Ravenhill–Saintfield Roads	Castlereagh Road
Upper Newtownards–Belmont Roads	Inner South Lough Shore
Outer South Lough Shore	

This suggests an overall sector distribution of density rather than a concentric one. However, while sectors can be distinguished, within any one sector the negatively sloped density gradient can still be distinguished, and is illustrated in figure 23.3A where density is shown along two high density and two low density sectors. The same gradient feature, though now positive, can be demonstrated for socio-economic status (Fig. 23.3B). The differences between sectors and the overall density gradient are both apparent.

Density (x) in Belfast is negatively correlated with distance (y) from the city centre (r log x. log y = — 0.72) but as noted above, with distinctive differences in density levels

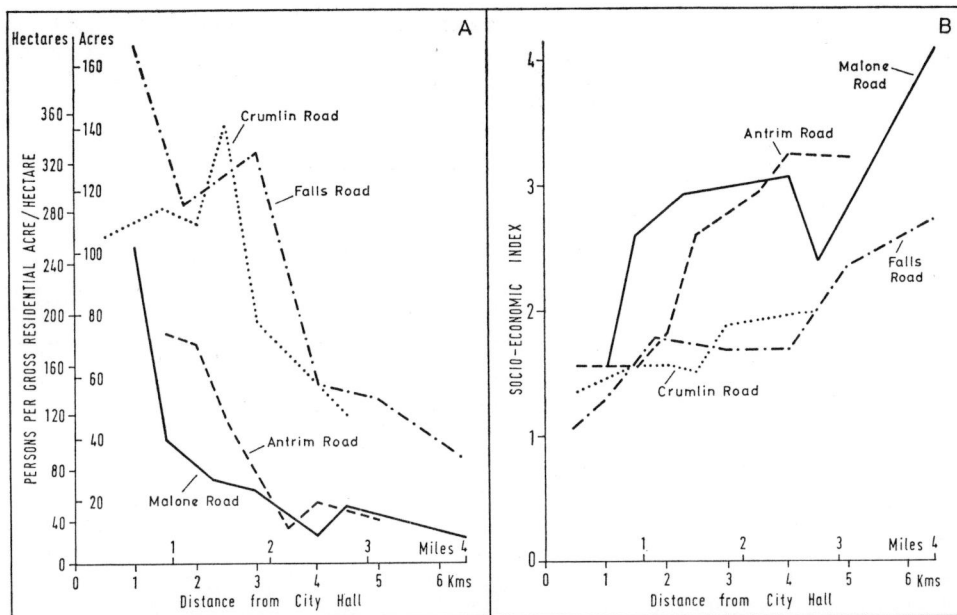

Fig. 23.3 Population density (A) and socio-economic status (B) measured along selected sectors in Belfast

between sectors. In European and North American cities there is also a high correlation between density and other socio-economic characteristics. Belfast is no exception, where, for instance, a general index of socio-economic status (a) based on occupation has a high negative correlation with density ($r_{a.x} = -0.70$), while there is a similar negative correlation between density and car ownership (b) ($r_{b.x} = -0.67$). If we take four general indicators of socio-economic status (density, occupational index[5], car ownership and male unemployment) and correlate them against a general array of variables for the 119 Belfast data zones, the correlation matrix shown in Table 2 is obtained.

The four general indicators are all highly intercorrelated. At the same time they are highly correlated with a number of other variables. It would seem possible, therefore, to substitute one of the indicators as a general socio-economic index. However, instead of using just one variable it was considered desirable to employ a technique that would involve the use of the full array of the 26 available variables. This number was finally reduced to 25 by the omission of the distance variable in case this had too strong a patterning effect on its own. The technique used was principal components analysis whereby linear combinations of variables are obtained which are uncorrelated, and whereby the first linear combination (component) is a normalized combination with maximum variance; the second component is uncorrelated with the first and has as large a variance as possible and so on. The initial data was standardized.

TABLE 2

Correlations between selected variables for the Belfast urban area. In addition the correlations between 25 variables and the first two components are also given
(data is untransformed)

	Density	Occupational Index[5]	Car Ownership	Male Unemployment	Correlation between variables and component Component 1	2
Per cent population ≤ 14 years						0.88
Per cent population ≥ 65 years						−0.92
Persons per household						0.73
Persons per room			−0.51	0.50	0.61	0.63
Distance from City Hall	−0.59	0.62	0.59		NA	NA
Gross residential density		−0.70	−0.67	0.72	0.78	
Gross dwelling density	0.92	−0.78	−0.72	0.57	0.81	
Occupational index	−0.70		0.86	−0.62	−0.88	
Cars per household	−0.67	0.86		−0.57	−0.89	
Per cent of population 15–19 years in full-time education	−0.64	0.70	0.75		−0.79	
Per cent of population with driving licences	−0.75	0.88	0.89	−0.65	−0.91	
Per cent of heads of household socio-economic group A_i	−0.75	0.70	0.77		−0.72	
Per cent of heads of household Socio-economic group A_{ii}	−0.50	0.66	0.53		−0.63	
Per cent of heads of household Socio-economic group B						0.62
Per cent of heads of household Socio-economic group C	0.62	−0.74	−0.74	0.54	0.83	
Per cent population over 15 years occupied						0.71
Per cent occupied males out of work	0.72	−0.62	−0.57		0.68	
Per cent workers employed in CBD						
Per cent journey to work by bus			−0.55		0.52	
Per cent journey to work by car	−0.75	0.88	0.91	−0.63	−0.92	
Per cent journey to work on foot	0.70	−0.72	−0.66	0.67	0.76	
Age of housing		−0.62			0.55	−0.73
Migrants as per cent of total population	−0.53	0.58	0.51		−0.61	
Internal area migrants						
In migrants from rest of Northern Ireland		0.58	0.50		−0.58	
Per cent of population Roman Catholic				0.57		

Only correlation coefficients ≥ 0.5 shown.   All coefficients significant at 0.01 level.   NA—not available

The first five principal components obtained absorbed 79 per cent of the total variance of the 25 variables as follows:

	Component					
	1	2	3	4	5	1–5
Percentage of Variance	41.4	18.0	8.8	6.4	4.5	79.1

The component scores were computed. The data zones were then ranked according to the value of their scores on each component, and then grouped by deciles. A map of the zonal groups derived from the first principal component is shown in figure 23.4. The component is most highly correlated positively with the following initial variables (see Table 2): persons per room, gross residential density, gross dwelling density, percentage of heads of household in socio-economic group C (semi-skilled and unskilled manual workers), percentage of normally occupied males out of work and percentage of people who journey to work on foot. The component is negatively associated with occupational index, car ownership, percentage of population with driving licences, percentage of population between 15 and 19 years in full time education, percentage of heads of household in socio-economic group A_i (managerial and professional), and percentage who make the journey to work by car. These variables are generally indicative of socio-economic status, and on this basis the first principal component has been named the socio-economic component.

The pattern displayed shows a close association with the pattern of residuals from the density analysis (Fig. 23.2) and the sectoral form is striking. Those zones that score highly on this component are areas of low socio-economic status, whereas at the other end of the scale are the high status areas. Particularly striking are the low status sectors along the inner parts of the north and south lough shores and the massive low status sector extending west and south-west from the city centre, along the Crumlin–Ligoniel and Falls–Springfield axes, with the Shankill Road in the middle. The most clearly defined high status sectors are on the lines of the Antrim, Malone, Ravenhill-Saintfield, and Upper Newtownards-Belmont Roads, together with the two outer lough shore areas.

One vital aspect of the low status sector extending west and south-west from the city centre is not included in the pattern derived from the first component—this is the high degree of religious segregation that exists.[6] Unfortunately, religious data was not obtained in the 1966 population census, necessitating the use of estimates derived from a series of surveys. This provides a sample cover for about 50 per cent of the urban area, but when considered with the pattern discussed by Jones[7] a fairly complete picture can be obtained. The main elements of the highly segregated religious area in the centre and western low status sector of the city is shown in figure 23.5, where a highly segregated area is defined as having more than 90 per cent Protestants or more than 90 per cent Roman Catholics. The main Roman Catholic concentration extends from the city centre south-westwards along the spine of the Falls Road for a distance of about 6 km (3.7 miles). There are separate and much smaller concentrations north of the middle Crumlin Road (Ardoyne), immediately west of the city centre, south-east of the centre (Cromac), and east of the centre (part of Ballymacarrett). Between Ardoyne and the Falls Road sector, there is the very well

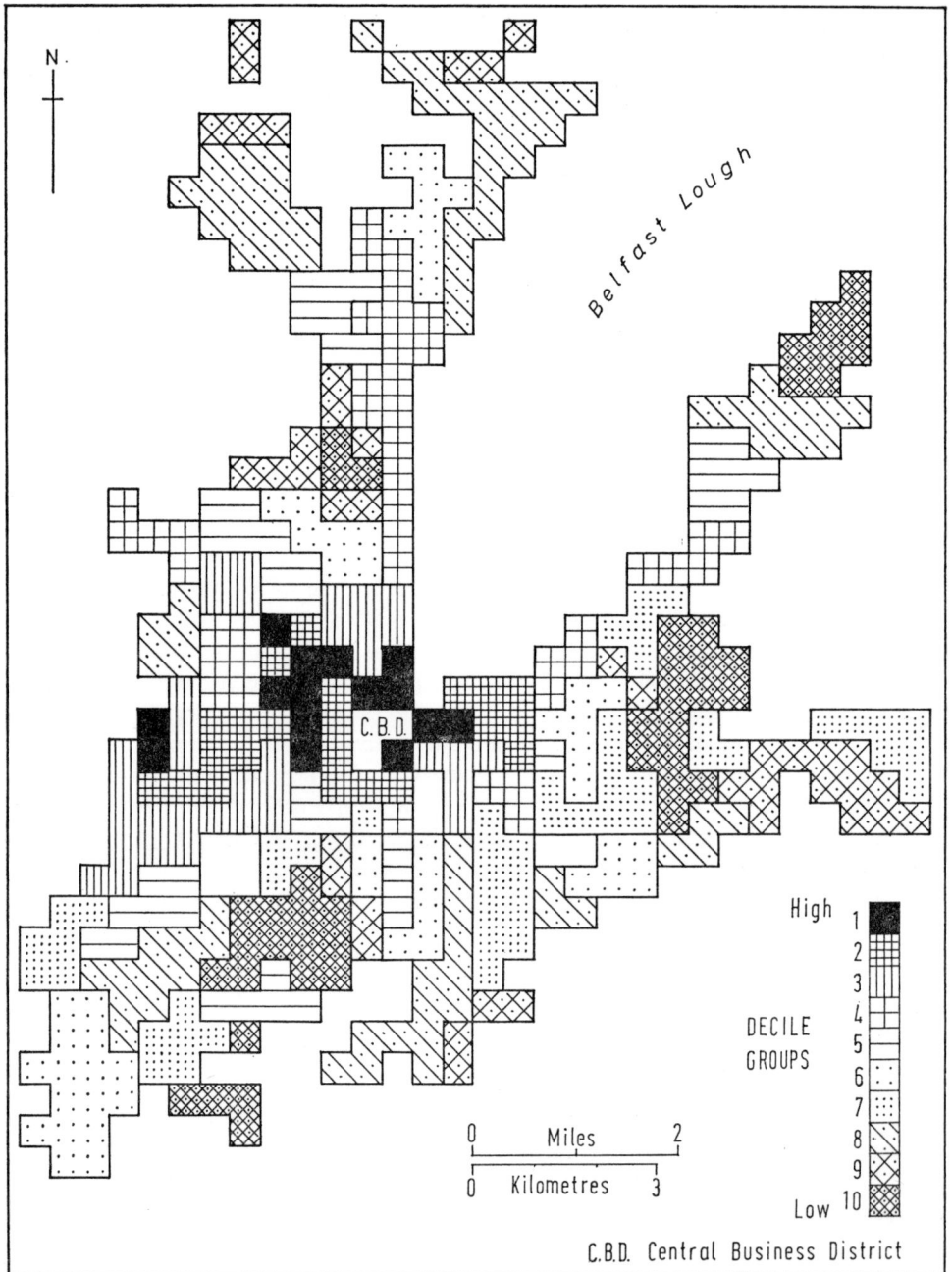

Fig. 23.4 Belfast urban area: census data zones ranked according to their component scores on the socio-economic component. The boundaries of the census zones have been adjusted to a grid format.

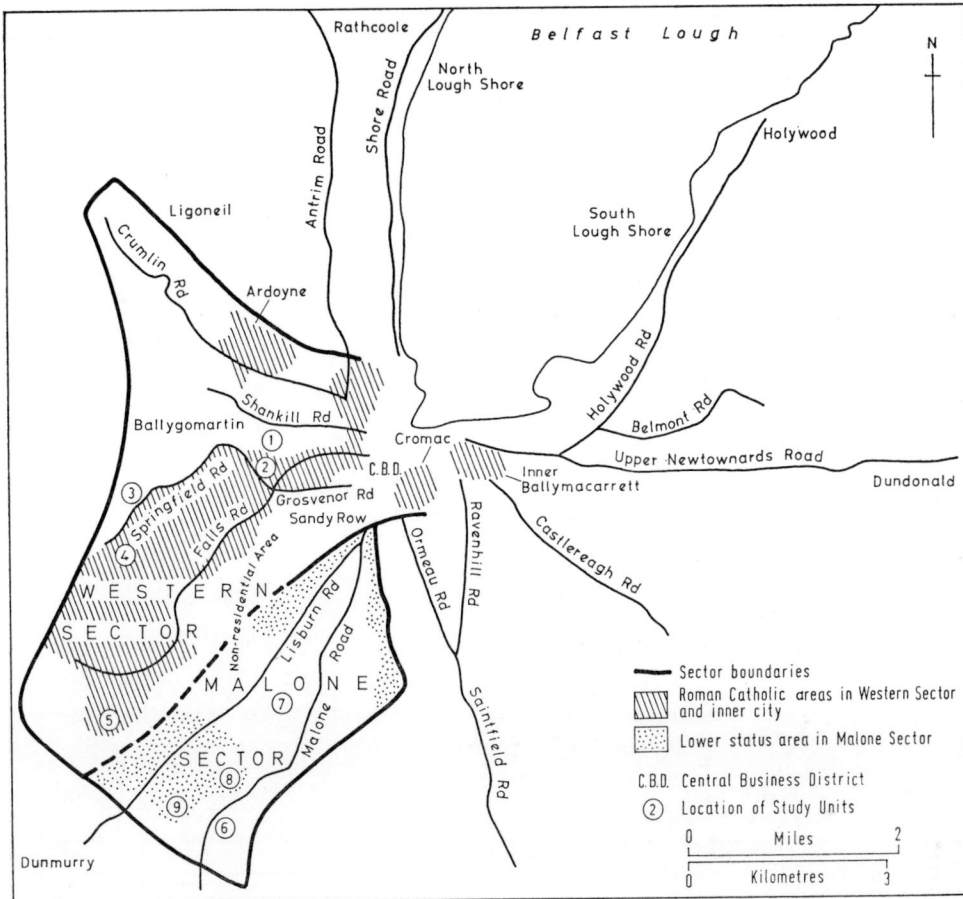

Fig. 23.5   Roman Catholic areas in central and west Belfast, and general key to locations mentioned in the text.   Study units: (1) Shankill; (2) Clonard; (3) New Barnsley; (4) Turf Lodge; (5) Ladybrook; (6) Upper Malone; (7) Inner Malone; (8) Taughmonagh; (9) Erinvale.

Note: Dock area excluded.

developed and almost entirely Protestant Shankill Road area, while lying south-east of the Falls sector is the equally predominantly Protestant Sandy Row area.

The result is that within the western low status area there is a Roman Catholic–Protestant alternation of sub-sectors. The actual divides between these sub-sectors are, almost without exception, very sharp. In some cases the division is composed of non-residential areas, such as factory sites and railway tracks, while in others, the residential areas come into direct contact with each other, and the transition from Protestant to Catholic occurs within the width of a street of houses. An example of this is shown in figure 23.6, on the divide between the Falls and Shankill sub-sectors.[8]

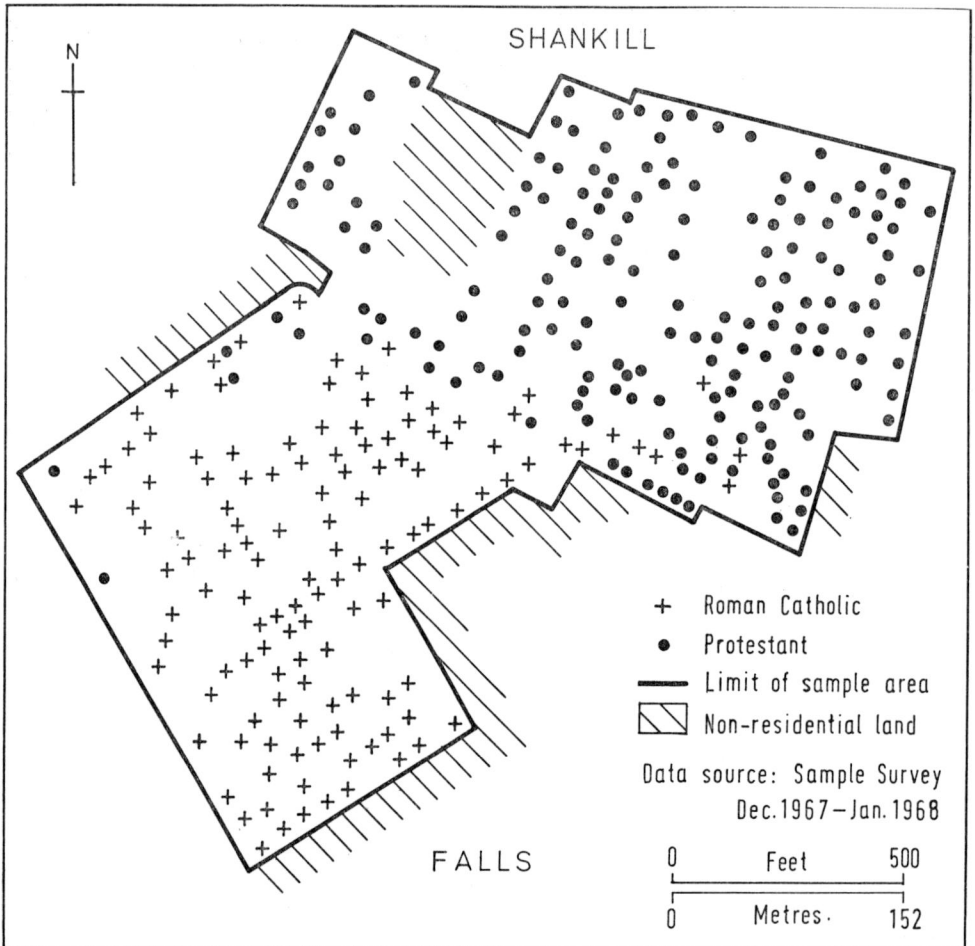

Fig. 23.6 Religious distribution in a small area of west Belfast at the contact of the Shankill and Falls sub-sectors. The map is based upon a ten per cent sample of persons over the age of twenty-one.

Thus far the basic socio-economic picture of the Belfast urban area we have obtained is one of a city centre focussed gradient, positively sloped in terms of social status, and negatively sloped in terms of density. Superimposed on this general surface are the alternating high and low status sectors, while the western low status sector displays a further set of internal sub-sectors distinguished on the basis of religion.

When the data zones are ranked on their scores for component 2 the pattern produced is much less sectoral in character. In fact, the highest scoring zones are the peripheral ones and the lowest scoring the central zones, with inner high status areas scoring lowest of all. The initial variables most heavily weighted in this component are those associated with demographic characteristics. Zones with high scores have large proportions of the population under 14, a low proportion over 65, and large households. A large proportion of the population has also been involved recently in a house move, and the houses occupied are relatively new. The component picks out the growing periphery of the urban area. This growth is of very mixed socio-economic character, in that there is Local Authority and Northern Ireland Housing Trust rental housing, low to medium cost private estates, and a limited development of high cost housing. Government developed housing (Local Authority and Housing Trust) is quite widespread on the periphery and has been constructed at the outer ends of a wide range of socio-economic sectors. However, there is a predominance of rental housing on the outer fringes of low status sectors. Where Government housing lies on the lines of higher status sectors, the population generally has a higher socio-economic status than for similar housing on the lines of the low status sectors. Thus, while the demographic characteristics of the urban area have a general concentric pattern, a strong sectoral influence can still be seen.

The presence of both sectoral and concentric residential patterns corresponds with the findings reported by Berry for American cities.[9] He notes that there are three dimensions of socio-economic variation: the sectoral variation of neighbourhoods by socio-economic rank, the concentric variation of neighbourhoods according to family structure and the localized segregation of particular ethnic groups. However, if we consider the religious groups as 'ethnic' the segregation pattern in the Belfast context is predominantly sectoral, as noted above. Thus, while Jones found a "sector residential pattern" in the west[10], the present analysis suggests the co-existence of 'sectors' and 'rings' over much of the urban area.

Before proceeding to the activity analysis it should be stressed that there is some loss of 'information' in the analysis of the Belfast data zones. This applies particularly to parts of the periphery, where the data zones are quite large and include a wide range of housing types. The general picture is not distorted greatly but locally considerable statistical homogenization has been imposed.

Activity analysis

Up to this point, the analysis has dealt with the whole urban area, and has concentrated on standard socio-economic data. An attempt will now be made to examine a series of sample areas in much greater detail, and in particular to carry out an analysis of some activity patterns to see how activity linkages are distributed and how activity is related to the basic socio-economic structure of the urban area outlined above.

Nine study units were selected and a random sample of persons over the age of 21 was interviewed in each area. The study units were selected from the western low status sector and the Malone high status sector. Pairs of units were also selected to allow comparison, while holding religion, socio-economic status and age of housing constant. The study units and certain of their characteristics are listed in Table 3 while their locations are shown in figure 23.5. The sharp differences of religion within the western sector and between the two semi-detached private housing areas, one in the western sector, the other on the outer edge of Malone, are evident.

TABLE 3

Study unit characteristics

Sector	Study Unit Name	Type of Housing	Persons per net residential hectare (acre)	Households per net residential hectare (acre)	Religion (per cent RC)	Size of Household	Occupational Index[5]	Persons Sampled
Western	Shankill I	Victorian terrace	438 (177)	138 (54)	1	3.3	1.68	158
	Clonard	Victorian terrace	353 (143)	90 (36)	98	3.9	2.27	113
	New Barnsley	Corporation estate*	195 (79)	34 (14)	12	5.7	2.47	101
	Turf Lodge	Corporation estate*	259 (105)	37 (15)	99	7.0	2.13	116
	Ladybrook	Semi-detached private	96 (39)	23 (9)	90	4.2	3.26	61
Malone	Inner Malone	Large detached	34 (14)	8 (3)	14	4.1	4.11	65
	Upper Malone	Large detached bungalows	30 (12)	8 (3)	8	3.7	4.20	66
	Erinvale	Mainly semi-detached private	125 (51)	33 (13)	10	3.8	3.32	77
	Taughmonagh	Corporation 'pre-fab' estate	107 (44)	19 (8)	13	5.7	2.58	92

*Maisonette areas excluded

Clearly, Shankill, Clonard, New Barnsley and Turf Lodge are low status areas, while Inner and Upper Malone are high status areas. On the other hand Ladybrook, Erinvale and Taughmonagh, do not conform to the particular low or high status characteristics of their respective sectors. In fact, these three areas lie on the flanks of the two sectors, Ladybrook being lower middle income and predominantly Roman Catholic, Erinvale being lower middle income and Protestant. Taughmonagh is a highly non-conforming insertion of Corporation housing on the central axis of the Malone sector. The non-conforming nature of these three study units is also evident in the activity analysis.

The activity analysis applied depends on the examination of a set of linkages within the Belfast urban area. The present residence of the interviewee forms one point and the links between that point and three other sets of points are established. The three other sets of points are the previous address of interviewee (if there is one), the origin points of social visits to interviewee or points interviewee visited during a one week period, and the pre-marriage addresses of interviewee and spouse (if applicable). The first step in the analysis required the establishment of the extent to which points associated with the three social attributes (previous address, visits and pre-marriage address) corresponded with each other for any one study unit. The extent to which the three point distributions were congruent for each of the study units is shown in figure 23.7, cells for which three or two attributes were congruent being indicated, together with the cells for which only one attribute was present.

If we confine our attention to those cells where two or three attributes are congruent a number of features emerge. Firstly, all the study units display 'core areas' where all three attributes are congruent. The simplest and most sharply developed are those for the inner low status areas of Shankill and Clonard. Secondly, we can note the more elongated well-developed cores for the outer housing estates of New Barnsley and Turf Lodge and the somewhat more fragmented core pattern for the private estate of Ladybrook. In the Malone sector two distinct patterns emerge, rather weakly developed elongated cores for the high status Upper and Inner Malone units, and more strongly developed but discontinuous cores for the Erinvale private estate and the Taughmonagh Corporation Housing area. Viewed differently we can say that all the low and middle status areas display well-developed cores while the high status units are weaker in this respect.

Well-developed cores indicate a closely knit spatial system wherein, for each study unit, there are a series of congruent linkages—the area or areas concerned are connected to the study unit in terms of visiting, an immediately previous address and the pre-marriage location of at least one partner. In the instances in which all these linkages occur within the same area, this is taken to indicate the existence of a tightly knit 'spatial community', which Fried claims is an indication of a standard working class community pattern, "an overlapping series of close knit networks".[11] The core areas occur either where there are old established fairly static groups (Shankill and Clonard) or where there has been movement from a small part of the inner city to new housing areas on the urban periphery (New Barnsley, Turf Lodge, Taughmonagh, which are Local Authority housing areas, and Ladybrook and Erinvale, which are higher status private housing areas deriving a significant

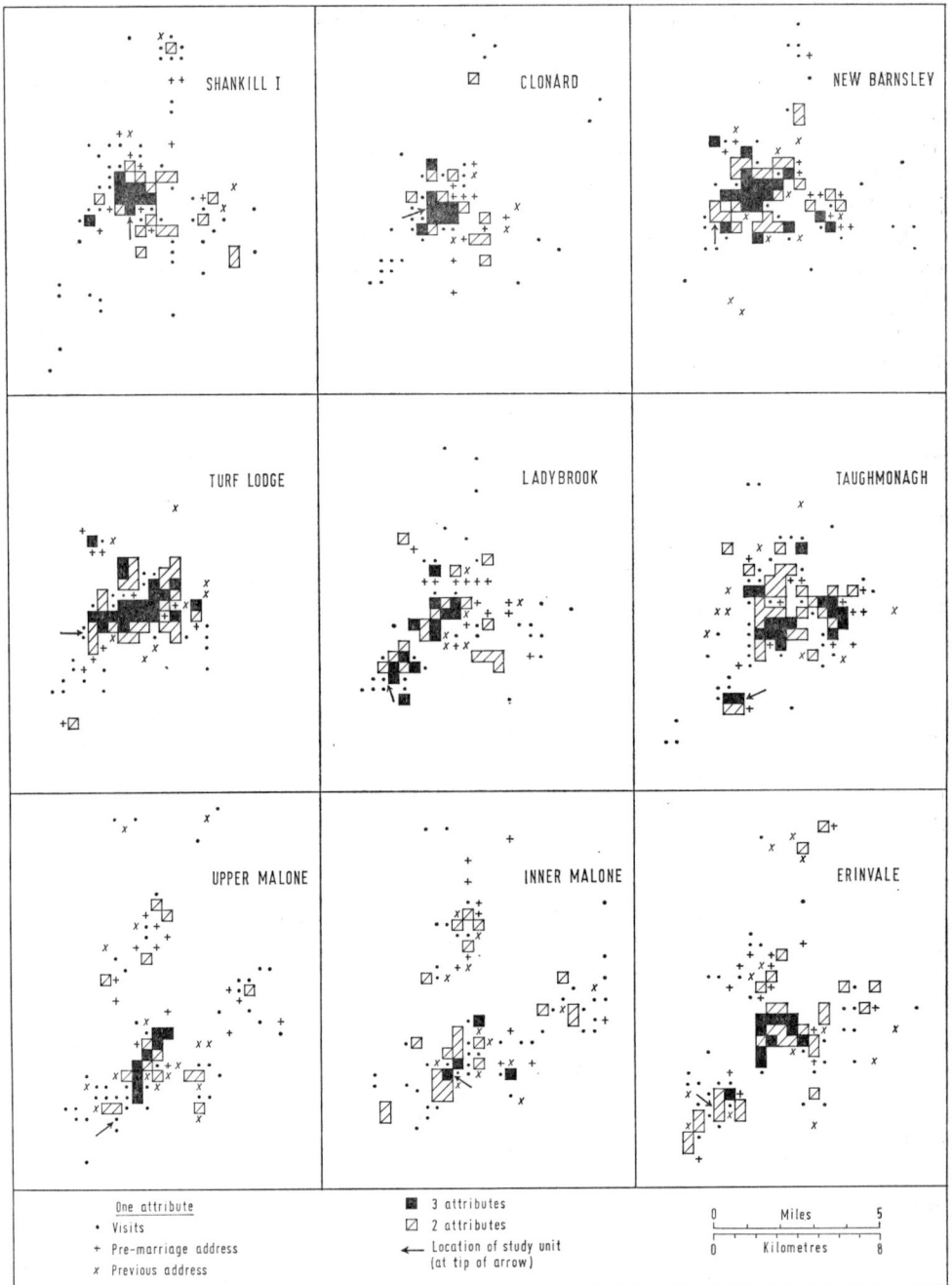

Fig. 23.7 Congruence of social activity attributes for sample residents in each of nine study units. The congruence is measured within a 0.5 km² grid superimposed on the Belfast urban area.

Note: the degree of concentration of attributes in the three and two attribute cells is not shown.

TABLE 4

Percentage allocation of previous addresses, pre-marriage addresses and visit connections for the Malone sector sample units.

	Sample Units	Malone sector (percentage of urban area connections)		Low Status sub-sector + Sandy Row (percentage of urban area connections)	Outside urban area (percentage of all connections)	
		Total	High Status sub-sector		Northern Ireland	Abroad
Previous address	Upper Malone	65	48	20	11	20
	Inner Malone	60	52	10	11	11
	Erinvale	25	4	35	20	12
	Taughmonagh	15	4	24	7	4
Pre-marriage address	Upper Malone	33	27	3	24	42
	Inner Malone	25	25	0	28	30
	Erinvale	24	7	30	33	9
	Taughmonagh	9	2	32	11	6
Visit connections	Upper Malone	71	66	9	17	4
	Inner Malone	63	58	6	22	5
	Erinvale	44	4	52	26	0
	Taughmonagh	27	1	36	6	3

proportion of their population from a restricted section of the inner city).

The two high status Malone areas do not show the close knit networks to the same degree, though even here reasonably well defined cores are evident. However, in these two cases, not only are the various social attributes less congruent within the Belfast urban area but they also show much stronger linkages outside the urban area altogether. This is shown in Table 4 where the percentage concentration of the various attributes is given for the Malone sector and also outside the urban area.

The five study units within the western sector show high levels of concentration for all three social attributes (Table 5). A very high proportion of total interaction is restricted to the western low status sector. A further degree of concentration can also be distinguished, in that the two predominantly Protestant study units (Shankill and New Barnsley) have very high levels of linkage within the Protestant sub-sectors, while the three Roman Catholic units have strong links within the Catholic sub-sectors. The different 'orientation' of the Protestant and Roman Catholic sub-sectors can also be indicated in terms of newspaper readership and support for certain football teams. In this case Catholic loyalties lie with

TABLE 5

Percentage allocation of previous addresses, pre-marriage addresses and visit connections for the western sector sample units

	Sample Units	Western Sector (percentage of urban area connections)			Outside Urban Area (percentage of all connections)	
		Total	Within Protestant sub-sectors	Within Catholic sub-sectors	Northern Ireland	Abroad
Previous address	Shankill	87	82	5	4	4
	Clonard	81	5	76	4	5
	New Barnsley	75	67	8	2	9
	Turf Lodge	85	5	80	0	2
	Ladybrook	87	11	76	9	14
Pre-marriage address	Shankill	91	89	2	5	1
	Clonard	85	7	78	7	8
	New Barnsley	79	71	8	7	4
	Turf Lodge	83	7	76	2	3
	Ladybrook	86	13	73	19	6
Visit connections	Shankill	83	79	4	3	1
	Clonard	93	5	88	3	2
	New Barnsley	84	76	6	5	1
	Turf Lodge	85	5	80	1	0
	Ladybrook	79	8	71	10	2

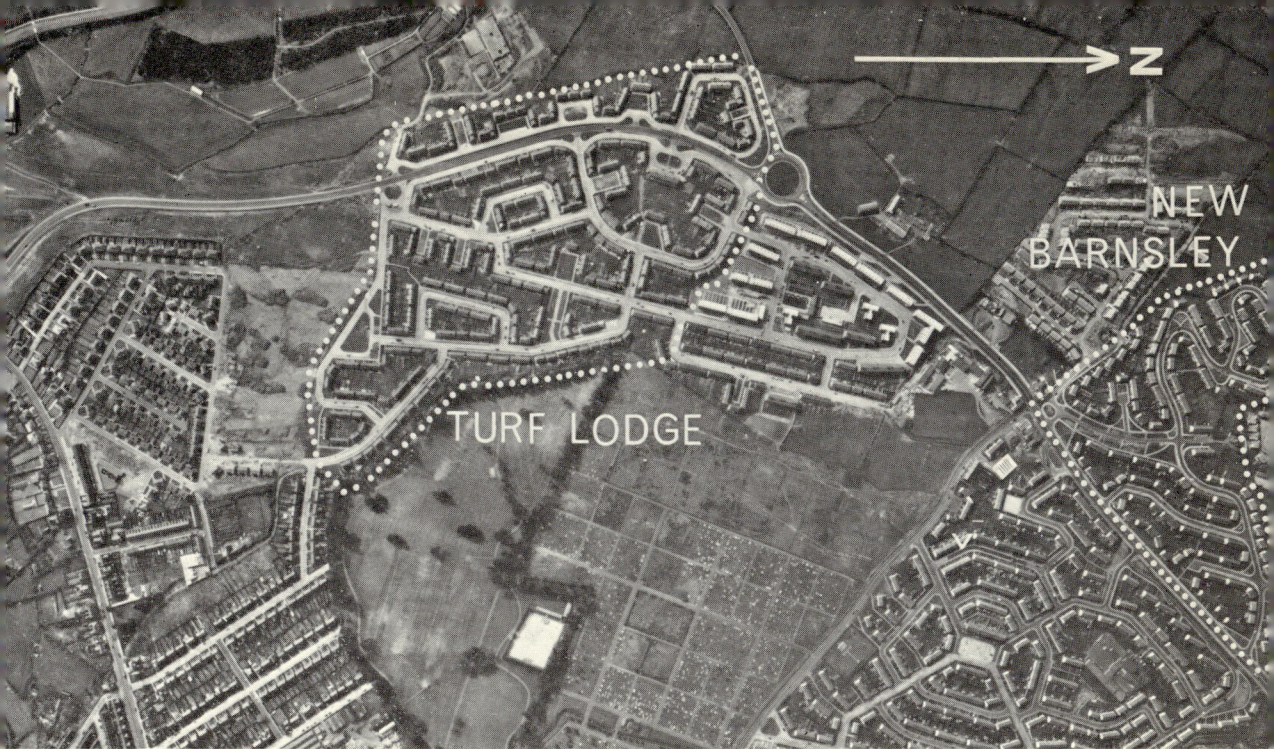

Crown Copyright Reserved

XXIX   Turf Lodge and New Barnsley study units. Both units are Belfast Corporation housing developed on the outer edge of the western sector.

XXX   Taughmonagh and Upper Malone study units. Taughmonagh is Belfast Corporation housing while Upper Malone is a private high income development. Both units lie at the outer edge of the Malone sector.

Approximate scale of both photographs 1:10560. The general locations of the study units are shown on Fig. 23.5 page 381.

Crown Copyright Reserved

Reproduced with the sanction of the Controller of H.M. Stationery Office. Crown Copyright Reserved

XXXI   The inner portions of the western low income sector. The principal Protestant sub-sector lies on either side of the Shankill Road, while the principal Roman Catholic sub-sector lies in the southern part of the area shown, centred on the Falls Road. The Shankill I study unit lies in the Protestant sub-sector while the Clonard unit lies in the Roman Catholic sub-sector. The CBD lies at the top edge of the plate.

Approximate scale 1:10560. The general locations of the study units are shown on Fig. 23.5 page 381

Glasgow Celtic and the Irish News, while Protestant loyalties lie with Linfield football club and there is an 'inverted' loyalty to the Irish News. Probably television and the Belfast Telegraph evening paper are the two news and cultural media that both sectors have in common but there is little else (Table 6).

The three outer units within the western sector (New Barnsley, Turf Lodge and Ladybrook) show clearly the centre-periphery nature of much interaction, for previous addresses are located in the inner parts of the subsectors as are pre-marriage addresses. The tendency towards out-migration along sectors has been noted previously by Jones[12], and is a generally observed feature of residential moves within the Belfast urban area. If a move to a new house is contemplated, people express a strong preference for a location in the outer reaches of the sector within which they already reside. This is clearly related to familiarity and ease of movement from the new housing area back to the 'home' district.

TABLE 6

Newspaper readership, football team support and presence of television sets, Western sector study units

	Percentage Roman Catholic	Percentage reading Irish News	Percentage supporting Glasgow Celtic	Percentage supporting Linfield	Percentage reading Belfast Telegraph	Percentage with TV sets
Clonard	98	83	73	0	58	77
Turf Lodge	99	74	63	0	70	97
Ladybrook	90	39	11	0	62	100
Shankill	1	3	0	74	68	86
New Barnsley	12	3	1	63	72	97

The study units in the Malone sector display a less concentrated set of linkages in terms of the sector itself. Even so the two high status units (Upper and Inner Malone) do show considerable degrees of sector concentration in terms of previous addresses and visit connections, even though there are significant linkages outside the urban area altogether. For these two areas the pre-marriage address is more dispersed, both within and outside the urban area, though the urban area distribution is almost entirely restricted to high status sectors.

The two lower status units in the Malone sector are the most weakly linked in terms of the sector within which they are present. This is because both units are non-conforming as far as the socio-economic characteristics of most of the sector are concerned. On social status grounds they have low probabilities of connection with the high status predominant portion of the sector. However, both study units show strong links with an inner low status area (Sandy Row), which until now we have considered part of the Western sector. In

CC

terms of potential interaction this interpretation needs to be relaxed because the innermost parts of all sectors west of the river are close to each other and it is questionable to which sector they should be allocated. From the restricted evidence available it would appear that Sandy Row is more strongly linked to the lower status outer parts of the Malone sector than to the outer parts of the Western sector, particularly since the outer parts of the western Protestant sub-sector are 'cut-off' from Sandy Row by the overwhelmingly Catholic sub-sector of Falls.

The non-conforming nature of Erinvale and Taughmonagh is further emphasized when the distances of the linked points from the study units are considered. For instance, the mean distance of visit links for Taughmonagh is not significantly different from that for Upper Malone, while it is significantly greater than that for Inner Malone ($p=0.05$) despite the considerable socio-economic differences between the units.

The pattern of connectivity which has been analysed would seem to be influenced by a number of factors. Firstly, linkages will occur predominantly with areas which are similar in socio-economic and religious characteristics. Secondly, the linkages are further constrained by distance, and by the general accessibility pattern of the various potential linkage areas to any particular study unit. Where there is a high dependence on walking and use of buses, distances are small unless movement is channelled in and out along a radial road where there is a good bus service. With the present radial arrangement of bus routes between city centre and periphery, lateral (inter-sector) movement is difficult, particularly where the spine roads of the sectors are far apart. As noted earlier, however, since the spine roads are much closer together in the inner parts of the city, inter-sector movement is easier here. The availability of a car and to some extent of a telephone also tends to free movement from the radial network. But all the low status study units have two-thirds to three-quarters of households without cars, and in the western sector there is no significant difference

TABLE 7

Mobility potential of households in the sample units

	Cars per household	Percentage of households with no car	Percentage of households with telephone
Shankill	0.14	85	2
Clonard	0.29	71	7
New Barnsley	0.19	82	5
Turf Lodge	0.24	77	2
Ladybrook	0.77	23	16
Upper Malone	1.55	2	96
Inner Malone	1.68	6	99
Erinvale	0.77	30	35
Taughmonagh	0.35	67	0

between the inner and outer low status areas (Table 7). Thus, in this case peripheral location is not compensated for by higher personal mobility using a car and consequently, movement by bus on the spine roads is a major constraint on linkage patterns.

At the other end of the spectrum lie the two high status Malone units where practically every household has at least one car, and about half the households have two or more cars available. About three quarters of the households in the middle status units (Erinvale and Ladybrook) have cars. The existence of a telephone is even more marked in the inequality of its distribution, ranging from just about saturation in the Malone units to almost insignificance in the low status areas. The telephone distribution pattern suggests a whole sub-system of interaction as far as the high status areas are concerned.

The lack of cars and to some extent of telephones in the low status units, together with the enforced radial nature of bus travel, suggests why so much social interaction is sectoral in nature, and the constraints of religion and social status further affect the pattern. In this context it is still striking to observe the degree to which the interaction for the Malone high status units is also restricted to a considerable extent to the Malone sector, despite much greater potential physical mobility. There are elements of Fried's "close knit networks"[13] present here too.

CONCLUSION

This analysis has disclosed the existence of clearly developed sectors in the Belfast urban area. The 'static' socio-economic sector pattern disclosed in the earlier part of the study is further emphasized by the sectoral congruence of selected activity systems. The sector pattern, when viewed both from a social pattern and activity analyses viewpoint, indicates very high levels of segregation, that is segregation by socio-economic group and by religious affiliation.

It remains to comment briefly on the significance of these sector-segregated patterns from a planning standpoint. Currently segregation based on religion is viewed with disfavour by external observers, while in the past, in many cities, segregation by class has been looked upon with equal disfavour, although these attitudes are not generally held in the segregated areas concerned. In fact, one could argue that highly segregated sectors are the most efficient form for the existing system of interaction. Where areas that are non-conforming in terms of the general character of the particular sector occur, this only seems to generate more extended linkages to other areas that do conform. On the other hand, it could be argued that the existing segregated activity patterns are a consequence of the homogeneous sectors or sub-sectors. In the Belfast area, in so far as people have any residential choice, they exercise it by moving from less segregated to more segregated housing groups or else they move within an existing highly segregated sector. In the case of one Corporation housing estate which initially was integrated in terms of religion, subsequent moves have produced an almost entirely Roman Catholic estate. The Ladybrook and Erinvale private estates are both highly segregated, with only ten per cent of the particular minority religious group present in each case. Catholic have opted for Ladybrook,

Protestants for Erinvale. This highlights a further factor in segregation, namely the availability of schools. As might be expected the voluntary (Roman Catholic) schools, and the Roman Catholic churches, are restricted to a large extent to the Catholic sectors. A Catholic family buying a house, or obtaining a rented housing allocation outside the Catholic sectors is faced subsequently with long and difficult school journeys, a particularly important factor in the case of primary schools.

Planning proposals for the Belfast urban area have been produced recently,[14] and these suggest that "the strengthening of the identity and sense of community of townships and city sectors is important socially". To achieve this a structuring of the urban area into a series of 'Districts' is proposed. While the 'Districts' may have meaning where they focus on pre-existing outlying settlements such as Dunmurry, Dundonald and Holywood (Fig. 23.5), the 'Districts' proposed for much of the rest of the area run quite counter to existing community identities. The findings of the current study indicate that well defined areas with marked identity already exist whereas the proposed new 'Districts' break right across these. This is particularly true for the proposed West Belfast District which would not allow the strengthening of existing communities. The only intention can be to completely restructure the western sector by attempting to link into one 'District' at least four sharply defined sub-sectors. This aim should have been stated unequivocally and the advantages and disadvantages of such a policy carefully assessed.

In the Belfast urban area physical segregation and social segregation are highly correlated. Whether physical desegregation, in terms of religion and social class, would lead to social desegregation (that is, social interaction) is open to question. The possible consequences of physical desegregation need to be examined in depth. In fact, actual experiment may be the most effective, though not necessarily the least painful way of providing the necessary data. Analyses such as the present study, or experiments as suggested above, cannot provide substitutes for judgement as to the desirability of desegregation, but they can provide a firmer basis on which the judgement can be made.

ACKNOWLEDGEMENT

The survey work on which part of the study is based was made possible by generous grants from the Frederick Soddy Trust, the James Munce Partnership and The Queen's University of Belfast. I would also like to thank Miss J. Orr, Mr W. McGaughey and Mr G. Bullock of the Department of Geography in the university for their assistance, and Building Design Partnership for providing data for the Belfast urban area.

NOTE

This chapter was completed in September 1968. The communal disturbances during 1969 and 1970, many of which occurred in the vicinity of the edges of the religious subsectors in the western part of the city, are, in consequence, not discussed here.

REFERENCES

1 E. Jones, *A social geography of Belfast,* (London, 1960)
2 E. Shefky and W. Bell, *Social area analysis,* (Stanford U.P., 1955)
3 E. W. Burgess, The growth of the city, in R. E. Park and E. W. Mackenzie eds., *The City,* (Chicago, 1927)
4 C. Clark, Urban population densities, *J. Roy. Stat. Soc.,* 114 (1951), 490–96
5 The Occupational Index is derived from the formula:
$(0.05 \times P_1) + (0.04 \times P_2) + (0.03 \times P_3) + (0.02 \times P_4) + (0.01 \times P_5)$ where P_1, P_2, ... P_n are percentages of heads of households in the given area whose socio-economic groups are 1, 2 ... n respectively. See R. Travers Morgan & Partners, *Travel in Belfast,* (Belfast, 1968), 188
6 See E. E. Evans, Belfast: the site and the city, *Ulster J. Arch.,* 3rd series, 7 (1944), 25–9, and E. Jones, op. cit., 172–206
7 E. Jones, op. cit., 196
8 F. W. Boal, Territoriality on the Shankill-Falls Divide, Belfast, *Irish Geography,* 6, No. 1 (1969), 30–50
9 B. J. L. Berry, Internal structure of the city, *Law and Contemporary Problems,* (Winter, 1965), 115
10 E. Jones, op. cit., 273
11 M. Fried, Functions of the working class community in modern urban society—implications for forced relocations, *J. Amer. Inst. Planners,* 33 No. 2 (March 1967), 92
12 E. Jones, op. cit., 145–6
13 M. Fried, op. cit., 92
14 Building Design Partnership, *Belfast Urban Area—Interim Planning Policy,* (Belfast, 1967), 72–106

PLACE-NAME INDEX

The Index is to place-names only, as the main
subjects are indicated in the chapter headings.

S. KAT   ES COLLEGE   L   ARY

123977